HANDS OF HUR

Dear Friend —

Thank you so much for purchasing this Hands of Hur print resource.

I am deeply grateful to be able to make a small contribution to your own spiritual journey and growth. What you are holding in your hand is part of the digital legacy that I have worked hard to leave after over forty years in public ministry. In fact, Hands of Hur itself was started in 2005 to hold-up the hands of those in ministry, just like Aaron and Hur held up Moses' hands in Exodus 17.

This ministry is committed to three primary goals: biblical integrity, cultural relevancy, and the restoration of shalom. Each resource, whether it's audio, video, or print, is the fruit of decades of study, editing, distilling, and prayerful arrangement. This particular book, *"The Fulness of Time"* represents the combined extended notes associated with the three, 13-hour Bible courses offered by Hands of Hur. They are available on the Hands of Hur print resources page (lulu.com/spotlight/Sciacca). Each of the three courses includes free access to 13 hours of audio lessons.

Finally, I want to let you know about some other Hands of Hur resources that can serve you, or the church, organization, or small group of which you are a part.

- *"What's Wrong With the World?"* — a two part video/print curriculum for one-on-one discipleship, small groups, or Sunday school classes that answers the questions: *"What is the gospel, and how far does it reach?"* And, *"What is a disciple, and what does one look like?"* The videos are available in streaming or DVD format. They are available at: https://fransciacca.com/category/video/
- *"The Road to Shalom"* - a podcast featuring Fran Sciacca and guests. It is available at this URL: https://buzzsprout.com/252313
- *"Knot or Noose? - Recovering the Mystery of Marriage* — a 9-session resource for singles, dating, engaged, or married couples exploring the place of marriage in the purposes of God. at: https://fransciacca.com/category/video/).
- My website: https://fransciacca.com

Thanks again for bringing this Hands of Hur resource into your life. If you'd like to stay abreast of all things Hands of Hur, please visit the website and subscribe to our updates.

In the Lamb,

Fran Sciacca

THE ONE STORY

THE "CLOCK"				THE SCRIPT
	Getting The Big Picture	**ACT I – Commencement**	Getting The Big Picture	
Prehistory				Genesis 1-2
c. 4000 B.C.		**ACT II – Conflict**		Genesis 3-11
c. 2300 - 425 B.C.		**ACT III – Complication**		Genesis 12 - Malachi 4
425 - 5 B.C.	Yeshua in 4D	**"INTERMISSION"**	Yeshua in 4D	*(no biblical record)*
5 B.C. - A.D. 33		**ACT IV – Climax**		Matthew - John
	Ends of the Earth	**ACT V – Consummation**	Ends of the Earth	
A.D. 33 - 90		✦ "The Apostolic Age"		Acts - 3 John
A.D. 90 - *the present*		✦ "This Present Age"		*(no biblical record)*
		✦ "The Age to Come"		Revelation

OF THE ONE GOD

"THE FULNESS OF TIME"

The Five Acts of Yahweh's Grand Drama

The Complete Teaching Notes
Hands of Hur Biblical Literacy Series

H
HANDS
of HUR

The Fullness of Time – The Five Acts of Yahweh's Grand Drama

©2019 Fran Sciacca

ISBN: 978-0-9859676-2-8

Cover photo by Jill Sciacca

Table of Contents

PART II: "Yeshua in Four Dimensions" — Act IV of God's Grand Drama

APPENDICES

PART III: "To The Ends of the Earth" — Act V-Scenes 1 & 3 of God's Grand Drama

APPENDICES

GETTING THE BIG PICTURE

Acts I-III of Yahweh's Grand Drama

Hands of Hur Biblical Literacy Series
Module One

UNIT I - INTRODUCTION: "Correctly Framing the Big Picture"

 A. "Pre-Flight Check-Up" — Item #1: *"My Own 'Big Picture' On The Bible, And Its Purpose?"*

  1. The Bible—creating a "3-Sided Coin":

   a. It is a Textbook of Truth — its words must be protected at all costs.

    (1) My responsibility is to know it, study it, and defend it.

    (2) This is the "traditional" view of the Bible; a carry-over from the Enlightenment.[1]

    (3) Emphasis on rational, scientific, and "objective" study, apologetics, and sound exegesis.

   b. It is a sort of *"Disciplopedia"* — a guide on how to live the Christian life.

    (1) My responsibility is to know it, study it, and use it.

    (2) This is "modern" view of the Bible; a carryover from the Sixties' enshrinement of the self.

    (3) Emphasis on personal success and fulfillment as fruits of right behavior, even "success" in the ministry.

   c. It is a Missional Narrative — God's divine revelation of His purposes.

    (1) My responsibility is to know it, study it, and submit to its Storyline.

    (2) This is the Bible's view of itself; and that held by Jesus and Paul.

  2. A Missional Narrative: The Testimony of Jesus: (cf. *The Mission of God*, C. Wright)

  [speaking to two on the road] *"And beginning with Moses and all the Prophets, he interpreted to them in all the Scriptures the things concerning himself."* [speaking to disciples in the upper room] *"Then he said to them, 'These are my words that I spoke to you while I was still with you, that everything written about me in the Law of Moses and the Prophets and the Psalms must be fulfilled.' Then he opened their minds to understand the Scriptures, and said to them, 'Thus it is written, that the Christ should suffer and on the third day rise from the dead, and that repentance and forgiveness of sins should be proclaimed in his name to all nations, beginning from Jerusalem.'"*   **— Luke 24:27,44–45**

   a. Jesus points to himself and his role as Messiah as the focus of the entire Hebrew canon (i.e. OT).

   b. This is what is known as the "Christological focus" of the Bible.

   c. In addressing the larger group, Luke tells us Jesus *"opened their minds"* to understand the Old Testament:

    (1) Greek *(syniēmi, "understand")* means to *"weave together," "to comprehend."* In other words, to "get the big picture."

   d. Jesus then tells these people whose minds had been "opened," that some things were "written" (Gk. perfect tense):

    (1) This is clearly a reference to the entire OT canon; Jesus is not citing the Old Testament here!

    (2) the Messiah would suffer, die and rise from the dead

    (3) repentance and forgiveness of sins would be "preached" (Gk. *kēryssō*; to "herald as a public crier," to "publish") in his name to "all nations (Gk. ethnos)."

   e. In Jesus' explanation of the Old Testament canon, he makes an inseparable connection between its Messianic focus and its Missional focus. *We must do the same!*

  3. A Missional Narrative: The Testimony of Paul:

   a. The apostle Paul also made the same connection in his testimony before Festus while imprisoned in Caesarea:

  "To this day I have had the help that comes from God, and so I stand here testifying both to small and great, saying nothing but what the prophets and Moses said would come to pass: that the Christ must suffer and that, by being the first to rise from the dead, he would proclaim light both to our people and to the Gentiles (Gk. ethnos, 'the nations')."   **— Acts 26:22–23**

---

[1] The *Geneva Bible* in 1560 by William Whittingham was the first English translation to have verse numbers. Robert Stephenus had given verse numbers to the Greek and Latin New Testaments in 1551.

4. Getting the Story Straight: Five Acts Not Two "Testaments"

    a. **ACT I -** "Commencement" *(Genesis 1-2)*

    b. **ACT II -** "Conflict" *(Genesis 3-11)*

    c. **ACT III -** "Complication" *(Genesis 12 - Malachi)*

    d. **INTERMISSION -** "The Blank Page" *(400 "silent" years)*[1]

    e. **ACT IV -** "Climax" *(Gospels)*

    f. **ACT V -** "Conclusion":

       (1) *Scene 1 -* "The Apostolic Age" *(Acts - Jude)*

       (2) *Scene 2 -* "The Present Age" *(Spirit-led improvisation)*

       (3) *Scene 3 -* "Conclusion and Credits" *(Revelation)*

B. "Pre-Flight Check-Up" — Item #2: *"Who Am I, In Relation To The Bible?"*

> *"The Abrahamic covenant is the overarching plan that unites God's dealings with his people and bridges the Old and New Testaments. This was God's unconditional plan for his people that he would see through to the end."* **The Journey From Texts to Translation, p 32**

1. Understanding this facet of my identity is the most crucial in shaping my view of Scripture, and my place *in it*.

2. Paul's "radical" theology—which threatened his life—was a statement about the temporary nature of the Mosaic covenant, *not* the Abrahamic covenant.

3. Paul taught that all believers (including us!), like Isaac, are "children of the promise," *not* children of the flesh: *"Now you, brothers, like Isaac, are children of promise."* **Galatians 4:28**

4. He also taught that by faith, believers are "children of Abraham, the man of faith." (cf. Galatians 3:7-9)

5. For Paul, to be a Christian is to be Abraham's "offspring."[2]

> *"There is neither Jew nor Greek, there is neither slave nor free, there is no male and female, for you are all one in Christ Jesus. And if you are Christ's, then you are Abraham's offspring, heirs according to promise."*
> **— Galatians 3:28–29**

6. The Jews' *limitation* of "Abrahamic" to themselves, mistakenly equates election with ethnicity.

7. Christians' *neglect* of the "Abrahamic" nature of *their* identity yields an anemic identity that mistakenly equates election with adoption.

8. Confusing ethnicity or adoption with election has devastating consequences:[3]

    a. no compelling sense of purpose and mission, neither corporate *nor* individual.

    b. alienation or even disdain towards "the nations," the very people for whom the elect exist![4]

    c. Peter and Paul (in Galatians) are clearly addressing *Gentile* audiences in their sweeping inclusion of them into the covenant descendants of Abraham. (1 Peter 1:14,18; 2:12; 4:3-5; Galatians 4:8)

    d. Peter captures this *"Two Testament - One People - One Purpose"* identity succinctly in two verses (see the graphic on the next page):

> *"But you are a chosen race, a royal priesthood, a holy nation, a people for his own possession, that you may proclaim the excellencies of him who called you out of darkness into his marvelous light. Once you were not a people, but now you are God's people; once you had not received mercy, but now you have received mercy."*
> **— 1 Peter 2:9–10**

    e. If we inherit Abraham's "blessing," we also inherit Abraham's *mission*!

---

[1] ACT III ends with a prophetic "trailer" pointing the coming of one like the prophet Elijah who would turn the hearts of the fathers back to the children, and the hearts of children back to their fathers. The INTERMISSION ends with the arrival of this "one like Elijah"—John the Baptizer, who is "the voice of one crying in the wilderness, 'prepare the way of the LORD, as the prophet Isaiah said'."

[2] It is significant that Paul does not see himself as "becoming a Christian" in any of the sense we understand conversion. He also does not see himself merely as a "disciple of Jesus" as we do. For Paul, this was what it really meant to be a "Jew" in the fullest sense of the word.

[3] In addition to the specifics outlined in 8a - 8e, to see "election" and/or "adoption" in any other context is not only selfish, it is *outside* the biblical Storyline.

[4] "The nations" (Heb - *goyim*; Gk - *ethnos*). *Ethnos* appears 162 times in 16 New Testament books, 54 by Paul alone. It is a major theme of the New Testament.

C. Getting The "Big Picture" On The Bible Creates A Missional Hermeneutic

   1. The Bible presents to us a God with a mission (Is. 46:8-12; 55:9-11; Eph. 1:3-10).

   2. The Bible presents to us a humanity with a mission (Gen. 1:28; 2:15).

   3. The Bible presents to us a nation with a mission (Gen 18:17-19; Deut. 7:6; Is. 41:8-9; 42:1).

   4. The Bible presents to us a Messiah with a mission (John 3:16; 12:32; Mark 10:45; 2 Cor. 5:19).

   5. The Bible presents to us a Church with a mission (Matt. 25:31-40; 28:18-20; Acts 1:8; 20:24).

TWO "TESTAMENTS" – ONE PEOPLE – ONE IDENTITY

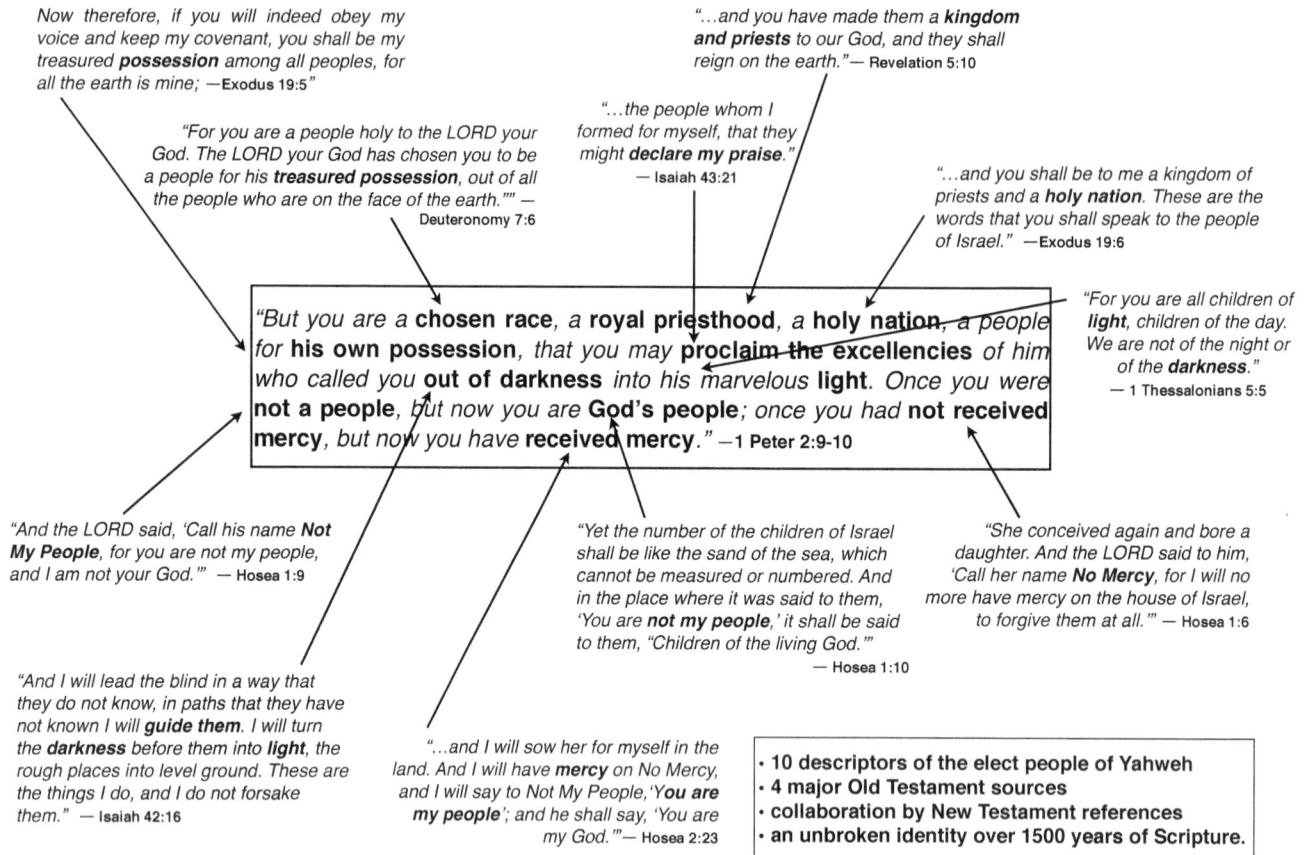

*Now therefore, if you will indeed obey my voice and keep my covenant, you shall be my treasured **possession** among all peoples, for all the earth is mine;* —Exodus 19:5"

*"...and you have made them a **kingdom and priests** to our God, and they shall reign on the earth."*— Revelation 5:10

*"For you are a people holy to the LORD your God. The LORD your God has chosen you to be a people for his **treasured possession**, out of all the people who are on the face of the earth."'* — Deuteronomy 7:6

*"...the people whom I formed for myself, that they might **declare my praise**."* — Isaiah 43:21

*"...and you shall be to me a kingdom of priests and a **holy nation**. These are the words that you shall speak to the people of Israel."* —Exodus 19:6

*"But you are a **chosen race**, a **royal priesthood**, a **holy nation**, a people for **his own possession**, that you may **proclaim the excellencies** of him who called you **out of darkness** into his marvelous **light**. Once you were **not a people**, but now you are **God's people**; once you had **not received mercy**, but now you have **received mercy**."* —1 Peter 2:9-10

*"For you are all children of **light**, children of the day. We are not of the night or of the **darkness**."* — 1 Thessalonians 5:5

*"And the LORD said, 'Call his name **Not My People**, for you are not my people, and I am not your God.'"* — Hosea 1:9

*"Yet the number of the children of Israel shall be like the sand of the sea, which cannot be measured or numbered. And in the place where it was said to them, 'You are **not my people**,' it shall be said to them, "Children of the living God."'* — Hosea 1:10

*"She conceived again and bore a daughter. And the LORD said to him, 'Call her name **No Mercy**, for I will no more have mercy on the house of Israel, to forgive them at all.'"* — Hosea 1:6

*"And I will lead the blind in a way that they do not know, in paths that they have not known I will **guide them**. I will turn the **darkness** before them into **light**, the rough places into level ground. These are the things I do, and I do not forsake them."* — Isaiah 42:16

*"...and I will sow her for myself in the land. And I will have **mercy** on No Mercy, and I will say to Not My People,'**You are my people**'; and he shall say, 'You are my God.'"*— Hosea 2:23

- 10 descriptors of the elect people of Yahweh
- 4 major Old Testament sources
- collaboration by New Testament references
- an unbroken identity over 1500 years of Scripture.

D. Getting The "Big Picture" On The Bible Also Means Getting The "Big Picture" On Ourselves

   1. The Bible is *not* primarily a textbook or a handbook (even though it *is* both of these).

   2. It is a Story Book; *the* Story Book:

"The Bible is nevertheless actually the story. This is the way it is. This is the grand narrative that constitutes truth for all [over against postmodernism's claims]. And within this story, as narrated or anticipated by the Bible, there is at work the God whose mission is evident from creation to the new creation." — **Christopher Wright**, *The Mission of God*, **p. 47**

"In short, a missional hermeneutic [interpretation] proceeds from the assumption that the whole Bible renders to us a story of God's mission through God's people in their engagement with God's world for the sake of the whole of God's creation." — **Wright, p. 51**

   3. The authority of the Bible is the authority of narrative (*indicative*), not of command (*imperative*):

     a. the majority of the biblical text is *not* commands.

b. This is illustrated in the lives of those who surrendered themselves to the Storyline:

(Mary the mother of Jesus) *"And Mary said, 'Behold, I am the servant of the Lord; let it be to me according to your word.'"*   **– Luke 1:38**

(Yeshua the Son of Yahweh) *"Father, if you are willing, remove this cup from me. Nevertheless, not my will, but yours, be done."*   **– Luke 22:42**

(Joseph the son of Jacob) *But Joseph said to them, "Do not fear, for am I in the place of God? As for you, you meant evil against me, but God meant it for good, to bring it about that many people should be kept alive, as they are today."*   **– Genesis 50:19–20**

(Esther the niece of Mordecai) *"Then I will go to the king, though it is against the law, and if I perish, I perish."*   **– Esther 4:16**

(Paul the apostle) *"But I do not account my life of any value nor as precious to myself, if only I may finish my course and the ministry that I received from the Lord Jesus, to testify to the gospel of the grace of God."*   **– Acts 20:24**

c. Discipleship (i.e., "Lordship") must be understood in terms of submission to the Story, *not* obedience to a set of rules.

"Not everyone who says to me, 'Lord, Lord,' will enter the kingdom of heaven, but the one who does the will of my Father who is in heaven."   **– Matthew 7:21**

d. The Bible contains a veritable litany of those whose purpose came from their place in The Story, such as Peter and John:

"Peter turned and saw the disciple whom Jesus loved following them, the one who also had leaned back against him during the supper and had said, 'Lord, who is it that is going to betray you?' When Peter saw him, he said to Jesus, 'Lord, what about this man?' Jesus said to him, 'If it is my will that he remain until I come, what is that to you? You follow me!'"   **– John 21:20–22**

e. Unfortunately, it also contains a long list of those who rejected The Story, and sought to "Choose Their Own Adventure," such as Esau:

"Once when Jacob was cooking stew, Esau came in from the field, and he was exhausted. And Esau said to Jacob, 'Let me eat some of that red stew, for I am exhausted!' (Therefore his name was called Edom.) Jacob said, 'Sell me your birthright now.' Esau said, 'I am about to die; of what use is a birthright to me?' Jacob said, 'Swear to me now.' So he swore to him and sold his birthright to Jacob. Then Jacob gave Esau bread and lentil stew, and he ate and drank and rose and went his way. Thus Esau despised his birthright...See that no one is sexually immoral, or is godless like Esau, who for a single meal sold his inheritance rights as the oldest son."
– Genesis 25:29–34 and Hebrews 12:16, NIV

E. The Story Did *Not* Get "Longer" With the New Testament…Only *Clearer*!

1. The "Story" was the legacy every Jew left to his offspring[1]:

a. it was their source of identity (e.g. Isaiah 49:9-10)

b. it was their source of worship (e.g. Pss. 105, 106)

c. it was their source of purpose (e.g. Jeremiah 29:11-13)

d. Yeshua demonstrated familiarity with Genesis 4 - 2 Chronicles 24:21 (e.g. Luke 11:51)[2]

e. NOTE: they only had the first *three* "Acts" and a host of "trailers"!!

2. For those of us with Acts IV and V, we should be even more passionate about knowing, living, and telling this Story!

---

[1] For example, Psalm 105 rehearses their national history from Abraham (vv 6-7) through Joshua (v 44); In other words, Genesis through Joshua. Psalm 106 references the time from the exodus event through the time of the judges. There are at least 13 clear references in the Psalms to the wilderness wanderings recorded in the book of Numbers. There are 34 references to Jacob in 27 different psalms. Moses is mentioned by name 8 times (77:20; 90:1; 99:6; 103:7; 105:26; 106:16, 23, 32). Aaron is mentioned 9 times (77:20; 99:6; 105:26; 106:16; 115:10, 12; 118:3; 133:2). There are 5 references to Joseph (77:15; 78:67; 80:1; 81:5; 105:17).

[2] This is evidenced in the sweep of his statement about the ancestral tendency to murder prophets in his blistering address to the religious leaders, *"...from the blood of righteous Abel to the blood of Zechariah..."* Considering that the books of Chronicles were likely compiled by Ezra, it would make Jesus' statement inclusive of the entire Old Testament "story."

    a.   The apostle Paul understood that because there was only *one* Story, there was also only *one* people of God:[1]

> *Know then that it is those of faith who are the sons of Abraham. And the Scripture, foreseeing that God would justify the Gentiles by faith, preached the gospel beforehand to Abraham, saying, "In you shall all the nations be blessed." So then, those who are of faith are blessed along with Abraham, the man of faith....for in Christ Jesus you are all sons of God, through faith. For as many of you as were baptized into Christ have put on Christ. There is neither Jew nor Greek, there is neither slave nor free, there is no male and female, for you are all one in Christ Jesus. And if you are Christ's, then you are Abraham's offspring, heirs according to promise.*   – **Galatians 3:7–9, 26–29**

    b.   The apostle Paul found himself on his face when he pondered the enormity and majesty of The Story:

> *Now to him who is able to strengthen you according to my gospel and the preaching of Jesus Christ, according to the revelation of the mystery that was kept secret for long ages but has now been disclosed and through the prophetic writings has been made known to all nations, according to the command of the eternal God, to bring about the obedience of faith— to the only wise God be glory forevermore through Jesus Christ! Amen.*   – **Romans 16:25–27**

F.   Three Primary Goals of This Module:

1.   To help us appreciate both the majesty of Yahweh, *and* the mystery of His Story.

2.   To help us attach ourselves to Yahweh the God of Abraham, Isaac and Jacob, who also happens to be the Father of Jesus and the God of all Christians.

3.   To help us paint a permanent "big picture" of Acts I-III of this missional narrative, in order to better understand our place in it, and it's place in the larger Story (i.e. ACTS I-V).

UNIT 2 - SCRIPTURE: Jews, Catholics, and Protestants – "All in the Family"

A.   What we Have in Common:

1.   Catholics, and Protestants both accept all the books of the Jewish Scriptures.

2.   There are no books of the Bible in the Jewish Scriptures that are *not* in those of Christians.

B.   Where We Differ:

1.   The *arrangement* of the Jewish Bible is different from the Christian Bible.

    a.   The 39 books of the Christian Old Testament comprise 24 "books" in the Jewish Bible.

    b.   The Jewish Bible consists of three major divisions, compared to four in the Christian Old Testament.

    c.   The Jewish Bible combines books that are separate in the Christian Old Testament.

2.   The *content* of the Catholic Old Testament is larger and different from that in the Protestant Bible.

    a.   The Catholic OT contains seven additional *books* *(see chart on page 8)*.

    b.   The Catholic OT also contains four other "books" that are actually *additions* to Esther and Daniel.[2]

    c.   Protestants consider these additions to be non-canonical; (hence, they are called the "Apocrypha").

    d.   Catholics consider them "deuterocanonical," and on equal par with the Hebrew canon.

    e.   This extra material *was* in the Greek Septuagint, but never recognized by Jews.[3]

C.   The Bible: Old and New Testaments — Old and New Understandings of the One Story

1.   See the illustrations on the next two pages.

---

[1] The idea of a single "people of God" dismantles forever any false grounds for "tribalism" among believers of any age. There is a single narrative whose storyline is already set. No one can legitimately inject the notion of a subplot.

[2] "Additions to Esther" (Esther 10:4-16:24), the "Songs of the Three Young Men" aka "Prayer of Azariah" (Dan 3:24-90), "Susanna" (Dan 13), and "Bel and the Dragon" (Dan 14).

[3] The larger (i.e. Catholic) canon is sometimes known as the "Alexandrian Canon," because the Septuagint was prepared there, and some allege that the Apocrypha was part of the canon. The shorter canon accepted by Jews and Christians is often known as the "Palestinian Canon," because it was allegedly established by the Jews. The whole issue of the place of the Apocrypha in the Christian canon came to a head during the Reformation because three of the key doctrines under dispute: prayers for the dead, purgatory, and indulgences stood or fell together. (There is a vague reference to praying for the dead in 2 Maccabees 12:44-45).

THE TANAKH

24 books

Torah - 5 books

Nevi'im - 8 books

Ketuvim - 11 books

· Genesis
· Exodus
· Leviticus
· Numbers
· Deuteronomy

First Prophets

· Joshua
· Judges
· Samuel (1 & 2)
· Kings (1 & 2)

Last Prophets

· Isaiah
· Jeremiah
· Ezekiel
· Trei Asar (minor prophets)

· Psalms
· Proverbs
· Job
· Song of Solomon
· Ruth
· Lamentations
· Ecclesiastes
· Esther
· Daniel
· Ezra-Nehemiah
· Chronicles (1 & 2)

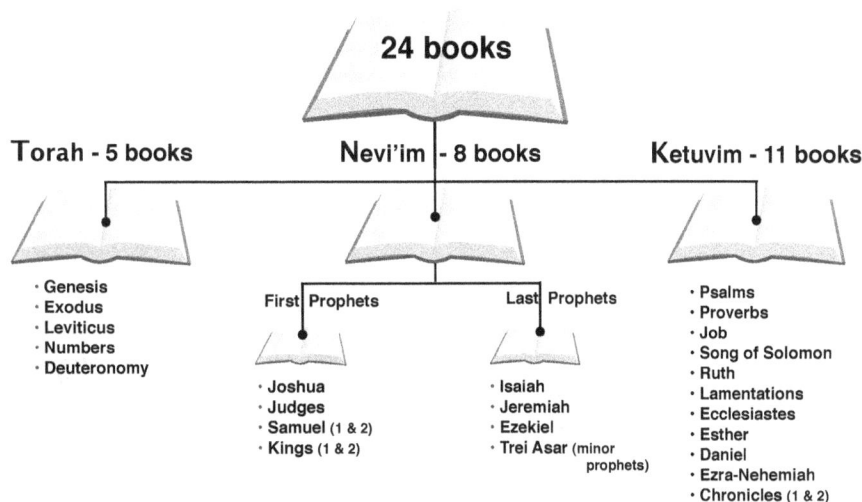

THE PROTESTANT OLD TESTAMENT

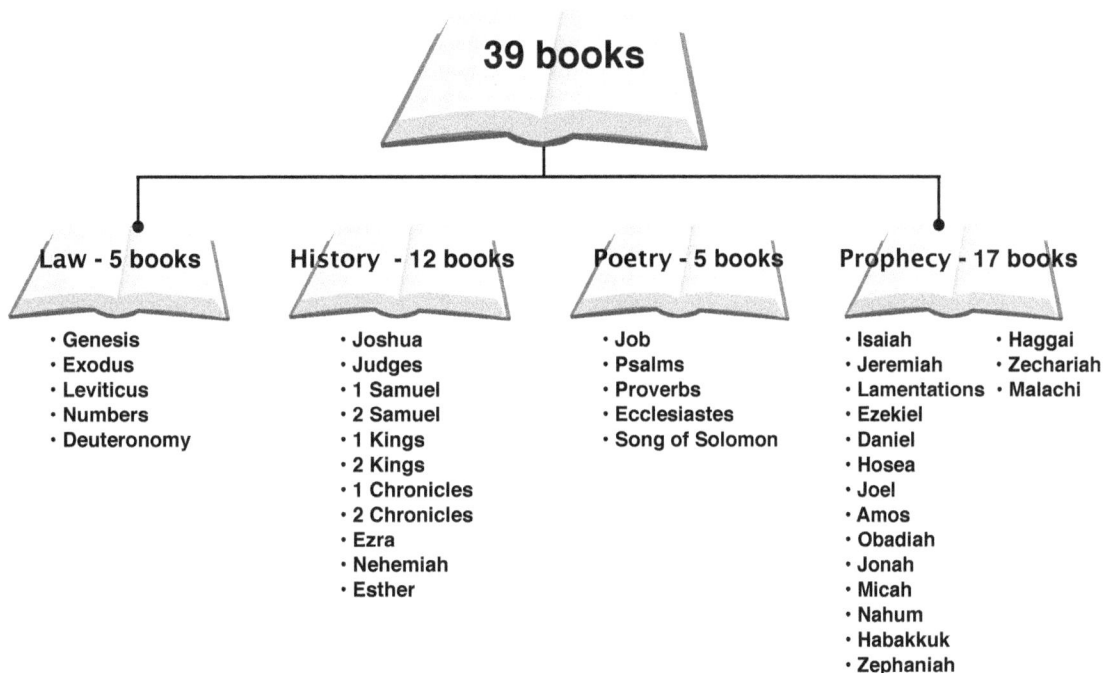

39 books

Law - 5 books

History - 12 books

Poetry - 5 books

Prophecy - 17 books

· Genesis
· Exodus
· Leviticus
· Numbers
· Deuteronomy

· Joshua
· Judges
· 1 Samuel
· 2 Samuel
· 1 Kings
· 2 Kings
· 1 Chronicles
· 2 Chronicles
· Ezra
· Nehemiah
· Esther

· Job
· Psalms
· Proverbs
· Ecclesiastes
· Song of Solomon

· Isaiah
· Jeremiah
· Lamentations
· Ezekiel
· Daniel
· Hosea
· Joel
· Amos
· Obadiah
· Jonah
· Micah
· Nahum
· Habakkuk
· Zephaniah

· Haggai
· Zechariah
· Malachi

The Catholic Old Testament

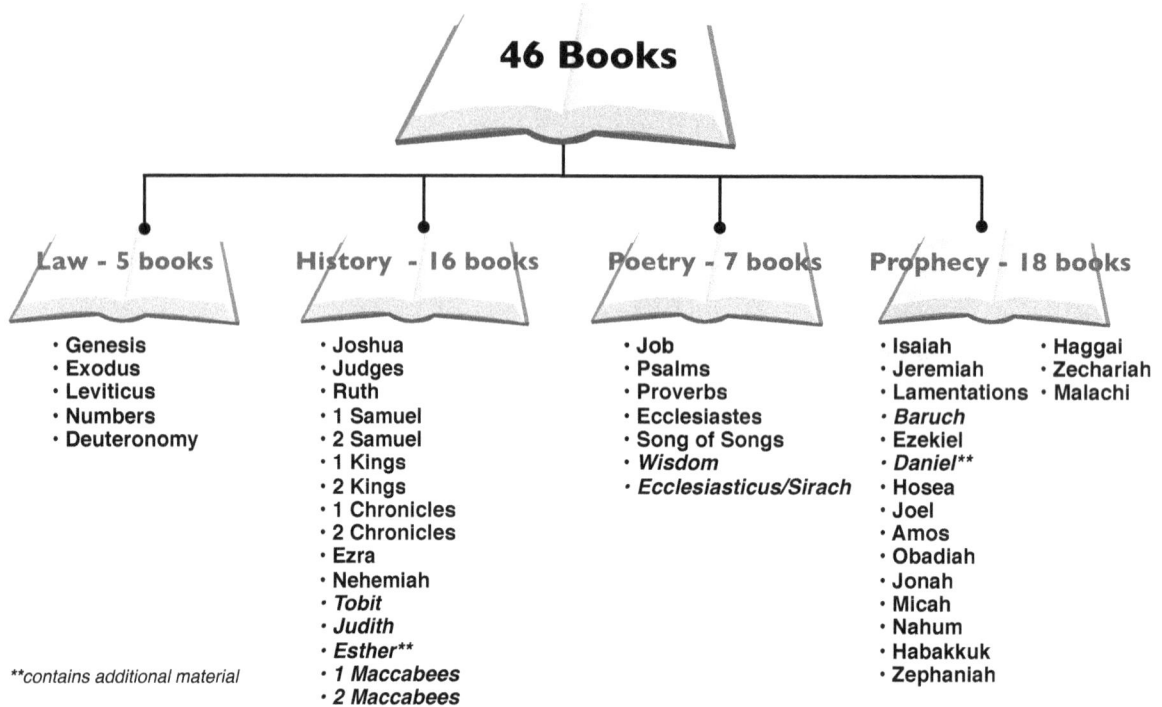

46 Books

Law - 5 books	History - 16 books	Poetry - 7 books	Prophecy - 18 books	
• Genesis	• Joshua	• Job	• Isaiah	• Haggai
• Exodus	• Judges	• Psalms	• Jeremiah	• Zechariah
• Leviticus	• Ruth	• Proverbs	• Lamentations	• Malachi
• Numbers	• 1 Samuel	• Ecclesiastes	• *Baruch*	
• Deuteronomy	• 2 Samuel	• Song of Songs	• Ezekiel	
	• 1 Kings	• *Wisdom*	• *Daniel***	
	• 2 Kings	• *Ecclesiasticus/Sirach*	• Hosea	
	• 1 Chronicles		• Joel	
	• 2 Chronicles		• Amos	
	• Ezra		• Obadiah	
	• Nehemiah		• Jonah	
	• *Tobit*		• Micah	
	• *Judith*		• Nahum	
	• *Esther***		• Habakkuk	
**contains additional material	• *1 Maccabees*		• Zephaniah	
	• *2 Maccabees*			

D. The "Twelve Word Tanakh"

   1. The Story of God in the Old Testament can be summarized using 12 words:

Twelve Words — One Story

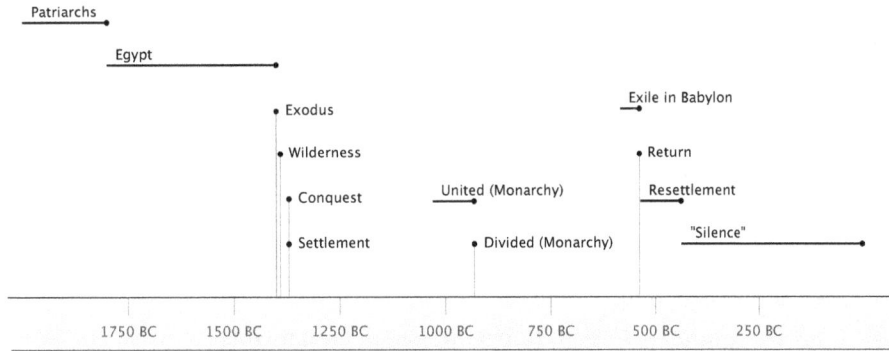

1750 BC	1500 BC	1250 BC

Patriarchs

Egypt

• Exodus

• Wilderness

Exile in Babylon

• Conquest

United (Monarchy)

• Return

Resettlement

• Settlement

• Divided (Monarchy)

"Silence"

1750 BC   1500 BC   1250 BC   1000 BC   750 BC   500 BC   250 BC

The Books of the "Twelve Words":

Patriarchs:	Conquest:	Exile:
Egypt:	Settlement:	Return:
Exodus:	United (monarchy):	Resettlement:
Wilderness:	Divided (monarchy):	"Silence":

Ancient And Modern Geographical Boundaries of the Biblical World

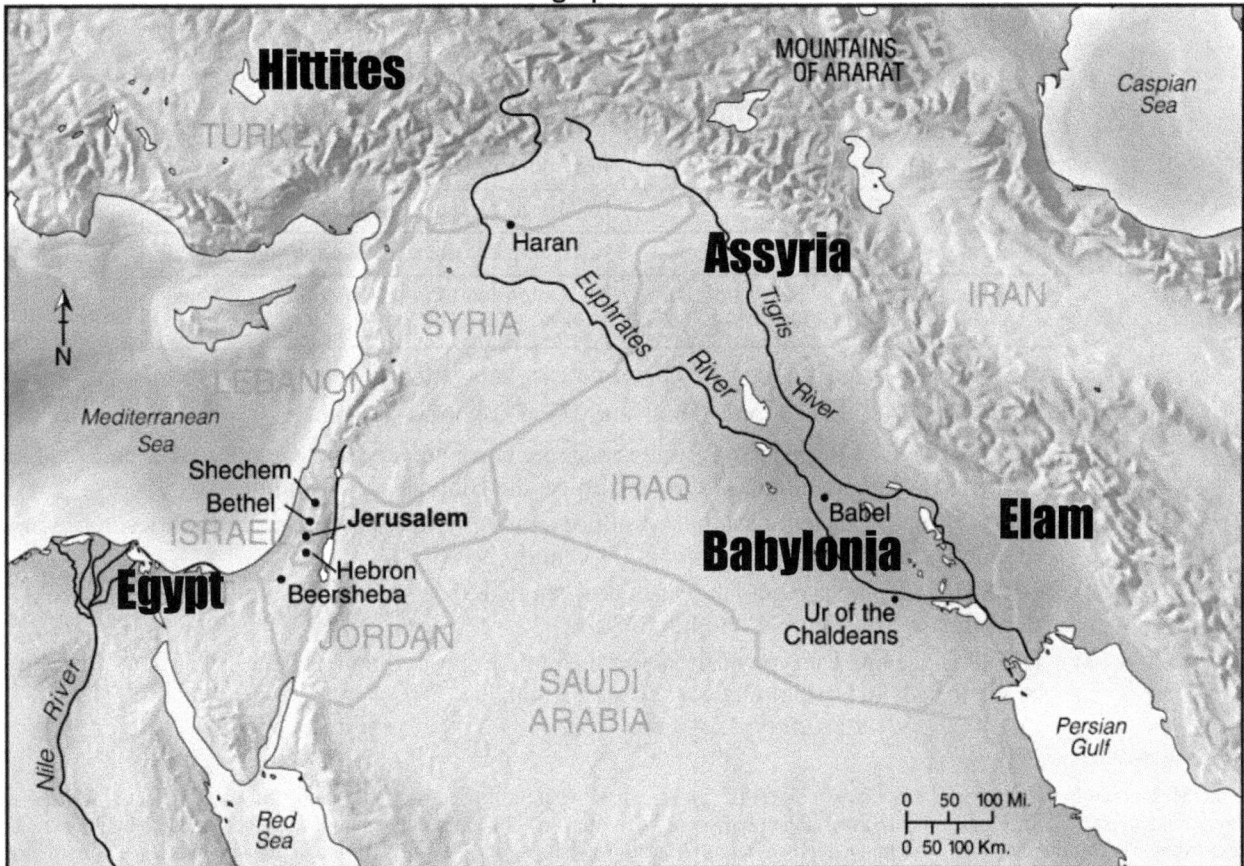

Modern names and boundaries are shown in gray.

This map adapted from *The Tyndale Handbook of Charts.*

UNIT 3 - GEOGRAPHY, GENRE, AND GENESIS

A. Geography: *Where* It All "Went Down"

  1. The "Ancient Near East"

    a. Four Main Regions

      (1) *Mesopotamia* ("between the rivers").[1]

      (2) *Syria* -Palestine

      (3) *Egypt* - the region of the Nile

      (4) *Anatolia* - the realm of the Hittites (Empire of Hatti)

    b. The Modern Near East — biblical lands today.

      (1) *Mesopotamia* = Iraq.

      (2) *Biblical Canaan* = Jordan, Lebanon, Israel, Golan Heights, West Bank.

      (3) *Hatti (Hittites)* = Turkey.

  2. The main events in the entire biblical "big picture" occur in a piece of property the size of the eastern half of the United States.

  3. The "centerpiece" of human history occupies a piece of real estate about twice the size of Rhode Island!
(aka "Palestine")

B. "Taking The Bible Literally"

  1. "Taking the Bible literally" means *literally* taking it the way it was originally *intended* to be "taken"!

  2. Some scholars divide the Old Testament into two types of literature: stories and poems:

"The Old Testament contains very little technical material. For the most part, its contents may be described under two rubrics: stories and poems...We encounter nothing quite like our modern history or scientific textbooks, and certainly nothing approaching a theological essay or confession."

           - Tremper Longman, *Introduction to the Old Testament*, page 26

"STORIES"		"POEMS"	
a.	long, complete sentences	a.	phrases and fragments
b.	built around paragraphs	b.	built on stanzas and cola
c.	little use of metaphor and imagery	c.	frequent use of metaphor and imagery
d.	more attention to *what* is said than *how* it is said	d.	attention to *how* something is said as well as *what* is said.

  3. Perspective: What we "bring" to the Bible determines what we take away.

    a. Four types of "lenses" I need to read and study God's Word responsibly:

      (1) **COHERENCE**: Because the Bible is a single narrative, my interpretation of what I read must always be weighed in light of the One Story; the Bible is *not* an anthology.

      (2) **HISTORY**: the ancient past that was once a modern present (geography, politics, religion, economics, etc.); The Bible is *not* a 21st century book![2]

      (3) **GRAMMAR**: the ancient languages now studied, then spoken (Hebrew, Aramaic, Greek); English is *not* the Bible's "mother tongue."

      (4) **GENRE**: the ancient type of literature the author chose; then familiar and obvious, now must be identified; all Scripture is *not* "created equal."

        • *narrative*

---

[1] Ur in the Mesopotamia of Abraham's day (known as Ur III) was a world where a prosperous and "high" culture flourished in many places. This was evidenced by a developed international trade (and spying!) framework, the existence of law codes that predate Hammurabi, 2-story homes, extensive commercial record keeping, highways, police stations, hotels, and schools. Thinking of Abraham as a sort of "country bumpkin" is contrary to the facts.

[2] The rough historical periods that the first five books of the Bible contain are: Early Bronze IV (2300-2000 BC; Ur III), Middle Bronze I-II (2000-1500 BC; patriarchs and bondage in Egypt), Late Bronze I-II (1500-1200 BC; exodus event thru the time of Judges), and the Iron Age (1200-586 BC; the rise and fall of the Jewish monarchy).

- *poetry*
- *genealogy*
- *chronicle*
- *law code*
- *proverb*
- *song*
- *epic*

C. Tanakh And Torah: The Books Of Law

1. Jesus acknowledged and recognized the Jewish 3-fold division of the Old Testament:

   Then he said to them, "These are my words that I spoke to you while I was still with you, that everything written about me in the Law of Moses and the Prophets and the Psalms must be fulfilled." Then he opened their minds to understand the Scriptures. —Luke 24:44-45

2. The Torah: Five Books of Law[1]

   a. Genesis
   b. Exodus
   c. Leviticus
   d. Numbers
   e. Deuteronomy

3. Genesis — The First "Fifth" of Moses

   a. *Approaching Genesis*: First Things First

   (1) I need to remind myself that Genesis' first hearers were the Jews who had come out of Egypt.[2]

   (2) Biblical *chronology* begins with Genesis, but biblical *historiography* began with Moses.

   (3) In truth, we should read Exodus *before* we read Genesis.

   (4) The primary purpose of this book was to educate an "illiterate" people about the one true God and their relationship to Him and His purposes. *(i.e., the Story and their place in it.)*

   (5) They were about to enter a land "famous" for its syncretism and polytheism (their continual nemesis!)

4. The "Big Picture" of Genesis

The Nature of God	The Nature of Man	The Nature of Nature
• monotheistic	• created	• created - not divine
• transcendent	• unique (Imago Dei)	• fallen - not neutral
• holy	• fallen	• serves God and man
• personal		
• missional		

5. Genesis: A Book of "Beginnings"

   a. the human race (1:26-27; 5:2)

   b. gender (1:26-27; 5:2)

   c. monogamous marriage (2:24-25; cf. Matt. 19:3-8)

   d. personal evil (6:5; 8:21)

   e. redemption (3:15)

   f. missions (ch. 12 & 17)

   g. a covenant people (ch. 17)

---

[1] In the Hebrew Bible, the names of the books are derived from the first word(s) of the book itself. For example, Genesis is *Bereishith* - "in the beginning," Exodus is *Shemoth* - "the names," Leviticus is *Vayikra* - "He called," Numbers is *Bamidbar* - "in the wilderness," and Deuteronomy is *Devarim* - "the words."

[2] The first eleven chapters of Genesis teach the first hearers of this story (i.e. the recently freed Jews) that their origins were in Mesopotamia, *not* in Egypt. This would have been their first "clue" that God had a plan in mind of which they were to play a key role. They had already "existed" in a sense, in the mind of Yahweh, even before they had a distinct identity as a people.

6. Genesis and the Christian

    a. It is from Genesis that we derive our fullest understanding of the beauty of shalom, the expansiveness of sin, and the extent of redemption.

    b. It is from Genesis that we derive our individual and corporate sense identity, purpose, and mission.

    c. It is from Genesis that we build our understanding of the "people of God" (i.e., the Church).

Snapshot of the Book of Genesis

The Human Race	*The Jewish "Race"*
Four Key Events	**Four Key People**
• creation — chapters 1-2	• Abraham — chapters 12-25
• the "fall" — chapters 3-5	• Isaac — chapters 25-26
• the flood — chapters 5-9	• Jacob — chapters 27-36
• the "Tower" — chapters 10-11	• Joseph — chapters 37-50*
	*Joseph is born in 30:24

KEY CHAPTER: *3 - the "fall" of humanity; 12 - the "call of Abram*

KEY WORD: *"beginnings"*

BASIC GEOGRAPHY: *Eden to Egypt*

BOOK SUMMARY: *Who God and humanity are, and how God plans to bless all the nations through one man, Abraham.*

UNIT 4: "KEEPING UP WITH THE JOBSES"

A. Ancient Poetry & Modern Minds

1. Hebrew poetry's most distinguishing difference from English poetry is that it "balances" ideas rather than rhyming words.

2. It's most popular tool for balancing ideas involves pairs of statements. It is called "parallelism."

3. Three types of parallelism dominate biblical poetry:[1]

    a. synthetic– the second line "completes" the idea begun in the first line.

    b. synonymous– the second line repeats the idea of the first line, using different words.

    c. antithetical– the idea in the second line stands in contrast to the idea in the first line.

Examples of Parallelism in Our Bibles:

Type of Parallelism	Example in Scripture
antithetical	*My flesh and my heart may fail, but God is the strength of my heart and my portion forever.* **—Psalm 73:26**

---

[1] This is a rather gross oversimplification of how elaborate and highly nuanced parallelism is in Hebrew poetry. For example, consider Isaiah 1:3, *"The ox knows its owner and the donkey its master's crib, but Israel does not know, my people do not understand."* The first and second stanzas are both synonymous parallelism, but taken as a whole, the verse is an example of *antithetical* parallelism.

Type of Parallelism	Example in Scripture
synthetic	*Cast your bread upon the waters, for you will find it after many days.* **—Ecclesiastes 11:1**
synthetic	*And the women sang to one another as they celebrated, "Saul has struck down his thousands, and David his ten thousands."* **—1 Samuel 18:7**
synonymous	*A poor man who oppresses the poor is a beating rain that leaves no food.* **—Proverbs 28:3**
antithetical	*An unjust man is an abomination to the righteous, but one whose way is straight is an abomination to the wicked.* **—Proverbs 29:27**
synonymous	*A garden locked is my sister, my bride, a spring locked, a fountain sealed.* **—Song of Solomon 4:12**
vs 3 - synonymous vs 4 - synthetic	*Who shall ascend the hill of the LORD? And who shall stand in his holy place? He who has clean hands and a pure heart, who does not lift up his soul to what is false and does not swear deceitfully.* **—Psalm 24:3-4**
synonymous	*Your steadfast love, O LORD, extends to the heavens, your faithfulness to the clouds.* **—Psalm 36:5**
synonymous	*…who does great things beyond searching out, and marvelous things beyond number.* **—Job 9:10**

4. Hebrew poetry is found in *every* type of Old Testament literature:

    a. Books of Law:

        Your right hand, O LORD, glorious in power, your right hand, O LORD, shatters the enemy.

        Exodus 15:6

    b. Books of History:

        God is not man, that he should lie, or a son of man, that he should change his mind. Has he said, and will he not do it? Or has he spoken, and will he not fulfill it?   **Numbers 23:19**

    c. Books of Prophecy:

        O LORD, how long shall I cry for help, and you will not hear? Or cry to you "Violence!" and you will not save?   **Habakkuk 1:2**

        For my thoughts are not your thoughts, neither are your ways my ways, declares the LORD.   **Isaiah 55:8**

    d. Only seven books in our Old Testament have little or no poetry sections in them (Leviticus, Ruth, Ezra, Nehemiah, Esther, Haggai and Malachi). That means that 82% of our OT contains Hebrew poetry.

5. Because Old Testament poetry is built around balancing ideas rather than rhyming words, it translates into prose in other languages with very little loss of meaning.

B. Hebrew Poetry and the Ancient World

    1. One type of ancient literature common to all peoples in the Ancient Near East (ANE) is known as "wisdom literature." It had several key characteristics:

        a. timeless and boundless in appeal and application.[1]

        b. written in experiential language (living life)

        c. consisted of general principles rather than specific precepts

    2. Two main types of wisdom literature:

        a. short, insightful sayings about life in general (E.g. our book of Proverbs)

        b. lengthy epics or dialogues grappling with life's difficult issues (E.g. Job and Ecclesiastes)

    3. For the Hebrew mind, "wisdom was for the journey of a life directed by God." He was its source.

    4. Job is a perfect example of the depth and universal appeal of ancient "wisdom literature":

---

[1] Consider, for example, when you read and seek to apply the life principles contained in our canonical book of Proverbs, you are engaging wisdom literature that is over 3,000 years old, yet still immensely relevant!

"Many reject Jesus, but no one rejects Job. Rather, the world respects Job, and not with the grudging respect accorded Christ, but with a deep affinity untinged by reserve or fear."
—Mike Mason , *The Gospel According to Job*

C. The Book of Job — Anonymous and Timeless

1. We do not know for sure who wrote this book, or when.

2. It was either written to appear old, or it records a story as ancient as Abraham:

   a. Job lived 140 years after his season of suffering. (cf. Job 42:16 and Gen. 25:7-8)

   b. Job's wealth was measured *primarily* in terms of livestock.[1] (cf. Job 1:3 and Gen. 13:5-7; 26:12-13)

   c. Job acts as a family "priest," offering sacrifices like Abraham and Jacob. (cf. Job 1:5 and Gen. 22:13; 31:54; 46:1)

   d. No references to Israel, Egypt, the Law, the Tabernacle or the Temple.

   e. Chaldeans who murder his children are marauding nomads, not settled in cities.

   f. Job uses Abraham's name, "Almighty" (*Shadday*) for God 31x in this book. It only occurs 17x in the rest of the Old Testament. (cf. Job 6:4 and Gen. 17:1; 35:11)

D. The Book of Job — A Literary Masterpiece

1. It is an epic ANE piece of wisdom poetry "framed" in narrative (ch 1-2 and 42:7-15); There are 220 references to conversation in this book!

2. It contains a "prequel" for the reader, unique in ANE literature.

3. It's arrangement is creative, intentional and unified:

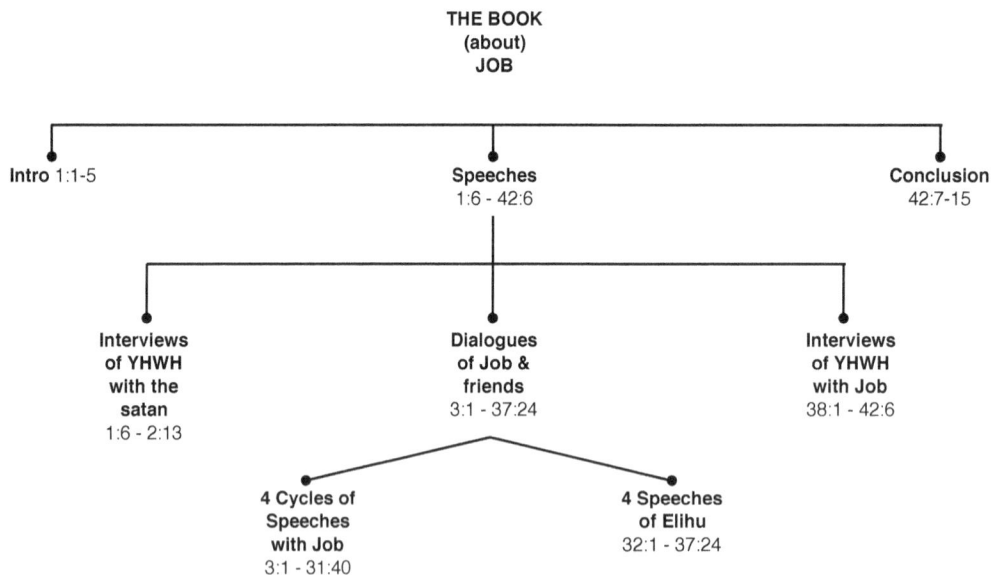

**THE BOOK
(about)
JOB**

Intro 1:1-5	Speeches 1:6 - 42:6	Conclusion 42:7-15

Interviews of YHWH with the satan 1:6 - 2:13	Dialogues of Job & friends 3:1 - 37:24	Interviews of YHWH with Job 38:1 - 42:6

4 Cycles of Speeches with Job 3:1 - 31:40	4 Speeches of Elihu 32:1 - 37:24

Adapted from: "Job" in the *Tyndale Old Testament Commentary Series*, pg. 20

E. "Going Backstage" — Keys to the Book of Job

1. This is a "courtroom" drama with arguments and counter-arguments.

   a. a *criminal* case from the perspective of Job's friends (I.e., guilt/innocence)

   b. a *civil* case from the perspective of Job (I.e., wrongful action)

   c. a *divine* case from the perspective of the reader (I.e., *Shadday* vs. the Satan)

2. Understanding exactly who is "on trial" is crucial to this book.

   a. It is not Job!

---

[1] Although Abraham *did* have precious metals as well (cf. Genesis 13:2).

(1) he is declared "blameless," "upright" "God-fearing" and "evil-shunning" twice by God in the opening scene.

(2) God describes him four times as "my servant" in the closing scene.

(3) for the reader, Job is "vindicated" before the story even opens.

    b. God is on trial and Job is merely circumstantial "evidence" in the case.

(1) "Satan" is literally "the satan" in Hebrew (14x; "the accuser," "the adversary" "the Prosecution")

(2) God is the one who needs to be "vindicated" in this drama

F. Getting Inside the Audience's Mind — *The "Payback Principle"*

    1. **Illustrated:** *"Remember: who that was innocent ever perished? Or where were the upright cut off? As I have seen, those who plow iniquity and sow trouble reap the same."* **[Eliphaz the Temanite], Job 4:7-8**

    2. Summarized: *"The wicked suffer and the righteous prosper...proportionally."*

    3. Not a real "issue" in ANE cultures, because their gods were capricious, unjust, and impersonal.

    4. A serious problem for *Jews* because of their theology of God's sovereignty and justice.

    5. In the Book of Job, *everyone* subscribes to the "Payback Principle":

        a. **JOB** - it's the root of his frustration with God and the basis of his defense.

        b. **FRIENDS** - they are demanding that Job "repent" of his hidden sin.

        c. **THE SATAN** - if God "blesses" the righteous with prosperity, then it's their greed, not their integrity that makes them seek His blessing. They are therefore *unrighteous*!

           (1) If Job "confesses" sins he didn't commit, to get his "blessings" back, Satan's point is proved.

           (2) if Job curses God to His face, then God's claim is false.

    6. Job exonerates God by wanting exoneration for himself rather than restitution:

        a. he is righteous for righteousness' sake, not for the "perks"

        b. the satan is silenced and the "sons of God" are enlightened:

"To me, though I am the very least of all the saints, this grace was given, to preach to the Gentiles the unsearchable riches of Christ, and to bring to light for everyone what is the plan of the mystery hidden for ages in God who created all things, so that through the church the manifold wisdom of God might now be made known to the rulers and authorities in the heavenly places." **- Ephesians 3:8-10**

    7. This book dismantles the *Payback Principle* forever as an "axiom" (something self-evident):

        a. the righteous sometimes suffer and the wicked sometimes prosper.[1]

        b. a person's temporal circumstances do not validate their spiritual condition or result from it.

G. Job and the Twenty-First Century

    1. From Job's friends we learn:

        a. God is bigger and different from even our best theology.

        b. He is not axiomatic and rejects being so portrayed.[2]

        c. The proper initial response to the suffering of others is silence, not speech.

        d. The "Payback Principle" is not mine to claim or proclaim, either for blessing or for justice.

    2. From Job we learn:

        a. The correct question in the face of suffering is *not* "Why...?" but "Whether...?"

           (1) is there evidence that God is wise?

           (2) is there evidence that God is competent?

---

[1] This demands an expansive understanding of the extent of sin's effects on one hand, and a profound trust in the justice of God on the other hand.

[2] This book teaches us, among other things, how the absence of humility in our theology produces a dogmatism in which being "right" becomes more valuable than people.

(3) is there evidence that God is benevolent?

    b. In facing suffering, for the Christian, the central issue is not God's justice, but His wisdom.[1]

3. The "bottom line" for this book is how it all turned out; but that is found in 42:1-6 *not* in 42:7-17!!

    a. Job repented of his faulty view of God, *not* any moral lapse on his part.

UNIT 5 - "GETTING ISRAEL OUT OF EGYPT"

A. EXODUS: Truth or Fiction?

1. The Challenge — Lack of *External* Evidence

    a. There is no mention of the exodus in Egyptian literature.

    b. There is no clear record of the Jews being in Egypt in ancient Egyptian literature.[2]

    c. No record of Moses in Egyptian literature.

    d. There is no clear archeological evidence of the exodus.

2. The Response — A Superabundance of *Internal* Evidence

    a. This is *not* a book about the Israelites. It is a book about the God of Israel. (How else do we explain the absence of the name of the current Pharaoh, but in inclusion of two Hebrew midwives?! - Ex. 1:15)

    b. The name of Moses appears 852 times in our Bibles; more than Abraham and Jacob combined! He is a central figure in the history of God's people and God's plan of redemption.[3]

3. Egypt is mentioned 600 times in our Old Testaments, compared to 671 for Jerusalem. It plays an enormous role in the history of God's people; always as a place from which they came and should not return.[4]

    a. There is an amazing number of references to Egyptian places names, vegetation, etc., and a veritable absence of references to the same in Palestine.[5]

4. The actual "exodus event" is mentioned clearly in 27 books of the Bible written by at least 19 different authors over a 1500 year period! *(see the chart below)*:

Book & Reference	Book & Reference
Exodus 12:51	Isaiah 10:26
Leviticus 11:45	Jeremiah 2:6
Numbers 9:1	Ezekiel 20:36
Deuteronomy 8:11-16	Daniel 9:15
Joshua 24:17	Hosea 11:1
Judges 2:12	Amos 2:10; 3:1
1 Samuel 8:8	Micah 6:4
2 Samuel 7:23	Haggai 2:5
1 Kings 9:9	*Matthew 2:15*

---

[1] This is true because at the end of the day, "faith" is always reduced to *trust.* Either I do or I don't.

[2] There *are* records of the "Habiru" or "Abiru" that appear in Egyptian writings, but scholars are not able to agree on whether these are ancient references to the "Hebrews." However, the Nile Delta where the Bible says the ancient Israelites lived has produced no historical or administrative documents that might shed light on any period."

[3] Removing Moses from Israel's history isn't possible, and removing the exodus event from *his* life destroys the only explanation for his significance in Jewish history.

[4] There is a specific prohibition against acquiring *Egyptian* horses in Deuteronomy 17 by the future king. Solomon's disobedience in this matter is actually highlighted in 1 Kings 10:28 and 2 Chronicles 1:16. God specifically addresses "returning to Egypt" as direct disobedience through the prophets (cf. Isaiah 31:1; Ezekiel 17:15, and Amos 4:10).

[5] This is apparent in descriptions of the climate and weather described in Exodus (e.g. the reference to crop rotation in connection with the plagues of hail in Exodus 9:31-32. The shittim (acacia) tree is indigenous to Egypt and the Sinai, but not to Palestine except around the Dead Sea. This was the tree that furnished much of the structural support for the Tabernacle. Also, the atmosphere and setting of a desert environs dominates these books.

Book & Reference	Book & Reference
2 Kings 17:7, 36	*Acts 7:40 (Stephen); 13:17-18 (Paul)*
1 Chronicles 17:21	*1 Corinthians 5:7; 10:1-4 (allusion)*
2 Chronicles 7:22	*Hebrews 3:6; 11:22*
Nehemiah 9:9-10	*Jude 5*
Psalms 105:38; 136:10-11	

5. The Exodus is the single most important event in the Old Testament, other than the Fall into sin.[1]

   a. It stands as an example of Yahweh's mission of redemption.[2]

   b. It illustrates the movement from slavery to covenant, *not* from slavery to freedom.[3]

   c. It illustrates Yahweh's desire to deliver from political, economic, social, and spiritual bondage.[4]

6. The writer of 1 Kings dates the building of Solomon's Temple by linking it to the exodus event. This passage also allows us to assign a date to the exodus:

   "In the four hundred and eightieth year after the people of Israel came out of the land of Egypt, in the fourth year of Solomon's reign over Israel, in the month of Ziv, which is the second month, he began to build the house of the LORD." **1 Kings 6:1**

7. Solomon's ascension year was 970 B.C. which puts the exodus at 1446 B.C. *(he started the Temple in 966 B.C.).*

8. The apostle Paul links the anointing of Saul as Israel's first king with the exodus event, using specific numbers of years (his "date" for the Exodus agrees with the 1 Kings passage above.)

   "And after destroying seven nations in the land of Canaan, he gave them their land as an inheritance. All this took about 450 years. And after that he gave them judges until Samuel the prophet." **Acts 13:19, 20**

9. What we know about Hatshepsut from Egyptian history, makes her a likely candidate for "hiding" Moses from Pharaoh. (That would make Thutmose III the Pharaoh when Moses fled and Ahmenhotep II the Pharaoh of the exodus event.)

B. Getting The big Picture of Exodus

   1. The Glory of God in Exodus[5]

      a. Seen in the victory of His "representative" (7:1)

      b. Seen in the demise of the pantheon of Egypt (12:12)

      c. Seen in the giving of the Decalogue (Deut. 32-34)

      d. Seen in the formation of a distinct people (Deut. 4:32-34)

      e. Seen in the Tabernacle (40:32-35)

   2. The Plagues of Egypt

      a. Were a statement to both the Egyptians and the Israelites that YAHWEH was the one true Lord.

---

[1] The observation of the sabbath is linked to the exodus event in Deuteronomy 5:12-15, along with the creation account. In a very real sense, Yahweh was "creating" Israel in the exodus. It is mentioned more than any other historical event in Israel's history and occupies a central place in the nation's worship hymnal, the Psalms.

[2] Even Luke's rather cryptic use of of the Greek word for "exodus" at the transfiguration to describe Yeshua's work on the cross makes the cross the fulfillment of God's model of redemption (cf. Luke 9:31).

[3] Misunderstanding this is at the heart of an enormous error in much modern evangelism. Being "set free" to serve Yahweh is very different from being "turned loose" to serve ourselves!

[4] This is evident in the choice of verbs describing Yahweh's involvement: *"God heard…remembered…saw…knew."* (Exodus 2:23-25)

[5] From beginning to end this is a book about the *kabod,* the "glory" of Yahweh.

b. The plagues themselves were clear "attacks" (I.e. polemics) on the false theology of Egyptian paganism.[1]

> *"For I will pass through the land of Egypt that night, and I will strike all the firstborn in the land of Egypt, both man and beast; and on all the gods of Egypt I will execute judgments: I am the LORD."*
> - **Exodus 12:12**

c. The magicians in Pharaoh's court were able to mimic Aaron's signs and the first two plagues through demonic power:

> *"For the mystery of lawlessness is already at work. Only he who now restrains it will do so until he is out of the way. And then the lawless one will be revealed, whom the Lord Jesus will kill with the breath of his mouth and bring to nothing by the appearance of his coming. The coming of the lawless one is by the activity of Satan with a ll power and false signs and wonders,"*
> - **2 Thess. 2:7-9**

Plague	Scripture	God of Egypt Vanquished	
Nile River	7:17-25	**Osirus** **Nu** **Hapi**	- God of the Nile - god of the life of the river - god of the flood; fertility
frogs (an epidemic of frogs could not be killed because they were sacred!)	8:2-14	**Heqet**	- frog goddess; Egyptians relied on her for protection in childbirth.
gnats	8:16-19	**Geb**	- god of the earth; these "gnats" came from dust
flies	8:21-31	**Beelzebub** **Kheprer**	- "Lord of the flies"; protector from natural disasters. - depicted often as a scarab beetle; the god of resurrection.
livestock (5th plague says "all" the livestock died, but in the 7th there is reference to livestock; some scholars allocate 18-24 months for the 10 plagues)	9:1-7	**Apis** **Isis**	- the chief bull-god - queen of the goddesses; depicted often with horns
boils	9:8-12	**Thoth** **Sekhmet**	- god of the healing arts (the magicians of Pharaoh's court belonged to this priesthood) - lion-headed goddess; power to start and stop disease (priests of this god were the "physicians" of Egypt)
hail	9:18-33	**Shu** **Nut** **Seth**	- god of the atmosphere - goddess of the vaulted sky - god of wind and storm
locusts (as recent as 2001 a report estimated 10,000 locusts per 10 feet!!)	10:3-19	**Anubis** **Senehem**	- guardian of the fields - protector against pests
darkness	10:21-23	**Amon-Re** **Aten** **Horus**	- creator god; main sun god (Pharaoh was regarded as the "son of Re" - god of midday - god of sunrise
firstborn	11:1 – 12:30	**Pharaoh himself:** the incarnation of Amon-Re	
Note: Egyptians believed Pharaoh had power to maintain ma'at (cosmic balance); his inability to control ma'at throughout the ten plagues would have put his own status as a deity in serious dispute.			

3. IN EGYPT: The First Passover

a. The context of the first Passover was the tenth plague.[2]

b. It became a vital educational vehicle for the the Jews, even to this day.

---

[1] Yahweh was as specific in his "attacks" as the 9/11 terrorists were in their choice of airlines (i.e., United and American). This fact is restated to the second generation in Numbers 33:4.

[2] We need to continually remind ourselves that this was *not* an ancient "communion service"! It was *not* a night of joy and celebration. It was a night of tremendous fear and apprehension. The joyous aspect of Passover would be a future reality.

    c.   We too often forget the Jewish nature of our own communion ceremonies. We are part of this "big picture" now too.

4.   AT SINAI: The Decalogue — "10 Words"

    a.   A covenant agreement, based on the exodus event.[1]

    b.   Written by the "finger of God," not given through Moses like the Law.

    c.   All the pronouns are singular.

    d.   All ten commandments are relational in nature: first 4 are with Yahweh, next 6 are within Israel.

    e.   It begins with the indicative and moves to the imperative; grace precedes law.

> *"I am the LORD your God, who brought you out of the land of Egypt, out of the house of slavery.* — **Exodus 20:2**

5.   AT SINAI: The Tabernacle

    a.   The abiding presence of the One True God in the midst of a people is a remarkable theme of Exodus.

> *"I will meet there with the sons of Israel, and it shall be consecrated by My glory. I will consecrate the tent of meeting and the altar; I will also consecrate Aaron and his sons to minister as priests to Me. I will dwell among the sons of Israel and will be their God. They shall know that I am the LORD their God who brought them out of the land of Egypt, that I might dwell among them; I am the LORD their God."* —**Exodus 29:43-46**

    b.   God's presence moves from the top of Sinai to their very center of the nation.

    c.   His presence becomes Israel's distinguishing characteristic.

> *Then he said to Him, "If Your presence does not go with us, do not lead us up from here. For how then can it be known that I have found favor in Your sight, I and Your people? Is it not by Your going with us, so that we, I and Your people, may be distinguished from all the other people who are upon the face of the earth?"* —**Exodus 33:15-16**

6.   Exodus and the Christian

    a.   Jesus is the Passover Lamb . (1 Cor. 5:7)

    b.   Jesus is our deliverer from bondage to sin and Satan. (Luke 9::29-31; 1 Pet. 1:18)

    c.   Jesus is the fulfillment of the Law. (Rom. 10:4)

    d.   Jesus is the "tabernacle" of God. (John 1:14)[2]

    e.   *We* are a new "chosen people." (1 Pet. 2:9-10)[3]

📷 Snapshot of the Book of Exodus

..................*about 3 months*.......................|.........*about 9 months*.........

Moses & Pharaoh	"Israel" in the desert	Moses & Yahweh
• bondage (chapters 1-6) • deliverance (chap. 7-12)	• traveling & trials (chap. 13-18)	• the Law (chapters 19-24) • the Tabernacle (chap. 25-40)

KEY CHAPTER: *12 - "exit us" (exodus); 20 - giving of 10 commandments*

KEY WORD: *"Exit!"*

BASIC GEOGRAPHY: *Egypt to Mount Sinai*

BOOK SUMMARY: *Yahweh delivers the Jews out of bondage in Egypt, and makes them into His unique covenant people.*

---

[1] Ten times in the Torah, Yahweh connects the covenant itself with the exodus event with the words, *"I am the YAHWEH who brought you up out of the land of Egypt…"* (Ex. 6:7; 20:2; Lev. 19:36; 22:33; 25:38; 26:13; Num. 15:41; Deut. 5:6; 8:14; 13:10)

[2] John uses *skenaō* in 1:14 in speaking of the Incarnation (i.e. "dwelt" among us is the word used in the LXX for the Tabernacle in the wilderness.

[3] Or more accurately, we are the *current expression* of the same group. Yahweh has always had *one* "chosen people"; the descendants of Abraham, of which we are the current expression according to Paul's repeated insistence in the Letter to the Galatians.

UNIT 6 - LEVITICUS: KEEPING CANAAN OUT OF ISRAEL

A. Two Books — One Story

    1. Leviticus begins with Hebrew word, *"and..."*

    2. Begins with the activities and people associated with worship in the Tabernacle God just occupied at the end of the book of Exodus.

    3. It is a *continuation* of the Law begun in Exodus 20.

B. Five Pieces in the "Big Picture"

    1. The Holiness of YAHWEH

    2. The Purity of the Covenant

    3. The Connection of Time to YAHWEH

    4. The Preparation For Canaan.

    5. The Theology of Atonement & Mediation

C. **Piece #1:** The Holiness of YAHWEH

    1. "Holy" means "separation"– (to *and* from)[1]

    2. "Holy" appears 90 times in Leviticus

    3. "Holy" appears most frequently in chapters dealing with those who approach God.

D. **Piece #2:** A Covenant Community

    1. Holiness was at the heart of the covenant; it was what the Jews were delivered *to*:

> *"For I am the LORD who brought you up out of the land of Egypt to be your God. You shall therefore be holy, for I am holy."*
> **Lev. 11:45**

    2. Maintaining holiness was the *purpose* of their ritual.[2]

       a. *Not* moral purity in itself.

       b. All their rituals were for the purpose of *restoring* broken holiness.

E. **Piece #3:** The Connection of Time to YAHWEH

    1. Establishment of a liturgical calendar.

    2. Primacy of the Sabbath:

      • connected their daily life to God as Creator

      • Deut. 5:12-16 links the sabbath to Creation and the Exodus event (i.e. God "created" Israel in the Exodus)

      • extended to their land and produce

      • extended to debts and real estate

      • made them "holy" among the nations

      • reminded them that time belonged to God *(and so did they!)*

---

[1] The word implies a "distinction" from the surrounding culture; being "in" it but it not being "in" them. They were to be as different in their values, worship, and lifestyle as Yahweh was "different" from the pantheon of gods in Canaan.

[2] *Not* moral purity, but covenant faithfulness. In fact, all the rituals were to *reestablish* holiness.

F. **Piece #4:** The Preparation For Canaan[1]

1. The god "El"

   a) 3 wives, all sisters!

   b) murdered son, decapitated daughter

      (1) Ugaritic texts describe his uncontrollable lust.

      (2) literature about him is the most sensuous of all ANE writings.

2. The god, "Baal" *(called Hadad in Amorite mythology)*[2]

   a) son of "El" *(considered the son of Dagon, an Amorite deity, in some literature)*

   b) married to his sister, Anat

   c) slain by Mot (winter)

   d) Anat slays Mot, "raises" Baal (spring)

   e) Baal celebrates victory with Orgy on "holy mountain" (engages in bestiality).

3. The goddess, "Anat"

   a) consort of Baal

   b) sacred prostitute.

   c) called the "holy one"[3]

   d) known as Asherah in Israel during time of Ahab & Jezebel[4]

   e) cult prostitutes were at her shrines (male *and* female)

G. **Piece #5**: The Theology of Atonement

Theological Idea	Biblical reference
Death: Sin results in death; the shedding of blood.	*"For the life of the flesh is in the blood, and I have given it for you on the altar to make atonement for your souls, for it is the blood that makes atonement by the life."* **Leviticus 17:11**

---

[1] The practices of the Canaanites were well-known even in the times of the Patriarchs. For example, Sodom and Gomorrah were described as places where the people were *"...exceedingly great sinners before the LORD"* (Gen. 13:13). The people of these two cities, we will learn from Ezekiel's further description 1,000 years later, were people who valued comfort and pleasure more than people. The sins of Samuel's two sons (Hophni and Phineas) in the early chapters of 1 Samuel with the women at the Tent of Meeting were clearly Canaanite in nature. Absalom's behavior on the roof of the palace with David's concubines was Canaanite in nature as well.

    Yahweh went "overboard" in erecting fences to keep Canaanite influence *out* of Israel's worship, (because He knew that people resemble what they revere): He forbade *any* statues or images of any kind, including any of Himself; there were no animal images allowed; in fact, all involvement with animals within the Jewish sacrificial system had to do with sin; He gave instructions for modest clothing for priests, and even the architecture of the Tabernacle and ultimately the Temple engendered modesty; He instituted a single-gender priesthood (unlike Canaanite worship), and made no provision for women to be associated with the all-male priesthood.

    We must never underestimate the immense cultural pressure upon the Israelites to succumb to the notion that Yahweh was a god of the wilderness, but *not* the valleys, rivers, and hills—their new source of food. These were all the regions "ruled" by Baal. (e.g., Elijah's "drought" is an attack on the gods of Canaan, not merely a punishment of Ahab; cf. 1 Kgs. 20:28)

[2] Baal means "master" or "Lord"; it is sometimes used in Hebrew proper names, such as Esh-Baal (Ish-Bosheth; cf. 1 Chron 9:39 and 2 Sam. 2:8), but even here as elsewhere, a connection of some degree to Canaanite influence is very likely. The name, Baal, appears alone or in compound form the most during the two darkest periods of Jewish history—the time of the Judges and 2 Kings. In fact, one third of all the occurrences of Baal in our Old Testament (67) appear in these two books! Frequently in the Old Testament narrative, the *plural* use of the name appears (i.e. "the Baals") because of the local nature of Canaanite deities (e.g., "the Baal of Peor" in Deut. 4:3); cf. Judges 3:7; Jer 9:14, and Hosea 2:13. Ahab and Jezebel made Baal worship the official "state religion" under their joint reign (cf. 1 Kgs 16:31). Baal worship was active even up to the end of the southern kingdom of Judah in the early 6th century B.C. Jeremiah tells us that the Jews were burning their children in sacrifices to Baal (Jer 19:5).

[3] Yahweh's insistence that this title be ascribed only to Him is as significant during this time period, as ascribing LORD to Jesus was during the first century, under Rome's domination and unwillingness to allow anyone to be "Lord" except the Emperor. In a very real sense, Yahweh was "starting a fight" and knew it.

[4] Baal and Asherah are frequently associated (cf. Judges 3:7).

Theological Idea	Biblical reference
Imputation: My guilt is "transferred" to someone or something else.	*"And when he has made an end of atoning for the Holy Place and the tent of meeting and the altar, he shall present the live goat. And Aaron shall lay both his hands on the head of the live goat, and confess over it all the iniquities of the people of Israel, and all their transgressions, all their sins. And he shall put them on the head of the goat and send it away into the wilderness by the hand of a man who is in readiness. The goat shall bear all their iniquities on itself to a remote area, and he shall let the goat go free in the wilderness."* **Leviticus 16:20-22**
Substitution: Someone or something must die in my place.	*"...when the sin which they have committed becomes known, the assembly shall offer a bull from the herd for a sin offering and bring it in front of the tent of meeting." "and shall lay his hand on the head of the goat and kill it in the place where they kill the burnt offering before the LORD; it is a sin offering."* **Leviticus 4:14, 24**
Mediation: Someone else must represent me before God	*"No one may be in the tent of meeting from the time he enters to make atonement in the Holy Place until he comes out and has made atonement for himself and for his house and for all the assembly of Israel."* **Leviticus 16:17**

H. The Theology of Mediation: Two High Priests Compared:

Characteristic	Old Testament High Priest	Jesus Christ
ELIGIBILITY:	Descendant of Aaron (Leviticus 16:3,32)	Son of God Himself (Hebrews 4:14)
LOCATION OF SACRIFICE:	Holy of Holies in Tabernacle (Leviticus 16:15,16)	the Presence of God (Hebrews 9:24)
FREQUENCY OF SACRIFICE:	Once Each Year (Leviticus 16:34)	Once For All Time (Hebrews 9:12)
SACRIFICE:	Blood of Bulls & Goats (Leviticus 16:14,15)	His Own Blood (life) (Hebrews 9:12)
BENEFICIARIES:	People of Israel (Leviticus 16:34)	All Who Come to God (Hebrews 7:25)
EFFICACY:	For One Year (Leviticus 16:34)	For All Eternity (Hebrews 9:12)
PREPARATION:	Atone For His Own Sin (Leviticus 6:16)	None – He is sinless (Hebrews 7:26-28)

"Therefore, since we have a great high priest who has gone through the heavens, Jesus the Son of God, let us hold firmly to the faith we profess. For we do not have a high priest who is unable to sympathize with our weaknesses, but we have one who has been tempted in every way, just as we are—yet was without sin. Let us then approach the throne of grace with confidence, so that we may receive mercy and find grace to help us in our time of need."
—Hebrews 4:14-16, NIV—

I. Leviticus and the Christian

   1. Biblical view of time

      a. our modern obsession with time compression is removing eternity from our thinking.

      b. our loss of a "sacred calendar" since the Reformation has removed God from our life rhythms and cycles.[1]

   2. The Legacy of Canaan: the hardening of our hearts

      a. a love of pleasure leads to social injustice[2]

      b. this is what happened to the Canaanite city of Sodom:

"Behold, this was the guilt of your sister Sodom: she and her daughters had pride, excess of food, and prosperous ease, but did not aid the poor and needy. They were haughty and did an abomination before me. So I removed them, when I saw it." **- Ezekiel 16:49, 50**

---

[1] This is somewhat less of a problem in liturgical churches that still follow an ancient calendar in which time is related to the events in salvation history rather than Hallmark's designations.

[2] A love of pleasure does two things: it anesthetizes the soul, and engenders a disdain for *dis*comfort of any kind, but most importantly, a disdain for personal discomfort, which of course the restoration of shalom (aka ministry) demands. As does discipleship itself.

3. Holiness is still God's standard because He has not changed.[1]

> "...but as he who called you is holy, you also be holy in all your conduct, since it is written, "You shall be holy, for I am holy."
> **- 1 Peter 1:15, 16**

4. Idolatry is accommodation to culture, that *results* in the worship of false gods.[2]

> "You shall not do as they do in the land of Egypt, where you lived, and you shall not do as they do in the land of Canaan, to which I am bringing you. You shall not walk in their statutes."
> **- Leviticus 18:3**

Snapshot of the Book of Leviticus

Holy Worship	The Day of Atonement	Holy "Walking"
• offerings, priests, and purity (chapters 1-15)	• chapter 16	• holy people and holy days (chapters 17-27)

KEY CHAPTER: *16 - the Day of Atonement*

KEY WORD: *"Holy"*

BASIC GEOGRAPHY: *at Mount Sinai (not moving)*

BOOK SUMMARY: *How God's covenant people must approach Him through sacrifices made by a mediator.*

UNIT 7 - NUMBERS "Do The Math!"

A. What's In A Name?

1. Book title comes from Greek Old Testament, "Arithmoi" (I.e. "Numbers"); reference to the two censuses in the book (Ch. 1, 26).

2. Hebrew title is *"be-midbar,"* which means, "in the wilderness"; a much more fitting title.

3. This title confusion is a great "parable" about our constant struggle to balance the Hebraic and Greek ways of thinking about God: abstract & practical vs. concrete & intellectual.

   a. A "Rusty" Hinge in History

     (1) This is a book of Transitions:

       (a) in priesthood: from Aaron to Eleazer *(Aaron dies immediately after this ceremony)*

       (b) in leadership: from Moses to Joshua

       (c) in demographics; age, etc.: parent generation to second generation

       (d) in lifestyle: nomadic to residential *(allotments to Gad and ½ tribe of Manasseh East of Jordan)*

---

[1] "Holy, holy, holy" is the perpetual song of the Seraphim in heaven right now (Isaiah 6:1-3; Rev. 4:6-8)

[2] The worship of false gods is the *result* of idolatry, not the cause of it. When someone accommodates to a culture that is in rebellion against God, it *results* in the institution of replacements for the one true God, or worship. God's clearest statement that connects idolatry, holiness, and accommodation to culture is in this book: *"You must not do as they do in Egypt, where you used to live, and you must not do as they do in the land of Canaan, where I am bringing you. Do not follow their practices."* **(Leviticus 18:3)** Other passages that support this idea are: Ex. 23:24; Lev. 18:30; Ps. 106:35; Jer. 10:2-3; Ezek. 20:7-8; 23:8; and Rom. 12:2.

(e)   in geography: from Egypt to Canaan[1] *(fulfillment of the promise)*

(2)   This is a book of rebellions[2]:

Scripture	Incident Recorded
11:1	People complain about misfortunes in general
11:4-6	People complain about their "diet"; wanted to return to Egypt
11:10-15	Moses complains about God's unreasonable task of leadership
12:1-16	Miriam & Aaron rebel against Moses' leadership
13:25-33	***Spies return and give a bad (majority) report***
14:1-4	Entire nation complains about the "impossibility" of taking Canaan
14:20-23	God indicates that there have been "ten rebellions" since leaving Egypt!
14:39-45	Rebel by "obeying" through disobedience
15:32-36	An individual Sabbath-breaker executed
16:1-40	Korah's rebellion (ground swallowed them up)
16:41ff	"all the congregation" is angry with Moses for the death of Korah and his companions.
20:1-9	Complaining over lack of water at Meribah near Kadesh; want to return
20:10-13	***Moses & Aaron usurp God's glory and draw attention to themselves***
21:4-9	Complaining over "diet" again; serpents punish them: brazen serpent
25:1ff	Baal worship, intermarriage and sexual immorality in Moab

4.   This is a book of warnings: (cf. 1 Cor. 10:9-12).

   a.   about the human capacity for sin.

   b.   about the human tendency to presume on God's provision.

   c.   About the impartiality of God's holiness (Korah *and* Moses).

   d.   This "dispensable" nature of God's servants (Aaron *and* Balaam)[3].

   e.   The unrelenting "pull" of culture (Baal of Peor in Moab).

5.   It is a book of "higher math!"

   a.   Non-sequential chronology[4]

   "The book of Numbers defies dissection into logical literary units, making it perhaps the most diffi-cult Old Testament book in which to identify order and structure."

   Andrew Hill, *Survey of the Old Testament*, p. 120

   b.   One researcher examined 46 commentaries and 24 different outlines for the book!

   c.   Contains huge gaps in the "storyline

   (1)   38 years are unaccounted for![5]

   (2)   of the 42 places mentioned in chapter 33, most are missing from the story.

---

[1] The book of Numbers explains the Jews' presence in Canaan; In other words, how they "got" there.

[2] Yahweh says in Number 14:22 that there had already been *ten* rebellions by the time the "big rebellion" of chapter 13 had occurred. We do not have a record of ten prior to this time, which is an excellent indicator that our narrative is smaller than the actual history of Yahweh's chosen people. This fact is true of *all* of Scripture. We're always "missing" something.

The rebellion recorded in chapters 13-14 is responsible for the 40 year wandering and the death of the entire first generation to come out of Egypt. The disobedience of Moses and Aaron in chapter 20 is the event that disqualified Moses from entering the Promised Land. This event should not be confused with a previous "no water challenge" at Rephidim, prior to arriving at Mt. Sinai (cf. Exodus17).

[3] Yahweh's "use" of Balaam is a sobering reminder that *who* He chooses, and for what purposes, are His prerogative.

[4] Looking at the "date stamps" (day, month, year) mentioned in 1:1; 7:1; 9:1, 15; 10:11; 20:1 will reveal quickly that the recorded narrative does *not* follow a strict chronology. For example, 9:1 clearly *precedes* 1:1 by a month, and 10:11 actually occurs soon after 1:1.

[5] Except in retrospect, cross-referencing 20:22-29 with 33:38.

      d.   Numbers has problems with "numbers"[1]

          (1)   Army's size doesn't "fit" history & culture, or Deuteronomy 7:7.

> *"It was not because you were more in number than any other people that the LORD set his love on you and chose you, for you were the fewest of all peoples…"*

          (2)   God typically works with few and weakness, rather than many and strength (cf. Judges 7:2; 1 Cor. 1:27-31).

B. Getting The Big Picture

    1. This is a book that validates God's revelation of Himself to Moses:

> *"The LORD descended in the cloud and stood with him there, and proclaimed the name of the LORD. The LORD passed before him and proclaimed, 'The LORD, the LORD, a God merciful and gracious, slow to anger, and abounding in steadfast love and faithfulness, keeping steadfast love for thousands, forgiving iniquity and transgression and sin, but who will by no means clear the guilty, visiting the iniquity of the fathers on the children and the children's children, to the third and the fourth generation.'"*   **- Exodus 34:5-7**

> *"And now, please let the power of the Lord be great as you have promised, saying, 'The LORD is slow to anger and abounding in steadfast love, forgiving iniquity and transgression, but he will by no means clear the guilty, visiting the iniquity of the fathers on the children, to the third and the fourth generation.' Please pardon the iniquity of this people, according to the greatness of your steadfast love, just as you have forgiven this people, from Egypt until now."*   **- Numbers 14:17-19**

    2. This is a book that constantly holds before us the dual aspects of God's nature that must be kept in view: His holiness and His love.

> *"Note then the **kindness** and the **severity** of God: severity toward those who have fallen, but God's kindness to you, provided you continue in his kindness. Otherwise you too will be cut off."*   **- Romans 11:22**

    3. This is a book about "testing"[2]

       a.   Leviticus was the "course," the book of Numbers was the "exam."

       b.   Israel "tests" God — this is always bad (Num. 20:13; Ps. 95:9).

       c.   God "tests" Israel — this is always good (Ps. 17:3; Isaiah 48:10).

    4. This is book about holiness.

       a.   Camp arrangement for peace and war (i.e., marching and camping) was designed to remind them of their need to stay close to God.

       b.   Ordination did not create holiness[3] (Korah and 250 others were all Levites).

       c.   Election did not excuse discipline (Ch. 20; Miriam, Moses, and Aaron).

       d.   Holiness is specific as well as corporate[4] (clan designations for labor within Levites; Num. 3:21-37).

    5. It is a book about faithfulness—Yahweh's.

       a.   The second census stands as a testimony to the covenant love of God.

       b.   No mention of a single death after the first generation is extinguished.

       c.   God's faithfulness to His covenant people repeatedly towers above their sin and *faithlessness.*

    6. It is a messianic book.

---

[1] Some Old Testament scholars think that the Hebrew for 1,000 (elep) could mean a "military unit" (allup). In this case, the actual number of fighting men would be closer to 6,000 rather than 600,000. Also, the Deuteronomic promise in Deut. 7:1 says Yahweh is going to use Israel to displace *"…seven nations more numerous and mightier than yourselves."* If Israel was 2 million in number, that would put the population of Canaan at the time of the conquest would be around 20 million. But, archaeological evidence suggests a population slightly over 1 million.

[2] In this regard, chapter 20 is a very eventful chapter. In a single chapter, Miriam dies and is given a single verse in remembrance! This woman was Moses' sister (likely the one who saved his life), a prophetess in her own right, and the lead singer at the exodus event (Exodus 15:20ff).

[3] Being "set apart" by God always involves a choice on the part of the one being "set apart." It is not merely a "calling" or a "position."

[4] In a very real sense, the same is true today among "the priesthood of believers," according to Paul. He asks the rhetorical question in 1 Corinthians 12. Diversity of function within a unity.

a. The sacrifice of the red heifer[1] is a clear prediction of Jesus' death (cf. Num. 19 and Heb. 13:12-13).

b. The brazen serpent is a prophetic picture of both the Cross and salvation by faith (cf. Num. 21:4-9; John 3:14).

C. Numbers and Our New Testament

1. Balaam is mentioned in 3 New Testament books; all indicting the manipulative nature of his character more clearly than it is in Numbers[2] (cf. 2 Peter 2:15; Jude 11; Rev. 2:13-14).[3]

2. Paul spends half of 1 Corinthians 10 connecting Israel's sin to the Corinthians' temptation, including:

a. idolatry (I.e. cultural accommodation; 1 Cor. 10:7 and Num. 25:1-9).

b. sexual immorality (1 Cor. 10:8 and Num. 25:1-9).

c. grumbling about life (1 Cor. 10:10 and Num. 14:2).

d. rejection of accountability (1 Cor. 10:9 and Num. 21:5).

3. Paul makes it clear that we are just as susceptible and even more culpable.[4]

4. The writer of Hebrews refers to Numbers at least three times, quoting Psalm 95[5]:

a. be alert - your heart can become hardened too.

b. be accountable - you cannot protect your heart alone.

c. be prophetic - you have an obligation for the protection of others' hearts too.

d. There is an eerie "silence" in Hebrews 11 regarding the book of Numbers.[6]

D. Numbers and the Christian

1. The Myth of Nostalgia- the temptation to "revise" our memories in the face of struggle.

2. The Grave Nature of Complaining - grumbling is always against God and "tests" His goodness.

3. Availability versus Ability - God used a talking jackass, he can use me.

4. Sovereignty versus Humanity - God will get the "job" done whether or not I "show up for work!" There are no "celebrities" in God's Story even though we seem determined to create them, and then to put our hope in them.

"Now these things happened to them as an example, but they were written down for our instruction, on whom the end of the ages has come. Therefore let anyone who thinks that he stands take heed lest he fall." **1 Corinthians 10:11 -12**

---

[1] There is significance in the fact that this is a heifer, *not* a bull like all the other ritualistic requirements. The heifer was also sacrificed "outside the gate," a clear marker pointing to the crucifixion outside the city of Jerusalem.

[2] Balaam is a key figure in the book of Numbers as well, his name appearing 53 times.

[3] We would do well to differentiate between the Balaam event in chapter 25 and the rebellions in the rest of the book. The incident involving Balaam was *not* merely "one more rebellion in a book of rebellions." The other "rebellions" involved complaining, grumbling, and a lack of trust in Yahweh. This incident was *idolatry;* the worship of a Canaanite god! There are two clear acts of idolatry in the corporate life of Israel prior to their entrance into the Promised Land. The first was at the base of Mt. Sinai in Exodus 32. Here they worshipped a god from the land they had just left (Apis, the bull). There is some *intimation* of sexual behavior in this first incident, as the Hebrew verb translated "laugh" in Exodus 32:6 is also translated "caress" in Genesis 26:8. But, a careful conflation of the available scriptures teach us that the incident with Balaam was very different. First and foremost, it was worship of the god of the land they were about to enter (as opposed to reverting *back* to Apis). Second, it was clearly sexual in nature. Yahweh uses sexual terminology to describe what happened: *"You (the men!) went whoring..."* It is sobering to hear Yahweh accuse the *men* of being prostitutes because they "joined themselves" to Baal. We learn from Rev. 2:14ff a fuller story of what happened that day. Finally, in Numbers 31:8,16 we learn that it was *Balaam* who was responsible for the immorality, and is killed by the Israelites in the end. He had figured out a way to get the daughters of Moab to do what the men of Moab could not in chapter 25. One commentator made this statement about chapter 25 of Numbers: *"It is the nadir of the book, the great sin at the end of the road."*

It is also worth mentioning that the geographical location of this incident (i.e. Shittim) is the "staging" area mentioned at the *end* of the book of Deuteronomy and the *beginning* of the book of Joshua. It is, in a real sense, the "end of the journey" for the Israelites, but what a miserable way to "end" 40 years of struggle and spiritual learning! (cf. Num. 36:13Deut. 34:1; Josh 2:1)

[4] *"Now these things happened to them* [those in the book of Numbers] *as an example, but they were written down for our instruction, on whom the end of the ages has come. –* **1 Corinthians 10:11**

[5] cf. Hebrews 3:7-11; 4:1-11

[6] One cannot ignore the fact that we get no "heroes" of the faith from the book of Numbers, even though names from the book of Judges make it into Hebrews 11 (e.g. Samson)!

📷 Snapshot of the Book of Numbers

The 1st Generation (chapters 1-14)	In the Wilderness (chapters 15-25)	The 2nd Generation (chapters 26-36)
• fighting men counted • arrangement of camp • spies report/rebellion	• wander 40 yrs • parents die • Aaron dies	• fighting men counted • transfer of leadership

KEY CHAPTER: *13 - spies' report & people's rebellion*

KEY WORD: *"wandering"*

BASIC GEOGRAPHY: *Mt. Sinai - Kadesh - Wilderness - Kadesh - Moab*

BOOK SUMMARY: *The first generation out of Egypt dies out during 40 years in the wilderness because of disobedience (didn't do what Yahweh required) and unbelief (didn't believe what Yahweh said about Himself).*

UNIT 8 - DEUTERONOMY "Don't Forget to Remember!"

A. What's In A Name?

   1. "Deuteronomy" comes from the *Septuagint* title, meaning "second law."

   2. This is a fitting but misleading title; it is so much more:

      a. It is more of a *renewal* than a restatement (cf. Deut. 29:1).

      b. It forms a central "link" in the primary history of the OT.

      c. It is a book about spiritual formation (relationship), not merely information (laws).[1]

      d. It is at the heart of the theology of the remainder of the Old Testament.[2]

B. Getting The Big Picture

   1. The Setting: Moab (Num. 36:13; Deut. 34:8).

      a. Takes place where Numbers left off

      b. Moab was one of the two sons born out of the affair between drunken Lot and his two daughters (Ammon was the other; cf. Gen. 19:30-38).

      c. Balak, who hired Balaam to curse Israel, was king of Moab.

      d. The Moabite Stone (9th century B.C.) is one of the most supportive archeological finds we have.[3]

   2. The Storyline: The "Flow" of Deuteronomy[4]

---

[1] Deuteronomy is very different from the previous four Books of Law. In Exodus and Leviticus we learn of the *stipulations* of the covenant (i.e., law, tabernacle, priesthood, calendar, sacrificial system). But in Deuteronomy the focus is on the *covenantal* nature of Israel's *relationship* with Yahweh. Or put another way, in Exodus and Leviticus we get the "letter" of the Law—what Yahweh *requires*. In Deuteronomy we get the "spirit" of the Law—what Yahweh *desires*.

[2] The occurrence of *berith* ("covenant") is central to this book, appearing nearly as many times as it does in Exodus, Leviticus, and Numbers combined. *Berith* is also a major theme in the writings of the prophets, whose message is essentially a call to "return" to covenant faithfulness (24x in Jeremiah, 18x in Ezekiel, 12x in Isaiah). It is very likely that "the book of the covenant" that was discovered during the reign of King Josiah was in fact this book—Deuteronomy (cf. Ex. 24:7; 1 Kgs 23:2,21 and 2 Chron. 34:30).

[3] It is also known as the "Mesha Stone" because Mesha, the King of Moab was responsible for its creation. On it he mentions the tribe of Gad by name, as well as 12 cities that are also mentioned in the biblical narrative.

[4] There is some similarity to Numbers in this regard, in that Deuteronomy also defies a strict organization and chronology.

a. Consists of 3 "sermons" by Moses and 3 appendices:

    (1) *"Remember Your Parents' Sin!"* - chapters 1-4 - look *back* on Israel's journey *to* Moab

    (2) *"Remember Your Parents' God!"* - ch. 5-28 - looks ahead to life under God in Canaan

    (3) *"Blessings or Curses?"* - ch. 29-31 - renewal of the Sinai Covenant

        (a) the Song of Moses[1] - ch 32

        (b) the Blessing of Moses - ch 33

        (c) the death of Moses[2] - ch 34

b. Follows the literary form of Hittite treaties of this era[3]:

The Deuteronomic Code and Hittite Treaties Compared

Deuteronomy	Treaty Section	Hittite Treaty (Example)
1:1-5	Preamble	*"These are the words of Mursilis, the great king of the Hittites, the valiant.*
1:6 - 3:29	Historical Prologue	*"When your father died, I did not drop you. Since your father mentioned your name to me with great praise, I sought after you. To be sure, you were sick and ailing. But I still let you replace your father and accepted your brothers, sisters, and your land i*
Chapters 4 - 26	The Stipulations	*"You shall remain loyal to me, the Hittite king, the Hittite land, and my sons and grandsons forever! The tribute imposed upon your grandfather and father (300 shekels of high quality gold) you will also present to me! Do not turn your eyes to*
31:9-13, 24-26	Provision for Deposit and Reading of Document *(where it was to be*	*"A duplicate of this document has been deposited before the god Tessub. At regular intervals they shall read it in the presence of the king and in the presence of the sons of the country.*
30:19; 31:19-22	List of Witnesses *(the many gods of Canaan vs. Yahweh)*	*"The Sun-god of Heaven, the Sun-goddess of Arinna, Ishtar, the gods and goddesses of the Hittites, the gods and goddesses of the Amorites, all the golden gods, the mountains, the rivers, heaven and earth, the winds and clouds – let these be witnesses to this treaty and this oath."*
Chapter 28	Curses & Blessings Formula *(this order is reversed in the Bible)*	*"Should Duppi-Tessub fail to honor this treaty, may these gods of the oath destroy Duppi-Tessub together with his wife, his son, his grandson, his house , his land and everything that he owns. But if Duppi-Tessub honors the treaty inscribed on this tablet, may these gods protect him together with his wife, his son, his grandson, his house and his country."*

3. The Cast: The "Stars" of Deuteronomy

    a. Monotheism[4] - Deuteronomy 6:4-5

        (1) Absolutely foreign to the ancient near east.

---

[1] This is a major part of this book, occupying 43 verses. It is also mentioned at the *end* of God's Story (cf. Rev. 15:3).

[2] Unlike some, Moses dies *not* of old age like the patriarchs, but because of his disobedience (i.e. He could just have easily died a few months later *in* Canaan.)

[3] The Hebrew word for "covenant" *(berith)* is the same as the word for "treaty." It appears 283 times in 27 of the 39 Old Testament books. The use of the suzerain-vassal Hittite treaty formulas in the composition of Yahweh's covenant with His people is an excellent illustration of a very real "problem" He faced when dealing with His people. How much of the surrounding culture, and *how* He used it, when relating to the Israelites, was something of a "tightrope act." At least from *our* vantage point. Yahweh needed to relate to them on terms that made sense in the context in which they found themselves. But, He also needed to do so in a way that did *not* draw them into the very culture they were supposed to be distinct from in the first place. It therefore reasonable that He would employ the mechanics of the Hittites' legal documents in His construction of the Law.

    There is also a clear difference between Assyrian and Hittite treaty structures. The *similarities* between the Israelite and Hittite treaties, and the *dissimilarities* between Assyrian and Israeli treaties actually enables scholars to more accurately date the book of Deuteronomy. The Hittites played a vital role in the history of the Ancient Near East up until around 1500 B.C. when their empire began to unravel. They were *not* Semites like the Jews, but rather Indo-Europeans whose major base of power was in the area that is modern Turkey. They were the first to develop iron technology in the ANE, which changed warfare forever because of its superiority over copper and bronze. Abram bought the Cave of Machpelah to bury Sara in, from Ephron, a Hittite (Gen. 23:4). Esau married two Hittite wives to deliberately displease his parents (Gen. 26:34-35; 27:46). The husband of Bathsheba was of Hittite descent (2 Sam 11).

[4] There are some who point to Ahkenaton in Egypt as the first "monotheist," however his religious system was actually a version of henotheism, which is a *family* choice to worship a single god out of many. This is very distinct from Yahweh's insistence that He is the only God, not because of the choices of people, but because He is.

(2) Was reflected in Israel's "Name/Place" theology[1].

    (a) Only one place of worship for the One God.

    (b) God said His "Name" would dwell in this one place.[2]

    (c) No graven images meant no other "places" *(iconography was blasphemy within Israel)*

    (d) Decentralization of worship always produced spiritual decay in their history.[3]

b. Revelation - Deuteronomy 32:39

    (1) The Law is not merely information, but revelation.

    (2) In Deuteronomy we meet a God who speaks about Himself not merely requirements

    (3) For the Jew, their very history was a form of revelation; a record of God's character and conduct.[4]

    (4) Knowing their history would create responsibility; one couldn't "know" it *and* ignore it!

c. Moses - Deuteronomy 34:10-12

    (1) He is mentioned by name 38 times in this book.

    (2) He is mentioned by name in 21 of the 39 OT books.

    (3) His name appears 852 times in our Bible!

    (4) He is mentioned in the last three verses of the Old Testament, along with Elijah.

    (5) He does not appear again in the pages of Scripture until the Transfiguration[5], again along with Elijah! (Mark 9:2-4).

    (6) We discover from Jude 8-9 that there was an angelic struggle over his body on Mt. Pisgah in Moab.

    (7) The final book of the Bible depicts celebrants in heaven singing two songs: the "song of Moses" and the "song of the Lamb"! (Rev. 15:3).

4. The Script: The Words of Deuteronomy

a. "fear" - there are 15 references in this book to "fearing" God compared to only 3 in the rest of the Torah.

b. "love" - there are 24 references to "loving Yahweh" in this book, compared to only 7 in the rest of Torah.

    (1) 8 are for God's love for *them*.

    (2) 10 are for *their* love for God.

    (3) the rest are for their love for *others*.

    (4) "Fear" *and* "love" are the basis for the biblical idea of obedience.

c. "Remember/forget" - there are 25 commands or references regarding this in Deuteronomy.[6]

    (1) This is a key danger for believers of *all* generations:

> *"Only take care, and keep your soul diligently, lest you forget the things that your eyes have seen, and lest they depart from your heart all the days of your life. Make them known to your children and your children's children."*   **Deuteronomy 4:9**

---

[1] We are living in the era that Jesus predicted in his conversation with the Samaritan woman in John 4. We are living on the other side of Pentecost and the fulfillment of the prophecies of Joel 2.

[2] Yahweh makes reference to this one "place that he would choose" 19x in this book, out of the 20 times this phrase appears in the Bible

[3] The wisdom of a central place of worship is demonstrated years later in the book of 1 Kings when Jeroboam sets up *two* shrines in the northern kingdom of Israel as its first king. He does so to minimize the migration of northerners back to the southern kingdom because that's where the one Temple was. What grew out of his decision was a culture of idolatry and perversion.

[4] That meant that one of the ways to truly "know" God was to know their own history; especially what we would likely call their "salvation history." This is radically different from the modern model of Christian education. We seem to spend our time trying to figure out what the Bible says to us about ourselves, rather than what it says to us about God.

[5] It's interesting, perhaps even significant, that Moses "disappears" from the Story on a mountain, and reappears in the Story on another mountain. And, in a rather poetic way, actually *does* get to "see" the Promised Land!

[6] Reflecting on Yahweh's past deliverance would be essential as war was ahead for them…lots of it.

Reference	What to Remember...What *Not* to Forget
Deut. 4:10	They were to remember the day they assembled at Mt. Sinai (Horeb) to receive the "Law" from the mouth of God.
Deut. 5:15	They were to remember their past bondage and how God miraculously delivered them.
Deut. 7:18	They were to remember God's past victories over their enemies.
Deut. 8:2	They were to remember God's faithfulness in leading them in the wilderness, even after they had so clearly disobeyed Him and were wandering as punishment.
Deut. 8:18	They were to remember that God is the One who enables them to succeed in whatever they do, once in the Promised Land.
Deut. 9:7	They were to remember their past sins and how God dealt with His people because of them.
Deut. 16:3	They were to remember (forever) their redemption from bondage in Egypt.
Deut. 32:7	They were to remind each other of the things their parents and grandparents had been through.

    d. The "Lord" (YHWH) - appears 550 times in 36 chapters! (average: 16 times per chapter).

    e. The "land" - 74 references in Deuteronomy; (average: 2 times per chapter).

C. Deuteronomy and The Old Testament

    1. The King- God gave specific commands regarding Israel's king long before they had one:

        a. He was NOT to accumulate horses from Egypt, wives and silver and gold (Deut. 17:14-17).

        b. He was to make a handwritten copy of "this law" and read from it daily (Deut. 17:15-20).

        c. It would keep his heart humble and his reign pure.

        d. Solomon violated everyone of these instructions (cf. 1 Kings 10:14 - 11:9).

    2. Josiah[1] and "the book" - 2 Chronicles: 34:1-28; 2 Kings 22:1-20

        a. There is a strong possibility that this was Deuteronomy because of *where* it was found.

        b. Josiah's "reform" movement after finding the "book" can all be linked to Deuteronomy[2]:

Josiah's Behavior	Record in 2 Kings	Command in Deuteronomy
The destruction of Canaanite "high places" and the centralization of worship.	2 Kings 23:4-20	Deuteronomy 12
Passover celebration in the Temple rather than in homes as prescribed in Exodus 12.	2 Kings 23:21-22	Deuteronomy 16
No divination, sorcery or witchcraft allowed.	2 Kings 23:24	Deuteronomy 18:14-22
The "book" given to Josiah had "curses" in it.	2 Kings 22:13,19	Deuteronomy 28
The kings of Israel were supposed to have their own copy of the law.	2 Kings 22:11; 23:2-3	Deuteronomy 17:18-19
It was called the "book of the covenant."	2 Kings 23:2	Deuteronomy 29:9,21
reflects "Name/Place" theology of Deuteronomy	2 Kings 23:27	Deuteronomy 12:5,11

D. Deuteronomy and the New Testament

    1. There are at least 43 direct quotations from 34 passages in Deuteronomy (perhaps as many as 40 more allusions)

    2. Some have cited Deuteronomy as Jesus' "favorite" book"

---

[1] Josiah is an amazing believer. He became king at age 8, and "got serious" with Yahweh at age 16. His "reforms" for which he is best known, began at age 20.

[2] The prohibition against sorcery and witchcraft by Josiah is *not* from Exodus or Leviticus, because neither book prohibits them. This prohibition first appears in the Deuteronomic law. Also the mention of "curses" refers back to Deuteronomy more clearly than Exodus. In Deuteronomy, Yahweh specifically pronounces "blessings" and "curses" over Israel (Deut. 29:11-13). The only two mention of "curses" in Exodus deal more with people than they do with Yahweh. (cf. Ex. 21:17; 22:28). Finally, 2 Kings 23:23-28, in rehearsing Josiah's greatness, cites from Deuteronomy's emphasis on the Name/Place theology to point to Judah's inevitable fall from fellowship with God after Josiah's death.

a. He quotes from it at least eleven times[1]:

PASSAGE IN DEUTERONOMY	JESUS' STATEMENT
"And he humbled you and let you hunger and fed you with manna, which you did not know, nor did your fathers know, that he might make you know that man does not live by bread alone, but man lives by every word that comes from the mouth of the LORD." **Deuteronomy 8:3**	*But he answered, "It is written, 'Man shall not live by bread alone, but by every word that comes from the mouth of God.'"* **Matthew 4:4**
"You shall not put the LORD your God to the test, as you tested Him at Massah." **Deuteronomy 6:16**	*And Jesus answered him, "It is said, 'You shall not put the Lord your God to the test.'"* **Luke 4:12**
"It is the LORD your God you shall fear. Him you shall serve and by his name you shall swear." **Deuteronomy 6:13**	*Then Jesus said to him, "Be gone, Satan! For it is written, "'You shall worship the Lord your God and him only shall you serve.'"* **Matthew 4:10**
"You shall not murder." **Deuteronomy 5:17**	*"You have heard that it was said to those of old, 'You shall not murder; and whoever murders will be liable to judgment.'* **Matthew 5:21**
"And you shall not commit adultery." **Deuteronomy 5:18**	*"You have heard that it was said, 'You shall not commit adultery.'* **Matthew 5:27**
"When a man takes a wife and marries her, if then she finds no favor in his eyes because he has found some indecency in her, and he writes her a certificate of divorce and puts it in her hand and sends her out of his house, and she departs out of his house, and if she goes and becomes another man's wife, and the latter man hates her and writes her a certificate of divorce and puts it in her hand and sends her out of his house, or if the latter man dies, who took her to be his wife," **Deuteronomy 24:1-3**	*"It was also said, 'Whoever divorces his wife, let him give her a certificate of divorce.'* **Matthew 5:31**
"If you make a vow to the LORD your God, you shall not delay fulfilling it, for the LORD your God will surely require it of you, and you will be guilty of sin." **Deuteronomy 23:21**	*"Again you have heard that it was said to those of old, 'You shall not swear falsely, but shall perform to the Lord what you have sworn.'* **Matthew 5:33**
"Your eye shall not pity. It shall be life for life, eye for eye, tooth for tooth, hand for hand, foot for foot." **Deuteronomy 19:21**	*"You have heard that it was said, 'An eye for an eye and a tooth for a tooth.'* **Matthew 5:38**
"Honor your father and your mother, as the LORD your God commanded you, that your days may be long, and that it may go well with you in the land that the LORD your God is giving you." **Deuteronomy 5:16**	*"For God commanded, 'Honor your father and your mother,' and, 'Whoever reviles father or mother must surely die.'"* **Matthew 15:4**
"A single witness shall not suffice against a person for any crime or for any wrong in connection with any offense that he has committed. Only on the evidence of two witnesses or of three witnesses shall a charge be established." **Deuteronomy 19:15**	*"But if he does not listen, take one or two others along with you, that every charge may be established by the evidence of two or three witnesses."* **Matthew 18:16**
"You shall love the LORD your God with all your heart and with all your soul and with all your might." **Deuteronomy 6:5**	*"And he said to him, 'You shall love the Lord your God with all your heart and with all your soul and with all your mind.'"* **Matthew 22:37**

E. Deuteronomy and the Christian

1. We may need to revisit our appreciation for Moses as a role model.

And there has not arisen a prophet since in Israel like Moses, whom the LORD knew face to face,
Deuteronomy 34:10

2. We need to balance "fear" and "love" as the grounds of our relationship with God in Christ.

You shall walk after the LORD your God and fear him and keep his commandments and obey his voice, and you shall serve him and hold fast to him.
Deuteronomy 13:4

---

[1] Matthew contains all eleven citations, which is understandable considering his Gospel is considered the most "Jewish" of the four, in terms of audience. Mark contains two: Jesus' response to the rich young ruler, and he recites the Shema in response to a scribe's question about the greatest commandment (10:19; 12:29-30). Luke has three, and they are all Jesus' response to Satan in the wilderness. John has none. There are two additional places where those speaking *to* Jesus cited Deuteronomy: the Pharisees in their question about Moses' provision for a certificate of divorce in Matt. 19:7, and the Sadducees question about the resurrection in the context of levirite marriage in Matt. 22:24).

3. We need to understand that God's revelation is always sufficient, though never exhaustive.

"The secret things belong to the LORD our God, but the things that are revealed belong to us and to our children forever, that we may do all the words of this law.   **Deuteronomy 29:29**

4. Christian leaders need to accept that success in ministry does not validate behavior.

That very day the LORD spoke to Moses, "Go up this mountain of the Abarim, Mount Nebo, which is in the land of Moab, opposite Jericho, and view the land of Canaan, which I am giving to the people of Israel for a possession. And die on the mountain which you go up, and be gathered to your people, as Aaron your brother died in Mount Hor and was gathered to his people, because you broke faith with me in the midst of the people of Israel at the waters of Meribah-kadesh, in the wilderness of Zin, and because you did not treat me as holy in the midst of the people of Israel. For you shall see the land before you, but you shall not go there, into the land that I am giving to the people of Israel."   **Deuteronomy 32:48-52**

📷 Snapshot of the Book of Deuteronomy

"Looking Back"   *"Looking Ahead"*

Sermon #1	Sermon #2	Sermon #3
• "Remember Your Parents' Sin" (1:1-4:43)	• "Remember Your Parents' God" (4:44-26:19)	• "Blessings or Curses?" (27:1-31:30) **3 "Appendices"** • "Song of Moses"(ch 32) • Blessings of Moses (33) • Death of Moses (ch 34)

KEY CHAPTER: *8 - a sobering reminder not to "forget" Yahweh*

KEY WORD: *"remember"/ "don't forget"*

BASIC GEOGRAPHY: *plains of Moab (not moving)*

BOOK SUMMARY: *Three sermons by Moses to the second generation east of the land promised to Abraham, Isaac, and Jacob.*

UNIT 9: JOSHUA - "POSSESSING YOUR POSSESSIONS!"

A. The Old Testament Books of History in Context

1. The 3 eras of our Old Testament

   a. **Transition:** *Joshua – Judges*; making the "switch" from being dessert nomads to a settled people with a distinct national identity.

   b. **Deterioration:** *Samuel thru Chronicles* – the story of the rise and fall of the kings of Israel and Judah

   c. **Restoration:** *Ezra thru Nehemiah* – the return of the exiles and the beginning of "Second Temple Judaism"

2. The Old Testament Panorama at a Glance: *(see chart on next page)*

B. The "Geography" of History
1. One crucial question: "What *is* history?"[1]
2. Two reasonable outcomes of our answer to this question:[2]
   a. It will determine how history is written.
   b. It will determine how history is read.

OLD TESTAMENT HISTORY...A GLANCE

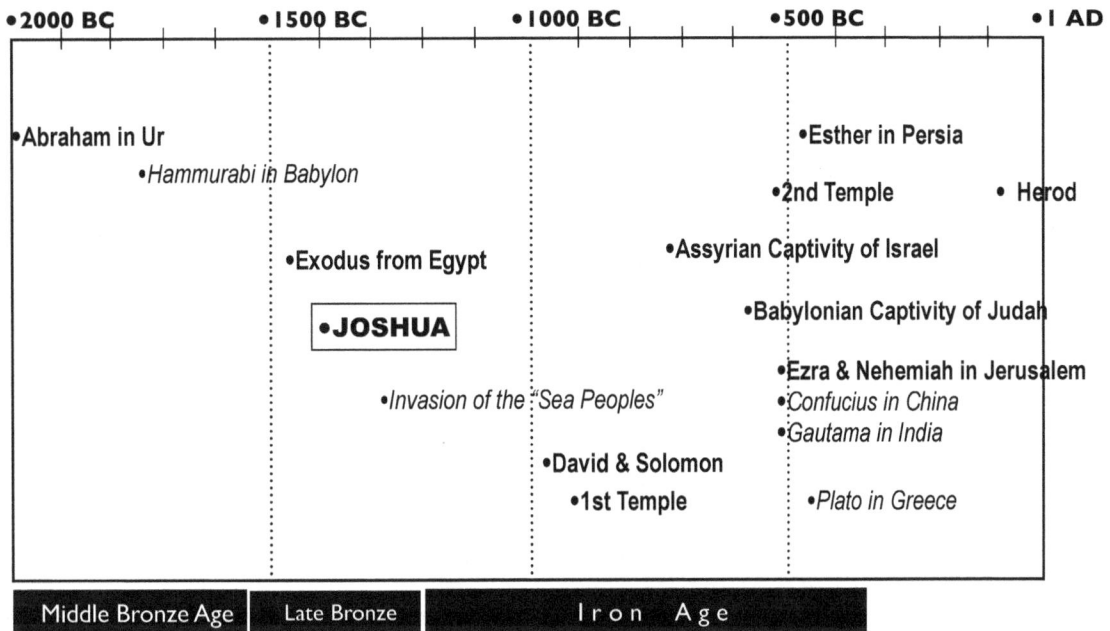

•2000 BC	•1500 BC	•1000 BC	•500 BC	•1 AD

•Abraham in Ur
  •Hammurabi in Babylon

•Esther in Persia

•2nd Temple   • Herod

•Exodus from Egypt

•Assyrian Captivity of Israel

•JOSHUA

•Babylonian Captivity of Judah

•Ezra & Nehemiah in Jerusalem
•Invasion of the "Sea Peoples"
•Confucius in China
•Gautama in India

•David & Solomon
  •1st Temple   *•Plato in Greece*

Middle Bronze Age	Late Bronze	Iron Age

*Historians divide and subdivide these periods of time in a variety of ways.

C. The "*Western*" View of History
1. *It is Secular:* it chronicles the affairs of people (we may have "religious" holidays, but we lack a spiritual view of time).[3]
2. *Cause & Effect:* occurs in a "closed system" of natural laws.
3. *It is Linear:* history is based on a continuum using an absolute chronology (I.e. "fixed" dates based on a common reference point)
4. "Time": refers to incremental marks along this continuum (E.g. the fall of Jerusalem occurred in 586 B.C.)
5. The "*Eastern*" View of History

---

[1] How we define "history" will determine a great deal. Most importantly, it will dictate how we *read* history, and what we expect from it. Unfortunately, we seem offended by the removal of prayer for our schools, and the manger from Christmas, yet fail to see that we have removed God from time itself.

[2] Both of these involve real people living in a real world. But, they are *not* contemporaries. The writing of history is a reflection of the era in which it was recorded, while the reading of history is influenced by the era in which it is read. Humility demands that we recognize, at least on the human level, that Joshua was writing for *his* grandchildren, not ours. And most importantly, Yahweh was fine with that.

[3] This stands in stark contrast to the ancient world where the word "atheist" referred to someone who was impious in the way they lived, and disregarded the gods. But, no one disbelieved that the gods were real. This is an important consideration when thinking of biblical history and the people who populate it. The struggles we face in the 21st century with neo-atheism would be totally foreign to the life and ministry of Paul. His burden was to turn people from *false* gods to the one true God. He never had to convince *anyone* of the divine!

    a. It is Religious: the gods are an integral aspect of all of life; they play an enormous role in the affairs of mankind.

    b. Cause & Effect: occurs in an "open system" of supernatural "laws" that control events and people.

    c. It is Cyclical: because the gods are responsible for the seasons, the passing of time is inseparable from the seasons. (E.g. the "Baal cycle")

    d. "Time": is understood in terms of the present; no absolute chronology; it is neither needed nor important. (E.g. 2 Kings 25:1 tells us that the Babylonian invasion of Jerusalem occurred "in the 9th year of Zedekiah's reign, on the 10th day of the 10th month.")

    e. Time needs to be "interpreted" more than recorded; there is a heavy reliance upon "reading" signs and omens in order to know what course of action to take.[1] The following passage is an excellent example:

> *"For the king of Babylon stands at the parting of the way, at the head of the two ways, to use divination. He shakes the arrows; he consults the teraphim; he looks at the liver."*   **–Ezekiel 21:21**

D. The *Hebrew* View of History

    1. *It is Sacred:* history is inseparably bound to God and the covenant.

        a. **the past** - always explained in terms of God dealing with them in response to obedience or disobedience; covenant-keeping or covenant-breaking.[2]

        b. **the present/future** - would be "written" (by Yahweh!) based on *their* response to the covenant and God's distribution of "blessings" or "curses."[3]

        c. this view of history is on virtually every page of the Old Testament historical books.

    2. *Cause & Effect:* understood in terms of obedience and disobedience

    3. *"Recurrence":* the cyclical nature of history is rejected; God can not be manipulated through sympathetic magic, or predicted by "reading" omens[4] (divination was prohibited! cf. Deut. 18:10)

    d. *Time:* there are recurring "patterns" that become opportunities to learn
        (E.g. *"He did evil in the eyes of the Lord as his father had done…"*)

    5. Distinctives of Hebrew History

        a. Joshua – Kings is in the "Former Prophets" section of the Tanakh.

        b. The Jews understood God to be "speaking" to them in and through these books because they are connected to the covenant blessings and curses.

        c. "Prophetic" had to do with the content, *not* the author (unlike our own day where we "follow" authors rather than ideas)

        d. Hebrew historical literature paints a distinctly blatant portrait of its own sin and weakness.

        e. ANE documents are often propagandistic in favor of the glory of nations and leaders.

        f. As an "elect" people, their own *faithlessness* in the face of God's unrelenting faithfulness is a dominant theme.[5]

E. Joshua: The Man & the Mystique

    1. He was an outstanding military general (cf. the battle with the Amalekites in Exodus 17)

---

[1] The name for the priests in the Early Bronze Age era (c. 3000-2000 BC) was *"baru"* which means "inspector," because of the important role inspecting the livers of animals was; especially sheep, which were typically sacrificial animals. "Live Omen Texts" were compiled supposedly correlating key events in a king's life with liver anatomy. These texts were passed down. Ezekiel's comment is not only the only reference in the Bible to this procedure, it was also one of the earliest references to it in history (until cuneiform was disciphered). The liver was believed to be the location of an animal's soul, and when the animal was sacrificed and therefore "accepted" by the god, their souls merged. Therefore, studying the "soul" (liver) of the animal properly, could reveal the "soul" of the god in question.

[2] The book of Deuteronomy set this in motion, and we see it played out in the books of Kings and Chronicles.

[3] In a very real sense, the Jews *knew* that they played a vital role in their own *children's* history, which was in reality, *their* own present.

[4] This is best understood as seeking to control one's own personal history, which at its root is a rejection of the existence of a Divine Narrative, or worse, a refusal to submit to its storyline in an attempt to create a new one.

[5] This would be an excellent thing to point out to Islamic followers who think we believe Israel itself is "special" rather than an object of undeserved, divine grace.

2. He was Moses' "assistant." (Exodus 24:13; 32:17; 33:11)

3. One of original 12 spies.[1] (Numbers 13)

4. He was a "temporary" figure":

   a. Of the 223 times he is mentioned in the Bible, 75% (203) are *before* Judges 3.

   b. He is only mentioned 2x in the NT (by comparison, Rahab is mentioned 3x)

   c. His absence in Hebrews 11 is very unusual (the wall falling *and* Rahab are mentioned, as well as the names of four judges).

   d. He is called "the servant of the Lord" *after* his death (Moses is called "the servant of the LORD 16x in this book, as well as in 1 Kings, Psalms, and Hebrews!)

5. Joshua: a "transitional" figure (he is the "link" between Moses and the future of Israel as a covenant people)

   a. God's promise to him: *"I'll be with you like I was with Moses."* (Joshua 1:5)

   b. Israel's promise: *"We'll obey you like Moses."* (Joshua 1:17)

   c. Israel's prayer: *"May God be with you like He was with Moses."* (Joshua 1:17)

   d. God's "proof" to both: *"Today, I'll exalt you in their eyes and show them I am with you like I was with Moses"* (Joshua 3:7)

       (1) Red Sea crossing and Jordan River crossing inaugurate their ministries (similar miracle in the eyes of the Israelites; both mark "leaving" the past and moving into their future)

       (2) removal of sandals in God's presence (cf. Joshua 5:5-15 and Ex. 3:5; cf. Rev. 19:11-16)

       (3) spies sent-in prior to invasion (cf. Joshua 2 and Num. 13)

       (4) led the nation in Passover celebration (cf. Josh 5:10-11; Ex. 12; Num. 9:2-12)

       (5) interceded for Israel's sin (cf. Joshua 7:7-9; Deut. 9:25-29)

F. "Building Blocks" and "*Stumbling* Stones"

   1. The Foundation Stone: The Theme of Covenant Faithfulness

      a. Joshua's "commission" is to usher in the covenant promise to Abraham to the covenant people of God (cf. Josh 1:6; Gen. 12:7), and hold them to the Law of the Covenant of Moses (Josh 1:8; ch 24)

      "Then the LORD appeared to Abram and said, "To your offspring I will give this land." So he built there an altar to the LORD, who had appeared to him.   **Genesis 12:7**

      b. "The land" is mentioned over eighty times in this book, and it is always linked to obedience to the covenant.

      c. God's "covenant" is mentioned 17 times in the book.

      d. There are 300 references to the God of Israel in this book and only 9 to the gods of Canaan (all in the final 2 chapters!)

      e. Considering that there were seven years[2] of warfare, there is very little *detail* about it.[3] *(the longest war narrative deals with the covenant offense at Ai)*.

      f. The first two events once in the land were both covenant celebrations: circumcision of the children born after the exodus, and Passover at Gilgal[4] (5:2-10).

      g. The military portion of the book opens with a sobering reminder that this is all about God, not them.

      h. The book closes with the reburial of Joseph's bones at Shechem, in fulfillment of God's promise to Abraham.

   2. The *Falling* Stones: Central Cities in Canaan

---

[1] Joshua was from the tribe of Ephraim; Caleb was a Judahite. Both must have bore the title of "nasi" (elder/chief) in the first place to have been selected to be part of the recognizance team.

[2] There is disagreement on the length of the conquest, as there is on many time periods during the days of the books of Joshua and Judges. Some suggest 17-20 years for the conquest. But, that longer time period may point to the fact that the warfare was a "quick defeat" followed by years of "clean-up" skirmishes. We will learn from the book of Judges that the Jews never *truly* conquered the land.

[3] The actual number of years of combat can be determined using Caleb's ages given in Deuteronomy 2:14 and Joshua 14:6-10.

[4] Gilgal was the spot where they camped after crossing the Jordan River. It remained their spiritual and military center for the entire conquest. Joshua moved the Tabernacle to Shiloh *after* the conquest (Joshua 18:1).

a. **Jericho**: • one of the oldest cities on earth.

• was continually inhabited for nearly 8000 years (6000 years before Joshua!).

• its remains predate the Pyramids by 4000 years

• "Joshua's walls" are gone; but there are "hints" of a 15th century upheaval.

• The tel is 10 acres, 70 feet high.

b. **Hazor**[1]: • the "head" of the northern cities in Joshua's "northern campaign"

• enormous city; 200 acres on a mound

• burn layers have been found at 1400BC and 1250BC

• had 21 occupations from 2700 - 150 BC

c. **Ai**[2] • there is great confusion over the location of the site

d. These are the only three cities burned (i.e., totally destroyed).

e. God's intention was to give His people cities, vineyards and houses, *not* ash and rubble.

> *"When the LORD your God brings you into the land he swore to your fathers, to Abraham, Isaac and Jacob, to give you—a land with large, flourishing cities you did not build, houses filled with all kinds of good things you did not provide, wells you did not dig, and vineyards and olive groves you did not plant—then when you eat and are satisfied,"* **Deuteronomy 6:10-11**

f. The archeological remains that address this book are *not* as plentiful as we would like.

3. *"Stumbling* Stones" — Difficulties in Joshua

a. "the ban" - *(kerem)* God ordered the total annihilation of the Canaanites in Deuteronomy 7:1-11 and Joshua instituted it in Joshua 6:17,21

(1) We do *not* have explanations for this that will fully satisfy our 21st century sensibilities (nor should we try to provide them to others).

(2) It is reasonable to say, however, that *no one* watching and experiencing the conquest (including the vanquished) thought it was "wrong" in the modern sense, no matter how much they feared it and suffered through it.[3]

(3) What we *do* have, is information concerning:

(a) the seriousness and depth of the Canaanites' sin (Deut. 9:5)

(b) the example of Rahab (6:17) indicating that God didn't "hate" Canaanites

(c) the example of Achan & his family, indicating that God didn't "favor" the Israelites

(d) the length of the conquest allowed repentance (16-20 years)

b. **solidarity** - Achan's entire family died because of his sin. But…

(1) 36 Israelites also died because of *Achan's* sin, which often goes unnoticed and doesn't seem to bother people as much as what happened to Achan and his family.

---

[1] Hazor was the capital of the northern alliance of kings; that's why it was a *vital* city for Joshua to conquer (cf. Josh 11:10); It was located about 14 miles north of the Sea of Galilee, and was on the Via Maris ("the way of the sea"); an important travel/trade. Deborah and Barak destroyed Jabin's (King of Hazor) army here in Judges 4 (note: the "Jabin" of the book of Joshua and that of Judges are two different people; archaeological remains have shown that "Jabin" was a dynastic name associated with numerous kings of Hazor). this story records the amazing valor of Jaal, the woman who killed Sisera, Jabin's commander; she drove a tent peg through his skull (cf. Judges 4:17ff). Solomon rebuilt and fortified a number of key military locations during his reign; Hazor was one of them (cf. 1 Kgs 9:15); his "classic" Solomonic triple gates are still standing!

Hazor was one of the key cities conquered by the Assyrians (Tiglath Pileasar) on his way to conquer the northern kingdom (cf. 2 Kgs 15:29). Nebachadnezzar conquered it 150 years later, according to Jeremiah, and left it desolate (cf. Jer 49:28-30, 33). Archaeologists have identified 21 occupational levels over 3000 years of history. Hazor is mentioned repeatedly by Egyptian pharaohs in Egyptian literature (e.g. Thutmose II, Amenhotep II, Seti I). Hazor was *the* Canaanite stronghold in the Fertile Crescent. Archaeology has uncovered three burn layers: 1400, 1300 and 1230 BC; after the 1230 destruction, there was apparently no occupation until the days of Solomon (c. 1000 BC)

[2] Joshua only burned *three* cities in Canaan during the conquest, according to the biblical record: Jericho, Ai, and Hazor (cf. Josh 6:24; 8:28; 11:13). We have to remind ourselves that Yahweh's intention was to provide the Israelites with cities to inhabit, with vineyards, fig trees, etc., *not* ashes and rubble (cf. Deut. 6:10-11).

[3] We even have evidence of this on a 9th century B.C. stele on which Mesha, King of Moab speaks of Israel's war with them being a result of their god Chemosh being angry with them.

(a) this was not unique to Israel; a similar incident is recorded on the Moabite Stone

(b) it is the foundation of our doctrine of imputation("in Adam" vs. "in Christ" 1 Cor. 15:22)

c. **"victory"** - the book records complete victory *and* incomplete victory (cf. 11:23; 21:43-35 with 13:1-6; 23:4-5)

(1) God had enabled Israel to conquer those with control; control then went to Israel.

(2) conquest and possession were not always synonymous in this book.

G. Joshua and The Christian

1. We need to be careful not to relegate YHWH to "supporting actor" in this drama. This is more than a book with great role models!

2. The Old Testament is *not* a "western" history book. It is an ANE document about a covenant-keeping sovereign God who creates history. *(He doesn't merely see to it that it's "recorded"!)*

3. We need to understand the delicate balance between "victory" and "possession" in our lives as Christians when it comes to the finished work of Christ.

4. We need to understand that God has no "sides" other than His own.

5. We need to see *ourselves* as "transitional" figures in an ongoing Story, not central characters of a current event.

Snapshot of the Book of Joshua

Entering Canaan (chapters 1-5)	Conquering Canaan (chapters 6-12)	Occupying Canaan (chapters 13-24)
• spies sent in (only 2!) • Jordan river crossing • same miracle that established Moses' leadership.	• 31 armies defeated • 3 military campaigns • Jericho the first victory • Ai the only defeat	• land divided-up by tribe • cities of refuged named • cities for priests named • Joshua's final plea: "Choose this day..."

KEY CHAPTER: *12 - summary of the nation's (Yahweh's) victories*

KEY WORD: *"victory!"*

BASIC GEOGRAPHY: *Moab - Canaan*

BOOK SUMMARY: *The second generation enters, conquers, and occupies the land Yahweh swore to give to Abraham, Isaac, and Jacob.*

UNIT 10: *"In Those Days…"* - The Books of Judges and Ruth

A. Understanding The Times[1]

    1. The Ancient Near East

        a. the time of the Judges falls within the Greek Heroic Age

        b. it was a time characterized by:

            (1) contests of champions (E.g. Hercules, Achilles, Jason and the Golden Fleece)

            (2) bloody violence, revenge and retaliation

            (3) aristocratic warriors (E.g. the Mycenaean Kings; "mighty men of valor")

            (4) demeaning view of women ("a womb for every man" - Judges 5:30)

        c. the Philistines were related to the "Sea Peoples" from the Aegean.

    2. Canaan in Particular

        a. Israel had failed to *fully* occupy the land (nine specific references):

> *And the LORD was with **Judah**, and he took possession of the hill country, but he could not drive out the inhabitants of the plain because they had chariots of iron.*   **Judges 1:19**

> ***Manasseh** did not drive out the inhabitants of Beth-shean and its villages, or Taanach and its villages, or the inhabitants of Dor and its villages, or the inhabitants of Ibleam and its villages, or the inhabitants of Megiddo and its villages, for the Canaanites persisted in dwelling in that land.*   **Judges 1:27**

> *But the people of **Benjamin** did not drive out the Jebusites who lived in Jerusalem, so the Jebusites have lived with the people of Benjamin in Jerusalem to this day.*   **Judges 1:21**

> ***Manasseh** did not drive out the inhabitants of Beth-shean and its villages, or Taanach and its villages, or the inhabitants of Dor and its villages, or the inhabitants of Ibleam and its villages, or the inhabitants of Megiddo and its villages, for the Canaanites persisted in dwelling in that land.*   **Judges 1:27**

> *And **Ephraim** did not drive out the Canaanites who lived in Gezer, so the Canaanites lived in Gezer among them.*   **Judges 1:29**

> ***Zebulun** did not drive out the inhabitants of Kitron, or the inhabitants of Nahalol, so the Canaanites lived among them, but became subject to forced labor.*   **Judges 1:30**

> ***Asher** did not drive out the inhabitants of Acco, or the inhabitants of Sidon or of Ahlab or of Achzib or of Helbah or of Aphik or of Rehob, so the Asherites lived among the Canaanites, the inhabitants of the land, for they did not drive them out.*   **Judges 1:31 -32**

---

[1] The Book of Judges falls roughly into three large "chunks": ***Part #1*** – the first few chapters; actually a summary of sorts and a sort of rubric for what follows. ***Part #2*** – chapter 2:6 thru chapter 16: this large section contains the stories of the 13 judges. ***Part #3*** – chapters 17-21: this reads much like a "postscript" and records a number of heinous deeds and godless behavior within Israel; of special note to me, is the obvious deterioration of the priestly tribe of Levi, as evidenced in the story of the family priest and that itinerant Levite whose concubine was raped and eventually dismembered by the Levite himself.

There is significant internal evidence that the books was compiled in its present form sometime during the time of King Solomon: **(1)** There is a repeated reference to the face that this story occurs at a time in the past; in particular, prior to the monarchy (*"In those days there was no king in Israel. Everyone did what was right in his own eyes."* 17:6; *"In those days there was no king in Israel. And in those days the tribe of the people of Dan was seeking for itself an inheritance to dwell in, for until then no inheritance among the tribes of Israel had fallen to them."* 18:1; *"In those days, when there was no king in Israel, a certain Levite was sojourning in the remote parts of the hill country of Ephraim, who took to himself a concubine from Bethlehem in Judah."* 19:1; *"In those days there was no king in Israel. Everyone did what was right in his own eyes."* 21:25; **(2)** There is a repeated reference to certain practices, etc. happening in the past, but still a present reality at the later time of composition: *"But the people of Benjamin did not drive out the Jebusites who lived in Jerusalem, so the Jebusites have lived with the people of Benjamin in Jerusalem to this day."* (6x total across the span of the book - 1:21; cf. 1:26; 6:24; 10:4; 15:19; 18:12).

The Book of Ruth ends with an abbreviated genealogy for King David, indicating a time of final redaction/editing/compilation sometime during or after his ascension to the throne (cf. Ruth 4:18-22)

> ***Naphtali*** *did not drive out the inhabitants of Beth-shemesh, or the inhabitants of Beth-anath, so they lived among the Canaanites, the inhabitants of the land. Nevertheless, the inhabitants of Beth-shemesh and of Beth-anath became subject to forced labor for them.*   **Judges 1:33**

> *The Amorites pressed the people of* ***Dan*** *back into the hill country, for they did not allow them to come down to the plain.*   **Judges 1:34**

    b. Israel had failed to *refrain* from inter-marriage[1]:

> *You shall not intermarry with them, giving your daughters to their sons or taking their daughters for your sons, for they would turn away your sons from following me, to serve other gods. Then the anger of the LORD would be kindled against you, and he would destroy you quickly.*   **Deuteronomy 7:3-4**

> *And their daughters they took to themselves for wives, and their own daughters they gave to their sons, and they served their gods.*   **Judges 3:6**

    c. Israel had failed to remain monotheistic[2]:

> *And God spoke all these words, saying, "I am the LORD your God, who brought you out of the land of Egypt, out of the house of slavery. "You shall have no other gods before me.*   **Exodus 20:1-3**

> *They abandoned the LORD and served the Baals and the Ashtaroth.* **Judges 2:13**

    d. Israel had broken the covenant they had sworn to Joshua[3] (Josh. 24:15-24).

3. God's Editorial Comments on the Time of the Judges

    a. from the time of the Temple (c. 1000 B.C.):

> *They did not destroy the peoples, as the LORD commanded them, but they mixed with the nations and learned to do as they did. They served their idols, which became a snare to them. They sacrificed their sons and their daughters to the demons; they poured out innocent blood, the blood of their sons and daughters, whom they sacrificed to the idols of Canaan, and the land was polluted with blood.*   **Psalm 106:34-38**

    b. from the time of Jeremiah (c. 586 B.C.):

> *And I brought you into a plentiful land to enjoy its fruits and its good things. But when you came in, you defiled my land and made my heritage an abomination.*   **Jeremiah 2:7**

    c. from the author of this book:

> *And the people of Israel did what was evil in the sight of the LORD and served the Baals. And they abandoned the LORD, the God of their fathers, who had brought them out of the land of Egypt. They went after other gods, from among the gods of the peoples who were around them, and bowed down to them. And they provoked the LORD to anger.*   **Judges 2:11-12**

B. The Book of Judges: Understanding The Participants[4]

  1. The Judges of Israel – the *saphat*

    a. What they *were:*

---

[1] This warning from Deuteronomy was given by Moses to the *second* generation of those coming out of Egypt. But, we are told in the preface to the book of Judges that this was the beginning of a generation that did not *"know Yahweh or what He had done for Israel."*

[2] This command was given to the *first* generation. They heard this from the lips of Moses. The second *generation* also heard it however in Deuteronomy 5:6. The repeated reference to "the Baals" in the plural is a reflection of the Canaanite belief in location-specific gods: Baal-Peor, Baal-Beruth, Baal-Timnah, etc.

[3] It is also very important to view the books of Judges thru 1 Samuel as very much a part of the same fabric; the moral and spiritual condition of the nation as evidenced in Eli's family life and the corruption of the priesthood is very consistent with that of the time of the Judges. In fact, Samson and Eli may have been contemporaries because of their constant struggle with the Philistines. Eli and Samuel were both judges and Eli's sons behaved in a fashion "typical" of the era.

[4] Judges is a "messy" book theologically because the agents of justice (i.e. the judges) were not pure or even just themselves! Yet, we are repeatedly told that it was Yahweh who "raised them up." Deborah and Othniel are the only two judges with a "clean" resumé; Yet, neither of them are mentioned in Hebrews 11. Othniel was Caleb's nephew. There were 12 judges for sure, but 13 if you include Barak in the list along with Deborah.

        (1)   military leaders and "deliverers"[1]

        (2)   agents of God's justice and faithfulness

        (3)   temporary and regional[2]

    b.   what they *weren't:*

        (1)   legal arbitrators: Deborah is the only exception (Judges 4:4-5)

        (2)   permanent: they were *not* elected, appointed, or anointed

        (3)   prophetic: they did *not* call the Israelites back to Yahweh

        (4)   priestly: they were *not* associated with Tabernacle or Shiloh

        (5)   "spiritual": only 3 even *mentioned* the Lord

        (6)   dynastic: they had *no* heirs

        (7)   "qualified": they had *no* previous resumé

        (8)   role-models: *reflected* their context more than *reformed* it (E.g. Gideon, Jephthah, and Samson; Deborah and Othniel are the only exceptions).

2.   Understanding the Book

    a.   It is thematic, *not* chronological[3]

        (1)   It covers the time period from the conquest to Saul's anointing (how you date the exodus determines the first date; the second is 1050 B.C.)

        (2)   the arrangement is *not* chronological (cf. Judges 18:1 with 1:34, and 22:28 with Josh. 22:13)

        (3)   the Judges are not strictly sequential or contemporaneous (410 years doesn't "fit")

    b.   Judges is a *prophetic* Book

        (1)   it *illustrates* the theology of the covenant (cf. Deut. 28)

        (2)   it illustrates the heart of the nation.

        (3)   it establishes the need for a king (but *not* for military purposes).

    c.   Judges is a *condemning* book[4]

        (1)   an angelic announcement the *opposite* of Joshua's (2:1-5)

        (2)   it begins with an historical review the *opposite* of Joshua's (ch. 1)

        (3)   a "sin cycle" that repeats itself six times!

        (4)   the book "closes" with idolatry, homosexuality, rape, mutilation, genocide and kidnapping within Israel!

        (5)   the book closes with stories indicating a corrupt priesthood.

    d.   Judges is a *spiritual* book!

        (1)   there are 22 references to the "Angel of the Lord"[5]

        (2)   there are 7 references to the "Spirit of the Lord"[6]

        (3)   four individuals are empowered by the "Spirit of the Lord"[7]

        (4)   there are 234 references to God

---

[1] In chapters 3-16, all the oppression is coming from *outside* the nation of Israel and the land of Canaan. But, there is no mention of outside oppression or of a judge after chapter 16. (Mesopotamia in 3:7-11; Hazor in ch 4-5; Ammonites in 10:6-12:7; Philistia in 3:31; Amalekites in ch 6-8; Moabites in 3:12-30; Midianites in ch 6-8)

[2] Shiloh is the only "central" location in the entire book.

[3] This is also reflected in the unbalanced "coverage" of the judges. Six of them receive a lot of "ink," the other six do not.

[4] Chapters 17-18 open with, *"In those days Israel had no king, and everyone did that which was right in their own eyes."* Chapters 19-21 opens and closes with a similar comment, thus setting the stage in the listener's mind that what Israel really needs is a king, which will come in the next book. Alfred Eidersheim holds that Canaan was a "hub" for spiritual darkness, and that in a very real sense, the Jews were moving into "hell." This sounds very similar to Jesus' statement about the ministry of the Church in Matthew 16:18.

[5] The Angel of the Lord is typically understood to be a pre-Incarnation appearance of the eternal Son of God.

[6] This phrase does not appear in our Bibles prior to this book.

[7] Othniel in chapter 3, Gideon in chapter 6, Jephthah in chapter 11, and Samson in chapter 14.

(5) the faithlessness of Israel serves as a foil for the loyalty and mercy of Yahweh.

(6) this is a book about one-sided covenant love.

3. Untangling The Problems

   a. Being Responsible Readers

     (1) the Bible's authentication is its unrelenting honesty about human sin.

     (2) this honesty is a record, *not a recommendation.*[1]

     (3) we must remind ourselves that we are *always* missing something (context, facts, etc.)

   b. Jephthah's Daughter

     (1) the act is *not* justifiable, but it *is* reasonable; we must remind ourselves of the context.

     (2) it was a foolish and rash vow; not the last during this time![2]

     (3) he was not expecting his daughter to come out from "the doors" of his house.

     (4) he was either ignorant of the Law, or had put her under *"cherem"* (cf. Lev. 27:1-8 and 27:29)

     (5) in *all* 286 occurrences of *olah* ("burnt offering") in the OT, the sacrifice is killed.

     (6) it is unreasonable to believe she lived.[3]

   c. Samson's Sensuality

     (1) he lived near the *end* of the era of the Judges (cf. Philistines and 1 Samuel)

     (2) he likely serves as a metaphor for Israel in this book.[4]

     (3) his behavior is consistent with Eli's two sons who were priests at the same time. (cf. 1 Sam. 2)

   d. Inclusion In Hebrews 11

     (1) a strong example of what we must be "missing" (inspiration vs. observation)

     (2) testifies to the connection between faith and the Story of God, rather than private salvation.[5]

     (3) testifies to the active nature of faith; true faith is always "in motion," it *does* the will of God.

4. Judges And The Christian

   a. We are always one generation away from apostasy![6]

     (1) the closing verse tells us what happened, but not why it happened

     (2) the beginning of the book tells us why (2:10)

     (3) the offspring of the 2:10 generation are the Jews of Judges 3-21

     (4) a king isn't what was missing; it was genuine "subjects"!

   b. Idolatry is accommodation to culture. It is loving what the culture serves.

   c. David was one of the "fruits" of the Book of Judges, showing God is always bigger than the obedience *or* disobedience of people.[7]

---

[1] This is a vital principle in interpreting the Bible correctly. Description is *not* prescription.

[2] Near the end of the book the Israelites voted to *not* give any of their daughters in marriage to Benjamites. This rash vow nearly led to the extinction of that tribe. In the book of 1 Samuel (similar time frame) Saul will make a rash vow that nearly leads to the execution of his own son. (cf. Judges 21:1; 1 Samuel 14:24)

[3] There are some who believe that her banishment to "perpetual virginity" was the sacrifice.

[4] In many ways, Samson is a personification of Israel as a nation: He is "set apart" by Yahweh, yet "marries" a Canaanite, which is exactly what Israel was and did.

[5] Redemption is a drama, not just a "declaration" of guilt absolved.

[6] Both Joshua and Judges end with the same statement: *"Every man went to his own inheritance."* (Josh. 24:28; Judges 21:24) But what a *different* inheritance!

[7] We learn this from the Book of Ruth. Imagine what we would be forced to conclude about the era of the judges *without* this book!

Snapshot of the Book of Judges

Explaining Israel's Sin (chapters 1-2)	Expunging Israel's Sin (chapters 3-16)	Exposing Israel's Sin (chapters 17-21)
• Joshua's generation dies • 3rd generation "forgets" Yahweh (the warning of Deuteronomy!)	• 13 judges • 7 "cycles" of sin	• idolatry • homosexuality • attempt at genocide • corrupt priesthood

KEY CHAPTER: *2 - a summary of Israel's "sin cycle"*

KEY WORD: *"self-defeat"*

BASIC GEOGRAPHY: *Canaan*

BOOK SUMMARY: *The story of Israel's departure from God's Story, from the death of Joshua up to their first king (Saul).*

C. The Book of Ruth — God's "Night Light"

    1. Uniqueness of the Book:[1]

        a. Presents an "op-ed" story of the time of the Judges.

        b. Demonstrates that God has "sheep" within all people groups.[2]

        c. Illustrates the *go'el* principle.[3]

        d. This is the only place in our Bible where the Hebrew "*go'el*" appears (23x).

        e. God had made provision in His Law to protect the covenant provision of land for His people.

        f. Both the family line and property rights were insured by the "*go'el*."

    2. The Message For Israel

        a. The covenant is kept alive by peasants, not heroes and kings.

        b. God is sovereign over the affairs of individuals (Naomi/Ruth) and nations (David).[4]

---

[1] Ruth and Jonah may be the two most *uncomplicated* books in our Old Testament. Both narratives are linear and clear.

[2] This shouldn't surprise us; it's the "nations" are the heart of the Abrahamic covenant, and the Abrahamic covenant is the explanation for the existence of Israel in the first place.

[3] The kinsman-redeemer (go'el) must fulfill three requirements in order to "redeem": (1) He must have the *right* to redeem. He must be a relative (cf. Deut. 25:5,7-20; Phil 2:5-8; Heb. 2:10-14); (2) He must have the *power* to redeem. He must be able to pay the redemption price (cf. Ruth 2:1; 1 Pet. 1:18-19; Heb. 9:120; (3) He must have the *desire* to redeem (cf. 2 Pet. 3:9; Heb. 10:7). The go'el was then responsible to preserve the family name when jeopardized through the death of a near relative. He was to buy back the property in question. He was also to avenge the unlawful death of a relative. Because family name and property went together, the first child born of the relationship from a levirate marriage would actually take the name of the deceased. In Ruth's case, the child born to her and Boaz was given to Naomi and took the her family name, thereby inheriting the property. (cf. Lev. 25:25-34 and Deut. 25:5-10)

[4]

      c.   God has an interest in the Gentiles[1] (Ruth 4:18-22)

      d.   Ruth stands as an example of a "virtuous woman," even though her origins are *not* from within Israel (e.g. the book of Ruth appears in the Hebrew Bible immediately *after* Proverbs 31)

  3. Ruth and the Christian

      a.   Ruth serves as a foreshadowing of the place of Gentiles in the Abrahamic promise, both as recipients of blessing, and conduits of grace.

      b.   The Book of Ruth illustrates the "remnant principle," that Yahweh always has faithful servants even in the darkest times and places (Is. 11:11; Jer. 23:3; Micah 2:12).

Snapshot of the Book of Ruth

"Scene I" **Ruth & Naomi** (chapter 1)	*"Scene II"* **Ruth** (chapter 2)	*"Scene III"* **Ruth & Boaz** (chapters 3-4)
• **setting:** time of Judges • Naomi returns with her daughter-in-law, "Ruth the Moabitess."	• Ruth "finds favor" with Boaz while working for him.	• Ruth marries Boaz and Naomi's family line is preserved. • Boaz & Ruth become the great-grandparents of King David

KEY CHAPTER: *4 - the redemption of Ruth (and Naomi) by Boaz*

KEY WORD: *"kinsman-redeemer"*

BASIC GEOGRAPHY: *Bethlehem - Moab - Bethlehem*

BOOK SUMMARY: *A story showing Yahweh's compassion towards one family, and His sovereignty and commitment to His Story (the line of David).*

UNIT 11: The Book of First Samuel — *"Give us a king!"*

  A. 1st SAMUEL[2]

    1. "God in a Box" — A Major But Hidden Theme

      a.   The Ark is one of the major "hidden" themes in the Books of Samuel.

---

[1] We need to remind ourselves that the Moabites were one of Israel's *oppressors* during the time of the judges! The story of Ehud as judge involves the brutal murder of Eglon, King of Moab who was oppressing the Israelites (cf. Judges 3:12-20). Also, Balak who hired Balaam to curse the Jews coming out of Egypt was King of Moab. In Deuteronomy 23, Yahweh specifically forbade a Moabite to "enter the assembly of the LORD" because of what they did under Balaam's influence in Number s 22. Even the marriage of Naomi's two sons to Moabite women while they were living there was forbidden by Yahweh in Deuteronomy 7:3. It is also likely that the famine in Ruth 1:1` that "drove"her family to leave Bethlehem was a judgment from God on the sin of the people (cf. Lev. 26:14-20).

Israel's history with Moab, and Yahweh's restrictions around relationships with them makes Ruth's willingness to love and serve Naomi, to return to Israelite territory, and to marry a Jew amazing evidences of a remarkable woman.

[2] It is worth pointing out at the onset that the two books of Samuel (a single book in the Hebrew Bible) are among the best know books of the Bible because of the stories they contain: Hanah's barrenness, David and Goliath, David and Saul, David and Bathsheba, David and Jonathan, and Absalom's rebellion against David.

(1) It is mentioned 40 times in 1 Samuel, more than any other book in the Old Testament.

(2) Over half of the references to it in the Old Testament appear in the Books of Samuel and 1 Chronicles.[1]

(3) Even when it is captured by the Philistines, it is *never* under anyone's control.

(4) The Ark has a greater sense of austerity and fierceness in the books of Samuel than it does even in Exodus.

(5) The Ark may be a "box" but Yahweh will *not* be manipulated.

2. Three Men – Three Destinies

  a. Samuel the Judge Samson the Judge: A Study of Contrasts[2] (chapters 1-19).

    (1) Both accounts begin, *"There was a man named..."*

    (2) The opening line is followed by:

      (a) Father's hometown, tribal affiliation and marital status.

      (b) Description of a barren wife[3].

      (c) Children who will be Nazarites from birth.[4]

      (d) Samuel stands as a stark contrast to Samson in the era of judges.

  b. Samuel the Prophet:

    (1) Perhaps the most important OT figure since Moses.

    (2) God *equates* him with Moses in Jeremiah 15:1

    (3) Of the tribe of Levi; he had a priestly ancestry.

    (4) He was born into a godly home like Samson; the third "light" in the dark pages of Scripture.[5]

    (5) Has a "call" to ministry that is as remarkable as Moses' burning bush.

    (6) Raised in a godless environment, typical of the *"days when the judges ruled..."*

      (a) Eli's two sons *were* what he assumed Hannah to be: ""worthless" (Heb: *belial*)" (cf. 1:16; 2:12).

      (b) the priesthood had been "Canaan-ized"

      (c) the Ark was seen more as a talisman than a tabernacle.

    (7) Samuel was the last of the judges and the first of "the prophets."[6]

      (a) The "word of the LORD was rare in those days" (Heb. *yaquar*; means "precious"; used mostly for jewels in the Old Testament; cf. 1 Kings 10:2).

      (b) With Samuel, Yahweh began "talking/speaking" to His people again.

    (8) Two new "offices" are initiated with Samuel: king *and* prophet.

---

[1] There are 194 references to the Ark in the Old Testament: 40 in 1 Samuel, 34 in 1 Chronicles, and 30 in Joshua (but all but 3 are in the context of the Jordan River crossing). Perhaps of even greater interest is that the Ark is only mentioned once in the book of Leviticus (16:2).

[2] Because of the anachronistic nature of the book of Judges, we know that chapters 17-21 actually occurred *before* the days of Samson. Samuel and Samson could very well have been contemporaries. It seems that the similarities in content and style of the two introductions is deliberate. One gets the distinct impression that Samuel is held up in contrast to Samson.

[3] Barrenness was one of the "curses" of covenant unfaithfulness. We see Yahweh's faithfulness demonstrated *both* in the barrenness itself, and "lifting" it from these two women (cf. Deut. 7:14). Contrary to our modern "way" of doing things, being barren and then having it miraculously lifted draws more attention to God than not being barren in the first place. Our temptation would be to be critical of Yahweh for making the two women barren in the first place, because we fail to see and know what God knows. And, this is *always* the case!

[4] "Nazarite" was really an "adult" thing; It was unusual to be called (i.e. told) to be a Nazarite from birth like both of these men. The only other person in the Bible to have this distinction, is John the Baptizer 1,000 years later.

[5] The other two were Boaz [Ruth], and Hannah.

[6] This designation, "the prophets," is different from someone being a "prophet." Aaron was a prophet, as was Moses. But here we have the introduction to a group of people with specific roles from Yahweh. The phrase, "the prophets" appears 156 times in scripture; 98 in the Old Testament and 58 in the New Testament. Luke accounts for over half of its uses in the New Testament, with 14 in each of his two books. Jeremiah and 2 Kings contain the most occurrences in the Old Testament, with 34 and 19 respectively. "The prophets" will eventually become synonymous with Yahweh trying to draw His covenant people back into the Story when they've left it.

        (a) We see in Samuel's first act as a prophet, a model of the prophetic office (a blistering rebuke to Eli).

        (b) The two sides of the "theocracy coin" are: prophets and kings.

        (c) If half of the "coin" became corrupt, the theocracy fell apart and God initiated judgment.

   c. The Place of Kings In The Story of God

     (1) God always planned on His people having a king.

     (2) Abraham was told "kings" would come from Sarah (Gen. 17:6).

     (3) Judah was told *"the scepter would not depart from his tribe, until it came to him to whom it belonged."* (Gen. 49:10-11).

   d. Kings & Prophets in Israel

     (1) In Israel, God was supreme, not the king!

     (2) Therefore, the prophet was more important than the king, because he spoke for God.[1]

     (3) The king's job was to carry out what God had spoken; to administer the covenant.

     (4) Kings were to be submitted to the Law *and* those who spoke for God.

   e. Saul the Weakling "King"[2] (chapters 9-31)

     (1) The People's Error:

        (a) The request for a king was not a sin, it was the type of king they wanted.

        (b) They wanted a king to lead them in battle, not in lead them in covenant faithfulness to Yahweh.

     (2) The "King's" Character:

        (a) Is more characteristic of a Judge than a king (strength in the midst of great weakness).

        (b) He is more influenced by the opinion of people than the Word of God. (1 Samuel 15:24-25)

        (c) Saul *failed* to do the very thing the Israelites "crowned" him for!

   f. David: the Warrior King[3] (chapters 16-31)

     (1) David sought to defend the name of Yahweh.

     (2) He understood theocracy, and what it required of a king.[4]

3. 1 Samuel and the Christian

   a. Obedience to the revealed *will* of God always has priority over the subjective "call" of God.

   b. For God, the "heart" always has priority over one's resume (cf. 1 Samuel 16:6-7, 11-12).

   c. God's leaders are "extruded" more than elected.

   d. A democracy can never be a theocracy. (There will never be a time when the "prophet" has more authority than the "king" in a government "by the people.")

---

[1] This is likely the reason behind Yahweh's harsh treatment of *false* prophets in the Old Testament (cf. Deut. 18:20). It is also noteworthy that nearly 25% of all occurrences of the word "king" appear in the prophetic books, and 40% of the word "prophet" appear in books that deal with kings.

[2] Saul stands forever as an example of squandered giftedness. It is noteworthy that although Saul receives a great deal of "ink" in 1 Samuel, he literally drops out of Yahweh's Story shortly after. His name appears 371 times in the Old Testament. 281 of them are in 1 Samuel, then it drops to 57 in 2 Samuel, and 27 in 1 Chronicles. After this, his name is never mentioned again in a direct reference to *him*. (There are 5 mentions of him in reference to David in the Psalms, and one reference to Gibeah as being his city.)

[3] Scripture calls David a "man after God's own heart." This is an Ancient Near Eastern concept that is not unique to the Bible. It's emphasis is on the *chooser*, not the one chosen.

[4] David knew and believed that Yahweh ruled His people, not him or Saul for that matter. David always referred to Saul as the "LORD's anointed," pointing to the source of his leadership.

Snapshot of the Book of 1 Samuel

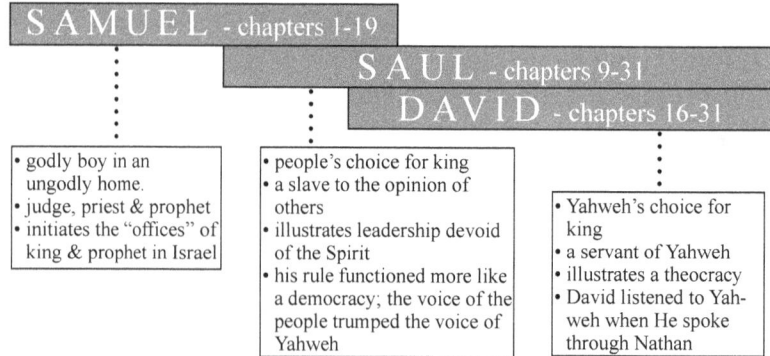

SAMUEL - chapters 1-19

SAUL - chapters 9-31

DAVID - chapters 16-31

• godly boy in an ungodly home. • judge, priest & prophet • initiates the "offices" of king & prophet in Israel	• people's choice for king • a slave to the opinion of others • illustrates leadership devoid of the Spirit • his rule functioned more like a democracy; the voice of the people trumped the voice of Yahweh	• Yahweh's choice for king • a servant of Yahweh • illustrates a theocracy • David listened to Yahweh when He spoke through Nathan

KEY CHAPTER: *16 - David anointed second king over Israel*

KEY WORD: *"Samuel, Saul, David"*

BASIC GEOGRAPHY: *Canaan (Israel)*

BOOK SUMMARY: *The transition from judges to kings in God's Story (i.e., Saul).*

UNIT 12 - The Book of Second Samuel — *"Israel's Sweet Psalmist"*

A. The "Cities of David"

1. Jerusalem *(aka: Jebus, Salem)*

    a. It was an *ancient* place.

    (1) Melchizedek was "King of Salem" during the days of Abram (I.e. *Jeru-Salem*; Gen. 14:18; Ps. 76:1-2).

    (2) Jebus (Jerusalem) was the capital of the "southern confederacy" in Canaan (1 Chron. 11:4-5).

    (3) Mount Moriah was here[1]; (Where Abraham was asked to "sacrifice" Isaac; cf. Gen. 22:2).

    (4) God met David at Mt. Moriah and stopped a judgment on his sin (2 Chron. 3:1).

    (5) Mt. Moriah was the site of Solomon's Temple (2 Chron. 3:1).

    b. It was a *strategic* place.

    (1) It sat at the junction of three valleys.[2]

    (2) It was easily defensible

    (3) It was more central to the nation than Hebron (20 miles south).

    c. It is a *holy* place.

    (1) all 3 of the world's major religions claim Jerusalem as their "holy city":

    (a) for Jews it is the "City of David."

    (b) for Christians it is the place where Jesus died *and* was raised.[3]

---

[1] Mt. Moriah and Mt. Zion are part of the same rock complex. Moriah was the Temple site, Zion was a former Jebusite stronghold where David built his palace and brought the Tabernacle prior to the construction of the Temple. (cf. Is. 66:20; 2 Sam. 5:6-9; 6:17; 1 Kgs 8:1)

[2] The three valleys were the Hinnom Valley where Gehenna was located, the Kidron Valley, which one crossed to get to the Mount of Olives and the Garden of Gethsemane, and the Tryopoean Valley.

[3] Making it more significant than Bethlehem in Judah or Nazareth or any other city in Galilee.

        (c)   for Muslims, it is the place from which Mohammed allegedly rose to Paradise.

  2. Hebron

      a. It is an ancient city in history – c. 3000 B.C. (cf. Num 13:22)[1].

      b. It is an "import" city in The Story:

          (1) it is where Abraham lived (Gen. 13:18).

          (2) it is where the angels appeared to Abraham, repeating God's promise of a son[2] (Gen. 18:1-9).

          (3) Abraham bought the "Cave of Machpelah" from Ephron the Hittite here as a family burial plot (Gen. 23:17).

          (4) Sarah, Abraham, Isaac, Rebekah, Leah and Jacob were all buried here.

          (5) Jacob's body was taken from Egypt to be buried here (Gen. 50:13).

          (6) For the Jew, Hebron actually had more sacred "history" than Jerusalem.

B. From Jesse's Shepherd in Bethlehem to God's Shepherd in Jerusalem.

  1. Ascending The Throne – 1 Samuel 16 - 2 Samuel 5

      a. He was anointed king privately in his own home by Samuel (1 Sam. 16) .

      b. He ministers to Saul in Gibeah (1 Sam. 16-17)

      c. He slays the Philistine giant, Goliath (1 Sam. 17).

      d. He runs for his life from Saul (1 Sam 18-27).

      e. He defeats Saul's remnant army (2 Sam. 2-4).

      f. He is anointed king over Judah at Hebron, and rules here for 7 ½ years (2 Sam 2:4; 5:5).

      g. He is anointed king over all Israel (2 Sam. 5:1-5).

  2. Building the "House" – 2 Samuel 6-10

      a. He conquers Jerusalem and makes it "the City of David," then rules from here for 33 yrs. (2 Sam. 5:5-13).

      b. He brings the Ark of the Covenant to Jerusalem (2 Sam. 6).

      c. Yahweh makes a covenant with David[3] (2 Sam. 7; 2 Chron. 21:7; Ps. 89:3):

          (1) David wants to build a "house" for God; He says "No!"[4]

          (2) Instead, Yahweh will build a "house" for *David* (dynasty).

          (3) Yahweh says He will make David's "name great" (2 Sam. 7:9).

          (4) This is in fulfillment of Yahweh's same promise to Abraham (Gen. 12:2)

          (5) It found its ultimate fulfillment in the *Son* of David, Yeshua the Messiah (Phil. 2:9-10).

      d. David secures his boundaries[5] (2 Sam. 8-10).

---

[1] This reference in Numbers speaks of Hebron build built "Seven years before Zoan (Tanis in Egypt)." This is more likely a reference to a *re-building* of Zoan rather than its original construction.

[2] Interestingly, this announcement comes in the context of another announcement: the destruction of the two cities of the plains: Sodom and Gommoreh.

[3] This puts David in a very elite "club," along with Noah (Gen. 6 and 8), Abram (Gen 15 and 17)), and Moses (Ex. 19 and 24).

[4] God's reason for refusing David's desire to honor Yahweh with a Temple is summarized for us later in But God said to me, *"You may not build a house for my name, for you are a man of war and have shed blood."* There are 63 references to fighting and the aspects of warfare and killing in 2 Samuel. Nine chapters out of 24 deal with bloodshed directly connected to David. There are only six chapters in the entire book where there is no mention of war and killing (5-7, 9, 16, and 19). There are ten instances when killing is either done by David, or ordered to be done: 1:11-15; 3:1,6; 4:1-12; 5:6-10, 17-20; 8:1-13; 10:1-18; 12:26-31; 20:1-22; 21:1-9).

[5] This involved the Philistines on the west coastal area, Moab and Edom to the south, the Ammonites in the east, and the Syrians and Arameans to the north.

C. David's "Fall" – 2 Samuel 11

   1. The "Anatomy of Adultery"[1]

      a. David was in the right place at the wrong time (vs. 1).

      b. He entertained what he should have exterminated (vs. 2).

      c. He twice *rejected* what he should have respected: his conscience[2] (vv. 2, 3).

      d. He *neglected* what he loved: the Law of the Lord (Ex. 20:17).

      e. He *concealed* what he should have revealed: his sin (Prov. 23:18)

      f. David "evolved" from pornographer to adulterer to deceiver to conspirator to murderer.[3]

D. David's "Fallout" – 2 Samuel 12-20 (see charts on page 50-51 for a detailed description of all involved)

   1. An unnamed child suffers and dies (11:16-18).

   2. His son rapes his daughter. (ch 13).

   3. One son murders another son. (ch 13)

   4. He refuses contact with a son for 5 years (13:34 - 14:32).

   5. A son forms a conspiracy and rebellion (ch. 15-17).

   6. His Prime Minister defects to the rebellion (15:12).

   7. His son disgraces Yahweh, David, and 10 women from David's harem (16:21-22).

   8. His military commander murders his son (ch 18).[4]

   9. His kingdom immediately faces another rebellion[5] (ch 20).

E. David and the New Testament

   1. The name of "David"

      a. occurs 60 times in our NT (compared to 74 for Abraham and 80 for Moses)

      b. the phrase "Son of David" occurs 16x times, but never outside the Gospels.

      c. all but 1 of the 60 occurrences of "David" in our NT center around two things:

         (1) him speaking/writing behalf of God (cf. Acts 2:29-30) I.e. a prophet, not a king!)

         (2) bearing children

   2. David and Jesus

      a. the prophecy of Isaiah 9:6 connects the coming Messiah to the "throne of David."

      b. the angelic announcement to Mary connects Jesus to the "throne of David"

      c. the "name" that God said He would "make great" to Abraham and David was to be finally fulfilled in the one who was a descendant of both—Jesus.

---

[1] David was home when he should have been involved in protecting those for whom he was responsible to Yahweh. This story is a classic example of the unintended consequences that happen when we put our own desires and passions ahead of the needs of others. In a very real sense, this is a 10th century B.C. version of Internet porn. It is an issue of "access," in that David had a vantage point into Bathsheba's private life that was inaccessible to common people. His palace was higher than her home. It is an ancient form of voyeurism. This is the one time in David's life when he would live like his son would daily in the future—Solomon. And sexual sin for Solomon became as common as the gold in his palace.

[2] Based on what we know of David's character, it is impossible to think that his own conscience did not prick him when he first saw Bathsheba. The second "warning" is a bit cryptic, but a careful and slow reading of his servants' response to his query, "Who is that?" shows that they were trying to "slap" him to alertness by connecting her to Uriah, a man who was risking his life to protect David's at that very moment.

[3] The idea that David did not "know" who this woman was is ridiculous. Her home was within visual distance of his palace, and her husband was one of David's elite fighting forces. His "mighty men" only numbered 30. To make matters even more complicated, Uriah, Bathsheba's husband fought alongside his father-in-law, Eliam, another "mighty man." A third factor is that Bathsheba's grandfather was Ohithophel, David's prime minister of sorts. It's likely that David's actions with Ohithophel's granddaughter are behind his quick desertion to Absalom when he rebelled against his David.

[4] Joab, David's military commander was also his nephew, the son of David's sister, Zeruiah (cf. 2 Sam 2:18 and 1 Chron. 2:16). She had three sons, all of which were involved with David. Joab was the commander, Abishai was commander of the "mighty men" (2 Sam 23:18; 1 Chron. 11:20-21), and Asahel who was one of the thirty "mighty men."

[5] There were some in the nation who were angry at David and refused to serve him. The leader of this group was named Sheba.

"The book of the genealogy of Jesus Christ, the son of David, the son of Abraham."
—**Matthew 1:1**

    d. David is the last human name mentioned in our Bible. Jesus says:

"I, Jesus, have sent my angel to testify to you about these things for the churches. I am the root and the descendant of David, the bright morning star."   —**Revelation 22:16**

F. 2 Samuel & The Christian

    1. God does not operate by the aphorism in "Field of Dreams" (*"If We Build It, They Will Come"*)

    2. David's "house" was destroyed by leisure, not by war.

    3. Who I am "at home" is who I am.

    4. A shepherd who becomes king is always grateful; I should be no different (2 Sam. 7:18)

    5. Sin's effects never end. Only God can stop them.

    6. I never choose for myself alone. I choose for my grandchildren.

Snapshot of the Book of 2 Samuel

David's Rise to Power	David's "Fall" *	David's "Slide"
• becomes king over a united Israel • makes Jerusalem the center of worship and of government	• commits adultery with Bathsheba, wife of Uriah, one of his "mighty men"	• David's sin begins to show-up within his own family and house
CH 1	CH 11 CH 13	CH 24

* his sin of adultery with Bathsheba is his most grievous sin (cf. 1 Kgs 15:5)

KEY CHAPTER: *11 - commits adultery with Bathsheba*

KEY WORD: *"King David"*

BASIC GEOGRAPHY: *Canaan (Israel)*

BOOK SUMMARY: *The story of Israel's greatest king, David.*

Connect the Dots…the Power of Sin

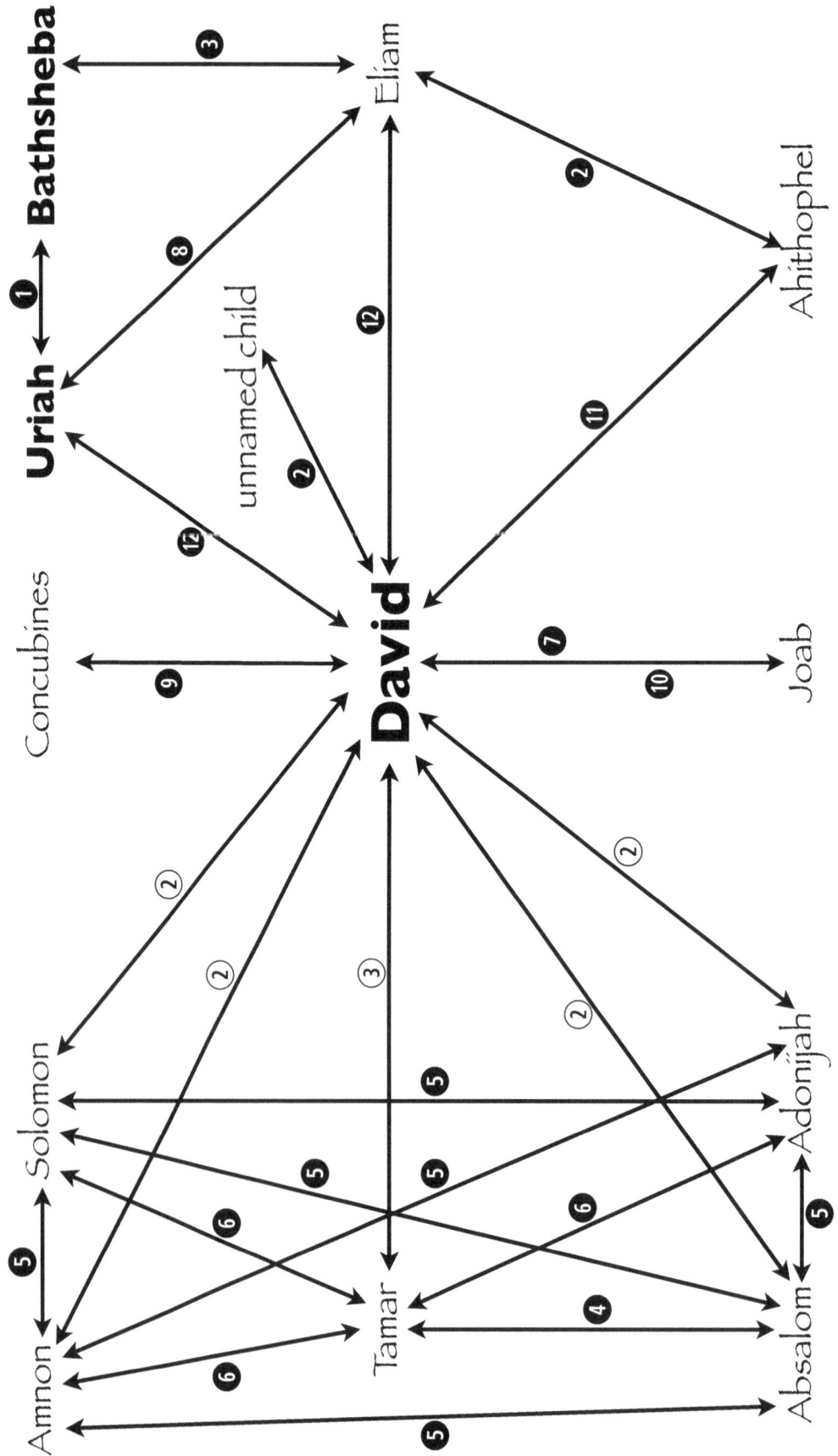

Bathsheba

Uriah

Eliam

Ahithophel

unnamed child

Concubines

David

Joab

Solomon

Amnon

Tamar

Adonijah

Absalom

❶ ❷ ❸ ❹ ❺ ❻ ❼ ❽ ❾ ❿ ⓫ ⓬

People Entangled in David's Web of Sin

Name	Relationship To David	Scripture ID	Other Key Scriptures	CODE
Bathsheba	Mistress	2 Samuel 11:27	2 Samuel 11-12; 1 Kings 1-2:25	❶
Unnamed Child	Son by Bathsheba	2 Samuel 11:27	2 Samuel 12:15b-23	❷
Solomon	Son by Bathsheba	2 Samuel 12:24	2 Samuel 12:24; 1 Kings 1:1- 1 Kings 14:24; 1 Chronicles 23:1, 28:1-29:30; 2 Chronicles 1:1-9:31	②
Amnon	Firstborn Son by Ahinoam	2 Samuel 3:2	2 Samuel 13:1-39; 1 Chronicles 3:1	② ❺ ❻
Absalom	Son by Bathsheba	2 Samuel 3:3	2 Samuel 13:1-20:7; 1 Chronicles 3:2	② ❹ ❺
Adonijah	Son by Haggith	2 Samuel 3:4	1 Kings 1:1-2:25; 1 Chronicles 3:2	② ❺ ❻
Tamar	Daughter by Maacah	2 Samuel 13:1	2 Samuel 13:1-13:32	③ ❹ ❻
Concubines	Harem	2 Samuel 5:13	2 Samuel 15:16, 16:21-22, 19:5, 20:3	❾
Joab son of Zeruiah	Nephew/Commander	2 Samuel 2:13	2 Samuel 2:8-39, 8:16, 11:1-27, 12:26-31,14-24; 1 Kings 1-2:34	❼ ❿
Uriah	"Mighty Men"	2 Samuel 23:39	2 Samuel 11-12:15, 23:23-39; 1 Kings 15:5	❶ ⓬
Eliam (father of Bathsheba)	"Mighty Men"	2 Samuel 23:34	2 Samuel 11:3, 23:23-39	❷ ❸ ❽ ⓬
Ahithophel (father of Eliam)	"Counselor" (advisor)	1 Chronicles 27:33	2 Samuel 15-17	② ⓫
Zeruiah (mother of Joab)	Sister	2 Chronicles 2:16	2 Chronicles 2:12-17	—

XIII. UNIT 13 — "PSALMISH 101" – THE BOOK OF PSALMS

A. "Singing In The Dark" — Stumbling Over The Psalms

   1. The Hebrew Psalter is *not* unique:

     a. Ancient near Eastern religious culture was saturated with music and song.

     b. A compilation of hymns, gods, and temples in Mesopotamia was done by an Akkadian high priestess before Moses' day.

     c. Paleographers have found anthologies, and individual hymns to specific deities and their temples, as well as to kings, etc.

     d. ANE hymns frequently contained superscriptions concerning musical instruments and rituals.

     e. The repetitive style of the Psalms is also a reflection of the culture in which they were written (e.g., Egypt, Mesopotamia, and Sumer).

     f. The similarity of imagery, structure, and content between pagan hymns and the Psalms is striking:

Hebrew Poetry	Sumerian Poetry	Egyptian Poetry
"Blessed is the man who walks not in the counsel of the wicked, nor stands in the way of sinners, nor sits in the seat of scoffers; but his delight is in the law of the LORD, and on his law he meditates day and night. He is like a tree planted by streams of water that yields its fruit in its season, and its leaf does not wither. In all that he does, he prospers. The wicked are not so, but are like chaff that the wind drives away. Therefore the wicked will not stand in the judgment, nor sinners in the congregation of the righteous; for the LORD knows the way of the righteous, but the way of the wicked will perish" **Psalm 1:1–6**	*"The man who knows fear of god…days will be added to his days, the name he has will become greater…The man who does not fear the gods… his old age will not last long. His inheritance will not be dear to him."*	*"[the silent man] he is like a tree grown in a meadow. It greens, it doubles its yield, it stands in the front of its Lord. Its fruit is sweet, its shade delightful, its end comes in the garden…. As for the heated man in the temple, he is like a tree growing indoors; a moment lasts its growth of shoots. Its end comes about in the woodshed."* **The Instruction of Amenemope**

   2. The Hebrew Psalter, *is* distinct:

     a. No other ANE hymn literature compares in terms of the variety of songs and internal organization.

     b. The entire collection is known as "Psalms."

       (1) Each unit is a "psalm," not a "psalms." (e.g. "Psalm 23" *not* "Psalms 23").

       (2) Superscriptions provide context but *not* interpretation (Pss. 3,7,18,30,34,51,52,54,56, 57,59,60,63,142).

     c. We must never forget that the Book of Psalms is Jewish in every possible way, and is literally "dripping" with covenant theology and steeped in covenant history.

       (1) The Psalms' theology is uncompromisingly monotheistic *and* monopolistic (i.e., one God, one Temple, and one ritual).

       (2) The *primary* purpose of the psalms was corporate praise, *not* private "worship" (the Hebrew title is, *cepher tĕhillîm* - "book of praises").

B. The "Books" *Within* The Book

   1. Psalms is an anthology, not a "book."

   2. It is the *only* anthology in a larger book that is itself *not* an anthology: The Bible.

   3. It is comprised of five "Books" that are also collections[1]:

     a. Book I ....Psalms 1 - 41

     b. Book II ....Psalms 42 - 72

     c. Book III..................Psalms 73 - 89

     d. Book IV ....Psalms 90 - 106

     e. Book V....................Psalms 107 - 150

C. The Book of Psalms had *multiple* authors:

   1. David – wrote 73 psalms

   2. Asaph – wrote 12 psalms (50, 73-83).

---

[1] There is no clear answer as to how and when these five divisions and their contents came to be. There is some evidence, according to scholars that they may have existed as separate collections for some time before being joined.

a. One of King David's three chief musicians (1 Chron. 15:29-16:6).

b. His four sons conducted the massive chorus at the dedication of the Temple in Jerusalem during Solomon's day (cf. 2 Chron. 20:5-19).

c. The "Sons of Asaph" formed a guild and played a prominent role during times of spiritual revival in Israel (cf. 1 Chron. 25:1).

3. The "Sons of Korah" – wrote 11 psalms (42,44-49,84,85,88,89).

a. Korah, their ancestor, died in the wilderness after a rebellion against Moses (Num. 16).

b. Korah's sons, however, did *not* die in the rebellion, and went on to become servants in the Temple (Num 26:11).

4. Solomon – Psalms 72 and 127

5. Moses – Psalm 90

6. Heman the Ezrahite – Psalm 88 (there is much debate regarding this man's ancestry; Levite vs. Judahite).

7. Ethan the Ezrahite – Psalm 89 (there is much debate regarding this man's ancestry; Levite vs. Judahite).

8. Unknown authorship – 49 psalms

D. It was "assembled" (not written), over about 1000 years (Exodus to Nehemiah).

1. Some scholars believe David has at least two separate "collections" within the book of psalms (Pss. 3-41 and Pss. 51-72).

a. Psalms 3-41 — "Yahweh" occurs 274x and "Elohim" occurs 49x

b. Psalms 52-72 — "Yahweh" occurs 23x and "Elohim" occurs 138x

c. Psalm 14 and Psalm 53 are "duplicates" except for the names of God used.

2. It was a "worship sourcebook" on some occasions (David's dedicatory prayer in 1 Chron 16:8-36 is taken from Pss. 105:1-15; 96:1-13; 106:1, 47-48).

3. The "Songs of Ascent" (Pss. 120-134) were specifically for pilgrims coming to Jerusalem who would be "ascending" the city and Temple mount.

4. The "Hillel Psalms" (Pss. 113-118) were sung during Israel's high holy days. (E.g. Passover, Tabernacles, Pentecost, Dedication).

5. Our present Book of Psalms most likely came into its present form around the 4th century B.C.

E. The Book *Above* All Books

1. Psalms is a book that speaks *for* us to God, instead of speaking *to* us from God, like the rest of Scripture:

> *"Here, for the most part, we find people addressing God in various ways—complaint in situations of distress and perplexity, thanksgiving in moods of liberation and joy, and hymnic praise in times of rejoicing in the goodness and wonder of of God's creation and providential care. In this sense, the Psalms may speak 'for' us by expressing the whole gamut of human responses to God's reality in our midst and thereby teaching us how to pray with others in the various times of our lives."* **Bernard W. Anderson, *Out of the Depths*, p. ix**

2. It reflects the hearts of individuals in a covenant relationship with Yahweh.[1] (There are over 2,400 references to "I, me, my, mine" as opposed to 350 for "we, us, our.")

3. But, its real focus in on God, *not* on man. (There are over 1200 references to Him in this book).

4. It was (and is!) primarily the "hymnal" of the covenant community, and only secondarily a private "prayer book"[2] (cf. 1 Cor. 14:26; Eph. 5:19; Col. 3:16)

5. It is the most extensive "teaching tool" on prayer in existence!

---

[1] Someone has wisely said that as a covenant child of Yahweh, I am always living in one of the psalms. They cover every human experience and reflect every human emotion for those caught up in Yahweh's grand Story. Some of the emotions captured in these exquisite prayers of old are: fear (Ps 56), love (Pss 91, 116), distress (Pss 31, 42, 120, 142), dismay (Ps 10), joy (Pss 98, 100, 117), impatience (Ps 13), gratitude (Pss 107, 118, 136), shame (Pss 25, 38, 44, 69), and guilt (Pss 32. 38, 51).

It was David's deep and personal familiarity with Yahweh's Law in the context of deep personal pain that yielded the psalms we have come to love and enjoy. The beauty of the psalms emerged out of the pressure and sorrow of life much like coal or a diamond. More than a great *writer*, we need to see that we have the fruit of a very *weak* human reflecting on a great God in the face of great pain. The greatness of both, exerting their pressure on a weak but devoted soul, produced the music of the psalms.

[2] We must continually remind ourselves that the Bible is an *ancient* book written to people much older than ourselves. God indeed wrote it *for* us too, but He did *not* write it to us.

F. Learning "Psalmish" — Figures of Speech and the Psalms

1. Figures That Compare

a. simile - an *explicit* comparison that uses the words, "like" or "as":

> *"He shall be like a tree planted by rivers of waters."* **(Psalm 1:3)**

b. metaphor - an *implicit* comparison in which one thing is said to be or to be represented by another:

> *"The LORD is my shepherd."* **(Psalm 23:1)**

c. implied comparison - similar to a metaphor, except the subject is not stated, and must be *inferred*. This figure requires care to determine the subjects before the interpretation:

> *"Dogs have surrounded me."* **(Psalm 22:17)**

d. personification - the attribution of human characteristics to non-human things (ideas, inanimate objects, even animals):

> *"Your rod and your staff, they comfort me."* **(Psalm 23:4)**

e. anthropomorphism - God is described in terms associated with humans. This is done to communicate some truth *about* God, not to actually describe what He is like (E.g. His "eyes" refer to His attentiveness, etc.):

> *"Hide your face from my sins."* **(Psalm 51:11 [9])**

f. zoomorphism - God is described in terms associated with animals or parts of animals. The intention here is the same as that of the personification:

> *"In the shadow of your wings I used to rejoice."* **(Psalm 63:8)**

2. Figures that Involve Substitution

a) paradox - An *apparent* contradiction.

> *"I have been crucified with Christ. It is no longer I who live, but Christ who lives in me."*
> **(Galatians 2:20)**

b. synecdoche - a whole is substituted for a part or a part for the whole.

> *"I will not trust in my bow, neither shall my sword save me."* **(Psalm 44:7 [6])**

c. merism - uses the opposite "ends" of something to represent everything in between:

> *"If I ascend to heaven, You are there; If I make my bed in Sheol, You are there."*
> **(Psalm 139:8)**

3. Figures Involving Addition or Amplification

a. parallelism - the repetition of an idea in the next line through contrast, completion or continuation:

> *"Oh, that my people would listen to me, that Israel would walk in my ways!"*
> **(Ps. 81:13)**

b. acrostic[1] - repetition of the same or successive letters at the beginning of words or clauses. (Psalm 119 is the best example of this literary device. Its 176 verses are comprised of twenty-two 8-verse stanzas, each line of which begins with the same letter of the Hebrew alphabet of 22 letters. E.g. vv. 1-8 all begin with the letter, "aleph," vv. 9-16 begin with "beth" and so on.)

c. inclusio - a literary unit (stanza, etc.) begins and ends with the same or similar word, phrase. It serves to "frame" the words in between and reiterates the theme of the section:

> *"O LORD, our Lord, how excellent is Your name in all the earth!"* **(Ps. 8: 1 and 9)**

d. hyperbole - deliberate exaggeration to emphasize a point. More is actually said than is really meant.

> *"I am worn out from groaning; all light long I make my bed swim with weeping and drench my couch with tears."* **[Ps. 6:6]**

G. Psalms and the New Testament

1. Next to Isaiah, Psalms is the most-quoted OT book in our New Testaments (approximately 155 direct quotes or allusions in 17 NT books!).

a. There are 55 references/allusions to the Psalms in the Gospels.

b. There are 23 in Revelation.

---

[1] This figure was especially helpful in an oral, illiterate culture. Much like the "preaching" done by stained glass windows in the cathedrals, the means by which the peasantry understood the gospel and the Scriptures, memory devices like acrostics served to aid those who could not read.

    c. There are 23 in Hebrews

    d. There are 17 in Romans

    e. There are 15 in Acts

    f. John quotes/alludes to Psalms the most (34x compared to Paul, 32x)

2. Jesus specifically said that the Psalms spoke about Him (Luke 24:44).

3. Jesus quoted Psalm 22 just before He breathed His last breath. (cf. Ps. 22:1 and Matt. 27:46)

H. Psalms and the Christian

1. The Psalms contain virtually every human emotion. There will never come a time when the Psalms do not minister to us.

2. It is worth noting that the "petitions" within the Psalms are strangely silent in regard to material wants and needs.

3. Even the "lament" psalms make up the largest portion of the Psalter, they invariably conclude with praise.

4. Writing psalms can be an excellent form of private worship.

5. In the face of the current "worship movement," we would do well to look to the Psalms for our model and our method of worship.[1]

I. PSALMS: Key Information

1. **Key Word:** "praise" (166x).

2. **Key Idea:** worship

3. **Book Summary:** Israel's Temple hymnal

4. **The Book of Psalms in the New Testament:**

*Then he said to them, "These are my words that I spoke to you while I was still with you, that **everything written about me** in the Law of Moses and the Prophets **and the Psalms** must be fulfilled."*
            Luke 24:44

Psalm	NT Citation	Psalm	NT Citation
2:1, 2	*Acts 4:25, 26*	37:11a	*Matthew 5:5*
2:7	*Acts 13:33; Hebrews 1:5 ; 5:5*	38:11	*Luke 23:49*
2:8, 9	*Revelation 2:26, 27; 12:5; 19:15*	40:6-8	*Hebrews 10:5-7*
4:4	*Ephesians 4:26*	41:9	*John 13:18*
5:9	*Romans 3:13*	41:13	*Luke 1:68*
6:3a	*John 12:27*	42:5	*Matthew 26:38; Mark 14:34*
6:8	*Matthew 7:23; Luke 13:27*	44:22	*Romans 8:36*
8:2	*Matthew 21:16*	45:6, 7	*Hebrews 1:8, 9*
8:4-6	*Hebrews 2:6-8*	48:2	*Matthew 5:35*
8:6	*1 Corinthians 15:27; Ephesians 1:22*	51:4	*Romans 3:4*
10:7	*Romans 3:14*	53:1-3	*Romans 3:10-12*
14:1c, 2b, 3	*Romans 3:10-12*	55:22	*1 Peter 5:7*
16:8-11	*Acts 2:25-28*	62:12	*Matthew 16:27; Romans 2:6*
16:10b	*Acts 13:35*	68:18	*Ephesians 4:8*
18:2b	*Hebrews 2:13*	69:4	*John 15:25*
18:49	*Romans 15:9*	69:9a	*John 2:17*
19:4	*Romans 10:18*	69:9b	*Romans 15:3*
22:1	*Matthew 27:46; Mark 15:34*	69:21	*Matthew 27:34, 48; Mark 15:36; Luke 23:36; John 19:28, 29*
22:7	*Matthew 27:39; Mark 15:29; Luke 23:35*	69:22, 23	*Romans 11:9, 10*
22:8	*Matthew 27:43*	69:25	*Acts 1:20*

---

[1] Unfortunately, it seems we draw more from the entertainment industry when it comes to how we do worship, how we construct our "worship centers," select sound systems, etc. In order to employ the Psalms in worship, one has to begin with an exalted view of God Himself. Otherwise, we may find ourselves singing to the mirror.

Psalm	NT Citation	Psalm	NT Citation
22:18	*John 19:24; cf. Matthew 27:35; Mark 15:24; Luke 23:34*	72:18	*Luke 1:68*
22:22	*Hebrews 2:12*	78:2	*Matthew 13:35*
24:1	*1 Corinthians 10:26 [28]*	78:24	*John 6:31*
31:5a	*Luke 23:46*	82:6	*John 10:34*
32:1, 2	*Romans 4:7, 8*	86:9	*Revelation 15:4*
34:8	*1 Peter 2:3*	88:8	*Luke 23:49*
34:12-16	*1 Peter 3:10-12*	89:10	*Luke 1:51*
34:20	*John 19:36*	89:20	*Acts 13:22*
35:19b	*John 15:25*	90:4	*2 Peter 3:8*
36:1b	*Romans 3:18*	91:11, 12	*Matthew 4:6; Luke 4:10, 11*
91:13	*Luke 10:19*	110:1	*Matthew 22:44; Mark 12:36; Luke 20:42, 43; Acts 2:34, 35; Hebrews 1:13. Cf.. Matthew 26:64; Mark 14:62; 16:19; Luke 22:69; 1 Corinthians 15:25; Ephesians 1:20; Colossians 3:1; Hebrews 1:3; 8:1; 10:12, 13; 12:2; 1 Peter 3:22*
94:11	*1 Corinthians 3:20*	110:4	*Hebrews 5:6; 6:20; 7:17, 21*
94:14	*Romans 11:1, 2*	111:9a	*Luke 1:68*
95:7-11	*Hebrews 3:7-11, 15, 18; 4:1, 3, 5, 7*	111:9c	*Luke 1:49*
97:7	*Hebrews 1:6*	112:9	*2 Corinthians 9:9*
98:3	*Luke 1:54*	116:10	*2 Corinthians 4:13*
102:25-27	*Hebrews 1:10-12*	117:1	*Romans 15:11*
103:17	*Luke 1:50*	118:6	*Hebrews 13:6*
104:4	*Hebrews 1:7*	118:22, 23	*Matthew 21:42; Mark 12:10, 11; Luke 20:17; Acts 4:11; 1 Peter 2:4, 7*
105:8, 9	*Luke 1:72, 73*	118:25, 26	*Matthew 21:9; 23:39; Mark 11:9; Luke 13:35; 19:38; John 12:13*
106:10	*Luke 1:71*	132:5	*Acts 7:46*
106:45	*Luke 1:72*	132:11	*Acts 2:30*
106:48	*Luke 1:68*	132:17	*Luke 1:69*
107:9	*Luke 1:53*	135:14a	*Hebrews 10:30*
109:8	*Acts 1:20*	140:3b	*Romans 3:13*
109:25	*Matthew 27:39*	143:2b	*Romans 3:20*

Copied from the appendix in A. F. Kirkpatrick, *The Book of Psalms*, The Cambridge Bible; Cambridge University Press, 1902; (*found online at:* http://www.jesuswalk.com/psalms/psalms-NT-quotations.htm); Only direct citations are listed. Allusions and indirect references are not.

XIV. UNIT 14 — "KEYS TO THE KINGDOMS" – An Introduction to the Prophets and I Kings

    A. First Things First: Getting a "*Bigger* Picture" of the Big Picture[1]

        1. **Picture #1:** The Book of Kings is a history of Israel's monarchy, highlighting "good" and "bad" kings.

---

[1] The two books of Kings in the English Old Testament comprise a single book in the Tanach, the Hebrew Bible. They record a period of world history that is nearly unprecedented. Much like the collision of tectonic plates, these books tell a story of murder, mayhem, near genocide, assassinations, wars, and rumors of wars. There is a veritable litany of nations and empires, foreign kings, and international battles. The book's time frame includes the rise and fall of Assyria, and the Neo-Babylonian empires, with intermittant warfare with Syria and Egypt. There are 41 different Jewish kings (including David and Solomon), and at least 22 prophets that minister during the time period of "the book of Kings." Of the 22 prophets, eleven left *no* writings. Of that eleven, there were 10 males and a lone female (Huldah - 2 Kgs. 22:14). The other eleven left writings, which we have in our Old Testament.

But perhaps most significant, is that the "book of Kings," which comprises 8% of our Old Testament, creates the historical context for nearly half of the books in our Old Testament.

The *Bigger* Picture: The Book of Kings is a record of the willingness or unwillingness of Israel's leadership to lead the nation in covenant faithfulness.[1]

2. **Picture #2:** The Book of Kings is a record of God's judgment of the sin of Israel and Judah.

   The *Bigger* Picture: The Book of Kings is a record of God's faithfulness to the covenant stipulations.[2]

3. **Picture #3:** It is important to know the history of the Ancient Near East during the 10th – 6th century BC to understand this book.

   The *Bigger* Picture: It is *more* important to know the covenant stipulations from the 15th century BC (I.e. Exodus and Leviticus) to understand this book!

4. **Picture #4:** The Book of Kings is only a small part of our Bible, comprising 47 of 1189 chapters (3% of the Bible and 5% of the Old Testament).

   The *Bigger* Picture: The scriptures associated with this time period comprise 36 % of the Bible and 46% (nearly half!) of the Old Testament.

5. **Picture #5:** The Book of Kings records primarily political activity; the political activity of kings.

   The *Bigger* Picture: The Book of Kings records a period of intense *prophetic* activity; the words of God! (375 of the 419 OT occurrences of *"thus says the LORD"* are associated with this time.)[3]

B. Four "P's" in the Puzzle

1. The "Powers" — Nations and Personalities Around Israel

   a. **Egypt** – a 3000 year old kingdom

      (1) *Solomon*— married a Pharaoh's daughter and built her a palace (1 Kings 7:1-8)

      (2) *Shishak*— Came against Rehoboam, Solomon's son in Jerusalem and took all the treasures of the House of the Lord as well as all the treasures of Solomon (1 Kings 14:21-26).

      (3) *Necco*— Killed King Josiah at Megiddo when Josiah interfered with a battle between Necco and the King of Assyria (2 Kings 23:29)

   b. **Assyria** – another ancient kingdom

      (1) *Tiglath Pileser III*— also known as Pul; wicked King Menahem of Israel taxed his people to provide tribute to Pul to keep him from destroying Samaria (2 Kings 15:19)

      (2) *Shalmaneser V*— Destroyed Samaria and conquered the Northern Kingdom of Israel in 722 BC and scattered the Israelites throughout the Assyrian empire. (2 Kings 18:9)

      (3) *Sennacharib*— came to Jerusalem eight years after Shalmaneser V had conquered Israel; Hezekiah gave him much tribute, but God caused him to return to Assyria where he was murdered. (2 Kings 18:13 - 2 Kings 19:36)

      (4) *Esarhaddon*— son of Sennacharib, became king in his place (2 Kings 19:37)

   c. **Babylon** – the "second coming" of an ancient people (i.e., the *Neo*-Babylonian Empire)

      (1) *Merodach Baladan* — was a constant threat to Assyria, but never succeeded. He also befriended King Hezekiah of Judah, and sent him gifts and a letter when he heard he was sick. (2 Kings 20:12-18; Isaiah 39:1-8)

      (2) *Nebuchadnezzar II*— the Babylonian king credited with the sack and destruction of Jerusalem. He attacked it on at least three occasions: 609, 597 and 586 BC (2 Kings 23:36-24:1; 24:8-11; 25:1-22)

2. The "Problems":

---

[1] The phrase, *"...he did what was right in the eyes of the LORD"* only appears 5 times in the "book of Kings," and all are in reference to kings from the southern kingdom of Judah (Joash, Amaziah, Azariah, Hezekiah, and Josiah).

[2] God's faithfulness is *always* to Himself. In other words, we must see His judgments upon sin as His faithfulness, not merely His care and deliverance. When it comes to His relationship with His covenant people, this becomes paramount. The execution of the "curses" of Deuteronomy 27-29 is as much of an expression of His faithfulness to the covenant, as the "blessings" are. This principle lies behind Paul's statement to Timothy over 1,000 years later: *"...if we are faithless, he remains faithful— for he cannot deny himself."* **2 Timothy 2:13**

[3] This period must be viewed as a time when Yahweh is *talking* to His covenant people about covenant faithfulness…especially their *lack* of it.

    a.   affluence[1] — *"As I live,"* declares the Lord GOD, *"Sodom, your sister and her daughters have not done as you and your daughters have done. Behold, this was the guilt of your sister Sodom: she and her daughters had pride, excess of food, and prosperous ease, but did not aid the poor and needy. They were haughty and did an abomination before me. So I removed them, when I saw it."* **(Ezekiel 16:48-50)**

    b.   accommodation to culture[2] (aka idolatry)— *"And this occurred because the people of Israel had sinned against the LORD their God, who had brought them up out of the land of Egypt from under the hand of Pharaoh king of Egypt, and had feared other gods and **walked in the customs of the nations** whom the LORD drove out before the people of Israel, and in the customs that the kings of Israel had practiced."* **(2 Kings 17:7-8)**

    c.   covenant *unfaithfulness* — *"Therefore the LORD said to Solomon, 'Since this has been your practice and **you have not kept my covenant** and my statutes that I have commanded you, I will surely tear the kingdom from you and will give it to your servant.'"* **(1 Kings 11:11)**

       *"They **despised his statutes and his covenant** that he made with their fathers and the warnings that he gave them. They went after false idols and became false, and they followed the nations that were around them, concerning whom the LORD had commanded them that they should not do like them."* **(2 Kings 17:15)**

  3.   The "Perps":

    a.   Solomon - the "grand-daddy" of Israel's idolatry (chapters 1-11)

       (1) "Mixed" marriages[3] - (1 Kings 11:3; Deut. 17:17)

       (2) Idolatry : cultural accommodation - (1 Kings 11:4-8; Deut. 12:1-5)

       (3) Confidence in his military rather than Yahweh[4] - (1 Kings 10:26,28; Deut. 17:16)

       (4) Security in his wealth rather than Yahweh - (1 Kings 10:14-21; Deut. 17:17)

       (5) **Summary:** He was unfaithful to the covenant (1 Kings 11:9-11; Deut. 12:18-20)

    b.   Jeroboam - the "gold standard" of evil[5] (1 Kings 12:26-33; he is mentioned all the way to 2 Kings 23:15!!)

       (1) moved worship out of Jerusalem

       (2) set-up "border shrines" at Bethel and Dan[6]

       (3) set-up his own priesthood

       (4) changed the days of sacred feasts

---

[1] Social justice is an inevitable fruit of covenant faithfulness. This is why Yahweh is able to use their treatment of the poor in their midst as a barometer of their faithfulness to the covenant, and therefore a possible grounds for blessing or judgment (cf. Hos 13:6; Is. 58; Zech 7:9-11). This blistering passage from Ezekiel highlights four evidences of covenant *unfaithfulness*: (1) too much "self" (pride), (2) too much food (gluttony), (3) too much "free time" (prosperous ease), and (4) too *little* mercy and compassion (did not aid the poor). The point here is that Yahweh judges them because He gave them more food, wealth, and time than they needed *so that* they'd share their excess with those among them who had less of all these things. Their refusal to do so violated the stipulations of the covenant, and therefore eventually brought judgment.

[2] Yahweh even extends this principle of accommodation to copying *each other* when one has abandoned the covenant. He accuses Judah of "imitating" Israel in her sin (2 Kgs. 17:19). Emulation was to be of Yahweh only. Seeking to be like anything or anyone else is accommodation rather than emulation. And Yahweh calls it "idolatry," and "whore-mongering."

[3] Solomon married a daughter of Pharaoh! Yahweh had forbade the Jews from ever returning to Egypt. Solomon "got around" that covenant stipulation by bringing Egypt into Jerusalem!

[4] "Nationalism" and "patriotism" have blinded Yahweh's people throughout the centuries from the call to be faithful to him above country.

[5] Jeroboam sought to keep the Jews in his northern kingdom away from Jerusalem because of the power of "place" in their national history. Jerusalem represented much more than simply a centralized capital city, it was the fulfillment of Yahweh's promises through Moses while they were still in the wilderness and very much *not* a nation. Also, Yahweh had built "fences" around worship by limiting worship of Him to a single shrine in a single city.

[6] Dan has been the longest continuous excavation in the holy land. It started as a salvage dig, but has continued ever since. It is a city rich in biblical history. Abraham began pursuing the 5 Mesopotamian kings and overtook them at Dan (also known as Laish or Leshem (cf. Gen. 14:144ff and Judges 18:7). The tribe of Dan, in its original allotment under Joshua moved to Laish and renamed it Dan. It was a place of great safety because of its location, and we are told that "there was no lack of anything on earth." (Jud. 18:10). But, also because of its location in the far north, Dan was usually the first city to fall to invaders. In fact, Dan was the first tribe to be carried away by the Assyrians when they invaded. This was captured poetically by Jeremiah: *"The snorting of their horses is heard from Dan; at the sound of the neighing of their stallions the whole land quakes. They come and devour the land and all that fills it, the city and those who dwell in it. —Jeremiah 8:16.*

    The site of Dan marks the northern limit of Israel in many biblical passages. The phrase, *"From Dan to Beersheba"* should be understood as a merism for the full length of the land (e.g. Judges 20:1; 1 Sam. 3:20). Archaeologically Dan has produced what is nearly universally accepted as the actual "high place" erected by Jeroboam (1 Kgs 12:24-33). Evidence of a four-horned altar has been found, as well as three iron shovels, a small horned altar, and an iron incense holder. A Greek inscription has also been found that reads, *"the god who is at Dan"* which helps identify the site with the biblical city, and provides some verification of the biblical account.

4. The "Plot"
    a. 1 Kings 1-11 — the "rise and fall" of Solomon
    b. 1 Kings 12 — the split of the nation
    c. 1 Kings 13 - 2 Kings 25 — the story of two kingdoms and one covenant.
C. God's Answer: The Prophets!
    1. "Pulpits and Pens" – Two types of prophets:
        a. "speaking" prophets — ("proto-prophets")[1]; left no writings (E.g. Elijah, Elisha, Shemaiah, and Huldah, the prophetess; cf. I kings 17:1; 2 Kings 6:12; 2 Chron. 12:5; 2 Kings 22:14).
        b. "writing" prophets — (classical prophets); writings have been preserved (E.g. Jeremiah, Isaiah, Nahum, et al.).
    2. Two "tests" of a genuine prophet:
        a. their present message cannot contradict the Story so far (Deut. 13:1-5).
        b. their predictive prophecies must be 100% accurate, 100% of the time (Deut. 18:21-22)
    3. Five characteristics of genuine prophets:
        a. they were "God-speakers " - they spoke *for* God; they were His "here-and-now voice" on earth.
            (1) the phrases, *"thus says the LORD,"* and *"...declares the LORD"* occur nearly 700x in the 17 books of prophecy.
            (2) in contrast to the priests, who spoke *to God* on behalf of the *people*, the prophets spoke to the people *on behalf of God*.[2]
        b. they were "forth-tellers" — they delivered God's word for the present hour.[3]
            (1) their ministry was primarily oral , not written (even though we have their writings).
            (2) they exposed the ""traitors"," those who had *abandoned* the covenant.
            (3) they spoke the Truth of God into the present hour, not preserving the words of God for posterity, like Moses).
        c. they were "fore-tellers" — they provided "trailers" for the Story, *(but always to reveal the will and word of God for the present)*.
            (1) the coming Messiah as the eternal kingdom of David, was a recurring theme of the prophets.
        d. they were "covenant guardians" — their messages were always connected to the covenant
            (1) they were constantly calling God's people back into the Story, and their covenant responsibilities in it (justice, mercy, faithfulness, and holiness).
            (2) they declared God's intentions to bless or judge them in response to covenant faithfulness or un-faithfulness
            (3) they predicted the future fulfillment of the Abrahamic covenant.
            (4) they emphasized the restoration of shalom, as the intention of Yahweh (Of the 234x "shalom" appears in our OT, one out of four are from the lips of Isaiah and Jeremiah).
D. The Book of Kings and the New Testament
    1. The last name mentioned in the Old Testament is the prophet, Elijah. But, he is mentioned nearly 30x times in the New Testament, seven times by Jesus himself.
    2. Elijah is one of the two Old Testament figures who meet with Jesus on the Mount of Transfiguration (the other one is Moses, the name mentioned along with Elijah's at the OT's close!).

---

[1] Samuel (to Saul) and Nathan (to David) are also early examples.

[2] In some ways, the prophets were not only *not* "interceders," they were in a very real way, *"interferers"!* King Ahab, when addressing Elijah, actually calls him the "troubler of Israel." (1 Kgs 18:17).

[3] In a very real sense, these two functions of "fore-tellers" and "forth-tellers" point to the fact that biblical prophecy's *primary* focus was always the present, not the future. The "fore-telling" (i.e. the "trailers") provided hope in the present because of the certain deliverance by Yahweh in the future. The "forth-telling" (i.e. dealing with the "traitors") also had its primary purpose in the present; calling wayward covenant breakers back to Yahweh and the covenant. It is indeed unfortunate that our modern perspective on prophecy essentially ignores this fact, and makes "prophecy" all about the future.

3. There are no references to the words of Elijah in the New Testament, compared to 22 references to the words of Isaiah.

4. The two references in the New Testament to Elijah speaking are *both* references to his prayer life!

5. Jesus' only mention of Elijah's (and Elisha's) ministry is in reference to him reaching out to those outside the covenant family[1] (Luke 4:24-30)

E. The Book of Kings and the Christian

1. We must constantly remind ourselves that the opposite of holiness is *not* sin. It is idolatry, because idolatry is accommodation to culture, and we are called to be "separate."

2. We too are in a covenant relationship with Yahweh. One secured by the death of His only Son. It too has responsibilities, not merely benefits. (John 13:34,35; 14:21; Luke 9:23, etc.)

3. We need to have or pray for, a love for the prophetic word of God. It's absence is a sign of judgment (Amos 8:11).

KEY INFORMATION - The Book of 1 Kings
Key Word: "Divided Kingdom"
Key Chapter: 12 — the nation divides in 931 BC
Geography: Canaan
Summary: How Israel became a divided kingdom.

• The 19 Kings of Israel •

King's Name	Dates	Length	Character	Manner of Death	Reference
Jeroboam	931-910	22 yrs.	bad	stricken by God	1 Kgs. 11:26-14:20
Nadab	910-909	2 yrs.	bad	murdered by Baasha	15:25-28
Baasha	909-886	24 yrs.	bad	died	15:27 - 16:7
Elah	886-885	2 yrs.	bad	murdered by Zimri	16:6-14
Zimri	885	7 days	bad	suicide	16:9-20
Omri	885-874	12 yrs.	bad	died	16:15-28
Ahab	874-853	22 yrs.	bad	wounded in battle	16:28 - 22:40
Ahaziah	853-852	2 yrs.	bad	fell through lattice	22:40 - 2 Kgs. 1:18
Jehoram (Joram)	852-841	12 yrs.	bad	murdered by Jehu	3:1 - 9:25
Jehu	841-814	28 yrs.	bad	died	9:1 - 10:36
Jehoahaz	814-798	17 yrs.	bad	died	13:1-9
Jehoash (Joash)	798-782	16 yrs	bad	died	13:10 - 14:16
Jeroboam II	793-753*	41 yrs.	bad	died	14:23-29
Zechariah	753-752	6 months	bad	murdered by Shallum	14:29 - 15:12
Shallum	752	1 month	bad	murdered by Manahem	15:10-15
Manahem	752-742	10 yrs.	bad	died	15:14-22
Pekahiah	742-740	2 yrs.	bad	murdered by Pekah	15:22-26
Pekah	752-731*	20 yrs.	bad	murdered by Hoshea	15:27-31
Hoshea	731-722	9 yrs.	bad	deposed to Assyria	15:30 - 17:6

*co-regency

[1] Yet, in a very real sense, they are "inside the covenant family" when one looks back now through the dual lenses of the Gospels and the writings of Paul. We now see that the Gentiles were always a part of the Abrahamic promise, and therefore the Abrahamic mission, which the Jews failed to recognize or fulfill.

• The 20 Kings of Judah •

King's Name	Dates	Length	Character	Manner of Death	Reference
Rehoboam	931-913	17 yrs.	bad	died	1 Kgs. 11:42-14:31
Abijam (Abijah)	913-911	3 yrs.	bad	died	14:31 - 15:8
Asa	911-870	41 yrs.	good	died	15:8-24
Jehoshaphat	873-848*	25 yrs.	good	died	22:41-50
Jehoram	853-841*	8 yrs.	bad	stricken by God	2 Kgs. 8:16-24
Ahaziah	841	1 yr.	bad	killed by Jehu	8:24 - 9:29
Athaliah	841-835	6 yrs.	bad	killed by army	11:1-20
Joash	835-796	40 yrs.	good	killed by servants	11:1 - 12:21
Amaziah	796-767	29 yrs.	good	murdered	14:1-20
Azariah (Uzziah)	792-740*	52 yrs.	good	stricken by God	15:1-7
Jotham	750-732	16 yrs.	good	died	15:32-38
Ahaz	735-716*	16 yrs	bad	died	16:1-20
Hezekiah	716 - 687	29 yrs.	good	died	18:1 - 20:21
Manasseh	697-643*	55 yrs.	bad	died	21:1-18
Amon	643-641	2 yrs.	bad	killed by servants	21:19-26
Josiah	641-609	31 yrs.	good	wounded in battle	22:1 - 23:30
Jehoahaz	609	3 months.	bad	deposed to Egypt	23:31-33
Jehoiachim	609-598	11 yrs.	bad	died during siege?	23:34 - 24:5
Jehoiachin	598-597	3 months.	bad	deposed to Babylon	24:6-16
Zedekiah	597-586	11 yrs.	bad	deposed to Babylon	24:17 - 25:30

Kingdoms in Contrast

ITEM	Israel *(North)*	Judah *(South)*
Number of Tribes in Kingdom	10	2
Capital City of Kingdom	Samaria	Jerusalem
Number of Kings During Kingdom	19	20
Good Kings	0	8
Number of Dynasties (ruling families)	9	1
First King	Jeroboam	Rehoboam
Last King	Hoshea	Zedekiah
King With Longest Reign	Jeroboam II (41 years)	Manasseh (55 years)
King With Shortest Reign	Zimri (7 days)	Jehoahaz and Jehoiachin (3 mos.)
Duration of Kingdom	approx. 210 yrs.	approx. 350 yrs.
Conquering Nation & Ruler	**Assyria** – Shalmaneser & Sargon II	**Babylon** – Nebuchadnezzar II
Result of Defeat	Dispersion throughout empire	Exile in Babylon
Date Kingdom Ended	722 B.C.	586 B.C.

XV. UNIT 15 — "Wise And Otherwise" – An Introduction to Wisdom Literature

A. Wising Up About Wisdom Literature

  1. "Wisdom Literature" is *Not* Unique to the Bible[1]

    a. Solomon's wisdom is highlighted by comparison, *not* uniqueness (i.e. a matter of degree, *not* novelty):

> *"And God gave Solomon wisdom and understanding beyond measure, and breadth of mind like the sand on the seashore, so that Solomon's wisdom surpassed the wisdom of all the people of the east and all the wisdom of Egypt."*   **–1 Kings 4:29-30**

    b. The Old Testament makes numerous references to "wise man" and "wise women":

      (1) Deborah speaks of the "wise princesses" living in Sisera's hometown (Judges 5:29)

      (2) a "wise woman" from Tekoa gave counsel to King David (2 Sam. 14:2-20).

      (3) a "wise woman" of Abel gave counsel to Joab (2 Sam. 20:16-22).

      (4) Jeremiah speaks of "prophet, priest and sage" as types of people living in Judah (Jer. 18:18).

    c. Archeological finds have revealed a wealth of wisdom literature in the Ancient Near East:

Location	Title	Description
Egypt	*The Instruction of Vizier Ptah-hotep*	Fifth Dynasty, (c. 2500-2350 B.C.); an aged counselor instructs his son on how he should conduct his life.

---

[1] The influence of Egyptian wisdom literature upon Hebrew writings should not surprise us. The Jews were *immersed* in Egyptian culture for nearly 10 generations (430 years according to Exodus 12:40). Also the author of the Torah (Moses) was educated "in all the wisdom (Gk - sophia) of Egypt" according to Luke and the author of Hebrews (cf. Acts 7:22 and Heb. 11:24). Finally, were are told in 1 Kings that Solomon actually *married* a daughter of an Egyptian king. (The identity of both her and her father are unknown, although some have suggested Pharoah Siamun, and early 10th century B.C. king who conquered the city of Gezar and may have given it to Solomon who fortified it later (cf. Josh. 10:33 and 1 Kgs. 9:15).

Location	Title	Description
Egypt	*The Instruction for Merikare*	Tenth Dynasty, c. 2106-2010 B.C.); A pharaoh (apparently Khety III) initiates his son in the principles of proper and effective ruling. This text, reflecting the social turmoil of the First Intermediate period, asserts that Merikare must earn the respect of the nobles through just governance in order to maintain his hold on the throne.
Egypt	*The Protests of the Eloquent Peasant*	Oldest copy dates to the Twelfth Dynasty,(c. 1963-1786 B.C.); A peasant who has been defrauded of his goods pleads for justice from high officials, eventually winning his case and gaining a high position for himself. The text reflect upon the nature of justice and the importance of eloquent speech. *(This text is often compared to the biblical book of Job by scholars.)*
Egypt	*The Instruction of Amenemope*	Oldest copy dates to between the 10th and 6th centuries B.C.; This text, which is remarkably similar to Proverbs 22:17-24:22, includes an introduction and 30 sections of teaching on wise behavior. *(Very similar in style to the biblical book of Proverbs.)*
Mesopotamia	*The Book of Ahiqar*	Found on a 5th century Aramaic papyrus but the setting is in Assyria and possibly composed originally in Akaddian.); This text describes how Ahiqar overcame the adversity of a scheming and ungrateful nephew, avoided execution on false charges and proved himself to be the wisest man of his age. The story was translated into Armenian and Arabic, and the apocryphal Book of Tobit alludes to it. The motif of the wise man who triumphs over adversity appears repeatedly in the Bible as well.
Mesopotamia	*The Babylonian Theodicy*	(c. 1100-1000 B.C.); A cynical sufferer enters into a dispute with a man who defends traditional notions of wisdom. The text originally included 27 stanzas each with 11 lines but not all remain intact. This writing is often compared to Job; there are in fact both clear similarities and sharp differences between the two.

2. Types of Wisdom Literature in the Ancient Near East

   a. "Universal" wisdom — monologues, dialogues, essays and epics about basic problems of human existence:[1]

   (1) the meaning of life

   (2) the problem of suffering

   (3) the path to success

   > *"My god has forsaken me and disappeared*
   > *My goddess has failed me and keeps at a distance*
   > *The benevolent angel who (walked) beside [me] has departed.*
   > *My protecting spirit has taken to flight, and is seeking someone else.*
   > *My strength is gone; my appearance has become gloomy;*
   > *My dignity has flown away, my protection made off."* **(Ludlul Bel Nemeqi, 1.43-48)**[2]

   > *"Behold, I go forward, but he is not there, and backward, but I do not perceive him;*
   > *on the left hand when he is working, I do not behold him;*
   > *he turns to the right hand, but I do not see him.*
   > *But he knows the way that I take;*
   > *when he has tried me, I shall come out as gold."* **(Job 23:8-10)**

---

[1] We of all people should expect this universal appeal and similarity of content within Ancient Near Eastern writings, including the Bible. Our doctrine of Creation, including the fall of humanity into sin, the suffering it produced, and the Imago Dei demand something of a "universal brotherhood" when it comes to pain.

[2] This is a hymn of thanksgiving to the god, Marduke. It is sometimes called, a "Babylonian Job." It is very different from the biblical Job in that it is only a monologue. In Job, a radically different theolgoy of suffering emerges because God actually engages everyone else in the story.

b. "proverbial wisdom" — short, pithy sayings which state rules for general happiness or distill life principles[1]:

"Do not associate to thyself the heated man, nor visit him for conversation..."

(Teaching of Amenemope, XI.12-14; XV.13-14)

"A man who bears false witness against his neighbor is like a war club, or a sword, or a sharp arrow."

(Proverbs 25:18)

3. Key Characteristics of Wisdom Literature
   a. It dealt with the concrete and practical (i.e. real life), not the abstract and theoretical (i.e. theology).[2]
   b. Was typically inclusive, not exclusive, in its intended audience[3].
   c. Was as much the *heart* of an oral culture as the "fruit" of it.

4. Uniqueness of Biblical Wisdom Literature
   a. It emanated *from* its theology but did not shape it.[4]

Biblical Wisdom Literature	Other Near Eastern Wisdom Literature
Education is centered in the family ("listen, my son...") and has the good of the individual in view.	Greek education was centered in the gymnasium and had the good of the city-state in view.
Education is directed primarily at moral and spiritual virtue rather than merely training for vocational success.	Some wisdom texts from Egypt are principally concerned with preparing a young man for work in the government or as a scribe.
Education in Proverbs does NOT focus on any one "class' of people, especially the upper or ruling class. It's focus is all the young men (and women) of the Israelite community.	Egyptian literature, was for the most part, directed toward the elite.
Wisdom is often personified, but never deified.	Wisdom is often represented as a god or goddess (E.g. Maat in Egyptian mythology)
Education in Proverbs begins with "fear of the LORD" as both the source and ultimate goal of all wisdom. It begins and ends with Yahweh, because HE is their reason to exist.	There is no parallel to this in any ANE wisdom literature. *(adapted from: Archeological Study Bible, p. 495)*

   b. It was founded on "the fear of the LORD":
      (1) this was a synonym for obedience (cf. 2 Chron. 19:9; Job 28:28; Prov. 8:13).
      (2) it linked wisdom to the covenant, and therefore to the Law.
      (3) for Israel, "wisdom" was understanding and living within the circumference of the stipulations of the covenant

---

[1] One of the accolades given to Solomon had to do with the prolific nature of his ability to write such sayings. 1 Kings 4:32 tells us that he wrote 3,000 proverbs. This is significant when you consider there are only 914 verses in the entire book of Proverbs.

[2] "Wisdom" is demonstrated in the ANE by the ability to say something *profound* in few words. An excellent example of this is the response of the King of Israel to the King of Syria who was predicting a greats victory for himself: *"And the king of Israel answered, 'Tell him, 'Let not him who straps on his armor boast himself as he who takes it off.'"* (1 Kings 20:11). This stands in stark contrast to our day when the multiplicity of words has produced a *lack* of genuine wisdom.

[3] Was written for "everyman" not the wealthy or privileged.

[4] Our modern view of Proverbs is totally foreign to the idea of covenant faithfulness (i.e. Storyline compiance). Our view is more likely the product of pop psychology in which we look for "principles" for help in relationships, parenting, finances, our feelings, etc. It turns Proverbs into something of a "self-help" book; It becomes more about *me* than it does about Yahweh. Even our perspective on the highly sensual piece of love poetry known as the Song of Solomon must be understood to be first and foremost a piece of ancient *Hebrew* poetry. It is inconceivable that it can be seen as a book about sexual love *outside* of marriage. It is implied and assumed by the culture that produced the document, and a non-negotiable for the ancient *reader* that the two lovers are married. Adultery was a capital offense within Israel!

XVI. The "Writings of Solomon" — Proverbs, Song of Songs and Ecclesiastes[1]

A. Authorship

1. All three books claim to be written by Solomon[2] *(directly or indirectly)*.

2. The books are consistent with the description of Solomon given to us in Scripture. (cf. 1 Kgs. 3:1-28; 4:29-33; 10:1-13).

B. *Proverbs* — Background

1. Three times in the book of Proverbs, Solomon is clearly stated to be the author (Prov. 1:1; 10:1; 25:1).

2. The Book of Psalms is clearly an "anthology" of worship hymns, designed to draw the individual or the whole community into honest communion with God, Proverbs is more of a "textbook" schooling young men (and women) on "right living."

3. The Proverbs are *not* promises or commands. Instead they are "*general* truths" that must be carefully weighed against the circumstances and the type of person they are describing. For example:

   *"Answer **not** a fool according to his folly, lest you be like him yourself."* — **Prov. 26:4**

   *"Answer a fool **according** to his folly, lest he be wise in his own eye."* — **Prov. 26:5**

4. Biblical wisdom literature is very similar to other Ancient Near Eastern writings, such as the *Teaching of Amenemope* from around 1000 BC[3]:

   "Numerous wisdom texts have been discovered in Egypt. Without doubt the most significant of these is a papyri document entitled the Teaching of Amenemope which was brought from Egypt by Sir. E.A.W. Budge in 1888. Amenemope was the administrator of the royal estates, serving in the court of Pharaoh in about 1 000 BC. Following the publication of a complete translation in 1923 the remarkable similarities between it and Proverbs 22:17-24:22 became apparent."   (http://www.biblicalstudies.org.uk/article_wisdom2.html#2.1)

The Proverbs of Solomon	The *Teaching of Amenemope*
"Incline your ear and hear my words, and apply your mind to my teaching." **(Prov. 2:2)**	*"Give thy ears, hear what is said, Give thy heart to understand them. To put them in thy heart is worth while..."* **(ch I)**
"Do not remove the ancient landmark that your ancestors set up... Do not remove an ancient landmark or encroach on the fields of orphans..." **(Prov. 22:28; 23:10)**	*"Do not carry off the landmark at the boundaries of the arable land, nor disturb the position of the measuring-cord; be not greedy after a cubit of land, nor encroach upon the boundaries of a widow..."* **(VII. 11-14)**
"Have I not written for you thirty sayings of admonition and knowledge, to show you what is right and true, so that you may give a true answer to those who sent you?" **(Prov. 22:20-21)**	*"See thou these thirty chapters: They entertain, they instruct: they are the foremost of all books; they make the ignorant to know. If they are read out before the ignorant, then he will be cleansed by them."* **(XXX)**
"Make no friends with those given to anger, and do not associate with hotheads..." **(Prov. 22:24-25)**	*"Do not associate to thyself the heated man, nor visit him for conversation..."* **(XI.12-14; XV.13-14)**

---

[1] These three books fall into the third major section of the Tanach, the Ketuvim ("the writings"). But, they are *not* the in the same "category" within this grouping. Provers is in the first subdivision known as the "Three Books of Truth" and are considered especially poetic (Psalms, Proverbs, Job). This title comes from the first letter of each of the books spells *emeth*, the Hebrew word for "truth." Song Of Solomon and Ecclesiastes are in the subdivision known as "Megillot" ("five scrolls"). Later Jewish tradition links this arrangement to the days in the Jewish calendar when each book was read in the synagogue. Song of Solomon was read in the spring, at Passover as a portrayal of Yahweh's covenant love for Israel. Ruth is read at Pentecost (early summer) at the time of the wheat harvest, like in the book of Ruth. Lamentations is read in late July and commemorates the final destruction of the second Temple. Ecclesiastes is read in the fall during the Feast of Tabernacles, which commemorates the wilderness wandering, or life without God as Ecclesiastes portrays. Passover, Pentecost, and Tabernacles are festivals established by Moses. The one post-exilic, post-Mosaic reading is Esther in early March, to celebrate the Feast of Purim, which was established as a result of what happened in that book.

[2] There is a great deal of debate about Solomonic authorship of Ecclesiastes and Song of Solomon. The debate orbits around Hebrew and Egyptian vocabulary, and the associated eras with the words. A later date (post-exilic) is frequently posited.

[3] Amenemope lived during "New Kingdom" Egypt (c. 1539-1075 B.C.). He was apparently a high official in what we might today call the Department of Agriculture. Like Solomon, he was writing these teachings for his son. This ancient document consists of an Introduction followed by 30 sections of teaching on "wise behavior." It is very similar in content and style to Proverbs 22:17 - 24:22.

The Proverbs of Solomon	The *Teaching of Amenemope*
"Do not wear yourself out to get rich; be wise enough to desist. When your eyes light upon it, it is gone, for suddenly it takes wings to itself, flying like an eagle toward heaven…" (Prov. 23:4-5)	*"Do not strain to seek an excess, when thy needs are safe for thee if riches are brought to thee by robbery, they will not spend the night with thee; At daybreak they are not in thy house: Their places may be seen, but they are not. The ground has opened its mouth… that it might swallow them up, and might sink them into the underworld. (Or) they have made themselves a great breach of their (own) size and are sunken down into the underworld. (Or) they have made themselves wings like geese and are flown away to the heavens…"* (X.4-5)
"Do not eat the bread of the stingy; do not desire their delicacies; for like a hair in the throat, so are they… You will vomit up the little you have eaten, and you will waste your pleasant words." (Prov. 23:6-8)	*"Be not greedy for the property of a poor man, nor hunger for his bread. As for the property of a poor man, it (is) a blocking to the throat… The mouthful of bread (too) great thou swallowest and vomitest up, and art emptied of thy goods…"* (XV.9-12)
"When you sit down to eat with a ruler, observe carefully what is before you, and put a knife to your throat if you have a big appetite. Do not desire the ruler's delicacies, for they are deceptive foods." (Prov. 23:1-3)	*"Do not eat bread before a noble, nor lay on thy mouth at first. If thou art satisfied with false chewings, they are a pastime for thy spittle. Look at the cup which is before thee, and let it serve thy needs…"* (XXIII. 13-20)

C. **PROVERBS — Purpose of the Book**
1. This is the only book in the Bible that was written specifically for children (I.e. the young).
2. The stated purpose of this book is to help children "see" all of life from God's point of view. This perspective is called "wisdom," and it is based on what Proverbs calls, *"the fear of the Lord."*[1]
3. The responsibility of instruction in the *"fear of the LORD"* (I.e. wisdom) within the covenant community, fell to the home, particularly the parents (cf. Prov. 1:8,10,15; 2:1; 3:1; 4:1-4; 5:1; 6:1, 20; 23:22; 7:1; 23:26)
4. The purpose of the Book of Proverbs is given in the first seven verses: *"…gaining wisdom"*
   a. **1:2** - Wisdom is not "automatic"; it must be acquired.
   b. **1:3** - Wisdom has to do with living, not just "knowing."
   c. **1:4** - Wisdom is actually "designed" for the young.
   d. **1:5** - Wisdom is cumulative, it should keep growing (One may *know* too much, but one can never be "too wise")
   e. **1:7-8** - Wisdom can be rejected or embraced; kept or forsaken.
   SUMMARY: Wisdom can be taught and learned. Unlike intelligence, one is not born with it, or endowed with it by God. It can be, and must be, acquired.
5. The Book of Proverbs covers and extremely wide range of topics, including:[2]
   - *wisdom & folly*
   - *parents & children*
   - *rich & poor (51x)*
   - *righteous & the wicked*
   - *words & speech*
   - *servants & rulers*
   - *laziness & diligence*
   - *planning & decisions*
   - *the family*
   - *friends & friendships*
   - *fear of God*
   - *anger & self-control*

D. **ECCLESIASTES — The "Journal" of Solomon's Journey *Outside* the Story**
1. The opening verse of the book fits the description of Solomon that we have from the book of 1 Kings.

---

[1] Attempting to make this a "practical living" textbook, teaching young people how to "live right" as Christians, without the connection to covenant faithfulness, will degenerate to legalism, which always produces self-righteousness or guilt that matures into pride or anger and bitterness.

[2] However, it must be reinforced that because of Yahweh's Story, the life of a covenant child must always be understood as a single fabric, not a collection of "principles."

2. The Hebrew word, (*Qoheleth*), translated "Preacher (ESV,NAS)" in our NIV Bibles, only occurs in this book, out of the entire Old Testament. (cf. 1:1,2,12; 7:27; 12:8-10)

3. In the Greek version of the Old Testament, a word is used to translate it (*ekklesiastou*), from which we get our title for the book, "Ecclesiastes."

4. The word "Yahweh" appears over 6,800 times in the Old Testament, 87x in Proverbs, but never in Ecclesiastes. "Elohim" is used instead.

5. Unlike Proverbs, which was written for "*anyman*," this book appears to have been written for the affluent elite.[1] (cf. 8:2-3; 10:4).

6. The book of Ecclesiastes is the "journal" of King Solomon's journey to find an answer to life's most penetrating question, *"What's the point?"*:

> *"What does man gain by all the toil at which he toils under the sun?"* **(Ecc. 1:3)**

7. Solomon tried to find meaning in life, *"under the sun"* (in other words, without God), by looking in all the wrong places:

> *"Then I considered all that my hands had done and the toil I had expended in doing it, and behold, all was vanity and a striving after wind, and there was nothing to be gained under the sun."* **Ecclesiastes 2:11**

8. Solomon's "Dead End Streets" on His Quest For Happiness "Under the Sun":

Reference	The "Street" Solomon Traveled
2:15-16	*wisdom* – what he knew
2:19-21	*work* – what he could accomplish "under the sun"
2:26	*money* – what he could buy that others couldn't
4:4	*status* – what others thought of him
4:7-8	*self-reliance* – how little he needed others
4:16	*fame* – how much he was known by others
5:10	*possessions* – what he owned & what it "proved"
6:6	*long life* – prolonging the search
6:7	*partying* – "forgetting" life's pain, with others
6:9	*passion/desire* – doing what "felt good"

9. Solomon finally realized that he could not separate God's purposes *for* him from his own purposes for himself:

> *"The end of the matter; all has been heard. Fear God and keep his commandments, for this is the whole duty of man. For God will bring every deed into judgment, with every secret thing, whether good or evil."* **Ecclesiastes 12:13,14**

10. Solomon realized the truth of 2 Kings 17:15, that we become like what we pursue:

> *"They rejected His statutes and His covenant which He made with their fathers and His warnings with which He warned them. **And they followed vanity and became vain,** and went after the nations which surrounded them, concerning which the LORD had commanded them not to do like them."*

E. Song of Songs

1. This piece of Scripture stands alone in its content and characteristics:

   a. No other book of the Bible has been read so differently from one age to the next.

   b. It was a "forbidden book" in Medieval times; excommunication was threatened!

   > The Spanish monk Fray Luis de Leon was imprisoned in 1562 by the Inquisition for composing an original translation of the Song of Songs directly from Hebrew, and for treating the text as if it were a non-allegorical pastoral poem. But as he observed in the introduction to his translation, "Nothing is more proper to God than love, and there is nothing more natural for love than to turn

---

[1] The lifestyle described in this book could never be experienced or sustained by the average Israeli peasant living a subsistence existence.

the lover to the conditions and character of the beloved."

(http://www.unc.edu/~cernst/articles/sosintro.htm#_edn5)

   c. The name of God is never mentioned (similar to the book of Esther)

   d. It contains references to 21 species of plants, 15 species of animals and 15 different geographical locations (including Tirzah in the North and Jerusalem in the South)

   e. It contains a multitude of descriptions of human anatomy and love-making

   f. Jewish allegorists see it describing the covenant "marriage" of Yahweh and Israel.

   g. Christian allegorists see it describing the covenant "marriage" of Jesus Christ and the Church.

   h. It comes close to a portrait of sexual love prior to the Fall (the "garden" is a key theme in this book.)

F. Wisdom Literature and the New Testament

   1. Ecclesiastes and Song of Solomon are never quoted in our New Testament.

   2. There are six clear citations from Proverbs in our NT:

> *Romans 12:20* ....*Proverbs 25:11-12*
> *Hebrews 12:5-6*...........................*3:11-12*
> *James 4:6*....................................*3:34*
> *1 Peter 4:18*................................*11:31*
> *1 Peter 5:5*..................................*3:34*
> *2 Peter 2:22*................................*26:11*

   3. The Book of James is wisdom literature (It's also most likely the first NT book penned.)

G. Solomon and the Christian

   1. Proverbs and Ecclesiastes from the same pen, testify that our biggest battles are moral, not intellectual. (*"Wisdom doesn't make me bullet-proof!"* – Dr. Allen Ross)

   2. Ecclesiastes is a sobering reminder in an affluent culture.

   3. The home is the place where wisdom is most effectively taught because it has to do with how to *live*, not how to make a *living*.

   4. The Song of Solomon is a sobering reminder of how much of our view of sexual love is shaped by Hollywood rather than Scripture.

H. **WRITINGS OF SOLOMON: Key Information**

   1. **KEY WORDS:**   **Proverbs**: "wise/wisdom"
                                Song of Solomon: "love/lover"
                                Ecclesiastes: "meaningless"

   2. **KEY IDEAS:** **Proverbs**: Living *inside* the Story
                                Song of Solomon: covenant marriage
                                Ecclesiastes: Living *outside* the Story

THE BOOKS OF ECCLESIASTES AND SONG OF SONGS

Arguments *Against* Solomonic Authorship	Arguments *in Favor of* Solomonic Authorship
The author of Proverbs uses "Yahweh" 87x and "Elohim" 5x but the author of Ecclesiastes uses "Elohim" 40x and never uses "Yahweh." *(Song of Songs never mentions God!).*	Scholars now know that *Aramaic* influence of Hebrew is much older than Solomon, and what has been considered *Aramaic* here may in fact be an unusual dialect of Hebrew.
There appear to be a high number of *Aramaic* words in Ecclesiastes, leading some to posit a *postexilic* date.	These words are actually *older* that Persian or Greek, going back to Sanskrit. Also, Solomon's numerous international trade agreements would have certainly put him in contact with other languages and cultures, and given him something of an "international vocabulary."
Some words in both books are allegedly said to be borrowed from Persian or Greek (cf. "park," "orchard," "carriage" in Ecc. 2:5; SS 4:13; 3:9).	This statement can just as easily be interpreted to be a "retrospective" statement such as, *"I have been king over Israel."*
The "Teacher" of Ecclesiastes says of himself, *"I, the Teacher, was king over Israel."* (1:12) is seen as evidence that the author was no longer the king.	We must remind ourselves that Jerusalem (aka *Salem* and *Jebus*) had a long history of kings "before" Solomon (e.g. Melchizedek was one, and the Jebusites before David had kings as well).
The statement, *"I have grown and increased in wisdom more than anyone who has ruled over Jerusalem before me."* is understood to point to a time when there had been many Judahite kings.	The books (especially *Song*) contain copious references to flora and fauna of the region, which is consistent with Solomon's keen interest in natural sciences (cf. 1 Kg 4:33).
	The author of *Song* was very familiar with exotic spices, vegetation, gold, alabaster, and jewels. This is a lifestyle consistent with Solomon's excessive tastes. It also points to a time in Jerusalem's history characterized by wealth, leisure, and peace. The tiny little settlement which was Judah *after* the exile hardly fits this description.
	Song mentions the city of Tirzah in parallel with Jerusalem seems to reflect a time *before* Tirzah was selected as the early capital of the Northern kingdom, sometime after Solomon's death. Also, the city of Tirzah did *not* exist after the exile, when many thing these books were composed.
	Both books speak without qualification, of locations like En Gedi, Jerusalem, Heshbon, Carmel, and Hermon, and others suggests a time *prior* to the divided kingdom of 931 B.C.

Adapted from, "The Authorship of Ecclesiastes and Song of Songs," in *The Archaeology Study Bible*, page 1021.

The Really "Big Picture"

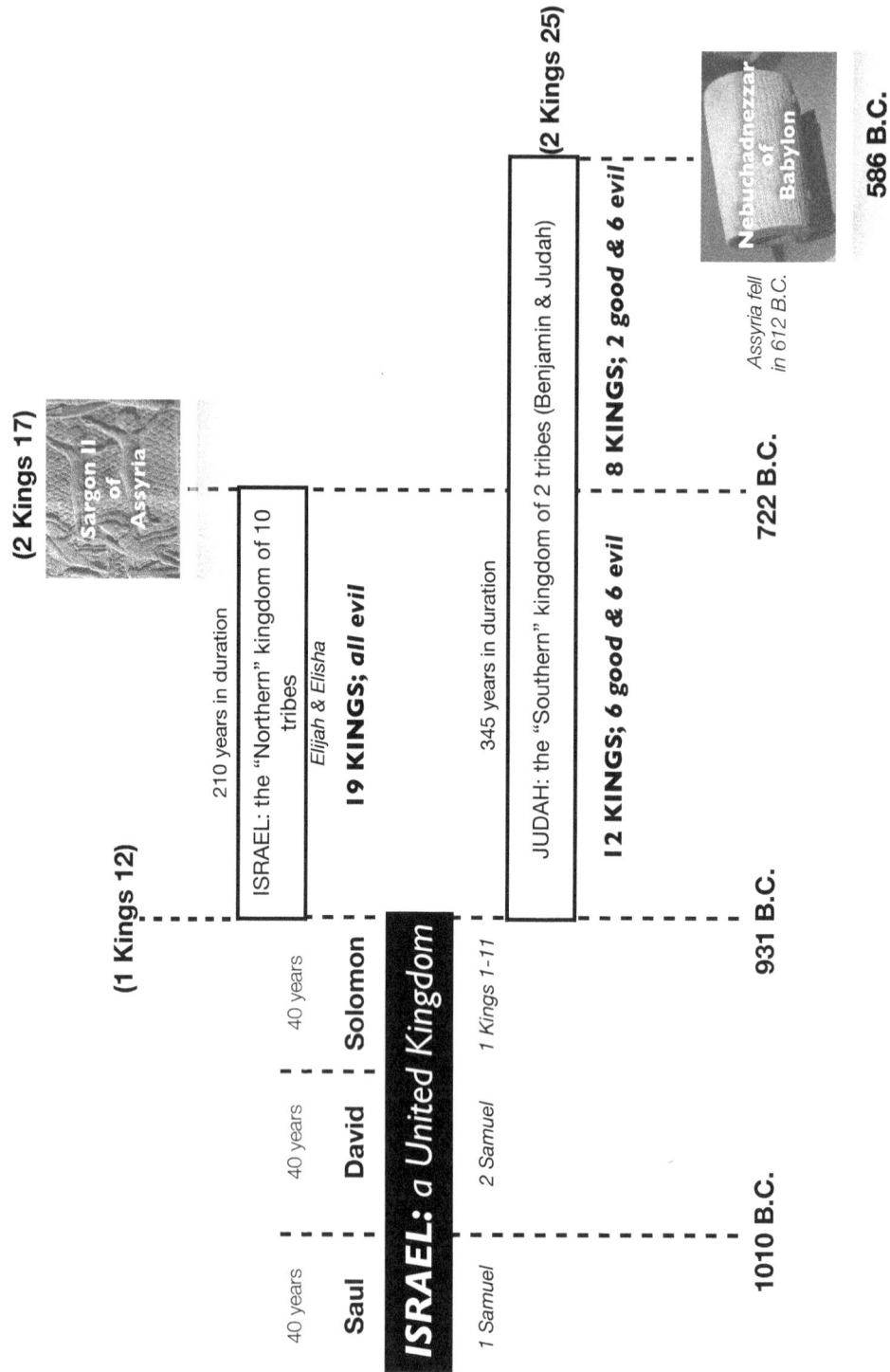

ISRAEL: a United Kingdom

Saul	David	Solomon
40 years	40 years	40 years
1 Samuel	2 Samuel	1 Kings 1-11

1010 B.C.

931 B.C.

(1 Kings 12)

ISRAEL: the "Northern" kingdom of 10 tribes
210 years in duration
Elijah & Elisha
19 KINGS; all evil

(2 Kings 17)

Sargon II of Assyria

722 B.C.

JUDAH: the "Southern" kingdom of 2 tribes (Benjamin & Judah)
345 years in duration
12 KINGS; 6 good & 6 evil   **8 KINGS; 2 good & 6 evil**

(2 Kings 25)

Nebuchadnezzar of Babylon

Assyria fell in 612 B.C.

586 B.C.

[1] Some additional facts that add "color" to this graphic are: (1) Saul was likely anointed as the first king around 1050 B.C. (2) Shalmanessar V began the siege against Samaria and the norther kingdom, even though he is not mentioned in our Bible. His son, Sargon II finished the job. (3) The division of the kingdom occurred in 931 B.C., the fall of the northern kingdom occurred in 722 B.C., and the fall of Jerusalem and the end of the monarchy occurred in 586 B.C. (Babylon had attacked Jerusalem on two other occasions that have deep biblical significance. The first, in 605 B.C. was when Daniel was taken captive. The second, in 597 B.C. is when Ezekiel was taken.)

XVII. UNIT 17 — *"At Many Times And In Many Ways"* – The Prophets

    A. The *Really* "Big Picture"

        1. "Framing" the Story *(see chart on previous page)*

            a. Four key books – 400 years: *(0 kingdoms —> 1 kingdom —> 2 kingdoms —> 1 kingdom —> 0 kingdoms)*

               (1) Samuel

               (2) Kings

               (3) Ezra

               (4) Nehemiah

            b. Three key periods – one pivotal event[1]:

               (1) **Before the Babylonian Exile:** the two "E's" and the *"Orange Juice Gang."*

               (2) **During the Exile:** Daniel & Ezekiel.

               (3) **After the Exile:** Haggai, Zechariah, and Malachi.

        2. Rolling the "Credits" – 17 Books from 16 Prophets

            a. Two *types* of prophets: Major (5) & Minor (12).

               (1) "Label" points to their length, *not* their importance.

               (2) The 12 Minor Prophets *combined* roughly equal Isaiah in length.

            b. Four prophet "pairs":

               (1) **Most prophecies about Jesus:** Isaiah *(major)* & Zechariah *(minor)*.

               (2) **Same audience, different message:** Jonah & Nahum.

               (3) **Different audience, same message:** Amos & Micah.

               (4) **Different message, same time:** Daniel & Ezekiel; Haggai & Zechariah.

            c. Three *main* audiences (who they addressed, primarily):

               (1) **Before the exile:** Israel & Judah.

               (2) **During the exile:** Jewish captives and pagan kings.

               (3) **After the exile:** Temple-builders and wall-repairers.

    B. Variations on Three Themes: The Message of the Prophets

        1. **Theme #1: The Covenant**

            a. The identity of the Jews as a nation and individuals was/is inseparable from the notion of covenant.[2]

            b. *This* covenant set them apart from the other ANE (Ancient Near Eastern) peoples.[3]

            c. Their purpose was tied to Yahweh's one grand Story for which they had been "chosen."[4]

            d. The role of the prophet must never be *(because it cannot be)* separated from these ideas.

            e. This is also true of our reading of the historical books of this time period.

            f. The nation's relationship to the covenant is the basis of the unrelenting call of the prophets to "return" to Yahweh's Repentance, (i.e. covenant faithfulness) *not* merely a change in their behavior.[5]

            g. Sticking to the Storyline (aka covenant faithfulness):

               (1) Manifested itself in dependence, openness and obedience to the Word of God, however it "arrived." (i.e., by scroll or in person)

---

[1] The Babylonian Exile, next to the exodus, may be the most important event in Jewish history. It marked the end of the monarchy to this day. It also marked the end of Israel being a major player on the world stage. The importance and centrality of this event can be seen in the opening verses of Matthew's Gospel where he arranges the three sets of names around the exile. It is the centerpiece of his genealogy.

[2] Their very existence, their customs, ritual, and theology make no sense apart from the covenant.

[3] Covenants were very common in the ANE. *Yahweh* is what is uncommon in this case! There is truly "no god like Him." This is shown as much by the *type* of covenant He establishes with Israel as it is in His character.

[4] There was a *reason* they existed. This is much more than an element of mere anthropology. They were "chosen" for a purpose, and were to be "holy" (different) by design. In both cases, it was Yahweh who took the initiative, not them.

[5] This idea is at the very heart of our modern understanding of the meaning of the Greek word, *metanoia* ("repentance"). What is actually happening is a person is leaving one Storyline to embrace another; Leaving their *own* story for Yahweh's and their place in it. This is just as true for what is involved in staying true to the covenant for ancient Israel.

    (2) Manifested itself in individual and corporate lives of holiness—the *opposite* of a cultural identity.

    (3) Manifested itself in "shalom": love, mercy, justice, and compassion to all whose lives intersected with theirs.

    (4) A restoration to "the way things are supposed to be."

  h. "Choose Your Own Adventure" (aka covenant *unfaithfulness*):

    (1) Manifested itself in a resistance and contempt for the word of God, especially through the prophetic ministry:

> *Thus says the LORD: "Stand by the roads, and look, and ask for the ancient paths, where the good way is; and walk in it, and find rest for your souls. But they said, 'We will not walk in it.'*
> **–Jeremiah 6:16**

> *"Thus says the LORD of hosts, Render true judgments, show kindness and mercy to one another, do not oppress the widow, the fatherless, the sojourner, or the poor, and let none of you devise evil against another in your heart." But they refused to pay attention and turned a stubborn shoulder and stopped their ears that they might not hear. They made their hearts diamond-hard lest they should hear the law and the words that the LORD of hosts had sent by his Spirit through the former prophets. Therefore great anger came from the LORD of hosts.*
> **–Zechariah 7:9 -12**

    (2) Manifested itself in a denial of their true condition and a desire for affirmation from the prophets:

> *"...who say to the seers, "Do not see," and to the prophets, "Do not prophesy to us what is right; speak to us smooth things, prophesy illusions,*
> **–Isaiah 30:10**

> *"Therefore, behold, I am against the prophets, declares the LORD, who steal my words from one another."*
> **–Jeremiah 23:30**

    (3) Manifested itself in the opposite of "shalom": injustice, indifference and oppression of the poor in their midst:

> *"For I know how many are your transgressions and how great are your sins—you who afflict the righteous, who take a bribe, and turn aside the needy in the gate."*
> **–Amos 5:12**

> *"Do you think you are a king because you compete in cedar? Did not your father eat and drink and do justice and righteousness? Then it was well with him. He judged the cause of the poor and needy; then it was well. Is not this to know me? declares the LORD."*
> **–Jeremiah 22:15-16**

2. Theme #2: The "Day of the LORD"

  a. The phrase appears 23x times in the Prophets; half of them in Joel and Zephaniah!

  b. *"The Day of the Lord"* appears 5x times in the New Testament

  c. Is a time of judgment or deliverance, depending on where one is in regard to the Story.

  d. Is a "now" and "later" reality, partial and ultimate

3. Theme #3: "The LORD'S *Anointed*"

  a. The Hebrew word is *"meshiach"* which means Messiah.[1]

  b. In Greek it is *"christos,"* which is transliterated, "the Christ".

  c. *Meshiach* appears 41x in the OT, most of which refer to kings and priests.[2]

  d. *Christos* appears 527x times in the NT, all referring to Jesus *the* Christ.

  e. The notion of a "deliverer" who would restore the Davidic Kingdom was an eschatological promise of the prophets:

> *"But you, O Bethlehem Ephrathah, who are too little to be among the clans of Judah, from you shall come forth for me one who is to be ruler in Israel, whose origin is from of old, from ancient days. Therefore he shall give them up until the time when she who is in labor has given birth; then the rest of his brothers shall return to the people of Israel. And he shall stand and shepherd his flock in the strength of the LORD, in the majesty of the name of the LORD*

---

[1] Unfortunately, because we are unfamiliar with the nature and use of this word, we tend to ascribe it only to Yeshua. But, in Isaiah 45:1, Yahweh calls the Persian king, Cyrus his "anointed" and uses this same word. The actual phrase that appears much more than "anointed" in the Bible is "my servant" (e.g. Isaiah 42 and 53).

[2] It only appears five times in the prophets; the clearest is Isaiah 61:1, which Yeshua *ascribed to himself* in Luke 4:18.

his God. And they shall dwell secure, for now he shall be great to the ends of the earth."
—Micah 5:2-4

"For to us a child is born, to us a son is given; and the government shall be upon his shoulder, and his name shall be called Wonderful Counselor, Mighty God, Everlasting Father, Prince of Peace."
—Isaiah 9:6

XVIII. UNIT 18 — PROPHETS OF THE EARLY YEARS: Obadiah

A. Obadiah: The Man & His Book

  1. His name means "Servant of Yahweh"

  2. We know nothing of his family, hometown or personal history.

  3. His book is the *shortest* book in the Old Testament — 21 verses!

  4. His book is one of the hardest books of Prophecy to date: scholars range from the 9th to the 5th century BC.

    a. Some prophets can be "dated" from the "outside-in":

      (1) The prophet is mentioned someplace else in the Bible? (E.g. Jonah, Jeremiah, Haggai)

    b. Other prophets can be "dated" from the "inside-out":

      (1) Specific names of rulers are mentioned in their prophecy (Judah, Israel, Assyria, etc.)

      (2) Specific locations are mentioned (Jerusalem, Nineveh, Babylon, the Temple)

      (3) "silence" about specific people, places or events (N. Kingdom, Temple worship, etc.)

    c. Dating Obadiah seems to hinge on when the events in verses 11-14 occurred:

    "On the day that you stood aloof, on the day that strangers carried off his wealth and foreigners entered his gates and cast lots for Jerusalem, you were like one of them. But do not gloat over the day of your brother in the day of his misfortune; do not rejoice over the people of Judah in the day of their ruin; do not boast in the day of distress. Do not enter the gate of my people in the day of their calamity; do not gloat over his disaster in the day of his calamity; do not loot his wealth in the day of his calamity. Do not stand at the crossroads to cut off his fugitives; do not hand over his survivors in the day of distress."

      (4) 848-841 BC — Philistines and Arabs attacked Jerusalem while Jehoram was king; during this time, Edom revolted against Judah (cf. 2 Chron. 21:8-20; 2 Kg 8:20-22).

      (5) 586 BC — Nebuchadnezzar attacked and destroyed Jerusalem (2 Kgs 25).

B. Obadiah: The Man and His Message

  1. His entire prophecy is directed against the Edomites.

    a. They are the descendants of Jacob's twin brother, Esau (Gen. 36:1, 8-9)

    b. They had periodic conflicts with Israel from the Exodus up through the Babylonian Exile (cf. 1 Sam. 14:47; 2 Sam. 8:13-14; 2 Chron. 20 and 25; Ezek. 25:12-14)

    c. In particular, they seem to have participated in one of the times Jerusalem was attacked and destroyed by foreign forces. (cf. vv. 11-14)

    d. Isaiah, Jeremiah, Ezekiel and Amos also preached against the Edomites.

    e. By New Testament times, they had moved further west in southern Judah and were called the Idumeans. Herod the Great was an Idumean. Some Idumeans appear to have been converted under Jesus' ministry (Mk. 3:7-8).

  2. Obadiah brings two "charges" against the Edomites

    a. Cruelty to Judah during a time of need. (vv. 11-14)

    b. Pride and the belief they were "beyond God's reach" because of their natural resources. (vv. 3-4)

  3. He *may* be the first prophet to speak of the "Day of the LORD" as a future event of God's justice. (vs. 15)

C. Obadiah and the Christian

  1. Covenant faithfulness to God always manifests itself in mercy, justice and compassion towards people.

  "He has told you, O man, what is good; and what does the LORD require of you but to do justice, and to love kindness, and to walk humbly with your God?"
—Micah 6:8

  2. God has expectations about how we view and treat other members of the "family of God."

"And let us not grow weary of doing good, for in due season we will reap, if we do not give up. So then, as we have opportunity, let us do good to everyone, and especially to those who are of the household of faith."
–Galatians 6:9-10

3. Trusting in our own national resources and strength is foolish and dangerous.

"Woe to those who go down to Egypt for help and rely on horses, who trust in chariots because they are many and in horsemen because they are very strong, but do not look to the Holy One of Israel or consult the LORD!"
–Isaiah 31:1

XIX. UNIT 19 — LOCUSTS & THE "LAST DAYS" — The Book of Joel

A. The "Details"

1. The prophet's name means "The Lord is God."
2. His prophecy begins with a parabolic use of an actual disaster (I.e. locust plague).
3. Joel was extremely familiar with Jerusalem and the Temple (I.e. a "Southern" prophet):
   a. Specific offerings are mentioned[1] (1:9).
   b. There are repeated references to "priests," "altar," "house of God," "Judah," and "Zion" (1:13-16; 2:15-17).

B. The "Difficulties"

1. A Puzzling Chronology: There are no internal "hooks" for dating this book.
2. A Biographical Vacuum: No information about the prophet other than his father's name.
3. A Broad Message: No specific sins are addressed; it is more of a "free-floating" prophecy.
4. A Messianic Silence: There are *no* prophecies about the future Messiah.
5. An Expansive Application: It provides prophetic details ranging from the 8th century BC to the Second coming of Christ.
6. It is not clear "who quoted whom" in this book* *(another dating issue)*:

...a day of darkness and gloom, a day of clouds and thick darkness! Like blackness there is spread upon the mountains a great and powerful people; their like has never been before, nor will be again after them through the years of all generations. **Joel 2:2**	*A day of wrath is that day, a day of distress and anguish, a day of ruin and devastation, a day of darkness and gloom, a day of clouds and thick darkness,* **Zephaniah 1:15**
Beat your plowshares into swords, and your pruning hooks into spears; let the weak say, "I am a warrior." **Joel 3:10**	*He shall judge between the nations, and shall decide disputes for many peoples; and they shall beat their swords into plowshares, and their spears into pruning hooks; nation shall not lift up sword against nation, neither shall they learn war anymore.* **Isaiah 2:4** *He shall judge between many peoples, and shall decide for strong nations afar off; and they shall beat their swords into plowshares, and their spears into pruning hooks; nation shall not lift up sword against nation, neither shall they learn war anymore;* **Micah 4:3**

*Scholars estimate that 27 phrases or expression from Joel appear in other Old Testament books.

C. The "Day" (of The Lord)

1. This phrase appears five times in this book (cf. 1:15; 2:1,11,31:3:14).
2. The "Day of the LORD" also appears in 6 other prophetic books (Obadiah, Amos, Isaiah, Zephaniah, Ezekiel, and Malachi)
3. The "Day of the LORD" is when YAHWEH reveals Himself as He really is.
4. It will be a day of judgment and/or blessing.

D. The "Declaration"

---

[1] Especially the "drink" and "grain" offerings which accompanied the two daily burnt offerings. Also, words that are typically associated with Jerusalem appear quite frequently: "Zion" (7x), "Judah" (6x), "Jerusalem" (6x), "house of the Lord" (5x), "priests," "grain offering," and "drink offering" each appear 3x. There is a reference to the "Valley of Jehoshophat" that may be a reference to the Kidron Valley.

1. Joel issues a timeless call to repentance that is rooted in the covenant revelation by YAHWEH about Himself:

Joel 2:12-13	Exodus 34:6,10
"Yet even now," declares the LORD, "return to me with all your heart, with fasting, with weeping, and with mourning; and rend your hearts and not your garments." Return to the LORD, your God, for **he is gracious and merciful, slow to anger, and abounding in steadfast love;** *and he relents over disaster."*	*The LORD passed before him and proclaimed, "The LORD, the LORD,* **a God merciful and gracious, slow to anger, and abounding in steadfast love and faithfulness,** *...And he said, "Behold, I am making a covenant. Before all your people I will do marvels, such as have not been created in all the earth or in any nation. And all the people among whom you are shall see the work of the LORD, for it is an awesome thing that I will do with you.*

E. Joel and the New Testament

1. Paul quotes Joel in his declaration about the inclusiveness of Grace:

   For "everyone who calls on the name of the Lord will be saved." **Romans 10:13**

2. Peter cites Joel extensively to introduce his first Pentecostal sermon.

3. Peter establishes forever an unbreakable continuity between God's elect ("chosen") people over the past 700 years an on into the future:

Acts 2:14-21	Joel 2:28-32
But Peter, standing with the eleven, lifted up his voice and addressed them, "Men of Judea and all who dwell in Jerusalem, let this be known to you, and give ear to my words. For these men are not drunk, as you suppose, since it is only the third hour of the day. But this is what was uttered through the prophet Joel: "'And in the last days it shall be, God declares, that I will pour out my Spirit on all flesh, and your sons and your daughters shall prophesy, and your young men shall see visions, and your old men shall dream dreams; even on my male servants and female servants in those days I will pour out my Spirit, and they shall prophesy. And I will show wonders in the heavens above and signs on the earth below, blood, and fire, and vapor of smoke; the sun shall be turned to darkness and the moon to blood, before the day of the Lord comes, the great and magnificent day. And it shall come to pass that everyone who calls upon the name of the Lord shall be saved.'	*And it shall come to pass afterward, that I will pour out my Spirit on all flesh; your sons and your daughters shall prophesy, your old men shall dream dreams, and your young men shall see visions. Even on the male and female servants in those days I will pour out my Spirit. "And I will show wonders in the heavens and on the earth, blood and fire and columns of smoke. The sun shall be turned to darkness, and the moon to blood, before the great and awesome day of the LORD comes. And it shall come to pass that everyone who calls on the name of the LORD shall be saved. For in Mount Zion and in Jerusalem there shall be those who escape, as the LORD has said, and among the survivors shall be those whom the LORD calls.*

4. This day is also an answer to the prayer of Moses in Number 11:29:

   "But Moses said to him, 'Are you jealous for my sake? Would that all the LORD'S people were prophets, that the LORD would put his Spirit on them!'"

5. God reversed the Jewish social order in this prophecy and in its fulfillment:

   "Blessed are you, Hashem [the name], our G-D, King of the Universe for not making me a gentile. Blessed are you for not making me a slave. Blessed are you for not making me a woman."

   (from the Jewish Talmud;

6. The first half of Joel's prophecy was fulfilled at Pentecost . The last half will be fulfilled in the "last days" of the "last days":

   "When he opened the sixth seal, I looked, and behold, there was a great earthquake, and the sun became black as sackcloth, the full moon became like blood, and the stars of the sky fell to the earth as the fig tree sheds its winter fruit when shaken by a gale.   **–Revelation 6:12-13**

XX. UNIT 20 — THIS AIN'T PREACHIN' TO THE CHOIR! — The Book of Jonah

A.   Cold Hearts Meet Cold Feet: The "Big Picture" on the Big Bully

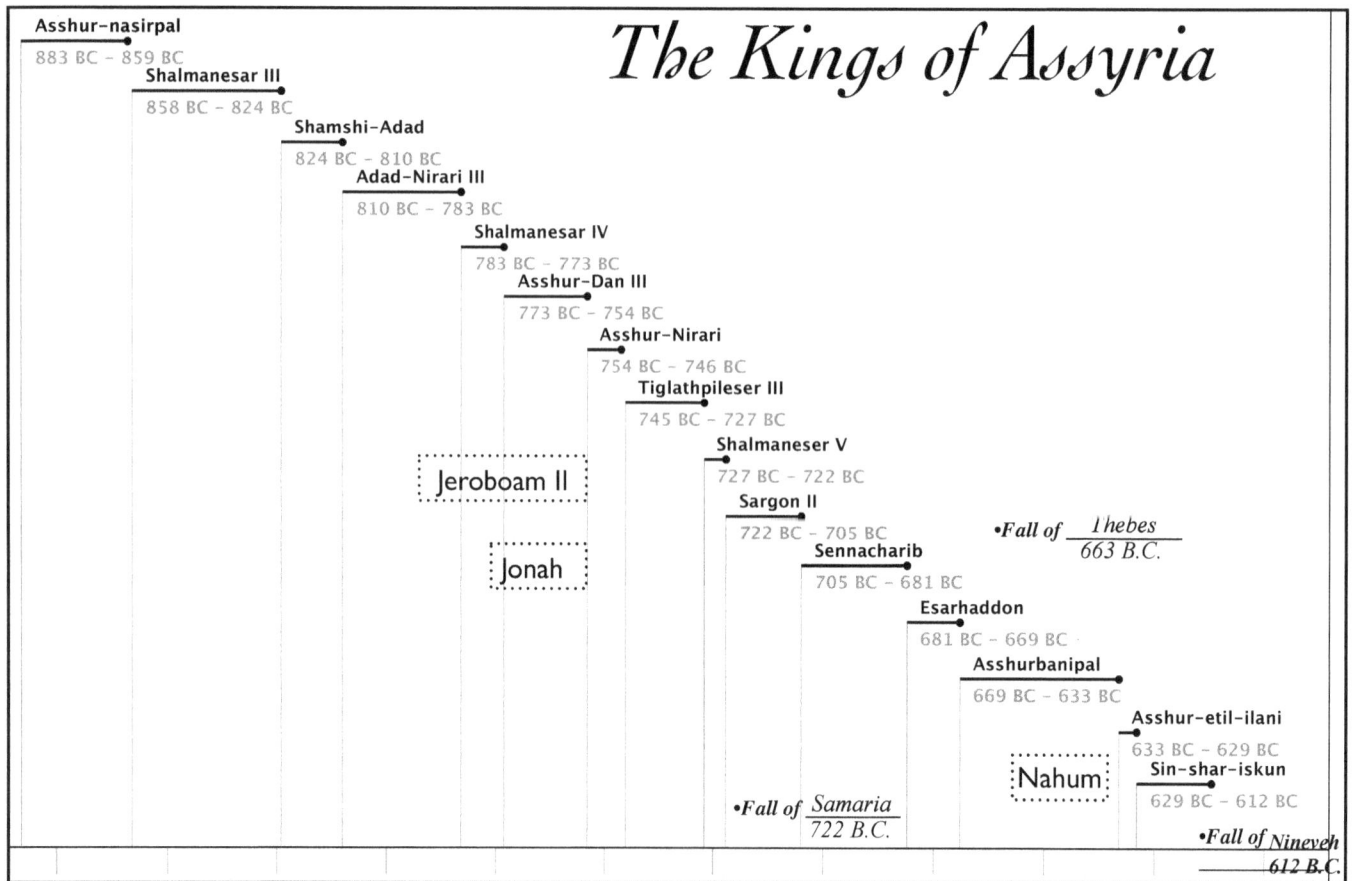

The Kings of Assyria

Asshur-nasirpal
883 BC – 859 BC
Shalmanesar III
858 BC – 824 BC
Shamshi-Adad
824 BC – 810 BC
Adad-Nirari III
810 BC – 783 BC
Shalmanesar IV
783 BC – 773 BC
Asshur-Dan III
773 BC – 754 BC
Asshur-Nirari
754 BC – 746 BC
Tiglathpileser III
745 BC – 727 BC
Jeroboam II
Shalmaneser V
727 BC – 722 BC
Sargon II
722 BC – 705 BC
Jonah
•*Fall of* Thebes 663 B.C.
Sennacharib
705 BC – 681 BC
Esarhaddon
681 BC – 669 BC
Asshurbanipal
669 BC – 633 BC
Asshur-etil-ilani
633 BC – 629 BC
Nahum
Sin-shar-iskun
629 BC – 612 BC
•*Fall of* Samaria 722 B.C.
•*Fall of* Nineveh 612 B.C.

1. The Assyrian "MO and Rap Sheet"

    a.   The Assyrians were cruel beyond imagination. Their treatment of captives of war included:

        (1) Leading captives by means of hooks in their lips.

        (2) Skinning captives alive

        (3) Cutting off body parts.

        (4) Tearing out tongues.

        (5) Making "pyramids" of human heads:

> *"Their men, young and old, I took as prisoners. Of some, I cut off the feet and the hands; of others I cut off the noses, ears and lips; of the young men's ears I made a heap; of the old men's heads I built a minaret."*
> **[Asshurnasirpal, King of Assyria 883-859 B.C.]**

2.   Assyria and Israel: Two Centuries of "Stormy Weather"

    a.   **853 BC** — Ahab (Israel) and Ben-Hadad (Syria) made a rare and brief alliance to fight Shalmanessar III (874-853 BC) at the Battle of Qarqar.[1]

    b.   **841 BC** — Jehu of Judah paid tribute to Shalmanessar.[2]

---

[1] This alliance is recorded in 1 Kings 22:1, although no explanation is given for its formation. Shalmannesar boasted of a total victory in this battle, but it is more likely a stalemate considering he went no further to dominate, which was the custom in those days.

[2] The "Black Obelisk" records 31 years of Shalmanessar's military victories. It has an actual relief of King Jehu of Judah kneeling prostrate before him. It says, *"Tribute of Iaua [Jehu], son of Humri [Omri]. From him I received silver, gold, a golden cask, golden beakers, golden pails, pewterware, a scepter, and puruhutu wood."*

c. **c. 745-727 BC** — Tiglathpileser III (745-727 BC) attacked Israel during the reign of Pekah[1] (2 Kg. 15:29)

d. **722 BC** — Shalmanessar V/Sargon II attacked and destroyed Samaria and *deported* Israel and repopulated the area with conquered peoples from other regions.. (2 Kings 17)

(1) The "Samaritan" people were the result of this invasion through inter-marriage with the people Assyria infused into the region.[2]

e. **701 BC** — Sennacharib attacked Lachish (Judah) and destroyed it.

(1) He fortified Nineveh and made it the capital of Assyria.

(2) He constructed the world's oldest aqueduct to bring water into Nineveh (30 miles!).

(3) Hezekiah built his famous "tunnel" to prepare for Assyrian attack. (Pool of Siloam).

f. **681-669 BC** — Esarhadden made Manasseh of Judah help him provide building supplies for Nineveh and perhaps even Babylon which he also refurbished:

"I called up the kings of the country Hatti and the region of the other side of the Euphrates, namely Ba'lu, king of Tyre, Manasseh, king of Judah . . . ; all these I sent out and made them transport under terrible difficulties to Nineveh, the city where I exercise my rulership, as building material for my palace: big logs, long beams" **(Ancient Near Eastern Texts, p. 29)**

"And at the beginning of my rule, in the first year of my reign, when I took my seat upon the royal throne in might, there appeared favorable signs in the heavens. ... Through the soothsayers' rites encouraging oracles were disclosed, and for the rebuilding of Babylon and the restoration of [the step-tower] Esagila they caused the command to be written down."

3. Nineveh "That Great City"

a. It is one of the oldest cities in the world, built by Nimrod the great-grandson of Noah! (Gen. 10:11)

b. Assyria is mentioned 146x in the Bible; over half are in the prophets (44x in Isaiah alone!)

c. Social reform occurred half-way through the reign of Ashur Dan III, which coincides with the lifetime of the prophet Jonah.

d. It was an intimidating city: 100' tall towers, 50' tall walls and 15 gates.

e. Two of its kings' palaces averaged 625,000 square feet![3]

4. Jonah: The Resume'

a. We know when and where he lived: Galilee (Gath-Hepher) 790-750 BC during the reign of Jeroboam II, the most powerful king of the northern kingdom. (cf. 2 Kings 14:25)

b. He was a prophet by "profession," not *"election."*

c. Hearing God speak and being faithful to His voice was nothing new to Jonah.

d. Jonah was the first (and only) prophet to the Gentiles in the Old Testament. *(i.e., He went to Nineveh).*

5. Jonah: The "Wreck"

a. This is a book about a prophet, not a prophecy about a people (of the 1300 words, 8 contain the prophetic message!)

b. Jonah is the only created thing in this book that disobeys Yahweh.

---

[1] Ahaz, the father of Hezekiah, is called the "son of Pul," a sign of vassalage and submission (2 Kgs 16:7).

[2] The Samaritan-Jewish hostility was "born" in this time frame. The inter-marriage of the northern Jews with the incoming pagans defeated by Assyria elsewhere in their empire, created a near hatred for these "covenant-breakers." However, the Samaritans believed that *they* not the southern Jews, were the true "chosen people." They claimed Mr. Gerazim as the true place of central worship, and built a rival temple there, citing the fact that when Joshua pronounced the covenant stipulations and "blessings" and "curses," Gerazim was the mountain of blessing. They believed that the move to Jerusalem by David was an act of apostasy, and would have nothing to do with the city. The still do not (there are about 1,200 Samaritans still living.) They only accept the Torah, and their version of it, known as the Samaritan Pentateuch, has 5,000 changes from the Hebrew Masoritic text. Most are minor, but not all of them. For example, in their account of the flood, they have Noah's ark landing on Mt. Gerazim rather than Aarat.

[3] By way of perspective, the Biltmore Estate outside Ashville, NC, one of America's largest private homes is 174, 240 square feet, three and a half times *smaller!*

      c.   Jonah's attempted "sailor-assisted suicide" was even used by Yahweh to convict/convert(?) the pagan sailors.

      d.   Jonah's sense of patriotism (if real) had degenerated to idolatry. He chose to disobey God for love of country.

      e.   Jonah was so committed to the "notion of nation" that he was blinded to God's passion for people.

6.   Jonah and the New Testament

      a.   This is perhaps the most "New Testament" book in our Old Testaments:

         (1) It is similar to Acts in its movement of Gospel Grace from Jew to Gentile

         (2) Peter's decision at Joppa stands in contrast to Jonah's decision in the same city.

         (3) This book establishes the fact that covenant love is available to those outside it.

7.   Jonah and the Christian

      a.   Jonah's anger over the repentance of his enemies stands in stark contrast to Jesus' sorrow over Jerusalem's refusal to repent (cf. Jonah 3:10-4:1 and Luke 19:41-44).

      b.   This is *not* a story about a fish or a failed prophet . It is a story about a covenant-keeping God who seeks to enlarge the boundaries of that covenant.

      c.   Jonah's patriotism drove him to seek the death of his enemies. Jesus tells us to love and pray for them. (Luke 6:27-28).

      d.   Jonah's "patriotism" was a disguise for his commitment to his own comfort. This is made clear in the ordeal with the plant and worm.

XXI. UNIT 21 — NAHUM: The Sequel to Jonah

A.   The Setting:

    1.   The Date

      a.   **3:16-17** — Nineveh appears to be at its zenith.

      b.   **3:8-10** — speaks of the fall of Thebes (No Amon) as past and Nineveh's demise as imminent.

         (1) Thebes fell to Ashurbanipal in 663 BC.

         (2) Nineveh fell to a coalition of Medes and Babylonians in 612 BC.

B.   The "Sequence": A Remarkable Prophecy

Passage	PROPHECY
1:10; 2:5	Inhabitants of Nineveh would be characterized by drunkenness prior to the fall of the city.
2:6	The river would overflow and wash away the city gates.
3:15-19	The palace would be burned; The Assyrian king burned himself alive in his palace.
3:12	Surrounding "palaces" would easily fall to the attackers; Asshur the religious center fell, Nimrud, the military center fell and finally Nineveh, the administrative center of the empire.
3:18-19	Destruction would be complete and permanent; Alexander the Great marched over the top of Nineveh and didn't even know its ruins lay beneath his feet!

C.   Yahweh: A Remarkable God — Nahum 1:7

    1.   "Buried" in the midst of this book on God's retributive justice is an amazing statement about His own character (perhaps an echo of Jonah?):

       "The LORD is good, a stronghold in the day of trouble; he knows those who take refuge in him.

                                                 Nahum 1:7

D.   Nahum and the Christian

    1.   Justice is an attribute of God. It is sure but not always immediate (I.e. 100+ years between Jonah and Nahum).

    2.   Moral decay is a more powerful enemy than military might.

XXII. UNIT 22: *"THE BEGINNING OF THE END"*: Amos & Micah

A. The Bigger Picture: Three Kings - Six Prophets

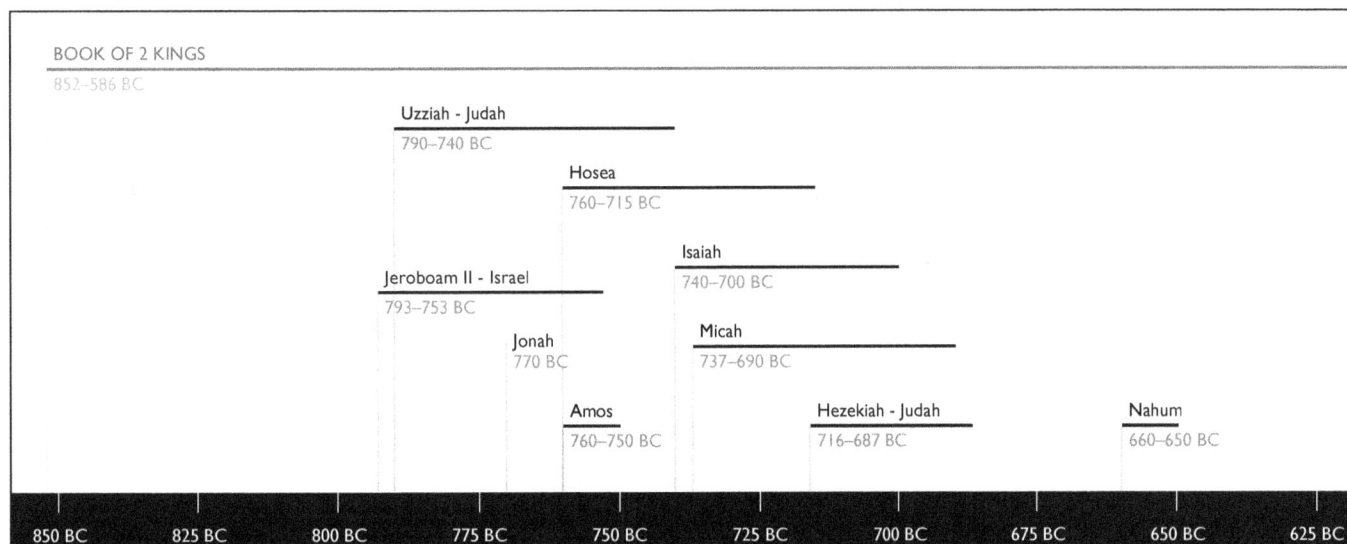

B. **Prophetic Reminders:** The prophets to Israel and Judah all had dual messages: judgment *and* hope; punishment *and* restoration; covenant-breaking *and* covenant-keeping; "now" *and* "later":

Judgment/Doom	Restoration/Hope
Amos 1:3 – 9:10	Amos 9:11-15
Micah 1:2 – 2:11 Micah 3 Micah 6:1 – 7:7	Micah 2:12-13 Micah 4 – 5 Micah 7:8–20
Hosea 1:2 – 2:13 Hosea 4:1 – 10:15 Hosea 11:12 – 13:16	Hosea 2:14 – 3:5 Hosea 11:1-11 Hosea 14

C. The prophetic message increases in intensity in proportion to God's heart breaking, and His wrath growing, as we move closer to the fall of Samaria (722 BC) and Jerusalem (586 BC).

D. **AMOS:** The Prophet to the "Suburbs"

1. Prophet or CEO?

  a. A "Southern boy" preaching to the North.

    (1) Amos' "hometown" was Tekoa, 12 miles *south* of Jerusalem.

    (2) He was "lay businessman," *not* a prophet or priest.

    (3) *"neither a prophet or a prophet's son"* may be a statement distancing him from their corruption (7:14).

  b. Amos is not a *"typical"* shepherd

    (1) The word used is *noqued*, not *ra'ah*

    (2) The word is only used here and for Mesha, King of Moab, whom the Scripture calls a "sheep breeder," *not* a shepherd:

      Now Mesha king of Moab was a sheep breeder, and he had to deliver to the king of Israel 100,000 lambs and the wool of 100,000 rams. – **2 Kings 3:4**

    (3) A similar word used *outside* the Bible (Ugaritic) refers to the owner of a sheep "operation"

    (4) His status as a businessman provided credibility to his ministry; the wealthy speaking to the wealthy class.

2. "Sodomites" in the Family of God

a. Jeroboam II and Uzziah both reigned during Israel and Judah's most prosperous and expansive time since Solomon and David.

b. It was a culture characterized by affluence and leisure:

(1) lounging women who oppress the poor (4:1).

(2) extravagant and multiple homes (3:15; 5:11).

(3) luxurious meals eaten on expensive furniture (6:4).

(4) sufficient leisure time to design instruments and sing "empty" songs (6:5).

(5) "happy hour" and "day spa" lifestyles (6:6).

(6) sexual promiscuity (2:7b; cf. Ex. 21:9).

(7) idolatry (2:8; 5:26).

(8) their lifestyles resembled that of Sodom (Ezek. 16:49-50).

3. It Was a Culture of Neglect

a. There are 10x as many references to "the needy" ('ebyan) in this book than any other book of prophecy.

b. "Things" were more valuable than people; (E.g. slave trade - 2:6).

c. The poor were neglected and taken advantage of (2:7; 8:4).

d. Dishonest pricing and products (8:5-6).

e. Injustice in the courts; bias for the wealthy (5:12).

4. A Culture Characterized By Spiritual Decay and Corruption

a. Empty ritual; worship that was disconnected from the covenant (5:21-24).

b. Bethel – where Jeroboam I set-up a golden calf is mentioned 7x in Amos as the center for religious apostasy (cf. 1 Kg 12:26-29 and Amos 3:13-14).

c. The "silence" of God's voice due to a refusal to listen (cf. 1:2 and 8:11).

E. MICAH: Same Song, Second Verse

1. His Resumé

a. His name is an abbreviation for Micaiah, which means, *"Who is Like Yahweh?"*

b. He was a country boy like Amos, not a "city boy" like Isaiah.

c. He preached prior to the fall of Samaria to Assyria in 722 BC (1:5-7).

d. Jeremiah knew of his ministry 150 years later (Jer. 26:17-19).

2. His Message

a. Spoke against injustice and corruption among civil leaders (3:1-3,9-11; 7:3).

b. Spoke against corruption and greed among spiritual leadership (3:5-11).

c. Spoke against social neglect and abuse (6:10-12).

d. Spoke against accommodation to culture, I.e. "idolatry" (6:16).

e. Pointed ahead to the fall of Jerusalem (4:10) like Amos did for Samaria (Amos 3).

3. The "Poet Laureate" of Moresheth

a. His skills as a writer are some of the best in the Old Testament:

"With what shall I come before the LORD, and bow myself before God on high? Shall I come before him with burnt offerings, with calves a year old? Will the LORD be pleased with thousands of rams, with ten thousands of rivers of oil? Shall I give my firstborn for my transgression, the fruit of my body for the sin of my soul?" He has told you, O man, what is good; and what does the LORD require of you but to do justice, and to love kindness, and to walk humbly with your God? —Micah 6:6-8

b. He "distilled" the Talmud's 613 requirements of the Torah down to 3:

(1) "do *justice*"

(2) *"love kindness"*

(3) *"walk with Yahweh in humility"*

   c. Some of Micah's writing skills are "buried" in the Hebrew language. Consider Moffatt's paraphrase of Micah 1:10-16:

E S V T r a n s l a t i o n	Moffatt Paraphrase
Tell it not in Gath; weep not at all; in Beth-le-aphrah roll yourselves in the dust. Pass on your way, inhabitants of Shaphir, in nakedness and shame; the inhabitants of Zaanan do not come out; the lamentation of Beth-ezel shall take away from you its standing place. For the inhabitants of Maroth wait anxiously for good, because disaster has come down from the LORD to the gate of Jerusalem. Harness the steeds to the chariots, inhabitants of Lachish; it was the beginning of sin to the daughter of Zion, for in you were found the transgressions of Israel. Therefore you shall give parting gifts to Moresheth-gath; the houses of Achzib shall be a deceitful thing to the kings of Israel. I will again bring a conqueror to you, inhabitants of Mareshah; the glory of Israel shall come to Adullam. Make yourselves bald and cut off your hair, for the children of your delight; make yourselves as bald as the eagle, for they shall go from you into exile.	*Tell it not in Tellington!* *Wail not in Wail!* *Dust Manor will eat dirt,* *Dressy Town flee naked.* *Safefold will not save* *Wallchester's walls are down,* *A bitter dose drinks Bitterton.* *(Towards Jerusalem, City of Peace, the Lord sends war)* *Harness the war-steeds O men of Barstead!* *(Zion's beginning of sinning, Equal to Israel's crimes)* *To Welfare a last farewell!* *For trapping Israel's trapped kings.*

   d. The beauty of this passage is further enhanced because the order of the cities is likely the route Sennachrib's military took in its assault on Jerusalem during Hezekiah's day!! (cf. 2 Kings 18:13ff).

F. Lessons From Samaria and Jerusalem (I.e. Amos and Micah)

  1. Amos and Micah both stand as warnings against separating our worship from our lifestyle.

  2. We need to understand that "social justice" is a misnomer because Injustice is a social outcome of covenant unfaithfulness, not a "social" issue or problem.

  3. The prophetic voice *to* the rich must come from *within*, not from outside.

   a. The truth of the message is validated by the life of the speaker more than the life of the hearers!

XXIII. HOSEA: GOD'S FINAL WORD TO AN UNFAITHFUL BRIDE

A. Hosea the Man

  1. A "Hometown Boy"

   a. His name means "*salvation*"; it is the second half of Je-shua *("God is salvation")*.

   b. Hosea is the only northern prophet who was *from* the North. ("Israel/Ephraim" - 81x; "Judah" - 15x).[1]

   c. He lived in the "last days" of the northern kingdom. There were 6 kings in 25 years, 4 were assassinated.[2]

B. "Guess Who's Coming to Dinner?"

  1. Hosea's "Problem Marriage": the options

   a. an allegory - describes in allegorical form the perennial problem of Israel's infidelity to Yahweh.

   b. symbolic - Gomer is a "harlot" in the same way Israel is: an idolater.

   c. a vision - this event never actually happened. Hosea simply wrote what he "saw."

   d. revisionist - Gomer had "tendencies" towards harlotry which she followed *after* she married Hosea (NIV leans in this direction)

   e. historical - God told Hosea to marry a "whore." The words *"whore/whoredom/adultery"* appear 27x in this book.

   f. Marrying a prostitute was *not* prohibited in Scripture unless one was a priest (Lev. 21:7,14); Would I marry a prostitute, if God told me to?

  2. The Importance of this Book

   a. It paints in the most painful language the meaning and cost of being in a covenant relationship.

---

[1] Hosea's northern heritage is apparent in the names of cities from norther Palestine that appear in this book: Mizpah and Tabor (5:1), Gilead (6:8), Schechem (6:9), Aram (12:12), and Lebanon (14:6).

[2] Hosea can be dated from the first verse. We are told his ministry was during the reigns of Jeroboam I, king of the northern kingdom of Israel (793-753 B.C.), and Uzziah king of the southern kingdom of Judah (792-740 B.C.).

b. It demonstrates the theological and relational nature of being God's covenant people.

c. It shows us that marriage is only an earthly illustration of a divine reality.

(1) Paul reinforces the "portrait" idea in Ephesians 5.

(2) This explains why marriage does not exist where a covenant is no longer needed (I.e. eternity)

(3) we have *deified* marriage (e.g. "family values") or denigrated it (e.g., same gender unions, polygamy, polyamorous unions) rather than honoring God *by* it.

C. God's Special Anger: The Failure of Leadership

1. They failed to be the guardians (kings), practitioners (priests) and proclaimers (priests) of the covenant.

2. Their failure resulted in spiritual darkness in the entire nation:

"My people are destroyed for lack of knowledge; because you have rejected knowledge, I reject you from being a priest to me. And since you have forgotten the law of your God, I also will forget your children." **–Hosea 4:6**

3. Their abandonment of the covenant was expressed by:

a. political "covenants" - Egypt is mentioned 13x, Assyria 9x (5:13;7:8-10)

b. Idolatry - Hosea uses a word-play with Bethel ("house of God") and Beth-aven ("house of sin"); Hosea 10:5, 15

D. Hosea's Use of "Flowers" (in his speech)

1. This book is saturated with figures of speech (similes and metaphors) describing both God and Israel:

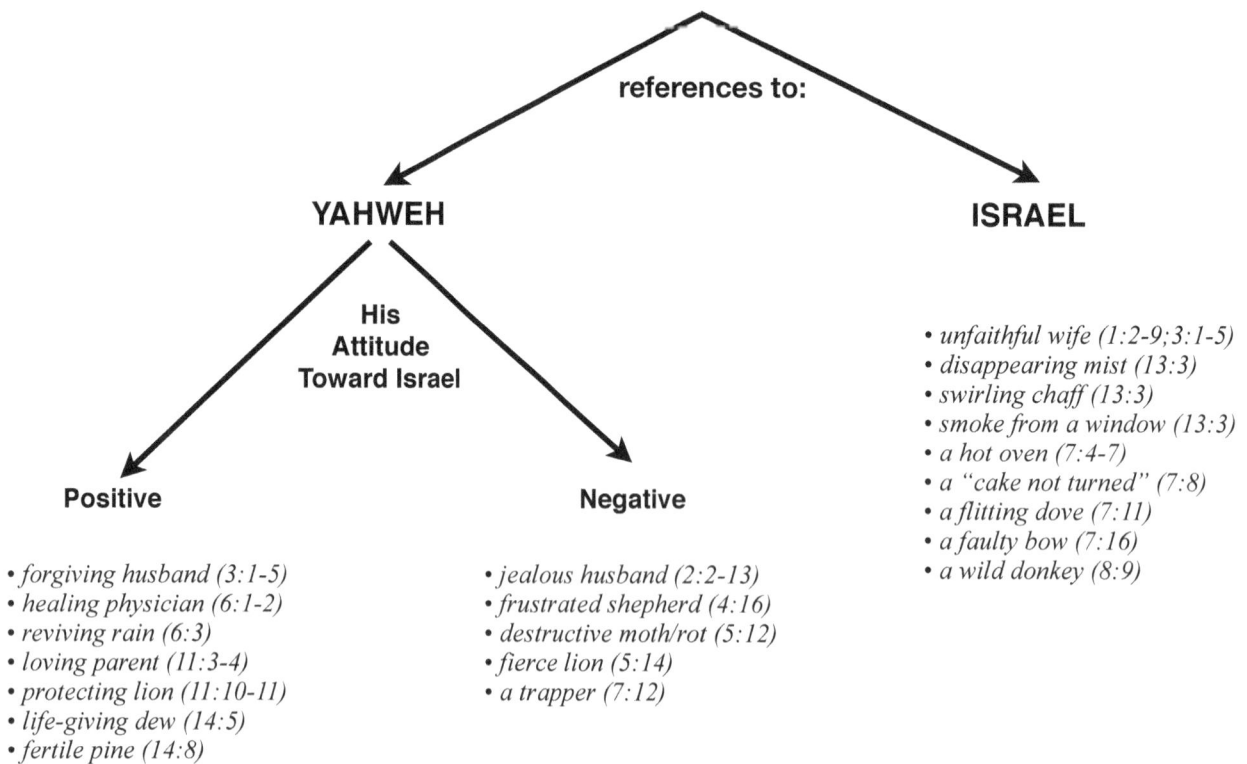

references to:

YAHWEH

ISRAEL

His Attitude Toward Israel

• *unfaithful wife (1:2-9;3:1-5)*
• *disappearing mist (13:3)*
• *swirling chaff (13:3)*
• *smoke from a window (13:3)*
• *a hot oven (7:4-7)*
• *a "cake not turned" (7:8)*
• *a flitting dove (7:11)*
• *a faulty bow (7:16)*
• *a wild donkey (8:9)*

Positive

Negative

• *forgiving husband (3:1-5)*
• *healing physician (6:1-2)*
• *reviving rain (6:3)*
• *loving parent (11:3-4)*
• *protecting lion (11:10-11)*
• *life-giving dew (14:5)*
• *fertile pine (14:8)*

• *jealous husband (2:2-13)*
• *frustrated shepherd (4:16)*
• *destructive moth/rot (5:12)*
• *fierce lion (5:14)*
• *a trapper (7:12)*

E. Hosea: The Old Testament *Scholar*

HOSEA	OLD TESTAMENT
Yet the number of the children of Israel shall be like the sand of the sea, which cannot be measured or numbered. And in the place where it was said to them, "You are not my people," it shall be said to them, "Children of the living God." **Hosea 1:10**	*I will surely bless you, and I will surely multiply your offspring as the stars of heaven and as the sand that is on the seashore. And your offspring shall possess the gate of his enemies,* **Genesis 22:17**

HOSEA	OLD TESTAMENT
Hear the word of the LORD, O children of Israel, for the LORD has a controversy with the inhabitants of the land. There is no faithfulness or steadfast love, and no knowledge of God in the land; there is swearing, lying, murder, stealing, and committing adultery; they break all bounds, and bloodshed follows bloodshed. But I am the LORD your God from the land of Egypt; you know no God but me, and besides me there is no savior. **Hosea 4:1-2; 13:4**	*And God spoke all these words, saying, "I am the LORD your God, who brought you out of the land of Egypt, out of the house of slavery. "You shall have no other gods before me. "You shall not make for yourself a carved image... "You shall not take the name of the LORD your God in vain... "Remember the Sabbath day, to keep it holy.... "You shall not murder. "You shall not commit adultery. "You shall not steal. "You shall not bear false witness against your neighbor. "You shall not covet your neighbor's house; you shall not covet your neighbor's wife, or his male servant, or his female servant, or his ox, or his donkey, or anything that is your neighbor's."* **Exodus 20:1-17**
How can I give you up, O Ephraim? How can I hand you over, O Israel? How can I make you like Admah? How can I treat you like Zeboiim? My heart recoils within me; my compassion grows warm and tender." **Hosea 11:8**	*the whole land burned out with brimstone and salt, nothing sown and nothing growing, where no plant can sprout, an overthrow like that of Sodom and Gomorrah, Admah, and Zeboiim, which the LORD overthrew in his anger and wrath* **Deuteronomy 29:23**
They shall not remain in the land of the LORD, but Ephraim shall return to Egypt, and they shall eat unclean food in Assyria. For behold, they are going away from destruction; but Egypt shall gather them; Memphis shall bury them. Nettles shall possess their precious things of silver; thorns shall be in their tents. **Hosea 9:3,6**	*for it is the LORD our God who brought us and our fathers up from the land of Egypt, out of the house of slavery, and who did those great signs in our sight and preserved us in all the way that we went, and among all the peoples through whom we passed."* **Joshua 24:17**
From the days of Gibeah you have sinned, O Israel; There they stand! Will not the battle against the sons of iniquity overtake them in Gibeah? **Hosea 10:9**	*So they passed along and went their way, and the sun set on them near Gibeah which belongs to Benjamin.... Then behold, an old man was coming out of the field from his work at evening. Now the man was from the hill country of Ephraim, and he was staying in Gibeah, but the men of the place were Benjamites.... While they were celebrating, behold, the men of the city, certain worthless fellows, surrounded the house, pounding the door; and they spoke to the owner of the house, the old man, saying, "Bring out the man who came into your house that we may have relations with him."* **Judges 19:14,16,22**

F. Hosea and the New Testament

   1. Both Peter and Paul utilize Hosea's children's names to testify to the expansive nature of the grace of Yahweh to include the Gentiles in the covenant:

> *As indeed he says in Hosea, "Those who were not my people I will call 'my people,' and her who was not beloved I will call 'beloved.'"*   **–Romans 9:25**

> *"Once you were not a people, but now you are God's people; once you had not received mercy, but now you have received mercy."*   **–1 Peter 2:10**

G. Hosea and the Christian

   1. Marriage is a tangible, visible portrait of a covenant-keeping God. I have an obligation to *Him* to protect His "image."

   2. Covenant faithfulness to Yahweh is the surest way to preserve a marriage.

XXIV. **UNIT 24: *"The Son of Amoz"*: ISAIAH**

A. THE MAN: "Isaiah ben Amoz"

   1. In both the English and Hebrew Bible, Isaiah stands first in his division.

   2. Isaiah ben Amoz has been called, "the Prince of Prophets."

   3. His book is considered the greatest piece of prophetic literature that we have.

   4. No other prophet has exerted so much influence on theology, especially soteriology and Christology.

   5. Isaiah ben Amoz is unique among the prophets for a number of reasons:

     a. The Jewish Talmud says he was Uzziah's cousin, i.e., of royal blood *(Meg. 10b)*.

     b. The author of Chronicles said that Isaiah wrote a history of Uzziah's reign *(2 Chron. 26:22)*.

      c.   Isaiah was married (to a prophetess; Is. 8:3).[1]

      d.   His two sons' names summarize his message:

         (1) **Maher-shalel-hash-baz** — *"quick to the plunder, haste to the spoil"* (8:1-3).

         (2) **Shear-Jashub** — *"a remnant will return"* (7:3).

      e.   The Apocryphal book, *The Assumption of Isaiah,* speaks of him being sawn in two by wicked king Manneseh (cf. Heb. 11:37).

B. THE "MESS": *"Will The Real Isaiah Please Stand?!"*

    1. Some scholars posit as many as three "Isaiahs" as contributors to this book.

    2. The book itself *does* "fall" into at least two very distinct parts: Chapters 1-39 and Chapters 40-66.[2]

      a.   The first section deals primarily with the present crisis with Assyria; the second section deals with the future and Babylon and Persia.

      b.   Isaiah is mentioned by name 16x in the first section, and not at all in the second.

      c.   First section consists largely of forth-telling, the second with fore-telling.

      d.   The phrase, *"the LORD says,"* appears 16x in the first section, and over twice that number in the second.

      e.   The second section mentions "Cyrus" by name, 200 years before he was born!

    3. However, there is strong evidence for a single author:

      a.   New Testament writers cite "Isaiah" by name 22x from 12 different chapters in both "halves" of his book.

      b.   The Ethiopian eunuch told Philip he was reading the "prophet Isaiah," and was reading in the second "half."

      c.   The 2nd century BC apocryphal book, Sirach (Ecclesiasticus) speaks of Isaiah as one who was a "fore-teller" not just a "forth-teller":

> *"For Ezekias [Ezekiel] had done the thing that pleased the Lord, and was strong in the ways of David his father, as Esay [Isaiah] the prophet, who was great and faithful in his vision, had commanded him. In his time the sun went backward, and he lengthened the king's life. He saw by an excellent spirit what should come to pass at the last, and he comforted them that mourned in Sion. He shewed what should come to pass for ever, and secret things or ever they came."*   **Sirach 48:22-25**

      d.   The Isaiah Scroll from Qumran (I.e. Dead Sea Scrolls) from the 2nd century BC begins Isaiah 40:1 on the last line of a column , showing no distinction from chapters 1-39.

C. THE MOTION: The World Was Shifting

    1. The Neo-Assyrian Empire was history's first truly "world" empire.

    2. The events around Jerusalem were cataclysmic and foreboding.

    3. Isaiah spoke during a time of great "covenant faith": either with pagan nations (7:1; 30:1-2; 39:1-7; E.g. Ahaz) or with Yahweh (37:14-21; E.g. Hezekiah).

D. ISAIAH ABRIDGED: 5 Key Themes

    1. **Theme #1** — "The Holy One of Israel[3]"

      a.   This is used for Yahweh 25x (in both "halves"!).

      b.   Outside the book of Isaiah, it only appears 6x (one of those is Isaiah himself speaking in 2 Kg 19:22!).

      c.   Holiness was at center of Isaiah's "call" to ministry and set the tone(6:1-3).

      d.   Holiness was the "centerpiece" of Israel's covenant relationship with Yahweh:

> *"You shall be holy to me, for I the LORD am holy and have separated you from the peoples, that you should be mine."*   **–Leviticus 20:26**

      e.   Isaiah describes Himself and all of his people as "unclean" (I.e. *"unholy"*; 6:1-3).

---

[1] The Hebrew word used here, *nev'a,* is the feminine form of *navi,* the word used for "prophet." This feminine form was also used for Miriam, Deborah, and Huldah (Ex. 15:20; Judges 4:4; 1 Kgs. 22:14)

[2] Proponents of multiple "Isaiahs" over a long period of time see these five points as "evidence" for multiple authorship.

[3] The phrase, "Holy, holy, holy" appears two times in our Bibles. Once in Isaiah 6:3, the other in Revelation 4:8, both scenes in God's throne room.

  f. God's holiness towards sin is judgment, a major theme in this book (E.g. the word "fire" appears 38x).

 2. **Theme #2** — The Gô'ēl, — "Kinsman Redeemer"

  a. Isaiah's own name means "Yahweh is Salvation."

  b. There are 71 references in this book to "saving":

   (1) "save/salvation" = 38x

   (2) redeem/Redeemer" = 26x

   (3) "savior" = 7x

 3. **Theme #3** — The Remnant"

  a. Yahweh as holy *and* Yahweh as Redeemer creates a tension in the face of Israel's unfaithfulness.

  b. The "remnant" in Isaiah refers to those who emerge from God's purifying fire of judgment to carry the covenant and repopulate the "chosen people":

  c. Isaiah uses a number of metaphors for this double motif:

"a shelter in the vineyard; a hut in a melon field" — **1:8-9**

"...like a terebinth or an oak, who stump remains when it is felled. The holy seed is its stump:
                           — **6:13**

"...Gleanings will be left in it, as when an olive tress is beaten—two or three berries in the top of the highest bough, four or five on the branches of a fruit tree, declares the Lord God of Israel."   — **17:6**

"A thousand shall flee at the threat of one; at the threat of five you shall flee, till you are left like a flagstaff on the top of a mountain, like a signal on a hill."   — **30:17**

"In that day the branch of the Lord shall be beautiful and glorious, and the fruit of the land shall be the pride and honor of the survivors of Israel..."   — **4:2**

"There shall come forth a shoot from the stump of Jesse, and a branch from his roots shall bear fruit. And the Spirit of the Lord shall rest upon him..."   — **11:1-2**

"In that day the remnant of Israel and the survivors of the house of Jacob will no more lean on him who struck them, but will lean on the Lord the Holy of of Israel in truth..." — **10:20**

"And the surviving remnant of the house of Judah shall again take root downward and bear fruit upward. "   — **37:31**

"For out of Jerusalem shall go a remnant, and out of Mount Zion a band of survivors. The zeal of the LORD of hosts will do this."   —**37:32**

 4. **Theme #4** — "The Servant of the LORD"

  a. This is one of the most enduring themes in Isaiah.

  b. There are specific passages known as the "Servant Songs" (41:1-4; 49:1-6; 50:4-9; 52:13 – 53:12).

  c. Sometimes, this "servant" is clearly the nation of Israel (41:8-9; 44:1-2,21; 45:4; 48:20;49:3-6).

  d. But, Isaiah clearly separates the nation from the remnant, so the "servant" can *not* always be the nation (cf. 49:5-6).

  e. This "servant" is also clearly spoken of as a *person* who addresses God's people (44.24; 46:3; 49:1).

  f. Ezra, after the Exile, says clearly that the "remnant" can not save itself(Ezra 9:13-15).

 5. **THEME #5** — The Sovereignty of Yahweh

  a. Yahweh's description of Himself in this book stands in stark contrast to the gods of the ANE.

  b. They scheme, seduce, manipulate and war with each other.

  c. Yahweh claims to be exclusive, omnipotent, omniscient and unique:

   (1) 13 times He says, *"I am He and there is no other."*

   (2) 7 of them are in one chapter! (ch. 45).

  d. This was a source of great comfort in the face of the global uncertainty of the Jews.

E. A LONG "HALF-LIFE": Isaiah and the New Testament

 1. Isaiah provided the New Testament writers with an amazing foundation for their Christology:

  a. John the Baptist's preparatory ministry for the coming glory of God (Is 40:3 and Matt. 3:3; Lk 3:4-6; John 1:23).

  b. The virgin birth of the Messiah (Isaiah 7:4 and Matt. 1:23; Lk 1:34).

    c. Israel's hardened heart causing Jesus to teach in parables(Is 6:9-10; 29:13 and Matt. 13:13-15; John 12:39-40; Act 28:24-27).

    d. Jesus is identified with the "Suffering Servant" in his suffering(Is. 53:1 and Jn 12:38; Acts 8:27-33)

    e. Jesus as the "Servant of the Lord" in his healing miracles (Is 53:4 and Matt 8:17).

    f. Jesus' ministry to the Gentiles was predicted by Isaiah (Is 9:1-2; Matt 4:13-16).

    g. Jesus justified himself in his hometown synagogue when challenged, by identifying himself with the one spoken of by Isaiah (Is. 6:1-3 and Luke 4:14-21).

    h. Jesus' "avoidance of notoriety" is justified in an appeal to Isaiah (Is. 42:1-4 and Matt 12:13-21).

    i. For John the apostle, he equates the glory of Isaiah's vision with Jesus (Is 6:1-3; John 12:41).

    j. For Paul, the inclusion of the Gentiles finds its basis in Isaiah (Is. 11:10 and Rom 15:12; Is 65:1 and Rom 10:20).

F. Isaiah and the Christian

    1. Holiness (i.e., cultural *non*-conformity) is still a covenant stipulation:

> *As obedient children, do not be conformed to the passions of your former ignorance, but as he who called you is holy, you also be holy in all your conduct, since it is written, "You shall be holy, for I am holy."*
> **—1 Pet. 1:14-16**

    2. We are still making "covenants" with pagan "nations."

        a. government

        b. science

        c. education

        d. Mammon

    3. For those of us at this stage of The Story, Isaiah 53 is *"Romans 1-8 in poetry."*

XXV. **UNIT 25: *"Southern Voices"* — Zephaniah & Habakkuk**

  A. The Bigger Picture

    1. The Final Days of Judah: 2 Kings 17-25

Chapter 17	• Ahaz is king in Judah • Hoshea is king in Israel • Shalmanessar V attacks Samaria – 725 BC • Samaria falls to Sargon II – 722 BC • Assyria relocates pagan population in Samaria	Chapter 22	• Josiah becomes king in Judah *(31 years)* • Temple renovation begun • Book of the Law discovered
Chapter 18	• Hezekiah is king of Judah *(29 years)* • Sennacharib attacks cities of Judah – 701 BC • Sennacharib besieges Jerusalem – 701 BC	Chapter 23	• Josiah institutes expansive spiritual reforms • Passover is celebrated (first time since Judges!) • Josiah dies at Megiddo against Pharaoh Neco in 609 BC • Jehoahaz is king in Judah *(3 months)* • Jehoahaz taken to Egypt by Neco • Jehoiachim is king in Judah *(11 years)* • Nebachadnezzar attacks Jerusalem & takes captives – 609 BC • Egypt defeated by Babylon at the Battle of Carchemish – 605 BC
Chapter 19	• Isaiah comforts Hezekiah & predicts death of Sennacharib • Sennacharib murdered by sons in Nineveh – 681 BC	Chapter 24	• Jehoiachin is king of Judah *(3 months)* • Nebuchadnezzar attacks Jerusalem & takes captives – 597 BC • Zedekiah is king in Judah (11 years)
Chapter 20	• Hezekiah becomes deathly ill • Isaiah brings news of healing for Hezekiah • Hezekiah shows national treasures to Merodach-baladan of Babylon	Chapter 25	• Nebuchadnezzar destroys Jerusalem & Temple – 586 BC • "Babylonian Captivity" begins • Gedaliah made governor of Judah • Gedaliah murdered in Mizpah
Chapter 21	• Manasseh becomes king of Judah *(55 years)* • Idolatry becomes rampant in Jerusalem • Amon becomes king of Judah *(2 years)*		

2. "Four Southern Voices": The Prophets in Their Time

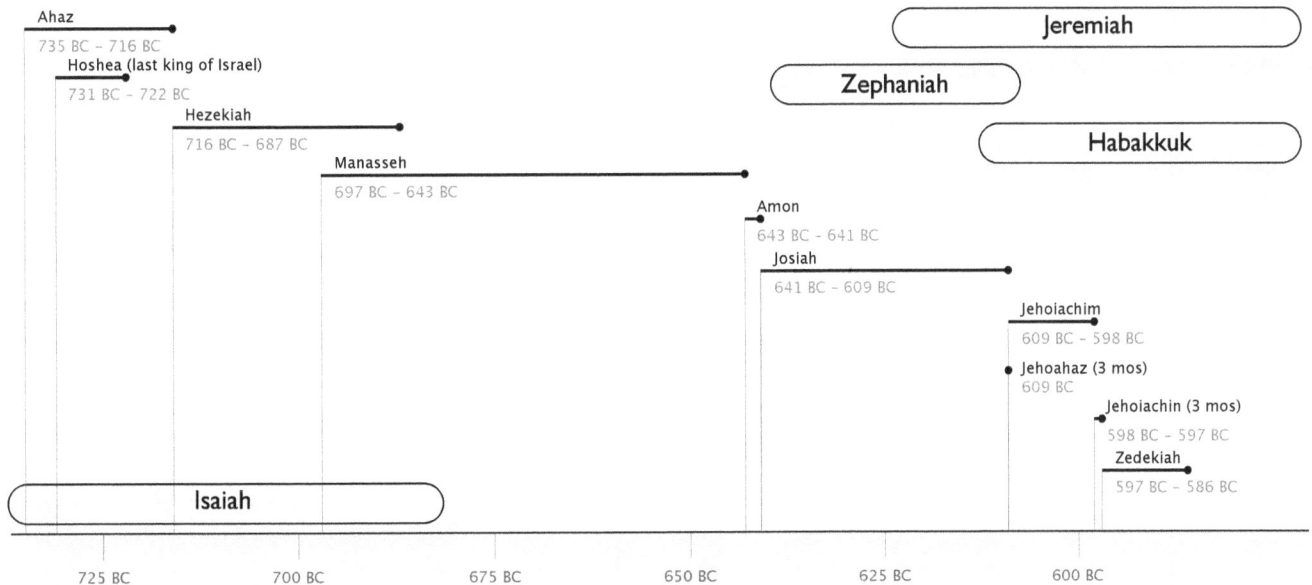

B. Zephaniah: *"The Mouse That Roared"*

1. "Dating" This Prophet

a. Zephaniah's message coincides with the spiritual climate surrounding the reforms under King Josiah:

(1) He uses the Hebrew word for *pagan* priests (*kahmar),* which is only used 3x in the Old Testament, and all during the time of Israel & Judah's demise (cf. 2 Kg 23:5; Hosea 10:5).

(2) He opens his book with phrases associated with ANE pagan worship : *"bow down on the roofs," "hosts of heaven," "Milcom," "leaps over the threshold."* etc. (cf. 1:4-5, 9).

(3) "The Book of the Law" (i.e. Deuteronomy) plays a central role in his message (see chart below)[1]:

D e u t e r o n o m y	Z e p h a n i a h
You shall betroth a wife, but another man shall ravish her. You shall build a house, but you shall not dwell in it. You shall plant a vineyard, but you shall not enjoy its fruit. (28:30)	*Their goods shall be plundered, and their houses laid waste. Though they build houses, they shall not inhabit them; though they plant vineyards, they shall not drink wine from them." (1:13)*
The LORD will strike you with madness and blindness and confusion of mind, and you shall grope at noonday, as the blind grope in darkness, and you shall not prosper in your ways. And you shall be only oppressed and robbed continually, and there shall be no one to help you. (28:28–29)	*I will bring distress on mankind, so that they shall walk like the blind, (1:17)*
...the whole land burned out with brimstone and salt, nothing sown and nothing growing, where no plant can sprout, an overthrow like that of Sodom and Gomorrah, Admah, and Zeboiim, which the LORD overthrew in his anger and wrath— (29:23)	Therefore, as I live," declares the LORD of hosts, the God of Israel, *"Moab shall become like Sodom, and the Ammonites like Gomorrah, a land possessed by nettles and salt pits, and a waste forever. The remnant of my people shall plunder them, and the survivors of my nation shall possess them." (2:9)*

---

[1] The "Book of the Law" (i.e., Deuteronomy) was discovered during Josiah's restoration of the Temple. Hilkiah the priest "discovered" it (2 Kgs. 22:8ff). There is at least the possibility that Hilkiah knew where the book was all along, but out of fear of Josiah's evil father, Amon, failed to bring it to the king's attention. When it was clear that Josiah was following Yahweh, perhaps it was time to "discover" the Book of the Law.

Deuteronomy	Zephaniah
"But if you will not obey the voice of the LORD your God or be careful to do all his commandments and his statutes that I command you today, then all these curses shall come upon you and overtake you. (28:15)	Woe to her who is rebellious and defiled, the oppressing city! She listens to no voice; she accepts no correction. She does not trust in the LORD; she does not draw near to her God. (3:1–2)
You shall not pervert justice. You shall not show partiality, and you shall not accept a bribe, for a bribe blinds the eyes of the wise and subverts the cause of the righteous. (16:19)	Her officials within her are roaring lions; her judges are evening wolves that leave nothing till the morning. (3:3)
But that prophet or that dreamer of dreams shall be put to death, because he has taught rebellion against the LORD your God, who brought you out of the land of Egypt and redeemed you out of the house of slavery, to make you leave the way in which the LORD your God commanded you to walk. So you shall purge the evil from your midst. (13:5)	Her prophets are fickle, treacherous men; her priests profane what is holy; they do violence to the law. (3:4)
They have made me jealous with what is no god; they have provoked me to anger with their idols. So I will make them jealous with those who are no people; I will provoke them to anger with a foolish nation. For a fire is kindled by my anger, and it burns to the depths of Sheol, devours the earth and its increase, and sets on fire the foundations of the mountains. (32:21–22)	"Therefore wait for me," declares the LORD, "for the day when I rise up to seize the prey. For my decision is to gather nations, to assemble kingdoms, to pour out upon them my indignation, all my burning anger; for in the fire of my jealousy all the earth shall be consumed. (3:8)
…and that he will set you in praise and in fame and in honor high above all nations that he has made, and that you shall be a people holy to the LORD your God, as he promised." (26:19)	At that time I will bring you in, at the time when I gather you together; for I will make you renowned and praised among all the peoples of the earth, when I restore your fortunes before your eyes," says the LORD. (3:20)

C. ZEPHANIAH: A Tiny Book With a Large Message
1. "the Day of the Lord"[1]
    a. Is used 20x in 53 verses, more frequently than any other prophet.
    b. Is a day of coming judgment for Judah (1:4ff)
    c. Is a day of coming judgment for all nations (2:1ff)
2. Unfaithfulness on Every Level
    a. The people – were worshipping Yahweh and the gods of Canaan (i.e. culture; 1:5).
    b. "princes" – (royal leaders) were driven by greed (1:8; 3:3).
    c. "judges" – (civil leaders) were predatorial in their dealings with people (3:3).
    d. "prophets" – adapted their message to please their listeners (3:4).
    e. "priests" – neglected the teaching and *protection* of Torah (their charge by Moses; 3:4):

        *And of Levi he said, "Give to Levi your Thummim, and your Urim to your godly one, whom you tested at Massah, with whom you quarreled at the waters of Meribah; who said of his father and mother, 'I regard them not'; he disowned his brothers and ignored his children. For they observed your word and kept your covenant. **They shall teach Jacob your rules and Israel your law;** they shall put incense before you and whole burnt offerings on your altar."*
        –Deuteronomy 33:8-10

3. A Comprehensive Promise of Restoration
    a. A remnant will be restored (3:12-13)
    b. A future day is coming when Gentiles will be included in the covenant (3:9-10).
    c. A future day is coming when Yahweh will "sing" over His people! (3:16-17).
D. Zephaniah and the Christian

---

[1] It appears in a number of variations: *"the day of the LORD"* (1:7), *"that day"* (1:9), *"the great day of the LORD"* (1:14), *"a day of…gloom, ruin, and wrath"* (1:15).

1. The theology of an "elect nation" can easily degenerate into an attempt to hold *Yahweh* "hostage" to the covenant, rather than ourselves being faithful to it![1]

E. Habakkuk — The Man

    1. We know nothing about him except his name.

    2. "Dating" his ministry can only be done from "clues":

        a. **2:20** – the Temple is still standing (i.e. prior to 586 BC).

        b. **1:5-11** – Babylonians are a *coming* threat, not a present one[2].

    3. Habakkuk functions more as a poet-philosopher, than a Hebrew prophet.

        a. Rather than speaking to the people on behalf of God, he speaks to God about his nation.

        b. Like Job, he has serious questions for God about justice and righteousness; or perhaps more accurately, about *in*justice and *un*righteousness.

        c. Unlike Job, he is not interested in why the righteous suffer, but why the wicked prosper.

        d. Unlike Job, God provides *him* with some *answers*.

F. Habakkuk — The Book

    1. Overview

        a. **Habakkuk's first complaint:** *"Why do You not judge the wicked in the covenant community?"* (1:2-4)

          (1) **God's Answer:** *"I am about to...using the (Neo)Babylonians!"* (1:5-11)[3]

        b. **Habakkuk's second complaint:** *"How can you reward their wickedness with victory?!"* (1:12-2:2)

          (1) **God's Answer:** *"I'm not. I always judge wickedness. I'm using theirs to judge yours. Then I'll judge theirs!"* (2:2-20)

        c. **God's Requirement** (in the meantime): *"The righteous shall remain faithful to the covenant."* (2:4)[4]

    2. The Uniqueness of the Book of Habakkuk

        a. The word "violence" (*chamas*) appears more times in this book than any other OT book except Psalms and Proverbs (6x).

          (1) It speaks of a "paralysis" of Torah (1:4) as the reason for the "violence."[5]

              (paralysis - Hebrew is "pug"; means to be numb, sluggish, to cease, to be feeble)

          (2) In the OT, "violence" was always expressed towards people.

          (3) Here it is the result of the corruption of those responsible for teaching and implementing Torah.

        b. The book concludes with a psalm, not merely a *"poem"*:

          (1) It uses the psalter term, *"Shigionoth"* (3:1)[6]

          (2) It uses the term "selah" three times (3:3,9,13)[7]

          (3) *"to the choirmaster"* (3:19) appears 56x in the OT; 55 are in Psalms.

          (4) It is written *"for stringed instruments"* (3:19; cf. Pss. 4:1; 6:1; 54:1)

G. Habakkuk and the New Testament

    1. Paul quotes Habakkuk 2:4 twice in his writings to illustrate:

        a. The universality of justification by faith in the Gospel:

---

[1] This unfortunate state of affairs is an inevitable consequence of losing sight of the fact that there was a *purpose* for our "election" in the first place. To fulfill the Abrahamic mission, now known as the Great Commission.

[2] This book predates 612 B.C. which marked the fall of Nineveh (Assyria) and a shift in world dominance to the Babylonians.

[3] I.e., the Chaldeans (1:6)

[4] This needs to be understood as the contrastive statement that it is. It begins with "But..." and could easily be translated, "But in contrast to the Babylonians, the righteous shall live, driven by his *emunah,* his "faithfulness." This is quite different from our popular understand of "faith." Yahweh is *not* talking about a mere belief or assent to the truth. He is referring to living in a way that is consistent with covenant faithfulness. *Emunah* appeaers 48 times in our Old Testament, nearly half (22) appear in the book of Psalms where it is translated, "faithfulness" (21x).

[5] The Hebrew word is *pug,* which means "to grow numb."

[6] Cf. "Shiggaion" in Psalm 7

[7] This word appears 74 times in our Old Testament, 71 of which are in the Psalms.

> *"For in it [the Gospel] the righteousness of God is revealed from faith for faith, as it is written, "The righteous shall live by faith."* –**Romans 1:17**

    b. The insufficiency of the Law to justify sinners:

> *"For all who rely on works of the law are under a curse; for it is written, 'Cursed be everyone who does not abide by all things written in the Book of the Law, and do them.' Now it is evident that no one is justified before God by the law, for 'The righteous shall live by faith.' But the law is not of faith, rather "The one who does them shall live by them."* –**Galatians 3:10-12**

    2. Unfortunately, our ignorance of the setting of Habakkuk leads us to turn Paul's *use* of this verse into its meaning.

H. Habakkuk and the Christian

    1. *"Living by faith"* should be understood as staying faithful to the covenant when *"Babylon is rising."*

> *"For you have need of endurance, so that when you have done the will of God you may receive what is promised. For, 'Yet a little while, and the coming one will come and will not delay; but my righteous one shall live by faith, and if he shrinks back, my soul has no pleasure in him.'"*
> **Hebrews 10:36–38**

    2. When "violence" (oppression) is addressed by God, it is always within the covenant community, not outside it.

    3. The "paralysis" of Torah and justice are *covenant community* problems, not pagan ones.

    4. God's judgment is linked to the degree of revelation given. (cf. Luke 12:48).

> *"For to everyone who has will more be given, and he will have an abundance. But from the one who has not, even what he has will be taken away."*
> **Matthew 25:29**

XXVI. UNIT 26: The *Books* of Jeremiah— *"He Who Wept"*

A. The bigger Picture: The World *Away* From Judah—"Babylon the Great!"[1]

    1. Babylon was a "living legend":

        a. There were 11 miles of walls, 85' high and 65' thick.

        b. Tops of walls had a roadway for chariots and an arial highway for troops.

        c. The moat in front of the wall had 10' of brick to prevent erosion of the wall.

        d. The Euphrates River divided the city, which was connected by a 30' wide bridge.

        e. The city had 8 gates, all named after Babylonian gods.

        f. The Ishtar Gate (goddess of fertility and war) has been preserved in Berlin.

    2. Babylon is mentioned 294 times in the Bible; 60% of them are in Jeremiah!

    3. The Neo-Babylonian Empire of Nebuchadnezzar (6th century BC) lasted less than 90 years!

    4. What we call the "Babylonian Exile" lasted 70 years (cf. Jer. 25:11-12; 29:10), from the exile under Jehoiachin to the first return under Zerubbabel (Ezra 1:1-2:2).

    5. Jeremiah: The Man and His Book

        a. He was a native of Anathoth, north of Jerusalem and near the former border of Israel.[2]

        b. He *may* have been a descendant of a line of banished High Priests (cf. 1 Kg 1:7; 2:26,35)[3].

---

[1] The reputation of Babylon far exceeded its borders. Even those who had never, and would never travel outside the environs of Jerusalem and Judah had *heard* of this great city from travelers passing through or Mesopotamian Jews in the city for the feasts. Its greatness was also known by comparison. After all, this was the city (empire) that had defeated Assyria, and destroy one of the most impenetrable cities on earth, Nineveh. In the Bible, Babylon is a synonym for evil and depravity. It is *never* spoken of in a positive fashion. Of the 12x it appears in the New Testament, 5 refer to the exile, and the other 7 are in the book of Revelation, and describe a city of perversion and wickedness.

[2] This is important because it means he would have been living very close to a population of apostates and Gentiles, *all* the fruit of the northern kingdom's (i.e. Israel) failure to listen to *her* prophet, Amos and Hosea nearly two centuries earlier. Judah's current rebellion and obstinace would have been very frustrating and painful for Jeremiah, because of the "lessons" that should have been learned from Israel's demise.

[3] Abiathar was the lone survivor of Saul's massacre of the priests at Nob in 1 Samuel 21-22. He became a priest to David, but supported Adonijah, David's son, when he tried to overthrow the rightful heir to the throne after David's death. Solomon banished Abiathar to Anathoth for his lack of loyalty to David, but refused to kill him because he had served as a priest before the Ark. The opening lines of Jeremiah *may* be a reference to this line of banned priests. All of this history, combined with the moral and spiritual decline of both Israel and Judah would have made Jeremiah passionate about the *purity* of worship of Yahweh. Jeremiah makes 16 references, directly or indirectly, to the "house" of Yahweh.

   c. Jeremiah is the prophet we know the most about.[1]
   d. His book is the *longest* book of prophecy in the Bible (40,500 words; cf. Isaiah = 35,288)
   e. Jeremiah's prophesies are *not* arranged in order:

Josiah	Jehoahaz	Jehoichim	Jehoiachin	Zedekiah
3:6	22:11	25:1 (4th year)	37:1	32:1 (10th year)
		36:1 (4th year)		39:1 (9th year)
		36:9 (5th year)		39:2 (11th year)
		45:1 (4th year)		51:59 (4th year)

6. The Hebrew (Masoretic Text) and the Greek (Septuagint, shorter) versions of Jeremiah differ by 2,700 words in length.
   a. But, *both* versions were in use in the Qumran community at the same time (i.e. Dead Sea Scrolls).

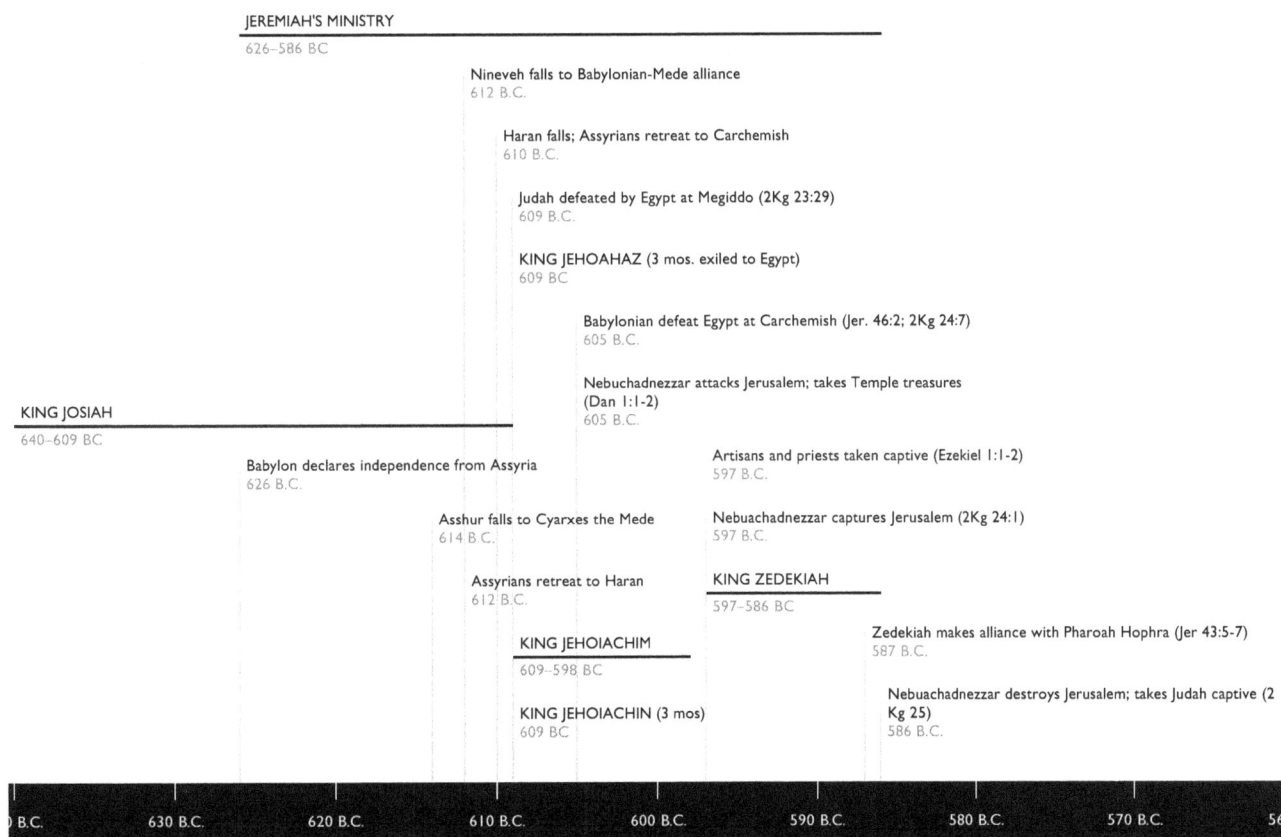

JEREMIAH'S MINISTRY
626–586 BC

Nineveh falls to Babylonian-Mede alliance
612 B.C.

Haran falls; Assyrians retreat to Carchemish
610 B.C.

Judah defeated by Egypt at Megiddo (2Kg 23:29)
609 B.C.

KING JEHOAHAZ (3 mos. exiled to Egypt)
609 BC

Babylonian defeat Egypt at Carchemish (Jer. 46:2; 2Kg 24:7)
605 B.C.

Nebuchadnezzar attacks Jerusalem; takes Temple treasures
(Dan 1:1-2)
605 B.C.

KING JOSIAH
640–609 BC

Babylon declares independence from Assyria
626 B.C.

Artisans and priests taken captive (Ezekiel 1:1-2)
597 B.C.

Asshur falls to Cyarxes the Mede
614 B.C.

Nebuachadnezzar captures Jerusalem (2Kg 24:1)
597 B.C.

Assyrians retreat to Haran
612 B.C.

KING ZEDEKIAH
597–586 BC

KING JEHOIACHIM
609–598 BC

Zedekiah makes alliance with Pharoah Hophra (Jer 43:5-7)
587 B.C.

KING JEHOIACHIN (3 mos)
609 BC

Nebuachadnezzar destroys Jerusalem; takes Judah captive (2 Kg 25)
586 B.C.

| B.C. | 630 B.C. | 620 B.C. | 610 B.C. | 600 B.C. | 590 B.C. | 580 B.C. | 570 B.C. | 56 |

1. The writings of Jeremiah are very similar to another "weeping prophet" that lived over a 150 years before him[2]:

---

[1] Most of what we know is from Lamentations. It is a highly personal book, giving us rare insights into the heart of this "weeping prophet," much like what we gain about Paul from his second letter to the Corinthians. There are 142 references to Jeremiah in our Bible, nearly three times as many as Isaiah. The majority of them in his own prophecy. However, he is also mentioned by Ezra, Nehemiah, Daniel and Matthew.

[2] Hosea and Jeremiah stand forever in the pages of Scripture as two faithful servants of Yahweh whose obedience was the cause of intense personal pain and suffering.

J E R E M I A H	H O S E A
Jeremiah pleaded with **Judah** to return to her *hesed* as a new bride in the wilderness (2:2)	Hosea repeatedly spoke of God's *hesed* in terms of His love for **Israel** (4:1; 6:4,6; 12:6)
Jeremiah describes **Judah** as an adulterous wife (3:1-5)	The entire story of Hosea and Gomer reflects this same idea for **Israel** (e.g. 2:14-15)
Judah became a whore (3:1-20)	**Israel** became a whore (8:8-9)
God promised to remain **Judah's** "husband" even though she was unfaithful (3:14).	God promised to be **Israel's** "husband," in spite of her un-faithfulness (2:2,16).
Jeremiah complained that there was widespread ignorance of the Law and of Yahweh (2:8; 4:22)	Hosea spoke of the lack of "knowledge of Yahweh" and its effects on the land (4:1,6)
Jeremiah linked the sin of **Judah** to a violation of the Law, especially the Decalogue (7:9)	Hosea described the conditions in **Israel** in terms of violations of the Decalogue (4:1-3)
Jeremiah spoke of a future day when God would institute an "new covenant" for ***all Israel*** (31:31-37)	Hosea spoke of a future day when ***all Israel*** would "know" Yahweh (2:16-23)

B. The World *Of* Jeremiah [1]

  1. He saw the total annihilation of the house of Josiah (2 Kg 23:30 - 25:30):

    a. A *good* king killed in battle with Egypt (Josiah).

    b. An *evil* king deported to Egypt (Jehoahaz).

    c. An *evil* king who dies during a Babylonian siege of Jerusalem (Jehoachim).

    d. An *evil* king and a priestly prophet deported to Babylon (Jehoiachin & Ezekiel).

    e. An *evil* king who was blinded after watching his sons slaughtered (Zedekiah)[2].

    f. A governor appointed by Nebuchadnezzar assassinated in Mizpah, the new capital city (Gedeliah).

  2. He predicted and witnessed three attacks on Jerusalem by Babylon.

  3. He saw two fellow prophets, Daniel and Ezekiel, taken captive to Babylon even though they were both righteous (Dan. 1:1-3; Ezek. 1:1-2).

  4. He was an eye-witness of the plundering and total destruction of the Temple and Jerusalem (2 Kg 24:14-16; 25:8-21).

  5. His prophetic ministry of nearly 40 years saw no visible fruit:

    a. He was beaten and put in stocks publicly (Jer. 20:2-3).

    b. He had his written prophecies mocked and burned by the king (36: 22-24).

    c. His prophecies to the exiles in Babylon were ridiculed and rejected (29:24-29).

    d. He was beaten and put in a dungeon (37:15-16).

    e. He was left to die in a unused cistern (38:6ff).

    f. He was taken captive to Egypt against his will *after* the destruction of Jerusalem (43:1-7).

  6. He witnessed the heinous fulfillment of God's promise for covenant *unfaithfulness* that Israel agreed to in Moab:

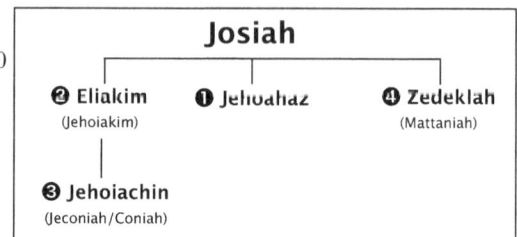

"The LORD will bring a nation against you from far away, from the end of the earth, swooping down like the eagle, a nation whose language you do not understand, a hard-faced nation who shall not respect the old or show mercy to the young. It shall eat the offspring of your cattle and the fruit of your ground, until

Josiah

❷ Eliakim (Jehoiakim)   ❶ Jehoahaz   ❹ Zedekiah (Mattaniah)

❸ Jehoiachin (Jeconiah/Coniah)

numbers refer to actual reignal order

---

[1] Any single one of these events would have the relative impact of 9/11 on the culture. They were cataclysmic in size and outcome. And, Jeremiah lived through all of them. Some only by hearing, but many of them happened in his lifetime to his own people as well as himself. Jeremiah lived to see and hear the horrors of Yahweh's curses in Deuteronomy being fulfilled in Jerusalem. Murder, rape, mothers eating their own children, and the Temple of Yahweh and the city destroyed. It is safe to say that we would not even be able to watch a movie of this, if it were portrayed accurately, so violent and heinous was the carnage and suffering.

[2] It's interesting, if nothing else, that the last "official" judge (Samson) and the last king both lost their eyes as a result of abandoning the covenant.

you are destroyed; it also shall not leave you grain, wine, or oil, the increase of your herds or the young of your flock, until they have caused you to perish. "They shall besiege you in all your towns, until your high and fortified walls, in which you trusted, come down throughout all your land. And they shall besiege you in all your towns throughout all your land, which the LORD your God has given you. And you shall eat the fruit of your womb, the flesh of your sons and daughters, whom the LORD your God has given you, in the siege and in the distress with which your enemies shall distress you. The man who is the most tender and refined among you will begrudge food to his brother, to the wife he embraces, and to the last of the children whom he has left, so that he will not give to any of them any of the flesh of his children whom he is eating, because he has nothing else left, in the siege and in the distress with which your enemy shall distress you in all your towns. The most tender and refined woman among you, who would not venture to set the sole of her foot on the ground because she is so delicate and tender, will begrudge to the husband she embraces, to her son and to her daughter, her afterbirth that comes out from between her feet and her children whom she bears, because lacking everything she will eat them secretly, in the siege and in the distress with which your enemy shall distress you in your towns." — **Deuteronomy 28:49-57** (cf. Jer. 19:9; Lam. 2:20; Ezek. 5:10)

C. Jeremiah And The New Testament

   1. There are nearly 40 direct quotations from Jeremiah in our New Testament, even though his name only appears 3 times.

   2. Most are references to "Babylon " in Revelation (e.g. Jer. 50:8 and Rev 18:4; Jer. 50:32 and Rev. 18:8).

   3. Jeremiah's "new covenant" to be written on human hearts was inaugurated by Jesus Christ at the Last Supper (cf. Heb. 8; Matt. 26"19-28).

   4. There are obvious similarities between Jeremiah and Jesus:

      a. Both wept over the city of Jerusalem because of its hardness of heart (Jer. 13:7; Lk 19:41).

      b. Both spoke of the destruction of the Temple (Jer. 7:4-14; Matt. 24:1-2).

      c. Both called the Temple a "den of robbers" (Jer. 7:11; Mk 11:17).

      d. Both of their harshest words were to those who "(mis)handled" the words of Yahweh (Jer. 23; Matt. 23).

D. Lessons From the Ashes – Jeremiah and the 21st Century

   1. True prophets (those Yahweh *uses*) are those who:

      a. Denounce *and* weep, not one or the other (13:16-17; 8:20–9:2; Lam 2:11).

      b. Stand "in the council of the LORD" (23:18,22; Heb. = sode: familiarity, intimacy, conversation).

      c. Speak *specifically* from God what He has given them for their audience (23:22; e.g. "words" not "Word.")

      d. Expose the sin of the covenant community (23:22).

   2. False prophets (those Yahweh *opposes*) are those who:

      a. Denounce *or* weep, but not both.

      b. Claim as revelation from God to them, what He has said to someone else (23:30).

      c. Copy the words of other prophets (23:30).

      d. Condemn the evil of the surrounding culture, but are silent about the sin of the covenant community (23:22).

      e. Seek a "celebrity" role rather than "supporting" role in the Story (e.g. 23:22).

   3. Jeremiah stands forever as an example of the tremendous personal cost of calling Yahweh's people *back* to the Story (cf. Lamentations 3).

   4. God can never be held "hostage" to His Word (18:6-10).

   5. Faithfulness in the motions of worship is no substitute for faithfulness to the God we worship (7:1-15).

   6. There can come a point where God will no longer "hear" prayer for a people (7:16; 11:14; 14:11).

   7. A "National Theology" (i.e. "God is on our side") is a very dangerous thing (7:1-34).

   8. Those of us "in" the Story often find ourselves personally affected when Yahweh deals with those "outside" the Story (e.g. Baruch, 45:2-5).

KEY INFORMATION - The Book of 2 Kings

Key Word: "Conquered Kingdoms"

Key Chapters: 17 — Israel taken by Assyria (722 B.C.); 25 — Babylonian captivity (586 B.C.)

Geography: Israel dispersed by Assyria; Judah taken to Babylon

Summary: Yahweh's judgment on Israel and Judah for covenant unfaithfulness.

XXVII. UNIT 27: The Books of Daniel & Ezekiel — *"Voices From Beyond the River"*

A. Our Unhealthy "Prophetic Diet"[1]

1. Every time Jesus was asked about the "end-times," his first answer was always, *"Take care that you are not led astray."* (cf. Matt. 24:3-4; Mk 13:3-5; Lk 21:8)

2. The last question Jesus answered on earth was in regard to the "end times."

   a. His two last earthly statements were in that context (Acts 1:6-9):

   "It's none of your business!" (It's His Story, not yours!)

   "On the contrary, you will receive power when the Holy Spirit has come upon you, and you will be my witnesses in Jerusalem and in all Judea and Samaria, and to the end of the earth." (I.e., be Story-dwellers and Story-tellers, not Story-hoarders)

3. We have developed an unhealthy and imbalanced view of biblical prophecy, evidenced by what we publish and read.

   a. Key words in modern Christian books reveal our bias:

   (1) "prophecy" – 2,640x

   (2) "the end times" – 1,643x

   (3) "the Tribulation" – 241x

   (4) "the Rapture" – 185x

   (5) "the Antichrist" – 175x

   (6) "repentance" – 8x

B. "The *End* of ACT III — The World of Daniel & Ezekiel and Beyond *(see chart on page 112)*

C. The Pens of the Fraternal Twins: "Reading Between the Lines"

1. One can discern their different audiences *and* messages from their vocabularies!

Word/Phrase	Daniel	Ezekiel	Word/Phrase	Daniel	Ezekiel
"Ezekiel"	0	*2*	*"Daniel"*	*75*	0
"say/says/saying"	4	*284*	*"king(s)/kingdom(s)"*	*234*	42
"priest(s)/Temple"	2	*50*	*"dream(s)"*	*27*	0
"whore, -ing"	0	*40*	*"vision(s)"*	*32*	21
"cherub(im)"	0	*31*	*"Nebuchadnezzar"*	*32*	4
"covenant"	7	*17*	*"Darius, Belshazzar, Cyrus"*	*19*	0
"glory"	6	*22*	*"time(s)"*	*48*	19
"Judah/Jerusalem"	18	*41*	*"Babylon"*	17	17
Israel	4	*186*			
"statute(s)/ordinance(s)"	1	*46*			
"appearance"/"like(ness")	38	*118*			
"…shall know that I am the LORD"	0	*74*			
"son of man"	2	*93*			
"beasts" (real/symbolic)	11/10	*28/0*			

D. Two Prophets: One "Famous" & One "Fuzzy" — *Both* Very "Future"

1. Ezekiel is typically avoided as one of the more difficult books of prophecy to understand.

   a. On one hand, it has the most "date-stamps" of any book of prophecy, at least 13[2].

   b. On the other hand, it is one of the most bizarre books in the Bible[3].

   c. His vision of a future Temple in chapters 40-48 is by far one of the most perplexing visions in prophecy, with at least *six* modern interpretations:

   (1) Three look back to the Temples of Solomon, Zerubbabel, or Herod.

   (2) Three look ahead: the Millennium, Eternity, or a purely symbolic Temple.

---

[1] One search on Christianbook.com resulted in over 1,500 "hits" for the phrase, "the end times" and over 2,500 for "prophecy," but only 8 for "repentance."

[2] 1:2; 8:1; 20:1; 24:1; 26:1; 29:1; 29:17; 30;20; 31:1; 32:1; 32:17; 33:21; 40:1

[3] Ezekiel is asked to bake bread over human dung, to make miniature sieges, cut and burn his hair, and even his wife is "taken away" and he is commanded not to weep! (4:1–5:17; 12:3–6; 24:16–18; 37:16–17)

(3) All six present serious difficulties with full biblical agreement[1].

2. Daniel is one of the most well-known and popular of all the prophets.

   a. His book falls "nicely" into two divisions:

      (1) Narrative "tales" - court stories *about* Daniel and his three friends:

         (a) **Ch 1** – Daniel's "experiment" with his diet.

         (b) **Ch 2** – Nebuchadnezzar's dream and his death threat.

         (c) **Ch 3** – The fiery furnace (Shadrach, Meshach, Abed-nego)

         (d) **Ch 4** – Nebuchadnezzar's temporary insanity.

         (e) **Ch 5** – Belshazzar's Feast.

         (f) **Ch 6** – Daniel in the lion's den.

      (2) Narrated visions - first person accounts of visions of his or others:

         (a) **Ch 7** – Daniel's vision of the "Four Beasts," and the "Ancient of Days."

         (b) **Ch 8** – Daniel's vision of the Ram and Goat.

         (c) **Ch 9** – Daniel's vision of the Seventy "weeks."

         (d) **Ch 10-12** – Daniel's vision of the final "conflict."

E. *Similarities* Between Daniel and Ezekiel:

   1. Both were members of the Judahite aristocracy

      a. Daniel was of noble blood and Ezekiel was a priest.

   2. Both were were in Babylon when Nebuchadnezzar destroyed Jerusalem.

   3. Both ministered exclusively in Babylon.

   4. Before being taken into captivity, both would have experienced:

      a. the impact of Josiah's reforms on the nation (623-609 BC).

      b. Josiah's untimely death at Megiddo (609 BC)

      c. the preaching of Jeremiah in Jerusalem.

      d. Judah's vacillation in allegiance between Egypt and Babylon (609-605 BC).

   5. Both prophets are quoted/alluded to extensively in our New Testament:

      a. There are 65 quotes from Ezekiel, 48 of them in the book of Revelation.

      b. Daniel is quoted by Jesus, and alluded to in Revelation.

F. *Differences* Between Daniel and Ezekiel

   1. Daniel's ministry was to the pagan *kings* of his captivity.

      a. There are 51 references to pagan kings *by name* in Daniel compared to only 4 in Ezekiel.

   2. Ezekiel's ministry was to his fellow *captives*; He was not a "dignitary" like Daniel, but a fellow captive.

      a. There are 227 references to Israel, Judah and Jerusalem in Ezekiel, compared to only 22 in Daniel.

   3. Daniel's focus in on God's sovereignty expressed in His control of all nations throughout all time.

      a. There are 234 references to "king/kingdoms" in Daniel compared to only 42 in Ezekiel (cf. Ch 7, 11-12).

   4. Ezekiel's focus is on God's sovereignty expressed in His dealings with His covenant people.

---

[1] None of the three past Temples fit the dimensions in Ezekiel, the tribal allotments and geography do not fit, and the "river" coming out of the Temple has *never* happened in history. Thinking of Ezekiel's Temple as existing during the Millennium doesn't help because it doesn't serve any biblically-sanctioned purpose. Sacrifices are no longer necessary *or* acceptable. That is the clear teaching of the book of Hebrews and much of Paul. Thinking of the Temple as a place to offer "commemorative" sacrifices, pointing back to Calvary as some propose violates the same principles mentioned above. Thinking of it as a sort of "Eternal Temple" allows for the presence of a healing river, but there is no mention of a new "Temple" in the new Jerusalem (Revelation 21:22), but there *is* mention of "the temple of my God" in Rev 3:12 in the context of the new Jerusalem. However, sacrifices fit less in eternity than they do in any earthly model. Thinking of the Temple of Ezekiel as a "symbolic" Temple does not fit the incredibly elaborate specifications in Ezekiel, especially Yahweh's instructions to Ezekiel to write it all down *and* to show it to His people (43:11).

(1) There are 40 references to "whore(ing)" in Ezekiel, but there are none in Daniel.

(2) There are nearly 100 references to priests, the temple, and the Law in Ezekiel compared to only 3 in Daniel).

5. Ezekiel's scope is national and *exclusive*; Daniel's is global and *inclusive*.

6. Daniel is a book of "dreams and visions" about kings and nations.

7. Ezekiel is a book of "visions" of Yahweh's glory and heaven[1].

    a. There are 31 references to cherubim in heaven in Ezekiel in contrast to the angelic *messengers* of Daniel (cf. Ezek. 1:28 and Dan. 7:15-18).

> *"Like the appearance of the bow that is in the cloud on the day of rain, so was the appearance of the brightness all around. Such was the appearance of the likeness of the glory of the LORD. And when I saw it, I fell on my face, and I heard the voice of one speaking."* **–Ezekiel 1:28**

8. Daniel's prophecy is mediated and written, Ezekiel's is direct and oral.[2]

    a. The words, *"say/saying"* appear 284 times in Ezekiel vs. 4 in Daniel.

G. *Highlights* of Daniel and Ezekiel

1. Daniel 2 contains a detailed prophecy about world history from the time of the Babylonian Empire down through the split of the Greek Empire after Alexander's death.

2. Ezekiel 37 is a masterful vision of Yahweh's faithfulness to the Abrahamic covenant and the reconstitution of Israel.

H. The Exilic Prophets and the Christian

1. Daniel stands forever as a model of a young man surviving—even thriving— and being used by God in the world of university, political, and foreign cultures.

2. His book is a clear reminder that Yahweh controls the plot of The Story.

    a. He is both the "Ancient of Days,"(ch 7) *and* the "Author of Days" (ch 8-12).

3. Daniel and his 3 friends illustrate the cost of faithfully fulfilling one's role in Yahweh's grand Drama.

4. Ezekiel stands forever as an model of the need and role of the prophetic "watchman" over the covenant community (cf. Ezek. 33:1-9 and Acts 20:26-27).

5. These two Exilic Prophets illustrate and reinforce the "trailer" nature of predictive prophecy in The Story, by pointing us to what it is we really need to know:

    a. Who is really the Author of The Story:

> *"Remember this and stand firm, recall it to mind, you transgressors, remember the former things of old; for I am God, and there is no other; I am God, and there is none like me, declaring the end from the beginning and from ancient times things not yet done, saying, 'My counsel shall stand, and I will accomplish all my purpose,...'"* **–Isaiah 46:8 -10**

    b. Who ultimately "wins" the battle between good and evil.

    c. How ought we to live in the meantime (2 Peter 3:8-14).

    d. Knowing the future for any other reason caters to our obsession for power, the centerpiece of our "Adamic residue," in this case, through knowledge (cf. Ezekiel 21:21).

---

[1] The book opens with a vision of the glory of God (1:1-28). God's glory "departs" in 11:22-25, and "returns" in 43:1-12.

[2] It's also noteworthy to point out the bilingualism in Daniel. Chapters 1:1 thru 2:4a are written in Hebrew, as are chapters 8-12, but the intervening chapters, 2:4b-7:28 are written in Aramaic.

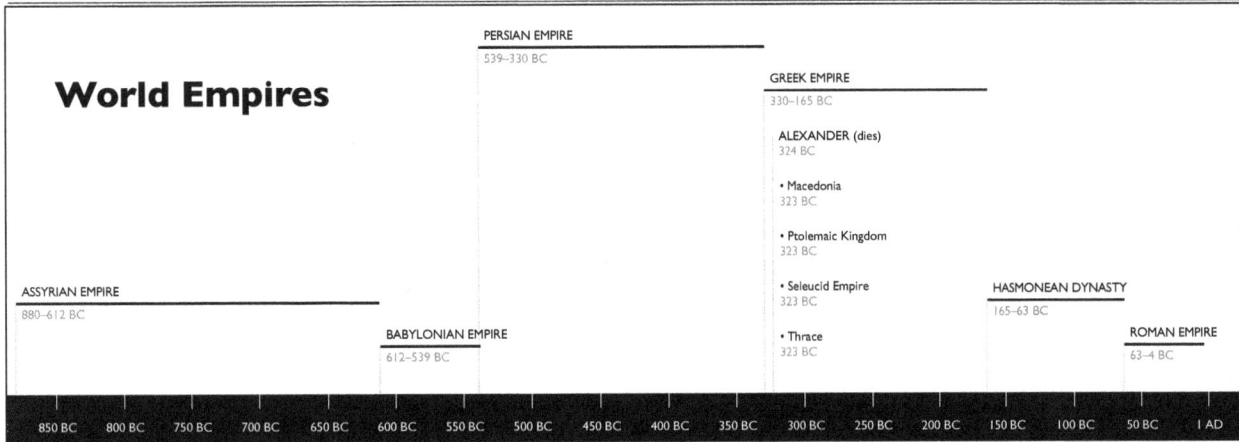

World Empires

PERSIAN EMPIRE
539–330 BC

GREEK EMPIRE
330–165 BC

ALEXANDER (dies)
324 BC

• Macedonia
323 BC

• Ptolemaic Kingdom
323 BC

• Seleucid Empire
323 BC

• Thrace
323 BC

HASMONEAN DYNASTY
165–63 BC

ROMAN EMPIRE
63–4 BC

ASSYRIAN EMPIRE
880–612 BC

BABYLONIAN EMPIRE
612–539 BC

850 BC   800 BC   750 BC   700 BC   650 BC   600 BC   550 BC   500 BC   450 BC   400 BC   350 BC   300 BC   250 BC   200 BC   150 BC   100 BC   50 BC   1 AD

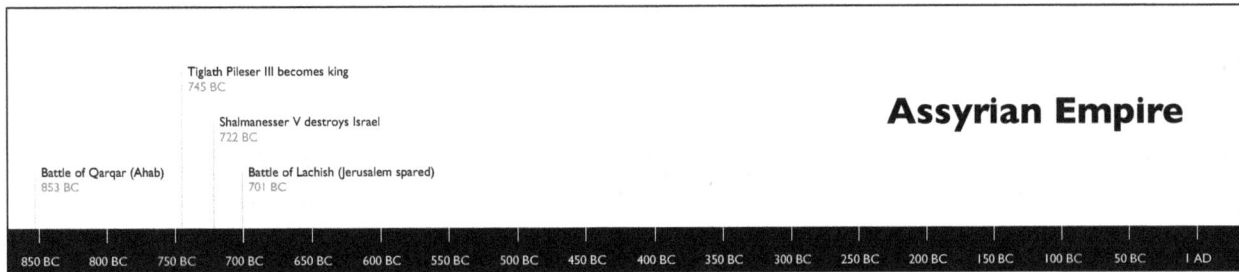

Assyrian Empire

Tiglath Pileser III becomes king
745 BC

Shalmanesser V destroys Israel
722 BC

Battle of Qarqar (Ahab)
853 BC

Battle of Lachish (Jerusalem spared)
701 BC

850 BC   800 BC   750 BC   700 BC   650 BC   600 BC   550 BC   500 BC   450 BC   400 BC   350 BC   300 BC   250 BC   200 BC   150 BC   100 BC   50 BC   1 AD

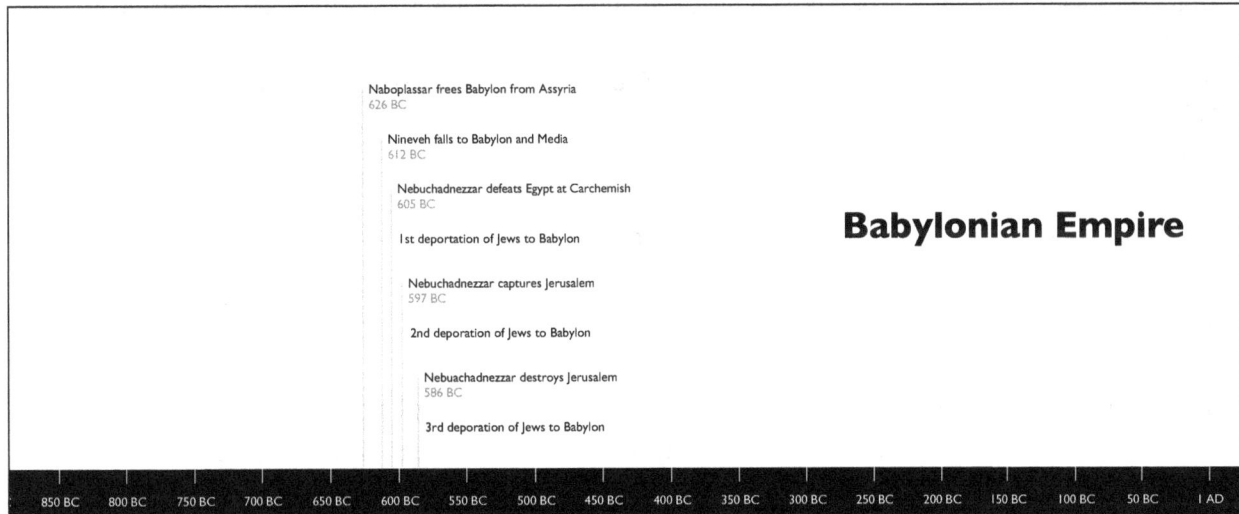

Babylonian Empire

Naboplassar frees Babylon from Assyria
626 BC

Nineveh falls to Babylon and Media
612 BC

Nebuchadnezzar defeats Egypt at Carchemish
605 BC

1st deportation of Jews to Babylon

Nebuchadnezzar captures Jerusalem
597 BC

2nd deporation of Jews to Babylon

Nebuachadnezzar destroys Jerusalem
586 BC

3rd deporation of Jews to Babylon

850 BC   800 BC   750 BC   700 BC   650 BC   600 BC   550 BC   500 BC   450 BC   400 BC   350 BC   300 BC   250 BC   200 BC   150 BC   100 BC   50 BC   1 AD

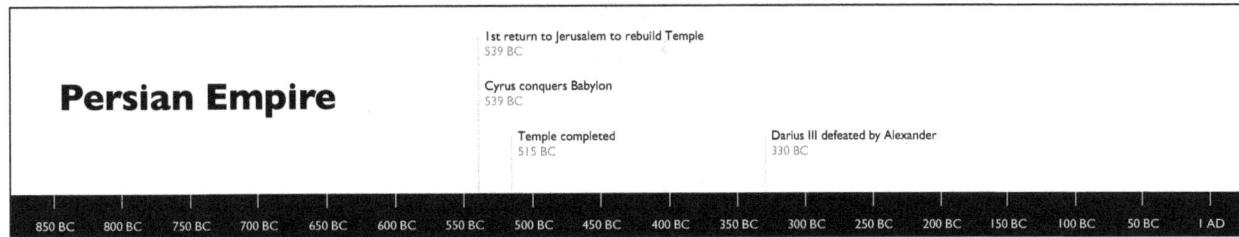

Persian Empire

1st return to Jerusalem to rebuild Temple
539 BC

Cyrus conquers Babylon
539 BC

Temple completed
515 BC

Darius III defeated by Alexander
330 BC

850 BC   800 BC   750 BC   700 BC   650 BC   600 BC   550 BC   500 BC   450 BC   400 BC   350 BC   300 BC   250 BC   200 BC   150 BC   100 BC   50 BC   1 AD

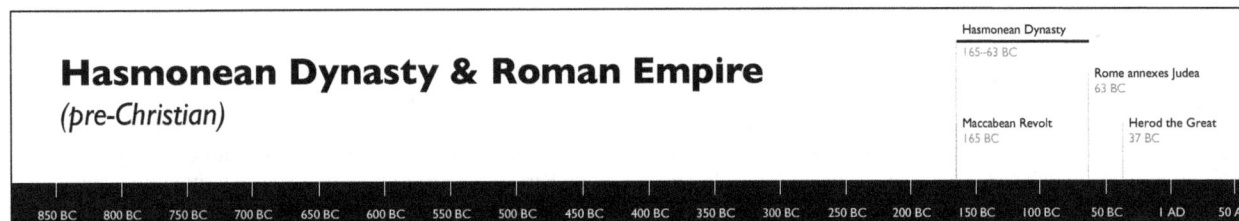

Hasmonean Dynasty & Roman Empire
(pre-Christian)

Hasmonean Dynasty
165–63 BC

Rome annexes Judea
63 BC

Maccabean Revolt
165 BC

Herod the Great
37 BC

850 BC   800 BC   750 BC   700 BC   650 BC   600 BC   550 BC   500 BC   450 BC   400 BC   350 BC   300 BC   250 BC   200 BC   150 BC   100 BC   50 BC   1 AD   50 A

XXVIII. UNIT 28: The Birth of Second Temple Judaism — *"Out of the Ashes"*

A. The "Post-Exilic Period As A Whole

   1. Occurs during the height of the Persian Empire[1].

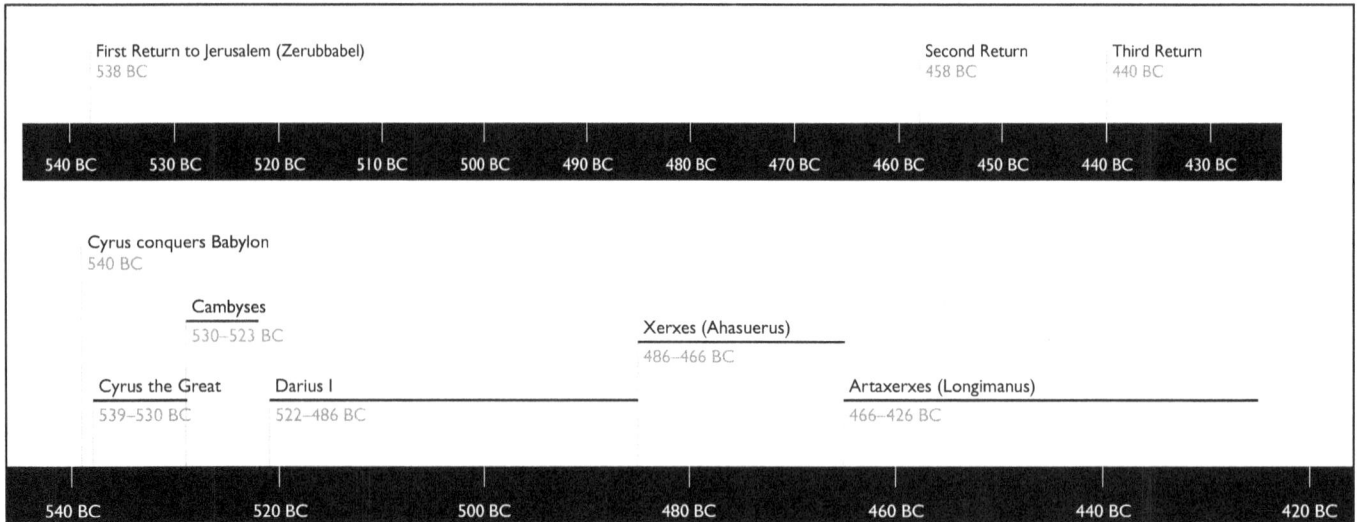

| First Return to Jerusalem (Zerubbabel) 538 BC | | | | | | | | | Second Return 458 BC | Third Return 440 BC |

540 BC · 530 BC · 520 BC · 510 BC · 500 BC · 490 BC · 480 BC · 470 BC · 460 BC · 450 BC · 440 BC · 430 BC

Cyrus conquers Babylon
540 BC

Cambyses
530–523 BC

Xerxes (Ahasuerus)
486–466 BC

Cyrus the Great
539–530 BC

Darius I
522–486 BC

Artaxerxes (Longimanus)
466–426 BC

540 BC · 520 BC · 500 BC · 480 BC · 460 BC · 440 BC · 420 BC

   2. Concludes with a prophecy about the coming of John the Baptist, 400 years before he actually arrives (cf. Malachi 4:5-6)!

   3. Many institutions and groups arose during this period (e.g. Pharisees, Sadducees, Herodians, scribes, Essenes, Sanhedrin, synagogues, the Feast of Purim, and the Feast of Dedication or Hanukkah).

   4. Includes eight Old Testament books:

     a. Three books of History: Ezra, Esther, & Nehemiah

     b. Three books of Prophecy: Haggai, Zechariah & Malachi

     c. One book of "editorial reflection": *our* 1 & 2 Chronicles

B. The Book(s) of Chronicles in *Context*

   1. Chronicles was written *after* the Babylonian Exile.[2]

   2. The actual date and author are unknown, although Ezra is a good candidate.[3]

   3. The *last* two verses of 2 Chronicles are almost identical to the *first* three verses of the book of Ezra:

In the first year of Cyrus king of Persia, in order to fulfill the word of the LORD spoken by Jeremiah, the LORD moved the heart of Cyrus king of Persia to make a proclamation throughout his realm and to put it in writing: "This is what Cyrus king of Persia says: 'The LORD, the God of heaven, has given me all the kingdoms of the earth and he has appointed me to build a temple for him at Jerusalem in Judah. Anyone of his people among you—may the LORD his God be with him, and let him go up.'" —**2 Chronicles 36:22,23**	*In the first year of Cyrus king of Persia, in order to fulfil the word of the LORD spoken by Jeremiah, the LORD moved the heart of Cyrus king of Persia to make a proclamation throughout his realm and to put it in writing: "This is what Cyrus king of Persia says: 'The LORD, the God of heaven, has given me all the kingdoms of the earth and he has appointed me to build a temple for him at Jerusalem in Judah. Anyone of his people among you—may his God be with him, and let him go up to Jerusalem in Judah and build the temple of the LORD, the God of Israel, the God who is in Jerusalem."* —**Ezra 1:1-3**

---

[1] **Supplemental notes to timeline:** Cambyses is not mentioned in the Bible. The Second Return of exiles in 458 BC was led by Ezra about a half century *after* the first group returned to rebuild the Temple. The Third Return of exiles in 440 BC was led by Nehemiah, from Persia.

[2] Some consider Chronicles, Ezra, and Nehemiah to be a single work of sorts.

[3] Ezra 4 is anachronistic. It contains a record of *all* the opposition the Jews faced from their return up to the time of Nehemiah, nearly 100 years. Much of it occurred *after* Zerubbabel's time (i.e., chapters 1-16). The letters to the Persian kins preserved in Ezra are written in Aramaic, the language of the Persian imperial court.

C. The Books of Chronicles in *Perspective*:

1 & 2 Chronicles in Perspective

I Samuel	2 Samuel	I Kings	2 Kings
Samuel, Saul David	King David	Solomon Divided Kingdom	Histories of Israel & Judah

	I Chronicles	2 Chronicles	
	King David	Solomon Divided Kingdom	History of Judah

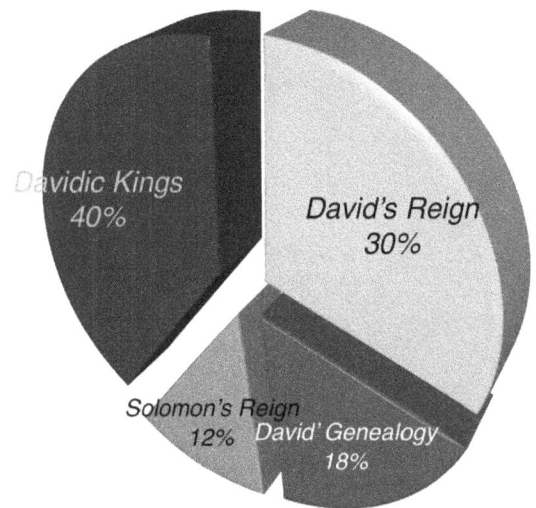

Davidic Kings 40%

David's Reign 30%

Solomon's Reign 12%

David' Genealogy 18%

The Content of Chronicles

D. The Books of Chronicles — a *Summary:*
1. The Books of Chronicles retell the spiritual history of the Southern kingdom of Judah from the time of 2 Samuel through 2 Kings.

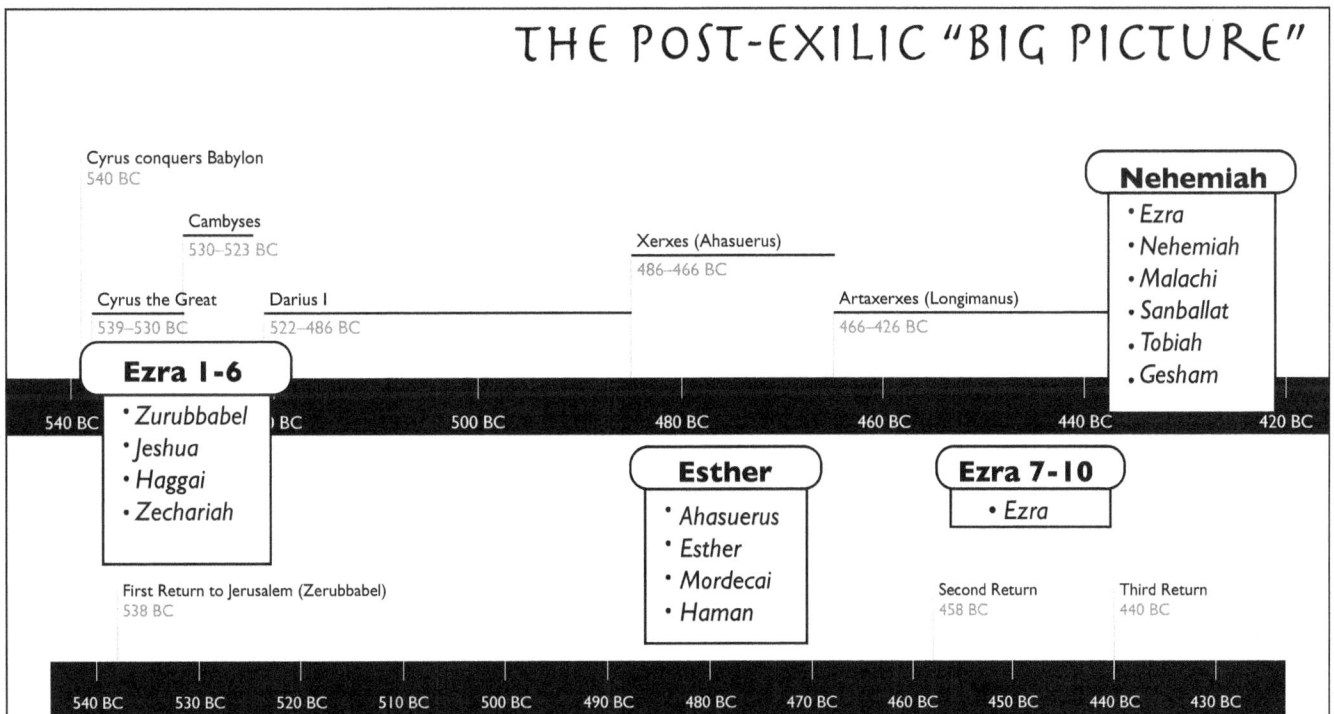

THE POST-EXILIC "BIG PICTURE"

Cyrus conquers Babylon
540 BC

Cambyses
530–523 BC

Xerxes (Ahasuerus)
486–466 BC

Cyrus the Great
539–530 BC

Darius I
522–486 BC

Artaxerxes (Longimanus)
466–426 BC

Nehemiah
• *Ezra*
• *Nehemiah*
• *Malachi*
• *Sanballat*
• *Tobiah*
• *Gesham*

Ezra 1-6
• *Zurubbabel*
• *Jeshua*
• *Haggai*
• *Zechariah*

540 BC   BC   500 BC   480 BC   460 BC   440 BC   420 BC

Esther
• *Ahasuerus*
• *Esther*
• *Mordecai*
• *Haman*

Ezra 7-10
• *Ezra*

First Return to Jerusalem (Zerubbabel)
538 BC

Second Return
458 BC

Third Return
440 BC

540 BC   530 BC   520 BC   510 BC   500 BC   490 BC   480 BC   470 BC   460 BC   450 BC   440 BC   430 BC

E. **Ezra 1 – 6:** The *First* Return From Captivity
1. Cyrus' policy of clemency was the *opposite* of Assyria and Babylon's oppression.
2. The Persian postal system would have allowed for good travel:
   a. There were 111 postal stations on 1,677 miles of roads from Susa to Ephesus.
   b. It was a 90 day journey on foot, but only 7 days for the king's couriers.
3. About 50,000 people made the 5-month trip from Babylon to Jerusalem.

4. The return of the exiles to Jerusalem was the fulfillment of many prophecies:

 a. Two hundred years earlier Isaiah had foretold this return under Cyrus *and* that the Temple and city would be rebuilt. (Is. 44:28)

 b. Jeremiah predicted the length of the exile, the return, and the final judgment of Babylon. (Jer. 29:10; 25:12)

 c. Daniel predicted the overthrow of Babylon and the rise of the Medo-Persian Empire. *(As well as the fall of Persia to Greece and the fall of Greece to Rome.)*

5. The exiles were led by two high-ranking Jewish leaders: Zerubbabel and Joshua.

 a. Zerubbabel, the *civil* leader[1]:

  (1) Is also known as Sheshbazzar in our Bibles. (Ezra 5:14,16; Hag. 1:1; 2:2; 3:2-8)

  (2) The son of Shealtiel and grandson of King Jehoiachin, king during the second deportation to Babylon of which Ezekiel was a part. (1 Chron. 3:17)

  (3) The appointed governor of Judah. (Hag. 1:14).

 b. Joshua, the priestly *spiritual* leader:

  (1) The son of Jehozadak the High Priest. (Ezra 2:2; hag. 1:1)

  (2) His father was one of those taken into exile by Nebuchadnezzar. (1 Chron 6:15)

6. Rebuilding the Temple:

 a. The altar is rebuilt and sacrificial system resumes.

 b. Foundation is laid in 535 BC, but is halted for nearly 15 years because of Samaritan opposition.

 c. It is completed in 515 BC and Passover is celebrated.[2]

7. Rebuilding the People:

 a. Haggai and Zechariah were used by God during this time.

 b. Haggai: The Man[3]:

  (1) Appears to have been a captive; familiar with the former Temple. (2:3)

  (2) Has a very brief ministry of about 4 months (cf. 1:1; 2:10, 20)!

  (3) His ministry was to the leaders, not the people .

 c. Haggai: The Message:

  (1) *"Quit building your own homes and get back to work on my 'House'!"*

  (2) Unfaithfulness to God's *revealed* will renders worship worthless.

 d. Zechariah: The Man[4]:

  (1) There are over 30 men in the Old Testament by this name!

  (2) His ministry begins two months after Haggai's.

  (3) His book consists of many visions (8 in one night!)

 e. Zechariah: The Message:

  (1) Haggai's message was a rebuke, Zechariah's was hope.

  (2) It contains the most Messianic prophecies of any minor prophet.

F. Yeshua in the Post-Exilic Prophets

 1. In the Prophet Haggai:

  a. He is the "latter glory of this house shall be greater than the former." (2:9a)

  b. He is "the shalom" that was to come to the Temple. (2:9b)

---

[1] His name drops out of the biblical narrative by the time of the Temple dedication and seems to be replaced by Tatani as the governor. Persia may have reorganized its political structure at this time, under Cambyses.

[2] Seven Passovers are recorded in the Bible: the first (Ex. 12), the 2nd year after the exodus (Num. 9:1-5), after entering Canaan (Josh. 5:10), Solomon (2 Chron. 8:13). Hezekiah (2 Chron. 30:15), Josiah (2 Kgs. 23:21), and Ezra (6:19; no names are mentioned, however Zerubbabel was prophesied in Zechariah 4:9 to both "start" and "finish" the Temple rebuild. If this was true, he should have been present at this Passover, because the Temple dedication was the context.)

[3] His name means "festive."

[4] His name means, "Yahweh remembers."

2. In the Prophet Zechariah:
  a. He is the "Righteous Branch." (3:8)
  b. He is the "King-Priest." (6:13)
  c. He is the "humble king, riding on a donkey." (9:9-10; cf. Matt 21:1-5)
  d. He is the "good shepherd, rejected and sold." ("potter's field," "30 pieces of silver"; 11:4-13; cf. Matt 26:14-15)
  e. He is the "one who was shepherd." (12:10; cf. Jn 19:37)
  f. He is the "smitten shepherd who was abandoned." (13:7; cf. Mk 14:27)
  g. He is the "cornerstone." (10:4; cf. 1 Pet 2:6)

G. Learning From the Exiles — The Second-Temple Prophets & The Christian
  1. The tendency to put my own "creature needs" ahead of Kingdom values did not perish in the rubble of Jerusalem. (Hag. 1:7-10; Matt. 6:31-33; Jer. 29:7)
  2. Bringing secular methods into the Kingdom may corrupt the Kingdom rather than sanctify the method.
  3. God's passion is *always* to bless and protect His covenant people (i.e. to uphold *His* end of the covenant).
  4. God is always willing to restore those who are willing to repent.
  5. The objective Word of God always trumps the subjective "call" of God, when it comes to declaring His "will" for His people.

XXIX. ESTHER: *"For Such a Time as This?"*

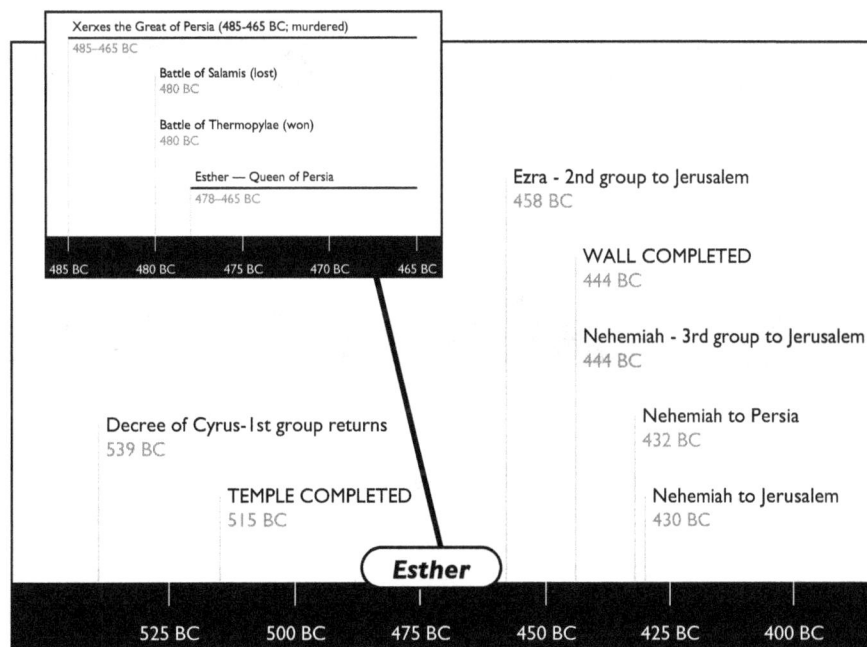

A. The Historical Context
  1. Xerxes had most likely just returned from his failed expeditions to conquer Greece.[1]
  2. Queen Vashti's insolence was met with royal rage guided by Divine sovereignty.
  3. Although God's name appears nowhere in Esther, His "fingerprints" are everywhere:
    a. Her parents had *not* died in the Babylonian destruction of Jerusalem because she was *born* in exile.
    b. She and her family had not returned with Zerubbabel when allowed to in 538 B.C.
    c. She had a wise and perceptive uncle.
    d. She was a *beautiful* woman.

---

[1] The battles of Thermopylae and Salamis

e. Esther's selection for Queen to replace Vashti (2:1-18).

f. Mordecai's intervention in the assassination plot (2:19-23).

g. Esther's life spared in approaching the king (5:1-8).

h. Xerxes' discovery of Mordecai's heroism on his "sleepless night" (6:1-4).

i. Haman's plot reversal[1] (6:7-7:10).

j. The Jews' preservation throughout the Empire (8:3-9:17).

XXX. EZRA & NEHEMIAH: The "Founders" Of New Testament Judaism

A. The Bigger "Big Picture"[2]

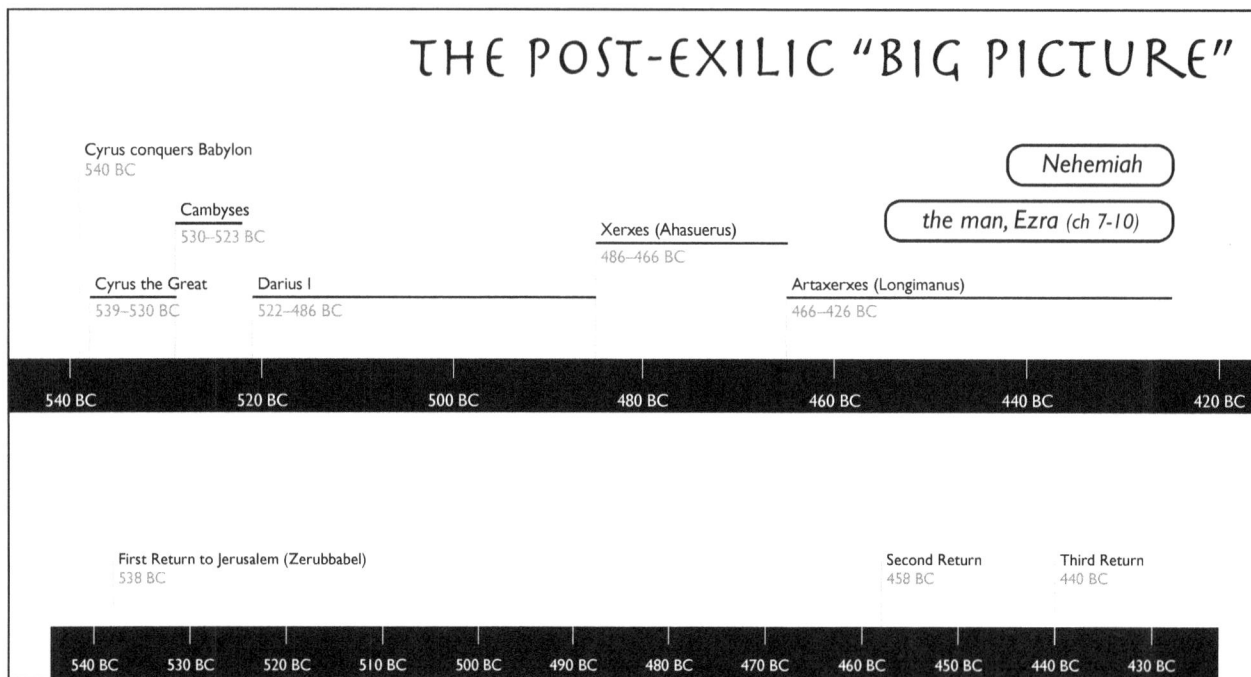

THE POST-EXILIC "BIG PICTURE"

Cyrus conquers Babylon
540 BC

Cambyses
530–523 BC

Xerxes (Ahasuerus)
486–466 BC

Nehemiah

the man, Ezra (ch 7-10)

Cyrus the Great
539–530 BC

Darius I
522–486 BC

Artaxerxes (Longimanus)
466–426 BC

| 540 BC | 520 BC | 500 BC | 480 BC | 460 BC | 440 BC | 420 BC |

First Return to Jerusalem (Zerubbabel)
538 BC

Second Return
458 BC

Third Return
440 BC

| 540 BC | 530 BC | 520 BC | 510 BC | 500 BC | 490 BC | 480 BC | 470 BC | 460 BC | 450 BC | 440 BC | 430 BC |

B. Ezra: *"Scribe of the Law of Moses"* (Ezra 7:1-11; Neh 8:2)[3]

---

[1] The logistics of *both* Haman's original decree being sent out and Xerxes second decree, are enormous. Consider that it was sent out to 127 provinces throughout the Persian Empire, ranging over 1,600 miles (on horseback!). Consider the scribal effort to record the decree in the different languages of the empire. And, the Persians had a courier system that allowed them to traverse the entire empire in 7 days. All in all, this was a massive effort, involving an enormous number of individuals, horses, and effort. Finally, we must remember that Judah would have received one of these letters. The exiles who had returned under Zerubbabel, and who had labored to rebuild the Temple, would have been recipients of these edicts.

[2] Dating these two reformers is quite difficult because there were *three* Persians kings named Artaxerxes: Artaxerxes I (Longimanus), who reigned 465-424 B.C., Artaxerxes II (Mneman), who reigned 404-359 B.C., and Artaxerxes III (Ochus), who reigned 359-338 B.C.

Cyrus the Great of Persia enters Yahweh's Story prophetically in the 8th century B.C. via the pen of Isaiah (44:28; 45:1), and in history in the exilic book of Daniel (1:21; 6:28; 10:1), and finally in the post-exilic books of 2 Chronicles (36:22) and Ezra (1:1; 4:5; et al). World history during the days of Ezra and Nehemiah was full and flourishing: Confucius in China (551-479 B.C.), Sidhartha Gutama (Buddha) in India (c. 563-483 B.C.), Socrates in Greece (469-399 B.C.), the construction of the Parthenon in Athens (447-438 B.C.), and the battles of Thermopylae and Salamis (land a sea, respectively in 480 B.C.). Shortly after our Old Testament ends, Darius III will suffer a crushing defeat at the hands of Alexander the Great at the Battles of Issus and Gaugamela in 333 and 331 B.C., respectively.

[3] There are 24 references to "the Law" in Ezra-Nehemiah, but *none* before Ezra's arrival in Jerusalem. There is not a single reference to Yahweh addressing his people in either of these two books (e.g. "the LORD said to…" or "the word of the LORD came to…" or "thus says the LORD." This stands in stark contrast to the book of Malachi where the phrase, "says the LORD" appears 25 times in 52 verses.

"And there went up also to Jerusalem, in the seventh year of Artaxerxes the king, some of the people of Israel, and some of the priests and Levites, the singers and gatekeepers, and the temple servants. And Ezra came to Jerusalem in the fifth month, which was in the seventh year of the king. For on the first day of the first month he began to go up from Babylonia, and on the first day of the fifth month he came to Jerusalem, for the good hand of his God was on him. For Ezra had set his heart to study the Law of the LORD, and to do it and to teach his statutes and rules in Israel." **–Ezra 7:7-10**

1. Scribes in the ANE[1]

   a. Grew out of the systematic development of writing systems

   b. *Pre-exilic* scribes were basically "secretaries" to kings, prophets and the public at large (2 Sam 8:16-17; 1 Kg 4:3; Jer 36:18).

   c. Ezra became the model of the *post-exilic* priest-scribe, dedicated to the copying, preservation and exposition of scripture.[2]

   d. By the time of the New Testament, the priests had abandoned this dual commitment (i.e. priest *and* scribe, in favor of political and economic concerns.[3]

C. Nehemiah: *"From Cupbearer to Wall Rebuilder"*[4] (Neh. 1:1 - 2:8; 4:15-20)

"When our enemies heard that it was known to us and that God had frustrated their plan, we all returned to the wall, each to his work. From that day on, half of my servants worked on construction, and half held the spears, shields, bows, and coats of mail. And the leaders stood behind the whole house of Judah, who were building on the wall. Those who carried burdens were loaded in such a way that each labored on the work with one hand and held his weapon with the other. And each of the builders had his sword strapped at his side while he built. The man who sounded the trumpet was beside me. And I said to the nobles and to the officials and to the rest of the people, "The work is great and widely spread, and we are separated on the wall, far from one another. In the place where you hear the sound of the trumpet, rally to us there. Our God will fight for us." **–Nehemiah 4:15-20**

1. Cupbearers in the Ancient Near East (ANE)

   a. Next to the king, the cupbearer was possibly the most important person in the Persian Empire.

   b. Xenophon tells us that the "cupbearer" tested everything before it reached the king.[5]

   c. He held the king's signet ring.

   d. Well-trained in court etiquette

   e. Was a "listening ear" for the king at all times.

   f. Had control over who had access to the king.

   g. Was supposed to be handsome, physically fit and of good temperament.

D. Ezra & Nehemiah: Two Men With One Mission[6]

1. Both Ezra and Nehemiah were driven by a deep commitment to the theology of the covenant.

   a. They both saw covenant renewal as a prerequisite to national health[7] (Neh 9:38 - 10:29).

   b. They both were committed to a purified and holy priesthood. (cf. Ezra 10:18-44; Neh. 13:4-9 and Malachi 2).

   c. They both were committed to observing the Sabbath and temple ritual. (Neh. 8:13-18; 10:3113:15-22).

   d. They both were committed to the reinstitution of the Law of Moses as the basis of all life within the community of faith (Neh. 8:1-12).

---

[1] There are 16 references to "scribe" in Ezra-Nehemiah (12 are for Ezra), but no mention of a "scribe" in Judah *prior* to Ezra's arrival in chap. 7.

[2] As Judaism moved from a prophetic (i.e. oral) religion to a document-driven religion (i.e. written; Torah, Mishnah, etc.), the role *and* status of "scribe" rose to enormous significance, notoriety, and power. By the time we get to the days of Jesus, they were powerful and respected men.

[3] In their zeal to build a "wall" around Torah and preserve it, scribes progressively removed themselves from the world of real people. The "spirit of the Law" was eclipsed and eventually replaced by the "letter of the Law."

[4] The book that bears his name is as much a memoir as it is a book of history. There are 84 references in this book to "walls," "gates," and "gatekeepers."

[5] Xenophon was a Greek historian and military leader, c. 435-354 B.C.

[6] It is worth noting that Ezra's name appears 14x in Ezra and 12x in Nehemiah, while Nehemiah's name appears 7x in Nehemiah but not at all in Ezra. Zerubbabel appears 6x in Ezra and 3x in Nehemiah, 7x in Haggai, and 4x in Zechariah. *both* Ezra and Nehemiah were loyal to the King of Persia, unlike the Judahite kings at the end of the life of the southern kingdom and the fall to the Babylonians.

[7] In truth, it was the only hope they had. No king, no "state," no real identity other than their covenant relationship to Yahweh. They were a remnant preserved by grace.

      e.   Both were committed to the spiritual purity of the covenant community, evidenced by separation from the pagan culture (Ezra 10:1-19; Neh. 9:1-5; 13:1-3).

      f.   They both were committed to reinstating "holiness" as the standard for all of life ("ceremonial purity" reflected in holy days, holy things, a holy race, the holy city, holy sabbaths, etc.; Ezra 8:28;9:2; Neh 9:14; 10:33; 11:1).

2.   Both Ezra and Nehemiah were "wall builders":

      a.   Ezra sought to rebuild the "wall" of the Law of Moses as the basis of personal and corporate holiness.

      b.   Nehemiah sought to rebuild the wall of the city to create and safeguard the covenant identity.[1]

E.   Ezra & Nehemiah: The "Grandfathers" of New Testament Judaism

1.   The role of king and state was replaced by priest and temple.

2.   The "voice" of God was Torah rather than prophet or king.

3.   The purity of the nation degenerated into a self-righteous exclusivity.[2]

4.   The *mission* of the nation degenerated to protection from Gentiles rather than bringing light *to* them (cf. Is 42:6; Lk 2:32).

5.   Their theology of sin was limited to what was *outside* the "walls" and blind to what was inside.

6.   The attraction of economic and political concerns (i.e. money and power) separated the priesthood from the spiritual responsibility of shepherding the covenant community.

7.   It is impossible to appreciate the Jerusalem and Judaism of Jesus' day without understanding the effect of Ezra and Nehemiah's ministries.

F.   Malachi: God's "Second To The Last" Prophetic Word

1.   The conditions in Malachi's day do not "fit" the prior *reforms* of Ezra and Nehemiah.

2.   Nehemiah's "leave of absence" (i.e. return to the court of Artaxerxes) most likely *preceded* Malachi's ministry (13:6).

3.   The sins that Malachi addresses in his prophecy mirror the conditions described by Nehemiah upon his return from Persia in 433 B.C.:

      a.   Offering God the "leftovers" for temple sacrifices (cf. Mal. 1:6-14 and Neh. 13:4-9).

      b.   Corruption within the priesthood (cf. Mal. 2:1-9 and Neh. 13:4-9).

      c.   Divorce and remarriage to pagan women (cf. Mal. 2:13-16 and Neh. 13:23-27).

      d.   Withholding of tithes and offerings[3] (cf. Mal. 3:8-12 and Neh. 12:44-47; 13:10-14).

      e.   Social injustice and absence of covenant compassion (3:5-6).

4.   Malachi ends with a call to covenant faithfulness *and* a promise of a future prophet like Elijah:

"Remember the law of my servant Moses, the statutes and rules that I commanded him at Horeb for all Israel."
                                                        –Malachi 4:4

"Behold, I will send you Elijah the prophet before the great and awesome day of the LORD comes. And he will turn the hearts of fathers to their children and the hearts of children to their fathers, lest I come and strike the land with a decree of utter destruction."
                                                        –Malachi 4:5-6

5.   Malachi is Yahweh's final word as the "curtain closes" on Act III of His grand Story.

6.   During the 400 year "Intermission," Yahweh will be drastically rearranging the "set" to prepare the way for the final prophet in the Story—John the Baptizer:

---

1 Our record of Nehemiah's original burden for the city is linked to Mosaic covenant language (cf. Neh. 1:7-11).

2 This danger still exists for any nation that massages notions of a "Christian" nation.

3 Nehemiah had put these things in motion before he left to return to Persia. In fact, Nehemiah had conducted a "lottery" of sorts in order to "tithe" people rather than money, to repopulate the under-populated city of Jerusalem (Neh. 7:4-5; 11:1-2)! What a powerful challenge to us today in the arena of church planting.

    The classic passage in Malachi about "tithing" is not about tithing! It's a call to return to covenant faithfulness. Jesus' statements about tithing in the New Testament must be understood as him saying it's possible to be a "law-keeper" and a "covenant-breaker." On top of the simplistic reduction of a larger covenant principle, tithing in the OT was complicated and extensive. The Deuteronomic Code "beefed up" the Levitical laws on tithing. Leviticus 27:30-33 required 1/10 of all grain, fruit, herds, and flocks. Deuteronomy 12:5-8; 14:22-27 required that annual tithes were to be eaten as families in Jerusalem to commemorate Yahweh's goodness (Levites too). Every three years, the entire tithe was taken to Jerusalem for a festival for the stranger, the fatherless, the widow, and the poor, as well as the Levites (Deut. 26:12-14; 14:28-29). There is debate among scholars over the number of tithes required. But most agree that the levitical tithe was separate from the festival tithes. In a community-based culture all this is very reasonable. But, not in a democratic culture that fosters individualism.

The beginning of the gospel of Jesus Christ, the Son of God. As it is written in Isaiah the prophet, "Behold, I send my messenger before your face, who will prepare your way, the voice of one crying in the wilderness: 'Prepare the way of the Lord, make his paths straight,'" John appeared, baptizing in the wilderness and proclaiming a baptism of repentance for the forgiveness of sins." **– Mark 1:1–8**

G. The End of Act III (i.e. the "Old" Testament) and the Christian

1. From Ezra we learn the vital need to be taught and *retaught* the true nature of the Story.

   "Who then is the faithful and wise servant, whom his master has set over his household, to give them their food at the proper time? Blessed is that servant whom his master will find so doing when he comes." **– Matthew 24:45–46**

2. From Esther we are reminded that all endowments are for the Story, *not* for the one possessing them.

   "For who sees anything different in you? What do you have that you did not receive? If then you received it, why do you boast as if you did not receive it?" **–1 Corinthians 4:7**

3. From Nehemiah we are reminded that for those of us in the Story, our most important choice is between holiness and accommodation to culture. Or, put another way, which "story" will we choose to "dwell" in?

   "Do not love the world or the things in the world. If anyone loves the world, the love of the Father is not in him. For all that is in the world—the desires of the flesh and the desires of the eyes and pride of life—is not from the Father but is from the world. And the world is passing away along with its desires, but whoever does the will of God abides forever." **– 1 John 2:15–17**

4. From Malachi we are reminded that "giving" is judged more by what we keep for ourselves and why, than what we give to Yahweh.

   "The point is this: whoever sows sparingly will also reap sparingly, and whoever sows bountifully will also reap bountifully. Each one must give as he has decided in his heart, not reluctantly or under compulsion, for God loves a cheerful giver. And God is able to make all grace abound to you, so that having all sufficiency in all things at all times, you may abound in every good work." **– 2 Corinthians 9:6–8**

CONTRIBUTIONS OF THE BOOKS OF THE BIBLE

BOOK	VERSES	WORDS	% of OT	% of BIBLE
Genesis	1,533	36,347	6.2%	4.8%
Exodus	1,213	30,901	5.3%	4.1%
Leviticus	859	23,461	4.0%	3.1%
Numbers	1,288	30,971	5.3%	4.1%
Deuteronomy	959	27,548	4.7%	3.6%
Joshua	658	17,984	3.1%	2.4%
Judges	618	18,287	3.1%	2.4%
Ruth	85	2,427	0.4%	0.3%
1 Sameul	810	24,137	4.1%	3.2%
2 Sameul	695	19,738	3.4%	2.6%
1 Kings	816	23,422	4.0%	3.1%
2 Kings	719	22,776	3.9%	3.0%
1 Chronicles	942	18,525	3.2%	2.4%
2 Chronicles	822	24,800	4.3%	3.3%
Ezra	280	6,893	1.2%	0.9%
Nehemiah	406	9,846	1.7%	1.3%
Esther	167	5,479	0.9%	0.7%
Job	1,070	17,610	3.0%	2.3%
Psalms	2,577	42,300	7.3%	5.6%
Proverbs	915	14,535	2.5%	1.9%
Ecclesiastes	222	5,339	0.9%	0.7%
Song of Solomon	117	2,533	0.4%	0.3%
Isaiah	1,292	35,267	6.1%	4.7%
Jeremiah	1,364	40,470	7.0%	5.3%
Lamentations	154	3,255	0.6%	0.4%
Ezekiel	1,273	37,206	6.4%	4.9%
Daniel	357	11,242	1.9%	1.5%
Hosea	197	4,966	0.9%	0.7%
Joel	73	1,895	0.3%	0.3%
Amos	146	4,048	0.7%	0.5%
Obadiah	21	605	0.1%	0.1%
Jonah	48	1,299	0.2%	0.2%
Micah	105	3,001	0.5%	0.4%
Nahum	47	1,111	0.2%	0.1%
Habakkuk	56	1,358	0.2%	0.2%
Zephaniah	53	1,557	0.3%	0.2%
Haggai	38	1,085	0.2%	0.1%
Zechariah	211	6,053	1.0%	0.8%
Malachi	55	1740	0.3%	0.2%
TOTAL	**23,261**	**582,017**	**100.0%**	**76.8%**

BOOK	VERSES	WORDS	% of NT	% of BIBLE
Matthew	1,067	22,647	12.9%	3.0%
Mark	673	14,351	8.2%	1.9%
Luke	1,149	24,617	14.0%	3.2%
John	878	18,891	10.8%	2.5%
Acts	1,003	23,471	13.4%	3.1%
Romans	432	9,492	5.4%	1.3%
1 Corinthians	437	9,282	5.3%	1.2%
2 Corinthians	257	6,072	3.5%	0.8%
Galatians	149	3,106	1.8%	0.4%
Ephesians	155	3,014	1.7%	0.4%
Philippians	104	2,147	1.2%	0.3%
Colossians	95	1,938	1.1%	0.3%
1 Thessalonians	89	1,844	1.1%	0.2%
2 Thessalonians	47	1,065	0.6%	0.1%
1 Timothy	113	2,317	1.3%	0.3%
2 Timothy	83	1,633	0.9%	0.2%
Titus	46	926	0.5%	0.1%
Philemon	25	460	0.3%	0.1%
Hebrews	303	6,908	3.9%	0.9%
James	108	2,319	1.3%	0.3%
1 Peter	105	2,393	1.4%	0.3%
2 Peter	61	1,549	0.9%	0.2%
1 John	105	2,499	1.4%	0.3%
2 John	13	300	0.2%	0.0%
3 John	15	302	0.2%	0.0%
Jude	25	604	0.3%	0.1%
Revelation	404	11,455	6.5%	1.5%
TOTAL	**7,941**	**175,602**	**100.0%**	**23.2%**

YESHUA IN FOUR DIMENSIONS

Act IV of Yahweh's Grand Drama

Hands of Hur Biblical Literacy Series
Part Two

UNIT 1: *"Now we see in a mirror dimly…"*

I. FIRST THINGS FIRST

A. Why a Course Called "*Yeshua…*"?

   1. The name, *"Jesus"* is the Greek rendering of the Hebrew name Joshua/Jeshua from the Old Testament language of the Jewish scriptures and Aramaic, the language of their common speech:

> *"Our fathers in turn brought it in with **Joshua** when they dispossessed the nations that God drove out before our fathers. So it was until the days of David…"* **Acts 7:45**

> *"For if **Joshua** had given them rest, God would not have spoken of another day later on."* **Hebrews 4:8**

   2. It is derived from the angel's announcement to Joseph in a dream, telling him that Mary's son was Israel's long-awaited savior[1] (keep in mind the angel likely spoke in Aramaic, *not* Greek):

> *Now the birth of Jesus Christ took place in this way. When his mother Mary had been betrothed to Joseph, before they came together she was found to be with child from the Holy Spirit. And her husband Joseph, being a just man and unwilling to put her to shame, resolved to divorce her quietly. But as he considered these things, behold, an angel of the Lord appeared to him in a dream, saying, "Joseph, son of David, do not fear to take Mary as your wife, for that which is conceived in her is from the Holy Spirit. She will bear a son, and you shall call his name **Jesus (Yeshua)**, for he will save his people from their sins."* **Matthew 1:18-21**

   3. The name includes the idea of God providing salvation, *"He (or Jah) saves."*[2]

   4. It is pronounced *"yeh-**shoo**-ah,"* and we transliterate this in English as *"Yeshua."*

B. Why a "Course" on Yeshua?

   1. Yeshua is the foundation of our faith[3], *not* the "founder" of it[4] (1 Cor. 3:11; Eph. 2:20)

   2. The "Gospel (i.e. "good news") of Yeshua the Anointed (i.e. Christ)" (Mk 1:1) is *not* a reference to *Yeshua's* "Good News"; He *is* the "good news"![5]

   3. Yeshua is the means of our *justification* (Acts 4:12; Rom. 3:22-24; 8:11).

   4. Yeshua is also the profile of our *sanctification* ; His likeness is what God wills to progressively transform us into. (Rom. 8:29; 2 cor. 3:18; 4:7-112).

   5. Yeshua is the One whose likeness should be the goal of the Church's vision of ministry to itself[6] (Col. 1:28-29; Gal. 4:19; Eph. 4:11-16; Phil. 2:12-15).

C. Avoiding the Two Extremes

   1. Over-simplification:

     a) Yeshua is merely a "savior" — focusing on his death and resurrection[7] (the conservative's tendency).

     b) Yeshua is merely a "sage" — focusing on his life and teachings[8] (the postmodern's tendency).

---

1 It is significant that Yeshua's name is associated with the salvation of the human race from conception!

2 "Yeshua" rather than "Jesus" also throws us immediately into the ancient past, rather than the "New Testament past," with which we are slightly more comfortable.

3 This is evidenced merely in the volume of textual information we have in our New Testament. Just including the Gospels and Acts 1:1-11, over 84,000 words deal with Jesus. That's 46% of our entire New Testament. He is not only the foundation of our faith, he is the centerpiece of our New Testament, textually, as well as the centerpiece of the entire Bible, thematically.

4 This is very important to distinguish. Jesus is *not* to Christianity what Mohammed is to Islam.

5 It is a bit of a startling fact that of the roughly 40 ministry encounters of Jesus with individuals in the four Gospels, only seven are mentioned by name! (Mary Magdalene - Luke 8; Zacchaeus - Luke 19; Lazarus - Jn 11; Thomas - Jn 20; Peter (reinstated) - Jn 21; Nicodemus - Jn 3; Bartemaeus - Mark 10). The late Brenning Manning said it best: *"The four evangelists never focus, in all their narratives, on another personality. Fringe women stay on the fringes; marginal men remain at the periphery. No one is allowed to take center stage. Various individuals are introduced only to interrogate, respond or react to Jesus. Nicodemus, Peter, Thomas, Martha, Mary, Caiphas, Pilate and a score of others are background to the person of Jesus. He dwarfs everyone else."* [Ruthless Trust, pp 136-137]

6 If we over-emphasize the role of Yeshua in our justification, we will inadvertently minimize not only his role in our sanctification, but the centrality of our sanctification in the overall purposes of God.

7 This view, for all practical purposes, negates the entire life of Jesus; the nearly forty years of interaction with the humanity he came to redeem. In so doing, it serves to castrate the gospel, reducing it to a means to personal safety rather than a call to personal sanctity.

8 C.S. Lewis rules out this possibility by telling us that Jesus was either a liar, or a lunatic on the level of someone who believes he is a poached egg, or he is Lord. The attribution of "sage" simply has no traction, given what Jesus claimed about himself.

2. Over-complication:

    a) Yeshua is reduced to a theological subject to be studied:[1]

        (1) His "hypostatic union": the relationship of Yeshua's two natures

        (2) His impeccability: whether or not Yeshua could sin and the nature of his temptations

        (3) The "kenosis": what exactly did the eternal Son "surrendered" in the Incarnation

        (4) The trinity: his place in the Godhead

II. THE TASK BEFORE US

A. The Difficulty of the Task

    1. The Material "problem":

        a) We have no tangible artifacts typical of many historical figures (E.g. Alexander, Caesar, Tutankhamen[2], etc.); perhaps because archeology is *not* the study of the ancient poor, but the ancient rich.

        b) Our most extensive sources are all documents written by followers of Yeshua.

    2. The literary "problem":

        a) The four Gospels, as literary sources:

            (1) They defy categorization by genre - what are they, really?[3] (I.e. If you were a librarian, where would *you* shelve them?)

            (2) They defy simple collaboration of composition:

                (a) This is one of the biggest areas of scholarly study of the Gospels.

                (b) No other section of Scripture (except Genesis 1-11) has undergone such scrutiny and criticism.

                (c) There are over 700 Christian books available that deal with "The Gospels."

            (3) They defy a clear chronology: the Gospels are not "blogs" or "journals" following a linear sequence:[4]

"Sermon on the mount" material	in Matthew	In Luke
beatitudes	5:3-12	6:20b-23
salt of the earth	5:13	14:34-35a
light of the world	5:14-16	8:16
law and the prophets	5:17ff	16:16ff
love for enemies	5:43-48	6:27, 32-36
Lord's Prayer	6:9-13	11:2-4
treasures in heaven	6:20ff	12:33ff
a tree and its fruit	7:16ff	6:43ff
the two builders	7:24-27	6:47-49

---

1 We don't want to minimize the incredible difficulty believers have had over the centuries since the Ascension, trying to understand the realities introduced via the Incarnation and resurrection. For example, there were at least 21 church councils in the roughly 1,600 years between AD 325-1965, with approximately 1,170 registered attendees. The Council of Nicaea was attended by 320 bishops, seeking to understand and solidify the nature of the relationship of the Son to the Father. The Council of Constantinople in AD 380 was essentially a trinitarian council, with more of a focus on the Holy Spirit than Nicaea. It was attended by 150 bishops. The Council of Ephesus in AD 431, attended by 200 bishops dealt with the dual natures of Jesus, as did the Council of Chalcedon in AD 451, which was attended by nearly 500 bishops. These are deep waters, and we have much to thank dedicated theologians for. However, our goal is to reflect Yeshua, not refract him.

2 Egyptian pharaoh of the 18th dynasty; reigned c. 1361– c. 1352 BC. His tomb, which contained a wealth of rich and varied contents, was discovered virtually intact by English archaeologist Howard Carter in 1922.

3 Even though the Gospels are not "biographies" in the modern sense, they DO follow some clear characteristics that scholars have attributed to an ancient genre called "lives." (Wenham, p. 50)

4 For example, when did Yeshua "cleanse" the Temple and how many times? If he cleansed it twice, why don't the Synoptics tell us? If he only cleansed it once, how do we explain the anachronism in John's account? Or consider that 60% of John's Gospel details only about 60 hours of Yeshua's life, and he spends 15 times as much writing about what Jesus taught during the Last Supper than he does the resurrection and what followed.

Excerpted from: *Exploring the New Testament: A Guide to the Gospels,* Wenham & Walton, page 65.

(4) They defy easy contextualization:

b) it takes serious work to understand them.[1]

(1) geography, climate, ethnicity, history, and language all shape the meaning of the text of the Gospels.

3. The "times" problem:

a) We are seeking to comprehend the life of someone who lived during a time of emperors and peasants.

b) We are dependent upon sources written in an illiterate, agricultural culture.

c) We are seeking to understand universally a story that is both provincial and parochial in its setting.

d) The world described in the Gospels was 2000 years old in Yeshua's day!

B. The Gravity of the Task

1. It is possible to have a wrong "Jesus": (in Greek, *allos* - "another," means *"another of the same kind,"* but *heteros* - "different," means *"another of a different kind altogether"*)

> *"But I am afraid that as the serpent deceived Eve by his cunning, your thoughts will be led astray from a sincere and pure devotion to Christ. For if someone comes and proclaims **another Jesus** than the one we proclaimed, or if you receive a **different spirit** from the one you received, or if you accept a **different gospel** from the one you accepted, you put up with it readily enough."* **2 Corinthians 11:3, 4**

> *"...not that there is another one [gospel], but there are some who trouble you and want to distort the gospel of Christ. But even if we or an angel from heaven should preach to you a gospel contrary to the one we preached to you, let him be accursed. As we have said before, so now I say again: If anyone is preaching to you a gospel contrary to the one you received, let him be accursed."* **Galatians 1:7-9**

a) The "Jesus" of Mormonism:

> *"That Lucifer, the son of the morning, is our elder brother and the brother of Jesus Christ..."* **Mormon Doctrine, pp. 163-64**

> *"Jesus got married at Cana and had many wives, Martha, Mary and others. He also had many children..."* **Journal of Discourses, Vol 1 345-346**

b) The "Jesus" of The Watchtower:

> *"Michael the archangel is no other than the only begotten son of God, now Jesus Christ..."* **New Heavens and New Earth, pp. 30-31**

c) The "Jesus" of Islam[2]:

> *O followers of the Book! do not exceed the limits in your religion, and do not speak (lies) against Allah, but (speak) the truth; the Messiah, Isa son of Marium is only an apostle of Allah and His Word which He communicated to Marium and a spirit from Him; believe therefore in Allah and His apostles, and say not, Three. Desist, it is better for you; Allah is only one God; far be It from His glory that He should have a son, whatever is in the heavens and whatever is in the earth is His, and Allah is sufficient for a Protector.* **Sura 4:171**

> *"...This means that unlike Christianity which teaches that all the children of Adam are sinful for Adam's sin, Islam teaches that all humans are innocent by birth and they become sinful only when they consciously commit a sin.... There is no need for salvation from sin, for there is no original burden. One's success in the hereafter lies in his living a righteous life in this world."* **[taken from Islamonline.net]**

d) The "Yeshua" of Judaism (*taken from:* http://www.jewfaq.org/looking4.htm):

> *"It is important to understand that Jesus is simply not a part of Judaism. He is irrelevant to our religion. To ask a Jew, "why don't you believe in Jesus?" is like asking a Christian, "why don't you believe in Zeus?"*

> *"...The Jews of Rome weren't looking for an incarnated god who would die and absolve them of their sins, because the idea of sin and its punishment and concern about salvation aren't at the heart of Judaism, the way they are in Christianity.*

> *"But though Jesus and his religion may be part of G-d's plan for the world, the general consensus among the rabbis regarding Jesus is not favorable. On the same page where he made the remark above, Rambam commented that Daniel 11:14 (regarding people who try to establish the vision but stumble and fall) is a reference to Christianity, saying:*

---

1 See "Types of Biblical Criticism" in the Appendix Section.

2 See the English translation in the Appendix Section of the Arabic script surrounding the Dome of the Rock's exterior and interior in Jerusalem for a startling understanding of the public theological position Islam takes against Christianity.

'Is there a greater stumbling block than [Jesus]? All the prophets foretold that the messiah would redeem the Jews, help them, gather in the exiles and support their observance of the commandments. But he caused Jewry to be put to the sword, to be scattered and to be degraded; he tampered with the Torah and its laws; and he misled most of the world to serve something other than G-d.'"

e) In an age of passion and emotion, it's vital to remind ourselves that we can be sincerely wrong about Yeshua *and* ourselves![1]

"And to the angel of the church in Laodicea write: 'The words of the Amen, the faithful and true witness, the beginning of God's creation. "'I know your works: you are neither cold nor hot. Would that you were either cold or hot! So, because you are lukewarm, and neither hot nor cold, I will spit you out of my mouth. For you say, I am rich, I have prospered, and I need nothing, not realizing that you are wretched, pitiable, poor, blind, and naked. I counsel you to buy from me gold refined by fire, so that you may be rich, and white garments so that you may clothe yourself and the shame of your nakedness may not be seen, and salve to anoint your eyes, so that you may see. Those whom I love, I reprove and discipline, so be zealous and repent. Behold, I stand at the door and knock. If anyone hears my voice and opens the door, I will come in to him and eat with him, and he with me.
Revelation 3:14-20

"Brothers, my heart's desire and prayer to God for them is that they may be saved. I bear them witness that they have a zeal [Gk = passion] *for God, but not according to knowledge."* **Romans 10:1, 2**

2. If Yeshua is, the "others" aren't!

a) The monotheism of Christianity excludes the monotheism of Judaism and Islam (and vice versa).

b) The common threads of these three religious streams blurs their exclusivity (E.g. ancestry, God's sovereignty, separation of God from nature).[2]

c) One's theology of Yeshua *affects* every doctrine of the Christian faith; it isn't merely one of them:

- God
- creation
- humanity
- sin

- Satan, angels and demons
- salvation
- eternity

C. "Yeshua in Four Dimensions"

1. Four ways of "looking":

a) The "world" behind the text: history and culture

b) The "world" of the text: language, vocabulary, grammar

c) The "world" around the text: implications and applications for the believing community.

d) The "world" before the text: personal application

2. Four things to "look" at:

a) Yeshua as Revelation: *"And the Word became flesh and dwelt among us, and we have seen his glory, glory as of the only Son from the Father, full of grace and truth."* **John 1:14**

b) Yeshua as Reconciler: *"...that is, in Christ God was reconciling the world to himself, not counting their trespasses against them, and entrusting to us the message of reconciliation.* **2 Corinthians 5:19**

c) Yeshua as Role Model: *For those whom he foreknew he also predestined to be conformed to the image of his Son, in order that he might be the firstborn among many brothers.* **Romans 8:29**

d) Yeshua as Rectifier: *"The Spirit of the Lord GOD is upon me, because the LORD has anointed me to bring good news to the poor; he has sent me to bind up the brokenhearted, to proclaim liberty to the captives, and the opening of the prison to those who are bound;"* **Isaiah 61:1**

3. Four "windows" to look through: Matthew, Mark, Luke, John

4. Forging a Four-Dimensional Method:

a) We are going to seek to use all four ways of looking.

b) We are going to look through *all four* windows.

c) We are going to look at *two* of the four things:

---

1 This is illustrated in the two passages in this point. The Revelation passage informs us of Christians "getting Jesus wrong," and needing correction. The Romans passage informs us of the fact that "zeal" (i.e. sincerity) can be uninformed or misinformed as well.

2 This is further complicated by shared sacred sites (e.g. Jerusalem), and shared histories (e.g. Abraham, Isaac, Ishmael, Moses, and David).

(1) Yeshua as Revelation
(2) Yeshua as Role Model

UNIT 2: *"In These Last Days"*

I. YESHUA: REVEALER *AND* REVELATION

A. MISSION IMPOSSIBLE: Yeshua as Revealer

1. God told Moses that no one could see Him face to face and live (Ex. 33:20).

2. This hasn't changed. Paul said the same thing nearly 1,500 years *after* Moses.[1]

3. Yeshua made it clear that only He could "unveil" (i.e. "reveal") the unseen, unapproachable God to the world of people. (Matt. 11:27).[2]

4. John tells us that's exactly what Yeshua has done:

    "No one has ever seen God; the only God, who is at the Father's side, he has made him known." **John 1:18**

    a) The word translated *"made him known"* (NIV,ESV) is the Greek verb *exegeomai,* from which our word, *"exegesis"* comes.

    b) It means "to explain in detail," or "to interpret."[3]

    c) It was used for Paul's "report" to the Church when he returned from his missionary journeys (Acts 25.12,14; 21:19), and the two men "telling" their story about seeing Yeshua near Emmaus (Lk. 24:35).

5. John also tell us *how* Yeshua *"exegeted"* God:

    "In the beginning was the Word, and the Word was with God, and the Word was God....And the Word became flesh and **dwelt** *among us, and we have seen his **glory**, **glory** as of the only Son from the Father, full of grace and truth."* **Jn. 1:1,14**

    a) The word *"dwelt"* (skenaō) is used for the Tabernacle in the Greek Old Testament. It means *"to pitch a tent."*

    b) The word, *"glory,"* (doxa) is used in the Greek Old Testament for God's presence in the Tabernacle (Ex. 25:9; 26:6 and 16:10; 24:16).

    c) John tells us that Yeshua of Nazareth was the habitation of the glory of the God of Israel![4]

    d) Yeshua himself said something no Jew ever dreamt he would hear:

    "Jesus said to him, "Have I been with you so long, and you still do not know me, Philip? Whoever has seen me has seen the Father. How can you say, 'Show us the Father'?" **John 14:9**

6. The author of the Book of Hebrews helps us understand what this means:[5]

    *"Long ago, at many times and in many ways, God spoke to our fathers by the prophets, **but** in these last days he has spoken to us by his Son, whom he appointed the heir of all things, through whom also he created the world. He is the radiance of the glory of God and the exact imprint of his nature, and he upholds the universe by the word of his power. After making purification for sins, he sat down at the right hand of the Majesty on high, having become as much superior to angels as the name he has inherited is more excellent than theirs."* **Hebrews 1:1-4**

    a) The variegated, perforated, and abbreviated revelation of God's will of "long ago," is a closed chapter. –vs. 1

    b) In *"these last days"* God has opened His final chapter of revelation and the medium (Yeshua) *is* the "message" (the Father). –vv. 2-3

---

1 Paul speaks of God dwelling in "unapproachable light" in 1 Tim. 6:15-16. This stands in very stark contrast to the nearly "recreational" view of God that persists in much of the American Church.

2 Peter's choice of words here is insightful. He uses the word, *apokaluptō*, which is the same word Jesus used speaking to him when Peter made his momentous confession, *"You are the Christ, the son of the living God."* Jesus told him that his Father had "revealed" this insight to Peter (Matthew 16:17).

3 It turns out that this is an *enormous* component of Yeshua's earthly ministry, and one of the primary purposes of the Incarnation in the first place. And, it is also a neglected facet of his life when it comes to modern teaching/preaching.

4 John's use of Old Testament language and imagery is clearly deliberate.

5 The contrastive "but" in this passage indicates the inauguration of a change in the manner and mechanism through which Yahweh is speaking to His people.

B. MISSION INCREDIBLE: The "Exegeted" God

1. He is a "Father" — He Has An "Only Son"[1]

   a) Of the nearly 900 times the word "Father" shows up in the Old Testament, only 8 are clear references to Yahweh!

   b) Of these 8, nearly all of them are metaphorical references to Yahweh's relationship to Israel as a nation (cf. Deut. 32:6; Is. 1:2; 30:19; 63:16; 64:8).

   c) God as "Father" in the Old Testament was always a reference to Him as the source or origin of the nation and only marginally in a relational sense.

   d) By contrast, God as "Father" appears over 180 times in the four Gospels alone:[2]

      (1) 5x in Mark
      (2) 20x in Luke
      (3) 43x in Matthew
      (4) 116x in John[3]

   e) Yeshua taught his followers to relate to Yahweh as their "Father." He said so 17x in the Sermon on the Mount alone (cf. Matt. 5-7)!

   f) Paul continues this beautiful picture of "Abba" that Yeshua began in Gethsemane (Mk. 14:36) in his own development of the doctrine of adoption (cf. Rom. 8:15; Gal. 4:6).

   g) Paul continues this description of God by opening every one of his 13 letters with a reference to God as "Father." (All but one are plural.)

   h) However, Yeshua also made it very clear that *his own* relationship to Yahweh as "Father" was one of equality, *not* mere familiarity.

      (1) 26x in John's Gospel Yeshua refers to "*my* Father."

      (2) Because he was the "Son of God," Yeshua claimed the authority to do what only God could do:[4]

         • give life, even to the dead (Jn 5:21)
         • judge all humans (5:22)
         • demand the honor given to God Himself (5:23)
         • will call the dead back to life in the resurrection (5:25-29)
         • that he is the source of eternal life (5:24, 39-40)

   i) We have to be careful to continually remind ourselves that Yeshua came to "exegete" the *Father*, not himself:

      (1) He came to do the *Father's* will, not his own:

      "For I have come down from heaven, not to do my own will but the will of him who sent me."   **John 6:38**

      (2) He spoke the *Father's* words, not his own:

      "For I have not spoken on my own authority, but the Father who sent me has himself given me a commandment—what to say and what to speak."   **John 12:49**

      (3) He came to reveal the *Father*, not himself:

      "All things have been handed over to me by my Father, and no one knows the Son except the Father, and no one knows the Father except the Son and anyone to whom the Son chooses to reveal[5] him."   **Matt. 11:27**

---

1 This is one of the most significant and powerful metaphors describing God that Jesus "exegetes."

2 This is a revolutionary change in the very nature of humanity's relationship with God. When Jesus instructed his followers to *"pray like this… our Father in heaven…"* it was a startling statement. We are given privileged insight into this aspect of Yeshua's own relationship with the Father in his prayers in Gethsemane, where he addresses him as "Abba," a term of familiarity and endearment.

3 It is no exaggeration to say that Yeshua's relationship to Yahweh as "Father and son" was at the very *heart* of the cause of the intense opposition he faced whenever he was in Jerusalem. In fact, John's Gospel is almost *more* about "the Father/my Father" than it is about Jesus! (cf. 116x versus 254x, by name)

4 John 5 is built around Yeshua's claim to have a unique relationship with Yahweh; One that, by definition, the religious leaders lacked, despite all their scrupulous attention to the Law of Moses.

5 Greek is *apokaluptō* .

(4) He was the exact representation of the *Father*:

> *"Jesus said to him, "Have I been with you so long, and you still do not know me, Philip? Whoever has seen me has seen the Father. How can you say, 'Show us the Father'?"*   **John 14:9**

C. MISSION INEVITABLE: The "Exegeting" Church

1. God has inseparably linked His "name" to His people:

> *"Because you are precious in my eyes, and honored, and I love you, I give men in return for you, peoples in exchange for your life. Fear not, for I am with you; I will bring your offspring from the east, and from the west I will gather you. I will say to the north, Give up, and to the south, Do not withhold; bring my sons from afar and my daughters from the end of the earth, everyone who is called by my name, whom I created for my glory, whom I formed and made."[1]*   **Isaiah 43:4-7**

2. It is possible for those "called by His name" to be arrogant, live in sin and turn their backs towards God:

> *"if my people who are called by my name humble themselves, and pray and seek my face and turn from their wicked ways, then I will hear from heaven and will forgive their sin and heal their land."*   **2 Chronicles 7:14**

3. It is possible for those "called by His name" to "exegete" God in a way that causes the world to hate Him:

> *"For, as it is written, "The name of God is blasphemed among the Gentiles because of you."*   **Romans 2:24**

4. Yeshua made it clear that the lives of those who call themselves by His name "exegete" the Father and affect what the world believes about Him:[2]

> *"I do not ask for these only, but also for those who will believe in me through their word, that they may all be one, just as you, Father, are in me, and I in you, that they also may be in us, so that the world may believe that you have sent me. The glory that you have given me I have given to them, that they may be one even as we are one, I in them and you in me, that they may become perfectly one, so that the world may know that you sent me and loved them even as you loved me."*   **John 17:20-23**

5. This is the clear expectation of God for His people:[3]

> *"Therefore be imitators of God, as beloved children."*   **Ephesians 5:1**

> *"I therefore, a prisoner for the Lord, urge you to walk in a manner worthy of the calling to which you have been called...,"*   **Ephesians 4:1**

> *"And so, from the day we heard, we have not ceased to pray for you, asking that you may be filled with the knowledge of his will in all spiritual wisdom and understanding, so as to walk in a manner worthy of the Lord, fully pleasing to him, bearing fruit in every good work and increasing in the knowledge of God."*   **Colossians 1:9, 10**

6. It is tragic that we have reduced the idea of a "testimony" to Christian *behavior* instead of the accurate "explanation" (i.e. exegesis) of the character of God.[4]

D. Incarnation, Apologetics and "Exegeting" God

1. Incarnation & Truth: a Two-Sided Coin

   a) Truth can be, and must be embodied:

   > *"In the beginning was the Word, and the Word was with God, and the Word was God.....And the Word became flesh and dwelt among us, and we have seen his glory, glory as of the only Son from the Father, full of grace and truth."* **John 1:1, 14**

   b) Truth can be seen and experienced, not just apprehended and believed.

   c) Propositional Truth (i.e. words) is judged by logical consistency, valid and true arguments.

      (1) What we call "evangelism" involves propositional Truth.

   d) Incarnational Truth (i.e. lifestyle) is judged by personal integrity, the congruence of words and conduct.

---

1 The Hebrew word for "formed" *(yatsar)*, is the word used in Genesis for the creation of humanity (Genesis 1:26-27). It is the word for the potter at the wheel. This is a beautiful metaphor, but also one that links the "creation" of a distinct people of God with the creation of humanity itself.

2 Or, in the words of one modern author, *"The Incarnation isn't over."*

3 The cumulative message of these texts is that God is our "Father" on one hand, but also that we, as His sons and daughters play an enormous and significant role in *representing* Him.

4 In the same way that the revelatory (i.e. "exegetical") ministry has been eclipsed or forgotten because of the propitiatory ministry of justification, so too we have abandoned *our* "exegetical" responsibilities in favor of focusing on the benefits of our own justification. Put another way, we seem to spend more of our time thinking and talking about what God has "done" for us (and wants to do for others), than we do seeking to "exegete" God by the way we talk and live. This is the unfortunate trickle down effect of having an anemic Christology to begin with.

(1) What we call a "witness" involves incarnational Truth—an observable, verifiable life.

e) Hypocrisy is incongruence between these two forms of Truth in the life of one who claims to be a son or daughter of God.

f) Yeshua's harshest words were towards those who neglected incarnational Truth yet defended propositional Truth!

"But woe to you, scribes and Pharisees, hypocrites! For you shut the kingdom of heaven in people's faces. For you neither enter yourselves nor allow those who would enter to go in." **Matthew 23:13**

g) His criticism was *not* because of their behavior as much as its fruit; They *misrepresented* God.[1]

h) Our passion should be the same as Yeshua,' to "exegete" the Father:

"I made known to them your name, and I will continue to make it known, that the love with which you have loved me may be in them, and I in them." **John 17:26**

UNIT 3: "The Bible on Yeshua's Nightstand"[2]

I. YESHUA AND OUR OLD TESTAMENT

A. Yeshua's Bible:

1. Yeshua accepted the three-fold division of the Jewish Bible:

THE TANAKH

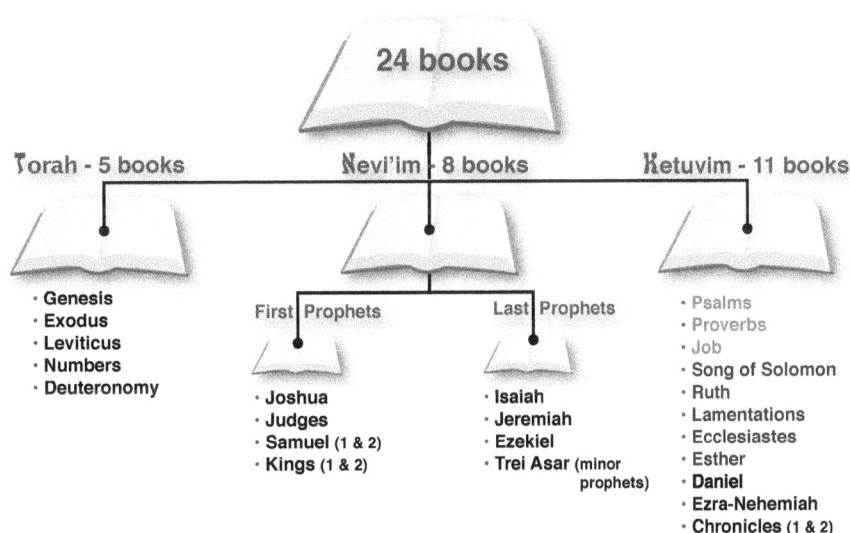

24 books

Torah - 5 books   **Nevi'im - 8 books**   **Ketuvim - 11 books**

- **Genesis**
- **Exodus**
- **Leviticus**
- **Numbers**
- **Deuteronomy**

First Prophets

- **Joshua**
- **Judges**
- **Samuel** (1 & 2)
- **Kings** (1 & 2)

Last Prophets

- **Isaiah**
- **Jeremiah**
- **Ezekiel**
- **Trei Asar** (minor prophets)

- Psalms
- Proverbs
- Job
- Song of Solomon
- **Ruth**
- Lamentations
- Ecclesiastes
- Esther
- **Daniel**
- **Ezra-Nehemiah**
- Chronicles (1 & 2)

a) He referred to it specifically in his instruction of the eleven after his resurrection:[3]

*Then he said to them, "These are my words that I spoke to you while I was still with you, that everything written about me in the **Law** of Moses and the **Prophets** and the **Psalms** must be fulfilled."* **Luke 24:44.**

---

1 *This* is the heart of hypocrisy and what makes it such a serious thing to God. Our glib cliché, "walking the talk" is an embarrassingly pale theology by comparison.

2 It's worth reminding ourselves from time to time that Jesus didn't *have* a "nightstand." He wouldn't even have had his own room! There were at least nine people in Yeshua's family, and first century rural Jews would have shared a small house, and likely the same sleeping quarters.

3 This needs to be understood as a statement from Jesus that says *all* the Scriptures speak of him, not merely some of them.

b) He alluded to two of the three divisions in a debate with the scribes and Pharisees:[1]

"Therefore I send you prophets and wise men and scribes, some of whom you will kill and crucify, and some you will flog in your synagogues and persecute from town to town, so that on you may come all the righteous blood shed on earth, from the blood of innocent Abel to the blood of Zechariah the son of Barachiah, whom you murdered between the sanctuary and the altar." **Matthew 23:34, 35.**

B. Yeshua's Use of the Tanakh[2]

1. Yeshua mentioned *at least* sixteen individuals from the Old Testament by name in his teaching, and from the breadth of names he uses, also gives evidence to an excellent familiarity with the revelation of Yahweh and salvation history itself.[3]

2. Those he mentioned also cover the entire range of the Tanakh (Genesis to 2 Chronicles):

Old Testament People Mentioned By Name in the Gospels

PERSON	Matthew	Mark	Luke	John	TOTAL	OT Books
Aaron	—	—	1	—	1	Exodus thru Numbers
Abraham	7	1	15	11	34	Genesis
Bathsheba	1	—	—	—	1	2 Samuel and 1 Kings
David	17	7	13	2	39	Ruth thru 2 Chronicles
Elijah	9	9	7	2	27	1 Kings
Elisha	—	—	1	—	1	2 Kings
Isaac	2	1	2	0	5	Genesis
Isaiah	6	2	2	4	14	2 Kings, Isaiah, 2 Chronicles
Jacob	6	1	4	3	14	Genesis
Jeremiah	3	—	—	—	3	2 Kings and Jeremiah
Jonah	5	—	4	—	9	2 Kings and Jonah
Lot	—	—	3	—	3	Genesis
Moses	7	8	10	13	38	Exodus thru Deuteronomy
Naaman*	—	—	1	—	1	2 Kings
Noah	2	—	3	—	5	Genesis
Queen of Sheba*	1	—	1	—	2	1 Kings
Rachel	1	—	—	—	1	Genesis
Rahab*	1	—	—	—	1	Joshua
Ruth*	1	—	—	—	1	Ruth
Solomon	2	—	3	—	5	2 Sam., 1-2 Kgs., 1-2 Chron. Ezra, Nehemiah
Uriah*	1	—	—	—	1	2 Samuel
Widow (at Zarephath)*	—	—	1	—	1	1 Kings
Zechariah	1	—	1	—	2	2 Chronicles
TOTAL	73	29	72	35	—	

*non-Jews whose inclusion is a clear indicator of familiarity with Israelite history.
People specifically mentioned by Jesus in bold.

---

1 Abel is in Genesis and Zechariah in 2 Chronicles 24:20-22, which was written *after* the Babylonian Exile (i.e. near the close of the Old Testament narrative.). Also, in the 2 Chronicles passage, Zechariah's father's name is given as Jehoida rather than Barachiah as it is in Matthew.

2 In a very real sense, the Gospel narratives are "Old Testament" history. We deceive or mislead ourselves by assigning them mentally to a new "division" we have created. We are stepping into a "river" of revelation at flood stage when we open our Gospel narratives. For this reason, it would be accurate to say that "Christianity" is Jewish.

3 Yeshua's extensive use of the Tanakh is even more significant when one considers that he assumes familiarity with all of it on the part of his listeners as well. He makes no effort to introduce or explain any of the characters he references in his teaching. For example, he makes reference to Lot and Lot's wife in a manner that assumes they knew of his connection to his uncle Abraham, the city of Sodom, etc. (Luke 17:28-32)

3. Yeshua *quoted* extensively from the Tanakh:

   a) Matthew attributes 45 of his 61 quotations from the OT to Yeshua.

      (1) Yeshua quotes from 19 of *our* 39 books! (11 of the 24 books of the Tanakh)

      (2) Yeshua quotes from all five Books of Law

      (3) Yeshua quotes from all four of the Major Prophets.

      (4) Yeshua quotes from 2 of the 5 Books of Poetry (Psalms, Proverbs)

      (5) Yeshua quotes from 8 of the 12 Minor Prophets (Joel, Jonah, Amos, Hosea, Micah, Zephaniah, Zechariah, and Malachi).[1]

   b) Mark attributes 28 of his 35 quotations from the OT to Yeshua.

      (1) Yeshua quotes from 11 of our 39 books!

      (2) Yeshua quotes from 4 Books of Law (exc. Numbers)

      (3) Yeshua quotes from all four of the Major Prophets.

      (4) Yeshua quotes from 1 of the 5 Books of Poetry (Psalms)

      (5) Yeshua quotes from 2 of the 12 Minor Prophets (Joel, Zechariah)[2]

   c) Luke attributes 23 of his 38 quotations from the OT to Yeshua.

      (1) Yeshua quotes from 10 of our 39 books!

      (2) Yeshua quotes from 3 Books of Law (Exodus, Leviticus, Deut.)

      (3) Yeshua quotes from all four of the Major Prophets.

      (4) Yeshua quotes from 1 of the 5 Books of Poetry (Psalms)

      (5) Yeshua quotes from 2 of the 12 Minor Prophets (Hosea, Malachi)

   d) John attributes 4 of his 14 quotations from the OT to Yeshua.

      (1) Yeshua quotes from 3 of our 39 books!

      (2) Yeshua does not quote from the Books of Law.

      (3) Yeshua quotes from 2 of the four Major Prophets (Isaiah, Jeremiah)

      (4) Yeshua quotes from 1 of the 5 Books of Poetry (Psalms)

      (5) Yeshua does not quote from any of the 12 Minor Prophets.

4. Yeshua made extensive reference to Old Testament people, places and events in his teaching throughout his entire ministry.

5. He *assumed* familiarity with Jewish history on the part of his listeners.[3]

6. Yeshua made reference to their past at least nineteen times in his teaching:

---

1 It's noteworthy to mention that these prophets contain intense preaching against social injustice and false spirituality.

2 He also quotes from Malachi, even though Mark attributes it to Isaiah (cf. Malachi 3:1 and Mark 1:2).

3 This is profound. Jesus *assumed* biblical literacy in a culture that was primarily *illiterate!* We have the opposite situation in the Church; biblical *illiteracy* in a culture that is nearly completely literate.

Old Testament People/Events Referred to by Jesus

Scripture Reference	PERSON, PLACE, OR EVENT
Matthew 5:11-12; 23:29-313	The repeated rejection of God's prophets by the nation of Israel.
Matthew 6:29	The wealth and splendor of King Solomon.
Matt. 11:13-14	The prediction of the return of the prophet Elijah.
Matt. 11:23	The fierce judgment of Yahweh on Sodom (and Gomorrah) for sin.
Matt. 12:2-4; Mk. 2:24-26	David's encounter with Abiathar the priest during the time of Saul's rampage against him.
Matt. 12:40-41	The story of the ministry of Jonah, including Nineveh's wickedness.
Matt. 12:42	The story of the Queen of Sheba's visit to Solomon and his splendor.
Matt. 22:29 - 23:1	Reference to Abraham, Isaac, Jacob, David and Moses in conversation.
Matt. 24:36-39	Reference to Noah, the ark and the flood.
Mark 7:6-8	The life and ministry of the prophet Isaiah, and Israel's resistance to his message.
Mark 12:26-27	Reference to Moses' first encounter with YHWH at the burning bush.
Luke 4:25-27	Elijah's ministry to the widow of Zarephath in Sidon.
Luke 4:25-27	Elisha''s healing of Naaman the Syrian.
Luke 10:13-14	The prophetic ministry of Ezekiel (his prophecies to Tyre and Sidon).
Luke 11:50-51	The murder of Abel (Genesis 4) and the priest Zechariah (2 Chronicles 24); this statement gives evidence of familiarity with the *entire* Old Testament!
Luke 17:28-29	The story of Lot living in Sodom.
John 1:51	Reference to Jacob's dream of the ladder to heaven with angels (at Bethel; Gen. 28).
John 3:14	The healing of the Israelites through the bronze serpent and Moses (Numbers 21)
John 6:31-32	Reference to the giving of the manna in the wilderness (Exodus 16:15).

C. Yeshua's Perspective on the Tanakh

    1. Yeshua believed and repeatedly taught that the Hebrew Bible's main subject matter was Him!

        a) He intimated it to his disciples early on:

And taking the twelve, he said to them, "See, we are going up to Jerusalem, and everything that is written about the Son of Man by the prophets will be accomplished."　**Luke 18:31**

        b) He said it clearly to the Pharisees near the end of his ministry:

"You search the Scriptures because you think that in them you have eternal life; and it is they that bear witness about me,…Do not think that I will accuse you before the Father; the one who accuses you is Moses, in whom you have set your hope."　**John 5:39, 45**

        c) He said it clearly to his disciples *after* his resurrection:

"…Was it not necessary that the Christ should suffer these things and enter into his glory?" And beginning with Moses and all the Prophets, he interpreted to them in all the Scriptures the things concerning himself.　**Luke 24:26, 27**

D. Twelve Words – One Story" – A Old Testament Outline

    1. The history of God's people can be summarized using 12 words:[1]

---

1 Genesis 1-11 is a sort of "history of the universe and the human race," whereas from Genesis 12 onward, the narrative focuses on a single people group, the Jews. The "Divided Kingdom" is a crucial element in Gospel history, for it marks the creation of Galilee and Judea, the Samaritans as a people group, and the association of idolatry and second-class Judaism with Galilee. The "Exiles" were a defining event in Jewish history. They lost their language, their power, and their monarchy. It is a pivotal event in their history. Even Matthew, in his genealogy of Jesus, uses the Babylonian Exile as a marking point for two of the three clusters of 14 generations in his list. When Jesus steps onto the scene of salvation history, the Story is already 2,000 years old! By contrast, Rome has only been on the scene for about 50 years by this time.

A "Twelve-Word Tanakh"

WORD	KEY INFO	OTHER INFO
Patriarchs	Abraham / Isaac / Jacob / Joseph	Genesis 12 c. 2000 BC
Egypt	Joseph / 400 years / 10 plagues	— —
Exodus	Moses / Red Sea	Exodus 12 c. 1500 BC
Wilderness	40 years / Moses dies	— —
Conquest	Jericho / Canaan / Joshua	Joshua 12
Settlement	12 tribes / Judges / chaos	— —
United (kingdom)	Saul / David / Solomon	40 years each c. 1000 BC
Divided (kingdom)	North (10) / South (2)	1 Kings 12 c. 931 BC
Exiles	North - Assyria South - Babylon	2 Kings 17 - 722 BC 2 Kings 25 - 586 BC
Return	Zerubbabel - 2nd Temple	— —
Resettlement	Ezra - the Law Nehemiah - the wall	— —
"Silence"	400 years	John the Baptizer (breaks the silence)

2. The "Twelve Word Tanakh" is charted to reflect the 39 books of our Old Testament on the following page:

Twelve Words — One Story

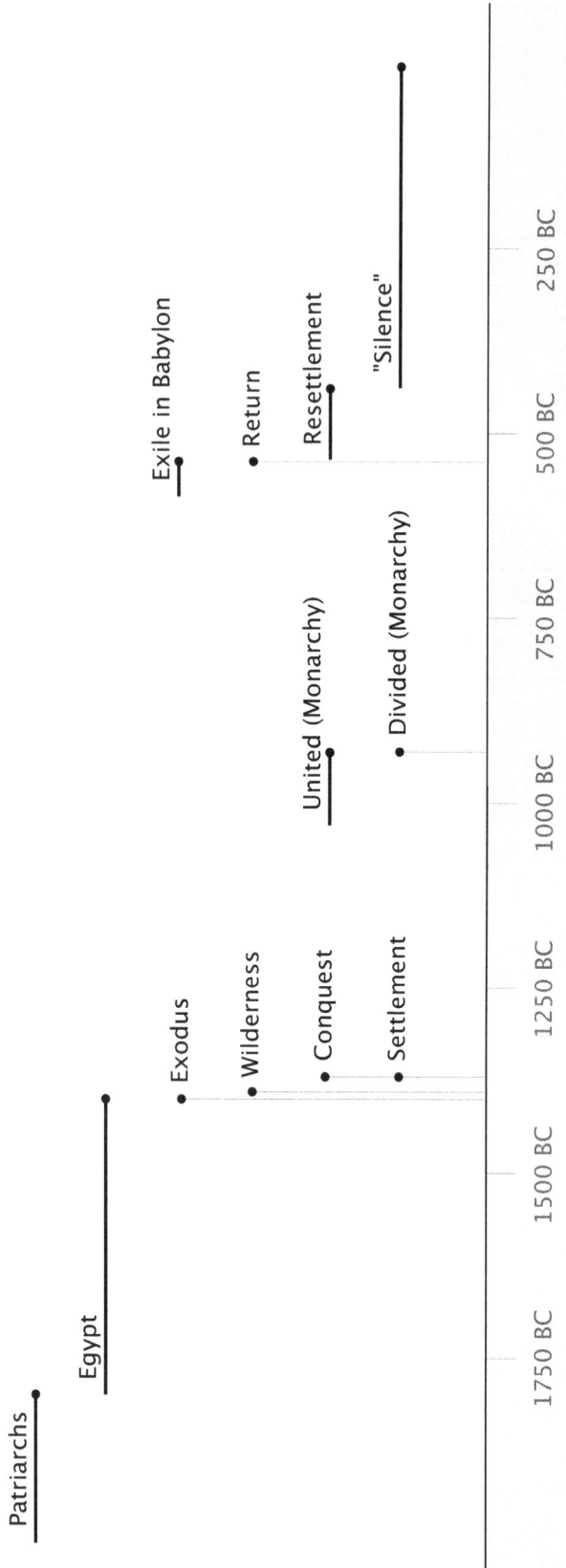

Patriarchs

Egypt

Exodus

Wilderness

Conquest

Settlement

United (Monarchy)

Divided (Monarchy)

Exile in Babylon

Return

Resettlement

"Silence"

| 1750 BC | 1500 BC | 1250 BC | 1000 BC | 750 BC | 500 BC | 250 BC |

The Books of the "Twelve Words":

Patriarchs: *Genesis 12-50*

Egypt: *Exodus 1-12*

Exodus: *Exodus 13-19*

Wilderness: *Exodus 19-40, Leviticus, Numbers, Deuteronomy*

Conquest: *Joshua*

Settlement: *Judges, Ruth, 1 Samuel 1-8*

United (monarchy): *1 Samuel 9-31
2 Samuel
1 Kg 1-11, 1 Chron.*

Divided (monarchy): *1 Kg 12-22, 2 Kings
2 Chronicles*

Exile: *2 Kings 25*

Return: *Ezra, Nehemiah*

Resettlement: *Ezra, Nehemiah*

"Silence":

E. Our "Old, Old Story" Isn't Old Enough!

    1. Three honest errors:

        a) We assume that because the Old Testament is a Hebrew story about the Jews that it is a "Jewish" book.

        b) Because Jews accept the Tankh and reject the New Testament, we assume that the New Testament is the "Christian" book—a sort of balanced equivalent of the Old Testament for Jews. In other words, we each have our "own" holy book.[1]

        c) Because Yeshua is the *centerpiece* of the Gospel, we assume that the description of him as *"the first and the last"* means the "old, old story" begins with Yeshua (cf. Rev. 1:18; 22:13-16).

        d) Yeshua tells us that he *is* the "hermeneutical key" to the Bible, but that the "old, old story" began much before Bethlehem (cf. John 5:39,45; 8:56; Luke 24:27,44; Matt. 5:17).[2]

    2. Yeshua tells us to study the Old Testament in light of what we now know about him and the Gospel:

> *And he said to them, "O foolish ones, and slow of heart to believe all that the prophets have spoken! Was it not necessary that the Christ should suffer these things and enter into his glory?" And beginning with Moses and all the Prophets, he interpreted to them in all the Scriptures the things concerning himself.*
>
> **Luke 24:25-27.**

        a) This gives the "big picture," creating one book, with one story broken into two "movements."[3]

        b) This provides us with a clearer sense of the purpose and direction of the Old Testament story.[4]

        c) This provides a "prophetic context" for the person and work of Yeshua the Anointed (I.e. the scope of his fulfillment).[5]

        d) It causes us to see ourselves in the same "old, old story" as King David, not Peter and Paul:

> *"Your father Abraham rejoiced that he would see my day. He saw it and was glad."*　　**John 8:56.**
>
> *"And if you are Christ's, then you are Abraham's offspring, heirs according to promise."*　　**Galatians 3:29.**

    3. A comprehensive, though not exhaustive list of the Old Testament's appearance and use in our four Gospels is in the Appendix Section. (scriptures are from the ESV)

UNIT 4: "The Bible's 'Blank Page'"

I.　THE BIBLE'S "BLANK PAGE"

A. Is Called The "Intertestamental Period" By Many Scholars[6]

    1. Is the time period between the voices of Malachi and John the Baptizer (c. 425 BC - 29 AD)

    2. Care must be given to to maintain the continuity of God's story, *not* insert an unbiblical "break." (God is actually fulfilling the Abrahamic covenant!)

---

1 This would be tragedy enough, except we unconsciously assume that what "really matters" began in the 1st century, *not* twenty centuries before that.

2 In John 17, Yeshua's prayer for "restored glory" goes back *prior* to the Incarnation, where the Story actually "began."

3 The physical divisions within our Bibles of chapters and verses were a product of the Enlightenment. They weren't even *in* our Bibles until the 15th century. Prior to that, it was *physically* more of a story than it is today.

4 When one begins to grasp the significance of all this, other things not only come into focus, but they take on a sense of meaning that is profound. For example, Jesus wept over Jerusalem when he entered it on Palm Sunday because *he* was the reason the city existed in the first place! That is what is behind his statement that he did not come to "abolish the Law and the Prophets, but to fulfill them." And as the Story unfolds, the Jewish authorities have Jesus put to death because they saw him as an *enemy* of their long and amazing history, when in fact, he was the intended culmination of it. And, we are no better when we separate *ourselves* from the history of the Jews (i.e. the Old Testament), because we do not see it as our own history.

5 The Tanakh was *not* merely Yeshua's Bible. And it also was *not* merely the history of his own people. The Scriptures are the Story of a massive and masterful plan of Yahweh to bring the reversal of Genesis 3 to humanity and all of Creation—to restore shalom—through Jesus. He, not they (or us!) was the whole point of their history!

6 "Blank Page" might be a much *better* descriptor because the "intertestamental" idea only serves to perpetuate a "two-testament" view of Scripture rather than a single narrative.

B. The Time Frame in Perspective

1. It is comparable to the length of the captivity in Egypt (c. 1840-1440 BC)

2. It is comparable to the period of the judges (c. 1406-1040 BC).

3. It is comparable to the length of the monarchy (c. 1040-586 BC).

4. *God* may have been "silent," but humanity certainly was not![1]

5. The truth is, all "roads" were leading to Bethlehem, not Rome.[2]

II. FOUR "HIGHWAYS" OF HEAVEN

A. **The Persian Period**: 536 – 330 BC

1. **539** – Cyrus of Persia conquered Babylon; his empire spread from India to Greece and from Egypt to the Caucasus Mountains.

a) Cyrus allowed conquered peoples to return, *with their gods,* to their native lands (the Jews brought back "utensils" but no images; Ezra 5:14!)

2. **536** – 1st group of Jews returned to Jerusalem (Daniel didn't!)

a) The Samaritans emerge as a distinct people group at this time (2 Kgs. 17:24,41; Ezra 4).

3. **525** – Cambyses conquers Egypt[3]; work on Jerusalem Temple stops due to Samaritan opposition.

4. **515** – the second Temple in Jerusalem is completed.

5. **480** – Greek navy destroys navy of Xerxes at Battle of Salamis (Esther is Queen of Persia)

6. **338** – Philip of Macedon and his son, Alexander, defeat Athens at the Battle of Arbela.

7. **336** – Darius III of Persia and Alexander ascend thrones.

8. **331** – Battle of Gaugemela ends the Persian Empire

B. **The Greek Period: 330 - 167 BC**

1. First time in history the "West" (i.e. Europe) was felt throughout the world.[4]

2. Alexander is called "the apostle of Hellenism" (even though he was not a Greek!):

a) He was educated by Aristotle.

b) He carried *The Illiad* and *The Odyssey* with him on campaigns.

c) He built the city of Alexandria in Egypt:

(1) its library was largest in the world

(2) the Septuagint was translated here

(3) Apollos (Paul's associate) was educated here (Acts 18:24)

(4) Stephen argued with Greek-Jews from here (Acts 6:9)

(5) both of Paul's ships to Rome were built here (Acts 27:6; 28:11)

(6) numerous "Church Fathers" taught here (Clement, Origen, Eusebius)

d) He brought Greek culture and the Greek language to the world.[5]

---

[1] For instance, during this "blank page" of *biblical* history, a flurry of human history was being forged. Among the people and events of this time window was the founding of Buddhism by Siddhartha Gautama, the founding of Jainism by Zao Tsu, the carving of the Rosetta Stone, the compiling of the Upanishads, the invention of parchment, the start of construction on China's Great Wall, the careers of Marc Antony, Cleopatra, and Caesar Augustus, and the exploits of the Carthaginian general, Hannibal, who took elephants over the Alps.

[2] God is quietly working in the midst of the din of human activity to create a "place" for Himself in the Incarnation.

[3] Cambyses actually called himself, "Son of Ra." Ra was one of the chief gods of the Egyptians.

[4] The "ripples" of this period on into our own lives in the present is impossible to over-emphasize. They're huge! *We* are more Aristotelian in our approach and interpretation of scripture than we are Hebraic. Paul himself is very "Greek" in his reasoning style in his letters.

[5] *God* didn't want the world to *be* Greek (like Alexander), but He did want the world to *know* Greek. Alexander's ambition was God's tool.

e) He paved the way for the notion of a "unified humanity."[1]

3. At his death in 323 BC the Empire was divided among his generals.

4. It was a period of constant conflict between the Seleucids (in Syria) and the Ptolemies (in Egypt).

5. Greek influence in Palestine hit an all time "high" (or *low*!) under the Seleucid ruler, Antiochus IV (aka Antiochus Epiphanes, "the illustrious"):

a) He was born and educated in Athens.

b) He spent 12 years as a hostage in Rome.

c) He had the passion to "Greek" the world, and a Roman sense of power and cruelty to "make it happen."

6. The descent into darkness:

a) He attacked Jerusalem on a sabbath.

b) He built a gymnasium, a theater, and a bathhouse in Jerusalem. (Greeks exercised naked).

c) He deposed the orthodox High Priest and appointed his own (a non Levite!)

d) He equated Yahweh with the Roman god, Jupiter. (Greek equivalent was Zeus)

e) He erected a statue of Jupiter on the Temple altar.

f) He sponsored pagan rituals in the Temple courts.

g) The drunken orgy of Bacchus was made compulsory.

h) Circumcision was made illegal upon penalty of death.

i) Sabbath and Jewish feasts were outlawed.

j) The Hebrew scriptures were destroyed.[2]

k) Pigs were sacrificed on the Temple altar.

7. Two factions solidified at this time, based on their association with Antiochus:

a) The Hasidim ("Pious Ones"— precursors to the Pharisees)

b) The Hellenists — precursors to the Sadducees.

C. **The Maccabean Period:** 167 – 63 BC

1. A rural priest and his 5 sons led a revolt against the paganism of Antiochus.

2. In 164 Palestine was retaken, the Temple cleansed and purified.

a) This became known as the Feast of Dedication (cf. Jn 10:22).

b) It is still celebrated as the Feast of Hanukkah.

3. Over time, the office of High Priest became increasingly political and corrupt.

a) On one occasion, a Priest/King murdered 800 Pharisees who had led a revolt.

b) During this time, one of the Priest/Kings named Hyrcanus had a powerful administrator named Antipater, who was the father of Herod the Great.

D. **The Roman Period:** 63 – 4 BC

1. In 63 BC, Pompey conquered Jerusalem and shattered the priestly dynasty that had controlled Palestine.

2. Antipater had supported Julius Caesar's part in Rome's war, and was given the title, "Procurator of Judea" in gratitude.

3. He appointed his 25-year old son, Herod, as ruler over Galilee.

---

[1] In 334 BC, Alexander crossed the Aegean and confronted a Persian army at the Granicus River in Western Asia (Turkey). He was near the point of being killed by a Persian horseman who had delivered such a shattering blow that it penetrated Alexander's helmet. As he was facing certain death, his friend, Clytus the Black rode in and either spared the Persian or cut off his arm. If this *hadn't* happened, Alexander would have gone down in history as a young and foolish king who reigned only 2 years and then died trying to overthrow Persia! The one moment during this one battle altered history forever.

[2] Antiochus was seeking to deny the Jews *both* their past *and* their future. "Modernity" and "progress" have been used throughout history to excuse cruelty.

4. In 37 BC, Herod formally conquered Jerusalem and established himself as "King of Judea."[1]

E. Herod the "Builder"[2]

1. Herod the Great is one of the most ambitious builders in antiquity.

2. In his 33 years as King, he built, enlarged or fortified a long list of cities and structures, including:

a) **Masada** – the desert fortress as old as King David on the SW coast of the Dead Sea.[3]

b) **Machaerus** – a citadel on the eastern side of the Jordan River; Josephus tells us that John was beheaded here.

c) **Jericho** – the legendary ancient city; he built an elaborate palace here.[4]

d) **Herodium** – another citadel 3 miles SE of Bethlehem:

(1) the only structure to bear his name

(2) had slaves "move" on hill on top of another!

(3) took four years to build (23-20 BC)

(4) upper and lower palaces; swimming pool for boats!

(5) used mirrors to signal from the Temple to here to Masada

(6) was Herod's burial site

e) **Caesarea** – one of the 2 largest ports in the Roman world[5]

(1) was an "anti-Jewish" city in every way possible; bath houses, theater, gymnasium, hippodrome, temples.

f) **Temple** – took 10,000 men ten years to complete.

(1) this 35-acre platform would hold 24-football fields.

(2) the "Wailing Wall" is what is left of the western side of this enormous "retaining wall" built to level the area.

g) **Caearea Philippi** – Roman city built by his son, Herod Philip

h) **Sephoris** – Roman city restored by Antipas; 4 miles from Nazareth; Made his capital.

i) **Tiberis** – pagan city built by his son Herod Antipas on the Sea of Galilee; made his capital instead of Sephoris.

F. Herod the "Butcher"[6]

1. Kept the vestments for the High Priest in a fortress in Jerusalem. He appointed the High Priests personally (after executing 46 members of the Sanhedrin!)

2. Arranged the drowning of his wife's brother, the execution of his "favorite" wife Miriam, and his own two sons.

3. On his deathbed, arranged for revolting Jewish leaders to be burned alive.

4. Arranged for the systematic execution of children under the age of two out of fear of news of another "King of the Jews." (Matt. 2:16).

5. Augustus purportedly said, *"It is better to be Herod's dog than his son!"*

---

[1] This is really the beginning of Herod's influence in Palestine that is associated with the Gospels and Acts, both dynastically *and* geographically.

[2] It would have been nearly impossible to have walked a "day's journey" (i.e. 20 miles) in any direction, without being confronted with the specter of Herod's shadow, cast by some magnificent building of his. His name is associated with at least 12 different building projects.

[3] Herod created reservoirs n the area and had slaves hand-carry water into the elaborate and enormous cisterns in Masada. There was actually more water at Masada (in the desert) than there was in the city of Jerusalem!

[4] Aristobulus, Herod's son, was drowned in the pool here. Herod had made him High Priest at age 17 and his growing popularity was seen as a political threat by Herod. In the last days of his life, Herod burned alive a large number of Jews who had torn down an idolatrous eagle he had erected.

[5] This building project is an excellent example of Herod's ability to "work both sides." He did a massive remodeling and expansion of the Jewish Temple in Jerusalem (Jews), and built this incredible man-made port on the Mediterranean coast and named it after Caesar, complete with a temple to Augustus in it! Caesarea could handle 200 ships, and was in effect, Jerusalem's "harbor."

[6] Herod's two besetting sins were (1) an addiction to pleasure, and (2) an addiction to power and a deep paranoia over losing it. Augustus is purported to have said, *"One would be better to be Herod's dog than to be his son."*

UNIT 5: The "Yeshua Road"

I.   GETTING AROUND IN THE GOSPELS

A. Yeshua's Life and Ministry

1. In the three years of Yeshua's ministry, he ministered in more than 20 specific towns and villages in seven different geographical regions: Judea, Samaria, Galilee, Iturea, Decapolis[1], Phoenicia[2], and Perea.

2. Yeshua's ministry saturated an area 150 miles from North to South:

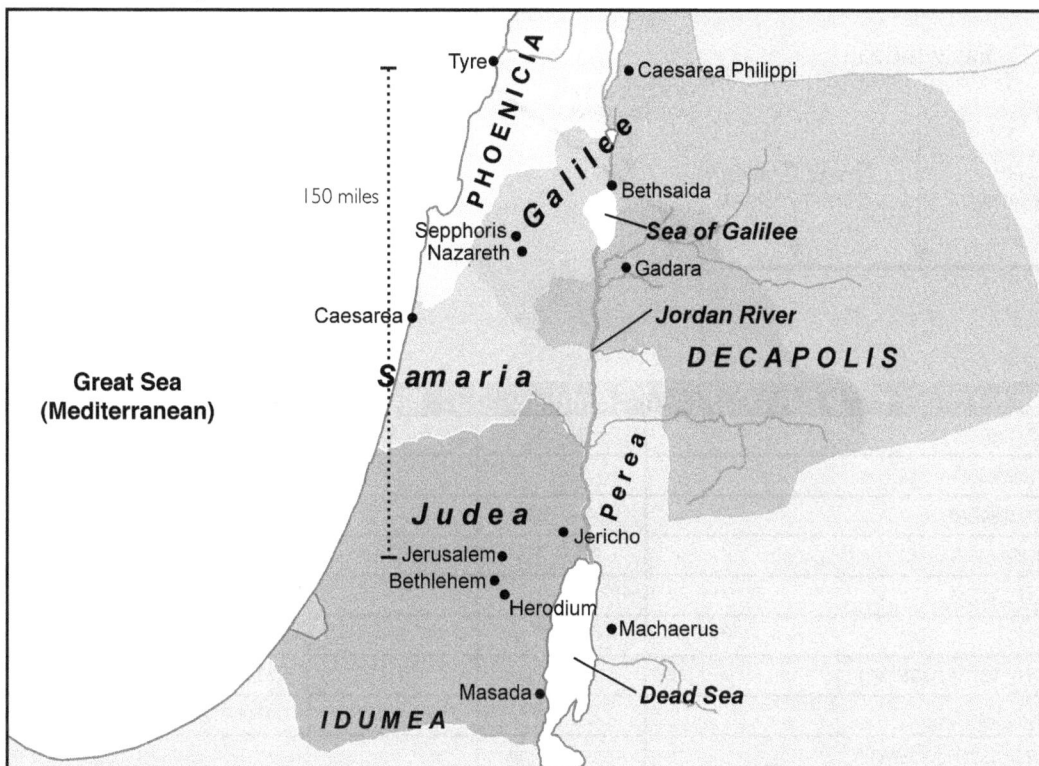

a) **Four Bodies of Water:** Sea of Galilee[3], Jordan River[4], Dead Sea, and the Mediterranean Sea.

b) **Five Geographical Regions:** Galilee, Samaria, Judea, Perea, and the Decapolis.

c) **Nine Cities:** Caesarea, Tyre, Sidon, Nazareth, Capernaum, Caesarea Philippi, and Jericho, Jerusalem, and Bethlehem.

---

1 The Decapolis (i.e. "10 cities") consisted of nine cities on the east side of the Jordan River, and one on the west side. The eastern cities included: Gerasa (in Jordan), Hippos (Syria), Gadara (Jordan), Pella (Jordan), Philadelphia (modern Amman, Jordan), Dion (Jordan), Raphana (Jordan), and Damascus (Syria). The western city was Scythopolis (Beth Shean in our Old Testament). It is likely that the "far country" that the prodigal wandered to in Luke's parable, was somewhere in the Decapolis.

2 Tyre and Sidon are two cities in this region. It was, in a very real sense, a totally Gentile area.

3 This body of water goes by multiple names in the four Gospels and the Old Testament. The Sea of Galilee (Matt 4:18), the Sea of Tiberius (Jn 21:1), Lake of Gennesaret (Luke 5:1), and the Sea of Chinnereth (Joshua 13:27). The Sea of Galilee was roughly 40,000 acres, or 62.5 square miles in area. It's dimensions are 13 miles by 7 miles, and it is 680' *below* sea level. By comparison, Lake Michigan is 22,400 square miles in area.

4 The Jordan River extends 75 miles from top to bottom, but consists of nearly 150 miles of waterway because of its circuitous path. And, today's river no longer flows all the way to the Dead Sea because water is siphoned off along the way for irrigation purposes.

UNIT 6: YESHUA IN FOUR DIMENSIONS

I.   THE "BIG PICTURE" OF Yeshua's LIFE AND MINISTRY

Yeshua's Life & Ministry

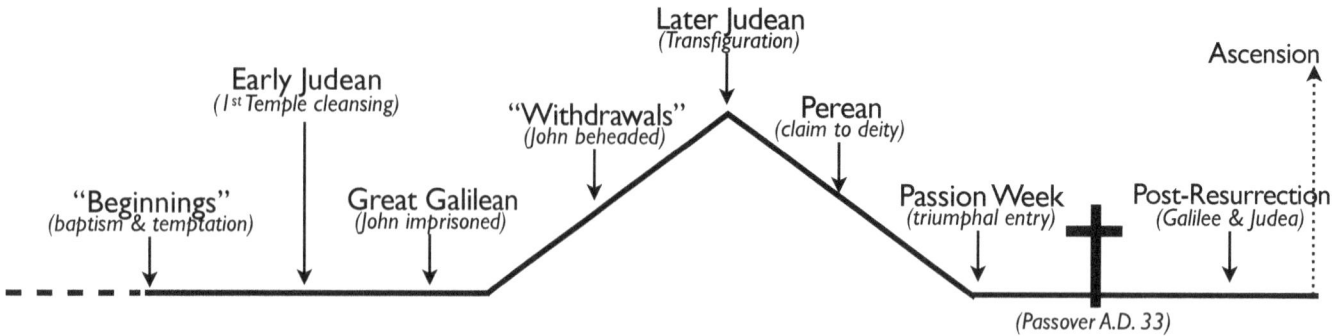

MINISTRY PERIOD	Matthew	Mark	Luke	John
Beginnings	1 – 4	1	1 – 4	1 – 2
Early Judean	–	–	–	2 – 3
Great Galilean	4 – 13	1 – 6	4 – 9	4*
"Withdrawals"	14 – 18	6 – 9	9	6
Later Judean	–	–	10 – 13	7 – 10
Perean	–	–	13 – 17	10 – 11
Journey to Jerusalem	19 – 20	10	17 – 19	–
Passion Week	21 – 27	11 – 15	19 – 23	12 – 19
Resurrection & Beyond	28	16	24	20 – 21

*chapter 5 contains brief trip to Jerusalem

II.   The Four Gospels: A "Collision" of Math and Literature

A. This is an ancient and on-going struggle:

1. Marcion – 2nd century heretic rejected all the Gospels except Luke.[1]
2. *Diatesseron* – 2nd century attempt by Tatian to "harmonize" the four Gospels by combining them.[2]
3. "The Jesus Seminar" – 20th century team of biblical researchers who "voted" on Yeshua's authentic sayings and deeds (15 & 10 respectively!)[3]

B. There are two primary ways scholars approach the four Gospel narratives:

1. By "addition" – 1+1+1+1 = 4 conflicting accounts
2. By "multiplication" – 1x1x1x1 = 1 complimentary composite

---

1 Marcion (c. A.D. 140-45) rejected the entire Old Testament. He developed his own list of accepted books which became known as the Marcionic Canon. From the four Gospels, he rejected all but Luke. He rejected Paul's Pastoral Epistles (Timothy and Titus) but accepted the remainder of Paul's writings. His final "canon" of Scripture ending-up being a highly reduced version of Luke's Gospel, and 10 of Paul's letters. He was condemned by the early Church.

2 Tatian's attempt is an excellent illustration of just how difficult it was to determine just what to *do* with the four Gospels. Keep them separate? Combine them? How do you go about harmonizing four distinct accounts that have more that is unique than the do in common? The parables of Jesus are a prime example. John has none! How do you present a "balanced" view of Yeshua's teaching without parables? These types of questions faced the early Church.

3 Our perspective on the Gospels is radically different from liberal scholars. We understand them to be God's final and most exquisite self-disclosure, *not* mere stories or biographies.

C. Some Foundational Building Blocks

1. We need to distinguish between *the* gospel and *a* Gospel.

  a) *The gospel* is the term we use for the body of truth surrounding God's work of redemption in Yeshua the Anointed (Rom. 1:16; Eph. 1:13).

  b) *A Gospel* is the term we use for one of four ancient documents accepted by the early Church as reliable records of the life of a real Yeshua.

2. We need to distinguish between the Gospels themselves.

  a) Matthew, Mark, and Luke though very different from each other, collectively are very different from John.

  b) These three Gospels are called the "Synoptic Gospels" (Gk *sunoptikos,* "together to see").

  c) Their similarities and differences make-up an entire field of study known as the "synoptic problem."

3. We need to anchor the Gospels in the redemptive purposes of God in the Incarnation.

  a) Each author, in his own style, sought to provide timeless answers to four crucial questions:*

   (1) "Who *was* this person?"

   Now it happened that as he was praying alone, the disciples were with him. And he asked them, "Who do the crowds say that I am?" **Luke 9:18.**

   (2) "Why was he rejected by his own people?"[1]

   Jesus answered them, "I have shown you many good works from the Father; for which of them are you going to stone me?" The Jews answered him, "It is not for a good work that we are going to stone you but for blasphemy, because you, being a man, make yourself God." **John 10:32-33.**

   (3) "What is *unique* about this man's death?"

   "Now is my soul troubled. And what shall I say? 'Father, save me from this hour'? But for this purpose I have come to this hour." **John 12:27.**

   (4) "What does this information have to do with *me*?"

   Pilate said to them, "Then what shall I do with Jesus who is called Christ?" **Matthew 27:22ᵃ.**

   Now when they heard this they were cut to the heart, and said to Peter and the rest of the apostles, "Brothers, what shall we do?" **Acts 2:37.**

   *adapted from: Frank Thielman's *Theology of the New Testament*, p. 181.

III. FOUR "PORTRAITS," OF ONE FACE

A. MATTHEW: The "Converted Crook"

1. Matthew was Jew, also known as "Levi" (Mark 2:14)

2. He was a "tax collector," who lived in Capernaum and worked for Rome.

3. Yeshua's "call" to him to be a disciple is recorded in all of the Synoptic Gospels.

4. It was at Levi's house (at a party he threw motivated by joy) that Yeshua made his famous statement about "coming for sinners and not for the righteous." (Lk 5:27-32; Matt. 9:9-12)

5. His name only appears where the names of the Twelve are given.

6. Matthew's Gospel contains over 30 references to wealth, money and taxes.

B. MATTHEW: The Kosher Gospel

1. Over 40% of the OT quotes in the four Gospels are in Matthew.

2. He cites 19 OT books, compared to 24 for the other three Gospels combined!

3. His Gospel is full of Jewish culture, but empty of explanations:

  a) Those in "the Seat of Moses" are to be obeyed (23:2ff)

  b) The commandments are to be observed (5:17-19; 23:23)

---

1 All four Gospel writers deal with this question. New Testament scholar, Frank Thielman holds that Jesus was killed because he *exceeded* their expectations for a Messiah, and they missed it.

    c)   Fasting, sacrifices and Sabbath are observed (6:16ff; 24:20)

    d)   The Temple tax is to be paid (17:24)

    e)   Yeshua's genealogy is traced to Abraham and arranged in rabbinic fashion (1:1ff).

    f)   He alone uses the phrase, "Kingdom of Heaven."[1]

    g)   There are 10 references to Yeshua as the "Son of David."[2]

C. **MATTHEW**: A Prophetic Book

    1.   There are nearly 30 references to prophecies being "fulfilled."[3]

    2.   It is the most "forward-looking" of the Gospels:

       a)   The "church" is mentioned as a divinely ordained entity with authority.

       b)   The "Great Commission" extends to "all nations." (28:19-20)

       c)   Yeshua's most extensive teaching on the "end times" is in this Gospel (ch. 24-25).

D. **MARK**: A "Chip Off The Old Rock"[4]

    1.   Mark had a very close association with Peter (e.g. "my son" in 1 Pet 5:13), even though not an apostle himself.[5]

    2.   The son of a wealthy Jerusalem family, cousin of Barnabas and traveled with Paul (Acts 12:12-14; 13:5).[6]

    3.   His Gospel opens with a statement almost identical to Peter's grand confession (cf. Matt. 16:16):

       The beginning of the gospel of Jesus Christ, the Son of God." **Mark 1:1**.

    4.   After John the Baptist, Peter is the first person to be introduced and his name is mentioned 21 times in this short Gospel (1:16).

    5.   Like Peter, this Gospel, even though the shortest, is *saturated* with action and passion:

       a)   The word "immediately" appears 40 times.

       b)   Unusual attention is given to Yeshua's emotions (e.g. compassion, anger, indignation, sorrow, tenderness, love; 1:41,43; 3:5; 8:12,33).

E. **LUKE**: The Grand, Gentile Gospel

    1.   He, like Mark, was a "non-apostle," but also a non-Jew!

    2.   His Gospel is the largest book in the NT, and combined with Acts, he is the major NT author.[7]

    3.   His Gospel is "grander" than the others:

       a)   Detailed birth narratives for John and Yeshua (i.e. names, dates, etc.; 1:5-2:52)

       b)   The only account of the ascension (24:50ff)

    4.   Luke's Gospel is the most "pastoral"

       a)   He gives detailed descriptions of individual people:

          (1)   His unique parables focus on people, *not* the "Kingdom" like Matthew.

          (2)   Zechariah and Elizabeth

          (3)   Elizabeth and Mary

---

1 The word "kingdom" appears 125 times in the four Gospels. But, Matthew alone uses the phrase "kingdom of heaven" (32x). The phrase, "kingdom of God" is used 4x by Matthew, 14x by Mark, 32x by Luke, and 2x in John.

2 Compared to 3 in Mark, 3 in Luke, and none in John.

3 Compared to 2 in Mark, 3 in Luke, and 6 in John.

4 Like Luke, Mark was not himself an apostle of Jesus.

5 Paul called Timothy his "son" (1 Tim 1:18; 2 Tim 2:1) and "my true child in the faith" (1 Tim 1:2); Paul uses this same phrase for Titus (Tit 1:4). In Peter's case, Mark may have been very *close* to Peter, "like a son," or perhaps Peter even led him to faith in Jesus.

6 This is the John (Mark) who was at the heart of a heated disagreement that erupted between Paul and Barnabas, and ultimately resulted in the two of them going separate ways at the onset of Paul's second missionary journey (Acts 15:36). Mark's mother, an obviously wealthy woman, had a large home within the city of Jerusalem. It was large enough for a large group to gather to pray for Peter's release from prison, and the presence of a servant indicates wealth as well (Acts 12:6-16).

7 This is typically not well known. Most Christians believe Paul was our primary contributor to the New Testament because of the larger number of books he wrote. But, in terms of actual words written, Luke is the clear leader, with Paul next in line.

        (4) Martha and Mary

        (5) Zacchaeus

   b) Luke gives the most attention to marginalized people:

        (1) The "woman of the city" (7:36-50)

        (2) The "transformation" of Zacchaeus (19:8-10)

        (3) The repentant thief on the cross (23:39-43)

        (4) Parables and stories of widows (7:11-17; 18:1-8)

        (5) He mentions 13 women not mentioned elsewhere.

        (6) Luke clearly highlights God's bias towards "the poor" and the rich's bias *against* them (4:17-21; 6:20, 24,30).

  5. Luke's Gospel is more "prayerful"

   a) 7 of the 9 prayers of Yeshua are unique to Luke.

   b) Three unique parables deal with prayer (11:5-13; 18:1-14)

   c) Luke alone records Yeshua's prayer for Peter (22:31-32), His first exhortation to pray in the garden (22:40), and His prayer on the cross (23:34).

F. **JOHN**: The Last Word on God's Final Word

  1. This is most likely the last Gospel written, penned by an aged apostle.

  2. John, like Matthew, writes to connect Yeshua to the Jews and their history.

  3. But, unlike Matthew, John highlights their *rejection* more than their association:

   a) 1:11 – Yeshua is rejected by "his own."

   b) 5:39 – the leaders are accused of "missing the point" of the entire Old Testament—him!

   c) 5:45 – Yeshua links true "Jewishness" (i.e. obeying Moses) with listening to him.

   d) 8:34-41 – Yeshua repeatedly appealed to and connected himself with Abraham (cf. 8:56-58).

   e) *"the Jews"* – A term John uses to refer to the leaders who rejected Yeshua (34 of his 63 uses are negative).

  4. John records more of Yeshua's theological teaching than the others:

   a) The role of the Holy Spirit in conviction, conversion, worship and guidance (e.g. Jn 3,4,14-16)[1]

   b) The relationship of the Son to the Father (of the 184 references to God as Father in the Gospels, 116 are here.)[2]

   c) John's Gospel has no parables. In fact, the *word* itself never appears (see chart on next page).

   d) The great "I AM" statements of Yeshua are in this Gospel:

        (1) *"I am the bread of life…"* (6:35,48,51)

        (2) *"I am the light of the world…"* (8:12; 9:5)

        (3) *"I am the gate of the sheep…"* (10:7,9)

        (4) *"I am the Good Shepherd…"* (10:11,14)

        (5) *"I am the resurrection and the life…"* (11:25)

        (6) *"I am the (only) way, the truth and the life…"* (14:6)

        (7) *"I am the true vine…"* (15:1,5)

        (8) *"I AM…"* (8;58-59 and Ex. 3:14)

  5. John records more of Yeshua's prayers, even though less of him actually praying (Jn 17).

IV. CONCLUSIONS

  A. We need to remind ourselves of the revelatory purposes of God in the Incarnation:

---

1 It is noteworthy that "truth" is a favorite word of John's, appearing 25 times in this Gospel, and an additional 20x in his three epistles. This stands in contrast to once in Matthew, twice in Luke, and three times in Mark.

2 Compared to 43 in Matthew, 5 in Mark and 20 in Luke.

1. The four Gospels are complimentary, but not comprehensive (Jn. 21:25).
2. Yeshua is God's final and fullest self-disclosure (Heb. 1:1-4; Jn 14:9).
3. We need to always be looking at Yeshua instead of the others in the "cast."
4. We need to be looking "beyond" Yeshua to the Father that He came to "exegete" (Jn. 1:14-18).

B. Four "Portraits" — One Face

1. In Matthew, we see a doubly "prophetic" Christ.
2. In Mark, we see a passionate and powerful Christ.
3. In Luke, we see a pastoral and prayerful Christ.
4. In John, we see a preeminent and priestly Christ.

UNIT 7: "IN THE BEGINNING"...

I. "IN THE BEGINNING...AND *BEFORE* THE BEGINNING"

A. The "Light Before Christmas"

1. John: An Eternal Son — John 1:1-18

   a) John tells us what was happening *in eternity* before Christmas.

   b) He uses Hebrew imagery from the book of Genesis:
      - *"in the beginning..."*[1]
      - creation
      - *"light and darkness"*

   c) John gives the "genealogy" of the eternal Son of God.[2]

   d) John gives us Incarnation, not merely "birth."[3]

2. Matthew: *"Yeshua the Messiah, the son of David the son of Abraham"*[4]

   a) Matthew and Luke give us the "human highway" to the Incarnation.[5]

   b) Matthew *begins* his Gospel with a genealogy, following the OT pattern of connecting significant people (e.g. Gen. 5,11; Ruth 4).[6]

   c) He draws a straight line from Yeshua to Abraham, but, he "names" the genealogy after Yeshua, *not* Abraham.

   d) He establishes "royal ancestry" for Yeshua through David, because his throne had ceased with the exile (1:1,20).[7]

   e) Matthew *appears* to give the legal genealogy of Yeshua through Joseph.

---

1 This is not only the opening line of the book of Genesis, it is also the actual Hebrew *name* of the book in the Torah.

2 John's "genealogy" actually *precedes* history. There's no mere baby at the end of his "genealogy"!

3 John uses Tabernacle language in his description of the Incarnation. The Greek verb, *skenaō* means "to pitch a tent." It is the word that is used extensively in the Greek version of the Hebrew Old Testament, the Septuagint, for the Tabernacle. All of this imagery is very, very "Jewish," but in this case it is for polemical purposes, *not* cultural purposes as with Matthew.

4 Matthew's genealogy provides us with 42 names in 16 verses.

5 Matthew and Luke give quite different genealogies. Their genealogies "split" after David. Matthew trades the line from Solomon, but Luke from Nathan. They were *both* sons of David by Bathsheba, but the royal dynasty was through Solomon. And, they each provide a different name for the father of Joseph, Mary's betrothed. Matthew names him Jacob, and Luke names him Heli. Some scholars posit that Matthew's genealogy passes through Joseph's family tree, and Luke's through Mary's. Other suggestions have been made, but the issue is not clear to us in the modern world.

6 The genealogy in Genesis 5 runs from Adam to Noah, and the next genealogy in Genesis 11 runs from Shem (Noah) to Abraham.

7 In a very real sense, *both* the Temple and the Palace were destroyed by the Babylonians. The "throne" never returned to Jerusalem, even though the Temple did.

  f) He breaks from Jewish custom by *including* four women in his genealogy, all of them associated with Gentiles (1:1-6)![1]

 3. Luke: *"Yeshua the son of Adam, the son of God"*[2]

  a) Luke's genealogy appears to be as much of an apologetic as a record:

   (1) He deliberately leaves out the four women, even though he knew about them (cf. 1:1-4).[3]

   (2) He sandwiches his genealogy between Yeshua's baptism and his temptation.

   (3) It stands between God's statement that Yeshua was His Son and Satan's challenge to that.

   (4) Luke uses the word "son" 146x in his Gospel; 80 of them are in this "sandwich"!

   (5) He seems to rearrange the three temptations so that this story opens and closes with Satan's challenge, *"if you are the son of God…"*

B. Heavenly Heralds: The Births of John and Yeshua[4]

 1. Both announcements were saturated with the supernatural:

  a) Both conceptions were announced by Gabriel, an angel known from the Book of Daniel (Dan. 8:16; 9:21; 10:21).[5]

  b) Zechariah's selection to offer incense was determined 1,000 years earlier by King David, and was a once-in-a-lifetime privilege (1 Chron. 24).[6]

  c) Zechariah's muteness substantiated his "story."[7]

  d) Neither woman *should* have been pregnant (Lk. 1:18,24)![8]

  e) God's "choices" defied human reason: an aged wife of a rural priest[9] (Lk. 1:23,39,65) and a Galilean peasant.

 2. Both accounts involve *amazing* believers:

  a) Zechariah, Elizabeth and Joseph are all said to have been "righteous" (Gk = *dikaios*) before the Lord (Luke 1:5-6; matt. 1:18-19).

---

8 This is as significant as Luke's omission of their names. Especially because Tamar and Rahab were both Canaanites, and Ruth was a Moabite. Matthew could just have easily used their fathers' names, like Luke did. For a Jew to include them points clearly to authorial purpose. And again, we are left with little more than speculation on our part as to why. But, with the combined oddities of Luke's omission and Matthew's inclusion of these four names, we have a powerful illustration of how authorial purpose trumps simplistic modern criticisms of the Bible in other places.

2 Luke's list consists of 75 names packed into the same number of verses as Mathew.

3 This had to be intentional. Luke was a "champion" for women, writing more about them than any of the other Gospel writers. His omission of their names must have fit his purposes.

4 Angels appear frequently in the four Gospels. Luke contains the most angelic activity with 24 references, Matthew has 19 (4 to Joseph alone). and Mark has 5.

5 Not only is Gabriel "well known" among the Jews, but his name is associated with the book of Daniel, a very messianic book. The fact that Gabriel is the message-bearer in both of these announcements points to something huge on the horizon. Something that will likely be messianic.

6 This is one of the most hidden, yet amazing details in the birth narratives of Luke's Gospel. A thousand years before this time, David set up an incredibly detailed template for worship and service in the Temple, even though Yahweh had forbidden him to build it. One of the things he did was to establish "courses" or lists of priests that would serve in the Temple rituals at set times during the year. The course of Abijah to which Zechariah belonged, was the 8th of 24 courses. About 50 priests served at any given time. The various roles were determined by casting lots. Lots were drawn to see who: cleaned off the altar, offered the morning sacrifice, and offer incense. The offering of incense was limited to once in a lifetime. The incense offerer was allowed to pick two priestly relatives to assist him. The first would clean off the coals and worship, always facing the Holy of Holies as he left the area. The second would put new coals on and light the fire. Zechariah would have offered the incense and prayers. Because of the word used to describe Zechariah's age, we can assume that he's around 60 years old. This means he's been going up to Jerusalem for a lifetime, and serving as a priest for about 30 years. What Zechariah was doing that day was a terrifying thing. People had been killed by Yahweh in the past for getting it wrong, or disregarding God's instructions (cf. Num 16:35; Lev. 10:1).

7 This is even more significant than meets the eye because Zechariah was *supposed* to pronounce the Aaronic blessing (Num 6:24-27) over those who had gathered and were waiting for him to come out of the Holy Place. His tardiness would have been eclipsed by his muteness. Instead of a priestly blessing, he could only make gestures and likely grunt. Those gathered *knew* something monumental had happened inside the Holy Place. What was typical and routine suddenly took on significance. Zechariah's once-in-a-lifetime opportunity had grown into a once-in-a-lifetime experience for everyone gathered that day to serve Yahweh. All fifty of them!

8 One was too old, the other too young.

9 The two main priestly "centers" in that day were Jericho and a section of Jerusalem known as Ophel. Zechariah would have been viewed with less respect than the "city priests."

b) Joseph chose *not* to "make an example" (Gk = *deigmatzō*) of Mary, even though he had a right to (Deut. 22:22).[1]

c) Mary's character is shown in the *opposite* results of her obedience to that of Zechariah and Elizabeth:

    (1) She nearly lost her pending marriage (Matt. 1:18-19).

    (2) The shame within her community was inevitable and inescapable (cf. John 8:39,41).[2]

d) Mary's public shame was transformed to honor as the story unfolded:[3]

    (1) The angelic rebuke of Joseph (Matt. 1:20-25).

    (2) The angelic announcement to the shepherds and the angelic choir (Lk. 2:8-20).

    (3) The testimonies of Simeon and Anna (Lk 2: 25-38).

    (4) The worship of the Magi (Matt. 2:1-12).

    (5) Herod's massacre (Matt. 2:1-18).

C. Hell's Howl: The Herods

  1. Prior to the "flight" to Egypt, Hell itself was paying its own "tribute":

    a) Magi visit (c. Feb, 4BC)

    b) Two revered rabbis and zealots are burned alive by Herod at Jericho (March).

    c) Massacre of the infants (March)

    d) Herod executes his son, Antipater (March)

    e) Jewish nobility incarcerated in hippodrome of Jericho, awaiting mass execution (March); (They were later freed.)[4]

    f) Herod changes will for 4th time, making Archaelus king (April).

    g) Herod dies, and Archaelus slaughters 3,000 Jews in the Temple area (April).[5]

    h) Mary and Joseph go to Nazareth from Egypt around this time (Matt. 2:19-23).

D. Yeshua & John: Lots of Years, Very Little "Ink"

  1. Matthew tells us nothing personal about Yeshua from his birth to his baptism (cf. 2:19-23 and 3:13).[6]

  2. Luke tells us about Yeshua's childhood, but nothing about the trip to Egypt:

    a) He grew in stature and strength (2:40,52).

    b) He matured in wisdom (2:40,52).

    c) His *outward* life was noteworthy (i.e. "righteous")[7] (2:52).

    d) He traveled to Jerusalem for nearly 20 Passovers (cf. 2:41 with 3:23).

    e) Yeshua's first trip to Jerusalem is the only "break" in the silence of his first thirty years (Luke 2:41-51).

    f) Both Matthew and Luke *intentionally* omit Yeshua early years, showing this is *not* a biography.[8]

  3. Nazareth in Galilee is where Yeshua spent his first 30 years (Matt. 2:22-23; Mark 1:9; Luke 2:39-40,51).

---

1 Joseph's character here stands in stark contrast to that of the religious leaders in John's Gospel who not only publicly humiliated the "woman caught in adultery," but were seeking her death.

2 There is even some evidence that Jesus was considered something of a "bastard" child by the religious leaders in Jerusalem. In one comment, there's a bit of a cryptic assault on Yeshua's parentage, *"...We were not born of sexual immorality..."* (John 8:41) in a chapter that deals intensely with Yeshua's relationship to Yahweh as his "Father."

3 It is clear that whatever others thought of the virginal conception, Mary certainly *never* saw it as a shameful thing. Rather, it was an honor for her to birth the Messiah. This is evident in her amazing song of praise, what we call "The Magnificat" in Luke 1:46ff.

4 We are told by historians that Herod's motivation for slaughtering the Jewish nobles was to make sure there was weeping on the day of his death. He feared the city would celebrate when he died.

5 Archaelus' ruled 4 BC - AD 6.

6 Even Matthew's birth narrative is cryptic — one verse!

7 In order to "grow in favor with men" in a first century Jewish culture, one would have to be righteous in character and conduct. Simply being the "best carpenter in Nazareth," or having the best ACT score in the local Jewish yeshiva (school) wouldn't have cut it back then! This short statement tells us volumes about Yeshua's visible, quantifiable life.

8 Children were a "big deal" in Jewish life. Of the 3,100 references to "sons, daughters, children" in our Bible, roughly 2,900 of them are in the Old Testament. The Jews had 8 *different* stages in a child's life, each designated by a different Hebrew word. *Yeled* was a newborn (Is. 9:6), *Yoneq* was a suckling (Is. 11:8), *Olel* was a suckling who also ate solids (Lam 4:4), *Gamul* was a weaned child (Is 28:9), *Taph* was a child who still clung to his mother (Jer 40:7), *Elem* was a child becoming "firm," *Naar* was sthe word for a child who was more independent ("the lad," "one who shakes himself free"), and *bachar* which meant "the ripened one," that last stage of childhood.

4. He was the *son* of a "laborer" *(not a carpenter; Gk = tekton)* and a laborer himself (Matt. 13:55; Mark 6:3).

5. Yeshua's step-father, Joseph, had been a faithful Jewish man. Every father was expected to:
    a) Circumcise his son.
    b) Redeem his firstborn son.
    c) Teach his son Torah.
    d) Teach his son a trade.

6. John: A Second Elijah *(see chart on following page)*
    a) John begins his ministry unannounced, like Elijah (Matt. 3:1; 1 Kgs 17:1).
    b) John dresses like Elijah (Matt. 3:4; 2 Kgs 1:8).
    c) John is uncompromising in courage and conviction, like Elijah (Matt. 3:7ff and 1 Kgs 18:17ff).
    d) John's baptism is "outlandish"; only converts to Judaism were baptized!
    e) John's ministry environment matched his message: harsh and uncomplicated.

7. John: The Expendable Servant[1]
    a) John's popularity was unprecedented for 400 years!
    b) Twenty years after his death, his disciples were found 500 miles from Jerusalem, in the Asian city of Ephesus (Acts 19:1-7)!
    c) John's baptism of Yeshua is unique:
        (1) It provides us with the only recorded conversation between two relatives who dearly loved one another (Matt. 3:13-15).
        (2) It appears to be a baton-passing ceremony of sorts.
        (3) In a very real sense, it marks the "end" of John and the "beginning" of Yeshua.
        (4) In The Wilderness: Yeshua the Last Adam
            (a) Yeshua, unlike Adam, faced Satan in a state of physical exhaustion.
            (b) Yeshua, unlike Adam, faced Satan in an environment of barren hostility.
            (c) Yeshua, like Adam, had no sin nature.
            (d) Yeshua, like Adam, chose for all humanity (cf. Rom. 5:14; 1 Cor. 15:21-22).
            (e) Yeshua, like Adam, was faced with the question of whose will would be served.
            (f) Satan's strategy was the same for both:
                i)   Question God's word:
                    (1) *"Did God say…"* (Gen. 3:1)
                    (2) *"If you are the son of God (as He said)…"* (Lk. 4:3,9).
                ii) Make *myself* the subject of God's Word rather than God Himself:
                    (1) *"He will command his angels concerning **you**, On their hands they will bear **you** up, lest you strike **your** foot against a rock."* – **Ps. 91:11,12**
                    (2) He omitted verse 9, *"Because you have made the LORD your dwelling place—the Most High, who is my refuge—"*
            (g) Yeshua's victory was the result of faithfulness to the will and Word of God.[2]
            (h) Yeshua began *and* ended his earthly ministry with the same prayer and conviction, *"Not my will, but thine be done…"*

---

[1] It is noteworthy that Luke devotes nearly as much ink to John's *parents* as he does to John! (1,035 words versus 1,185 words, respectively). Mark has 651, Matthew 1,117, and John 795.

[2] Yeshua's mastery of Torah is shown in this encounter. All three of his responses to Satan were citations from Deuteronomy, from memory in the face of extremity.

JOHN THE BAPTIZER

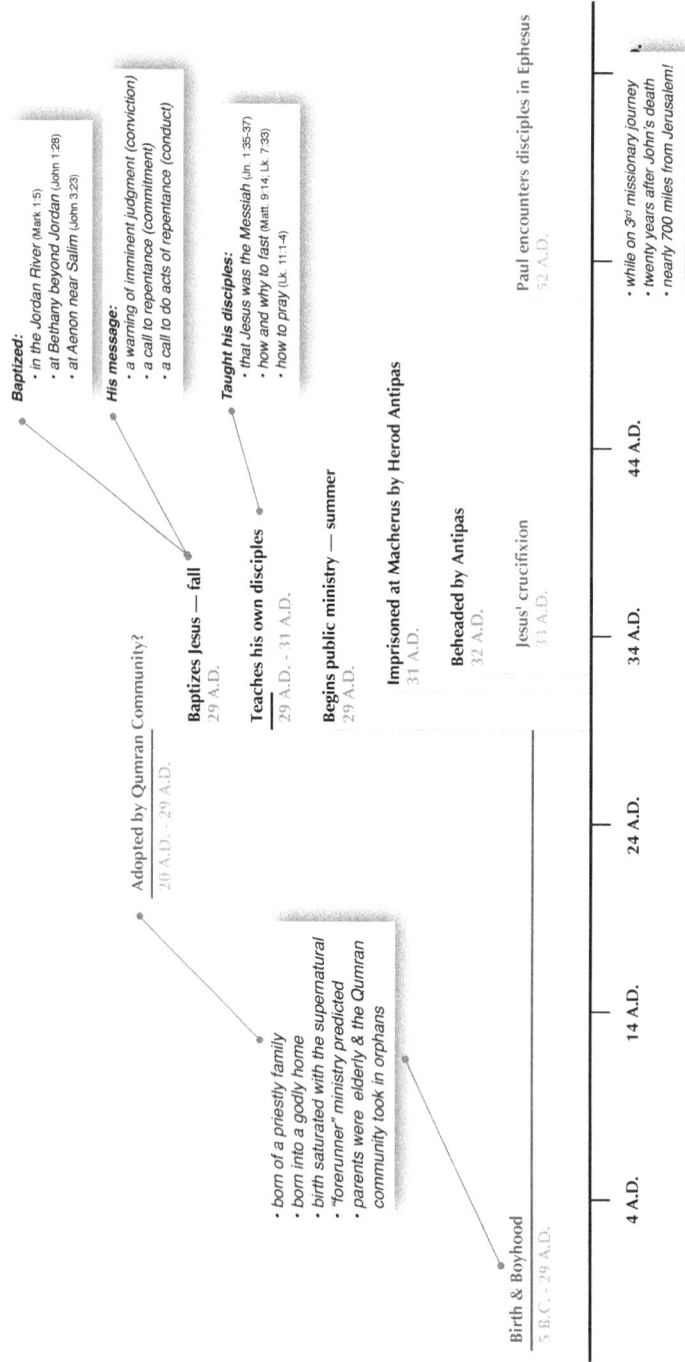

Birth & Boyhood
5 B.C. - 29 A.D.

- born of a priestly family
- born into a godly home
- birth saturated with the supernatural
- "forerunner" ministry predicted
- parents were elderly & the Qumran community took in orphans

Adopted by Qumran Community?
20 A.D. - 29 A.D.

Baptizes Jesus — fall
29 A.D.

Teaches his own disciples
29 A.D. - 31 A.D.

Begins public ministry — summer
29 A.D.

Imprisoned at Macherus by Herod Antipas
31 A.D.

Beheaded by Antipas
32 A.D.

Jesus' crucifixion
33 A.D.

Baptized:
- *in the Jordan River* (Mark 1:5)
- *at Bethany beyond Jordan* (John 1:28)
- *at Aenon near Salim* (John 3:23)

His message:
- *a warning of imminent judgment (conviction)*
- *a call to repentance (commitment)*
- *a call to do acts of repentance (conduct)*

Taught his disciples:
- *that Jesus was the Messiah* (Jn. 1:35-37)
- *how and why to fast* (Matt. 9:14; Lk. 7:33)
- *how to pray* (Lk. 11:1-4)

Paul encounters disciples in Ephesus
52 A.D.

- *while on 3rd missionary journey*
- *twenty years after John's death*
- *nearly 700 miles from Jerusalem!*

4 A.D. 14 A.D. 24 A.D. 34 A.D. 44 A.D.

UNIT 8: *"He Must Increase…"*

I. "BEGINNINGS" — Overview

Event in the Gospels	Matthew	Mark	Luke	John
"genealogy" of the Eternal Son	—	—	—	1:1-5
genealogy of Yeshua of Nazareth	1:1-17	—	3:23-38	—
angelic announcement to John's father	—	—	1:5-25	—
angelic announcement to Mary	—	—	1:26-38	—
Mary visits Elizabeth	—	—	1:39-56	—
birth & early years of John	—	—	1:57-80	—
angelic announcement to Joseph	1:18-25	—	—	—
birth of Yeshua	—	—	2:1-7	(1:14ᵃ)
angelic announcement to shepherds and their visit	—	—	2:8-20	—
circumcision of Yeshua and his presentation in the Temple	—	—	2:21-38	—
visit of magi	2:1-12	—	—	—
flight to Egypt; Herod's massacre	2:13-18	—	—	—
journey from Egypt to Nazareth	2:19-23	—	—	—
childhood in Nazareth			2:39-40	
special Passover story at age 12	—	—	2:41-50	—
18 "quiet years" in Nazareth	—	—	2:51-52	—
John the Baptist begins his ministry	3:1-12	1:1-8	3:1-18	(1:6-8)
Yeshua is baptized by John	3:13-17	1:9-11	3:21-23	—
Yeshua is tempted in the wilderness	4:1-11	1:12-13	4:1-13	—
John the Baptizer's "confession"	—	—	—	1:19-34
Yeshua's first five disciples	—	—	—	1:35-51
Yeshua's first "sign" (i.e. miracle)	—	—	—	2:1-11

II. "BEGINNINGS PART II — John 1:15 – 2:12

A. "Full Calendar" — A Busy Week

1. Day 1: John's "confession" to "the Jews" (1:19-28).
2. Day 2: John's profession before the crowds (1:29-34).
3. Day 3: John's persuasion of his own disciples (1:35-3).

    Two of John's disciples transfer allegiance to Yeshua (1:37-39).

4. Day 4: Andrew, the first evangelist (1:40-42).
5. Day 5: Yeshua makes the "call" — Philip (1:43-51).
6. Day 6: travel?
7. Day 7: wedding in Cana (2:1-11).

B. The World *Behind* the Text

1. *"…priests and Levites from Jerusalem"* (1:19)

  a) John's *parents* were both from priestly families (Lk 1:5).

  b) John was *immensely* popular:

    "Then Jerusalem and all Judea and all the region about the Jordan were going out to him…" **Matthew 3:5**

  c) John was immensely *unorthodox—baptizing Jews!* (Luke 3:7ff).

  d) This is the only place in all four Gospels were the Levites are mentioned.

e) John *never* mentions "scribes," "Sadducees" or "Herodians."

f) It is very *likely* (though not certain) that this first group contained scribes[1] and Sadducees.

2. *"Pharisees (from Jerusalem)…"* (1:24)

    a) They were "major players" in the "Yeshua story" *(i.e. the four Gospels)*:

•*"priest"* - 97x (total)	•*"chief priests"* - 54x	•*"Sadducees"* - 9x
•*"Pharisee"* - 89x	•*"high priest"* - 29x	•*"Herodians"* - 3x
•*"scribe"* - 59x	•*"elders"* - 24x	•*"Zealot"* - 3x (all the same man, Simon)

    b) Their heritage:[2]

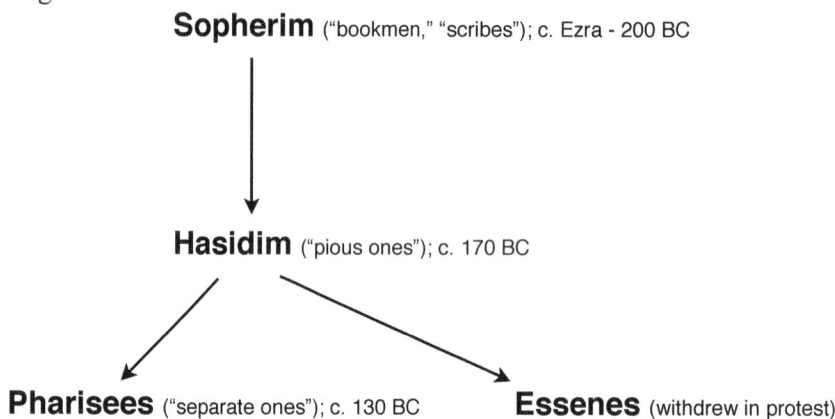

Sopherim ("bookmen," "scribes"); c. Ezra - 200 BC

↓

Hasidim ("pious ones"); c. 170 BC

Pharisees ("separate ones"); c. 130 BC   **Essenes** (withdrew in protest)

    c) Their influence:

        (1) The most populous and popular of the various groups. [3]

        (2) "Middle class" in status, between peasants and aristocracy; were scattered throughout the land (cf. Lk 5:17).

    d) Their theology

        (1) Meticulous observance of the Law[4] (Lk. 11:39-42).

        (2) Conservative, protective, and devotional; wanted to please Yahweh and protect His word.

        (3) Believed in, and adhered to the "Oral Law," (i.e. *"the traditions of the elders"*; cf. Matt. 15:1-2).[5]

---

1 Scribes are frequently mentioned in the context of our religious groups and individuals (e.g. "scribes and Pharisees" - Matt 5:20; "chief priests and scribes" - Matt 20:18; "scribes and elders" - Matt 26:57)

2 The Essenes are never mentioned in the Bible. Our knowledge of them comes from outside sources, especially the community living at Qumram, where the Dead Sea Scrolls were discovered.

3 Josephus puts their number at roughly 6,000. They were the religious conservatives, committed to protecting the Law. It is likely as evangelicals we would have been in this group.

4 An excellent example of this is the regulations that grew out of trying to properly apply and obey the Law regarding the sabbath. How far can someone walk on the sabbath? The result was the creation of a "sabbath's day journey," the distance one could walk on the sabbath without "breaking" the sabbath (i.e. violating the Law of Moses). The distance was set at 2,000 cubits, or about 3,000 feet. This number was arrived at using a complicated application of how far the Tabernacle was from the people of Israel as per instructions in the book of Joshua! A "sabbath's day journey" appears to be roughly the distance from Jerusalem to the Mount of Olives. This is significant in that it would have allowed Jesus to honor the Law during Passion Week.

5 "The traditions of the elders" (i.e. the oral Law) as a whole, was seen as a "fence" around the Law, to protect it.

A page from Babylonian Talmud's nearly 6,000 pages. The actual scripture passage is in the small box. The rest is commentary. (c. 500 AD)

"The words of the scribes are lovely beyond the words of the law; for the words of the law are weighty and light, but the words of the scribe are all weighty."
[Hierus. Berac. fol. 3]

3. Sadducees: a Small Group With An Enormous Influence
   a) Everything we know about them comes from their *opponents*; they left no writings. (Acts 23:6-8)
   b) They are almost always associated with Temple leadership (cf. Acts 4:1; 5:17).
   c) They were urban, wealthy aristocrats.
   d) They were distinct from, and antagonistic towards Pharisees. In fact, there was a history of "bad blood" between these two groups (cf. Acts 23:6-8).
   e) Their theology was the *opposite* of the Pharisees and the common people (Acts 23:8).
      (1) They *denied* the resurrection of the dead.[1]
      (2) They *denied* the existence of anything beyond the material world.
      (3) They *denied* the authority of the "Oral Law."
4. Essenes — The First "Monastics"
   a) A group attested to by Roman (Pliny[2]) and Jewish (Josephus) historians, but not mentioned in our Bibles.
   b) Ascetics committed to simplicity, purity, community and austerity.
   c) Very possibly, John the Baptist was associated with this group:
      (1) He came "out of the wilderness" preaching (Lk 1:80).
      (2) Area around Qumran was likely an Essene community.

---

1 The apostle Paul played on this facet of their theology when he was being questioned before the Sanhedrin in Jerusalem. He cried out, *""Brothers, I am a Pharisee, a son of Pharisees. It is with respect to the hope and the resurrection of the dead that I am on trial."* (cf. Acts 23:6-7)
2 Pliny accompanied the Roman general Titus in AD 70 in his attack on Jerusalem. Pliny spoke of the Essenes living in Qumran. What we know about the residents of Qumran comes largely from the Dead Sea Scrolls that were discovered in the caves nearby. They lived rigorous and austere lives characterized by disciplined living and punishment for non-compliance. The Dead Sea Scrolls inform us about their diets, their rituals, etc. They refused to visit Jerusalem and rejected the legitimacy of the High Priest. Initiates were subjected to a year-long probationary period before they were allowed entrance into the community, or allowed to eat the communal meals. They were also apparently bee-keepers and raised honey.

(3) He baptized near Qumran (Jn. 1:28).

(4) He was likely "orphaned" young (cf. Lk 1:5ff).

(5) His "style" fits this group (e.g. Mk 1:6; documents in Qumran indicate that locusts were a dietary item).

5. Scribes: The Last Word

   a) *Not* a religious or political group; more of a professional guild.

   b) Very influential because they were the "treasurers of knowledge" in an oral/illiterate culture (I.e. they could read and write, which put them in a place of incredible power and possible abuse and deception).

   c) They contributed to Midrash, the oral commentary on Scripture which eventually became part of the "oral Law."

6. Bethsaida — The "House of Fishing"[1]

   a) David's "princess bride," Maacah, came from this area (2 Sam. 3:3).

   b) Absalom fled here after killing his half-brother, Amnon, and lived with his grandfather for three years (2 Sam. 13:37).

   c) The (original) home of Andrew, Peter and Philip (Jn, 1:44).

   d) Yeshua healed a blind man outside this city (Mk. 8:22-26).

   e) It was one of the three cities that saw "most of Yeshua mighty works," yet were cursed by him! (Matt. 11:20-24).

   f) Herod Philip rebuilt it and renamed it after the Emperor's daughter, Julia. He was also buried here.

   g) Josephus, the priestly Pharisee and military commander, fought against Rome here (c. 66 AD).

7. "Cana of Galilee…"[2]

   a) Mentioned only by John (3x) in all the NT, and always as "Cana in Galilee."[3] (2:1; 4:46; 21:2).

   b) A town about 8 miles north of Nazareth; an obscure place.

   c) Yeshua's first miracle is done here[4]:

     (1) Yeshua saved the groom's family from great embarrassment, and even perhaps great cost.[5]

     (2) The water he used for this "sign" had been set apart for "holy" purposes to begin with (Jn. 2:6).[6]

     (3) He may have given the new couple a "wedding gift" by means of the excess wine![7]

     (4) Yeshua makes a clear "break" with his mother (Jn. 2:3-5; John never calls her by name in his Gospel!).

     (5) Four of his five disciples "believe" because of this "sign."[8] (cf. 1:50 and 2:11).

C. The World *Of* The Text

1. *"the world" — kosmos* - (John 1:29)

   a) John uses this word 105x in his writings; 78x in this Gospel.

   b) By comparison: Matthew - 8, Mark - 3, Luke - 3

---

1 The city of Geshur in the Old Testament is located in this area.

2 The Jewish general who eventually became one of our most extensive sources of information for first century Palestine, Josephus, made his home in Cana. When the Romans began their assault on Palestine which would eventually end with the destruction of the Temple and Jerusalem, and Masada to the south of Jerusalem, they began in Galilee at a place called Gamla in AD 66. Josephus was a general at that battle and eventually surrendered to the Romans. It is a rather unknown fact that more Jews committed suicide at Gamla than did at Masada four years later.

3 Some scholars believe there may have been more than one city by this name, and this was a distinguishing detail.

4 John never actually uses the word "miracle" to describe the works of Jesus. Instead, he uses the word "sign." John is always "pointing" his readers to Yeshua's identity. His use of the miracles must be framed within this intention.

5 The party in question would have been at the home of the groom.

6 The Jews purified themselves always. In this case, there was no way to know for sure where the food had all come from. The water used for the wine was for miqveh, the ceremonial bathing/hand-washing that Jews performed.

7 Wine was typically diluted 3:1, so depending upon whether the jars were "two measure" or "three measure," the total wine yield would have been between 420 - 630 liters, or in modern terms between 600-820 bottles! However, we need to remember that a Jewish wedding was a 7-day feast, so this was *not* a drunken orgy similar to a Dionesian or Bacchus festival.

8 Nathaniel had already confessed belief in Jesus as Messiah in John 1:47-50.

      c)   *Kosmos* can mean a "place" (e.g. John 3:17; 16:33 - *"in the world you will have tribulation…"*).

      d)   But, it most often points to a "perspective" (i.e. an ideology).

      e)   *"the world"* is human society seeking to exclude God (cf. 1 Jn 4:4-6; 2:15-17).

  2.   *"the Jews"* — (1:19)

      a)   71 of the 78 uses of this phrase in the Gospels are John.

      b)   It is *not* an "anti-Semitic" Gospel!

      c)   This is John's term for the Jewish version of the *"kosmos,"* those opposed to Yahweh's Messiah. This opposition most frequently came from the *leaders* of the Jews in Jerusalem.

  3.   *"witness"* - *"marturia"* or *martureō-* (1:6 contains both the noun and verb form)

      a)   John uses these words more than any NT writer (47x).

      b)   By comparison: Matt. - 1, Mark - 3, Luke - 2

      c)   It means a *"report"* or *"to be a report"* of something you know to be true.

      d)   It is the root of our English word, "martyr," but it's use in our New Testament is devoid of this focus on death and dying. The focus is on "speaking" or "pointing" to something that is known.

  4.   *"follow me"* — *akoloutheō* – John 1:43

      a)   John uses this phrase more than the other Gospels (18x).

      b)   The word includes an ancient Greek word for "road."

      c)   It carries the meaning of being on the same journey, *not* being behind someone (cf. Amos 3:3).

D. The World Around & Before the Text

  1.   *"Who are you?"* (John 1:19)

      a)   John's identity was rooted in his conviction of who he *wasn't*! (John 1:20-22).

      b)   John made absolutely sure *they* knew what he knew about himself:

          (1) The "awkward" 3-verb statement in verse 20 (*"He confessed, and did not deny, buy confessed, I am not the Christ."*).

          (2) Terse answers with no self-disclosure.

          (3) Quoted Scripture for his identity.

      c)   John had no identity, no purpose, and no mission apart from Yeshua.

          (1) He was a "voice," but *not* "the Word"; a messenger, but *not* the "message." In short, he was a *marturia.*

          (2) He was less than the servant of a disciple of a rabbi:

              "Every service which a slave performs for his master shall a disciple do for his teacher, except the loosing of his sandal thong."

  2.   *"Andrew…first found his brother."* (Jn.1:40-41)

      a)   Every time Andrew appears in John's Gospel, he is bringing someone to Yeshua (Peter, boy with a lunch, Greeks at the feast: Jn. 1:40-41; 6:8; 12:22).

  3.   In John's Gospel, Yeshua's "glory" is first revealed at a wedding in an obscure village, yet he omits the Transfiguration! (Jn. 2:11).

  4.   Questions for Today:

      a)   How much of my sense of identity (i.e. *"Who I am"*) is connected to Yeshua (i.e. his *values, character, and* mission*),* and how much is connected to "Christianity" as a religious *faith*, or "church" as a religious *affiliation*?

      b)   "Glory" is the accurate representation of who God is. Paul said:

         "So, whether you eat or drink, or whatever you do, do all to the glory of God."   **1 Corinthians 10:31**

      c)   Is God "accurately reflected" in my life?

UNIT 9: John's Unique Recollections

I. THE EARLY JUDEAN MINISTRY OF YESHUA — John 2:13 – 4:42

A. The World *Behind* the Text

   1. Yeshua's Ministry "Strategy"

     a) Yeshua had two "hubs" from which his ministry radiated like spokes (see maps on next page):

     b) Capernaum in Galilee (i.e. the "North")

     c) Bethany in Judea (i.e the "South")

B. Three Key Cities

1. Capernaum

     a) Was nearly 200 years old by the time Yeshua ministered here.[1]

     b) Located on the *Via Maris*, one of two major trade routes.[2]

     c) Population estimate: 15,000 in Yeshua's day.

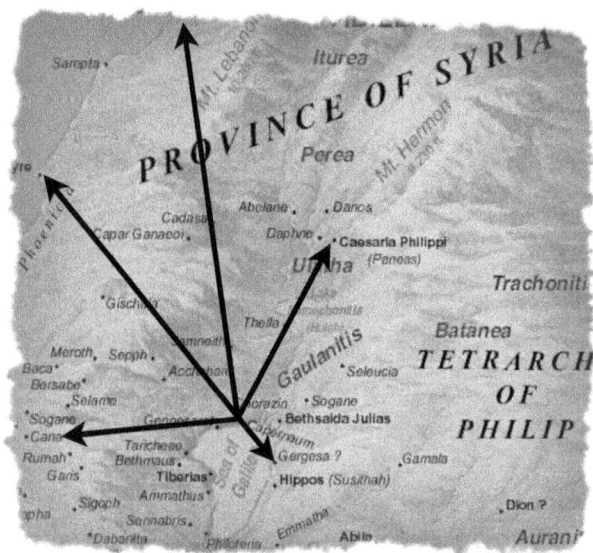

Galilee in the North

Judea in the South

     d) Had a military garrison and its own centurion[3] (Luke 7:1-10).

     e) Had an assigned tax collector (Mark 2:14).

     f) At least two synagogues were built here; one prior to the 1st century, and one in the 3rd or 4th century.[4]

     g) Peter, Andrew, James and John lived here, and were "called" by Yeshua here (Matt. 4:13-22).

     h) The tax collector, Matthew, lived here, and was "called" by Yeshua (Matt. 9:9).

     i) Yeshua preached often in the synagogue here (Mark 1:21-27).

     j) Yeshua healed the servant of the centurion stationed here (Matt. 8:5-13).[5]

---

1 This makes it a relatively "new" city in the Ancient Near East. Jericho by contrast, was over 5,000 years old by this time.

2 The other major road, "The King's Highway," was more inland than the Via Maris (i.e. "The Way of the Sea").

3 "Centuries" were appointed by Rome and were responsible to lead 100 soldiers.

4 The ruins of the synagogue today are from a later period. This is quite obvious because of the type of stone that was used. It is *not* indigenous to the area. We know there was an extant synagogue here in Yeshua's day because he preached in it.

5 There were many healings in this city (e.g. the nobleman's son, the man with the withered hand, etc.).

      k)   *"I Am the bread of Life"* sermon was delivered here (John 6:16-59).[1]

      l)   Yeshua was eventually rejected here and pronounced "woes" on it (Matt. 11:20-24).

2. **Jerusalem** — The City of God's Name

    a) The Scene of Desecration — Passover, A.D. 27

       (1) **Setting:** "Bazaars of the sons of Annas"[2]

       (2) **Characters:** opportunists and thieves.

       (3) **Plot:** Yeshua may have really "turned the tables"[3]

    b) The Day of Preparation[4]

       (1) preceded the Passover

       (2) a solemn family ritual of removing leaven.

       (3) Yeshua may have cleansed His "Father's House" of leaven!

3. **Sychar** — A "Hot" Meeting Place!

    a) Shechem — A Hallowed Site With a Holy History

       (1) God appeared to Abram here (Gen. 12:6)

       (2) Jacob bought land here, and dug a well. (Gen. 33:19)

       (3) Joseph looked for his brothers here (Gen. 37:12)

       (4) Moses set it as the "mountain of blessing" (Deut. 11:29)

       (5) Joshua renewed the covenant here (Josh. 8:33-35)

       (6) One of the 6 "cities of refuge" (Josh. 21:21)

       (7) Joshua buried Joseph's bones here[5] (Josh. 24:32)

       (8) Sychar & Jacob's well were in this area (Jn. 4:1-2)

       (9) Samaritans built their rival temple here, on the "Mount of Blessing."

       (10)Yeshua and Jacob drank from the same well! (Jn. 4:12)

       (11)Samaritans, Jews, Christians & Muslims all agree that this is the location of Jacob's well.

4. **Samaria:** a "Hostile" Site With a Heated History!

    a) Samaria the city was built by Omri, father of King Ahab (1 Kg. 16:24-28).

    b) Became the capital of Northern Kingdom and a synonym for evil.

    c) Ahab built a "house" for Baal here and a palace for himself "made of ivory."

---

1 Jesus lost many of his followers after this sermon. He even pushed the question with his disciples and asked them, "Are you also going to leave?"

2 Annas the High Priest had turned the Court of the Gentiles into a first century "flea market" and was making a profit from all the vendors who set up shop. There is even some evidence that Annas had a group of "henchmen" who extorted payments from the vendors, often using violence. Yeshua's anger and subsequent actions were motivated by the injustice and hypocrisy that had found its way into the very courts of Yahweh. Rabbi Abba Shaul of Jerusalem actually pronounced a curse on the "sons of Annas" (i.e. the high priestly family). Another scholar estimated that his income, just on money changing, was nearly $18,000 during a single Passover. The "half sheckel" Temple tax was a *Judean* sheckel. A "Galilean" sheckel was unacceptable. Women and children were exempted from paying the Temple tax. Though it is difficult to estimate with accuracy the number of Jewish pilgrims from all over the known world in Jerusalem during the high holy days, some have suggested that the city's population may have swelled to nearly half million.

3 The Gospel accounts of these events vary considerably. John provides us with the most detail, mentioning twice the presence of pigeons for sale (the poor used these), oxen, sheep, the money changers, and the making of a whip by Jesus. Matthew and Mark mention the money-changers and the "seats" of those who sold pigeons. Luke tells us Jesus "drove out all who sold…", but he also tells us that Jesus wept over Jerusalem before the Temple cleansing.

4 The "cleasing of the Temple" occurred *after* the Day of Preparation. Priests would have taken the "desecrated cakes" (i.e. leaven) *outside* the Temple, then blew the shofar (ram's horn) to announce the beginning of Passover. Families performed a similar ritual in their homes, going from room to room, removing anything that contained leaven. The ritual included prayers, and "searching" for leaven using a candle. All leaven was gathered and burned.

5 Depending on how one reads Stephen's comments in Acts 7:15-16, there is at least the possibility that the remains of more people that merely Joseph were brought to the Promised Land by the Jews who left Egypt under Moses.

d) Fell to Assyria in 722 B.C. and its population displaced by gentiles (2 Kg. 17:6,24)

e) The resulting people were idolatrous and hostile to the Jews returning from exile. (2 Kg. 17:41; Neh. 4:1-2; Ezra 1-6)

f) The city was destroyed by Alexander the Great in 331 B.C. and made a station for a garrison of troops.

g) Samaritan Temple destroyed by John Hyrcanus (a Jew) c. 128 B.C.

h) Samaria was rebuilt by Pompey in 63 B.C.

i) Was also rebuilt by Herod the Great and renamed Sebaste in honor of Augustus Caesar, following a foiled assassination attempt on Herod's life.

j) Herod married and murdered his wife Marianne and her two sons here.

k) Ruins were sill sitting there in Yeshua's day.

l) By Yeshua's day, the conflict between the Jews and Samaritans was over 400 years old! (cf. Jn. 6:9 and Ezra 4)

m) Yeshua was rejected by a Samaritan village because they were traveling to Jerusalem (Luke 9:52).

n) The Jewish leaders called Yeshua a "Samaritan" and demon-possessed! (John 8:48)

o) The parable of the "Good Samaritan" would have incensed the Jews! (Luke 10)

p) There are 600 Samaritans sill living today.

C. Two Amazing Encounters

1. Nicodemus: A Night of Revelation

a) Nicodemus may have witnessed much of what happened that day:[1]

*"Now when he was in Jerusalem at the Passover Feast, many believed in his name when they saw the **signs** that he was doing. But Jesus on his part did not entrust himself to them, because he knew all people and needed no one to bear witness about man, for he himself knew what was in man....no one could do these **signs** that you do unless God was with him."*   **John 2:23 - 3:2**

b) A meeting of opposites:

(1) high-ranking influential teacher vs. a common laborer.[2]

(2) a formally trained teacher vs. a man with no credentials. (Jn 3:1)

(3) an elder vs. a younger man

(4) Jerusalem vs. Galilee (cf. John 7:50-52)

c) Nicodemus' two shocking discoveries

(1) the Kingdom can't be physically perceived (Jn. 3:3; 19:36-37)

(2) Nicodemus was not in the Kingdom! (Jn. 3:5)

2. The "Woman at the Well" — Sychar: a Blessed Site With a Bright Future

a) This woman was "unclean" to everybody, not just Yeshua.[3]

b) She was a lonely and estranged person.[4]

---

1 The context for Yeshua's evening encounter with Nicodemus is Passover Week. The Temple cleansing occurred during this same time frame.

2 The Greek word used in the Bible to describe Jesus is *tekton,* which is not a reference to a "carpenter," but rather to what we would call in the modern era, a "general laborer." It would be likely that Jesus was skilled in working with wood, but also with stone, plaster, and brick. Some scholars believe that he and his father Joseph walked the relatively short distance from Nazareth to Sephoris nearby for work.

3 If her lifestyle was as promiscuous as some scholars assume, we need to remind ourselves that she would have been considered "unclean" by her own Samaritan religious leaders and her community for her lifestyle, not just by the Jews visiting the well that day because she was a Samaritan. She was truly a woman without a people.

4 This is implied both by the time of her arrival at the well, and the fact that she came alone. The town well was the "social media" of Yeshua's day. Women in the towns and neighboring villages would exchange gossip and family news while drawing water, or waiting. The fact that she came alone is very significant. Also, the time to normally draw water was early in the morning before the heat of the day. This woman came at noon, a time when she was guaranteed there would *not* be anyone there who knew her. Strangers traveling the road near the well would have to stop as needed, but 'locals' would schedule their trips to the well when it best suited them.

      c) Yeshua violated at least 4 cultural "norms":

        (1) geography[1]

        (2) ethnicity[2]

        (3) gender[3]

        (4) social status

      d) This story is about total "immersion," not a mere encounter.[4] (John 4:40)

D. The World *Of* The Text - Words & Meanings

  1. John's Peculiarities & Nicodemus' Story

    a) *"truly, truly"*- appears 25 times in New Testament; all are in this Gospel! The first use is with Nicodemus (3x)

    b) *"Kingdom of God"* - only twice in John; both here

    c) *"Israel's teacher"* - literally "**the** teacher of Israel" (the definite article is present in the Greek)

  2. Two Ways of knowing

    a) **Nicodemus**: *"we know you are a teacher come from God"* (John 3:2)

      (1) *"know"* - means to be in a "state" of knowing (i.e. it is in the Perfect tense).

      (2) literally: *"we have become* convinced"

    b) **Yeshua**: *"...you are Israel's teacher and yet you do not understand?"* [John 3:10]

      (1) literally: *"...and you are not knowing these things?"*

    c) **Yeshua**: *"You know, but you don't know!"*[5]

---

1 Devout Jews traveling *North* would have gone east after leaving Jerusalem, and gone to Jericho. From there, they would have traveled further north, skirting the hills of Judea *and* Samaria just west of the Jordan River. When Mt. Gilboa came into sight, they would soon come to Scythopolis (Old Testament Beth Shan), then travel west up the Jezreel Valley towards Galilee.

2 The "mixed race" nature of being a Samaritan also was compounded by distinct differences in theology. The last three of the "Four Principles of Faith" held by the Samaritans were at odds with classic first century Judaism. (1) one God, the God of Israel, (2) one prophet, Moses the son of Amram, (3) one holy book, the Penteteuch, the Torah handed down by Moses. (4) one holy place - Mt. Gerizim. Jews and Samaritans shared a common hope of a coming Messiah, which Jesus used as his point of contact in the conversations that day.

3 This encounter would have been highly uncomfortable for his disciples, who likely were already shocked because he was talking with a woman, which was culturally forbidden for any rabbi. In fact, some sources indicate that a rabbi was specifically not to talk with a woman about theology, as it was the privilege of Jewish men to discuss Torah. Finally, some traditions indicate that conversation with women at wells in general were to be avoided by rabbis because it might "send a message" that the rabbi was interested in the woman. This is supposedly linked to the stories in their history of significant encounters at wells between men and women that ended in marriage (e.g. Moses and Keturah - Exodus 2:15-21, Jacob and Rachel - Genesis 29:1-19, Abraham's servant and Rebecca - Genesis 24:1-51)! There is also at least the possibility that the woman's response, *"I have no husband..."* was a statement of "availability" on her part. If so, Jesus doesn't allow this ambiguity to to stand. His response would have been as much a clear statement of what he was *not* interested in, as it was a prophetic revelation of her past life.

4 The ongoing narrative informs us that Jesus actually visited the village of the woman after many "came out" to see him. He spent two days in this Samaritan village. This is a highly significant inclusion by John because it tells us of Jesus reaching out to non-Jews very early in his ministry. In fact, nearly half of all references to Samaritans in the New Testament appear in this story (5/11). The others are: Matt 10:5 - Jesus instructs his disciples to *not* "go into any of the villages of the Samaritans..."; Luke 9:52 - Jesus sends his disciples ahead to a Samaritan village to secure lodging, but they are refused because they are traveling to Jerusalem, Luke 17:16 - one of the 10 lepers Jesus healed, the only one to thank him, was a Samaritan, Luke 10:33ff - that parable of the "Good Samaritan"; John 4 - the woman at the well, John 8:48 - Jesus is accused of being demon-possessed and being a Samaritan; Acts 8 - the gospel spreads to "many of the villages of the Samaritans."

5 The Greek word used for "know" by Nicodemus in this narrative is *oida,* which has to do with a purely mental "perception". In other words, Nicodemus was thinking theologically and abstractly. It is also in the perfect tense, pointing to a "state" of sorts. The word used for Jesus, on the other hand, is *ginoskō* which refers to knowledge grounded in personal experience. Yeshua's verb is in the present tense, indicating an ongoing *not* "knowing."

3. Two Ways of Living

    a) **Yeshua**: *"you must be born from above"*[1] (John 3:3,7)

        (1) used for where Yeshua is "from" (John 3:31)

        (2) was the word Yeshua used to refer to the source of Pilate's authority (John 19:11)

        (3) James tells us this is the source of true wisdom (James 3:17)

    b) The Kingdom can't be entered by birth or behavior, but only by belief.

        (1) Kingdom subjects must be transformed

        (2) Yeshua equated himself with the brazen serpent (Numbers 21:9)

        (3) Yeshua linked "eternal life" to belief in Him![2] (John 3:14-15)

        (4) This flew in the face of Pharisaism and Judaism!

4. Yeshua's Noontime Theology Class - An Unlikely Student

    a) *"worship"* - used 12x in John; 10 are here!

      • Yeshua's most extensive recorded teaching on worship is here, not chapter 3!

    b) *"spirit & truth"* - genuine worship's two "pillars"

      • Jerusalem had it wrong; no "spirit."

      • Gerizim had it wrong; no "truth."

      • God is actively seeking those with *both*!

    c) *"seek"* - used 32 times in John's Gospel![3]

      • a Gospel about what people "seek" or are "looking for."

      • used 12x for "the Jews" desire to kill Yeshua.

      • Yeshua said elsewhere he *"came to seek and save that which was lost."* (Lk 19:10)

      • John's Gospel opens with, *"What are you seeking?"*[4] (1:17-18)

      • It closes with, *"Whom are you seeking?"*[5] (20:14-15)

      • Yeshua's disciples enter this story with the thought, *"What are* you *seeking?"* (4:27)

      • Yeshua explodes their theology with the idea of a "seeking God"! (4:23-24)

E. The World *Before* The Text - Nicodemus and *Me*

  1. Nicodemus' dilemma is ours too!

    a) being "convinced" does not convert.

    b) no place for mystery means no place for God!

    c) no place for the Spirit means to place in the Kingdom.

  2. Two Abiding Questions:

    a) How much mystery?

    b) How much Spirit?

"Oh, the depth of the riches and wisdom and knowledge of God! How unsearchable are his judgments and how inscrutable his ways! "For who has known the mind of the Lord, or who has been his counselor?" "Or

---

1 The word here frequently translated "again," is the Greek word *anōthen,* which is used 13 times in our New Testament. Eight of those 13 refer to "above" or from a "higher place." Because Nicodemus stumbled over the metaphor, it is easy for modern readers to think he was having difficulty with being "born again" only. The "second" birth was very much in his mind, but he likely understood that Jesus was primarily referring to the *type* of rebirth, not merely the fact of it. In fact, "born again" was a term used by the Jews for conversion to Judaism. Nicodemus, if he was thinking of "again," wouldn't have been confused as much as simply disagreed with Jesus regarding whether this even applied to him.

2 This phrase appears 17 times in John, compared to only 8 in the three other Gospels combined.

3 It is the Greek word, *zeteō,* which implies a seeking with intent to find. It is used 199x in the New Testament, 85 of which are in the four Gospels (Matt - 15; Mark - 11, Luke - 24, John - 32). Paul uses the word 20x and Luke uses it 10 more in Acts.

4 This is the question Jesus poses to Andrew and "the other disciple" of John the Baptizer who were following Jesus.

5 This is the question the angel asked the women when they came to the empty tomb.

who has given a gift to him that he might be repaid?" For from him and through him and to him are all things. To him be glory forever. Amen."

Romans 11:33-36

F. The World Before The Text - The Samaritan Woman and *Me*

1. A Conversational Christ

   a) Yeshua was not afraid to ask for help from an unbeliever.

   b) **QUES:** How often have I said to an unbeliever, *"Would you have time to help me with...?"*

2. A Controversial Christ

   a) Yeshua rejected social categories that violated the will of God.

   b) **QUES:** How closely does my view of "family" match Yeshua's in Matthew 12:47-50?

3. A Conciliatory Christ

   a) Yeshua wanted *this* woman to know that God was "looking" for her!

   b) **QUES:** Do I think to myself, *"God is looking for you."* when I look into the eyes of an unbeliever?

4. A Conditional Christ

   a) Yeshua made it clear that worship is *always* on God's terms, not ours.

   b) **QUES:** Is my worship built on truth or my own opinion? On Spirit-led passion or human emotion?

UNIT 10: The Great Galilean Ministry

I. THE GREAT GALILEAN MINISTRY

A. The "Bigger Picture"

1. "Looking *Back*" — Beginnings & Early Judean Ministries

   a) Yeshua is baptized by John. **(MML)**

   b) Yeshua is tempted by Satan. **(MML)**

   c) Yeshua turns water into wine at Cana. **(J)**

   d) Yeshua "cleanses" the Temple in Jerusalem. **(J)**

   e) Pharisees become jealous of Yeshua's popularity. **(J)**

   f) John is arrested by Herod Antipas. **(MML)**

   g) Yeshua leaves Judea for Galilee. **(MML)**

   h) Ministry in Samaria. **(J)**

2. The "Divisions"

   a) "Setting up Shop" — establishing a home base in Capernaum.

   b) "Recruiting" — selection of the Twelve

   c) "Mentoring" — training as He teaches

   d) "Soloing" — Yeshua sends out the Twelve in twos & follows

P O R T I O N	Matthew	Mark	Luke	John
"Setting Up Shop"	4 & 8*	1*	4-5*	4+
"Recruiting"	4-12*	1-3	4-7*	5
"Mentoring"	12-13*	3-6	8	—
"Soloing"	9-11, 14	6	9	—

* *narrative is non-sequential*

3. "Looking *Ahead*" — Great Galilean Ministry: Phase I

   a) Heals nobleman's son in Cana. **(J)**

   b) Rejection in Nazareth. **(L)**

    c) Ministry in Capernaum (ML):

       (1) *teaching & exorcism in synagogue*

       (2) *healing Peter's mother-in-law & multitudes*

       (3) *"calls" four fishermen to fish for men*

B. The World *Behind* The Text — History and Culture

  1. The "Great" in Galilean

    a) This is Yeshua's longest, largest, and most lasting ministry segment:

       (1) About 15 months; c. Feb. AD 31 — end of April, AD 32

       (2) Josephus tells us that there are nearly 240 cities and villages in Galilee!

       (3) The majority of Yeshua's twelve apostles are Galileans.

       (4) Matthew uses very expansive language to describe this portion of Yeshua's ministry:

> *"And he went throughout all Galilee, teaching in their synagogues and proclaiming the gospel of the kingdom and healing every disease and every affliction among the people."* **Matthew 4:23**

> *"And Jesus went throughout all the cities and villages, teaching in their synagogues and proclaiming the gospel of the kingdom and healing every disease and every affliction.* **Matthew 9:35**

  2. Yeshua's Synagogue Strategy[1]

    a) Yeshua made it a ministry principle to teach in places of Jewish community:

> *The high priest then questioned Jesus about his disciples and his teaching. Jesus answered him, "I have spoken openly to the world. I have always taught in synagogues and in the temple, where all Jews come together. I have said nothing in secret."* **John 18:19, 20**

    b) A synagogue could be formed wherever 10 Jewish men could assemble.

    c) Josephus tells us that there were 480 synagogues in Jerusalem alone! (E.g. Jn. 9:22; 12:42).

    d) Matthew tells us that Yeshua taught in the synagogues throughout "all of" Galilee (Matt. 4:23).

    e) Prior to the destruction of the Temple, synagogues were used for much more than worship:

       (1) A place of study, prayer and exposition of scripture.

       (2) Community building for social and business purposes.

    f) From a variety of Scriptures, we can assemble a partial picture of first century synagogue worship:

       (1) There was a specific structure called the "Seat of Moses" from which leaders taught (Matt. 23:2,3).

       (2) Prayers were offered (Matt. 6:5).

       (3) Moses (Torah) was read at least every Sabbath (Acts. 15:21).

       (4) The Prophets were read (Lk. 4:16-30).

       (5) There was a time and place for brief homilies after the reading of the Prophets (Acts 13:15-43; Luke 4:21-27).[2]

       (6) Synagogues were "run" by multiple elders called "rulers" (Gk = archisunagōgos; Acts 13:15; Mk 5:22).

       (7) Synagogues also had "attendants" who looked after the building and cared for the Torah scrolls (Gk = *huperētes*, "under-rower"; Lk 4:20).

       (8) Early Christians continued to attend synagogue worship until Jews made it impossible.

       (9) James describes a synagogue seating arrangement and even uses the word, *sunagōgē* in his letter (Jms 2:2).

       (10) Our modern services are model after the synagogue model: prayer, worship, scripture, sermon.[3]

---

1 The Gospels tell us of an extensive ministry in synagogues throughout the entire region. We have the synagogues at Nazareth and Capernaum mentioned by name, but it is safe to assume that Jesus also preached in those in Chorazin and Bethsaida, two cities that he denounced because of their failure to listen to him.

2 Both Jesus and later Paul were given the opportunity to "preach" in synagogues.

3 The similarities between synagogue worship and modern church services would have become more pronounced after the Temple was destroyed and a central place of ritual and worship was no longer possible.

II. PHASE I — "SETTING UP SHOP"

A. The "Healing" of a Household — John 4:46-54

1. John alone gives us this story.

2. Yeshua reputation arrived in Galilee before he did:

> *So when he came to Galilee, the Galileans welcomed him, having seen all that he had done in Jerusalem at the feast.*
> *For they too had gone to the feast.* **John 4:45**

3. This "official" obviously was one of those who had heard, or perhaps even "seen." (Jn. 4:47)

4. He progressed from hearing, to believing, just like everyone else in John's Gospel (E.g. Nathaniel, Cana, Jerusalem, Sychar).[1]

5. This man was very likely linked in some way to Herod Antipas (Gk word for "official" is basilikos, which has kingly connotations)[2]:

   a) Some have suggested that this is Chuza, Herod's "steward," whose wife, Joanna was a disciple of Yeshua.[3]

   b) This would explain her wealth *and* great generosity (Lk. 8:1-3).[4]

B. The Rejection of a Rabbi — Luke 4:16-30

1. Luke alone gives us this account.

2. Luke reminds us of Yeshua's familiarity with this building and its occupants:

> *And he came to Nazareth, where he had been brought up. And as was his custom, he went to the synagogue*
> *on the Sabbath day, and he stood up to read.* **Luke 4:16**

3. The population of Nazareth in Yeshua's day is thought to have been less than 150.

4. It is safe to say that Yeshua was known by *everyone* in this village!

5. Yeshua deliberately reads from two messianic passages and then applies them to himself! (Isaiah 61:1-2; 58:6)

6. Yeshua *knew* they thought contextually, *not* particularly, like we do (I.e. Isaiah 60:15 - 61:10)

7. Yeshua's behavior in this narrative must be understood to reveal an attitude or motive in Nazareth unknown to us.

C. "Setting Up Shop" in Capernaum — **Matt. 4:13-22; Mark 1:14-34; Luke 4:31-5:11**

1. Matthew tells us that this relocation is a fulfillment of messianic prophecy, but he doesn't provide us with an explanation as to *why.* Luke gives us that. (Matt. 4:14-16).

2. Luke informs us that Yeshua's teaching in the synagogue was unparalleled in its power and authority (Lk 4:32).

3. The word "astonished" is the Greek word, *explēssō*, which can mean *"to strike with a blow."*

4. The confrontation with the demoniac was loud, emotional, and "evangelistic":

   a) It was *not* a "healing," per se.

   b) The demoniac was *screaming* in a synagogue!

   c) The verb tense for the report "going out" is ongoing, and the verb itself is like the waves of the sea; we get our English word, "echo" from it (cf. Lk 4:37; 21;25).

5. From Luke's account we discover some vital information:

   a) Peter is married (Lk 4:38).

   b) His home was Capernaum even though he was "from" Bethsaida (cf. Jn. 1:43-44; Lk 4:38).

   c) Yeshua used Peter's boat as a "pulpit" from which to teach (5:1-3).

---

1 This man *came* because he believed Jesus "could" heal his son, but he *left* because he believed what Jesus *said.* In other words, this man's faith grew from belief in an ability to belief in an identity. He came to believe who Jesus was.

2 This Greek word appears only twice in our New Testament; both of them in this narrative.

3 cf. Luke 8, where we also learn that Mary Magdalene and Joannah were disciples as well.

4 If, in fact, Jesus had healed their son, it would be completely reasonable that they would become disciples. Their wealth, in the face of obvious need, would also be a reasonable explanation for becoming benefactors as well.

      d) Yeshua won four fishermen over by proving to them he knew more about fishing than they did! (5:4-10).

      e) Peter and Andrew were business partners with James, John and their father, Zebedee (cf. Lk 5:9-10; Matt. 4:18-22).

  D. The World *Of* The Text[1]

    1. The Gospel According to Yeshua[2] — Luke 4:14-20

> *And the scroll of the prophet Isaiah was given to him. He unrolled the scroll and found the place where it was written, "The Spirit of the Lord is upon me, because he has anointed me to proclaim good news to the poor. He has sent me to proclaim liberty to the captives and recovering of sight to the blind, to set at liberty those who are oppressed, to proclaim the year of the Lord's favor." And he rolled up the scroll and gave it back to the attendant and sat down. And the eyes of all in the synagogue were fixed on him.* **Luke 4:14-20**

      a) *"The Spirit of the Lord is upon me…"[3]*

         (1) He claimed to be speaking on behalf of God; He had God's message.

      b) *"He has anointed (chriō) me to preach (euaggelizō) the Gospel[4] to the poor (ptōchos)…"*

         (1) He claimed to be the "Anointed One"; we get the title "Christ" and our verb, "evangelize" from these words.

         (2) There are two Greek words for "poor," one is for those who must work *(penēs)*, the other for those who must beg *(ptōchos)*.

      c) *"He has sent (apostellō) me to proclaim (kerussō)…"[5]*

         (1) The verb for "sent" is in the perfect tense; Yeshua is saying that this is his *mission*.

         (2) The word for "proclaim" means to herald with authority and to expect a response.

      d) *"…release (aphēsis) to the captives (aichmalōtos)…"*

         (1) "Release" means liberty from bondage and imprisonment; the cancellation of debt.

         (2) "captives" is a unique word meaning *"to be taken captive at spear point."[6]*

      e) *"[He has sent me] to free those who are oppressed (thrauō)…"*

         (1) "Oppressed" is in the perfect tense; a state of being shattered and broken. Only time in the New Testament.[7]

      f) *"…to proclaim the favorable year of the LORD…"*

         (1) A clear reference to the messianic hope of the Year of Jubilee.

         (2) The final "fresh start," and cancellation of all debts.

         (3) A year of simplicity and humility (Lev. 25:8-17).[8]

---

1 This narrative is sometimes called Yeshua's "Nazareth Manifesto," because in it he announces the coming of the Kingdom, which implies the arrival also of the King.

2 Jesus calls it the "gospel of the kingdom" and the "gospel of the kingdom of God." It is also known as "the gospel of God," "the gospel of Christ/Jesus Christ," "the gospel of our Lord Jesus Christ," "the gospel of the grace of God," "the gospel of his Son," "the gospel of the glory of Christ," "the gospel of your salvation," and "the gospel of peace" (cf. Matt. 9:35; Luke 16:16; 1 Thess 3:2; Acts 20:24; Rom 1:9; 2 Cor 4:4; Eph 1:13; Eph 6:15).

3 The spirit of the LORD "came upon" people in the Old Testament primarily to empower them for service to Yahweh, especially in regard to *speaking* on his behalf. Examples include Moses (Num. 11:17,25), Samson (Judges 14:6), David (1 Sam 16:3), Isaiah (Is 59:21), and Ezekiel (Ez 11:5). The phrase that Jesus employs here, is sometimes called the "prophetic formula" by scholars, preparing the hearers for a word from Yahweh.

4 The "good news" and its proclamation is a repeated idea in Isaiah. He speaks of it 7 times, compared to 9 times in our New Testament, 2 of which are in reference to Isaiah.

5 Kerussō is used twelve times in our New Testament alongside the noun, euggelion.

6 It is very possible that this is an indirect reference to the healing of the demoniac in the synagogue at Capernaum.

7 The word that is used here is typically used to describe broken pottery.

8 We lose much of the significance of the Year of Jubilee if we merely taut the whole issue of debt forgiveness and real estate restoration, but fail to take into account the fact that the land laid fallow for two years! Also, the third year was a time of sowing *not* reaping. This meant that they harvested in the 6th year of the regular sabbatical cycle (48th year of the Jubilee cycle), but not again until the 2nd year of the *eighth* sabbath cycle (i.e. the "ninth year").

E. The World *Before* The Text

    1. What kinds of "signs" do I demand of Yeshua?

    2. Is the Gospel I preach honestly "good news" for the poor? If not, what is wrong with my Gospel?[1]

    3. The Gospel Yeshua preached was a message that connected him to those who heard it. How connected am I to the message I proclaim?

III. PHASE II — "RECRUITING"

A. The Key Events

    1. Healings (leper, cripple in Peter's home[2]).

    2. the "call" of Matthew in Capernaum.

    3. Sabbath controversies (including one in Jerusalem recorded only by John).

    4. Selection of "The Twelve." apostles.

    5. The "Sermon on the Mount."

B. HEALINGS: The World *Behind* The Text

    1. Yeshua's Healing Ministry (Matt. 4:23; 9:35)

        a) Yeshua had two ministry foci:

            (1) "touching" (i.e. healing)

            (2) teaching

        b) *Both* were "moved" by compassion[3] (Mark 1:40-41 and 6:34).

        c) Yeshua's compassion always "moved" him in the same way and direction:

            (1) engagement *with* people[4]

            (2) not merely *talking to* people (Yeshua reserved this for the "mockers")

        d) This was what gave Yeshua's teaching more "authority" than the religious leaders. (Luke 4:32; Matt. 7:28; Mk 1:22).[5]

    2. Yeshua & Lepers: "Getting Under Their Skin" — Matt. 8:2-4; Mk. 1:40-45; Luke 5:12-16

        a) Yeshua's healing of this man is a *theological* event, not merely a medical one![6]

---

1 One has to wonder what the implications are if we as Christians are *not* known as people of "compassion." And, what is the relationship between "weeping" and showing "compassion"? Can I weep and still *not* be truly compassionate? Can I be compassionate and not weep?

2 Regarding the healing of the paralytic in Peter's home (Mark 2): The text says "the whole town" was present. This is most likely a hyperbole as the largest house that has been excavated had a span of 18 feet, making a maximum occupancy for a meeting such as this around fifty people. Single story homes in the first century often had outside staircases, making access to the roof not too difficult. Roofs were typically strong enough to walk on. They were made of branches and rushes overlaid with mud. Beneath this outer surface would have been a series of wooden beams.

3 The word in both of these verses is, *splagchnizōmai, "compassion."* It is this that "moved" Jesus. It is the same word for what "moved" the good Samaritan and the father of the prodigal (cf. Luke 10:33ff and 15:20). The Gospels tell us that Jesus was "moved" to heal (Mt 14:14), teach (Mk 6:34), feed the hungry (Mt. 15:32), give sight to the blind (Mt. 20:34), exercise demons (Mk 9:22), cleanse lepers (Mk 1:40-41), and raise the dead (Lk 7:13-14). This must always be understood as ministry to the *living.* It is significant that this word is not used outside the synoptics Gospels; it is in a very real sense a "Jesus word." But, lest we conclude that "compassion" is a New Testament attribute, we are confronted with the stark significance that of the 91 times the word appears in the Old Testament, 67 are in the pre-exilic prophets; a time when Yahweh was chastising his people for neglecting the poor.

4 Eidersheim reminds us that whenever and wherever God (in Jesus) met misery, disease, and suffering, he *did something about it.* It was the exception when he didn't. He also points out that "deeds" became the distinguishing companion to Yeshua's teaching. In fact, the absence of deeds of mercy became a point of criticism for Jesus later when he accused the religious leaders of "not lifting a finger" to help those with burdens (Matt 23:3-4, 23).

5 This raises an interesting question for us 21st century believers: What "impresses" us most about *our* teachers: content, delivery, passion, or their credibility?

6 The Hebrew (i.e. Old Testament) word for leper and leprosy contain the root idea of being "struck" or "smitten" because the disease was understood to come directly from God in judgment. (E.g. Moses' sister, Miriam in Num 12:10-15, and Hezekiah in 2 Chron 26:1921). It was only in Jewish culture were lepers were quarantined *and* stigmatized. Consider that when Hezekiah was stricken, his son had to represent him. Miriam too was put "outside the camp" when she was stricken. Yet, the Syrian, Naaman, was able to maintain his political position and public movement even though he had leprosy. The word never appears again in our Bibles after the Gospels, and John never mentions the disease or those having it. It only appears 8 times in the Synoptics, compared to 44 times in the Old Testament.

b) Yeshua's healing of this man is a *revelatory* event, not merely a historical one!

 (1) We learn more about the nature of God from this story than perhaps any other.[1]

c) In Israel, leprosy was *not* a disease one was healed of, but a *defilement* one was "cleansed" from (cf. Leviticus 13-14).[2]

 (1) of the 61 different ways a Jew could become defiled, contact with a leper was second.

 (2) If a leper entered a house, the *entire* house up to the rafters was "unclean."

 (3) Lepers were to stand at least 6 feet away from people.

 (4) They had to dress like a mourner and cry out "unclean" to those approaching (this was a *moral* statement).[3]

 (5) They were banned from the Temple and were to remain outside walled cities (e.g. 2 Kgs. 7:1-11).[4]

 (6) Some Rabbis stayed 150 feet away from lepers if they were "upwind"!

 (7) The fact that the leper *approached* Yeshua tells us a great deal about Yeshua.[5]

 (8) Yeshua's behavior here would have *stunned* everyone:[6]

 *Moved with compassion, Jesus stretched out His hand and **touched him**, and said to him, "I am willing; be cleansed."* **Mark 1:41**

3. HEALINGS: The World *Before* the Text — Leprosy and the Christian

a) The word "cleanse" occurs 28 times in the New Testament.

 (1) Fourteen are in the Synoptics; 13 deal with leprosy.[7]

 (2) Twelve of the remaining 14 are clear references to dealing with sin.

b) We are never "healed" of sin in this life, only cleansed.[8]

c) We are "declared clean" (forever), and are commanded to continually *be* cleansed:

 "Since we have these promises, beloved, let us cleanse ourselves from every defilement of body and spirit, bringing holiness to completion in the fear of God." **2 Corinthians 7:1**

 "Therefore, if anyone cleanses himself from what is dishonorable, he will be a vessel for honorable use, set apart as holy, useful to the master of the house, ready for every good work." **2 Timothy 2:21**

 "If we confess our sins, he is faithful and just to forgive us our sins and to cleanse us from all unrighteousness" **1 John 1:9**

d) Yeshua's insistence that the leper go to Jerusalem for "cleansing" was for *restoration* to the covenant community, not healing.

e) Confession to one another is for cleansing and restoration also[9]:

 "If we say we have fellowship with him while we walk in darkness, we lie and do not practice the truth. But if we walk in the light, as he is in the light, we have fellowship with one another, and the blood of Jesus his Son cleanses us from all sin." **1 John 1:6, 7**

---

1 We need to remind ourselves of the Incarnation. This is *Yahweh* who is welcoming, touching, and cleansing those society has ostracized and marginalized.
2 Jesus "heals" individuals of many sicknesses and even blindness, but never "heals" anyone of leprosy. They are "cleansed."
3 Their hair was to be disheveled, their clothes torn, and their faces covered.
4 We have no instances of Jesus cleansing a leper inside the walls of Jerusalem. The four lepers in the 2 Kings narrative were living *outside* the city walls, and their conclusions about what might happen to them by sneaking into the Syrian camp are predicated on the fact that they didn't have much of a life to begin with!
5 This was first century Ancient Near Eastern culture in general, and *Jewish* society in particular. Jesus couldn't have gotten too much further "outside the box" on this one!
6 In light of the cultural shock associated with Yeshua's actions, it becomes even more significant that all three of the Synoptics record this story. It made a significant impression on all three of them.
7 The other lone reference deals with a Pharisee cleansing *himself* after being in the market! And this is because he *may* have been around Gentiles…hardly lepers!
8 Our misunderstanding of the biblical portrait of leprosy combined with our often anemic understanding of the nature and persistence of sin leads us to think of sin as something "curable" or even manageable.
9 Unfortunately, we have reduced sin and confession—like most every other facet of spirituality—to private, democratic principles rather than covenant and community issues.

C. "CALL" OF MATTHEW: The World *Behind* the Text - (Matthew 9:9-13; Mark 2:14-17; Luke 5:27-32)[1]

    1. *"Rendering Unto Caesar…"* — Rome, Taxes, and Life in Yeshua's Day[2]

        a) The IRS Code of Rome

           (1) Roman citizens did *not* pay taxes; it was the *non-citizen* provincials who generated the tax revenue for Rome (cf. Matt. 17:24-27).[3]

           (2)

           (3) Non-citizens paid two types of *direct* taxes to Rome:

               (a) *tributum soli* – fixed rate property tax on real estate, slaves and ships.

               (b) *tributum capitis* – "head" or "poll" tax of 1 denarius/year/adult.

                   i) Rome utilized censuses for this purpose.

                   ii) obviously, this "flat tax" favored the wealthy.

           (4) There were also many *indirect* taxes imposed by Rome as well as local cities (e.g. customs, bridge tolls, produce, etc.).[4]

           (5) Some scholars estimate the total tax burden as high as *50%* at times![5]

---

1 Conflating these three accounts provides some interesting insights. From Luke we learn that a very large (Gk = "mega") part was thrown after Matthew's conversion, and it was *in Matthew's home!* He threw a party at which Jesus was the guest of honor. From Mark and Luke we learn that Matthew's Jewish name was Levi, a tribal pointer. Both Matthew and Mark mention "tax collectors and sinner" among those in attendance. The Pharisees also isolated these two distinct groups. But, in Luke's account, rather than using the word "sinners," he uses the word, "others." And, he uses the Greek word, *allos* rather than *heteros*. Luke says there were "others of the same kind" present, and in so doing identifies himself and everyone else with those who *weren't* "tax collectors." In other words, Luke puts *everyone* in the "sinner" category.

2 Taxation was not unique to or created by Rome. A full millennium before Jesus, Solomon was likely the first to tax Israel (although there is disagreement on this point). To maintain his lavish lifestyle and court, he created 12 "districts" each under an officer who was responsible to provide food and support for the king and his household for 1 month out of every year (1 Kg 4). His extravagant lifestyle is summarized for us in a few verses: *"Solomon's provision for one day was thirty cors of fine flour and sixty cors of meal, ten fat oxen, and twenty pasture-fed cattle, a hundred sheep, besides deer, gazelles, roebucks, and fattened fowl."* (1 Kings 4:22–23). The primary form of income for Solomon was known as "tribute": *"Solomon ruled over all the kingdoms from the Euphrates to the land of the Philistines and to the border of Egypt. They brought tribute and served Solomon all the days of his life."* (1 Kings 4:21).

    In the later days of Judah, she found herself paying tribute to other overlords as her own influence and power waned. The scripture tells us that Sennacharib of Assyria took 300 talents of silver, 30 talents of gold as tribute, and also stripped gold from the doors of the Temple (2 Kgs 18:14-16). Neco of Egypt about 100 years later took 100 talents of silver and a talent of gold (2 Kgs 23:33). Finally, Nebachadnezzar of Babylon tall *all* the Temple treasure and palace treasure, 10,000 captives, *all* the craftsmen, and 100 smiths (2 Kgs 24:13-16). The Persians, who eventually displaced Babylon as the world power, instituted a "definite and regular tax system" in which the satraps ruling each province was required to make payments into the Persian Treasury. There were 127 satraps in the Persian Empire during the days of Xerxes, according to the book of Esther. Artaxerxes banned the taxation of priests (cf. Ezra 7:4). Persian governors were given food, wine, and 40 shekels of silver to maintain their households (cf. Neh. 5:14-15). But, Nehemiah apparently did *not* claim this allowance for himself because the tax burden on the poor was already so great. (Nehemiah 5:3-4 is an excellent passage on the principle of enslavement to others over money.). Finally, when Alexander's empire collapsed after conquering the Persians, his generals who took over his empire instigated taxation procedures that prevailed all the way down to Roman times. The "office" of tax collector was created and sold to the highest bidder, who in turn exacted the maximum payment possible from the people and built up his own personal wealth from the surplus it generated.

3 People who were born citizens, lived in Roman colonies, or bought their citizenship were exempt from taxes. They were also exempt from crucifixion and were entitled to legal counsel. Roman colonies were considered to be Roman "soil" that was in a distant place. And, there was no tax on Roman "land." The city of Philippi, visited numerous times by Paul, was a Roman colony and enjoyed all the benefits of being truly "Roman." It would have had a local Roman government, and not merely the presence of Roman military. That is why Paul's statement, "our citizenship is in heaven…" (Phil 3:20) is so significant in this letter and would not have carried the same force if he had said it to the Colossians.

4 The revenue under Claudius alone (AD 41-54) was estimated to have been around 12 million denarii, or roughly $500,000,000 in modern currency.

5 We have to remind ourselves that there was no "middle class" in the Ancient Near East. There were only the rich and the poor. And, the poor were living at subsistence standards. Taxing them at this rate would have been devastating. That's why Yahweh's provisions for the poor in the Deuteronomic Code is so significant.

TAXES LEVIED IN NEW TESTAMENT TIMES

T A X	Description	NT Word	NT Occurrences
tributum soli	• direct "property" tax • levied annually • real estate, slaves • paid in produce	*phoros*	• 5x • *"tribute," "taxes"* • Lk 20:22; 23:2; Rom. 13:6,7
tributum capitis	• direct "poll" tax • levied annually • 1 denarius (or 2 Greek drachmas) • males 14-65 years • females 12-65 yrs	*kēnsos*	• 4x • *"poll tax," "taxes"* • Matt. 22:15-22; Mk. 12:13-17; Lk. 20:21-26
customs tax	• *indirect* taxes • merchandise that was "moving." • roads, bridges, harbors had "booths." • some cities had *their own* customs booths!	*telos*	• 3x • *"custom"* • Matt. 17:25; Rom. 13:7
Temple tax	• half shekel, equal to: • 2 Greek drachmas, or • 1 Alexandrian drachma • 1 Roman denarius • levied on Jewish males 20+ years to support the Temple. • *"voluntary"* (expected) • due each March (Adar) • "money changers" had a windfall of profit here!	*didrachma*	• 2x (both in Matthew 17:24, he was a tax collector himself!) • *"two drachma tax," "half shekel tax"* • cf. Exodus 30:13

*adapted from: *Thayer's Greek-English Lexicon* and the *International Standard Bible Encyclopedia*

"TAX COLLECTORS" IN NEW TESTAMENT TIMES

Roman Name	Location	NT Word	Additional Information
*publicanus***	Rome	*does not appear*	• was of the Equestrian order • "bidded" for taxes of a province • responsible directly to Emperor for amount.
submagistri	province	*archtelōnēs*	• had a *share* of territory in a province • hired workers to work under him. • accountable to the *publicanus* for fixed amount • 2x in our New Testament • *"chief tax collector"* • Zacchaeus in Jericho • Luke 19:1-2
portitores	city	*telōnēs*	• 22x • *"tax collector"* • had a customs "booth" • did the "grunt" work of collecting taxes • accountable to *submagistri* for a fixed amount • Matthew was one of these.

***the KJV incorrectly renders the Greek word telōnēs as "publican"*

MONETARY UNITS IN OUR NEW TESTAMENT

Talent*	Mina*	Aureus	Denarius*	Sestertii	As*	Quandrans*	Lepton*
1 =	60	240	6,000	24,000	96,000	384,000	768,000
	1 =	4	100	400	1,600	6,400	12,800
		1 =	25	100	400	1,600	3,200
			1 =	4	16	64	128
				1 =	4	16	32
					1 =	4	8
						1 =	2
*appears in one or more of the Gospels							1

OCCURRENCES OF MONEY UNITS IN OUR GOSPELS

Unit of Money	NT Usage	Additional Information	Modern Equivalent
talent	Mt. 18:23-35	Yeshua's parable of the "unjust steward" involved *10,000* talents vs. 100 denarii!!	$240,000.00
mina	Lk. 19:13-15	Yeshua's parable of the "wicked tenants" involved 10 minas *each*.	$4,000.00
stater	Mt. 17:27	• equivalent to 4 *drachmas* (denarii) • used to pay the *tributum capitis* for Peter and Yeshua (actual Greek word used here)	$160.00
denarius	Mt. 20:2; 22:19 Lk 10:35; 15:8-9	• a generous "one day's wage" in 1st cent. • cost of one's day's lodging at an inn, based on the parable of the "Good Sa-maritan." • approximate cost of 1 sheep; 5 for an ox • 200 could "buy" lunch for 5,000 people according to Mk. 6:37 (approx. 1 As per lunch) • coin used for the *tributum capitis*. • word appears 16x in NT; 14 in Gospels • Judas' suggested the perfume used on Yeshua's feet was worth 300 *denarii*, or about $12,000! • Roman soldiers received 225 *denarii*/yr. • A Roman citizen seeking Senatorial status had to have a net worth greater than 250,000 *denarii* ($10 million)!	$40.00 (approx.)
as	Mk. 10:29 Lk. 12:6	• Greek word is *assarion* • 2 asses would buy 4 or 5 "sparrows" • the cost of a sparrow = $1	$2.00
half-shekel	Mt. 17:24; 21:12	• the cost of the annual "voluntary" tax for Jewish males 20 years and older • the "money changers" exploited this cur-rency exchange • equal to two *denarii* or Greek *drachmas*.	$80.00
quadrans	Mk. 12:42	• translated *"a cent"* in the story of the "widow's mite" • Greek is *kodrontēs*	$0.60 (approx.)
lepton	Mk. 12:42	• translated *"two copper coins"* in the story of the "widow's mite" • Greek is *leptos*	$0.30 (approx.)

NOTE: *It should also be remembered that the "purchasing power" of any monetary unit was also controlled in a very real way by the locale's idiosyncrasies and its exchange rate.*

2. The "son of Alpheus — a son of God"[1]

a) Matthew lived in one of the three "collection cities" for Roman taxes: Capernaum (Jericho[2] and Caesarea were the other two).

b) By occupation, Matthew was a despised and solitary figure:

(1) Orthodox Jews believed the Roman denarius itself was a sacrilegious coin (see figure and inscriptions below):

Roman
Denarius of
Yeshua's day

Obverse: *"Tiberius Caesar, August Son of the Divine Augustus"* (abbreviated in Latin)
Reverse: *"Pontifex Maximus"* (high priest of the Roman religion); showed a picture of Tiberius' mother, Liva, holding a branch and scepter.

c) Yeshua, in quoting his opponents, gives us a clear picture of the public consensus about tax collectors:

"...tax collectors and sinners..." **Mark 2:15-16**

"...the tax collectors and harlots..." **Matthew 21:31**

"...let him be to you as a tax collectors and a Gentile..." **Matthew 18:17**

"...behold a glutton and a drunkard, a friend of tax collectors and sinners..." **Luke 5:34**

d) Yet, Yeshua uses a tax collector in one of His chief parables about the nature of true repentance (Luke 18:9ff).

e) Yeshua repeatedly honored tax collectors because of their total *lack* of self-righteousness (the prerequisite for *God's* righteousness; Matt. 21:31; Lk. 15:1).

D. "CALL" OF MATTHEW: The World *Of* the Text – Matt. 9:9-13; Mk. 2:13-17; Lk 5:27-32

a) Three Thirds Equals One: A Combined Portrait of a Tax Collector

(1) From the Synoptics we learn that:

(a) Matthew and Levi are the same person (Matt. 9:9; Lk. 5:27).

(b) Matthew's father is a man named Alpheus (Mk. 2:14).

(c) Matthew's "booth" (Gk. *telonian*) was near the Sea of Galilee on the route from Syria to the Mediterranean (Mk. 2:13).

(d) The Pharisees "statement" was either a conversation or a sermon: (Gk for *"saying"* is in Imperfect tense in all 3 Gospels!).[3]

(e) Luke uses a word for "grumbling under one's breath" (*gogguzō*).

(f) Matthew alone, the author and subject, tells us of Yeshua's biblical rebuke from Hosea, unveiling the Pharisees' false spirituality (cf. Hos. 6:6 and Mt. 9:12-13).

b) "Money" is a key topic for Yeshua:

(1) There are nearly 140 references in the Gospels to money, wealth, and greed.

(2) This is compared to 100 to prayer and fasting, combined.

(3) The Pharisees loved money, but hated those with it who weren't like them. (cf. Lk 16:14 and 18:9-11)

---

1 Matthew is one of only three disciples associated with money in the Gospels. The other two are the tax collector, Zacchaeus, and Judas Iscariot.

2 The home base of the tax collector Zacheus. It is interesting that the only tax collectors mentioned by name in the Gospels become disciples of Jesus.

3 Yeshua's use of the phrases, "Go and learn what this means…" and "Have you not read…?" that appear here and elsewhere in the Gospels are what are known as rabbinic formulas. They were phrases that rabbis used when engaging people and teaching. It is also worth noting that the "call" of Matthew actually occurred *before* the Sermon on the Mount, even though Matthew places it after it in his Gospel.

(4) The parable of the 10 minas was Yeshua's response to those who criticized Yeshua for eating with Zacchaeus. (Lk. 19:1-27)

E. "CALL" OF MATTHEW: The World *Before* the Text

1. Tax Collectors and the 21st Century Christian

    a) The parable of the tax collector and the Pharisee was told to *"...some people who trusted in themselves that they were righteous..."*

    b) The word for "trusted" *(Gk - peithō)* means *"to convince oneself; to have faith in..."*. It is also a *condition* (Perfect tense).

    c) The Pharisee's prayer was: *"God, I thank you that I'm not like other people..."*[1]

        (1) Who do *I* identify with in this parable?

        (2) Which of the two am I *"...grateful I am not like...?"*

        (3) **The truth:** I am *both* a sinner *and* self-righteous. I am so damned it's scary!

    d) The tax collectors' sin was *neither* their occupation nor their wealth.

    e) The sin of tax collectors was a "legal-but-unethical greed":[2]

        (1) They used a system they did not create to generate revenue they did not need or deserve.

        (2) Their guiding principle was to collect as much as *"the market will bear."*

        (3) Yeshua was speaking to both the Pharisees *and* Levi when He quoted from Hosea (in Levi's home).[3]

        (4) *Both* needed to exercise *"chesed"* (loving kindness)![4]

F. "RECRUITING" (continued)

1. "Fighting in Church"—Sabbath Controversies[5]—The World *Behind* the Text

    a) The "Sabbath" became a theological weapon in the hands of Yeshua:

        (1) There are 50 references to the "sabbath" in the four Gospels.

        (2) All of them, in one way or another, involve Yeshua.

        (3) Of the fifty, forty-two of them also involve Yeshua engaged in some type of ministry.[6]

        (4) Of that forty-two, Yeshua is engaged in controversy in 38 of them![7]

    b) John's "Sabbath Strategy" — John 5:9ff; 7:19-24; 9:1ff

        (1) John's 3 "controversies" involve 2 healings unique to his Gospel (lame man and man born blind).

        (2) John devotes nearly *100 verses* to these two events and their outcome!

        (3) John's intentions here are consistent with his purposes in writing:

---

1 It is ironic and tragic that this was an incorrect conclusion! And, his statement is the evidence.

2 We would be wise, as we examine the lives of Levi and Zacheus to be careful that we do *not* merely see them as great examples of "true repentance" or the "kinds of people Jesus associated with." Although both of these insights are true, we must not lose sight of who and what they were *before* their conversion. In many ways, both of them stand as ancient caricatures of much of our modern business ethic: "fair" is what the market or the law will allow. Paul will later equate greed with idolatry, raising the ante on how serious it really is (cf. Eph 5:5; Col. 3:5).

3 *"Go and learn what this means: I desire mercy and not sacrifice."* (Hosea 6:6)

4 "*Chesed*" is a beautiful Hebrew word that is difficult to translate into English. It is rendered, "loving kindness," "faithfulness," and "mercy" among other words. It appears 248 times in the Old Testament, in 28 of the 39 Old Testament books, 127 of which are in the Psalms, in reference to Yahweh. The Greek word in Matthew's Gospel that is in the Hosea citation, is *eleos*. This is the same word that is used in the Greek translation of the Hebrew Bible (i.e. the Septuagint) in Hosea 6:6. It is a word that always involves action. Jesus is *not* speaking of mere sentimentality or sympathy here. He is referring to an attraction to and involvement with the object of mercy.

5 The "sabbath" appears 171 times in our Bible: 110 in the Old Testament, and 61 in the New Testament, 50 of which occur in all four Gospels. In the Old Testament, there are 46 occurrences in the books of Law, 31 in the books of History, and 1 superscription in Psalm 92:1. But, the significant thing is that there are 33 references to the sabbath in the Prophets, a very clear "clue" that the sabbath *must* have a great deal more to do with how one lives than merely whether or not we rest on a certain day.

6 "Ministry" for John in these sabbath battles is *always* healing. In the Synoptics, it is both healing and teaching. The other 8 references have to do with the resurrection, which, in a very real way involve the Father "working" on those days.

7 E.g. Matthew 12:1-8, 10; Mark 1:21ff; Luke 13:10ff; 14:1ff; John 5:9ff; 9:1ff

(a) to validate Yeshua's identity[1] (unity with Yahweh) and mission (sent vs. "rose up"; John 5:19-47)

(b) to clarify the nature and intensity of Jewish hostility (5:16-18)

c) Yeshua's "Sabbath Theology" — John 5:9ff; 7:19-24

(1) "Resting" on the Sabbath must be understood in light of God, not Moses!

(2) God "rests," but is never idle (the universe depends on this!).

(3) Mercy, compassion, and justice are *not* "work" from which Kingdom subjects are to take a "sabbath."

(4) Yeshua *does* what his Father does, which includes compassion on the Sabbath.

(5) Yeshua uses this "controversy" to expose the Jews' "*ancient* postmodernism"[2]:

(a) they circumcise on the 8th day, *even if it's a Sabbath!*[3]

(b) they believe God wants *some* things done, even on the Sabbath.

(c) their *real* problem is *not* Yeshua "working" on the Sabbath, but *what* that work is.

(d) their conflict then, is between Yeshua's theology and theirs (or so they originally think)[4]

(6) John establishes the *root* of Yeshua's rejection (and ultimate murder):

(a) the Jews finally realized that the "problem" was *not* Yeshua's behavior, but his "theology" about himself.[5]

(b) suddenly, Yeshua was no mere "Sabbath-breaker"

(c) Yeshua is seen as a demon-possessed blasphemer who deserved to die (5:18;7:20)

(d) this is *all* galvanized very early in Yeshua's ministry, and John alone alerts us to this.[6]

d) Two "Pools of Great Price" — John 5:9ff; 7:19-24; 9:1ff

(1) John's two Sabbath "controversies" both involve healings at pools in Jerusalem.

(2) The lame man of chapters 5 & 7 is healed at the Pool of Bethesda in the north of Jerusalem.

(3) The blind man in chapter 9 is healed at the Pool of Siloam in the south of the city.

(4) Both healings launch Yeshua into irreversible conflict with "the Jews" (I.e. hostile Jewish leadership).

(5) At least a year separates these two healings, and "the Jews" are *still* upset about the first one a year later! (7:19-24 is a year after ch. 5)

(6) These two men are polar opposites and defy categorization:

(a) one "tattles" and one testifies (5:11,15 & 9:30-33)

(b) one didn't know Yeshua, one did (5:11 & 9:10-11)

(c) one was a "sinner," the other wasn't (5:14 & 9:1-3)

(d) one came to faith, the other didn't (5:14 & 9:38)

> *"Christianity founds hospitals, and atheists are cured in them, never knowing that they owe their cure to Christ."*
> **William Temple**

2. "Fighting in Church" — Sabbath Controversies — The World *Of* the Text

a) *"you are well…"* – (5:14; Greek - *hugiēs*); word stresses *restoration to* something *good.*

(1) John uses the perfect tense here, indicating the permanence of the healing.

(2) John uses this word six times in his Gospel, all in reference to this incident!

---

1 John is not the only Gospel writer to record Yeshua's repeated and varied claims to deity. But, John always seems to wed those claims to the sabbath in some way (cf. Jn 5:17-18)

2 They were interpreting the Law to suit their own bias, rather than subjecting and submitting themselves to it.

3 The Mishnah actually *required it!*

4 Or perhaps more accurately, Yeshua's "hermeneutic" on Moses versus theirs. He is accusing them of getting it wrong on the very foundation upon which they thought they stood.

5 In a very real way, Jesus is claiming to be the "sabbath *Maker*" not a mere sabbath "breaker."

6 We need to be very careful to connect John 7 with John 5, which occurred *very* early in the Great Gali

(3) Luke *never* uses this word; he uses *sōzō,* which stresses deliverance *from* something; a "taking away" rather than "bringing back."

    b) *"doing..."* – (5:16); Greek is in the imperfect tense

       (1) this was Yeshua's "M.O." not an isolated event

    c) *"seeking...breaking...calling..."*

       (1) (5:16); these are all in the present tense

       (2) John is stressing the intensity of this conflict

       (3) John uses the word for *"tried..."* 8x in his Gospel in regard to Yeshua's life being endangered.

3. "Fighting in Church" — Sabbath Controversies — The World *Before* the Text

    a) When *you* think of the word, "Sabbath," what do you think of *first*:

       (1) God?

       (2) others?

       (3) church?

       (4) yourself?

    b) From the beginning, God's intention was that the "Sabbath" would always point people towards Him, not us:

> *"Cry out and wail, son of man, for it is against my people. It is against all the princes of Israel. They are delivered over to the sword with my people. Strike therefore upon your thigh."*   **Ezekiel 21:12**

4. "Making the Cut"—Choosing the Twelve[1]—The World *Behind* the Text

    a) Of the four Gospels, only Mark and Luke record this selection[2] (Mk. 3:13-19; Lk 6:10-16).

    b) Luke alone tells us it was preceded by a night spent in prayer.[3]

    c) Luke "sandwiches" this account between a hostile confrontation and the "Sermon on the Plain" (5:6-11 and 6:17-49).

    d) Mark tells us the dual purpose of apostleship: intimacy and authority

> *"And he appointed twelve (whom he also named apostles) so that they might be with him and he might send them out to preach and have authority to cast out demons."*   **Mark 3:14, 15**

    e) All three Synoptists inform us of the *impermanence* of apostleship in their description and placement of Judas[4] (Mt. 10:4; Mk 3:19; Lk 6:16).

    f) Luke is "fondest" of the word "apostle," using it 6 of the 8 times it appears in the Gospels, and 29x in Acts.

    g) Luke's concern for "the Twelve" can be seen in his sole record of Judas' replacement by Matthias (Acts. 1:12-20).

    h) Yeshua establishes an unmistakable, but unexplained connection between Israel's 12 tribes and His 12 apostles[5] (Mt. 16:17-19; cf. Rev. 21:14; Eph. 2:20).

---

1 Among other things, the "selection of the Twelve" was Jesus pulling a dozen men out of "the multitudes" that were following him. There are 146 references to "the crowds" and "the multitudes" in the four Gospels. The Greek word is *ochlos,* and it is always used for what we would consider the "common man," in contrast to the "chief priests, elders, and rulers" that also populate the pages of the Gospels. Mark uses the word with the greatest frequency, over twice per chapter. Matthew uses it the most; 49 times. And, as one would expect, John uses it the least (20x) because his Gospel is clearly about the identity of Jesus more than what he did.

2 The *list* of the names of the twelve apostles appear in all three Synoptics.

3 (cf. Luke 16:12) There are 57 references to the word "prayer" in the four Gospels. Matthew has 19, five of which are Jesus praying, and the others are references to others praying or about prayer in general. Mark has 12, five of Jesus praying. Luke has the most with 26 references, nearly half of which are Jesus (12). John, who provides us with Yeshua's longest recorded prayer (ch 17) does not use the word "pray" or "prayer" in his entire Gospel! He *does* mention "giving thanks" twice in reference to the miracle of the feeding of the 5,000.

4 Judas' name appears last in the list in all three of the Synoptics. One does have to wonder what was going on that night as Jesus prayed. Somewhere in the mix, Judas was also chosen after a night in prayer.

5 However, Luke also informs us that Jesus seems to place apostleship above tribal Israel, for he says they "will sit on twelve thrones judging the twelve tribes of Israel." (Lk 22:30)

    i) Yeshua makes a clear statement that the Twelve *represent* Him, they don't merely *reference* Him (Lk 10:16; Mt 10:40).

    j) Paul uses the word, "apostle" 36x in his writings; 9x to refer to himself.[1]

5. "Making the Cut"—Choosing the Twelve—The World *Of* the Text

    a) The word, "*apostolos*" (a representative with authority) is sometimes differentiated from "*angelos*" (a messenger) in classical Greek.

    b) The LXX translates Isaiah 6:8 and 1 Kings 14:6 with the verb, form of "*apostolos*":

      *"And I heard the voice of the Lord saying, "Whom shall I **send**, and who will go for us?" Then I said, "Here am I! **Send** me."*
      Isaiah 6:8

      *But when Ahijah heard the sound of her feet, as she came in at the door, he said, "Come in, wife of Jeroboam. Why do you pretend to be another? For **I am charged** with unbearable news for you."*
      1 Kings 14:6

    c) Paul includes "*apostoloi*" in his lists of the gifts of the Holy Spirit (1 Cor. 12:28; Eph. 4:11).

6. "Making the Cut"—Choosing the Twelve—The World *Before* the Text

    a) Both Paul and Yeshua spoke of "pseudo-apostles," (2 Cor. 11:13; Rev 2:2).

    b) The characteristics of "false apostles" include:

      (1) adulterating the Word of God for financial gain (2 Cor 2:17; Gk - *kapeleuō*)[2]

      (2) adulterating the Word of God for theological gain (2 Cor 4:2; Gk - *doloō*)[3]

    c) Any "messenger" of God who puts himself above the message is *not* functioning as a true *apostolos*, regardless of his/her theology.[4]

G. The "Sermon" That *Wasn't* a "Sermon" — Matthew 5-7; Luke 6:17-49

1. Matthew and Luke are the only two Gospel writers who offer us this material as a "sermon."[5]

2. But, their "offerings" are immensely different:

    a) In Length: Matthew is 2, 476 words; Luke is 851 *(reading, Matthew "sermon" lasts 14¹ᐟ² min; Luke's 5 min. if they are read)*.

    b) Matthew has nine "blessings" and no "woes"; Luke has four "blessings" balanced by four "woes."

    c) Luke mentions the "kingdom" once out of 45x in his Gospel (2%); Matthew mentions the "kingdom" 9x out of 55 occurrences in his Gospel(16%)

    d) Luke focuses on the *outer* world of people in the present; Matthew focuses on the inner world of motivations and one's life before God.

    e) Both "sermons" begin and end similarly, but Luke "scatters" throughout His Gospel what Matthew "gathers" here.

"Point" Being Made in the Sermon	Matthew	Luke
"Blessed are the poor in spirit/poor…"	5:3	6:20
"Blessed are those who mourn/weep…"	5:4	6:21
"Blessed are the meek…"	5:5	—
"Blessed are those who hunger and thirst for righteousness/hunger…"	5:6	6:21

---

1 Considering the significant contrast of use of the word *outside* the Gospels (8x vs 73x), we are led to conclude that "apostleship's" greatest era was post-ascension. Some scholars differentiate between the spiritual gift of apostle and the "office" of apostle. Because of the meaning of *apostolos*, the spiritual gift is equated with a "missionary." One "sent" by God to bring the message of God. There is some support for this in the New Testament, as James and Barnabas both are called *apostolos* (cf. Acts 14:14 and Gal. 1:19).

2 The word Paul uses here translated "peddler" was from the Greek version of a Flea Market, where hucksters and thieves would stack fresh fruit on top of poorer quality. It is a word meaning to present something to be other than what it really is, all for gain.

3 This is an old Greek word, and is used only here in the entire New Testament. It carries with it the meaning of *ensnaring*. One scholar renders is, *"to corrupt with error."*

4 An excellent example of this from the pen of John is Diotrophes in 3 John 1:9, who "loves to be first." The Greek word used to describe him is *philprotos*, a combination of *phileō* ("to love") and *protos* ("first"). Or, "a lover of being first in importance."

5 Mark contains a few isolated verses from this teaching corpus; John is totally silent.

"Point" Being Made in the Sermon	Matthew	Luke
"Blessed are the merciful..."	5:7	6:36
"Blessed are the pure in heart..."	5:8	—
"Blessed are the peacemakers..."	5:9	—
"Blessed are those who are persecuted..."	5:10	—
"Blessed are you, when you are persecuted..."	5:11-12	6:22-23
"Woe to you who are rich (now)..."	—	6:24
"Woe to you who are full now..."	—	6:25
"Woe to you who laugh now..."	—	6:25
"Woe to you when all speak well of you (now)..."	—	6:26
"You are the salt of the earth..."	5:13	*14:34-35* *
"You are the light of the world..."	5:14-16	*8:16; 11:33*
Yeshua's commitment to the Law and the Prophets	5:17-20	*16:16-17*
ANGER: "You have heard that it was said..., but I say to you..."	5:21-26	*12:57-59*
LUST: You have heard that it was said..., but I say to you..."	5:27-30	—
DIVORCE: You have heard that it was said..., but I say to you..."	5:31-32	*16:18*
OATHS: You have heard that it was said..., but I say to you..."	5:33-37	—
"An eye for an eye"	5:38-42	—
"Love your enemies..."	5:43-48	6:27-36
GIVING: genuine vs. "the hypocrites"	6:1-4	—
PRAYER: genuine vs. "the hypocrites" & Gentiles	6:5-8	—
THE LORD'S PRAYER	6:9-15	*11:1-4*
FASTING: genuine vs. "the hypocrites"	6:16-18	—
Treasures in heaven, eye is "lamp," "serving two masters"	6:19-24	*11:34-36; 16:13*
Anxiety over food & clothing vs. seeking first His Kingdom & righteousness	6:25-34	*12:22-23*
Judging others	7:1-6	6:37-8,41-2
Blind leading the blind	—	6:39-40
"Ask, seek, knock..."	7:7-11	*11:9-13*
THE GOLDEN RULE	7:12	6:31
Narrow and wide gate	7:13-14	*13:23-24*
By their fruits you will know them...	7:15-23	6:43-46
"On that day, many will say to me, 'Lord, Lord...'"	7:21-23	*13:25-27*
Wise and foolish builders	7:24-27	6:47-49

f) This "sermon" may be the best known, most studied and debated, yet least obeyed of all Yeshua's teaching!

(1) Who we believe this sermon was "for" controls both our hermeneutic (interpretation) *and* our application of it.

"Is it not true to say of many of us that in actual practice our view of the doctrine of grace is such that we scarcely ever take the plain teaching of the Lord Jesus Christ seriously? We have so emphasized that it is all

of grace and that we ought not to try to imitate His example in order to make ourselves Christians, that we are virtually in the position of ignoring His teaching altogether and of saying that it has nothing to do with us because we are under grace. Now I wonder how seriously we take the Gospel of our Lord and Saviour Jesus Christ. The best way of concentrating on that question is, I think, to face the Sermon on the Mount." **Martin Lloyd Jones, *Studies in the Sermon on the Mount*, pp. 12-13**

    (2) If we believe it is for "kingdom subjects" in the future, we will ignore it.[1]

    (3) If we believe it was primarily for first century Jewish peasants, we will reinterpret or minimize it.[2]

    (4) If we believe it is for true disciples of Yeshua of all ages, we must *do something* with it.

3. The "Sermon" And Modern Believers

    a) Much of the impotence of Western Christianity can be traced to our ignorance, neglect, or minimization of this core teaching of Yeshua:

"It is the failure to understand Jesus and his words as reality and vital information about life that explains why, today, we do not routinely teach those who profess allegiance to him how to do what he said was best. We lead them to profess allegiance to him, or we expect them to, and leave them there, devoting our remaining efforts to 'attracting' them to this or that…" **Dallas Willard, *The Divine Conspiracy*, xiv**

*"More than any other single thing, in any case, **the practical irrelevance of actual obedience** [emphasis the author's] to Christ accounts for the weakened effect of Christianity in the world today, with its increasing tendency to emphasize political and social action as the primary way to serve God. It also accounts for the practical irrelevance of Christian faith to individual character development and overall personal sanity and well-being."* **ibid, xv**

    b) There is more to be gained from Matthew that the "sermon" itself:

       (1) Of the 23,554 words in his Gospel, 57% of them fall from the lips of Yeshua.

       (2) This "sermon" constitutes 20% of all of Yeshua's teaching, and 10% of the entire Gospel of Matthew.[3]

       (3) The very *ink* "cries out," both in color and volume (i.e. "red letter" editions), that this teaching should be taken seriously.

    c) Luke's account must be used as ballast, not merely as contrast.[4]

       (1) To neglect his account's variations and additions is to violate God's purposes for giving us more than one Gospel.

    d) Our perspective on, and commitment to the teachings of Yeshua in this "sermon" will dictate the passion *and* the content of however we seek to obey the Great Commission:

Go therefore and make disciples of all nations, baptizing them in the name of the Father and of the Son and of the Holy Spirit, teaching them to observe all that I have commanded you. And behold, I am with you always, to the end of the age." **Matthew 28:19, 20**

    e) If we are teaching people how to evangelize, but not the core of this "sermon," we are *disobeying* the Great Commission, no matter how large our ministries are.

4. Some Worthwhile "Sermon Notes" (thanks to Martin Lloyd-Jones)

    a) What does the Sermon on the Mount mean to me? (I.e. Where does it "fall" on my list of vital passages?)

    b) Where does it come in my life? (E.g. How often to I refer to it, actually or mentally?)

    c) What place does the Sermon on the Mount have in my thinking and outlook? (E.g. What effect is it having on my choices?)

    d) What is my current relationship to it? (I.e. How aggressively am I seeking to implement/emulate?)

---

1 Some strains of Dispensationalism see it this way.

2 Some Liberal theologians believe that this "sermon" as the core of the gospel itself; that Yeshua's main concern was teaching people how to treat others.

3 Matthew's Gospel contains four "sermons": (1) the Sermon on the Mount; ch 5-7, 2,445 words. (2) the Commissioning Sermon for the Twelve; ch 10, 819 words. (3) Sermon of Parables; ch 13, 1,138 words. (4) The Olivet Sermon on the End Times; ch 24, 2,021 words.

4 I.e., we should *add* Luke's words and Matthew's together, not merely compare and contrast them in a detached, academic exercise. Thus, when Matthew speaks of "the poor in spirit," and Luke speaks of "the poor," we need to understand Jesus addressing *both*, not one versus the other. Or, *"blessed are those who hunger and thirst for righteousness,"* versus *"blessed are those who hunger."*

IV. PHASE III — "MENTORING" (the Twelve)
A. Reminding Ourselves of Two "Gospel Guides"
1. The writers' *choice* of material is determined by their purpose:[1]

Events Of The Great Galilean Ministry	Matt	Mark	Luke	John
1. *Healing of nobleman's son at Cana.*				✓
2. *Jesus' 1st rejection at Nazareth.*			✓	
3. *Jesus moves his "home base" from Nazareth to Capernaum.*	✓			
4. The calling of the four fishermen on the Sea of Galilee.	✓	✓	✓	
5. Jesus heals a demoniac on a sabbath.		✓	✓	
6. Healing of Peter's mother-in-law in Capernaum.	✓	✓	✓	
7. Healing of a leper in Capernaum.	✓	✓	✓	
8. Man lowered through roof and healed in Capernaum.	✓	✓	✓	
9. The "calling" of Matthew/Levi.	✓	✓	✓	
10. *Healing of a lame man on a sabbath in Jerusalem.*				✓
11. Controversy with Jews: grainfield 'work' on the Sabbath.	✓	✓	✓	
12. Healing of a man with a withered hand on a sabbath.	✓	✓	✓	
13. Healing of the "multitudes" by the Sea of Galilee.	✓	✓		
14. The selection of "The Twelve."		✓	✓	
15. The "Sermon on the Mount."	✓		✓	
16. Healing of the centurion's servant.	✓		✓	
17. *Widow's son is raised from the dead at Nain.*			✓	
18. John the Baptizer sends a group with questions of Jesus.	✓		✓	
19. Jesus pronounces "woes" on, Chorazin, Bethsaida, & Capernaum.	✓		✓	
20. *Jesus' feet anointed by "sinful woman" in Pharisee's home.*			✓	
21. Jesus is accused of being in partnership with Beelzebub.	✓	✓		
22. *Scribes and Pharisees demand a "sign" of Jesus' authority.*	✓			
23. Jesus' family tries to "take him home."	✓	✓	✓	
24. Parable of the "Sower/Soils."	✓	✓	✓	
25. *Parable of the "seed growing by itself."*			✓	
26. *Parable of the "tares" and its explanation.*	✓			
27. Parable of "mustard seed."	✓	✓		
28. Parable of the "leaven."	✓	✓		
29. *Parable of the "hidden treasure."*	✓			
30. *Parable of the "Pearl of Great Price."*	✓			
31. *Parable of the "net."*	✓			
32. *Parable of the "householder and his treasury."*	✓			
33. Jesus stills the storm on the Sea of Galilee.	✓	✓	✓	
34. Healing of the Gadarene demoniac (pigs rush into sea).	✓	✓	✓	
35. Woman with the "flow of blood" healed.	✓	✓	✓	
36. Jairus' daughter raised from the dead.	✓	✓	✓	
37. *Healing of two blind men and a dumb demoniac.*	✓			
38. Jesus' final visit to Nazareth.	✓	✓		
39. Jesus sends out the Twelve in pairs.	✓	✓	✓	
40. Herod's superstitious fears that Jesus is John raised from dead.	✓	✓	✓	

NOTE: Bold items appear in all three Synoptics; *Italicized items are unique to one Gospel.*

---

1 We have to constantly remind ourselves of the actual *genre* of the four Gospels, and lean against our natural tendency to force them into the genre of simple historical narrative. And, of the four writers, only *two* actually inform us of their purpose in writing: John (20:30-31) and Luke (1:1-4).

---

2. The writers' *arrangement* of material is determined by their purpose:[1]

The Great Galilean Ministry — Chronological vs. Thematic

E V E N T	Matt	Mark	Luke
Jesus "calls" four fishermen.	4	1	5
Jesus heals Peter's mother-in-law.	8	1	4
The man is lowered through the roof and healed.	9	2	5
Controversy over "work" in grainfields on Sabbath.	12	2	6
Healings by the Sea of Galilee.	12	3	—
Sermon on the Mount	5-7	—	6
Healing of centurion's servant.	8	—	7
Jesus' family seeks to "take him home."	12	3	8
Parable of the "Sower."	13	4	8
Stilling of the storm on the Sea of Galilee.	8	4	8
Woman healed by "touching the hem of his garment."	9	5	8
Herod's fears about Jesus and John.	14	6	9

B. Redrawing The "Big Picture"

1. Yeshua's Great Galilean ministry is "framed" by similar events involving the same individual, his cousin, roughly 18 months apart:

   a) It *begins* with the imprisonment of John the Baptist (Matt. 4:12,23).[2]

   b) It "ends" with the beheading of John the Baptist (Mk. 6:14-29).

2. Yeshua's Great Galilean ministry consists of three "preaching tours":

   a) The first one *before* "the Twelve." (Matt. 4:23-25; Mk. 1:35-39).

      (1) Peter, Andrew, James and John accompany Yeshua.

      (2) People from Galilee, Judea, the Decapolis, Jerusalem, Idumea and the regions around Tyre and Sidon hear.[3]

      (3) Levi is "called" at the end.

   b) The second one *with* "the Twelve." (Luke 8:1-3)

      (1) This tour occurs *after* the selection of the apostles.[4]

      (2) It also includes a significant number of women, including Mary Magdalene and Joanna, Chuza's wife.

      (3) The ministry has "costs" associated with it by this time.

   c) The final one *following* "the Twelve." (Matt. 9:35-11:1; Mk. 6:6-13)

3. Yeshua's popularity with the people goes down as the "cost" of discipleship goes up:

   a) John the Baptist asks for "clarification" of Yeshua's credentials, from prison (Lk. 7:18-35).[5]

   b) Yeshua's friends and family come to "take him home," thinking he has lost his mind! (Mk. 3:21,31-35)

   c) Yeshua begins to use parables as a primary teaching method (Matt. 13:1-3)

---

1 Matthew, for instance, groups his parable about the *nature* of the Kingdom in chapter 13. Of the 52 times the word "kingdom" appears in Matthew, 12 of them are in 42 verses in this chapter! Luke on the other hand, places many of his parables later, when Yeshua's ministry has "heated up" in terms of opposition. And, his parables have more to do with the *subjects* in the Kingdom (e.g. rich fool, persistent widow, evil tenants, good Samaritan, prodigal son, etc.). Mark's Gospel, by contrast, is much more *sequential,* indicating his purpose is less thematic than the other two.

2 *Where* this even actually occurred will dictate where the beheading most likely happened as well. And, whether this was at Tiberius in Galilee or Macherus near Judea is itself dependent upon where John was doing his baptizing at the time.

3 cf. Matthew 4:25

4 Luke differentiates between "the Twelve," and "disciples."

5 From this narrative, we learn that the Baptizer still has disciples of his own. They all have not yet made the migration to Jesus.

4. The hostility of the religious leaders enlarges as Yeshua's mission narrows:

   a) Yeshua's claim to forgive sins attracts the "fire" of the Pharisees in Galilee (Lk. 7:36-50)

   b) Yeshua is accused of being empowered and in partnership with Beelzebub by scribes *from Jerusalem!* (Mk. 3:19-30)

   c) The scribes and Pharisees demand to see Yeshua's "credentials" via a "sign." (Matt. 12:38-45)

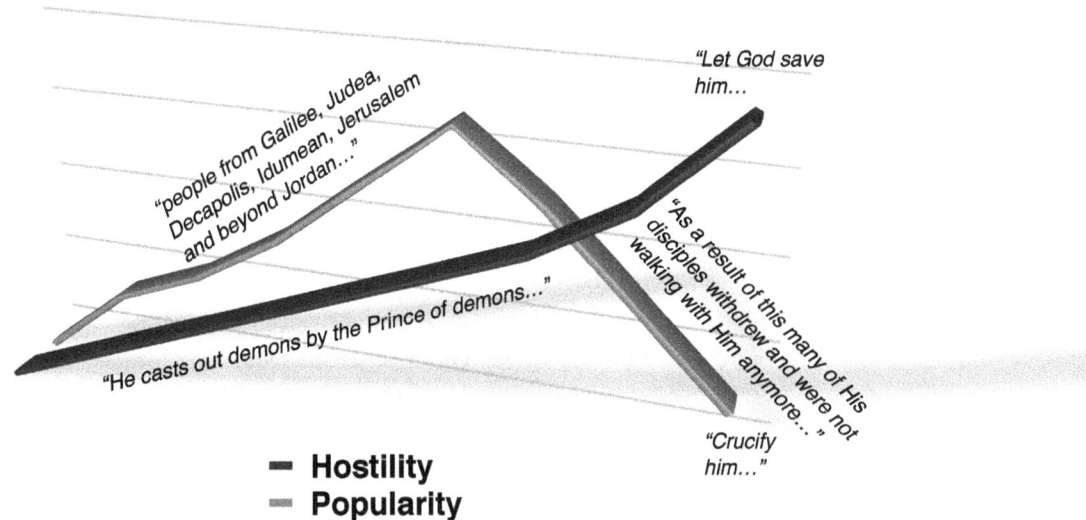

- **Hostility**
- **Popularity**

C. "Mentoring the Twelve": The High Points — Luke 7:1-9:9; Matt. 11:2-14:12

   1. Four controversial ministry choices.

   2. Popularity decreasing; hostility increasing.

   3. Parabolic teaching becomes the "norm."

   4. Yeshua sends out the Twelve without him.

   5. Yeshua "closes up shop" in Galilee.

D. "MENTORING"—Four Controversial Choices—The World *Behind* the Text

   1. The healing of the "Centurion's servant" (Matt. 8:5-13; Lk. 7:1-10).[1]

      a) "Centurion" (Gk = *hekatontarchos*) appear 23x in our NT; 16 of them by Luke.[2]

      b) The centurion was over 100 men and was the "backbone" of the Roman military.[3]

         (1) 2 Centuries = 1 Maniple (200 legionnaires)

         (2) 3 maniples = 1 Cohort (600 men; led by a Tribune)

         (3) 10 Cohorts = 1 Legion (6,000 men; led by a general)[4]

      c) It is likely that this "centurion" was *not* a Roman, but was employed by Herod Antipas.

      d) He, like Cornelius in Acts 10, is a "god-fearing" Gentile who comes to faith:

      "Now there was a man at Caesarea named Cornelius, a centurion of what was called the Italian cohort, a devout man and one who feared God with all his household, and gave many alms to the Jewish people and prayed to God continually."
      Acts 10:1

---

1 These two accounts of the same event are very different, but they are not contradictory. This is an issue of perspective and purpose on the part of each of the writers. Matthew has the centurion coming directly to Jesus, but Luke has a group of Jews representing him coming to Jesus on his behalf first.

2 He uses the word 3 times in his Gospel, but 13 times in Acts.

3 Roman officers were not allowed to marry. They could retire after 20 years of service.

4 This word is never used in the New Testament to refer to a military unit; it *is* used by Jesus in reference to angels, and by the demoniac in reference to the large number of demons that had possessed the demoniac. The Roman Empire had a total of 9 or 10 legions.

2. The raising of the widow's son (Luke 7:11-17)

   a) Nain was about 25 miles SW of Capernaum.

   b) Culturally, this death was a devastating blow to this woman.

   c) This is the first of three resurrections that Yeshua performs (Jairus' daughter & Lazarus).

   d) Elijah and Elisha are the only two OT prophets to have raised someone from the dead (1 Kgs 17:17-24; 2 Kgs 4:16-37).

   e) Yeshua violates some of the most stringent Jewish laws of purity:[1]

     (1) By touching the funeral bier, Yeshua "contracted" one day's uncleanness (Num. 19:21-22).

     (2) By touching the corpse, Yeshua "contracted" corpse-unclean-ness, the most severe form of ritual impurity in Judaism (Num. 5:2-3; 19:11-20).

3. The "healing" of the "woman of the city" (Luke 7:36-50)

   a) "Reclining at table" was a phrase used for *banquets*, not daily meals. Yeshua was a guest of honor (Lk. 7:37).

   b) Her "perfume" would have been viewed as a "tool of the trade"!

   c) She endured the public judgement of others to secure the forgiveness of Yeshua. (E.g. loose hair was improper for women in public)

4. The scandal of a co-ed mentorship (Luke 8:1-3)

   a) Yeshua violated all the "rules" by allowing women to not only travel with them, but to be "disciples." *("with him..." vs. 1-2).*

   b) From Luke we learn the details of Mary of Magdala's conversion.

   c) We learn of the penetration of the Gospel into the palace of Herod Antipas.

E. "MENTORING"—Four Controversial Choices—The World *Of* the Text

  1. *"healed...gone out..."*

    a) these are both perfect tenses in Greek

    b) not an event, but a condition; not a healing, but a healed *woman*!

  2. *"providing"* — imperfect in Greek; ongoing support, not a gift

  3. *"manager"* – epitropos; official of a king responsible for finances.

  4. The wife of a politician and a former demonized woman are working side-by-side for the Kingdom!

F. "MENTORING"—Four Controversial Choices—The World *Before* the Text

  1. Mary's loyalty was the fruit of her gratitude to Yeshua for delivering her from what she was destined to become.

    a) **Question:** Have I ever thanked the Lord, not for what he saved me out of, but from what I would have become?

  2. Mary's commitment to support Yeshua's ministry was the fruit of witnessing that ministry firsthand.

    a) **Question:** Is my support of the Gospel the fruit of personal involvement or someone's appeal?

  3. Yeshua's rejection and hostility from religious people was the result of who he touched and who touched him.

    a) **Question:** Is who I "touch" and who "touches" me the fruit of my relationship with Yeshua or my relationships with religious people?

---

1 Everyone Jesus touches, things "flow" in the opposite direction they are "supposed" to go in terms of clean and unclean. Instead of Jesus becoming "unclean" by touching unclean people and things, those he touches are healed and/or cleansed.

G. "MENTORING"—Preaching in Parables—The World *Behind* the Text

1. Words that "winnow" instead of words that "win." (Mt. 13:1-53; Mk. 4:1-34; Lk. 8:4-18)

   a) Yeshua's first use of parables was in self-defense against the Pharisees (Matt. 9:14-17).[1]

   b) Yeshua's use of parables is actually a fulfillment of the Baptizer's description of His ministry:[2]

   "I baptize you with water for repentance, but he who is coming after me is mightier than I, whose sandals I am not worthy to carry. He will baptize you with the Holy Spirit and with fire. His winnowing fork is in his hand, and he will clear his threshing floor and gather his wheat into the barn, but the chaff he will burn with unquenchable fire." **Matthew 3:11, 12**

   (1) Parables were for those who were "looking" for the Kingdom.[3]

   (2) Parables contained truths about the Kingdom that had previously been *hidden*[4] (Gk = *musterion*).

   (3) The "mysteries" created three groups:

      (a) those who wanted to hear but were told "no" (Matt. 13:17)

      (b) those who *didn't* want them and missed them (Matt. 13:13)

      (c) those who wanted them and were blessed to get them (Matt. 13:16)

      (d) the "parable of the soils" illustrates this relationship between the ears and the heart

   (4) Yeshua's parabolic method was a fulfillment of a prophecy uttered 700 years earlier! (Isaiah 6:9,10).

   c) Yeshua *use* of parables is reflected in the Synoptics *record* of them:

   (1) Matthew records 12 of his 17 uses of the word "parable" in a single chapter, out of a total of 5.

   (2) Matthew's parables deal primarily with the *nature* of the Kingdom itself.

   (3) Luke spreads Yeshua's use of parables out over 11 chapters.

   (4) Luke's recorded parables deal primarily with the *conduct* of Kingdom subjects.

2. Words that "wander" — Interpreting the Parables

   a) *How* we "take the Bible literally" will dictate what we do with the parables.

   b) **Question 1:** "What *are* the parables?" (i.e., what is their *genre*?)

   (1) allegory? — the popular view of the ancient past

      (a) each element had its own "hidden meaning"

      (b) "parable of the soils" seems to support this.

   (2) aphorism? — each parable is believed to teach one point.

      (a) most popular modern view.

   (3) "narrative fiction" — recent view of conservative scholars.

      (a) compares parables to short-stories:

      "...to communicate meaning through their main characters. They encourage readers t identify with one or more of these characters and experience the plot of the story from their various points of view." **Introduction to Biblical Interpretation, pg. 338**

      (b) suggests a correlation between the number of characters and the number of "points":
      i) prodigal son - 3 characters
      ii) lost sheep - 3 characters/groups
      iii) good Samaritan - 3 characters/group
      iv) wicked servant - 3 characters
      v) Pharisee & tax collector - 2 characters
      vi) wise & foolish builders - 2 characters

---

1 This is the parable of new wine and wine skins. Old wineskins are *not* useless, but they are not suited for anything that is still fermenting (i.e. "new"). They have lost their ability to flex and adapt to what is happening within them, much like the religious leaders of Yeshua's day.

2 Yeshua's "winnowing" is not simply an issue of judgment on the Great Day (Matt. 25), or the division that will ensue between members of the same family. Yeshua's very teaching will divide people by their responses to it. This will happen *during* his earthly ministry not after the ascension.

3 We are actually given the name of one such person, Simeon in Luke 2:22ff.

4 Most versions of the New Testament translate this word as "secrets." The NASB translates it "mysteries" in Matthew 13:11.

    c) **Question 2:** "What do we *do* with the parables?"

        (1) We must remind ourselves of their dual purpose: to winnow and give wisdom.

        (2) Look *first* for the literary context of the parable; Many of them were told as a *response* to something or someone. (E.g., the parable of the Good Samaritan was told in response to the question, *"Who is my neighbor?"* The parable of the Pharisee and tax collector was told to *"...some people who trusted in themselves that they were righteous, and viewed others with contempt..."*)

        (3) Be careful to learn as much cultural/historical background as possible (E.g. Samaritans, relative value of coins, etc.)

        (4) Maintain a high degree of humility and tentativeness towards the meaning.

        (5) Do *not* build theology from the parables!

        (6) Use them for "big picture" insight rather than detailed application.

V. PHASE IV — "SOLOING" (Matt. 9:35-11:1; Mark 6:2-29; Luke 9:1-9)

  A. Matthew's Account: The Good and the Bad *(for us!)*

    1. **The Bad:** He "places" Yeshua's *third* tour of Galilee *before* His first and second!

    2. **The Good:** Matthew provides us with a wealth of unique information about this phase of Yeshua's ministry.

      a) Matthew *may* provide us with the actual "pairs" that only Mark tells us were sent out (Mk 6:7; Matt. 10:1-5):[1]

        (1) Simon and Andrew

        (2) James and John

        (3) Philip and Bartholomew

        (4) Thomas and Matthew

        (5) James the son of Alphaeus and Thaddaeus

        (6) Simon the Cananaean (Zealot) and Judas Iscariot

      b) Matthew gives us a detailed record of their "ordination sermon":

        (1) 38 verses, 819 words

        (2) Luke's "version" is 3 verses, and only 53 words

      c) Matthew's use of the word "go" in verse 7 is a Greek word for an *"army on the march."*[2]

        (1) Luke uses this word 53x and almost always in the sense of going on a "mission," i.e. having a "purpose" rather than merely traveling.

        (2) Yeshua uses this same word in *both* His first and last "commissioning" of the Twelve (cf. Matt. 10:7 and 28:19).

    3. Matthew's account of Yeshua's "commissioning sermon" provides us with an amazing list of the elements of genuine discipleship:

      a) Specificity of audience (vv. 5-6; it is *not* the "world" at large)

      b) Specificity of message (vs. 7)

      c) Mercy and acts of compassion; (vs. 8; "cleanse," "heal," "give")

      d) Generosity - they were not to "charge" for what was given to them for free (vs. 8b)

      e) Simplicity (absence of "extra" sandals, money, clothing)[3]

      f) Urgency (leave an unresponsive city and go to a responsive one; vs 11-15)

---

1 It appears that this list is arranged from greatest to least notoriety.

2 Matthew has nine different Greek words in his "go" vocabulary, and uses them in his Gospel.

3 Probably the best way to reconcile the differences between the Synoptics here. Jesus is likely *not* telling them to go "barefoot," but rather not to bring extras of necessities.

g) Expectancy (persecution, rejection, betrayal; all the things that have happened to Yeshua and will happen to him in the next few months; vv. 17-28)

h) Difficulty - discipleship requires a daily commitment to die; (vv. 38-39; this is the famous "he who seeks to save his life will loose it…" passage.)

4. Mark's account provides us with an additional encouragement about ministry:

"And he called the twelve and began to send them out two by two, and gave them authority over the unclean spirits."
Mark 6:7

a) The phrase, *"began to send them out…"* is a combination of an aorist and an infinitive, but *"gave them authority"* is an imperfect.

b) Mark tells us that Yeshua continually gave them authority after the event of sending them out!

B. "He Must Increase, I Must Decrease" — the death of John the Baptizer

1. The four Gospel writers place differing emphases on the death of John:

a) Matthew - 213 words (0.9%)

b) Mark - 399 words (2.7%)

c) Luke - 73 words (0.3%)

d) John - 0 words (0%)

2. Mark's account provides us with the richest details about John's relationship with Herod Antipas:

"For John had been saying to Herod, "It is not lawful for you to have your brother's wife." And Herodias had a grudge against him and wanted to put him to death. But she could not, for Herod feared John, knowing that he was a righteous and holy man, and he kept him safe. When he heard him, he was greatly perplexed, and yet he heard him gladly."
Mark 6:18-20

a) Mark's verbs for "feared" and "knowing" are both in the *perfect* tense, indicating that Herod had arrived at a "state" of fearing and knowing.

b) In other words, he was completely convinced of John's holy and righteous character.

c) The verb for "kept him safe" is in the *imperfect* tense, which alerts us to two things:

(1) John's life had often been in danger.

(2) Herod had protected John *more than once prior to this incident!*

(3) From Mark we learn that John's *real* adversary was *not* Herod, as Matthew indicates, but Herodias.

d) Mark also gives us the "guest list" for Herod's birthday party:

(1) "nobles" — *(Gk - megistanes)*; superlative of "megas" meaning of enormous importance.

(2) "military commanders" *(Gk - chiliarchos)*; a tribune, commander of cohort (1000 men).

(3) "leading men of Galilee" *(Gk - protos)*; first in imminence.

e) Mark provides us with one final insight, that Salome was *not* planning on her mother's response to her question!

(1) The verb means "to ask *for* a gift" (rather than to ask a *person*)[1]

(2) It is in the middle voice, meaning "to ask for oneself."

(3) She said to her mother, *"What kind of gift to you think I should ask for myself, having such a wonderful opportunity?"*

C. "SOLOING" — The World *Before* The Text

1. Which of the seven characteristics of genuine discipleship above am I reluctant to embrace:

a) **Specificity** of audience and of message.

b) **Mercy** and acts of compassion.

c) **Generosity** - they were not to "charge" for what was given to them for free.

---

1 There are two primary Greek verbs in the New Testament for "asking." One is *aiteō,* which means to ask a person, but to do so much like a demand. The second is *erōtaō,* which means to ask for a *thing.* In this story, the force of a "demand" is absent.

d) **Simplicity** (absence of "extra" sandals, money, clothing)

e) **Urgency** leave an unresponsive person and go to a responsive one

f) **Expectancy** (persecution, rejection, betrayal; all the things that have happened to Yeshua and will happen to me.

g) **Difficulty** - discipleship requires a daily commitment to die to self.

2. Do I believe Yeshua's last word, "go" is still operative? If so, where am I "going?"

UNIT 11: Yeshua's "Retirement" Year

I. THE 1st WITHDRAWAL OF YESHUA FROM GALILEE

A. Understanding the "Pieces" on the Board

And when Peter saw it he addressed the people: "Men of Israel, why do you wonder at this, or why do you stare at us, as though by our own power or piety we have made him walk? The God of Abraham, the God of Isaac, and the God of Jacob, the God of our fathers, glorified his servant Jesus, whom you delivered over and denied in the presence of Pilate, when he had decided to release him." **Acts 3:12, 13**

1. The "Christ"

a) Yeshua's identity, which was the focal point of conflict in Jerusalem earlier, begins to be an issue in Galilee.

b) Who Yeshua truly *is* will determine what various people will expect him to *do*.

c) For some, this has to do with expectations, for others with fears.

2. The "Crowns"

a) There are two political figures at work in this drama:

(1) Herod Antipas – the representative of Rome in the region where Yeshua spends most of his time (i.e. Galilee).

(2) Pontius Pilate – the representative of Rome in the city which is the "heart" of Judaism in the world.

3. The "Crowds"

a) Range from those who are confused and uncommitted to those who are angry and disillusioned (Jn. 6:60,66).

b) The "swing voters" among the Jews in Syro-Palestine.

c) This is the peasant majority.

4. The "Conspirators"

a) The recently formed confederacy of Jerusalemite Jews united only by their shared enmity towards Yeshua.

b) This includes the Pharisees, Sadducees, Herodians, scribes, elders and priests. (Matt. 15:1; 16:1; Mk. 3:6)

c) This is the aristocratic minority.

5. The "Core"

a) Those who are willing to constantly readjust their theology to align with that of Yeshua. (Matt. 16:13-20)

b) This is the "Church" yet unborn.

B. Understanding What Was "Moving" the Pieces

1. The death of John the Baptizer was a cataclysmic, not merely unfortunate event.

2. Yeshua growing resistance to accommodate popular expectations was reducing his following, from "the ground up."

3. Yeshua growing clarity of teaching about his identity and the decayed state of Judaism was increasing the hostility "from the top down."

4. Yeshua's response to this was to spend six months "beneath the radar" of the "crowds" and the "crowns":

a) He withdraws to "the other side" of the Sea of Galilee.

b) He withdraws to the Gentile boundaries of Israel.

c) He withdraws into Phoenicia and the Decapolis.

d) He withdraws to Caesarea Philippi.

5. All of these journeys kept him away from Tiberius and Herod Antipas.

C. The First Withdrawal Key Events: (Mt. 14:13-15:20; Mk. 6:30-7:23; Lk. 9:10-17; Jn. 6:1-7:1)

1. Death of the Baptizer

2. "The Twelve" return from their ministry in pairs.

3. Yeshua feeds the 5,000.

4. Yeshua shuns attempts to make him king.

5. Yeshua "walks on the water."

6. Healing ministry at Genneseret.

7. Bread of Life sermon at Capernaum.

8. Yeshua confronts Jerusalem scribes on a "spy" mission.

D. The Feeding of the 5,000 — The World *Behind* the Text

1. This is the first and only *miracle* other than the resurrection, that is recorded in all four Gospels!

2. A list of the other events recorded in all four Gospels is below:

E V E N T	Ministry Segment
Feeding of the 5,000	Withdrawals
Triumphal Entry ("Palm Sunday")	Passion Week
Yeshua identifies Judas as the betrayer	Passion Week
Yeshua predicts Peter's denial	Passion Week
Yeshua's arrest in Gethsemane	Passion Week
Yeshua before the Sanhedrin	Passion Week
Peter's denial	Passion Week
Yeshua's 1st appearance before Pilate	Passion Week
Yeshua 2nd appearance before Pilate	Passion Week
Journey to Golgotha (Good Friday)	Passion Week
Crucifixion and 1st three hours on cross (Good Friday)	Passion Week
Darkness from noon-3pm (Good Friday)	Passion Week
Joseph of Arimathea requests and obtains body	Passion Week
Joseph buries Yeshua	Passion Week
Women at empty tomb & angelic announcement	Post Resurrection

3. The total numbered "served" could have been as high as 10,000.

a) This is the seating capacity of the theater at Ephesus!

b) It is four times the seating capacity of the theater at Sephoris.

c) From John we learn that *"the time of the Passover was at hand…"* which would account for the enormous number in this crowd (Jn. 6:4).

d) This is substantiated by a tiny comment made only by Mark:

"Then he commanded them all to sit down in groups on the green grass."   **Mark 6:39**

4. Matthew's account has apparent contradictions about the time of day:

"Now when it was evening, the disciples came to him and said, "This is a desolate place, and the day is now over; send the crowds away to go into the villages and buy food for themselves."   **Matthew 14:15**

*And after he had dismissed the crowds, he went up on the mountain by himself to pray. **When evening came**, he was there alone…"*   **Matthew 14:23**

a) The Jews had two "evenings" that they reckoned in a 24-hour period.

b) The "1st evening" began with the decline of the sun, and lasted until around 3 pm.

    c) The second began with the appearance of the first star and lasted until the appearance of the 3rd star.

    d) The "night," from which the following day was reckoned, began after the second evening.

E. The Feeding of the 5,000 — The World *Of* the Text

  1. John bursts into the story with the most detail and insight about this incident of all the Gospels (this is his first entry since early in the Galilean ministry!); Jn. 6:15

    a) John leaves out important details that the Synoptics provide:

      (1) Yeshua had sought to "get away" with the Twelve after their mission trip (Mk 6:30-31).

      (2) Yeshua had spent the entire day teaching and healing prior to the feeding miracle (Mt. 14:14; Mk. 6:34; Lk. 8:10-11).

      (3) That the feeding took place "in the evening."

    b) John uses three Imperfect tense verbs to tell us the intensity of the following Yeshua was accumulating: *"following him," "saw"* and *"doing."*

    c) From John we learn very important details about this "meal":

      (1) The loaves were "barley" loaves, the grain of the very poor.

      (2) The Greek word John uses for "fish" is the Greek word, *opsarion,* not *ichthus,* the normal word for a "fish."

      (3) *Opsarion* is the word for a small, salted fish similar to our sardines. A snack more than a meal!

      (4) This adds credibility to the story, because it contains the detailed knowledge of a skilled fishermen.

      (5) But, this is the identical word for the "fishes" that Yeshua served the apostles after the resurrection, on the shores of Galilee (contrasted to the 153 *ichthon megothon,* "large fishes" in their nets!)

      (6) John calls this miracle a "sign," which in his Gospel always points to Yeshua's identity more than his power.

      (7) John alone tells us why Matthew and Mark's account has Yeshua hurrying the disciples to get into the boat and leave:

        "When the people saw the sign that he had done, they said, "This is indeed the Prophet who is to come into the world!" Perceiving then that they were about to come and take him by force to make him king, Jesus withdrew again to the mountain by himself. When evening came, his disciples went down to the sea,"   **John 6:14-16**

      (8) John alone tells us that this miracle was the basis of Yeshua's sermon in Capernaum that "tanked" his popularity (cf. Jn. 6:22-7:1)

    d) The Greek word for "basket" used by all four writers is the word, *kophinos,* the bread-bag of the poor. (This is likely the reason there were twelve!)

    e) The solitude Yeshua sought for them was real, he took it himself!

F. Walking on the Water — The World *Of* the Text

  1. Luke omits this incident from his Gospel completely!

  2. Matthew *alone* records the detail about Peter's short adventure on the water.

  3. Matthew alone also records the response of *"those in the boat"* (most likely *not* the Twelve) as "worship" (Mt. 14:33).

    a) There are only 5 instances of Yeshua being worshipped in the Gospels:

      (1) The magi (Mt. 2:2,11)

      (2) The "man born blind" (Jn. 9:37-38).

      (3) *"Those in the boat"* (Mt. 14:33).

      (4) Disciples at his ascension into heaven (Mt. 28:9,17; Lk. 24:52).

  4. This was their *second* trial of faith with Yeshua on the Sea of Galilee.

    a) In the first one, he was asleep in the boat (Mk. 4:35-41).

    b) In this one, he is in prayer on the shore (Mk. 6:47-52).

      c)   In both cases, they were convinced that they were on their own.

G. The World *Before* the Text

   1. How much of my commitment to the Christian faith is a product of its popularity and safety?

   2. When I'm on the "seas," do I think about the fact that Yeshua is praying on the shore, if I don't sense him with me in the boat?

   3. How often do I *"dismiss the crowds"?*

II. THE FINAL WITHDRAWALS OF YESHUA FROM GALILEE (cont'd)

A. Syro-Phoenecia: The Word *Behind* the Text

   1. Israel's long history with these "neighbors" was long and unpleasant.

      a) Syria (aka Aram) had been an enemy of Israel from the time of the Judges to the post exilic period.

      b) Phoenicia was the region from which Jezebel, Ahab's wicked wife had come:

"And Ahab the son of Omri did evil in the sight of the LORD, more than all who were before him. And as if it had been a light thing for him to walk in the sins of Jeroboam the son of Nebat, he took for his wife Jezebel the daughter of Ethbaal king of the Sidonians, and went and served Baal and worshiped him." **1 Kgs 16:30, 31**

      c) Syro-Phoenicia was the region where Elijah hid from Ahab, and from which Naaman came to be healed of leprosy by Elisha.

      d) Yeshua's first mention of ministry in this area nearly cost him his life in Nazareth (Lk. 4:16-30).

   2. Yeshua already had disciples in this Gentile area (Mk. 3:7-12).

      a) Residents of Tyre and Sidon had actually *seen* Yeshua heal and cast out demons.

      b) Likely, one of these people is whose home Yeshua stayed in (Mk. 7:24).

   3. Weaving this tale of wonder together

      a) Luke does not even mention this segment of ministry.

      b) Mark informs us that her daughter is *not* with her (Mk. 7:30)

      c) Matthew tells us that she believed Yeshua to be the Jewish Messiah (e.g. "son of David" in 15:22).

   4. Of the 16 times "son of David" appears in the Gospels, 14 of them are in a messianic context.

B. Syro-Phoenicia: The World *Of* The Text

   1. This was an on-going drama, not an event:

      a) The woman's *"crying,"* the disciples *"urging,"* and her *falling before him…"* are all *Imperfect* tenses in Greek.

      b) Yeshua's treatment of *her* is unusual (cf. Caiphas, Pilate, Herod), but also similar to his treatment of the Twelve!

      c) The word for "dog," *(kunarion)* is a house pet, *not* the stray, savage "dog" *(kuon)* of the street (cf. Matt. 7:4; 1 Kgs. 21:23).

      d) This story is the only place in our NT where the word, *kunarion* is used.

      e) There is at least the possibility that this whole ordeal was for the benefit of the Twelve as much as the woman.

C. From Tyre to the Decapolis: The World *Behind* The Text

   1. Yeshua's Gentile ministry may have been as prophetic as it was compassionate:

   2. Yeshua's path of travel *may* have been predicted by Isaiah 700 years earlier:

"But there will be no gloom for her who was in anguish. In the former time he brought into contempt the land of Zebulun and the land of Naphtali, but in the latter time he has made glorious the way of the sea, the land beyond the Jordan, Galilee of the nations." **Isaiah 9:1**

D. From Tyre to the Decapolis: The World *Of* The Text

   1. Luke omits this segment of ministry from his account.

   2. Mark indicates that he was in this area for a while, *"In those days…"* (Mk. 8:1)

3. Matthew implies that Yeshua's healing and exorcism ministry was mostly to Gentiles:

> *"...so that the crowd wondered, when they saw the mute speaking, the crippled healthy, the lame walking, and the blind seeing. And **they glorified the God of Israel**."*   **Matthew 15:31**

4. The "feeding of the 4,000" is *not* a reinterpretation of a prior event:

   a) The word for "basket" *(spuris)* here is a large "hamper," big enough for Paul to escape a walled city in one (Acts. 9:25).

   b) Yeshua specifically refers to two separate miraculous feedings, to make a point (Mk. 8:19-20).

5. The contrast in responses by people in this account is chilling.

   a) Those "in the dark" (Gentiles):

   > *And they were astonished beyond measure, saying, "He has done all things well. He even makes the deaf hear and the mute speak."*   **Mark 7:37**

   b) Those "in the light" (religious leaders):

   > *"The Pharisees came and began to argue with him, seeking from him a sign from heaven to test him. And he sighed deeply in his spirit and said, "Why does this generation seek a sign? Truly, I say to you, no sign will be given to this generation." And he left them, got into the boat again, and went to the other side."*   **Mark 8:11-13**

E. Caesarea Philippi: The World *Behind* The Text

1. This region has a rich history...all of it pagan!

   a) It was known as Baal-Hermon during the Old Testament era (Jdg. 3:3; 1 Chron 5:23).

   b) It's name was changed to Paneas in Hellenistic times (c. 200 BC) in honor of the goat-man god of fertility, Pan.

   c) The remains of a temple to Pan are still visible today.

   d) Herod's son, Philip, built an administrative center there and changed its name to Caesarea Philippi.

   e) It did not become a true "city" until AD 54, during the days of Herod Agrippa II.

   f) When Yeshua visited this area, it was largely pagan and *not* an actual city:

   > *"Now when Jesus came into the **district** of Caesarea Philippi, he asked his disciples, "Who do people say that the Son of Man is?"*   **Matthew 16:13**

   g) The highest mountain in Israel, Mount Hermon is in this area (9,232 ft.).

   h) The events in this region mark a indisputable turning point in the ministry and mission of Yeshua.

F. Caesarea Philippi: The World *Of* The Text

1. Matthew gives us the fullest account (cf. Mt. 16:13-20; Mk. 8:27-30; Lk. 9:18-20)

   a) *"You are the Christ, the son of the living God."*

   b) Simon's name is *officially* changed to "Peter" here, and he is to be a central leader (cf. Jn 1:42 and Mt. 16:18).

   c) Yeshua speaks of a new group, the *ekklesia* (church) that belongs to *Yeshua*, who is its "builder."

   d) The rulers and authorities (e.g. "gates") in spiritual realms will *not* be able to stop what is coming.

   e) Peter's confession is emphatic: there are four Greek articles in a sentence of only ten words!

   "You are [the] Christ, [the] son of [the] living [the] God."

2. Yeshua's questions are *strategic*:

   a) The Greek plural pronoun, *"you"* appears first in the sentence.

   b) The verb, *"say"* is in the present tense.

   c) Yeshua is at the beginning of a progression that will end shortly on Mount Hermon:

   (1) *"Who do men say that I am?"*

   (2) *"Who do you say that I am?"*

   (3) *"Who do I say that I am?"*

   (4) *"Who does Yahweh say that I am?"*

   (5) *"Who do you NOW say that I am?"*

d) Yeshua shifts their focus from function (a prophet) to identity (the Son of God).

e) From this point on, *everything* will focus on the *second* half of Yeshua's stated mission:

For even the Son of Man came not to be served but to serve, and to give his life as a ransom for many." **Mark 10:45**

f) From this point on, Yeshua begins to speak of suffering and death, both his and theirs (Lk. 9:21-23).

g) Peter's rejection of Yeshua's suffering is *not* a denial of Yeshua's Messiahship. It is a reflection of bad *theology,* not weak faith.

G. Mount Hermon: The World *Behind* the Text

1. The four Gospel writers use this event in very different ways, evidenced by how many chapters *follows* the event itself:

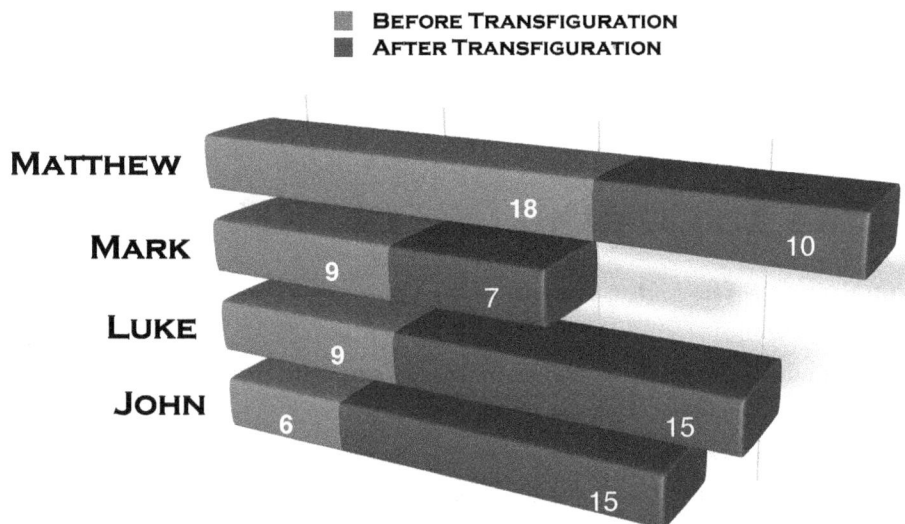

■ **BEFORE TRANSFIGURATION**
■ **AFTER TRANSFIGURATION**

MATTHEW — 18 / 10
MARK — 9 / 7
LUKE — 9 / 15
JOHN — 6 / 15

2. Luke provides the fullest setting:

a) Yeshua went up on the mountain to *pray* (9:28).

b) This "transfiguration" occurred while *he* was praying and Peter, James and John were *sleeping!* (9:29,32)

c) The cloud *enveloped them,* and God spoke to them *in* the cloud (9:34-35).

d) Elijah and Moses were talking with Yeshua about his "departure *(Gk - exodus)* which he was to accomplish at Jerusalem." (9:30)

3. Re-Examining the Obvious

a) Yeshua's glory was *inherent*, not reflected.

b) Moses had been through this before (Ex. 34:29).

c) This was Moses' first visit to the Promised Land.

d) Elijah had no "experience" with death.

e) Both of these men already knew the eternal Son of God.

4. Explaining the *Odious*

a) It was *after* this event that the posturing over being "the greatest" began (cf. Mt. 18:1-5; Mk. 9:33-34; Lk. 9:46).

b) Their experience was unprecedented in all of the Bible:

(1) They were hand-picked out of an already elect group (9 others did *not* have this experience!)

(2) They were eye-witnesses of the glory of the Son of God (no one else living saw this).

(3) They were eye-witnesses of the conversation between Yeshua, Elijah and Moses.

(4) They *met* Elijah and Moses!

(5) Yahweh *spoke* to them! (They did not "overhear" Him speaking to Yeshua.)

(6) Yeshua makes them swear to secrecy until *after* the resurrection. (This is similar to Paul's thorn in the flesh.)

5. A Permanent Lesson

a) When Yeshua revisits the theme of his coming suffering right after this, Peter is silent (Mt. 197:9-13).

b) Both Peter and John write of this event near the end of their lives (cf. Jn. 1:14; 2 Pet. 1:16).

c) Peter, James and John *knew* Yeshua was not the enemy of Moses or the Law after this event! (cf. Jn. 9:28-31).

H. The World *Before* The Text

1. The Syro-Phoenician woman is an excellent example of the heart of prayer. She first prayed for her daughter, then, in exasperation, she said, "Help *me!*" How attached to the pain am I of those I pray for?

2. The "Yeshua on the mountain" is the Yeshua of the Second Coming. Do I think of him in those terms?

3. The apostles battle with "greatness" was always relative to others rather than Yeshua. To whom do I cast my comparative glances?

UNIT 12: COMING *OUT* OF "RETIREMENT"

I. Yeshua's "Comeback" – The Later Judean Ministry

A. Getting the *Bigger* Picture[1]

1. This segment begins the final six months of Yeshua's ministry prior to Golgotha.

2. The "Later Judean" segment occupies about 3 months.

3. Our sources:

a) Matthew and Mark are *silent* about this segment and beyond (cf. Lk. 9:51–18:14 and Jn. 7:2–11:54).

b) Luke gives us nearly 4,200 words! (9:51-13:21).

c) John gives us nearly 3,900 words! (7:10-10:39).

d) Luke and John have only *one verse* in common for this entire period! (Lk. 9:51 and Jn. 7:1).

e) Luke alone tells us of Yeshua's prophetic determination to go to Jerusalem and complete His mission:

> "When the days drew near for him to be taken up, **he set his face** to go to Jerusalem."　　　　**Luke 9:51**

> "I gave my back to those who strike, and my cheeks to those who pull out the beard; I hid not my face from disgrace and spitting. But the Lord GOD helps me; therefore I have not been disgraced; therefore **I have set my face like a flint**, and I know that I shall not be put to shame."　　　　**Isaiah 50:6, 7**

f) Luke "splits" this fixation on Jerusalem into three distinct "returns" to the city (cf. 9:51; 13:22; 18:31).

4. The Main Events of this period:

a) Yeshua's family "encourages" him to travel to Jerusalem for the Feast of Tabernacles and "reveal" himself (Jn. 7:2-9).

b) He does go, later, and travels through Samaria with the Twelve, where he is rejected by the Samaritans and refused hospitality (likely because he was a Jew going to Jerusalem to worship; Lk. 9:51-56; Jn. 7:10).

c) Arrives in Jerusalem for the Feast of Tabernacles; great excitement among the people (Jn. 7:11-52).

d) Woman "caught" in adultery brought to Yeshua (Jn. 7:53 - 8:11).

e) Yeshua claims to be "the light of the world" and creates animosity with leaders (Jn. 8:12-59).

f) Healing of the man born blind and the ensuing dialogues with him and his parents (Jn. 9:1-41).

---

1 This is a period of growing hostility, misunderstanding, and rejection. Jesus goes from losing followers in Galilee following the "bread of life" sermon in Capernaum, to the disbelief of his own family, to the rejection in Samaria, to the posturing over "greatness" among the Twelve. And, all of this occurs *before* he arrives in Jerusalem for the most difficult week of his life! John's summary statement, *"He cam to his own, but his own people did not receive him."* is about to be fulfilled. (John 1:11)

g) Teaching (parable?) on the Good Shepherd, especially his willingness to die for the sheep (Jn. 10:1-21).

h) Yeshua sends out "the seventy" on a similar mission as the Twelve (Lk. 10:1-24).

i) Parable of the Good Samaritan in response to question about eternal life (Lk 10:25-37).

j) Yeshua in the home of Martha and Mary (Lazarus does not appear to be present; in Jerusalem?; Lk. 10:38-42).

k) Series of parables about Kingdom subjects (e.g. Rich Fool, Wise Servant, Barren Fig Tree; Lk. 11:1-13:21).

l) Yeshua attends the Feast of Dedication 2 months after Feast of Booths (Jn. 10:22-39).

B. The World *Behind* The Text

  1. The Rejection in Samaria (Luke 9:51-56)

    a) Yeshua's *"direction"* indicated his devotion.

    b) The Samaritans were more critical of Jerusalem than Judaism The Greek here is literally, *"because his face was going to Jerusalem…"* (cf. Jn. 4:1-29 and this account).

    c) It is likely that Yeshua was more discouraged by James and John than the Samaritans!

  2. The Tumult at Tabernacles (John 7)

    a) The Jews had 8 annual festivals; six were Mosaic and *two were post-exilic (in italics):*

      (1) Unleavened Bread (Passover — 15th-22nd Nisan

      (2) Feast of First Fruits (Pentecost) — 6th Sivan

      (3) Feast of Ingathering (Tabernacles/Booths) 15th - 22nd Tishri

      (4) Solemn Assembly (Octave of Ingathering) — 23rd Tishri

      (5) Feast of Trumpets (Rosh Hashanah)— 1st Tishri

      (6) Day of Atonement (Yom Kippur)[1] — 10th Tishri

      (7) *Feast of Dedication (aka Chanukah) — 25th Chislev*

      (8) *Feast of Purim — 14th - 15th Adar*

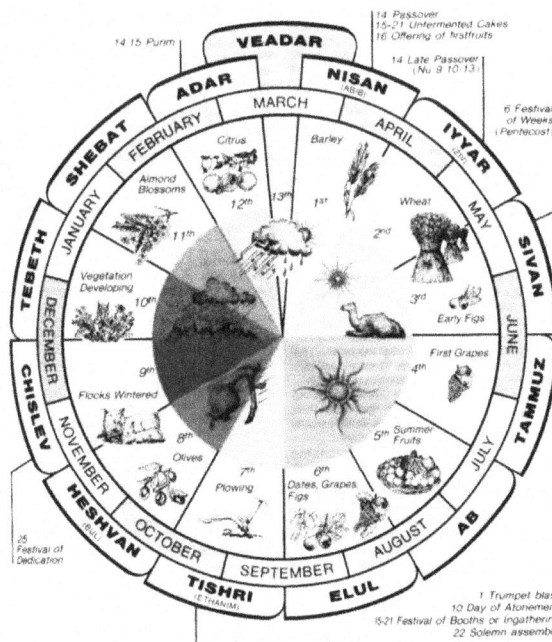

    b) Of these eight, three were *"pilgrim festivals"* because native-born Jewish males were required to travel to Jerusalem (Ex. 23:14-17).

---

1 The days *between* Rosh Hashanah and Yom Kippur were known as "the days of awe," a time for deep personal introspection.

(1) Unleavened Bread (Passover) commemorated the barley harvest *and* the exodus from Egypt (Nu. 28:16-25; Dt. 16:1-8).

(2) First Fruits (Pentecost) commemorated the wheat harvest *and* the giving of the Law at Sinai (Ex. 34:26; Lev. 23:1-14; Nu. 28:26-31).

(3) Ingathering (Tabernacles) celebrated the final harvest (fruits) *and* the beginning of the 40-year wilderness wandering (Lev. 23:43; Neh. 8:9-18).

(4) It is amazing that God built their liturgical celebrations on covenant theology wedded to the agricultural seasons (cf. Deut. 28).

3. A closer look at the "feast of feasts" (Num. 29:12-38)

   a) The Feast of Ingathering was the most elaborate and celebratory of all the Jewish feasts:

      (1) It lasted *eight* days (7+1).

      (2) 182 animals were sacrificed during the week (70 bulls, 14 rams, 98 lambs).

      (3) It required nearly 500 priests (*not to mention Levites!*) to service all the sacrifices.

      (4) It is known as the *"Feast of Yahweh"* in Leviticus 23:39.

      (5) In Sabbatical years, the Law was to be read during this week as a reminder and as an evangelistic tool (Deut. 31:10).

      (6) Solomon picked *this feast* for the dedication of the first Temple he had built (most likely because of its length *and* celebratory nature).

      (7) It is the one feast singled out by Josephus *and* the Rabbis as most important.

      (8) It is the only feast that is associated with the ingathering of the *Gentiles* and the end of the age (cf. Zech. 14:16-21).

   b) It was the most community-building feast of the year:

      (1) It marked the end of the agricultural year (change of seasons; approach of rain, winter equinox)

      (2) It followed five days after the Day of Atonement in which the sin of Israel has been removed, and its covenant relation to God restored.

      (3) The temple treasury boxes were opened and emptied for the final time that year, which would remind the pilgrims of all their brethren scattered throughout the world, who, from time to time during the year had come and brought their "temple tax" to support the daily offerings and priests. It would have been a time of tremendous national identity.

      (4) Living in booths for a week also galvanized their sense of identity in the world and in history. They alone did something like this, and the reason was to commemorate the fact that the God of Heaven created a new nation by bringing them out of Egypt.

      (5) The city of Jerusalem and the roads, courtyards, balconies, streets and yards would have been *saturated* with people. within a "Sabbath's day journey" (i.e. 2,000 paces; one-way) and booths that were set-up the previous day.

   c) The liturgy of the Feast was very significant, considering the events of Yeshua's life that week given to us by John:

      (1) The altar of burnt-offering would have been cleansed during the first watch of the night (c. 9pm).

      (2) The gates of the Temple were thrown open immediately after midnight.

      (3) The priests made preparations all night and into the morning, getting ready for the first morning sacrifice.

      (4) While the sacrifice was being prepared, a priest "accompanied by a joyous procession, went down to the Pool of Siloam, where he drew water into a golden pitcher (except on Sabbath, when the water was drawn the day before).

      (5) While this first procession was headed to the Pool, a second joyous procession went to the Kidron Valley to gather willow branches to be placed as a canopy over the altar of burnt-offering.

(6) The procession from Siloam timed their procession perfectly to arrive at the altar just as the sacrifice was being laid on the altar (they came through the "Water Gate" which got its name from this ritual).

(7) There were two small funnels on the side of the altar into which he poured the water (and some wine).

(8) It was this portion of the ceremony (among others) which the Sadducees did not believe should be followed; Alexander Jannaeus (a Macabbean) poured the water on the ground to spite the Pharisees, and the Jews began pelting him with the *ethrogs* (fruits) they had been carrying in their left hands. A riot broke out and 6,000 Jews were killed in the Temple area!

(9) The Hillel Psalms (113-118) were sung when the water and wine were poured out.

(10) Every day the priests made a procession around the altar singing, *"O then, now work salvation, Jehovah! O Jehovah, give prosperity!"* (Ps. 118:25). But, on the seventh day, "that great day," they made this circuit seven times, remembering how the walls of Jericho had fallen after seven circuits, symbolizing the collapse of heathenism and the triumph of God's redemption of all "nations" (Goyim; Gentiles).

d) It is in *this* context that Yeshua interrupts this ceremony on the "great day," and shouts, *"If anyone thirsts, let him come to me..."*

    (1) Jewish scholar Alfred Eidersheim's description of a plausible scene is chilling:

> *"It obtained this name, although it was not one of 'holy convocation,' partly because it closed the feast, and partly from the circumstances which procured it in Rabbinical writings the designations of 'Day of the Great Hosannah,' on account of the sevenfold circuit of the altar with 'Hosannah'; and 'Day of Willows,' and 'Day of Beating the Branches,' because all the leaves were shaken off the willow boughs, and the palm branches beaten in pieces by the side of the altar. It was on that day, after the priests had returned from Siloam with his golden pitcher, and for the last time poured its contents to the base of the altar; after the 'Hallel' had been sung to the sound of the flute, the people responding and worshipping as the priests three times drew the threefold blasts from their silver trumpets—just when the interest of the people had been raised to its highest pitch, that from amidst the worshippers, who were waving towards the altar quite a forest of leafy branches as the last words of Psalm 118 were chanted—a voice was raised which resounded through the Temple, startled the multitude, and carried fear and hatred to the hearts of their leaders. It was Jesus, who 'stood and cried, saying* **"If anyone is thirsty, let him come to Me and drink. "He who believes in Me, as the Scripture said, 'From his innermost being will flow rivers of living water.'"** (John 7:37, 38)

e) It is also likely (*if* John 7:53-8:11 is an addition) that later that same evening Yeshua made his first unmistakable *"I Am"* statement in the context of the climax of the Feast of Tabernacles:

> *Again Jesus spoke to them, saying,* **"I am the light of the world.** *Whoever follows me will not walk in darkness, but will have the light of life."*
>
> John 8:12

f) Eidersheim's comments on this incident serve to amplify just how volatile the environment surrounding Yeshua was becoming:

> *"Jerusalem, the City of Solemnities, the City of Palaces, the City of beauty and glory, wore quite another than its usual aspect; other, even, than when its streets were thronged by festive pilgrims during the Passover week, or at Pentecost. For this was pre-eminently the Feast of the foreign pilgrims, coming from the farthest distance, whose Temple contributions were then received and counted. Despite the strange costumes of Media, Arabia, Persia, or India, and even further; or the Western speech and bearing of pilgrims from Italy, Spain or the modern Crimea, and the banks of the Danube...They would come at this season of the year—not during the winter for the Passover, nor yet quite so readily in summer's heat for Pentecost. But now, in the delicious cool of early autumn, when all harvest operations, the gathering of luscious fruit and the vintage were past, and the first streaks of gold were tinting the foliage, strangers from afar off, and countrymen from Judea, Perea and Galilee, would mingle in the streets of Jerusalem, under the ever-present shadow of that glorious Sanctuary of marble, cedar wood, and gold, up there on high Moriah, symbol of the infinitely more glorious over-shadowing Presence of Him, Who was the Holy One in the midst of Israel. How, all day long, even till the stars lit up the deep blue canopy overhead, the smoke of the burning, smoldering sacrifices rose in slowly-widening column, and hung between the Mount of Olives and Zion; how the chant of Levites, and the solemn responses of the Hallel were born on the breeze, or the clear blast of the Priests' silver trumpets seemed to waken the echoes far away! And then, at night, how all these vast Temple buildings stood out, illuminated by the great Candelabras that burned in the Court of the Women, and by the glare of torches, when strange sound of mystic hymns and dances came floating over the intervening darkness! Truly, well might Israel designate the Feast of Tabernacles as 'the Feast' (haChag), and the Jewish Historian [Josephus] describe it as 'the holiest and greatest."*   **Life and Times of Jesus the Messiah, pg. 577**

4. Yeshua's "Identity Crisis" – The *Original* Purpose Driven® Life

   a) From this point on, Yeshua's main "battle" with the Jewish authorities is centered around two insepa-rable conflicts:

      (1) his identity (I.e., *who* He is)

      (2) his mission (*why* He's here)

   b) John introduces these conflicts at the *beginning* of his Gospel:

> *"The true light, which enlightens everyone, was coming into the world. He was in the world, and the world was made through him, yet the world did not know him. He came to his own, and his own people did not receive him. But to all who did receive him, who believed in his name, he gave the right to become children of God, who were born, not of blood nor of the will of the flesh nor of the will of man, but of God. And the Word became flesh and dwelt among us, and we have seen his glory, glory as of the only Son from the Father, full of grace and truth."*
> **John 1:9-14**

   c) The use of personal pronouns in the four Gospels reveals John's uniques emphasis on *who Yeshua is* as opposed to what he did or said:

      (1) *"I, me, my, mine"* appears nearly 800x in John's Gospel (compared to 395 in Matthew, 179 in Mark and 415 in Luke), and nearly 200 in the Later Judean segment alone.

   d) Only John records the *"I Am..."* statements of Yeshua, and the majority of them are during *this seg-ment* of Yeshua's ministry (Jn. 7:56-10:39):

      (1) *"I am the bread of life..."* – **John 6:35,41,48,51**

      (2) *"If anyone is thirsty, let him come to Me and drink."* – **John 7:37**

      (3) *"I am the Light of the world..."* – **John 8:12; 9:5**

      (4) *"Truly, truly I say to you, before Abraham was, I am."* – **John 8:58**

      (5) *"Truly, truly, I say to you, I am the door of the sheep."* – **John 10:7**

      (6) *"I am the door..."* – **John 10:9**

      (7) *"I am the good shepherd..."* – **John 10:11**

      (8) *"...I and the Father are one."* – **John 10:30**

      (9) *"...I said, 'I am the Son of God..."* – **John 10:36**

      (10)*"I am the resurrection and the life..."* – **John 11:25**

      (11)*"I am the way, and the truth, and the life..."* – **John 14:6**

      (12)*"I am the true vine..."* – **John 15:1**

   e) All but *"I am the bread of life"* were made in Jerusalem, and *all* were made in the face of opposition.

   f) Yeshua's claim to a unique relationship to Yahweh is also a distinctive of John's "portrait" of Yeshua:

      (1) Yeshua's refers to Yahweh as *"Father"* 123x in 14 chapters of John's Gospel (compared to 44 in Matthew, 5 in Mark and 21 in Luke).

      (2) Of those 123x, 26 are references to *"My Father..."*

> *But Jesus answered them, "My Father is working until now, and I am working."*   **John 5:17**

> *They said to him therefore, "Where is your Father?" Jesus answered, "You know neither me nor my Father. If you knew me, you would know my Father also."*   **John 8:19**

> *My sheep hear my voice, and I know them, and they follow me. I give them eternal life, and they will never perish, and no one will snatch them out of my hand. My Father, who has given them to me, is greater than all, and no one is able to snatch them out of the Father's hand. I and the Father are one."*   **John 10:27-30**

      (3) It is Yeshua's *claim* to this relationship that causes the Jews in Jerusalem to seek to *stone him* twice surrounding the healing of the man born blind, during this segment of his ministry (cf. Jn. 8:54-59; 10:24-33).

5. Yeshua's Two "Worlds": Jerusalem and Bethany

   a) The final months of Yeshua's life will be spent around two "centers," one hostile and the other "home."

b) It is during this segment of Yeshua's life and ministry when he meets the family that will become the source of stability in the most volatile season of his life: Martha, Mary, and Lazarus.

c) In a very real sense, Bethany is what Capernaum was in Galilee:

(1) He is welcomed into the home of Martha and Mary when he first arrives (Lk 10:38-42).

(2) It is from here that he rides the donkey into Jerusalem (Mk. 11:1-2)

(3) It is here, in the home of "Simon the leper," that he was "anointed" for his burial (Mk. 14:3ff).

(4) It is his "home" during Passion Week (Mk. 11:11-12).

(5) It is from this vicinity that he ascended into heaven (Lk. 24:50-51).

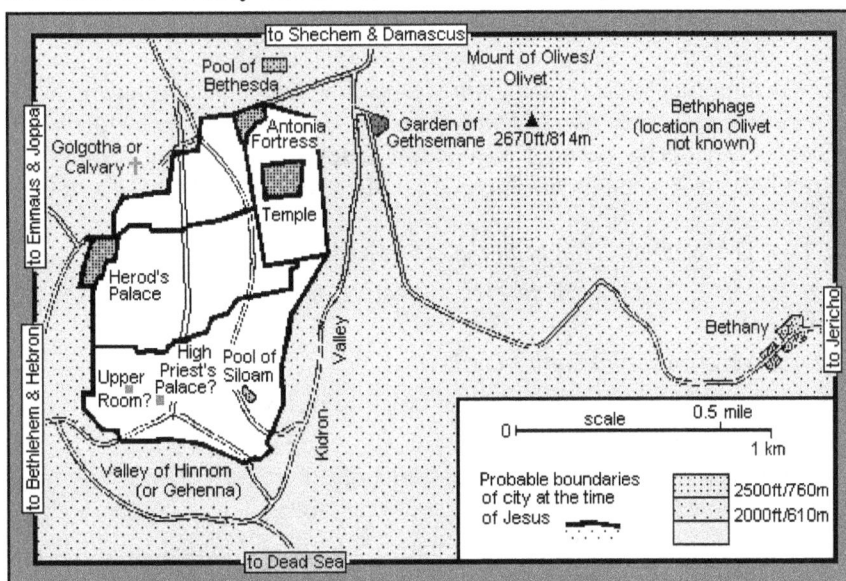

(*Image taken from:* http://www.ccel.org/bible/phillips/CN091MAPS.htm)

C. The World *Of* The Text—The Later Judean Ministry

1. John 7:37-38 — The word here for Yeshua's speech, "cried out" (Gk - *krazō*) is a verb for a harsh, almost instinctual crying out.

a) It is the same verb used for the responses of demoniacs upon encountering the Son of God (Mt. 8:29)

b) Of Peter when he was sinking beneath the waves (Mt. 14:30).

c) Of the crowds when Yeshua entered Jerusalem on Palm Sunday (Mt. 21:9) and the crowds who demanded Yeshua's crucifixion (Mk. 15:13).

2. John 7:39 — "*Now this he said about the Spirit, whom those who believed in him were to receive, for as yet the Spirit had not been given, because Jesus was not yet glorified.*"

a) The Greek here is arresting. The English rendition, *"had not yet been given"* is actually not present. The literal Greek is: *"For it was (*imperfect of *eimi) not yet Spirit."*

b) John uses the verb, *doxazō* (to glorify) for the first time here; In all, he uses it 23x in his Gospel, 14 of which are from the time of the Passover meal onward.

c) By comparison, Luke uses the word 9x, Matthew 4x and Mark only once.

3. John 7:47 — The officers answered, "*Never has a man spoken the way this man speaks.*" The Pharisees then answered them, "*You have not also been led astray, have you?*

a) The verb here, *"led astray,"* is a perfect passive; they obviously saw Yeshua as a deceiver, and a successful one at that!

b) It is the verb, *planaō*, which stresses the process of going astray, or being led astray (passive); it particularly is used for error.

c) It is interesting that in John 7:41ff, there are three negative references to Yeshua being from Galilee, and point to that fact prohibiting him from being the Messiah! These statements come from both the pilgrims in the city for the feasts *and* the Jewish leadership (cf. 7:41, 52).

d) The biting discrimination of the religious leaders comes through in a statement made to the Temple police who failed to arrest Yeshua as ordered, *"Has any of the rulers or of the Pharisees believed in him? No! But this mob that knows nothing of the law — there is a curse on them!"* (7:48-49)

e) Nicodemus (whose name does not appear in another Gospel) makes his *second* of three appearances in this Gospel, and makes a weak "defense" for Yeshua, asking if they have followed due process in their condemnation of him (referencing their law). He is rebuked with a scriptural "proof" that because Yeshua is a Galilean, he is automatically eliminated from consideration as a candidate for Messiah.

f) It is very interesting that these leaders, who despise the uneducated pilgrims in the city for the feast, as *"under a curse,"* and who *"do not know the Law,"* are shown to be people who do *not* know the Law themselves! That is the point of Nicodemus. They were violating the law they claimed to know so well in not hearing Yeshua themselves.[1] Also, the prophet Jonah was from Gath Hepher, in *Galilee*! (2 Kg 14:25)

4. John 7:53 - 8:11 — The woman *"caught in the act of adultery."*

  a) *"...has been caught..."* is a perfect passive indicative of the verb *"caught"*; the stress here is on the certainty of the charge.

  b) *"...go, and from now on sin no more."* **(Jn. 8:11b)**

  (1) Although Yeshua does not condemn her, he also does not condone her conduct. The verb here is an imperative of "to sin."

  (2) The literal Greek rendering is: *"continue your life [imperative] and from this [sin] stop sinning [imperative], now."*

  (3) Interestingly, Yeshua is in effect telling her to "continue, but discontinue!" To "resume your journey, but change its direction."

  c) The real target here was *not* the woman, it was Yeshua.

  d) The opening and closing phrases in the Pharisees' question to Yeshua reveal their true intent: *"Now, in the Law, Moses commanded...what then do you say?"* **(vs 5)**.

5. John 9:41 – the man born blind

  a) *"blind"* - of the 62 references to blindness in the Gospels, nearly ¼ are in this story!

  b) Of the 17 references to blindness in John's Gospel, 13 are in this story!

  c) There are 30 statements about *"seeing"* in this story!

  d) This is a story about a blind man and a blind *mob*! (There are 10 references to the blind man, but also 17 references to the Pharisees.)

  e) Yeshua says there are two kinds of people:

  (1) Those who want to see and keep on seeing.

  (2) Those who think they already see (9:39-41).

D. The World *Before* The Text

1. The three sins of James and John that emerged *after* the most spiritual experience of their lives (i.e., the transfiguration), are still with us today:

  a) The sin of *celebrity*; loosing track of the Master because of the "fame" of the servant.

  b) The sin of *"partiality"*; being more committed to my own "team" than the mission itself.

---

1 It is possible to know the "letter" of the Law flawlessly, and yet be ignorant of the Prophets. But, it is *not* possible to truly know the Prophets and be ignorant of the true meaning and purpose of the Law. This is why Jesus repeatedly accused "the Jews" (i.e. religious leaders) of *not* knowing their own scriptures (cf. Mark 12:24), and would have angered them by his use of the phrase, *"have you not read...?"* (cf. Matt 12:3,5; 19:4; 22:31; Mark 12:26).

c) The sin of *hostility*; being more angry at sinners than sin.

2. The sins of the Pharisees in Jerusalem are still with us today:

a) When I hear the word, "sinner," do I think of myself or others?

"We know that this man is a sinner…" **John 9:24**

b) Who/what will I "allow" to teach me?

"They answered him, 'You were born in utter sin, and would you teach us?' And they cast him out."

John 9:25

UNIT 13: Moving Toward The "Flame"

I. The Perean Ministry of Yeshua

A. Key Events of This Segment:[1]

E V E N T	Matthew	Mark	Luke	John
Dedication in Jerusalem; Jesus' life threatened	–	–	–	10:19-38
Jesus retreats outside the boundaries of Judea; "Bethany beyond the Jordan"	–	–	–	1:28; 10:40-42
Jesus teaches on Yahweh's love for sinners (parables of the Lost Sheep, Coin, Son)	–	–	15:1-32	–
Jesus teaches on Kingdom living (parables of the dishonest steward, rich man and Lazarus, unprofitable servants;	–	–	16:1-17:10	–
Illness, death and raising of Lazarus (Bethany)	–	–	–	11:1-44
Jesus leaves the Jerusalem area and heads "northeast"	–	–	–	11:54
Heals 10 lepers on journey back to Jerusalem	–	–	17:11-21	–
Encounter with the "rich young ruler"	19:16-30	10:17-31	18:18-30	–
Jesus' third prediction of death	20:17-19	10:32-34	18:31-34	–
Healings at Jericho	20:29-34	10:46-52	18:35-43	–
Conversion of Zacchaeus in Jericho	–	–	19:1-10	–
Arrival back at Bethany and anointing by Mary	26:6-13	14:3-9	–	11:55-12:11

Matthew and Mark are "silent" for most of this period (December through early to mid-March)

B. The Raising of Lazarus — the World *Behind* the Text (John 11)

1. The "Logistics" of Grieving

a) Yeshua had gone to "Bethany beyond Jordan" for temporary safety (cf. Jn 1:28 and 10:40).

b) Lazarus would have been buried the same day he died (Acts 5:6-10).

c) Yeshua was most likely about 60 miles from "Martha's Bethany."

d) Martha and Mary were "sitting shiva" (cf. Jn 11:20-29 and page 119).

e) Martha was again in Yeshua's face and Mary was again at his feet (cf. Lk 10:38-42 and Jn 11:17-32).

f) Yeshua ministers to *both of them*, right where they each are:

(1) To Martha with *words* (Jn. 11:21-27).

(2) To Mary with *weeping* (Jn 11:32-36).

---

1 The opposition against Jesus is growing on every side. This is best understood by thinking of two primary groups who will eventually be responsible for Yeshua's death. One is the aristocratic *minority*, and the other is the peasant *majority*. Both groups, divided by animosity towards one another in normal life, found themselves standing on opposite sides of the same cross on Golgotha. The peasantry hated Rome for economic reasons; they were being taxed to death. They wanted a political Messiah to deliver them from Rome's oppression. They slowly became disenchanted with Jesus because he failed to meet those expectations. This is even evident in the statement by one of Yeshua's intimate followers after the resurrection: *"We had hoped he was the one to redeem Israel."* (Luke 24:21). The aristocracy on the other hand, hated Rome for theological reasons; they were pagan in every sense of the word. They were looking for a "convenient" Messiah, one who would allow them to continue their way of life. They were *threatened* by the possibility of losing all this because of Yeshua's revolutionary message and following: *"If we let him go on like this…the Romans will come and take away both our place and our nation."* (John 11:48)

C. The Raising of Lazarus — the World *Of* the Text (John 11)

1. Yeshua's "weeping" was private, theirs was public:

    a) Mary and the others were *"crying as children, audibly" (Gk = klaiō)*

    b) Yeshua was *"weeping silently; shedding tears" (Gk = dakruō)*

2. Yeshua's indignation was public, *not* private!

    a) *"deeply moved"* - (2x) comes from a verb meaning, *"to snort with anger"* (Jn 11:33,38).

        (1) this same verb is used for the apostles anger over the "waste" of nard on Yeshua's head (Mk 14:5).

        (2) it is translated "enraged" in Daniel 11:30 (LXX).

    b) *"troubled"* - this verb means to be *"distressed, agitated, or disturbed."*

        (1) there is also a reflexive pronoun in this sentence; Yeshua was doing this *to Himself!*

        (2) it is the same verb He uses to describe His own emotions about being betrayed (Jn 13:21).

3. Yeshua "loving" was unique:

    a) The word used for Yeshua's "love" for this family is an *imperfect* in the Greek.

        (1) John is highlighting the quality of a *relationship* here, not the reality of a *commitment* (Jn 11:5).

        (2) This love was obvious enough for the residents of Bethany to have seen it (Jn 11:36).

        (3) This resurrection is very different from Jairus' daughter and the widow's son (Mk 5:22,35-43; Lk 7:11).

    b) This verb construction is unique to Yeshua *and* to John:

        (1) No other NT author uses an imperfect with *agapaō*.

        (2) This is the same verbal construction used 5x in this Gospel to speak of *"the disciple that Jesus loved…"* (13:23; 19:26; 21:7,20 and phileō in 20:2).

D. The Sanhedrin: The World *Behind* the Text (John 11:45-52)

1. This is the first mention of this "Council" in the Gospel narrative (even though it has been made reference of; cf. Mt 5:22).

2. The Sanhedrin (from Greek *sunedrion*) had existed for nearly 200 years by this time.

3. The first record of the "Sanhedrin" is Josephus' account of Herod's insolent and intimidating appearance before it *(Ant. 14.9.3-5)*.

4. During the Hasmonean era (I.e., Maccabean) it emerged as both a court of justice *and* a guardian of the "traditions of the elders."

5. The influence of this austere group extended into Syria (e.g. Damascus; Acts 9:2; 22:5) and apparently into Galilee (cf. Mk 3:22; 7:1).

6. The Sanhedrin had come to be composed of three primary groups of people:

    "On the next day their rulers and elders and scribes gathered together in Jerusalem, with Annas the high priest and Caiaphas and John and Alexander, and all who were of the high-priestly family."   **Acts 4:5, 6**

    a) **"rulers"** - those of the high priestly families

        (1) mostly Sadducean in background and very wealthy

        (2) there may even have been an "inner circle" of ten most powerful families based on references in Josephus to other similar councils *(cf. Ant. 20.8.11)*.

    b) **"elders"** - priestly and economical aristocracy in Jerusalem

        (1) Joseph of Aramathea was in this group (Mk 15:43; Mt. 27:57; Jn. 19:38).

    c) **"scribes"** - historically, this group was the most recent addition to the old structure.

        (1) were predominately Pharisees

        (2) Gamaliel, Paul's mentor, was in this group

        (3) most likely, Nicodemus, *"the teacher in Israel…"* was in this group as well (Jn. 3:10).

7. This "Council" (Sanhedrin) appears 22x in our NT, but never after Acts.

a) 8x in the Gospels

b) 14x in the Book of Acts: Peter & John, Stephen, Paul are all tried by this group (Acts 4:15; 6:12-60; 22:30-24:20).

E. The True Enemy of Yeshua and Judaism: *"the traditions of the elders"*

1. In order to understand the incredible and blind hostility towards Yeshua, we must understand an earlier conversation of Yeshua:

> *And the Pharisees and the scribes asked him, "Why do your disciples not walk according to **the tradition of the elders**, but eat with defiled hands?" And he said to them, "Well did Isaiah prophesy of you hypocrites, as it is written, "'This people honors me with their lips, but their heart is far from me; in vain do they worship me, teaching as doctrines the commandments of men.' **You leave the commandment of God and hold to the tradition of men.**" And he said to them, "You have a fine way of rejecting the commandment of God in order to establish **your tradition!** For Moses said, 'Honor your father and your mother'; and, 'Whoever reviles father or mother must surely die.' But you say, 'If a man tells his father or his mother, Whatever you would have gained from me is Corban' (that is, given to God)-- then you no longer permit him to do anything for his father or mother, thus **making void the word of God by your tradition** that you have handed down. And many such things you do."* **Mark 7:5-13, emphasis added**

2. In Yeshua's day, there was a body of teaching collectively known as *"the traditions of the elders."*

a) It is also called the "Oral Law."

b) It was believed to have been given to Moses at Sinai and passed down over the generations.

c) It emerged as an attempt to interpret and apply the *written Law* in contexts and cultures that were always changing.

d) For example, the law against "working" on the Sabbath does *not* explain what it actually *means* to "work."

e) We see the first record of this with Ezra ("the scribe"!) exegeting the Law:

> *And Ezra blessed the LORD, the great God, and all the people answered, 'Amen, Amen,' lifting up their hands. And they bowed their heads and worshiped the LORD with their faces to the ground. Also Jeshua, Bani, Sherebiah, Jamin, Akkub, Shabbethai, Hodiah, Maaseiah, Kelita, Azariah, Jozabad, Hanan, Pelaiah, the Levites, helped the people to understand the Law, while the people remained in their places. They read from the book, from the Law of God, clearly, and they gave the sense, so that the people understood the reading."* **Nehemiah 8:6-8**

f) This "running commentary" on the law was known as midrash.

g) The Oral Law actually became more important than the written law because it was deemed necessary for understanding Moses.

h) Over time, the Rabbis took on an almost divine status in the eyes of the leadership and the people:

> *"'Know then, that "the words of the Scribes" are more lovely than the words of the law: for, says R. Tarphon, if a man does not read, he only transgresses an affirmative; but if he transgresses the words of the school of Hillell, he is guilty of death, because he hath broke down a hedge, and a serpent shall bite him. It is a tradition of R. Ishmael, the words of the law have in them both prohibition and permission; some of them are light, and some heavy, but "the words of the Scribes" are all of them heavy-- המורים דברי זקנים, "weightier are the words of the elders", than the words of the prophets."* **T. Hieros. *Beracot*, fol. 3. 2**

i) Eventually, all this midrashic teaching was compiled into a single volume, known as the "Mishna" which became the basis for the two Jewish Talmuds[1] (see chart on next page):

---

1 The Jewish Talmud ("the study") is considered by many Jewish scholars as the pinnacle of rabbinic Judaism. It is based on (and includes) the Mishnah in its entirety, but also the Gemara ("the completion"), which is much longer and actually makes up the majority of the Talmud. The Gemera is the combined effort of Jewish scholars in Babylon and Galilee during the 3rd through the 6th centuries A.D. There are actually *two* Talmuds, the Babylonian and the Palestinian. The Babylonian Talmud is longer, and more studied. The Palestinian Talmud is shorter and more difficult. The study of Talmud is fundamental to Jewish scholarship today.

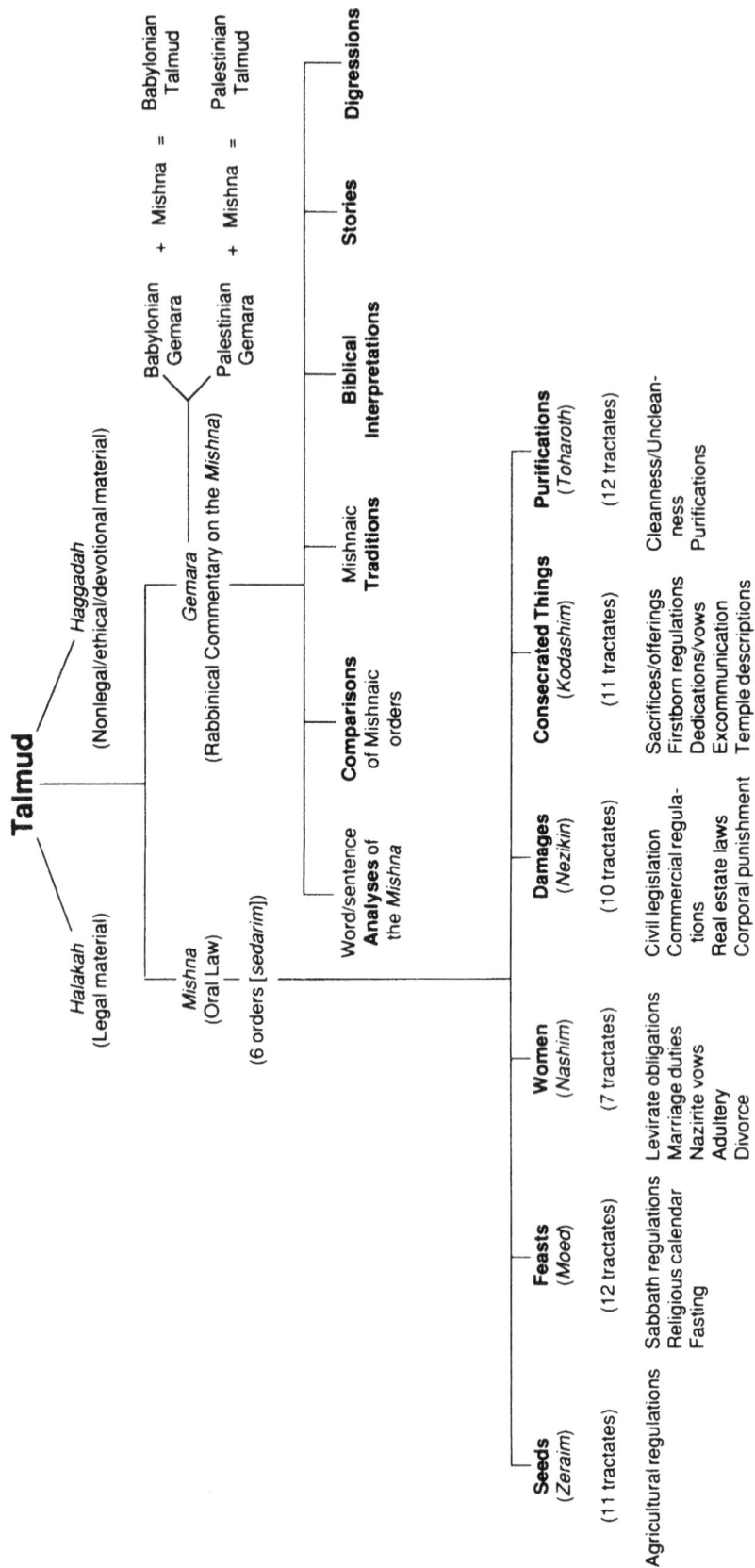

Talmud

Halakah
(Legal material)

Haggadah
(Nonlegal/ethical/devotional material)

Mishna
(Oral Law)

(6 orders [*sedarim*])

Gemara
(Rabbinical Commentary on the *Mishna*)

Seeds (*Zeraim*)	**Feasts** (*Moed*)	**Women** (*Nashim*)	**Damages** (*Nezikin*)	**Consecrated Things** (*Kodashim*)	**Purifications** (*Toharoth*)
(11 tractates)	(12 tractates)	(7 tractates)	(10 tractates)	(11 tractates)	(12 tractates)
Agricultural regulations	Sabbath regulations Religious calendar Fasting	Levirate obligations Marriage duties Nazirite vows Adultery Divorce	Civil legislation Commercial regulations Real estate laws Corporal punishment	Sacrifices/offerings Firstborn regulations Dedications/vows Excommunication Temple descriptions	Cleanness/Uncleanness Purifications

Word/sentence Analyses of the *Mishna*

Comparisons of Mishnaic orders

Mishnaic **Traditions**

Biblical Interpretations

Stories

Digressions

Babylonian Gemara + Mishna = Babylonian Talmud

Palestinian Gemara + Mishna = Palestinian Talmud

3. The development of *"the traditions of the elders"* can be understood graphically[1]:

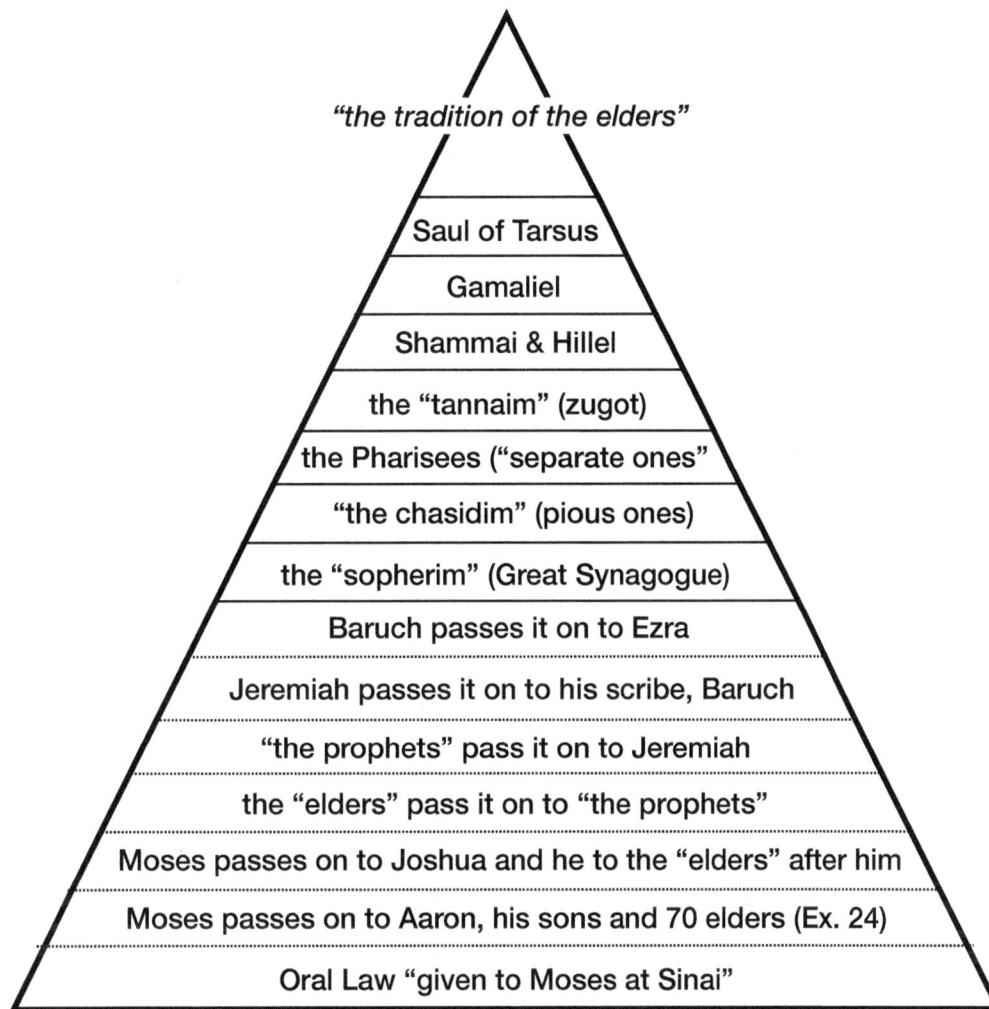

"the tradition of the elders"

Saul of Tarsus
Gamaliel
Shammai & Hillel
the "tannaim" (zugot)
the Pharisees ("separate ones"
"the chasidim" (pious ones)
the "sopherim" (Great Synagogue)
Baruch passes it on to Ezra
Jeremiah passes it on to his scribe, Baruch
"the prophets" pass it on to Jeremiah
the "elders" pass it on to "the prophets"
Moses passes on to Joshua and he to the "elders" after him
Moses passes on to Aaron, his sons and 70 elders (Ex. 24)
Oral Law "given to Moses at Sinai"

4. But, its "fruit" was an oppressive system that promoted self-righteousness, the enemy of grace.

5. Yeshua repeatedly attacked the "traditions of the elders" and in so doing poisoned the minds of those who valued systematic theology over biblical theology.

"But you say, 'If anyone tells his father or his mother, What you would have gained from me is given to God, he need not honor his father.' So for the sake of your tradition you have made void the word of God."
Matthew 15:5, 6

"You have heard that it was said, 'You shall love your neighbor and hate your enemy.'   **Matthew 5:43**

"They tie up heavy burdens, hard to bear, and lay them on people's shoulders, but they themselves are not willing to move them with their finger."   **Matthew 23:4**

[Peter, speaking of the relationship of the Law to Gentile converts] *"Now, therefore, why are you putting God to the test by placing a yoke on the neck of the disciples that neither our fathers nor we have been able to bear? But we believe that we will be saved through the grace of the Lord Jesus, just as they will."*
Acts 15:10–11

---

1 "The traditions of the elders" is mentioned by Jesus in Matthew 15:2. Gamaliel is mentioned twice by Paul in Acts 5:34 and 22:3. Shammai and Hillel are considered the last of the *zugot,* and their two "schools" of theology were both very influential during the ministry years of Jesus. Evidence of this is seen in the questions posed to Jesus about divorce. These two men held very differing views on divorce. The tannaim ("pairs") were typically the President and Vice-President of the Sanhedrin. The "Sopherim" are likely in view in Ezra 7:10 and Nehemiah 5:7; 8:7-8.

6. What the "traditions of the elders" had *become* by the days of Yeshua:

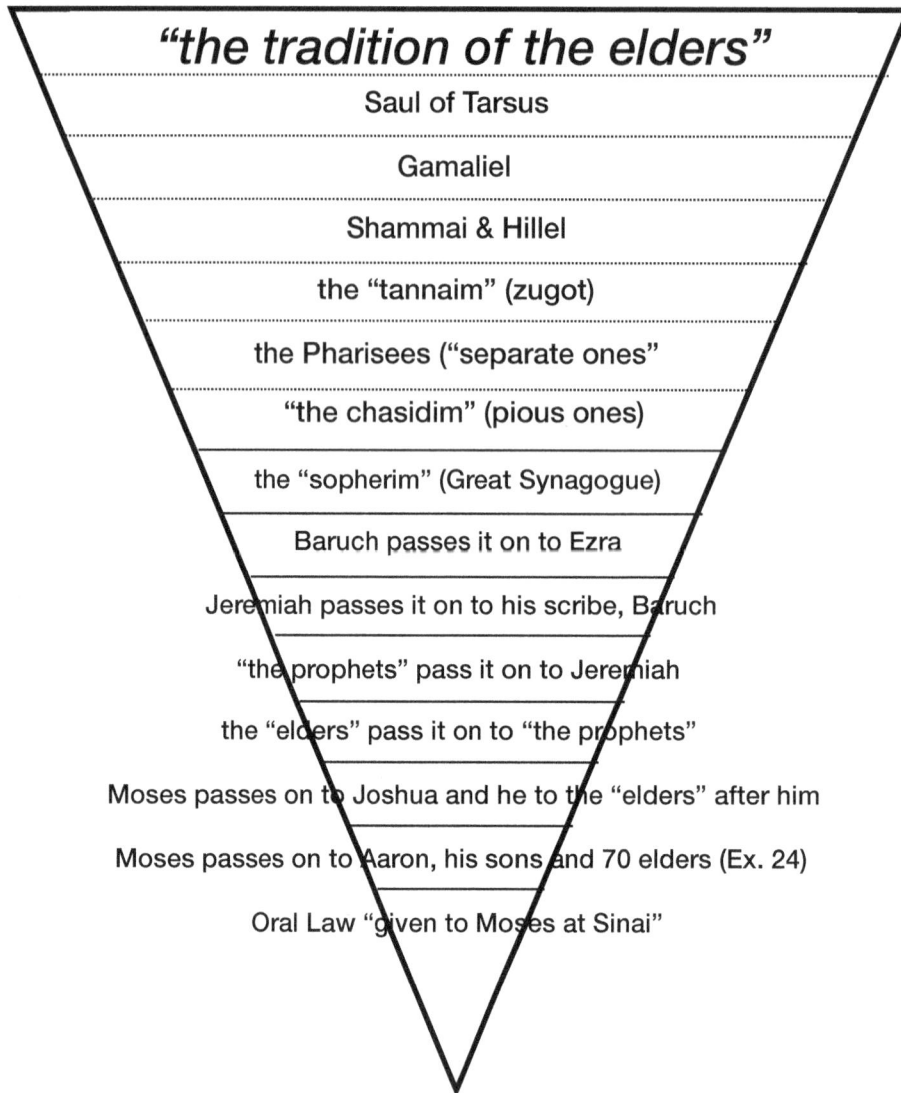

"the tradition of the elders"

Saul of Tarsus

Gamaliel

Shammai & Hillel

the "tannaim" (zugot)

the Pharisees ("separate ones"

"the chasidim" (pious ones)

the "sopherim" (Great Synagogue)

Baruch passes it on to Ezra

Jeremiah passes it on to his scribe, Baruch

"the prophets" pass it on to Jeremiah

the "elders" pass it on to "the prophets"

Moses passes on to Joshua and he to the "elders" after him

Moses passes on to Aaron, his sons and 70 elders (Ex. 24)

Oral Law "given to Moses at Sinai"

F. The World *Before* the Texts
   1. Yeshua wants us "at His feet" more than "in His face." Are you "at His feet" in times of prosperity, or only in times of need?
   2. Yeshua's anger was *always* directed against sin, not sinners (unless they claimed to be righteous).
   3. How much of my theology comes from the words of *Yeshua* rather than the thoughts of *people*?

UNIT 14: Daniel's 69th "Week"

I. DANIEL'S SIXTY-NINTH "WEEK": Yeshua's Final Days

A. Synchronizing our "Watches" — Einstein's Maxim

"A man with a watch knows what time it is. A man with two watches is never sure." – **Einstein** *(attributed)*

B. The World *Behind* the Text: "Passion Week," A Flurry of Blur

1. What we conveniently call "Passion Week" is *not* as neat and tidy as our Church calendar proposes. Consider the variations suggested by these four scholars:

D A Y	Allan Ross[1]	Harold Hoehner[2]	Wayne H. House[3]	Alfred Eidersheim[4]
Friday	traveling	traveling	arrival at Bethany; anointed by Mary	arrival at Bethany; anointed by Mary
Saturday	arrival at Bethany; anointed by Mary	arrival at Bethany; anointed by Mary	—	—
Sunday	crowds at Bethany	crowds at Bethany	"triumphal entry" – Jerusalem	"triumphal entry" – Jerusalem
Monday	"triumphal entry" – Jerusalem	"triumphal entry" – Jerusalem	curses fig tree; Temple cleansed	curses fig tree; Temple cleansed
Tuesday	curses fig tree; Temple cleansed	curses fig tree; Temple cleansed	Jesus' authority challenged; anointing by Mary at Bethany	Jesus' authority challenged; teaching on end times on Olivet
Wednesday	Jesus' authority challenged; teaching on end times on Olivet Judas' betrayal arrangements with Sanhedrin	Jesus' authority challenged; teaching on end times on Olivet Judas' betrayal arrangements with Sanhedrin	"quiet" day; Judas' betrayal arrangements with Sanhedrin	"quiet" day; Judas' betrayal arrangements with Sanhedrin
Thursday	Passover meal, Upper Room teaching, Gethsemane and betrayal	Passover meal, Upper Room teaching, Gethsemane and betrayal	Passover meal, Upper Room teaching, Gethsemane and betrayal	Passover meal, Upper Room teaching, Gethsemane and betrayal
Friday	Crucifixion and burial	Crucifixion and burial	Crucifixion and burial	Crucifixion and burial
Saturday	in the tomb	in the tomb	in the tomb	in the tomb
Sunday	Resurrection	Resurrection	Resurrection	Resurrection

1 — Class notes from *Biblical Archeology,* Dr. Allan Ross
2 — *Chronological Aspects of the Life of Christ,* Harold Hoehner (adaptation cited by Wayne H. House)
3 — *Chronological and Background Charts of the New Testament,* H. Wayne House
4 — *Life and Times of Jesus the Messiah,* Afred Eidersheim (distilled from Table of Contents)

2. The sequence of events and the days associated with them during "Passion Week" are dependent upon the actual day that Yeshua *died*.

3. This is complicated by the fact that the Synoptics and John *appear* to present two very divergent, almost contradictory records:

Synoptic Gospels	John's Gospel
He said, "Go into the city to a certain man and say to him, 'The Teacher says, My time is at hand. I will keep the Passover at your house with my disciples.'" And the disciples did as Jesus had directed them, and they prepared the Passover. When it was evening, he reclined at table with the twelve...And when they had sung a hymn, they went out to the Mount of Olives." **Matt. 26:18-20, 30**	Peter again denied it, and at once a rooster crowed. Then they led Jesus from the house of Caiaphas to the governor's headquarters. It was early morning. They themselves did not enter the governor's headquarters, so that they would not be defiled, but could eat the Passover. **John 18:27, 28**
And on the first day of Unleavened Bread, when they sacrificed the Passover lamb, his disciples said to him, "Where will you have us go and prepare for you to eat the Passover?" And he sent two of his disciples and said to them, "Go into the city, and a man carrying a jar of water will meet you. Follow him, and wherever he enters, say to the master of the house, 'The Teacher says, Where is my guest room, where I may eat the Passover with my disciples?' And he will show you a large upper room furnished and ready; there prepare for us." And the disciples set out and went to the city and found it just as he had told them, and they prepared the Passover...And when they had sung a hymn, they went out to the Mount of Olives. **Mark 14:12-16, 26**	So when Pilate heard these words, he brought Jesus out and sat down on the judgment seat at a place called The Stone Pavement, and in Aramaic Gabbatha. Now it was the day of Preparation of the Passover. It was about the sixth hour. He said to the Jews, "Behold your King!" They cried out, "Away with him, away with him, crucify him!" Pilate said to them, "Shall I crucify your King?" The chief priests answered, "We have no king but Caesar." So he delivered him over to them to be crucified. So they took Jesus, and he went out, bearing his own cross, to the place called the place of a skull, which in Aramaic is called Golgotha. There they crucified him, and with him two others, one on either side, and Jesus between them. **John 19:13-18**

Synoptic Gospels	John's Gospel
Then came the day of Unleavened Bread, on which the Passover lamb had to be sacrificed. So Jesus sent Peter and John, saying, "Go and prepare the Passover for us, that we may eat it." They said to him, "Where will you have us prepare it?" He said to them, "Behold, when you have entered the city, a man carrying a jar of water will meet you. Follow him into the house that he enters and tell the master of the house, 'The Teacher says to you, Where is the guest room, where I may eat the Passover with my disciples?' And he will show you a large upper room furnished; prepare it there." And they went and found it just as he had told them, and they prepared the Passover. **Luke 22:7-13**	*Since it was the day of Preparation, and so that the bodies would not remain on the cross on the Sabbath (for that Sabbath was a high day), the Jews asked Pilate that their legs might be broken and that they might be taken away.* **John 19:31**

4. There are a variety of suggestions on how to "reconcile" this apparent contradiction among scholars, but one seems to provide the greatest number of answers with the least number of difficulties.

5. Old Testament language scholar Allan Ross "solves" this dilemma by proposing *two* Passover meals rather than one.

6. The Galileans (Gentile region) reckoned their days differently than did Judeans (Jewish region), according to Ross[1].

   a) *"Galileans reckon days from sunrise; so Nisan 14 began in the morning and their lambs would be killed between 3-5pm on Thursday, explaining a Thursday night Passover meal of Yeshua and his disciples."*

   b) *"Judeans reckon days from sunset, so Nisan 14 began on sunset on Thursday; therefore the High Priests would have had to wait until Friday at 3pm to begin sacrificing the Paschal Lamb—the precise time of Yeshua's death."*[2]

7. Allan Ross postulates *two* Passovers, both observed on the 14th Nisan:

   a) Yeshua and his disciples, following the tradition of the north, would have eaten their Passover meal late on Thursday evening.

   b) The Judean leadership and populace would have been hurrying to get the "Yeshua business" wrapped up, so they could eat *their* Passover.

8. This is further substantiated by astronomical data telling us that 14th Nisan (Lev. 23:5; Num. 9:4; Josh. 5:10) fell on a Friday during two years that both fit within the time frame given to us in the Gospels[3]:

   a) April 3, AD 33 (with the new moon occurring on March 19)

   b) April 7, AD 30 (with the new moon occurring on March 22)

9. The "key" verse for establishing the sequence of events and days for "Passion Week" is John 12:1

   Six days before the Passover, Jesus therefore came to Bethany, where Lazarus was, whom Jesus had raised from the dead. So they gave a dinner for him there. Martha served, and Lazarus was one of those reclining with him at the table. Mary therefore took a pound of expensive ointment made from pure nard, and anointed the feet of Jesus and wiped his feet with her hair. The house was filled with the fragrance of the perfume. ..." **John 12:1-4**

   a) In Jewish reckoning, any portion of a day is considered a "day."

   b) Counting backwards six days from the *Judean Passover* (John's reckoning) brings us to a Saturday arrival in Bethany.

   c) Given the events involving the "crowds" from Jerusalem and the surrounding areas, it seems likely that Yeshua's actual "triumphal entry" *may* have happened on the third day, not the second.[4]

---

1 These citations are taken from Fran Sciacca's class notes from Allan Ross' Biblical Archaeology class, Beeson Divinity School.

2 This puts the eating of the Passover meal *after* the crucifixion. The geographical focus of John's Gospel is consistently Jerusalem and the surrounding environs, so his description of the event seems to fit nicely with Ross' dual-Passover model.

3 There is actually a *third* possibility, AD 27, but that is too early to allow for sufficient time for Yeshua's life and ministry.

4 It seems reasonable to assume that John was only "working" off of *one* Passover meal, and that *has* to be the Judean (i.e. Friday) meal.

10. Using Ross' arguments and chronology, "Passion Week" looks like this:

Day	Events of the Day
Saturday	arrival in Bethany and anointing at "a dinner for him there" (at home of Simon the leper); Jn. 12:1-3; Mk. 14:3-9
Sunday	gathering of the crowd of "the Jews" from Jerusalem, at Bethany (hostile crowd)
Monday	rides into Jerusalem, praised by "the crowd that had come for the feast" (enthusiastic crowd; Jn. 12:12-15)
Tuesday	cursing fig tree, temple cleansing, healing, discourse on unbelief (Mt. 21:12-19; Jn. 12:20-50)
Wednesday	day of controversy with Jews, teaching on Mt. of Olives, fig tree withers, Judas makes betrayal arrangements; (Mt. 21:19-26:16; Mk. 11:19-14:11; Lk. 20:1-22:6)
Thursday	Passover prep and meal, Upper Room teaching, events in Gethsemane; (Mt. 26:17-56; Mk 14:12-52; Lk 22:7-51; Jn.13:1-18:12)
Friday	trials, crucifixion, burial; (Mt. 26:57-27:60; Mk. 14:53-15:46; Lk. 22:54-23:54; Jn. 18:13-19:42)
Saturday	watch at the grave (Mt. 27:61-66; Mk. 15:47; Lk. 23:55-56)
Sunday	resurrection, appearances to women, disciples w/o Thomas, road to Emmaus (Mt. 28:1-20; Mk. 16:1-20; Lk. 24:1-53; Jn. 20:1-25)

11. There are also strong arguments in favor of the disciples' meal being a true Passover meal:

a) The clear statements in the Synoptics that this meal was, in fact, a Passover meal.

b) The meal took place at night, whereas typical Jewish evening meals were eaten earlier.[1]

c) Those "at the table" reclined, rather than sitting. Sitting was the posture for "normal" meals, and "reclining" was the posture for special meals/banquets.[2]

d) The "breaking of bread[3]" did not come first in the meal, like it does in a normal Jewish meal. There were some dishes served and eaten prior to it (although some argue that the *silence* regarding the specific Passover items—such at bitter herbs—speaks *against* a Passover seder.)

e) Red wine was drunk, as is prescribed in the Passover.

f) The meal ended with the singing of a hymn[4], most likely the Hillel psalms (Pss 113-118) as prescribed for Passover.

g) After the meal, Yeshua went to Gethsemane, not Bethany; The first was within the prescribed perimeter for travel on Passover, the other was outside it.[5]

h) Yeshua's "introductory" remarks, explaining the significance of the bread and cup is very similar to the comments made by the leader during a Passover seder.

i) The statement about giving something to the poor in John 12:5 fit the customary generosity that surrounded Passover.

C. The World *Behind* the Text: "Passion Week," The Players

1. Love in a Leper's Lodging: Mary's anointing of Yeshua (John 12:1-8)

a) Lazarus is there…alive!

b) Martha is there…silently serving.

---

1 This is substantiated by the fact that it was very late (i.e. dark; "torches") when they went from the upper room to the Garden of Gethsemane.

2 This is the same posture assumed by the guests at the "feast" (i.e. *not* a typical meal) given in Yeshua's honor in John 12.

3 For the Jew, "bread" represented both Yahweh's covenant faithfulness to them in the provision of grain, rain, and harvest, *and* was evidence of their own faithfulness to the covenant, of which fruitful harvests were the resultant "blessing." Besides being a daily staple in the Jewish diet, bread was also symbolic of Yahweh's unique love for them as a people.

4 It is noteworthy that all four Gospels record this fact.

5 A "Sabbath's day journey" in the Old Testament era was considered to be the distance between the Ark of the Covenant and the camp proper (Josh 3:4). During the settlement period, it was the distance between the levitical cities and their pasturelands Num 35:4-5). In the days of Jesus, it was the distance between the Mount of Olives and the Temple (Acts 1:12). In all three cases, it was 2,000 cubits, or approximately 3,000 feet. Bethany was *outside* this perimeter.

    c) Mary is there…at Yeshua's feet for a third time.

2. *"The Son of Man has no place to lay his head."* – another borrowed item[1]

> *"And Jesus found a young donkey and sat on it, just as it is written, "Fear not, daughter of Zion; behold, your king is coming, sitting on a donkey's colt!"*   **John 12:14, 15**

    a) John and Matthew identify this event as a fulfillment of clear Messianic prophecy (cf. Zech. 9:9)[2].

    b) It also reveals the *type* of Messiah Yeshua was to be, even though most missed it[3]:

      (1) the donkey was *not* used by a warlike or conquering king.

      (2) it was the typical "vehicle" for priests and prophets[4] (cf. 1 Kg. 13:11-13; 2 Pet. 2:15-16).

      (3) A conquering king would ride on a war horse[5] (like Pilate's first entrance!) or march at the head of his army.

      (4) Yeshua was making a very clear statement of what He was *not* as much as what He was.

3. *"The crowds…"* (John 12:1-19)

    a) There were *five* different "crowds"[6] involved in this event:

      (1) The Twelve and all those associated with them (Simon the Leper, Lazarus, et. al).[7]

      (2) The hostile Jewish leaders from Jerusalem who intended to put an *end* to all this, including killing Lazarus (vv 9-11).

      (3) A group of pilgrims most likely passing *through* Bethany on their way to Jerusalem to be purified *before* Passover (vv 12-16).

      (4) The "locals" who had witnessed Lazarus' resurrection (vs. 17).

      (5) A mixed group who had previous *heard* about this miracle, but never had a chance to actually *see* Lazarus (vs. 18).

    b) The combination of all this is evidenced by the exasperation of the Pharisees: *"You see that you are not doing any good; look, the world has gone after Him!"* **John 12:19**

    c) John follows this tumult with an even more startling element: Greeks who are asking to have an "audience" with Yeshua (Jn 12:20-36).

D. The World *Of* the Texts

> *"When the large crowd of the Jews learned that Jesus was there, they came, not only on account of him but also to see Lazarus, whom he had raised from the dead. So the chief priests made plans to put Lazarus to death as well, because on account of him many of the Jews were going away and believing in Jesus."*   **John 12:9-11**

1. The phrase, *"going away"* (hupagō) carries with it both the idea of "departing" *and* leaving *with* someone.[8]

---

1 The "poverty" of Jesus and his dependence upon others as an expression of his identification with humanity in the Incarnation can be seen from birth to death. He was born in a "borrowed" manger, lived in the home of Peter, was supported financially by a number of wealthy women, entered Jerusalem on a borrowed donkey's colt, ate his final Passover in a borrowed room, and was buried in a "borrowed" tomb.

2 Zechariah, like Isaiah, is "dripping" with Messianic references. It is in Zechariah that we read of Messiah entering Jerusalem on a donkey, of the Jews "looking upon him whom they've pierced," and the Mount of Olives splitting at the return of the Messiah.

3 It is likely that they were so mesmerized by the *idea* of a messiah, that they missed the actual *identity* of him when he finally appeared! They spent little time wondering what he'd be like, and most of their time wondering when he would come; not unlike today. In a very ironic way, Jesus had come to deliver the Jews from the oppressive burden of Judaism more than the taxation of Rome.

4 Balaam rode a donkey on his journey to curse the Israelites (cf. Numbers 22).

5 This is the significance of Yeshua's glorious description in Revelation 19 as riding on a white horse. His entrance into the world as it's saviour was on a donkey. His return to the world as its King is on a white horse.

6 One needs to picture two large groups. One traveling from Jerusalem *towards* Bethany, and one traveling *away from* Bethany towards Jerusalem.

7 It is very reasonable to assume that Zacheus the converted tax collector, and Bartimaeus the healed blind man would be among this group. Not to mention any who had attached themselves to both of these men because of the radical transformation that had occurred to each of them; one moral, the other physical. Make no mistake, this is an excited group of people.

8 There is also a sense of "submission" to the one the departing person is leaving with.

2. Both of these verbs (*"going"* and *"believing"*) are in the imperfect tense, indicating an ongoing "defection" in Yeshua's direction.[1]

3. This probably explains the sense of urgency on the part of the Jewish leaders. They wanted to reduce the collateral damage, to stop the "bleeding," so to speak. Things were spinning out of their control

4. The NIV does *not* translate the definite article (i.e. *"the"*) in verse 9, even though it *does* translate it in verse 11. This neglects John's strategic use of that phrase, *"the Jews"* throughout his Gospel.

5. There are *two* crowds in this passage: one is hostile, the other "hungry." It is this *second* crowd that proclaims him king in the rest of the account.

> *"Now among those who went up to worship at the feast were some Greeks. So these came to Philip, who was from Bethsaida in Galilee, and asked him, "Sir, we wish to see Jesus." Philip went and told Andrew; Andrew and Philip went and told Jesus. And Jesus answered them, "The **hour** has come for the Son of Man to be glorified. Truly, truly, I say to you, unless a grain of wheat falls into the earth and dies, it remains alone; but if it dies, it bears much fruit. Whoever loves his life loses it, and whoever hates his life in this world will keep it for eternal life. If anyone serves me, he must follow me; and where I am, there will my servant be also. If anyone serves me, the Father will honor him."*   **John 12:20-26**

1. Yeshua statement, *"the hour has come"* is in the perfect tense.[2]

2. He is speaking of an irreversible arrival; *"We are here for good!"*

3. Yeshua's statement that those who "love" their life will "lose it" is explosive:

   a) The word for *"lose"* (apollumi) means *"to destroy"* not to misplace or no longer "own."[3]

   b) It is in the *present tense*. Yeshua is talking about a cause-and-effect relationship happening *while* they are "loving" their lives.[4]

   c) It is the same word used for Herod's intentions with the baby Yeshua; he wanted to destroy Yeshua (Mt. 2:13).

   d) It is the same word used for what happens to an old wineskin when new wine is put into it (Mt. 9:17).

   e) It is the same word used by the demons for what they were afraid Yeshua was going to do to them (Mk. 1:24).

E. The World *Before* the Texts

1. Who do I relate to more, the "crowds" (fellowship with others), or to Mary (intimacy with Yeshua)?

2. What type of Messiah am I drawn to, one on a donkey or one on a white horse?

3. If I was the donkey, would I have thought the people were cheering for me?

4. Where have I truly "died" and seen fruit come from it?

II. THE *ORIGINAL 'JESUS SEMINAR'*: A Day of Conflict & Teaching

A. WEDNESDAY: The Key Events[5] (Mt. 21:19 - 23:39; Mk. 11:19 - 12:44; Lk 20:1 - 21:4)

1. The "parable" of a withered fig tree.[6]

2. Chief Priests, Scribes, and Pharisees all challenge Yeshua's "authority."

---

1 We have to ask ourselves, just *what* was it the Jews were "leaving"? In this case, they are "leaving" rabbinic Judaism for this new teaching and its teacher.

2 Yeshua's use of "hour" (Gk - *kairos*) in John's Gospel is worth noting. *Kairos* is a word pointing to a very specific period of time, contrasted to *chronos* which is the word for time in general. In John 2:4, at the wedding in Cana, Jesus tells his mother that his "hour" had not yet come. He makes a very similar statement to his disciples in John 7:6. John, in an editorial comment in John 7:30 on one incident of Jewish opposition says that the Jew could not kill Jesus because "his hour had not yet come. There is the incident recorded in the passage above when Jesus was sought by the Greeks. Finally, John announces a change in John 13:1, and says Jesus *knew* that "his hour had finally come."

3 This is *not* like losing one's car keys. It's more akin to wrecking the car!

4 We could actually say that Jesus is warning, *"The one who is loving himself is destroying himself."* This is the inevitable outcome of narcissism, and an important and vital warning in our era of self-promotion and personal branding.

5 This is by far Yeshua's hardest day; it may also have been his longest day of ministry as well.

6 The two Gospels that record this event, Matthew and Mark, do not agree in their presentation. Mark places it both before *and* after the Temple cleansing. A sort of prophecy and fulfillment motif. Matthew places it *after* the Temple cleansing. The immediacy of the "withering" in Matthew's account may be a record of the blossoms only. Again, we have to remind ourselves that the Gospel authors are *not* embedded journalists seeking to provide a piece of investigative journalism.

3. Three parables of judgment (2 sons, wicked tenants, wedding feast).

4. Yeshua is attacked by every religious group in Jerusalem.

5. Yeshua publicly denounces Pharisaism.[1]

6. Yeshua privately teaches on the "last days."

7. "The Jews" privately craft a conspiracy of murder.

B. WEDNESDAY: The Larger Issues

1. Everything Yeshua said and did publicly that day was built upon three unavoidable truths:

   a) Israel was "barren" because she had created her own "kingdom theology."[2]

   b) The Kingdom of Heaven was going to be offered to *non-Jews!*[3]

> *"Therefore I tell you, the kingdom of God will be taken away from you and given to a people producing its fruits."*
> **Matthew 21:43**

     (1) The phrase, *"a people"* is the Greek word, *ethnos.*[4]

     (2) Matthew uses it 15 of the 39 times it appears in the Gospels.

     (3) He *always* uses it to refer to Gentiles.

     (4) John's five uses are *all* in reference to Israel as a distinct people.

   c) Yeshua is playing "hardball" from this point on:[5]

     (1) Of the 18 times Yeshua said, *"Woe to you…"* in Matthew and Luke, 14 of them are on this day![6]

     (2) Yeshua used the Greek word, "hypocrite" ,(Gk - *hupokritas; an impostor; to impersonate*) 18x, *all* in reference to Jewish religious leaders. Half are on this day!

C. WEDNESDAY: Unmasking the Opposition

1. Shared hatred is almost as powerful as shared love.[7]

   a) All the powerful groups in Jerusalem agreed on at least two things:

     (1) They held the "country people" in disdain and "accursed."[8] (Jn. 7:49)

     (2) They believed Yeshua was a serious threat to their personal way of life.[9]

---

1 It is worth noting that Jesus does *not* attack or humiliate any individuals. Rather, he attacks institutional rabbinic Judaism. If someone *was* humiliated, it would be because of their association with what Jesus denounced, *not* because he called them out publicly.

2 Most everybody "missed it" when it came to Jesus. John the Baptizer even seemed to be confused and had doubts shortly before he was murdered by Herod Antipas.

3 Jesus uses three parables of judgment to make and reinforce the future inevitability. We have to continually guard against forgetting that Yeshua's entire message was about a *kingdom* coming. You simply do not disrespect or disregard a king like we tend to do in a democracy.

4 This Greek word can mean any group of people in general, or it can refer specifically to "non-Jews." This second usage is most frequent in our New Testament.

5 Interestingly, his focus from this point on is *not* evangelism or even preaching the gospel. Yeshua's focus is now on his own identity and his mission, and the unbreakable connection between these two things.

6 The other four are references to judgements on cities. Mark and John do not have a single "woe." And, the four times it appears in Luke's Gospel are all in his record of the Sermon on the Mount of Matthew 5-7. And, Luke's "woes" are essentially cryptic assaults on the religious leaders: *"woe to you who are…rich, full, laughing, and having all men speak well of you."*

7 All the groups involved in orchestrating Yeshua's crucifixion and death *hated* each other! In fact, one rabbinic source said the Pharisees were *grateful* for Rome's presence in Jerusalem because it prevented everyone from killing each other! Sharing hatred (i.e. co-belligerency) is not the same as being an ally.

8 This was especially true of the scrupulously ritualistic Pharisees. The inevitable uncleanness due to their way of life, and their presumed ignorance, made the peasantry not only distasteful to the religious leaders, but also "unclean." It is interesting that *our* Latin word, "pagan" comes from *paganus* which originally meant "villager," or "country dweller."

9 He still is! In fact, if he's *not* a threat to the way I'd like to live in my natural self, then perhaps it's not Jesus that I'm "following."

Word Frequencies of Religious Groups in Jesus' Day:

W O R D	Matthew		Mark		Luke		John		Gospels
"chief priests"	18	*2*	14	*1*	12	*2*	10	0	54
"elders"	12	*1*	7	*1*	5	*1*	0	0	24
"high priest"	7	*0*	8	*0*	3	*0*	11	0	29
"Herodian"	1	*1*	2	*1*	0	*0*	0	0	3
"Pharisee"	30	*13*	12	*1*	27	*0*	20	0	89
Sadducee"	7	*2*	1	*1*	1	*1*	0	0	9
"the Jews"	5/4*		6/5*		4/3*		63/6*		78/18*
T O T A L S (w/o "the Jews")	75		44		48		41		208
T O T A L S (incl. "the Jews")	76		45		49		98		268

NOTES: (1) Numbers in **bold italics** correspond to occurrences during the "Day of Controversy."
(2) Numbers marked with "*" are the occurrences of the phrase, "King of the Jews."
(3) The second TOTALS columns include the phrase, "the Jews" but not those with "King of the Jews."

2. The "Coalition of Darkness"

a) HERODIANS: the "Religious Right" – a *political* group

(1) Believed the house of Herod was "God's choice" for king.

(2) Herod had appointed Joazar, son of a wealthy Alexandrian Jews, Boethus, to be High Priest shortly before he died.[1]

(3) The house of Boethus held the priesthood for 23 years from 23 BC - AD 42.

(4) The Boethusian family founded a new political party in Jerusalem — the Herodians!

(5) Herodian *theology* was similar to that of the Pharisees, but their allegiance to Herod was unique among Jews.

b) SADDUCEES: the Conservatives

(1) They sought to be more "biblical" than the Pharisees.[2]

(2) Stuck to what the scriptures said, no more, no less.

(3) Their power was social, but not spiritual.

(4) In *spiritual* matters however, they were forced to submit to the dominant theological view—that of the Pharisees[3]:

c) PHARISEES: the Fundamentalists

(1) The Pharisees' theology gravitated around three "centers":

(a) a hyper-scrupulousness about ceremonial cleanness

(b) a hyper-scrupulousness about tithing.[4]

---

1 Yahweh had given specific instructions regarding the office of High Priest in the Old Testament books of Exodus and Leviticus. The High Priest was to be of the tribe of Levi, a direct descendent of Aaron, and held office for life. But, by the time of Jesus, the office and its management had undergone comprehensive corruption. Over the 400-year period following the Babylonian captivity and destruction of the Temple, there had been nearly fifty High Priests, of which approximately 35 had been "appointed" by a Gentile ruler!

2 For instance, they only accepted as authoritative the writings of Moses. They also held that any behavior that was not *prohibited* my Moses was acceptable, and if something was not *mandated* by Moses, it was not required as necessary. They also dismissed the "traditions of the elders," or what has been called the "Oral Law." The Oral Law is supposedly what Yahweh said to Moses on Mt. Sinai that he did *not* write down. It was purportedly passed down orally over many generations, and then finally codified in the Talmud.

3 When it came to issues of the Sanhedrin or the Temple, Pharisaical theology always prevailed.

4 Yeshua's attack on the Pharisees around the topic of tithing actually had *nothing* to do with tithing. He was furious with them for how they *used* their "faithful commitment to tithe" as an excuse for neglecting mercy, compassion, and justice.

(c) a professedly higher commitment to the "elders" than scripture.

(2) The Pharisee was focused on the *outer* person to the neglect of the "heart":[1]

> *"Woe to you, scribes and Pharisees, hypocrites! For you tithe mint and dill and cumin, and have neglected the weightier matters of the law: justice and mercy and faithfulness. These you ought to have done, without neglecting the others. You blind guides, straining out a gnat and swallowing a camel! "Woe to you, scribes and Pharisees, hypocrites! For you clean the outside of the cup and the plate, but inside they are full of greed and self-indulgence. You blind Pharisee! First clean the inside of the cup and the plate, that the outside also may be clean. "Woe to you, scribes and Pharisees, hypocrites! For you are like whitewashed tombs, which outwardly appear beautiful, but within are full of dead people's bones and all uncleanness. So you also outwardly appear righteous to others, but within you are full of hypocrisy and lawlessness."* **Matthew 23:23-28**

(3) The Pharisee added to the requirements of God (justice, kindness and humility) a host of "required" behaviors, including:

(a) phylacteries – compartments with scriptures, worn on head and on the wrist. (cf. Ex. 13:9; Deut. 6:8):

(b) showy "religious" clothing – they lengthened their "tassels" to draw attention to themselves (cf. Num. 15:38).

(4) Yeshua attacked this spiritual arrogance without mercy:

> *"They do all their deeds to be seen by others. For they make their phylacteries broad and their fringes long, and they love the place of honor at feasts and the best seats in the synagogues and greetings in the marketplaces and being called rabbi by others."* **Matthew 23:5-7**

d) CHIEF PRIESTS: the Upper Class

(1) Of the 50 High Priests from 350 BC to AD 70, 35 were appointed by Gentiles!

(2) Of the 14 High Priests from ten families, during the time from Herod the Great to Yeshua's crucifixion, half of them came from two families:[2]

(a) the family of Boethus

(b) the family of Annas

(c) the "house of Annas" held control for 35 years between AD 6-43.

(3) The corruption and power of the high priestly families is evident from this second century talmudic excerpt:

> *Woe is me because of the house of Boethus;*
> *Woe is me because of their staves!*
> *Woe is me because of the house of Hanin (Annas);*
> *Woe is me because of their whisperings.*
> *Woe is me because of the house of Kathros*
> *Woe is me because of their pens!*
> *Woe is me because of the house of Ishmael the son of Phabi;*
> *Woe is me because of their fists!*
> *For they are High Priests and their sons are [temple] treasurers and their sons-in-law are trustees and their servants beat the people with staves.* **[b. Pesah. 57a=t.Menah.13.21]**

---

1 This is very similar to some modern beliefs among Christians; a sort of "negative righteousness," that believers should be known for what they *don't* do, where they *don't* go, etc. For many Christians, we are known for what we're "against" and what we "don't do," rather than what we're "for," and "do." The "white-washed tombs" is a reference to Jerusalem during the pilgrim festivals when the city would triple in size. The tombs were painted so those unfamiliar with the city would not be ceremonially unclean through accidental contact with the dead.

2 Given normal lifespans, there should only have been *one High Priest* who outlived Jesus!

LIST OF HIGH-PRIESTS FROM THE ACCESSION OF HEROD THE GREAT TO THE DESTRUCTION OF JERUSALEM

Appointed by

Herod the Great . . *(37 – 4 BC)*.
1. Ananel.
2. Aristobulus.
3. Jesus, son of Phabes.
4. Simon, son of Boethos.
5. Matthias, son of Theophilos.
6. Joazar, son of Boethos.

Archelaus . . . . . . *(4 BC – AD 6*
7. Eleazar, son of Boethos.
8. Jesus, son of Sie.

Quirinius . . . . . . *(AD 6 – 12*
(Governor of Syria)
9. Ananos (Annas).

Valerius Gratus . . *(AD 15 – 26)*
(Procurator of Judea)
10. Ishmael, son of Phabi.
11. Eleazar, son of Ananos.
12. Simon, son of Camithos.
13. Joseph (Caiaphas).

Vitellius . . . .
14. Jonathan, son of Ananos.
15. Theophilos, son of Ananos.

Agrippa I. . . . . . . *(AD 41 – 44)*
16. Simon Cantheras, son of Boethos.
17. Matthias, son of Ananos.
18. Elionaios, son of Cantheras.

Herod of Chalcis . . . .
19. Joseph, son of Camithos.
20. Ananias, son of Nedebaios.

Agrippa II. . . . .
21. Ishmael, son of Phabi.
22. Joseph Cabi, son of Simon.
23. Ananos, son of Ananos.
24. Jesus, son of Damnaios.
25. Jesus, son of Gamaliel.
26. Matthias, son of Theophilos.

The People during the last war
27. Phannias, son of Samuel.

NOTE: Herod Antipas was tetrarch of Galilee from the death of his father in 4 BC until AD 39. He was the "Herod" of the entirety of Jesus' earthly ministry.

This list is adapted from, Life and Times of Jesus the Messiah, by Alfred Eidersheim.

D. WEDNESDAY: The "Prequel" to the Main Event

1. This is Yeshua longest and most difficult day of teaching, ever.

2. Every strand of "the Jews" weave themselves together in a single day.

   a) The "chief priests, elders and scribes" challenged his "authority":[1]

And when he entered the temple, the chief priests and the elders of the people came up to him as he was teaching, and said, "By what authority are you doing these things, and who gave you this authority?" **Matthew 21:23**

   b) The Herodians challenged his political loyalty:

Then the Pharisees went and plotted how to entangle him in his talk. And they sent their disciples to him, along with the Herodians, saying, "Teacher, we know that you are true and teach the way of God truthfully, and you do not care about anyone's opinion, for you are not swayed by appearances. Tell us, then, what you think. Is it lawful to pay taxes to Caesar, or not?" **Matthew 22:15-17**

   c) The Sadducees challenged his knowledge of Torah:

The same day Sadducees came to him, who say that there is no resurrection, and they asked him a question, saying, "Teacher, Moses said, 'If a man dies having no children, his brother must marry the widow and raise up children for his brother.' Now there were seven brothers among us. The first married and died, and having no children left his wife to his brother. So too the second and third, down to the seventh. After them all, the woman died. In the resurrection, therefore, of the seven, whose wife will she be? For they all had her." **Matthew 22:23-28**

---

1 In the rabbinic system, one's "authority" was derived. You inherited it, in a sense, from the "authority" of the rabbi who taught you. So, in effect, they were asking Jesus, *"Who is your rabbi?"* Yeshua's consistent answer was that Yahweh was his rabbi, or the source of his "authority." Again, we see Jesus, once in Jerusalem, forcing every conversation back to the question of his identity.

    d) The Pharisees challenged his commitment to the covenant:

> *But when the Pharisees heard that he had silenced the Sadducees, they gathered together. And one of them, a lawyer, asked him a question to test him. "Teacher, which is the great commandment in the Law?"* **Matthew 22:34-36**

    3. What Yeshua was about to accomplish in Heaven on Golgotha that Friday, he accomplished on earth in Jerusalem on Wednesday:

> *And no one was able to answer him a word, nor from that day did anyone dare to ask him any more questions.* —**Matthew 22:46**

E. WEDNESDAY: The World *Before* the Text

  1. What is my perspective on the place, power and purpose of government? Have I deified it? *(Am I a Herodian?)*

  2. What do I do with the "silence" of Scripture? Is it a license for sin? *(Am I a Sadducee?)*

  3. Is my "barometer" of true spirituality based on what is seen, or what is unseen, in regard to my behavior? *(Am I a Pharisee?)*

  4. Do I believe justice and mercy are more important than tithing?[1]

III. A Day of Conflict & Teaching — continued

A. Yeshua's Olivet Discourse: The *Real* "Sermon on the Mount" (Matt. 24:1–26:2; Mk. 13:1-37; Lk. 21:5-38)

  1. This is Yeshua's most comprehensive teaching on the "end times."

  2. The contributions by the four Gospels *varies* dramatically:[2]

    a) John is totally "silent."

    b) Mark and Luke omit *all* of the material of Matthew 25:

      (1) Yeshua's two "end times" parables (10 virgins, 10 talents; Matt. 25:1-30).

      (2) Yeshua's "parable" of the Final Judgment (sheep, goats, *"least of these ... "*; 25:31-46).

      (3) Matthew precedes this with the "woes" to the Pharisees (Mt. 23).

      (4) Mark and Luke precede it with the *"widow's mite"* and teaching about sacrificial giving (Mk. 12:41-44; Lk. 21:1-4).

  3. The contributions by the Synoptic Gospels *agree* dramatically:

    a) All three of the Synoptic Gospels precede the teaching segment with statements of awe by the disciples about the Temple Mount (Mt. 24:1; Mk. 13:1; Lk. 21:5).

    b) All three record Yeshua's alarming statements about the total destruction of the Temple and the city.[3]

    c) All three present Yeshua's teaching as His response to two questions posed by the disciples[4]:

      (1) *"When will all this be?"*

      (2) *"What will be the signs that show it's really here?" (i.e. How will we know for sure?")*

---

1 In a technological era, we need to be reminded that there is no such thing as *virtual* mercy, virtual justice, virtual righteousness. They can only be administered face-to-face, life-to-life. Also, tithing never excuses me from obedience to the clear teaching of Scripture. Otherwise, it's *not* tithing, it's "bribing."

2 Looked at in terms of percent of contribution, 58% of the teaching in the Gospels on the end times is in Matthew, 22% in Mark, 20% in Luke, and 0% in John.

3 Their amazement at the beauty and architecture of the Temple mount and its associated buildings mustn't be underestimated by modern Christians. The Temple was the center of the universe for devout Jews, the dwelling place of the Lord of Hosts, the one city out of all the world where He chose to dwell. It's total destruction as described by Jesus would have been terrifying and traumatic. This is even more so the case when one considered that the Jews had already gone through the trauma of total devastation in their history once before. Six centuries earlier, after years of siege warfare, the Babylonians leveled the Temple and the city. This event was a permanent part of their national memory. The very thought of it repeating itself would have stricken Yeshua's disciples with dread and sorrow.

4 It is significant that *all three* of the Synoptics record Yeshua's startling response: *"Be careful that you are not led astray..."* A plain reading of this statement, and its repetition, is a clear indicator that left to ourselves, we have a natural proclivity to be misled. We would do well to pay attention to this fact, especially when it comes to the interest of modern believers in "end times" teaching, and our attraction to conspiracy theories.

d) All record Yeshua making an undeniable connection between Himself and the messianic figure in the Book of Daniel, *"the Son of Man."*[1]

> **Daniel 7:13,14** — *I saw in the night visions, and behold, with the clouds of heaven there came one like a son of man, and he came to the Ancient of Days and was presented before him. And to him was given dominion and glory and a kingdom, that all peoples, nations, and languages should serve him; his dominion is an everlasting dominion, which shall not pass away, and his kingdom one that shall not be destroyed.*

> **Matthew 24:30, 31** — *Then will appear in heaven the sign of the Son of Man, and then all the tribes of the earth will mourn, and they will see the Son of Man coming on the clouds of heaven with power and great glory. And he will send out his angels with a loud trumpet call, and they will gather his elect from the four winds, from one end of heaven to the other.*

> **Mark 13:26, 27** – *And then they will see the Son of Man coming in clouds with great power and glory. And then he will send out the angels and gather his elect from the four winds, from the ends of the earth to the ends of heaven.*

> **Luke 21:25-27** — *"And there will be signs in sun and moon and stars, and on the earth distress of nations in perplexity because of the roaring of the sea and the waves, people fainting with fear and with foreboding of what is coming on the world. For the powers of the heavens will be shaken. And then they will see the Son of Man coming in a cloud with power and great glory.*

e) All record Yeshua describing His "coming" in language from the Old Testament "Day of the Lord" (Mt. 24:29-30; Mk. 13:24-25; Lk 21:25-26):[2]

> *"Behold, the day of the LORD comes, cruel, with wrath and fierce anger, to make the land a desolation and to destroy its sinners from it. For the stars of the heavens and their constellations will not give their light; the sun will be dark at its rising, and the moon will not shed its light."*   **Isaiah 13:9, 10.**

> *"And I will show wonders in the heavens and on the earth, blood and fire and columns of smoke."*   **Joel 2:30**

B. Yeshua's Olivet Discourse: The World *Behind* the Text

1. Yeshua's description of the Temple Mount fits the final destruction of Jerusalem perfectly.

   a) In AD 66 the First Roman War began in Caesarea and spread to Gamla in Galilee.[3]

   b) By AD 69, the Roman commander, Vespasian was at the gates of Jerusalem.

   c) When Nero died, and Vespasian was made Emperor, he transferred power to his son, Titus, who "finished the job" in AD 70.

   d) Yeshua's description of the sufferings of "the end" as unimaginable is amplified by Josephus' description of the Roman siege:

   > *"The best of friends wrestled with each other for even the shadow of food. Others, mouths agape from hunger like mad dogs, staggered along, beating on the doors like drunken men...They put their teeth into everything, swallowing things even the filthiest of animals would not touch. Finally, they devoured even belts and shoes or gnawed at the leather they stripped from their shields."*   **Josephus,** *The Jewish War*, **6.194ff**

   e) The chilling fact that this Temple was destroyed *on the exact day as Solomon's Temple*—August 30th—must have sent a chill into the hearts of devout Jews.

---

1 All of Yeshua's teaching about his return in the four Gospels has to do with what we call the "Second Coming." There is no mention of a separate "rapture" as a distinct event. Even the teaching in Matthew 24 about "one taken and one left" (cf. Matt. 24:39) and its parallel passage in Luke 17 is in the context of the "coming of the Son of Man," which throughout the Gospels is clearly a reference to the Second Coming.

2 The "Day of the Lord" in Old Testament prophetic literature is a *terrifying* event. The return of Jesus is *not* going to be comparable to the finalé of a grand Christian conference. Paul's description of it in 2 Thessalonians 1:5-12 is sobering. The two "comings" of Jesus serves as an excellent example of what is known as "multiple fulfillment" in biblical prophecy. In such a case, a prophecy has more than one facet to it, and so is "fulfilled" either in multiple events, or one event spread over a length of time. In the case of Jesus, his first "coming" was as a humble servant, born as a peasant, growing up as a carpenter, and arriving in Jerusalem on a donkey, coming in peace. In his second "coming," he arrives from heaven as the King of Kings, riding a white horse, arriving to execute judgment. In cases of multiple fulfillment, typically the second fulfillment is *worse* than the first if it is judgment, and *better* than the first if it is blessing.

3 Vespasian landed in Caesarea with three legions of Roman soldiers (9,000 - 18,000 men). His conquest took him on a march from north to south; Galilee to Jerusalem, and finally to Masada south of Jerusalem. The total campaign lasted from AD 66-73. Titus was eventually made Emperor when his father Vespasian died. What is known as the Second Jewish Revolt, or the Bar Kochba Rebellion occurred roughly 60 years later, in AD 132. The Emperor Hadrian made circumcision illegal, built a temple to Zeus on the Temple mount and a temple to Aphrodite on Golgotha. Between 600,000 - 1 million Jews were killed during this second, brutal war.

f) This event marked the replacement of Temple Judaism by "synagogue" Judaism, which is still with us today.[1]

g) This also marked the beginning of 19 centuries of foreign domination of the Jewish homeland!

2. This "sermon" cannot be understood apart from the Book of Daniel, to which *both* Yeshua and Matthew refer (cf. Mt. 24:15,30-31 and Dan. 9:27; 11:31; 12:3).

3. Yeshua laid-out some "non-negotiables" about his "coming":[2]

a) The exact *timing* of His coming was, and will remain, unknown[3] ("day and hour"; Mt. 24:36,42-44).

b) His "coming" will be spectacular and public, not "secret" (Mt. 24:26-27)

c) The "Great Desolator" of Daniel would arise before His "coming"[4] (Mt. 24:15; cf. Dan 9:27;11:36ff; 3x in 12:11).

d) The Gospel will be preached to all the Gentiles[5] (i.e. "nations") prior to His "coming" (Mt. 24:14).

e) A time of great tribulation will precede His "coming"(Mt. 24:9-22).

C. Yeshua's Olivet Discourse: The World *Of* the Text

1. **"led astray"** – Greek *planaō; "to seduce, to lead astray, to deceive"*[6]

a) This is the word used for sheep when they "go astray" (Mt. 18:12-13).

b) Yeshua repeats this warning four times in this sermon (vv. 4, 5,11, 24).

c) He says "many" *will be misled,* by false prophets (teaching), false messiahs (people) and false proofs ("signs")[7] Mt. 24:5,11, 24.

2. **"coming"** – Greek *parousia; "coming, arrival, advent"*

a) The word is used 22 times in the NT, 15 of which are for Yeshua.

b) Matthew is the only Gospel writer to use this word; 4x, all here.

c) Paul uses it 14 times, seven of which are in his Thessalonian correspondence.[8]

d) Peter uses it 3 times and John only once (2 Pet. 1:16; 3:4,12; 1 Jn 2:18).

e) It is a technical term for, *'...the arrival of a king or ruler who expects to receive his 'crown of coming.'"* **(Deissmann, *Light from the Ancient East*, pp. 372ff).**

---

1 It also marked the end of what we could call "Hebraic Christianity," the portion of the early believing community that still was quite "Jewish" in its approach to life and scripture. After the destruction of the Temple and the resulting dispersion of Jews, the Greek and Roman "flavors" of Christianity rose to prominence, and are still with us today.

2 Yeshua's admonition to "watch" (cf. Matt 24:44) is predicated on two facts: (1) We must be ready because of the *certainty* of his return (It was promised by Jesus and prophesied in the Old Testament), which we will recognize *generally* by the fulfillment of the preliminary signs. And, (2) We must be watchful because we do *not* know the *exact* time of his return. But perhaps even more importantly, we should live godly lives *not* out of fear of embarrassment at his unexpected arrival, but because of our convictions of the *certainty* of it, *and* the temporal nature of this life. Peter says we "look forward" to his return because of the hope of our redemption, not fear of our embarrassment.

3 By giving a "list" of sorts of preliminary events that will precede his return, Jesus is telling us we *can* know some things in regard to the "when." Also, the words *hēmera* ("day") and *hōra* ("hour") are words that are customarily used for things that deal with predicability and/or repeatability. The popular idea that Jesus can return "at any moment," if true today, at least was not always true. For example, Jesus told Paul (via Ananias) that he would carry the gospel to *"before the Gentiles and kings and the children of Israel."* (Acts 9:15-16). He also told Paul during the shipwreck of Acts 27 that he would testify in Rome (Acts 27:22-26). Even while on earth, he predicted to the Twelve that they would suffer in the future, as his disciples (Lk 21:12-19). If the "any moment" return of Jesus wasn't *always* true, it's at least likely that it was *never* true.

4 This is clearly a historical reference to Antiochus IV in the 2nd century B.C. But, Daniel 11 paints the portrait of an "abomination" that over-shadows all of the historical figures and points to one final desecrator at the end of time.

5 In Matthew, the 15 occurrences of the Greek word *ethnos* always refers to the Gentiles; 8 of the 15 are actually *translated* "Gentiles." (Contrasted to John, for whom *ethnos* is a reference to the nation of Israel in his 5 uses of the word.

6 This verb is *passive* here, indicating someone or something outside me is "leading me astray." This is *not* self-deception here. Luke's account provides us with two *types* of people to avoid: (1) those who say, *"I am he."* and (2) those who say, *"the time of his coming is at hand."* (Luke 21:8).

7 The Greek word for "signs" here (*sēmeion*) is the same word John uses throughout his Gospel to refer to Yeshua's miracles as "convincing proofs" of his deity. The Scripture tells us that God has "put eternity on men's hearts" (Ecc 3:11), so it is understandable that we have a longing to know the future. But, in our fallen state, we tend to want to know for reasons of personal power, so *where* we look (i.e. horoscopes) and *why* we look (biblical prophecy) are often skewed by this selfishness.

8 While Paul uses *parousia* in 1 Corinthians and Philippians to refer to various *people* "coming," in his Thessalonian correspondence, six of the occurrences are references to the return of Jesus, and the final reference is to the "coming of the lawless one." (i.e. the Antichrist).

IV. Yeshua's LAST PASSOVER

A. The Four Gospels provide a panoramic perspective of the events of "The Last Supper":

ITEM IN NARRATIVE	Matthew	Mark	Luke	John
1. *Securing & preparation of room in city for Passover*	*26:17-19*	*14:2-16*	*22:7-13*	—
2. Statement of intense "longing" for this meal.	—	—	22:15	—
3. Passover meal	**36:20**	**14:17**	**22:14-16**	**(13:1-14:31)**
4. Washing of disciples' feet.	—	—	—	13:1-20
5. Jesus predicts the betrayal.	**26:21**	**14:18**	**22:21-23**	**13:21**
6. The betrayer is identified.	26:23-25	14:20-21	—	13:22-30
7. Judas departs.	—	—	—	13:30-31ª
8. Argument and teaching of true "greatness" in the Kingdom.	—	—	22:24-30	—
9. Jesus gives the "new commandment" *(Maundy Thursday)*.	—	—	—	13:34-35
10. Prediction of Peter's coming "sifting" by Satan.	—	—	22:31-32	—
11. 1st prediction of Peter's denial.	—	—	22:33-34	13:36-48
12. *Institution of "the Lord's Supper."*	*26:26-29*	*14:22-25*	*22:17-20**	—
13. The "Upper Room Discourse." •*"I go to prepare a place for you…"* • *"I will send another Helper…"* •*"I am the vine…you are the branches…"* •*"The Spirit of Truth will lead you into all Truth…"*	—	—	—	14:1-16:33
14. Jesus' prays (aloud) His "High Priestly prayer."	—	—	—	17:1-26
15. They sing a "hymn" (the Hallel).	26:30	14:26	—	—
16. Leave the city and go to the Mount of Olives.	**26:30**	**14:26**	**22:39**	**18:1**
17. Peter's denial is predicted a 2nd time.	26:31-35	14:27-31	—	—
18. *Jesus warns the disciples to "watch and pray."*	*26:36-38*	*14:34*	*22:40,46*	—
19. *The agony in the garden.*	*26:39-46*	*14:35-42*	*22:41-45*	—
20. Jesus is strengthened by an angel.	—	—	22:43	—
21. Actual betrayal and arrest.	**26:47-57**	**14:43-53**	**22:47-54**	**18:2-12**
22. High Priest's servant (Malchus) ear is cut-off, then healed.	—	—	22:50-51	18:10-11

*anachronistic
Entries in italics appear in all the Synoptics.
Bold entries appear in all four Gospels.

1. John provides the *least* amount of narrative and the *greatest* amount of unique material (Mt. 305 words, Mk. 352 words, Lk. 658 words, Jn. 3,589 words)![1]

2. John has 28 references (direct or indirect) to the Holy Spirit in this section.

3. This is one of the few historical events in the life of Yeshua (other than crucifixion and resurrection) specifically addressed by Paul:[2]

   For I received from the Lord what I also delivered to you, that the Lord Jesus on the night when he was betrayed took bread, and when he had given thanks, he broke it, and said, "This is my body which is for you. Do this in remembrance of me." In the same way also he took the cup, after supper, saying, "This cup is the new covenant in my blood. Do this, as often as you drink it, in remembrance of me."   **1 Corinthians 11:23-25**

B. The "Last Supper" — The World *Behind* the Text

1. Yeshua is drawing the Jewish worlds of "covenant" into their final fulfillment:

   a) Passover commemorated the beginning the fulfillment of the Abrahamic covenant of one people blessing the nations:

   When Abram was ninety-nine years old the LORD appeared to Abram and said to him, "I am God Almighty; walk before me, and be blameless, that I may make my covenant between me and you, and may multiply you greatly."

---

1 Interestingly, this is also the Gospel that gives us virtually *nothing* about Yeshua's second coming. This is an excellent example of authorial intent differing from writer to writer. The second coming was either unimportant to John at the time of his writing, or it didn't warrant enough significance for his purposes to include it.

2 Comparing Paul's account of his direct revelation from Jesus to the accounts in the three Synoptics, we discover that Matthew and Mark do not mention the idea of "remembrance," and Luke attaches it only to the bread, but not the wine (Lk 22:19). Also, Luke is the only Gospel writer who attaches the adjective "new" to the word "covenant." And, as with Paul, he chooses the Greek word *kainos*, which means "new of a new kind" rather than "most recent." But, the fact that both Luke and Paul use this same phraseology shouldn't surprise us because of the long and significant relationship between these two men.

Then Abram fell on his face. And God said to him, "Behold, my covenant is with you, and you shall be the father of a multitude of nations. No longer shall your name be called Abram, but your name shall be Abraham, for I have made you the father of a multitude of nations. I will make you exceedingly fruitful, and I will make you into nations, and kings shall come from you."
Genesis 17:1-6

And Moses wrote down all the words of the LORD. He rose early in the morning and built an altar at the foot of the mountain, and twelve pillars, according to the twelve tribes of Israel. And he sent young men of the people of Israel, who offered burnt offerings and sacrificed peace offerings of oxen to the LORD. And Moses took half of the blood and put it in basins, and half of the blood he threw against the altar. Then he took the Book of the Covenant and read it in the hearing of the people. And they said, "All that the LORD has spoken we will do, and we will be obedient." And Moses took the blood and threw it on the people and said, "Behold the blood of the covenant that the LORD has made with you in accordance with all these words."
Exodus 24:4-8

b) The "Last Supper" component that Yeshua inaugurated that night marked the merger of Abraham, Moses and the fulfillment of the prophetic covenant of Jeremiah:

And likewise the cup after they had eaten, saying, "This cup that is poured out for you is the new covenant in my blood."
Luke 22:20

But this is the covenant that I will make with the house of Israel after those days, declares the LORD: I will put my law within them, and I will write it on their hearts. And I will be their God, and they shall be my people. And no longer shall each one teach his neighbor and each his brother, saying, 'Know the LORD,' for they shall all know me, from the least of them to the greatest, declares the LORD. For I will forgive their iniquity, and I will remember their sin no more."
Jeremiah 31:33, 34

"And I will give you a new heart, and a new spirit I will put within you. And I will remove the heart of stone from your flesh and give you a heart of flesh. And I will put my Spirit within you, and cause you to walk in my statutes and be careful to obey my rules."
Ezekiel 36:26, 27.

2. Yeshua may have followed the traditional Passover seder liturgy:

Preliminary Course:
• Word of dedication or blessing over the day and the offering of the first cup of wine.
• Preliminary dish of green herbs, bitter herbs and fruit puree sauce is eaten.
• Meal proper is served, but not eaten.
• 2nd cup is mixed.

Passover Liturgy:
• An account of the Passover event and an interpretation is given by the head of the family unit.
• First part of the Hallel (Pss. 113-118) is sung in Hebrew.
• The second cup is drunk, the haggadah or cup of interpretation.

Main Meal:
• Grace (thanks) is said over the unleavened bread.
• *It is likely that Yeshua made his comments about His body being the bread that was broken for them, here.*
• The meal is eaten: lamb, unleavened bread, bitter herbs, fruit puree, wine
• Grace (thanks) is said over the third cup, the cup of blessing.
• *It is likely that this is the point where Yeshua would have introduced the "blood of the new covenant."*

Conclusion:
• Second part of the Hallel is sung in Hebrew
• Praise over the fourth cup, the hallel cup, the cup of consummation.
• *It is likely that this is the cup that Yeshua said he would "not drink again until he drank it in the kingdom." (Lk 22:18).*

3. There is a strong likelihood that the "Last Supper" took place in the home of Mary, the mother of John Mark.[1]

a) Yeshua *apparently* had made prior contact with "a certain man" in the city for using his "guest room" (Mt. 26:18).

b) It would have had to be a room large enough for *at least* 13 people (and perhaps more).

c) We learn from Luke later, that immediately *after* the ascension, the disciples and a large company returned to *"the upper room where they were staying"* (Acts 1:13-15).

d) We know that the home of Mary was a central meeting place for prayer and worship (Acts 12:12; Peter went immediately here after his release from prison).

---

1 Two factors lead us to this likely conclusion. First, Mary's home was within the city of Jerusalem. Second, it was a liturgical requirement that Passover be eaten with the walls of Jerusalem.

    e) Eidersheim suggests that it was to *this home* that the Temple guards were first taken by Judas, and that Mark followed them to the garden after they had visited his home.[1]

  C. The "Last Supper" — The World *Of* the Text

    1. *"new"* – Greek *kainos; "new of a different kind; unused, unworn"* (not *neos*, new in time)

      a) This is the word used for "new" wineskins, for "new" cloth (Mk. 2:21-22).

    2. *"I have earnestly desired to eat…"* – Greek *epithumia epethumēsa*

      a) This is the word normally translated "lust" or "covet" (Mt. 5:28; Acts 20:33)

    3. *"Helper"* – Greek *paraklētos; "advocate, one called alongside"*

      a) This word appears 5x in our NT, all by John.

      b) Four are for the Holy Spirit, and one is for Yeshua (Jn 14:16,26; 15:26; 16:7;1 Jn 2:1).

      c) The word family basically means: *"To keep someone on their feet, who, if left alone, would collapse."*

      d) Our words, *comforter, encourager* have lost their original meaning of empowerment, and have been replaced by "sympathy."

  D. The Olivet Discourse: The World *Before* the Text

    1. Yeshua's answer to the questions of *"When?"* and *"How?"* are still relevant today:

      a) *Be alert!* Don't allow yourself to be led astray by deceptive teaching or deceptive teachers (Mt. 24:5,25:1-3).

      b) *Be faithful!* Make it your goal to being *serving* the Master who has left, until He "comes" (Mt. 24:45-46; 25:14-30).

      c) *Be holy!* The *purpose* of predictive prophecy is motivation for sanctified living, not fear or distraction (2 Pet. 3:9-11; Is. 46:9-10).

  E. The "Last Supper": The World *Before* the Text

    1. We are part of that amazing promise God gave to Moses:

> *Now therefore, if you will indeed obey my voice and keep my covenant, you shall be my treasured possession among all peoples, for all the earth is mine; and you shall be to me a kingdom of priests and a holy nation. These are the words that you shall speak to the people of Israel."*   **Exodus 19:5, 6.**

> *And they sang a new song, saying, "Worthy are you to take the scroll and to open its seals, for you were slain, and by your blood you ransomed people for God from every tribe and language and people and nation, and you have made them a kingdom and priests to our God, and they shall reign on the earth." Then I looked, and I heard around the throne and the living creatures and the elders the voice of many angels, numbering myriads of myriads and thousands of thousands, saying with a loud voice, "Worthy is the Lamb who was slain, to receive power and wealth and wisdom and might and honor and glory and blessing!" And I heard every creature in heaven and on earth and under the earth and in the sea, and all that is in them, saying, "To him who sits on the throne and to the Lamb be blessing and honor and glory and might forever and ever!" And the four living creatures said, "Amen!" and the elders fell down and worshiped.*   **Revelation 5:9-14**

---

1 The Greek word used to describe the "linen cloth" (*sindōn*) that a young man was wearing who, when assaulted by the guards in the garden, left it and fled away naked, is a word that refers to *expensive* cloth. It's the same word used in the Greek Old Testament for the cloth that the woman of Proverbs 31 made and sold. Also, the location and size of Mark's mother's home would suggest that she was a wealthy woman. That would explain her son (if it was indeed him in the garden) having an expensive night shirt. This notion is further supported by the fact that the story of the anonymous "young man" only appears in the Gospel written by Mark. Eidersheim suggests that Judas, familiar with the home used for the Last Supper, would have led the Temple guards and Jewish authorities there first, considering that was the last place Judas has seen Jesus. After discovering that Jesus had already left, he would have then led them to Gethsemane, where Mark would have followed.

UNIT 15: Yeshua's "24"

I. Yeshua's "24": Gethsemane to the Grave

A. Twenty Four "Stops" in 24 Hours[1]

E V E N T	Matthew	Mark	Luke	John
1. Jesus is arrested in Gethsemane	26:47-57	14:43-53	22:47-54	18:2-12
2. Jesus is taken to Annas the "high priest"[1]	—	—	—	18:13-24
3. John & Peter follow Jesus to high priest's house	—	—	—	18:15
4. John is allowed access to high priest's courtyard & secures Peter's access	—	—	—	18:15-16
5. Peter's first denial (specific)	—	—	—	18:17
6. Peter is sitting in "the company of the enemy"	26:58	14:66	22:55	18:18
7. Jesus is brought before Annas[1] the "high priest" (Trial" #1)	—	—	—	18:13-24
8. Jesus is taken to appear before Caiaphas[2] the high priest ("Trial" #2)	26:57-68	14:53-65	22:54	—
9. Peter's "denials" (general)	26:69-75	14:67-72	22:56-65	18:25-27
10. Jesus appears before the Sanhedrin ("Trial #3)	27:1	15:1	22:66-71	18:19-24
11. Jesus' first appearance before Pilate ("Trial #4)	27:2-14	15:1-5	23:1-5	18:28-38
12. Judas returns "blood money" and commits suicide[3]	27:3-10	—	—	—
13. Jesus is sent to Herod Antipas by Pilate ("Trial" #5)	—	—	23:6-12	—
14. Jesus' second appearance before Pilate ("Trial" #6)	27:15-26	15:6-15	23:13-25	18:39 – 19:16
15. Pilate's wife tries to dissuade him	27:19	—	—	—
16. Pilate "washes his hands"	27:24	—	—	—
17. Jesus is mocked and abused by the Roman soldiers	27:27-30	15:16-19	—	—
18. Jesus travels the "Dia Dolorosa" to Golgotha	27:31-34	15:20-23	23:26-33	19:17
19. The women of Jerusalem lament	—	—	23:27-31	—
20. Jesus is offered wine with myrrh on Golgotha	27:34	15:23	—	—
21. Crucifixion: the first three hours (9am - noon)	27:35-44	15:24-32	23:33-43	19:18-27
• *the soldiers cast lots for Jesus' clothes*	—	—	—	19:23-24
• *the Jews mock Jesus on the cross*	27:39-43	15:29-32	23:35	—
• *the thief's "confession"*	—	—	23:39-43	—
• *Jesus "transfers" Mary's care to John*	—	—	—	19:25-27
22. Crucifixion: the final three hours (noon- 3pm)	27:45-54	15:33-39	23:44-47	19:28-30
• *3 hours of darkness in the land*	27:45-50	15:33-37	23:44-46	19:28-30
• *Temple curtain torn/graves opened*	27:51-56	15:38-41	23:47-49	—
• *the Centurion's "confession"*	27:54	15:39	23:47	—
23. Jesus' body obtained from Pilate by Joseph of Aramathea	27:57-58	15:42-45	23:50-52	19:31-38
24. Jesus is buried by Joseph and Nicodemus	27:59-60	15:46	23:53-54	19:39-42

[1] - High Priest, AD 7-15   [2] - Mark & Luke do *not* mention him by name   [3] - see also Acts 1:18-29

B. The World *Behind* the Text: The "Stops" From Gethsemane to the Grave (aka Golgotha)

1. Starting Point: Gethsemane — *"Olive Press"*[2]

   a) The area where David wept, while running from *his* betrayer, his own son (2 Sam. 15:30-32).

   b) An unknown site, unmentioned by any other sources.[3]

   c) A favorite place of Yeshua according to Luke (Lk 22:29).

---

1 It is worth pointing out that the large gaps of days, even months that characterized the four Gospel accounts for the previous three years of Yeshua's life are not evident here. There is a very tight chronology in all four Gospels for this week of Yeshua's life. The number of words is quite similar also. That's because the death and resurrection of Jesus has been the core of the gospel message since Pentecost (cf. Acts 2:22-24; 1 Cor 15:3-4). This central message has been called the *kerygma* by some, drawing on the Greek verb *kērussō* , "to preach."

2 Some of the olive trees in the location today are over 500 years old! It took many years before an olive tree even *began* to bear fruit. Trees were in families for generations. That's why there was profound psychological damage done in AD 132 when Hadrian squashed the Bar Kochba rebellion; he destroyed all the trees in Jerusalem.

3 In the Ancient Near East, "sacred sites" have a long history. In some ways, they are about as trustworthy as textual evidence. Sacred sites might even be viewed as a "genre" in themselves because of what is signified to occupy a *previously* "sacred site." This is most obvious in the layer upon layer of temple, mosque, church, mosque, etc. Each time power shifted in an area, it was important to "prove" the victory by building a new sacred site on the ruins of the previous one just conquered.

d) A "Sabbath Day's journey"[1] from Jerusalem (Acts 1:12).

2. Stop #1: The "Herodian Quarters" on Mount Zion

  a) Yeshua was likely taken to a "gated community" owned by priestly families.[2]

  b) It was here that he was interrogated first by Annas[3], then by Caiaphas, his son-in-law, denied by Peter, and beaten with *fists*[4] [Gk = *kolaphos*] (Jn 18:13-27; Mt. 26:57-68).

  c) Recent excavations have isolated the "Herodian Quarters" in Jerusalem's Jewish Quarter.

  d) These palatial mansions (5,500 ft[2]) were worth $20 million in today's market![5]

3. This housing arrangement very closely supports the Gospel descriptions:

  a) Multi-story (Peter was *"below"* Yeshua according to Mk 14:66-68).

  b) Interconnected, allowing easy movement from Annas to Caiaphas.

18 The Herodian Quarter in Jerusalem

- 5,500 ft[2] mansion
- imported glass from Sidon
- multiple miqv'ot
- plastered walls
- multiple frescoes
- "bar Kathros" stone found here

General plan of the buildings in the Herodian Quarter.

---

1 see footnote #93

2 From John's account, it is obvious that he is both known *and* trusted by the priestly families and their servants, for him to have both access *and* influence (it was through his request that Peter was allowed access to the proceedings.).

3 John's account is the only one that provides us with this insight. Annas was the "mastermind" behind everything that happened to Jesus. And was, in fact, the real High Priest in terms of influence and power, even though his son-in-law was the *acting* High Priest.

4 This word implies a *closed* fist, whereas the Roman soldiers used an *open* fist, or a slap in their abuse of Jesus.

5 A glass vase made by Ennion of Sidon was discovered in these villas. This is the "Gucci of glass" in the 1st century. A stone weight, with the owner's name was also found: "bar Kathros," or "son of Kathros." This was the name of one of the most powerful priestly families in Jerusalem at the time of Jesus.

     c) It is consistent with both rabbinic and Gospel descriptions of the wealth and corruption of the priestly families (cf. b. *Pesah.* 57a=t. *Menah.* 13:21).

  4. Stop #2: "Chamber of Hewn Stone" on the Temple Mount? (m. *Mid.* 5:4)

     a) This is a "daytime" event, following the evening "trials" (cf. Luke 22:66).

     b) This is *not* a uniform consensus; Jews do not want to incriminate the *entire* Great Sanhedrin, yet allow for corruption in its midst.[1]

> *"A Sanhedrin that puts someone to death in a week* [i.e. 7 years] *is called 'destructive.' Rabbi Eleazar ben Azariah says: 'Even one person in seventy years.' Rabbi Tarfon and Rabbi Akiva say: 'If we had been members of the Sanhedrin, no one would ever have been put to death.'"*   **(m. Miksh. 1:10)**

     c) The Gospels speak of the "Sanhedrin," but Luke later uses that same term to refer to a *place* rather than a *"people"* (cf. Luke 22:66a and 22:66b; Acts 4:15;5:27).

  5. Stop #3: "Trial" #1 With Pilate at "The *"Palace"* of the Governor[2] (Mk 15:16)

     a) This has traditionally been thought to be the Antonia Fortress on the Temple Mount.

     b) It is now believed to have been Herod the Great's Palace, near the Jaffa Gate on the Western Hill.

     c) Mark's description, *"...the soldiers led him away inside the palace (that is, the governor's headquarters* [Gk = praetorium]*"* (Mk 15:16) agrees with Luke's description of *"Herod's praetorium"* in Caesarea (Acts 23:35).

     d) That means the journey from Caiaphas to Pilate was a 5-minute walk; about 500 yards, "as the crow flies."

  6. Stop #4: Herod Antipas, "Trial" #5 (Lk 13:31-33; 23:8-12)

     a) Josephus tells us that Herod was staying in the "Hasmonean Palace" in Jerusalem (*Ant.* 20:190). It's exact location is still unknown.

  7. Stop #5: Back to Pilate for "Trial" #6 (Jn 18:39-19:16)

     a) Pilate tries desperately to free Yeshua, but turns him over to the will of "the Jews."[3]

     b) It is here where Yeshua is scourged, mocked and delivered to be crucified.

  8. Stop #6: Golgotha — "Outside the City" (Lev. 16:27; Heb. 13:11-12)

     a) John tells us that the location of the crucifixion and burial of Yeshua were in the same proximity:

> *"Now in the place where he was crucified there was a garden, and in the garden a new tomb in which no one had yet been laid".*   **John 19:41**

     b) The present day Church of the Holy Sepulcher is an ancient and likely place (even though it is *inside* the modern walls of Jerusalem[4]).

C. The World *Behind* the Text: The "Stars" From Gethsemane to the Grave

  1. Peter: The "Star" in the Group Satan Demanded to "Sift Like Wheat" (Lk 22:31-32)

     a) Peter believed *he alone* was incapable of deserting Yeshua (Mk 14:43-50).

     b) Peter believed he was *incapable* of denying Yeshua (Mk.14:43-50).

     c) Yeshua told him their desertion was as inevitable as his crucifixion (Mt. 26:30-35).

  2. Annas: A Not-So-Happy "Reunion"?

---

1 Some scholars see a smaller, highly influential group operating here, rather than the Great Sanhedrin of 71 men. The families of Kathros and Annas would have certainly been a part of the smaller, more powerful group.

2 Herod Antipas' father, Herod the Great *built* this palace, but Pilate trumps Herod in the Roman chain of command, so he rather than Herod is staying in it during the feast. John gives us the most detail about Yeshua's conversations with Pilate. In each of the three Synoptics, we are limited to four words in English, *"You say I am"* (only 2 in Greek!). Whereas in John, we are given 123 words in English.

3 Surely part of this panic on Pilate's part is due to the insistence of the Jews that Jesus deserved to die because he *"made himself to be the son of God."* Romans were superstitious, and this statement would have terrified Pilate.

4 This is significant because it is *impossible* to have a graveyard *inside* a city in the ancient world. We have excellent indirect evidence here that the city walls were closer in then than they are now.

a) Annas was appointed High Priest in AD 7, and would have been there the year Yeshua first came to Jerusalem.[1]

b) It is likely he remembered this "child prodigy" from Galilee[2] (Lk 2:46-49).

c) He, and the rest, sold their conscience for *power*[3] (Jn 19:15).

d) He certainly remembered Yeshua "closing up shop" on his corrupt operations in the Court of the Gentiles 2-3 years earlier (Jn 2:13-22).

e) Annas' influence was immense and continued long after the crucifixion. He was the interrogator of Peter and John after Pentecost (Acts 4:6-21).

3. Pilate: *"Failing* Theology 101"

a) Pilate was given the most extended, detailed "theology lesson" ever extended to a Gentile by Yeshua.

b) Pilate sold his conscience[4] for *peace* (Jn 19:7-16).

D. The World *Of* the Text: From Gethsemane to the Grave

1. Peter's "Purified" Pen: Lessons From Being "Sifted"[5] (Lk 22:31-32)

"Simon, Simon, behold, Satan demanded to have you, that he might sift you like wheat, but I have prayed for you that your faith may not fail. And when you have turned again, strengthen your brothers."

a) **"you"** — in verse 31, both are *plural;* Yeshua is addressing *them all* about Satan.

b) **"you"** — in verse 32, both are *singular;* Yeshua is talking to *Peter* about "falling" and "rising."

(1) Thirty years later, a much humbler Peter warns others, in the context of submission and humility, to "be alert" for Satan's devastating attacks (1 Pet 5:5-8).

c) **"strengthen"** — word means to help others be "rooted and established"

(1) Thirty years later, Peter uses this word to encourage suffering Christians (1 Pet 5:10, the word translated, *confirm*).

2. Pilate's "One Verse Theology Course" (John 18:37)

Then Pilate said to him, "So you are a king?" Jesus answered, "You say that I am a king. **For this** *purpose* **I was born** *and* **for this** *purpose* **I have come** *into the world to bear witness to the truth. Everyone who is of the truth* **listens** *to my voice."*

a) **"I was born…I have come…"** — both verbs are *Perfect tense.*

(1) Yeshua is stressing the fact that he is now *here,* more than how he got here.

b) **"for this…"** — the Greek is literally, *"for this I was born…for this I have come…"*

(1) Yeshua's deliberate repetition makes one thing clear: *"I have a mission!"*

c) **"listens to my voice…"** — Present tense in the Greek

(1) Yeshua is talking about a *lifestyle* here, not simply "paying attention."

(2) He's speaking of *"hearing"* with the intention of *doing* (i.e. obeying)[6].

---

1 He was High Priest AD 7-15, but was then deposed by Rome.

2 Scholars point to a particular place in Jerusalem were the elders used to gather to talk and argue Torah, Mishnah, and theology.

3 Jewish men recited the "18 Benedictions" each day. Benediction #11 was: *"We have no king by you, O Lord."* These men had all recited this benediction already that day, or would do so before they retired for the evening! When they told Pilate, *"We have no king but Caesar"* (John 19:5) it was a profound blasphemy designed to secure Yeshua's death by charging him with insurrection. If anyone should have been stoned that day for blasphemy, it should have been these men! The irony is that Jesus was charged with blasphemy for telling the truth.

These men all played the Roman government *and* their own religious system to support and validate their own values and lifestyle. Woe to us if we do the same!

4 Pilate's repeated efforts to free Jesus all point to the fact that he was convinced of his innocence.

5 They will *all* "turn" from Jesus that night. Jesus here is speaking of Peter's *re*-turn; his repentance.

6 John 10:27 has the same verb in the same tense: *"My sheep hear my voice, and I know them, and they follow me."* Clearly "hearing" here is a synonym for "obeying."

3. "The Jews" One Word Confession (John 18:31-32)

*Pilate said to them, "Take him yourselves and judge him by your own law." The Jews said to him, "It is not lawful for us to **put anyone to death**." This was to fulfill the word that Jesus had spoken to show by what kind of death he was going to die.*

    a) This verb *apokteinō*, "to kill," is distinguished from *lithoboleō*, "to stone" in the Gospels (Mt. 21:35; 23:34).

    b) Stoning was the punishment for blasphemy (Lev. 24:16).

    c) "The Jews" are admitting that they want Yeshua *dead*, not punished!

E. The World *Before* the Text: From Gethsemane to the Grave

  1. What sin do you believe you are incapable of, that others aren't?

Peter said to him, "Even though they all fall away, I will not." And Jesus said to him, "Truly, I tell you, this very night, before the rooster crows twice, you will deny me three times." But he said emphatically, "If I must die with you, I will not deny you." And they all said the same.   **Mark 14:29-31**

  2. What is *your* response when reviled?

"For to this you have been called, because Christ also suffered for you, leaving you an example, so that you might follow in his steps. He committed no sin, neither was deceit found in his mouth. When he was reviled, he did not revile in return; when he suffered, he did not threaten, but continued entrusting himself to him who judges justly."   **1 Peter 2:21-23**

  3. What is your commitment to *"strengthening your brothers"*?

"Simon, Simon, behold, Satan demanded to have you, that he might sift you like wheat, but I have prayed for you that your faith may not fail. And when you have turned again, strengthen your brothers."   *Luke 22:31-32*

UNIT 16: "He is Not Here"

I. LOOKING BACK:

JESUS' LIFE & MINISTRY

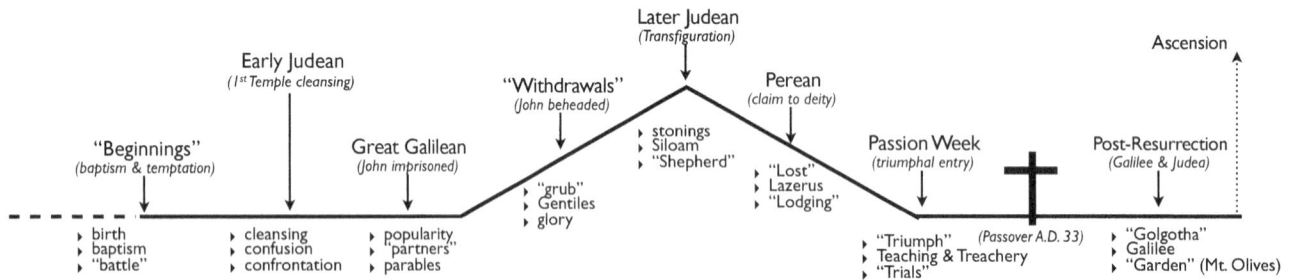

II. "HE IS NOT HERE!" — THE RESURRECTION

A. Our Greatest Hope: A Stumbling Block to Jews and Foolishness to Gentiles

  1. The resurrection narratives are a critic's "goldmine"!

  2. There is no account in the Bible that has greater difficulties associated with it than that which is at the heart of the Christian faith.

  3. Our information comes from six New Testament books, and five historical accounts, none of which give *all* the information, *and* whose accounts contain serious apparent difficulties :

    a) **Books:** Matthew, Mark, Luke, John, Acts, 1 Corinthians

    b) **Accounts:** Matthew, Mark, Luke, John, Acts

4. A summary of the difficulties:

    a) ***Number of women:*** Luke at least 5, Mark 3, Matthew 2, John 1, Paul 0

    b) ***Time of the visit:*** John still dark, Mark sun had risen

    c) ***Number and nature of messengers:*** Mark one man, Luke two men, Matthew one angel, John two angels.

    d) ***Location of messengers:*** Mark, Luke, and John inside; Matthew out then in (sitting/standing)

    e) ***Telling the disciples:*** Matthew and Luke yes; Mark no (also translation, maybe "over-awed")

    f) ***Appearance of Christ:*** John at the tomb, Matthew after tomb visit

    g) ***Holding of Christ by woman(en):*** Matthew *un*rebuked, John rebuked

5. Crafting a solution

    a) What I bring *to* these accounts will determine what I take away from them.

    b) The apparent disagreement lends itself to authenticity more than duplicity or ignorance.

      (1) The fact that all the accounts record women as the initial visitors, and Mary Magdalene as the first eyewitness go against everything we know about Jewish legal culture.

      (2) We know clearly that it is *our ignorance* of details and cultural values that is more to blame than error, when it comes to misperception and misunderstanding of Scripture.

    c) John Wenham, in his book, *Easter Enigma,* has compiled an amazing, yet believable attempt to reconcile all the accounts (a summary of it is at the end of this unit).

B. The World *Behind* the Text: The Resurrection and the Early Church

  1. It was the centerpiece of apostolic preaching:

    a) Peter's first four sermons were built around the resurrection of Yeshua

      (1) Peter preached the resurrection to Jews of every ethnicity at Pentecost in Jerusalem (Acts 2:14-41).

      (2) Peter' preached the resurrection on at least two occasions to the leading religious minds of his day (Acts 4:1-22; 5:27-42).

      (3) Peter's preached the resurrection to Cornelius, the Gentile at Joppa (Acts 10:25-42).

      (4) Paul's makes *four* references to the resurrection, preaching to foreign Jews in a synagogue in Antioch of Pisidia on his first missionary journey (Acts 13:14-41).

      (5) Paul preached the resurrection on the Areopagus in Athens, to pagan philosophers (Acts 17:22-33).

  2. Luke's account of Pentecost in Acts 2 is more about the *resurrection* than the Holy Spirit (402 words vs. 379 words).

  3. Paul was more concerned about the *implications* of the resurrection than the verification of it:

    a) He only uses the word "resurrection" 9x in his writings, 6 of which are in debate with the authorities involving theology! (Acts 23:6-24:21).

    b) However, he uses the word, "raised" (Gk = *egeirō*) 39x in his writings to refer to the resurrection in the plan and purposes of God:

      (1) 26 are in reference to what God did to Yeshua.

      (2) 13 refer to the implications of the resurrection for believers.

  4. Paul makes it clear that Yeshua's resurrection was *not* simply a "coming back from the dead" like the widow's son, Jairus' daughter, and Lazarus (Lk 7:11-15; Mk 5:21-24; Jn 11:1-44).

    a) *"The resurrection from the dead"* was a key element of Jewish theology (cf. Lk 20:35; Acts 4:2; 26:23; Rom 1:4).

    b) He refers to Yeshua as the *"first fruits"* of the "resurrection from the dead." (1 Cor 15:20,23).

  5. The resurrection of Yeshua provided the foundation for many New Testament doctrines:

    a) The total transformation of the cowardly apostles (cf. Jn 20:19 and Acts 4:13-30).

    b) The total reversal of Saul of Tarsus (Acts 9:1-5).

    c)   Yeshua's abiding presence in the Church's missionary activity (Matt 28:19-20).

    d)   Their confidence in addressing Yeshua in prayer (Acts 7:59)

    e)   Yeshua's Second Coming (Acts 1:11; Col 3:1-4; Phil 3:10, 20-21).

    f)   Their own resurrection (1 Cor 15:12-23).

    g)   The physical (perfect) nature of their eternal state (2 Pet 3:13; Rom 8:21).

C. The World *Of* the Text: A Sampling of Resurrection Texts

    1. **John 20:22** — *And when he had said this, he breathed on them and said to them, "Receive the Holy Spirit. If you forgive the sins of anyone, they are forgiven; if you withhold forgiveness from anyone, it is withheld."*

       a)   ***"breathed"*** – *(Gk = emphuasō);* This word is only used twice in the LXX, in Genesis 2:7 for the creation of Adam, and Ezekiel 37:9 for God "breathing" into the valley of dry bones!

       b)   ***"forgive…withhold"*** – both of these verbs are plural, speaking of the new community of faith, the Church.

       c)   ***"forgiven…withheld"*** – the verbs referring to the condition of the sins themselves are both in the Perfect tense.

          (1) the verbs have the idea of "letting go" and "hanging onto"

          (2) the is an excellent portrait of forgiveness within the covenant community.

    2. **John 20:1-23** — *…He said to him the third time, "Simon, son of John, do you love me?" Peter was grieved because he said to him the third time, "Do you love me?" and he said to him, "Lord, you know everything; you know that I love you." Jesus said to him, "Feed my sheep.….Jesus said to him, "If it is my will that he remain until I come, what is that to you? You follow me!"*

       a)   ***"love"*** - Yeshua questions Peter the same number of times he denied Him.

          (1) Yeshua switches words for "love" the 3rd time.

          (2) this question caused Peter great "grief."

          (3) Peter switched his words for "know" from mere certainty to experience in his last response.

       b)   ***"grieved"***   - same word used for Yeshua in Gethsemane (Matt. 26:37).

          (1) used for the apostles' response to hearing of their own betrayal (Matt. 26:22).

       c)   ***"follow me"***   - command with no end (present imperative; ongoing).

          (1) comes from a word for "road"; *"Get on my road and stay on it!"*

D. The World *Before* the Text: Resurrection and the Christian

    1. It is the basis of my own spiritual rebirth:

       "Blessed be the God and Father of our Lord Jesus Christ! According to his great mercy, he has caused us to be born again to a living hope through the resurrection of Jesus Christ from the dead,"   **1 Peter 1:3**

    2. It is the basis of my progressive victory over the power of sin in my life:

       "…that I may know him and the power of his resurrection, and may share his sufferings, becoming like him in his death,"   **Philippians 3:10**

       "We were buried therefore with him by baptism into death, in order that, just as Christ was raised from the dead by the glory of the Father, we too might walk in newness of life. So you also must consider yourselves dead to sin and alive to God in Christ Jesus. For sin will have no dominion over you, since you are not under law but under grace."   **Romans 6:4, 11, 14**

    3. The certainty of my resurrection is to be the basis of my hope in ministry:

       "Therefore, my beloved brothers, be steadfast, immovable, always abounding in the work of the Lord, knowing that in the Lord your labor is not in vain."   **1 Corinthians 15:58**

    4. The certainty of my resurrection is to be the basis of my value system as a believer:

       "If then you have been raised with Christ, seek the things that are above, where Christ is, seated at the right hand of God. Set your minds on things that are above, not on things that are on earth. For you have died, and your life is hidden with Christ in God. When Christ who is your life appears, then you also will appear with him in glory."   **Colossians 3:1-4**

5. The resurrection of Yeshua touches every facet of my redemption:
   a) It is meaningless without Golgotha, which accomplished my justification.
   b) The power that raised Yeshua from the dead is available to me for my sanctification.
   c) The body Yeshua assumed is the "first fruits" of my glorification.
6. A Christian who is *not* growing, or engaged in redemptive ministry is denying the resurrection of Yeshua.

"Nevertheless, I tell you the truth: it is to your advantage that I go away, for if I do not go away, the Helper will not come to you. But if I go, I will send him to you. And when he comes, he will convict the world concerning sin and righteousness and judgment: concerning sin, because they do not believe in me; concerning righteousness, because I go to the Father, and you will see me no longer; concerning judgment, because the ruler of this world is judged. "I still have many things to say to you, but you cannot bear them now. When the Spirit of truth comes, he will guide you into all the truth, for he will not speak on his own authority, but whatever he hears he will speak, and he will declare to you the things that are to come. He will glorify me, for he will take what is mine and declare it to you. All that the Father has is mine; therefore I said that he will take what is mine and declare it to you." **John 16:7-15**

"But you will receive power when the Holy Spirit has come upon you, and you will be my witnesses in Jerusalem and in all Judea and Samaria, and to the end of the earth." **Acts 1:8**

"Him we proclaim, warning everyone and teaching everyone with all wisdom, that we may present everyone mature in Christ. For this I toil, struggling with all his energy that he powerfully works within me." **Colossians 1:28, 29**

"Now the Lord is the Spirit, and where the Spirit of the Lord is, there is freedom. And we all, with unveiled face, beholding the glory of the Lord, are being transformed into the same image from one degree of glory to another. For this comes from the Lord who is the Spirit.' **2 Corinthians 3:17, 18**

The Post-Resurrection Appearances of Jesus*

APPEARANCE	Matthew	Mark	Luke	John	Acts	1 Corinth.
Mary Magdalene (after Peter and John had left)	—	16:9	—	20:16-18	—	—
"The women" (Salome and Mary of Clopas)	28:5-10	—	—	—	—	—
Simon Peter (Cephas)	—	—	24:34	—	—	15:5
Cleopas and one other on the road to Emmaus	—	—	24:31	—	—	—
"The Eleven" (without Thomas)	—	16:14	24:33-39	20:19	—	—
"The Eleven" (with Thomas) a week later	—	—	—	20:26	—	—
"The seven" on the sea of Galilee; Peter reinstated	—	—	—	21:1	—	—
"more than 500 brethren" (most likely in Galilee)	—	—	—	—	—	15:6
James, the half-brother of Jesus	—	—	—	—	—	15:7
"The Eleven" in Galilee	28:16-17	—	—	—	—	—
"The Eleven" in Jerusalem (debatable passage in Mark)	—	16:14-15	—	—	—	—
Possible separate meeting of "The Eleven"	—	—	24:44	—	1:4	—
"The Eleven" throughout a forty day period	—	—	—	—	1:1-5	—
At his ascension from the Mount of Olives	—	—	24:50	—	1:9-12	—

*Using the chronology of John Wenham, from *Easter Enigma*, Grand Rapids: Baker Books. ©1992

The Post-Ascension Appearances of Jesus

A P P E A R A N C E	Acts	New Testament Letters	Revelation
To Stephen as he was being stoned	7:55	—	—
To Saul of Tarsus on his way to Damascus	9:5	1 Corinthians 15:8	—
To Paul in the Temple on his first visit to Jerusalem	22:17-21*	—	—
Paul is caught up into the "3rd heaven" and taught (14 years before writing 1 Corinthians)	—	2 Cor. 12:1-9 (cf. 1 Cor. 11:23; Gal. 1:11-12)	—
To Paul in Corinth in a night vision	18:8-11	—	—
To Paul in Roman barracks after his arrest in Jerus.	23:9-11	—	—
To Paul in Rome just prior to his execution (c. AD 67)	—	2 Timothy 4:16-18	—
To John on the island of Patmos (c. AD 92)	—	—	1:9-18
To the human race at his Second Coming (predictions)	1:11	Col. 3:4; 1 Thess. 1:7-10; 4:15-17 1 Tim. 6:14; 2 Tim 4:8; Titus 2:13; 1 Pet. 1:7	1:7

*This is a recollection in Paul's defense before the Sanhedrin 20 years later.

APPENDICES

"Yeshua In Four Dimensions" Glossary

MAJOR GEOGRAPHICAL REGIONS

Decapolis............The region located on the Southeast of the Sea of Galilee, East of the Jordan River largely populated by Greeks consisting of ten cities (Deca-10, Polis-City) united by a trade/defense alliance.[1] According to Matthew's Gospel, people from this region were present at the Sermon on the Mount.[2] Mark records Yeshua's exorcism of Legion and His healing of the mute man in this region.[3]

Galilee.................The region bordered on the east by the Sea of Galilee and Jordan River extending from Samaria north of the Sea of Galilee into the northern mountains. Though largely populated by Gentiles, this was the region of Yeshua's birth, childhood, and much of his early ministry.

Judea...................The hilly region located west of the Jordan River and Dead Sea largely populated by Jews. With Jerusalem as its main center, Israelite worship centered around the Temple located in this region. It is also the region of Yeshua's trial, crucifixion and resurrection.

Samaria...............The territory located between Galilee and Judea, west of the Jordan River composed of people of mixed race (Jew/Gentile) shunned by the Jews. This is the region in which Yeshua's conversation with the woman at the well occurred.

Perea...................The region located east of the Sea of Galilee, south of the Decapolis reaching south to the northeast shore of the Dead Sea.

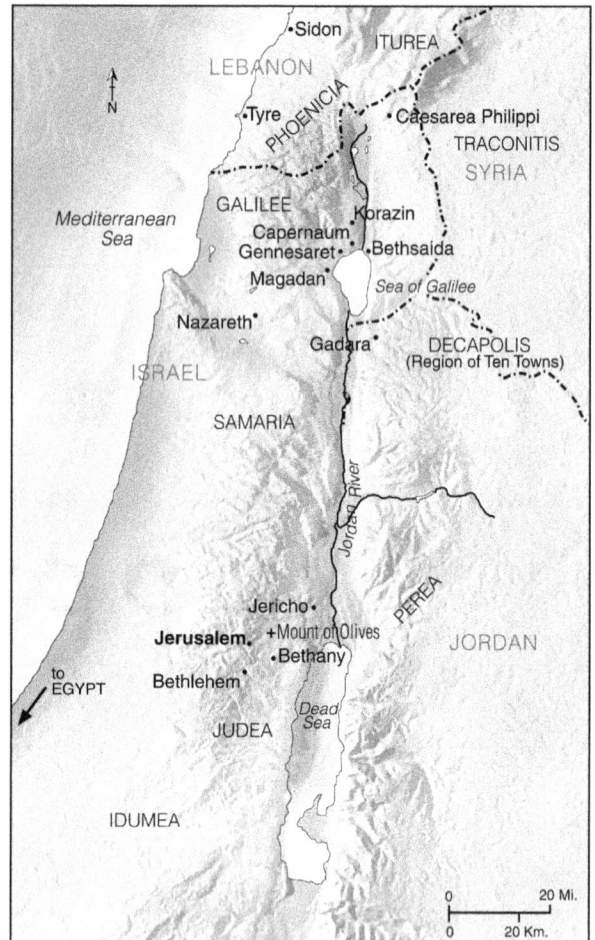

The broken lines (·—·—·) indicate modern boundaries.

1 Adapted from the *New Bible Dictionary*, 268.
2 Matthew 4:25
3 Mark 5:20; 7:31

SOURCES OF WATER

Dead Sea...............A body of water at the mouth of the Jordan River southeast of the city of Jerusalem. Due to its high salt content, the Dead Sea contains no living organisms. The surface of the Dead Sea is more than 1300 feet below sea level and at its deepest is more than 2300 feet below sea level making it the lowest point on Earth! This is in contrast with the city of Jerusalem located only a few miles away is 2550 ft above sea level.

Mediterranean Sea........The largest body of water in the Middle East located to the west of Jerusalem and the majority of the Fertile Crescent. The apostle Paul traveled this sea during his missionary journeys.

Sea of Galilee ....The sea on the northern part of the Jordan river. Much of Yeshua's Galilean ministry occurred around this sea. It is 630 ft. below sea level. It is also referred to as the Sea of Tiberias and the Lake of Gennesaret in the Gospels.

Jordan River........The river that flows from Lake Haleh through the Sea of Galilee and empties into the Dead Sea providing a means of life for much of the western fertile crescent. It is the most mentioned river in the Bible beginning with its first mention in Genesis 13 when Lot chose the well-watered valley of the Jordan for himself. Yeshua's baptism by John occurred in this river.

TOPOGRAPHICAL DIVISIONS

Mount of Olives ....The mountain ridge adjacent to the east side of the Temple mount in Jerusalem. The Mount of Olives sits roughly 200 ft. higher than Jerusalem and is separated from it by the Kidron Valley. It was a place Yeshua frequented with his disciples and was the site of Yeshua's arrest.

Temple Mount ....The portion of Land on the east side of Jerusalem on which Solomon's temple stood. After its destruction in 586 B.C., the second temple built by Zerubbabel, was reconstructed on this site. During the rein of Herod the Great, the courtyard was expanded to 35 acres over a period of 83 years. This final mount covered hills and filled valleys making a large flat platform over what otherwise was hilly terrain. It was this elaborate structure that Yeshua and his disciples frequented and referred to in John 2:19-20. While the temple mount is still visible in Jerusalem today, in the place of the Temple which was destroyed by the Romans in 90 AD, stands the Muslim mosque, Dome of the Rock.

Mt. Hermon ....Located north of the Sea of Galilee, it is the highest mountain in the entire region. With a height of 9,320 ft, it is covered with snow during the winter and water runs down the mountain and out through the springs forming the headwaters of the Jordan River. Mentioned with significance throughout the Scriptures, it is the probable site of the Transfiguration of Yeshua.

Mt. Tabor ....A significant mountain in the Scriptures beginning with the battle against the Canaanites in Judges 4:12. It is located southeast of the Sea of Galilee. An early tradition claimed it was the site of the transfiguration, however the Scriptures record the location of the transfiguration near the town of Caesarea Philippi,[1] a long way from Mount Tabor.

---

1 Mark 8:27-9:14

SIGNIFICANT CITIES

Bethany .... A city roughly 2 miles outside the city of Jerusalem near the Mount of Olives where Yeshua and his disciples frequently stayed, especially while visiting Jerusalem. This is the home of Mary and Martha, site of the raising of Lazarus, and the place where the woman anointed Yeshua feet with perfume.[1]

Bethlehem .... An ancient city originally called Ephrath in Abraham's day, later "Bethlehem Ephrathah" in the time of the prophets. It was the birth place of Kind David thus it gets its title, "the city of David." Messianic prophesies identified this as the Messiah's birthplace and thus was the location of Yeshua birth.[2]

Caesarea Philippi .... A city north of the Sea of Galilee at the foot of Mount Hermon. Herod the Great originally built the city and Philip the Tetrarch added on and named the city in honor of Augustus Caesar. This was the site of Peter's confession of Yeshua as the Christ, the Son of God and was the city nearest the Mount of Transfiguration (probably Mt. Hermon).[3]

Capernaum .... A city located on the northwest shore of the Sea of Galilee. Yeshua made his home here for a time and was the center of Yeshua's Galilean ministry. This also was the home of Peter and Andrew. [4]

Jericho .... A very ancient city (7000 BC) located northeast of Jerusalem, west of the Jordan River. It is first mentioned in the Bible in the context of the Israelites entering the promised land of Canaan. It was here that Yeshua healed Blind Bartimaeus.[5]

Jerusalem .... An ancient city west of the Dead Sea built on a high plateau, forming a strategic natural defense barrier. It is first mentioned in Genesis when it titles Melchizedek "king of Salem." The city did not become the capital of Israel until King David defeated the Jebusites. Solomon built the temple here making it the center of the Jewish life. Though under Roman occupation, Yeshua visited Jerusalem many times during his life and it was the site of his trial and sentencing.[6]

Hippos .... One of the 10 cities forming the Decapolis in the eastern hills of the Sea of Galilee.

Nazareth .... A city located southwest of the Sea of Galilee in the region of Galilee near Mount Tabor. Yeshua spent lived here from childhood through the beginning of his adult ministry.

Scythopolis .... A Greek city built on the ancient Jewish city of Bethshan. It is located west of the Jordan River, South the Sea of Galilee and a member of the Decapolis.

Sephoris .... A city located outside of Nazareth. It is likely Yeshua spent time working here with Joseph as a youth.

FROM:	Jerusalem	Capernaum
Bethany	2 miles	83 miles
Bethlehem	6	91
Bethsaida	91	6
Caesarea	57	—
Caesarea Philippi	105	27
Cana	—	16
Capernaum	85	—
Dead Sea	6	85
Emmaus	16	—
Jericho	15	70
Jordan River	21	25
Mediterranean Sea	37	28
Nazareth	70	20
Sychar (Samaria)	31	55
Sea of Galilee	70	0
Sidon	144	59
Tyre	120	35
Corinth (Greece)	840	—
Egypt (border)	100	185
Ephesus (Asia)	650	—
Rome	1450	—

1 Matt 21:17 & John 11:1
2 Gen 35:19, 1 Sam. 17:12, Micah 5:3 & Matt 2:1
3 Matt 16:13
4 Matt 4:13, 8:14
5 Num 22:1, Mark 10:46
6 Gen 6:18, 2 Sam 5:7

Shechem .... The ancient Jewish city located in the hill country near Mt. Gerizim, It was first visited by Abram in Genesis 12 where he built and alter to the Lord. After the exile, this was the center of the Samaritan region. The city was destroyed by John Hyrcanus in 108 BC. It is conjectured that the city of Sychar was built on top of this city.[1]

Sidon .... An ancient pagan city located along the Mediterranean Sea north of Tyre in the region of Phoenicia. Yeshua referred to this city in the Gospels and visited it on occasion.

Sychar .... A Samaritan city possibly built on the ancient city of Shechem. This was the location of Yeshua's dialogue with the Samaritan woman at the well.

Tyre .... An ancient fortified city along the Mediterranean Sea south of Sidon in the region of Phoenicia. Yeshua made reference to and visited this city on occasion. It was during his stay here that he healed a Syrophoenician woman.

INFLUENTIAL PEOPLE

Essenes .... An ultra conservative Jewish religious sect in existence from the 2nd Century BC till 70 AD when the temple was destroyed. They adopted a very communal lifestyle and they held strictly to the Scriptures. It is very likely that a large portion of the Qumran community (site of the Dead Sea Scrolls) were Essenes. This word does not actually appear in the Bible.

Herodians .... A Jewish sect mentioned in the Gospels characterized by their loyalty to rule of the Herod.

the Herods .... A Jewish ruling family of Idumaean lineage who, beginning with Herod Antipater in 47 BC, governed much of the Land of Israel under Roman authority until Herod Agrippa II's death in 100 AD. This family was ruling the time of Yeshua and throughout the early church.

Pharisees .... A Jewish sect whose members constantly opposed Yeshua in the Gospels. They were the religious conservatives of their day and placed emphasis on strict observance of the law.

Pontius Pilate .... The Roman appointed governor of Judea from 26-36 AD. He was the legal representative responsible for Yeshua's trial and execution.[2]

priest .... One set apart as representative of God to/for the people. In Israel, only the descendants of the tribe of Levi were set apart to fill the office of the priest by genealogical perpetuation. The priests primary functions were to teach the people, pray for the people, and makes sacrifices for the people. While their were many priests within the nation of Israel, only one would serve as the high priest making the sacrifices in the temple at a time. Jewish festivals were an exception to this rule.[3]

Sadducees .... A Jewish sect whose members opposed Yeshua in the Gospels. They tended to be the theological liberals of their day. They denied any physical resurrection of the body and did not believe in angels or spirits.[4]

Samaritan .... A person from the region of Samaria who's racial make up was only partially Jewish. These people were a product of the forced integration of the Assyrian invasion of 722 and were despised by the Jews. They had their own temple on Mt. Gerizim to worship separate from the Jews.[5]

---

1 *New Bible Dictionary,* 1090.
2 Matt 27:2, Mark 15:1, Luke 3:1, & John 18:29
3 Ex 28, Lev 8, & Deut 33:10
4 Acts 23:8
5 John 4:9

Sanhedrin............The Jewish ruling council in Jerusalem composed of 71 religious leaders responsible for for judging the important civil and religious cases. This council had enough power to condemn someone to death with Roman approval. It was before this council that Yeshua appeared and was condemned before being handed over to pilate. Paul was also brought before this council in the book of Acts.[1]

scribe...................One known as a "counter" who meticulously translated the scriptures. Their devotion to the Scriptures set them up as religious leaders and teachers in the Jewish community. Like the Pharisees and Sadducees, the Scribes also conflicted with Yeshua.[2]

tax collector.........A person in charge of collecting Roman taxes known for their greed and unjust practices. Matthew and Zacchaeus are two mentioned by name in the Gospels. Because of their evil practices, they were considered scum by the Jewish religious authorities.[3]

Zealot...................A member of the sect of Jewish "Zealots" who exhibited extreme zeal for the law and outwardly opposed Roman occupation and imposition particularly in their worship practices.

MAJOR JEWISH OBSERVANCES

Feast of Dedication......................Mentioned only in John's Gospel[4], it was an annual celebration of the purification of the temple that occurred during the Maccabean period.

Feast of Tabernacles...................Also known as the Feast of Booths. It was the final of three required festivals for which Jews traveled to Jerusalem. The feast was celebrated the seventh month of every year requiring the Israelites to live in booths for seven days in remembrance of the time the Lord caused the people to live in booths in the wilderness following the exodus from Egypt. During this period, certain offerings were to be brought into the sanctuary. The week long feast began and ended with a day of rest. Over all, this was a time of joy and celebration.[5]

Feast of Unleavened Bread........A feast observed in conjunction with the Passover in which all yeast is to be removed from the house and only unleavened bread is to be eaten for seven days culminating with a feast on the seventh day. This feast commemorates the haste in which the Lord was faithful to bring the Israelites out of Egypt not giving their yeast time to rise.[6]

Feast of Weeks...........................Also known as Pentecost. The second of the three great feasts occurring in the third month celebrating the first fruits of the wheat harvest. It was during this pilgrim feast that all were gathered in Jerusalem when the Holy Spirt came in Acts 2.[7]

Passover ....The first of the three great feasts in the Jewish calendar occurring in the first month of the year. The annual feast commemorates the preservation of the Israelite families with the lambs blood over their door as the death angel killed the first born son in all the houses in Egypt while passing over the Israelites. This feast also marked the beginning of the Feast of Unleavened Bread. Yeshua and his disciples were gathered in the upper room celebrating the Passover shortly

---

1 *New Bible Dictionary,* 1060; Mark 15:1
2 Matt 5:20
3 Matt 10:13 & Luke 19:2
4 John 10:22
5 Lev 23:34; John 7:37
6 Ex 12-13,
7 Num 28:26

before his arrest. Paul taught that Christ is our Passover lamb and we are to go on living unleavened (without sin) lives.[1]

sabbath...The seventh day of every week set aside for rest and enjoyment of the Lord. Patterned after God's rest on the last day of Creation, the Israelites were to rest from all their work on the Sabbath and set it aside as a holy day to the Lord. During the time of Yeshua, the religious leaders had added many extra prohibitions relating to this observance which Yeshua contradicted and acted against.[2]

1 Ex 12; John 13; 1 Cor 5:7
2 Gen 2:3; Ex 20:8-10; John 5

The Old Testament in Matthew

chap	verse	New Testament Excerpt	OT Ref	Context Summary
1	23	"Behold, the virgin shall conceive and bear a son, and they shall call his name Immanuel" (which means, God with us).	Isaiah 7:14	Joseph's vision relating to the coming birth of Jesus
2	6	"And you, O Bethlehem, in the land of Judah, are by no means least among the rulers of Judah; for from you shall come a ruler who will shepherd my people Israel.'"	Micah 5:2	Response to Herod as to the prophesied location of the Messiah
2	15	He remained there until the death of Herod. This was to fulfill what had been spoken by the Lord through the prophet: "out of Egypt I called my son."	Hosea 11:1; Numbers 24:8; Exodus 4:22f	Fulfilled prophecy concerning Mary and Joseph taking Jesus to Egypt
2	18	"A voice was heard in Ramah, weeping and loud lamentation, Rachel weeping for her children; she refused to be comforted, because they are no more."	Jeremiah 31:15	Fulfilled prophecy relating to Herod's slaughter of the male babies after the Magi's departure
3	3	"For this is he who was spoken of by the prophet Isaiah when he said, "The voice of one crying in the wilderness: 'Prepare the way of the Lord; make his paths straight.'"	Isaiah 40:3	Fulfilled prophecy relating to John the Baptist as the forerunner preaching repentance
4	4	But he answered, "It is written, "'Man shall not live by bread alone, but by every word that comes from the mouth of God.'"	Deuteronomy 8:3	Jesus response to the temptation to turn stones to bread
4	6	... and said to him, "If you are the Son of God, throw yourself down, for it is written, "'He will command his angels concerning you,' and "'On their hands they will bear you up, lest you strike your foot against a stone.'"	Psalms 91:11-12	The devil quoting scripture during Jesus' second wilderness temptation
4	7	Jesus said to him, "Again it is written, 'You shall not put the Lord your God to the test.'"	Deuteronomy 6:16	Jesus response to the temptation to test God by throwing himself from the temple
4	10	Then Jesus said to him, "Be gone, Satan! For it is written, "'You shall worship the Lord your God and him only shall you serve.'"	Deuteronomy 6:13, 10:20	Jesus response to Satan's final temptation to worship him
4	15-16	"The land of Zebulun and the land of Naphtali, the way of the sea, beyond the Jordan, Galilee of the Gentiles— the people dwelling in darkness have seen a great light, and for those dwelling in the region and shadow of death, on them a light has dawned."	Isaiah 9:1-2	Fulfilled prophecy relating to Jesus beginning his Galilean ministry
5	21	"You have heard that it was said to those of old, 'You shall not murder; and whoever murders will be liable to judgment.'	Exodus 20:13; Deuteronomy 5:17	Jesus Sermon on the Mount teaching regarding the "spirit" of the law
5	27	"You have heard that it was said, 'You shall not commit adultery.'	Exodus 20:14; Deuteronomy 5:18	Jesus Sermon on the Mount teaching regarding the "spirit" of the law
5	31	"It was also said, 'Whoever divorces his wife, let him give her a certificate of divorce.'	Deuteronomy 24:1,3; Jeremiah 3:1	Jesus teaching on divorce in the Sermon on the Mount
5	33	"Again you have heard that it was said to those of old, 'You shall not swear falsely, but shall perform to the Lord what you have sworn.'	Leviticus 19:12; Numbers 30:2; Deuteronomy 23:21, 23	Jesus teaching on the taking of oaths in the Sermon on the Mount
5	35	or by the earth, for it is his footstool, or by Jerusalem, for it is the city of the great King.	Psalms 48:2	Jesus teaching on the taking of oaths in the Sermon on the Mount
5	38	"You have heard that it was said, 'An eye for an eye and a tooth for a tooth.'	Exodus 21:24; Leviticus 24:20; Deuteronomy 19:21	Jesus teaching on turning the other cheek in the Sermon on the Mount

5	43	"You have heard that it was said, 'You shall love your neighbor and hate your enemy.'	Leviticus 19:18	Jesus teaching on loving your enemies in the Sermon on the Mount
7	23	And then will I declare to them, 'I never knew you; depart from me, you workers of lawlessness.'	Psalm 6:8	Jesus teaching in the Sermon on the Mount on those who falsely claim to know him
8	17	This was to fulfill what was spoken by the prophet Isaiah: "He took our illnesses and bore our diseases."	Isaiah 53:4	The healing of Peter's mother-in-law and others ill and demon possessed
9	13	Go and learn what this means, 'I desire mercy, and not sacrifice.' For I came not to call the righteous, but sinners."	Hosea 6:6	Jesus response to the Pharisees regarding eating with "sinners"
10	35-36	For I have come to set a man against his father, and a daughter against her mother, and a daughter-in-law against her mother-in-law. And a person's enemies will be those of his own household.	Micah 7:6	Jesus teaching on the cost and division of true discipleship
11	5a	...the blind receive their sight and the lame walk, lepers are cleansed and the deaf hear, and the dead are raised up,	Isaiah 33:5	Jesus response to John the Baptist's prison inquiry
11	5b	...and the poor have good news preached to them.	Isaiah 61:1	Jesus response to John the Baptist's prison inquiry
11	10	This is he of whom it is written, "'Behold, I send my messenger before your face, who will prepare your way before you.'	Malachi 3:1	Jesus' discussion on the greatness of John the Baptist
11	29	Take my yoke upon you, and learn from me, for I am gentle and lowly in heart, and you will find rest for your souls.	Jeremiah 6:16	Jesus teaching on knowing the Father and His easy yoke
12	7	And if you had known what this means, 'I desire mercy, and not sacrifice,' you would not have condemned the guiltless.	Hosea 6:6	Jesus response to the Pharisees questions regarding the Sabbath
12	18-21	"Behold, my servant whom I have chosen, my beloved with whom my soul is well pleased. I will put my Spirit upon him, and he will proclaim justice to the Gentiles. He will not quarrel or cry aloud, nor will anyone hear his voice in the streets; a bruised reed he will not break, and a smoldering wick he will not quench, until he brings justice to victory; and in his name the Gentiles will hope."	Isaiah 42:1-3	Fulfillment of prophecy concerning justice and the Gentiles in the context of Jesus healing on the Sabbath
12	40	For just as Jonah was three days and three nights in the belly of the great fish, so will the Son of Man be three days and three nights in the heart of the earth.	Jonah 1:17	The only sign given to the Pharisees was the sign of Jonah
13	14-15	Indeed, in their case the prophecy of Isaiah is fulfilled that says: "'You will indeed hear but never understand, and you will indeed see but never perceive." For this people's heart has grown dull, and with their ears they can barely hear, and their eyes they have closed, lest they should see with their eyes and hear with their ears and understand with their heart and turn, and I would heal them.'	Isaiah 6:9-10	Jesus fulfillment of prophecy regarding his teaching in parables
13	32	It is the smallest of all seeds, but when it has grown it is larger than all the garden plants and becomes a tree, so that the birds of the air come and make nests in its branches."	Ezekiel 17:23, 31:6; Psalm 104:12; Daniel 4:12	Jesus teaching on the kingdom of heaven and the mustard seed
13	35	This was to fulfill what was spoken by the prophet: "I will open my mouth in parables; I will utter what has been hidden since the foundation of the world."	Psalm 78:2	The fulfillment of prophecy regarding Jesus speaking in parables
13	43	Then the righteous will shine like the sun in the kingdom of their Father. He who has ears, let him hear.	Daniel 12:3	Explanation of the parable of the Tares among the wheat
15	4	For God commanded, 'Honor your father and your mother,' and, 'Whoever reviles father or mother must surely die.'	Exodus 21:17; Leviticus 20:9	Jesus refuting the Pharisees breaking the Tradition of the Elders

Ch	Vs	Quotation	Reference	Description
15	8-9	"'This people honors me with their lips, but their heart is far from me; in vain do they worship me, teaching as doctrines the commandments of men.'"	Isaiah 29:13	Jesus relating Isaiah's prophecy to the Pharisees and their question regarding the Tradition of the Elders
16	27	For the Son of Man is going to come with his angels in the glory of his Father, and then he will repay each person according to what he has done.	Psalm 62:12; Proverb 24:12	Jesus' teaching on costly discipleship and His judgment of the deeds of man
18	16	But if he does not listen, take one or two others along with you, that every charge may be established by the evidence of two or three witnesses.	Deuteronomy 19:15	Jesus' teaching on church discipline
19	4	He answered, "Have you not read that he who created them from the beginning made them male and female,	Genesis 1 27, 5:2	Jesus' response to the Pharisee's question regarding divorce
19	5	and said, 'Therefore a man shall leave his father and his mother and hold fast to his wife, and the two shall become one flesh'?	Genesis 2:24	Jesus' response to the Pharisee's question regarding divorce
19	7	They said to him, "Why then did Moses command one to give a certificate of divorce and to send her away?"	Deuteronomy 24:1-4	The Pharisee's question to Jesus regarding divorce
19	18-19	He said to them, "Because of your hardness of heart Moses allowed you to divorce your wives, but from the beginning it was not so. And I say to you: whoever divorces his wife, except for sexual immorality, and marries another, commits adultery."	Exodus 20:12-16	The Rich Young Ruler
21	5	"Say to the daughter of Zion, 'Behold, your king is coming to you, humble, and mounted on a donkey, on a colt, the foal of a beast of burden.'"	Isaiah 62:11; Zechariah 9:9	Fulfillment of prophecy concerning the mode of entry during the triumphal entry
21	9	And the crowds that went before him and that followed him were shouting, "Hosanna to the Son of David! Blessed is he who comes in the name of the Lord! Hosanna in the highest!"	Psalm 118:26	The Crowds cry at the triumphal entry
21	13	He said to them, "It is written, 'My house shall be called a house of prayer,' but you make it a den of robbers."	Isaiah 56:7	Jesus' words at the cleansing of the temple
21	16	and they said to him, "Do you hear what these are saying?" And Jesus said to them, "Yes; have you never read, "Out of the mouth of infants and nursing babies you have prepared praise'?"	Psalm 8:2	Jesus' response to the Pharisee's question regarding the children's praise during the cleansing of the temple
21	33	"Hear another parable. There was a master of a house who planted a vineyard and put a fence around it and dug a winepress in it and built a tower and leased it to tenants, and went into another country.	Isaiah 5:1	Jesus' parable of the Landowner
21	42	Jesus said to them, "Have you never read in the Scriptures: "The stone that the builders rejected has become the cornerstone; this was the Lord's doing, and it is marvelous in our eyes'?	Psalm 118:22f	Jesus' quotation regarding the Jewish leaders' rejection of him in the context of the parable of the landowner
22	24	saying, "Teacher, Moses said, 'If a man dies having no children, his brother must marry the widow and raise up offspring for his brother.'	Deuteronomy 25:5	The Sadducees question regarding marriage and the resurrection
22	32	'I am the God of Abraham, and the God of Isaac, and the God of Jacob'? He is not God of the dead, but of the living."	Exodus 3:6	Jesus response to the Sadducees question regarding the Resurrection of the dead
22	37	And he said to him, "You shall love the Lord your God with all your heart and with all your soul and with all your mind.	Deuteronomy 6:5	Jesus' response to the lawyer regarding the greatest commandment
22	39	And a second is like it: You shall love your neighbor as yourself.	Leviticus 19:18	Jesus' response to the lawyer regarding the second most important commandment
22	44	"'The Lord said to my Lord, "Sit at my right hand, until I put your enemies under your feet'?	Psalm 110:1	Jesus' response to the Pharisees answer regarding the messiah "the son of David"

Chapter	Verse	New Testament Excerpt	OT Reference	Context Summary
23	39	For I tell you, you will not see me again, until you say, 'Blessed is he who comes in the name of the Lord.'"	Psalm 118:26	Jesus lament over Jerusalem
24	15	"So when you see the abomination of desolation spoken of by the prophet Daniel, standing in the holy place (let the reader understand),	Daniel 9:27, 11:31, 12:11	Jesus' response to his disciples question regarding the time of his return
24	29	"Immediately after the tribulation of those days the sun will be darkened, and the moon will not give its light, and the stars will fall from heaven, and the powers of the heavens will be shaken.	Isaiah 13:10, 24:23; Ezekiel 32:7; Joel 2:10; Amos 5:20, 8:9; Zephaniah 1:15	Jesus' discussion of the tribulation and his Second coming
24	30	Then will appear in heaven the sign of the Son of Man, and then all the tribes of the earth will mourn, and they will see the Son of Man coming on the clouds of heaven with power and great glory.	Daniel 7:13	Jesus' discussion of the tribulation and his Second coming
24	31	And he will send out his angels with a loud trumpet call, and they will gather his elect from the four winds, from one end of heaven to the other.	Exodus 19:16; Deuteronomy 30:4; Isaiah 27:13; Zechariah 9:14	Jesus' discussion of the tribulation and his Second coming
26	31	Then Jesus said to them, "You will all fall away because of me this night. For it is written, 'I will strike the shepherd, and the sheep of the flock will be scattered.'	Zechariah 13:7	Jesus' prediction of the disciples unfaithfulness after the last supper and at the Mount of Olives
26	64	Jesus said to him, "You have said so. But I tell you, from now on you will see the Son of Man seated at the right hand of Power and coming on the clouds of heaven."	Psalm 110:1	Jesus defense before Caiaphas, the high priest
27	9-10	Then was fulfilled what had been spoken by the prophet Jeremiah, saying, "And they took the thirty pieces of silver, the price of him on whom a price had been set by some of the sons of Israel, and they gave them for the potter's field, as the Lord directed me."	Zechariah 11:12-13	Fulfillment of the prophecy of Jesus' betrayal with 30 pieces of silver
27	43	He trusts in God; let God deliver him now, if he desires him. For he said, 'I am the Son of God.'"	Psalm 22:8	The mocks of the chief priest while Jesus hung from the cross
27	46	And about the ninth hour Jesus cried out with a loud voice, saying, "Eli, Eli, lema sabachthani?" that is, "My God, my God, why have you forsaken me?"	Psalm 22:1	Jesus' cry from the cross

The Old Testament in Mark

Chapter	Verse	New Testament Excerpt	OT Reference	Context Summary
1	2	As it is written in Isaiah the prophet, "Behold, I send my messenger before your face, who will prepare your way,"	Malachi 3:1	The beginning of Mark's gospel relating OT prophecy
1	3	the voice of one crying in the wilderness: "Prepare the way of the Lord, make his paths straight,"	Isaiah 40:3	The beginning of Mark's gospel relating OT prophecy
4	12	"... so that "they may indeed see but not perceive, and may indeed hear but not understand, lest they should turn and be forgiven."	Isaiah 6:9f	Jesus' parable of the sower and the soils
4	32	"....yet when it is sown it grows up and becomes larger than all the garden plants and puts out large branches, so that the birds of the air can make nests in its shade."	Ezekiel 17:23; Psalm 104:12; Ezekiel 31:6; Daniel 4:12	Jesus' parable of the mustard seed

7	6-7	And he said to them, "Well did Isaiah prophesy of you hypocrites, as it is written, "'This people honors me with their lips, but their heart is far from me; in vain do they worship me, teaching as doctrines the commandments of men.'	Isaiah 29:13	Jesus' answer to the Pharisees regarding the "tradition of the elders"
7	10a	For Moses said, 'Honor your father and your mother'	Exodus 20:12; Deuteronomy 5:16	Jesus' answer to the Pharisees regarding the "tradition of the elders"
7	10b	For Moses said, ... 'Whoever reviles father or mother must surely die.'	Exodus 21:17; Leviticus 20:9	Jesus' answer to the Pharisees regarding the "tradition of the elders"
8	18	"Having eyes do you not see, and having ears do you not hear? And do you not remember?"	Jeremiah 5:21; Ezekiel 12:2	Jesus' rebuke to the disciples over worrying about food after they had already fed the 4000 and the 5000
9	44	"And if your hand causes you to sin, cut it off. It is better for you to enter life crippled than with two hands to go to hell, to the unquenchable fire."	Isaiah 66:24	Jesus' teaching regarding causing others to stumble (NOT IN EARLY MSS.)
9	46	"And if your foot causes you to sin, cut it off. It is better for you to enter life lame than with two feet to be thrown into hell."	Isaiah 66:24	Jesus' teaching regarding causing others to stumble (NOT IN EARLY MSS.)
9	48	"....where their worm does not die and the fire is not quenched."	Isaiah 66:24	Jesus' teaching regarding causing others to stumble
10	4	They said, "Moses allowed a man to write a certificate of divorce and to send her away."	Deuteronomy 24:1	The Pharisees question Jesus regarding divorce
10	6	But from the beginning of creation, 'God made them male and female.'	Genesis 1 27, 5:2	Jesus answers the Pharisees concerning divorce
10	7-8	'Therefore a man shall leave his father and mother and hold fast to his wife, and the two shall become one flesh.' So they are no longer two but one flesh.	Genesis 2:24	Jesus answers the Pharisees concerning divorce
10	19	"You know the commandments: 'Do not murder, Do not commit adultery, Do not steal, Do not bear false witness, Do not defraud, Honor your father and mother.'"	Exodus 20:12-16; Deuteronomy 5:16-20	Jesus' interaction with the rich young ruler
11	9	And those who went before and those who followed were shouting, "Hosanna! Blessed is he who comes in the name of the Lord!"	Psalm 118:26	Shouts of the people at The Triumphal Entry
11	17a	And he was teaching them and saying to them, "Is it not written, 'My house shall be called a house of prayer for all the nations'?	Isaiah 56:7	The Clearing of the Temple
11	17b	".... But you have made it a den of robbers."	Jeremiah 7:11	The Clearing of the Temple
12	1	And he began to speak to them in parables. "A man planted a vineyard and put a fence around it and dug a pit for the winepress and built a tower, and leased it to tenants and went into another country.	Isaiah 5:1-2	Jesus' parable of the vine growers and the rejection of the cornerstone
12	10-11	Have you not read this Scripture: "'The stone that the builders rejected has become the cornerstone; this was the Lord's doing, and it is marvelous in our eyes'?"	Psalm 118:22-23	Jesus' parable of the vine growers and the rejection of the cornerstone
12	19	"Teacher, Moses wrote for us that if a man's brother dies and leaves a wife, but leaves no child, the man must take the widow and raise up offspring for his brother."	Deuteronomy 25:5	Sadducees question Jesus concerning marriage and the resurrection
12	26	And as for the dead being raised, have you not read in the book of Moses, in the passage about the bush, how God spoke to him, saying, "I am the God of Abraham, and the God of Isaac, and the God of Jacob'?"	Exodus 3:6	Jesus responds to the Sadducees' question concerning marriage and the resurrection

Chapter	Verse	New Testament Excerpt	OT Reference	Context Summary
12	29-30	Jesus answered, "The most important is, 'Hear, O Israel: The Lord our God, the Lord is one. And you shall love the Lord your God with all your heart and with all your soul and with all your mind and with all your strength.'"	Deuteronomy 6:4-5	Jesus answers to the Scribes concerning the greatest commandment
12	31	"The second is this: 'You shall love your neighbor as yourself.' There is no other commandment greater than these."	Leviticus 19:18	Jesus answers to the Scribes concerning the second greatest commandment
12	32	And the scribe said to him, "You are right, Teacher. You have truly said that he is one, and there is no other besides him."	Deuteronomy 4:35	The intelligent scribe responds to Jesus answer regarding the greatest commandment
12	33	"And to love him with all the heart and with all the understanding and with all the strength, and to love one's neighbor as oneself, is much more than all whole burnt offerings and sacrifices."	Deuteronomy 6:5	The intelligent scribe responds to Jesus answer regarding the greatest commandment
12	36	David himself, in the Holy Spirit, declared, "The Lord said to my Lord, 'Sit at my right hand, until I put your enemies under your feet.'"	Psalm 110:1	Jesus teaching in the temple regarding the scribes and the messiah of David
13	14	"But when you see the abomination of desolation standing where he ought not to be (let the reader understand), then let those who are in Judea flee to the mountains."	Daniel 9:27; 11:31; 12:11	Jesus teaching on the return of Christ
13	24	"But in those days, after that tribulation, the sun will be darkened, and the moon will not give its light,"	Isaiah 13:10; Ezekiel 32:7, Joel 2:10, 31; 3:15	Jesus teaching on the return of Christ
13	25	"…and the stars will be falling from heaven, and the powers in the heavens will be shaken."	Isaiah 34:4	Jesus teaching on the return of Christ
13	26	"And then they will see the Son of Man coming in clouds with great power and glory."	Daniel 7:13	Jesus teaching on the return of Christ
14	27	"And then he will send out the angels and gather his elect from the four winds, from the ends of the earth to the ends of heaven."	Zechariah 13:7	Jesus predicting the scattering of the disciples at the Lord's supper
14	62a	And Jesus said, "I am, and you will see the Son of Man seated at the right hand of Power…"	Psalm 110:1	Jesus' answer to the High Priest during his trial
14	62b	"…and coming with the clouds of heaven."	Daniel 7:13	Jesus' answer to the High Priest during his trial
15	34	And at the ninth hour Jesus cried with a loud voice, "Eloi, Eloi, lema sabachthani?" which means, "My God, my God, why have you forsaken me?"	Psalm 22:1	Jesus cry on the cross

The Old Testament in Luke

Chapter	Verse	New Testament Excerpt	OT Reference	Context Summary
1	17	"…and he will go before him in the spirit and power of Elijah, to turn the hearts of the fathers to the children, and the disobedient to the wisdom of the just, to make ready for the Lord a people prepared."	Malachi 4:6	An angel speaks to Zecharias regarding the birth of John
1	50	"And his mercy is for those who fear him from generation to generation."	Psalm 103:17	The Magnificat of Mary during her stay with Elizabeth while she was pregnant with Jesus
1	53	"….he has filled the hungry with good things, and the rich he has sent away empty."	Psalm 107:9	The Magnificat of Mary during her stay with Elizabeth while she was pregnant with Jesus

Ch	Vs	Quote	Reference	Description
1	71	"...that we should be saved from our enemies and from the hand of all who hate us;"	Psalm 106:10	The prophecy of Zecharias after the birth of John
1	76	"And you, child, will be called the prophet of the Most High; for you will go before the Lord to prepare his ways,"	Malachi 3:1	The prophecy of Zecharias after the birth of John
1	79	"...to give light to those who sit in darkness and in the shadow of death, to guide our feet into the way of peace."	Isaiah 9:2	The prophecy of Zecharias after the birth of John
2	23	(as it is written in the Law of the Lord, "Every male who first opens the womb shall be called holy to the Lord")	Exodus 13:2; Numbers 3:13; 8:17	Fulfillment of prophecy by Jesus' presentation at the temple on the 8th day
2	24	...and to offer a sacrifice according to what is said in the Law of the Lord, "a pair of turtledoves, or two young pigeons."	Leviticus 5:11; 12:8	The offering made at the temple during Jesus presentation at the temple
2	32	"...a light for revelation to the Gentiles, and for glory to your people Israel."	Isaiah 9:2, 42:6; 49:6,9; 51:4; 60:1-3	Simeon's blessing of Jesus in the temple
3	4-6	As it is written in the book of the words of Isaiah the prophet, "The voice of one crying in the wilderness: 'Prepare the way of the Lord, make his paths straight. Every valley shall be filled, and every mountain and hill shall be made low, and the crooked shall become straight, and the rough places shall become level ways, and all flesh shall see the salvation of God."	Isaiah 40:3-5	Fulfilled prophecy concerning the ministry of John the Baptist
4	4	And Jesus answered him, "It is written, 'Man shall not live by bread alone.'"	Deuteronomy 8:3	Jesus' response to the first wilderness temptation of Jesus
4	8	And Jesus answered him, "It is written, 'You shall worship the Lord your God, and him only shall you serve.'"	Deuteronomy 6:13	Jesus' response to the second wilderness temptation of Jesus
4	10-11	"...for it is written, 'He will command his angels concerning you, to guard you,' and "'On their hands they will bear you up, lest you strike your foot against a stone.'"	Psalm 91:11-12	Satan's use of Scripture to tempt Jesus the third time in the wilderness
4	12	And Jesus answered him, "It is said, 'You shall not put the Lord your God to the test.'"	Deuteronomy 6:16	Jesus' response to Satan's third wilderness temptation
4	18-19	"The Spirit of the Lord is upon me, because he has anointed me to proclaim good news to the poor. He has sent me to proclaim liberty to the captives and recovering of sight to the blind, to set at liberty those who are oppressed, to proclaim the year of the Lord's favor."	Isaiah 61:1-2	Jesus' reading the Isaiah in the synagogue on the Sabbath in Nazareth
7	22	And he answered them, "Go and tell John what you have seen and heard: the blind receive their sight, the lame walk, lepers are cleansed, and the deaf hear, the dead are raised up, the poor have good news preached to them."	Isaiah 35:5; Isaiah 61:1	Jesus' report to the those sent from John concerning Himself
7	27	This is he of whom it is written, "Behold, I send my messenger before your face, who will prepare your way before you."	Malachi 3:1	Jesus' testimony concerning the importance of John
8	10	...he said, "To you it has been given to know the secrets of the kingdom of God, but for others they are in parables, so that 'seeing they may not see, and hearing they may not understand.'"	Isaiah 6:9	Jesus' explains the purpose of His parables in the context of the parable of the sower
10	27	And he answered, "You shall love the Lord your God with all your heart and with all your soul and with all your strength and with all your mind, and your neighbor as yourself."	Deuteronomy 6:5; Leviticus 19:18	The Lawyers response to Jesus' question concerning what the Law said concerning inheriting eternal life

Chapter	Verse	Quote	Reference	Description
10	28	And he said to him, "You have answered correctly; do this, and you will live."	Leviticus 18:5	Jesus' response to the Lawyer's answer
13	19	"It is like a grain of mustard seed that a man took and sowed in his garden, and it grew and became a tree, and the birds of the air made nests in its branches."	Ezekiel 17:23	Jesus' parable of the mustard seed
13	27	"But he will say, 'I tell you, I do not know where you come from. Depart from me, all you workers of evil!'"	Psalm 6:8	Jesus' teaching concerning the judgment and entering the kingdom of heaven
13	35	"Behold, your house is forsaken. And I tell you, you will not see me until you say, 'Blessed is he who comes in the name of the Lord!'"	Psalm 118:26	Jesus responds to the Pharisees concerning Herod and the Jerusalem
18	20	"You know the commandments: 'Do not commit adultery, Do not murder, Do not steal, Do not bear false witness, Honor your father and mother.'"	Exodus 20:12-15	Jesus' conversation with the rich young ruler
19	38	...saying, "Blessed is the King who comes in the name of the Lord! Peace in heaven and glory in the highest!"	Psalm 118:26	The shouts of the crowds at the triumphal entry
19	46	...saying to them, "It is written, 'My house shall be a house of prayer,' but you have made it a den of robbers."	Isaiah 56:7; Jeremiah 7:11	Jesus' cleansing of the temple
20	17	But he looked directly at them and said, "What then is this that is written: 'The stone that the builders rejected has become the cornerstone'?"	Psalm 118:22	Jesus' parable of the vine-growers and the rejection of Him as the chief cornerstone
20	28	...and they asked him a question, saying, "Teacher, Moses wrote for us that if a man's brother dies, having a wife but no children, the man must take the widow and raise up offspring for his brother."	Deuteronomy 25:5;	The Sadducees question to Jesus concerning Moses' command concerning marriage and the resurrection
20	37	"But that the dead are raised, even Moses showed, in the passage about the bush, where he calls the Lord the God of Abraham and the God of Isaac and the God of Jacob."	Exodus 3:6	Jesus responds to the Sadducees question concerning Moses' command concerning marriage and the resurrection
20	42-43	For David himself says in the Book of Psalms, "The Lord said to my Lord, "Sit at my right hand, until I make your enemies your footstool."	Psalm 110:1	Jesus responds to the Sadducees question concerning Moses' command concerning marriage and the resurrection
21	27	"And then they will see the Son of Man coming in a cloud with power and great glory."	Daniel 7:13	Jesus' teaching concerning the his second coming
22	37	"For I tell you that this Scripture must be fulfilled in me: 'And he was numbered with the transgressors.' For what is written about me has its fulfillment."	Isaiah 53:12	Jesus response to the his disciples when departing for the Garden of Gethsemane
22	69	"But from now on the Son of Man shall be seated at the right hand of the power of God."	Psalm 110:1	Jesus' response to the Sanhedrin
23	30	"Then they will begin to say to the mountains, 'Fall on us,' and to the hills, 'Cover us.'"	Hosea 10:8; Isaiah 2:19,20	Jesus' response to the mourners following him on the way to Golgotha
23	46	Then Jesus, calling out with a loud voice, said, "Father, into your hands I commit my spirit!" And having said this he breathed his last."	Psalm 31:5	Jesus' final cry from the cross

The Old Testament in John

		Scripture text	Old Testament reference	Description
1	23	He said, "I am the voice of one crying out in the wilderness, 'Make straight the way of the Lord,' as the prophet Isaiah said."	Isaiah 40:3	John the Baptist's self description
2	17	His disciples remembered that it was written, "Zeal for your house will consume me."	Psalm 69:9	The disciples remembrance of OT during Jesus' early cleansing of the temple
6	31	"Our fathers ate the manna in the wilderness; as it is written, 'He gave them bread from heaven to eat.'"	Psalm 78:24; Exodus 16:4,15	The question of the crowd concerning a sign from Jesus after the feeding of 5000 and in the context of the "I am the Bread of Life" statement
6	45	"It is written in the Prophets, 'And they will all be taught by God.' Everyone who has heard and learned from the Father comes to me."	Isaiah 54:13; Jeremiah 31:34	Jesus' response to the Jews further questions regarding the Bread of Lifeq
10	34	So the Jews gathered around him and said to him, "How long will you keep us in suspense? If you are the Christ, tell us plainly."	Psalm 82:6	Jesus' response to the Jews desiring to stone Him when He said He and the father are one
12	13	So they took branches of palm trees and went out to meet him, crying out, "Hosanna! Blessed is he who comes in the name of the Lord, even the King of Israel!"	Psalm 118:26	The cries of the crowd during the triumphial entry
12	15	"Fear not, daughter of Zion; behold, your king is coming, sitting on a donkey's colt!"	Zechariah 9:9	The scripture fulfilled when Jesus rode in on a donkey at the triumphal entry
12	38	...so that the word spoken by the prophet Isaiah might be fulfilled: "Lord, who has believed what he heard from us, and to whom has the arm of the Lord been revealed?"	Isaiah 53:1	Fulfilled prophecy regarding the people's rejection of Jesus prior to the Upper room
12	40	"He has blinded their eyes and hardened their heart, lest they see with their eyes, and understand with their heart, and turn, and I would heal them."	Isaiah 6:10	Fulfilled prophecy regarding the people's rejection of Jesus prior to the Upper room
13	18	"I am not speaking of all of you; I know whom I have chosen. But the Scripture will be fulfilled, 'He who ate my bread has lifted his heel against me.'"	Psalm 41:9	Jesus quotes this scripture regarding Judas' betrayal
15	25	"But the word that is written in their Law must be fulfilled: 'They hated me without a cause.'"	Psalm 35:19; 69:4	Jesus in the upper room describes the rejection they will experience because of him
19	24	"...so they said to one another, 'Let us not tear it, but cast lots for it to see whose it shall be.' This was to fulfill the Scripture which says, "They divided my garments among them, and for my clothing they cast lots." So the soldiers did these things,	Psalm 22:18	Fulfilled Scripture regarding the division of Jesus' garments
19	36	For these things took place that the Scripture might be fulfilled: "Not one of his bones will be broken." (John 19:36)	Exodus 12:46; Numbers 9:12; Psalm 34:20	Fulfilled Scripture regarding preservation of Jesus' bones from breaking during His crucifixion
19	37	And again another Scripture says, "They will look on him whom they have pierced."	Zechariah 12:10	Fulfilled Scripture regarding those seeing Jesus pierced

The Parables of Yeshua in the Four Gospels

TOPIC/PARABLE	Matthew	Mark	Luke	John
Parables About the Kingdom				
Parable of the soils	✓	✓	✓	
Parable of the weeds	✓			
Parable of the mustard seed	✓	✓	✓	
Parable of yeast ("leaven")	✓		✓	
Parable of the treasure	✓			
Parable of the great pearl	✓			
Parable of the net of fish	✓			
Parable of the growing seed	✓			
Parable of cloth/wineskins	✓	✓	✓	
Parables About Discipleship				
Parable of the harvest workers	✓			
Parable of the talents	✓			
Parable of the good Samaritan			✓	
Parable of nobleman's servants			✓	
Parable of the servant's role			✓	
Parables About Prayer				
Parable of friend at midnight			✓	
Parable of the persistent widow			✓	
Parables About Humility				
Parable of the wedding feast			✓	
Pharisee and tax collector			✓	
Parables About Wealth				
Parable of the rich fool			✓	
Parable of the great festival			✓	
Parable of the shrewd manager			✓	
Parable of the rich man & Lazarus			✓	
Parables About God's Love				
Parable of the lost sheep	✓		✓	
Parable of the lost coin			✓	
Parable of the lost son			✓	
Parables About Gratitude				
Parable about two debtors			✓	
Parables About Yeshua's Return				
Parable of the 10 virgins	✓			
Parable of the faithful servants	✓		✓	
Parable of the man on journey		✓		
Parables About God's Will				
Parable of the two sons	✓			
Parable of the evil farmers	✓	✓	✓	
Parable of the unproductive fig			✓	
Parable of the wedding garment	✓			
Parable of unforgiving servant	✓			
TOTAL / UNIQUE (to this Gospel)	18/11	5/1	22/17	0/0

The Jewish Way of Mourning — by Rabbi Maurice Lamm *(In this wisely conceived, graduated process of mourning, Judaism raises up the mourner from the abyss of despair to the normalcy of daily life.)*

Judaism, with its long history of dealing with the soul of man, its intimate knowledge of man's achievements and foibles, his grandeur and his weakness, has wisely devised a system of graduated mourning periods. During this time, the mourner may express his or her grief and release, with calculated regularity, the built-up tensions caused by bereavement.

The Jewish religion provides a beautifully structured approach to mourning which is divided into five stages.

1. The first stage — *aninut*.

This is the period between death and burial when despair is most intense. At this time, not only the social amenities, but even major positive religious requirements are canceled in recognition of the mourner's troubled mind.

2. The second stage — *lamentation*.

This period consists of the first three days following burial, days devoted to weeping and lamentation. During this time, the mourner does not even respond to greetings, and remains in his home (except under certain special circumstances). It is a time when even visiting the mourner is usually somewhat discouraged, for it is too early to comfort the mourners when the wound is so fresh. During this time, the mourner remains within the house, expressing his grief through the observances of wearing of a torn garment, sitting on the low stool, wearing of slippers, refraining from shaving and grooming, and recital of the Kaddish (see below).

3. The third stage — *shivah*.

This stage covers the seven days following burial and includes the three-day period of lamentation. During this time, the mourner emerges from the stage of intense grief to a new state of mind in which he is prepared to talk about his loss and to accept comfort from friends and neighbors.

The world now enlarges for the mourner. He continues the observances outlined in the second stage above, but he is able to interact with acquaintances who come to his home to express sympathy in his distress.

A sacred obligation devolves upon every Jew — no matter his relationship to the deceased or to those mourning — to comfort the survivors — these being father, mother, wife (or husband), son, daughter, (married or unmarried), brother, and sister (or half-brother and half-sister) of the deceased.

In Judaism, exercising compassion by paying a condolence call is a mitzvah, considered by some of our greatest scholars to be biblically ordained. It is a person's duty to imitate God: as God comforts the bereaved, so man must do likewise.

The fundamental purpose of the condolence call during shivah is to relieve the mourner of the intolerable burden of intense loneliness. At no other time is a human being more in need of such comradeship.

The inner freezing that came with the death of his relative now begins to thaw. The isolation from the world of people and the retreat inward now relaxes somewhat, and normalcy begins to return.

4. The fourth stage — *sheloshim*.

This period consists of the thirty days (counting the seven days of shivah) following burial. The mourner is encouraged to leave the house after shivah and to slowly rejoin society, always recognizing that enough time has not yet elapsed to assume full, normal social relations.

Shaving and haircutting for mourners is still generally prohibited, as is cutting the nails, and washing the body all at once for delight (as opposed to washing for cleanliness which is required).

5. The fifth stage — *a year of mourning*.

The fifth stage is the twelve-month period (counted from the day of burial) during which things return to normal, and business once again becomes routine, but the inner feelings of the mourner are still wounded by the rupture of relationship with the loved one.

The observance that most affects the daily life of the mourner during the twelve-month period is the complete abstention from parties and festivities, both public and private. Participation in these gatherings is simply not consonant with the depression and contrition that the mourner experiences.

It borders on the absurd for the mourner to dance gleefully while his parent lies dead in a fresh grave.

Thus, the Sages decreed that, while complete physical withdrawal from normal activities of society lasts only one week, withdrawal from joyous, social occasions lasts thirty days in mourning for other relatives, and one year in mourning for one's parents. Joy, in terms of the mourning tradition, is associated largely with public, social events rather than with personal satisfactions.

At the close of this last stage, the bereaved is not expected to continue his mourning, except for brief moments when yizkor or yahrzeit (see below) is observed. In fact, Jewish tradition rebukes a man for mourning more than this prescribed period.

SAYING KADDISH

The Kaddish is recited at every prayer service, morning and evening, Shabbat and holiday, on days of fasting and rejoicing.

The period that the mourner recites the Kaddish for parents is, theoretically, a full calendar year. The deceased is considered to be under Divine judgment for that period. Some communities, therefore, adhere to the custom that Kaddish be recited for twelve months in all cases.

However, because the full year is considered to be the duration of judgment for the wicked, and we presume that our parents do not fall into that category, the practice in most communities is to recite the Kaddish for only eleven months.

The Kaddish is to be recited only in the presence of a duly constituted quorum, a minyan, which consists of ten males above the age of Bar Mitzvah. If there are only nine adults and one minor present, it is still not considered a quorum for a minyan.

YIZKOR AND YAHRZEIT

Yizkor is a ceremony recalling all the deceased during a communal synagogue service. Yahrzeit is a personal memorial anniversary; it may be observed for any relative or friend, but it is meant primarily for parents.

The Yizkor service was instituted so that the Jew may pay homage to his forebears and recall the good life and traditional goals. This service is founded on a vital principle of Jewish life, one that motivates and animates the Kaddish recitation.

It is based on the firm belief that the living, by acts of piety and goodness, can redeem the dead. The son can bring honor to the father. The "merit of the children" can reflect the value of the parents.

This merit is achieved, primarily, by living on a high ethical and moral plane, by being responsive to the demands of God and sensitive to the needs of one's fellow man. The formal expression of this merit is accomplished by prayer to God and by contributions to charity.

Yahrzeit is a special day of observances to commemorate the anniversary of the death of parents. Though the word is of German origin, the custom is outlined in the Talmud.

This religious commemoration is recorded not as a fiat, but as a description of an instinctive sentiment of sadness, an annual rehearsing of tragedy, which impels one to avoid eating meat and drinking wine — symbols of festivity and joy, the very stuff of life.

Author Biography: Rabbi Maurice Lamm is the author of *The Jewish Way of Death and Mourning*, *The Jewish Way in Love and Marriage*, *Becoming A Jew*, and many other books. A professor at Yeshiva University's Rabbinical Seminary, he lectures nationally to Jewish and Christian audiences.

This article can also be read at: http://www.aish.com/literacy/lifecycle/The_Jewish_Way_of_Mourning.asp

The Herodian Genealogy

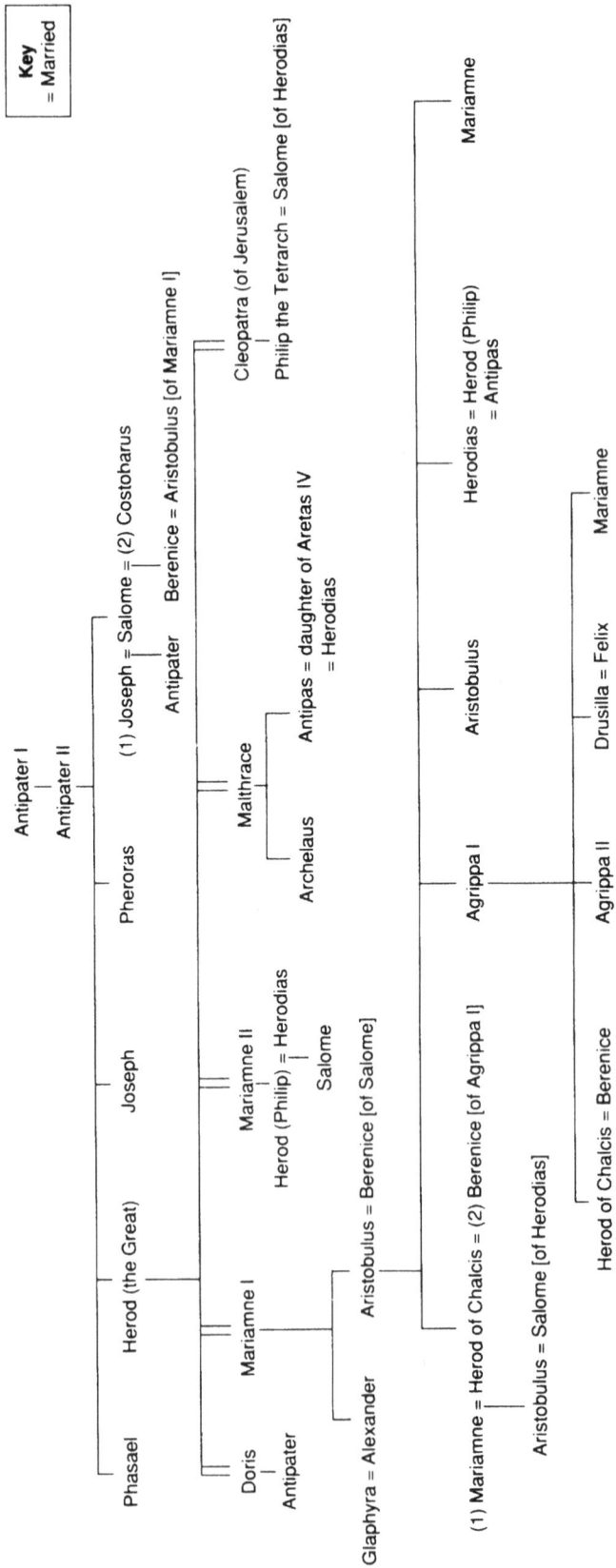

Key
= Married

Phasael

Herod (the Great)

Joseph

Pheroras

Antipater I

Antipater II

Doris
Antipater

Mariamne I

Mariamne II

Malthace

(1) Joseph = Salome = (2) Costoharus

Antipater

Berenice = Aristobulus [of Mariamne I]

Cleopatra (of Jerusalem)

Philip the Tetrarch = Salome [of Herodias]

Herod (Philip) = Herodias

Salome

Archelaus

Antipas = daughter of Aretas IV
= Herodias

Herodias = Herod (Philip)
= Antipas

Mariamne

Glaphyra = Alexander

Aristobulus = Berenice [of Salome]

(1) Mariamne = Herod of Chalcis = (2) Berenice [of Agrippa I]

Aristobulus = Salome [of Herodias]

Agrippa I

Aristobulus

Herod of Chalcis = Berenice

Agrippa II

Drusilla = Felix

Mariamne

The Herodian Genealogy

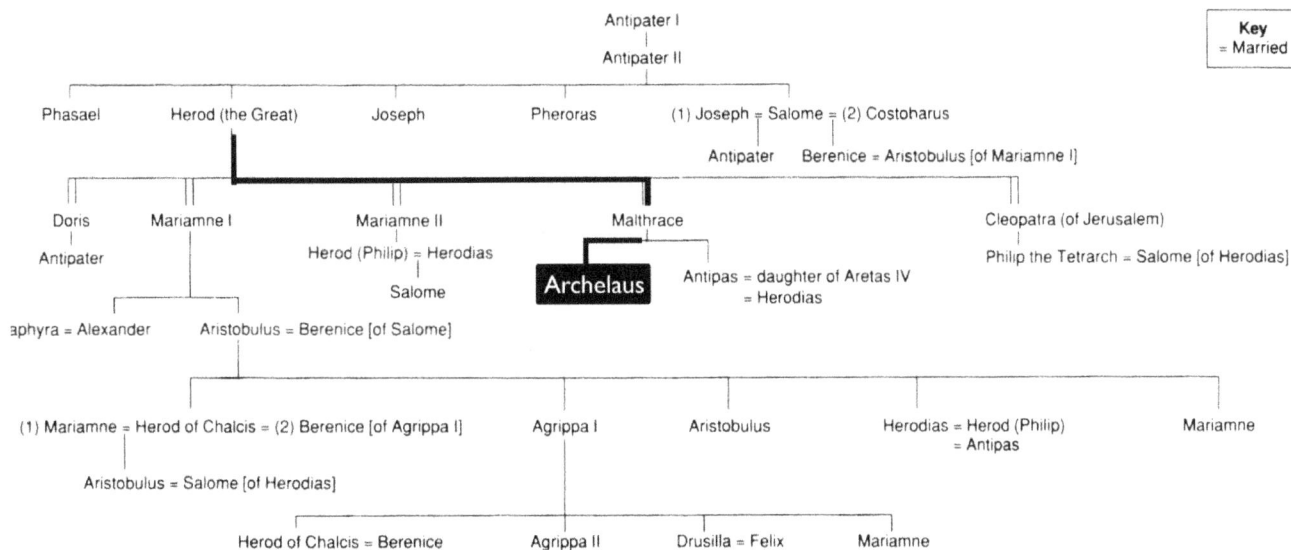

Herod Archelaus — 4BC - AD 6

1. Born 22 BC to Herod's fourth wife, Malthrace (a Samaritan).

2. Herod the Great named him "King" in his sixth will, made 5 days before he died.

3. Gave his father a glorious funeral that ended at Herodium.

4. Killed 3,000 Jews the day of his father's death, to quell a riot in Jerusalem.

5. Traveled to Rome to have his father's will ratified, but so did two other sons of Herod (Antipas and Philip)!

6. While in Rome a second riot erupted; Romans burned and looted the Temple.

7. The governor of Syria responded in force; burned Sephoris and took Jews captive and crucified 2,000 rebels.

8. An envoy of Jews went to Rome to protest while Archelaus was there.

9. Augustus (Octavian) ratified a compromise will, making Archelaus "Ethnarch" of Judea (i.e "ruler of a people"), but not king…yet.

10. Upon returning to Palestine, he continued his reign of terror (cf. Matt. 2:19-23; the only NT reference to Archelaus).

11. His rule was so offensive, Samaritans *and* Jews joined forces and sent an envoy to Rome.

12. Archelaus was stripped of his ethnarchy and banished to Lyons (France) in AD 6.

13. Judea then became a Roman province, under the rule of a Roman prefect until AD 41.

14. It was again a "client" kingdom under Herod Agrippa I from AD 41-44, after which it was ruled by Roman procurators such as Felix and Festus before whom Paul was tried in Caesarea (cf. Acts 24-25).

The Herodian Genealogy

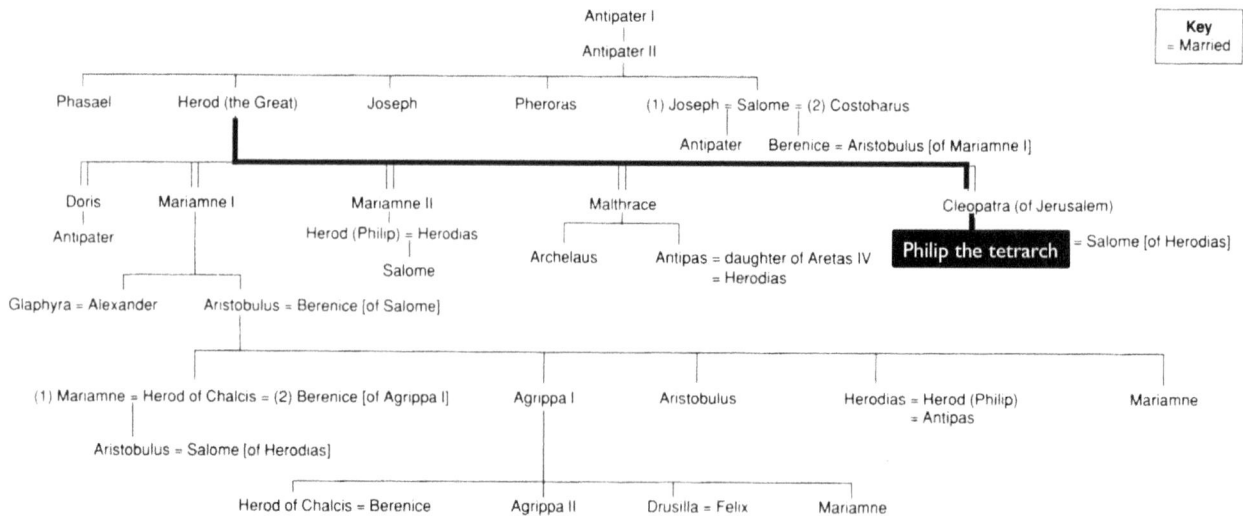

Philip the Tetrarch — AD 50-100

1. Born 21 BC, the son of Herod the Great and Cleopatra of Jerusalem.

2. Herod's final will gave the tetrarchy in the North (Galaunitis, Auranitis, Batanea, Trachonitis and Paneas; cf. Luke 3:1).

3. Because his subjects were mostly Syrians and Greeks, he is the only Herod to have his image on a coin.

4. Is remembered for two cities he built that play heavily into the Gospel narrative:

    a. He rebuilt and enlarged Paneas and renamed it Caesarea Philippi

    b. It was near here that Peter made his great confession about Jesus' identity and Jesus made his profound statement about the nature and success of the yet-unheard-of Church (Matt. 16:13-20; Mk. 8:27-30).

    c. He later rebuilt and enlarged Bethsaida and renamed it Julias.

    d. It was here that Jesus healed a blind man, and near where he fed the 5,000 (Mk. 8:22-26; Lk. 9:10-17).

5. Philip is known as the "softer, gentler" Herod according to Josephus.

6. After his death in AD 34, his territory was annexed by Syria and then later given to Agrippa I when Caligula became Emperor in AD 39.

The Herodian Genealogy

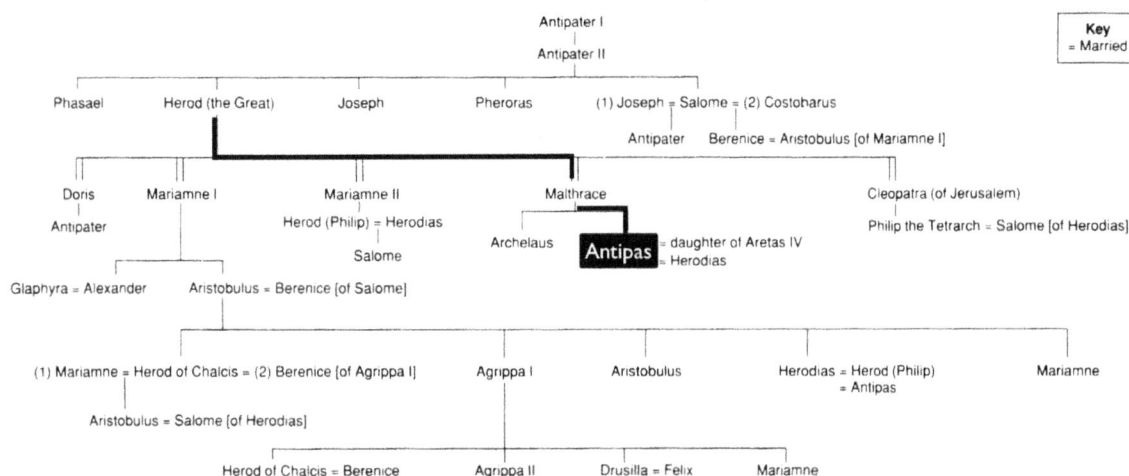

Antipater I
|
Antipater II

Phasael	Herod (the Great)	Joseph	Pheroras	(1) Joseph = Salome = (2) Costobarus	Key
					= Married

Antipater   Berenice = Aristobulus [of Mariamne I]

Doris	Mariamne I	Mariamne II	Malthrace	Cleopatra (of Jerusalem)
Antipater		Herod (Philip) = Herodias		Philip the Tetrarch = Salome [of Herodias]
		Salome	Archelaus **Antipas** = daughter of Aretas IV	
			= Herodias	

Glaphyra = Alexander   Aristobulus = Berenice [of Salome]

(1) Mariamne = Herod of Chalcis = (2) Berenice [of Agrippa I]	Agrippa I	Aristobulus	Herodias = Herod (Philip)	Mariamne
Aristobulus = Salome [of Herodias]			= Antipas	

Herod of Chalcis = Berenice	Agrippa II	Drusilla = Felix	Mariamne

Herod Antipas— 4BC - AD 39

1. Born 20 BC, the younger brother of Archelaus.

2. The most "mentioned" Herod in the New Testament (most likely because of his realm more than his "rule": Galilee and Perea, the ministry centers for Jesus and John the Baptist).

3. The most similar to Herod the Great in his vision and ambition:

    a. Began his rule by seeking to restore order to the chaos caused by Archelaus.

    b. Rebuilt the recently destroyed Sephoris near Nazareth and made it his capital. (It is almost certain that Joseph and Jesus would have worked on this reconstruction project.)

    c. Built the city of Tiberius, the first Jewish city built on the Greek *polis* model, and moved his capital there.

    d. Gave tax incentives and free homes and land to those moving there the first few years.

4. Was given the dynastic title, "Herod," which smoothed his political relations with Rome.

5. Married the daughter of King Aretas IV of the Arab kingdom of Nabatea, most likely as a political alliance.

6. Later fell in "love" with Herodias, the wife of his step-brother, Philip (and his own niece!).

7. Herodias agrees to marry him *if* he divorces the daughter of Aretas, which he does.

8. This new marriage was a flagrant violation of Mosaic Law and infuriated the Jews (Lev. 18:16; 20:21).

9. This is the union John the Baptizer publicly denounced, was imprisoned for, and eventually lost his life over (Mark. 6:14-29).

10. Herod Antipas apparently was threatened by Jesus' popularity and revealed an intent to kill him (Luke 13:31-33).

11. This is the Herod Jesus was interrogated and humiliated by just before his crucifixion (Luke alone; 23:6-12).

12. Herod and Pilate's "friendship" was galvanized through this mutual event (Luke 23:11-12).

13. In AD 36, Aretas seeks revenge for his daughter's honor and attacks Antipas.

14. In AD 37, Caligula becomes Emperor and makes Agrippa, Antipas' nephew, *King* over Philip's land.

15. Herodias convinced Antipas to petition Rome for the title, "King," like her brother.

16. Caligula responds by banishing Antipas to France, and gives his territories to Agrippa!

The Herodian Genealogy

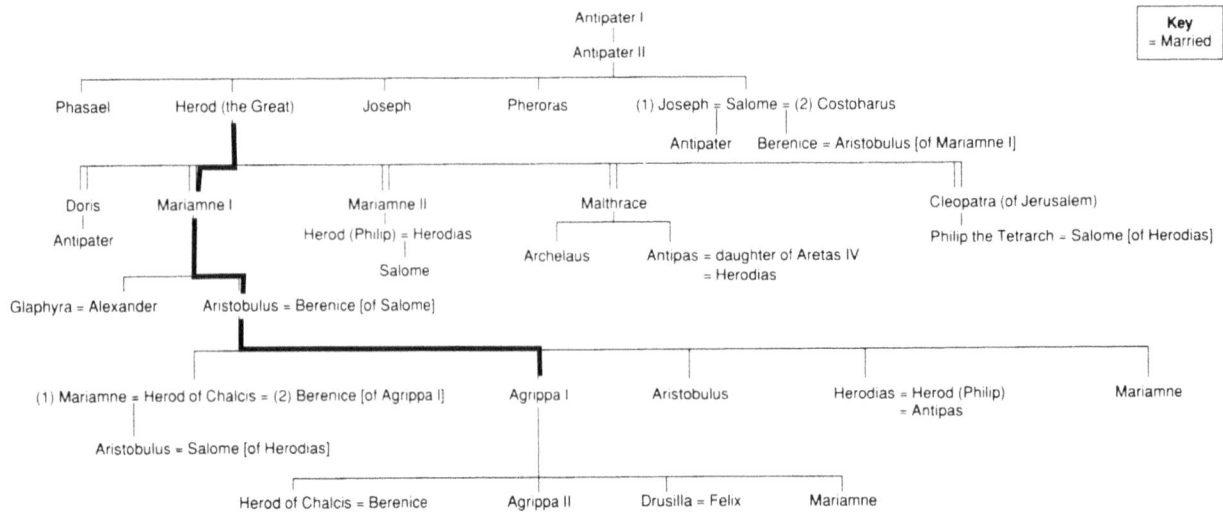

Herod Agrippa I — AD 37-44

1. Born 10 BC, the son of Aristobulus, Herod the Great's son by Miriamne I.

2. His sister is Herodias, the first wife of Herod Philip who became Antipas' second wife.

3. Was educated in Rome, like all the Herods, and lived the life of a spoiled brat away from home.

4. While in Rome he became friends with Caligula *before* he became Emperor (He was actually imprisoned by Tiberius for saying he'd rather Caligula be Emperor than Tiberius!).

5. When Tiberius died, Caligula released Agrippa and gave him the title, "King" as well as the territories that had belonged to Philip the tetrarch.

6. In AD 39 when Antipas sought the title "King" for himself, Agrippa was given *his* territories and his property.

7. In AD 41 Caligula died and Agrippa found favor with Claudius, the new Emperor, who gave him rule over Judea and Samaria.

8. Agrippa I now had control over all the territory once ruled by his grandfather, Herod the Great.

9. Agrippa I is best known in the New Testament as a fierce persecutor of the infant Church.

10. He is the King who had James, the brother of John, beheaded and imprisoned Peter (Acts 12:1-5).

11. He executed the sentries on duty when Peter was miraculously released from prison (Acts 12:18-19).

12. Agrippa's arrogance cost him his life, when he accepted the worship of people who called him a "god" at Caesarea (Acts 12:20-23).

13. Agrippa was survived by three daughters, Bernice, Mariamne, and Drusilla, and a son, Agrippa II who was too young to rule at the time.

14. Agrippa's territory was temporarily made back into a province by Rome.

The Herodian Genealogy

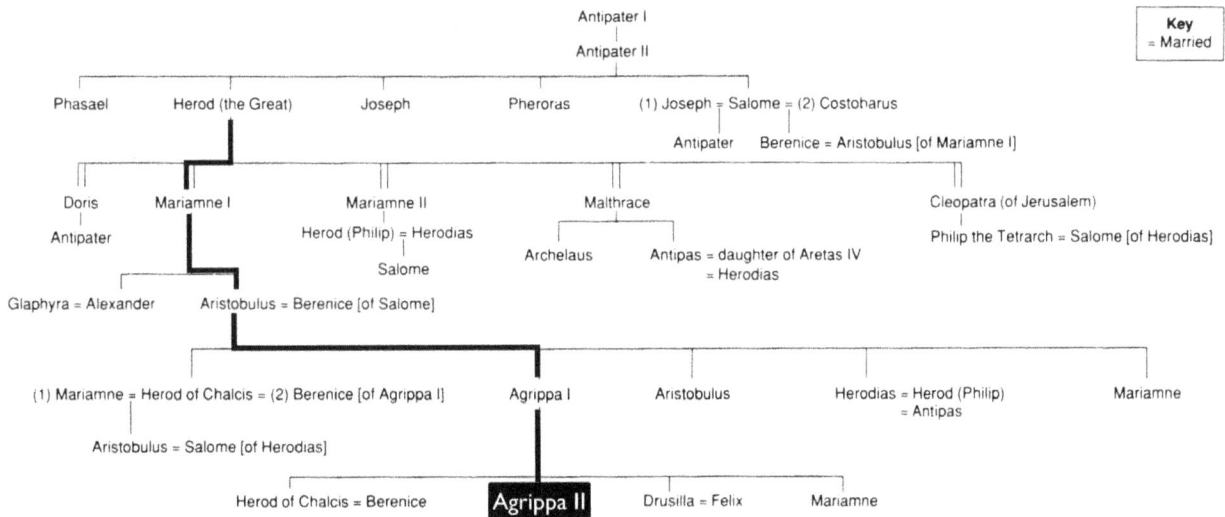

Antipater I
Antipater II

Key
= Married

Phasael | Herod (the Great) | Joseph | Pheroras | (1) Joseph = Salome = (2) Costobarus

Antipater | Berenice = Aristobulus [of Mariamne I]

Doris | Mariamne I | Mariamne II | Malthrace | Cleopatra (of Jerusalem)

Antipater | Herod (Philip) = Herodias | Philip the Tetrarch = Salome [of Herodias]

Salome

Archelaus | Antipas = daughter of Aretas IV
= Herodias

Glaphyra = Alexander | Aristobulus = Berenice [of Salome]

(1) Mariamne = Herod of Chalcis = (2) Berenice [of Agrippa I] | Agrippa I | Aristobulus | Herodias = Herod (Philip) | Mariamne
= Antipas

Aristobulus = Salome [of Herodias]

Herod of Chalcis = Berenice | **Agrippa II** | Drusilla = Felix | Mariamne

Herod Agrippa II — AD 50-100

1. Born AD 27, the son of Agrippa I and Cypros; was 17 when his father died in AD 44.

2. Although he had been educated in Rome, he had not totally forgotten his people, like the Herods before him.

3. He brought the Jews' case to Rome, to have control and possession of their High Priestly vestments returned to them.

4. In AD 50, upon death of his uncle, Claudius made him "King of Chalcis."

5. In AD 53 he was given the tetrarchy of Philip in exchange for Chalcis.

6. In AD 54, when Nero became Emperor, he was given properties in Galilee and Perea. In appreciation, Agrippa enlarged his capital city of Tiberius and renamed it, Neronius.

7. He was consulted by Rome on religious matters concerning the Jews.

8. This is evidenced in the procurator, Festus, asking him to listen to a political prisoner named Paul in AD 59 (Acts 24:27-26:32).

9. The account in Acts is indirect proof of Agrippa's incestuous relationship with his sister, Bernice, which was well-attested to in ancient literature.

10. The first Jewish Revolt began in AD 66, and Agrippa's failure to quell it resulted in him becoming a staunch supporter of Rome against his own people.

11. During the war (Ad 66-70), Nero committed suicide, and eventually Vespasian came to power. His son, Titus, was the military commander who destroyed Jerusalem for the final time in AD 70.

12. Agrippa remained a ruler through the reigns of Vespasian and his son, Titus who became Emperor in AD 79.

13. Agrippa wrote Josephus and after purchasing a copy of his, *Jewish War,* praised him for it.

14. His death in AD 100 marked the end of the Herodian dynasty. He was the last Hasmonean to rule the Jews.

YESHUA vs THE STATE": A Case Study on the *Illegalities* of Yeshua's "Trials"

JEWISH "RULE"	WHAT ACTUALLY HAPPENED	Primary Source	Secondary Source
No trials were to occur during the night hours (before the morning sacrifice).	Yeshua was taken to Annas, Caiaphas, and the Sanhedrin at night.	Mishnah: Sanhedrin 4:1	Laurna L. Berg. "The Illegalities of Yeshua's Religious and Civil Trials," (Bibliotheca Sacra, Vol. 161, No. 643, July–September, 2004), 330–342.
Trials were not to occur on the eve of a Sabbath or during festivals.	The trials occurred at night during the Passover celebration.	Mishnah: Sanhedrin 4:1	Berg, ibid.
All trials were to be public; secret trials were forbidden.	Yeshua was taken before the Sanhedrin at night for questioning and was immediately declared "guilty." Only his official sentencing took place during the day.	Mishnah: Sanhedrin 1:6	Berg, ibid.
All trials were to be held in the Hall of Judgment in the temple area.	Yeshua was first taken to Annas then Caiaphas before put before the Sanhedrin.	Mishnah: Sanhedrin 11:2	Berg, ibid.
Capital cases required a minimum of twenty-three judges.	We don't know how many judges were present. The trials took place at night during a festival.	Mishnah: Sanhedrin 4:1	Berg, ibid.
An accused person could not testify against himself.	The Sanhedrin convicted Yeshua on His own words and did not see the need for witnesses.	Mishnah: Sanhedrin 3:3–4	Berg, ibid.
Someone was required to speak on behalf of the accused.	No one spoke for Yeshua, and when He objected to the illegality of the proceeding, He was struck in the face.	Darrell L. Bock, "Jesus v. Sanhedrin: Why Jesus 'Lost' His Trial," (Christianity Today, Vol. 42, No.4, April 6, 1998), 49.	—
Conviction required the testimony of two or three witnesses to be in perfect alignment	The prosecution sought witnesses against Yeshua, but their testimony conflicted.	Deuteronomy 17:6–7, 19:15–20	—
Witnesses for the prosecution were to be examined and cross-examined extensively.	Witnesses were sought against Yeshua for the purpose of conviction, not to acquit Him or even find the truth.	Mishnah: Sanhedrin 4:1	—
Capital cases were to follow a strict order, beginning with arguments by the defense, then arguments for conviction.	No one spoke in Yeshua's defense, neither before the accusations, nor after.	Mishnah: Sanhedrin 4:1	Berg, ibid.
All Sanhedrin judges could argue for acquittal, but not all could argue for conviction.	The chief priests and the council sought witnesses against Yeshua.	Darrell L. Bock, ibid	—
Each witness in a capital case was to be examined individually, not in the presence of other witnesses.	We don't know how many witnesses were brought to testify at any given time.	Mishnah: Sanhedrin 3:6	Berg, ibid.
The testimony of two witnesses found to be in contradiction rendered both invalid.	The testimonies of those who testified against Yeshua did not agree.	Mishnah: Sanhedrin 5:2	Berg, ibid.

JEWISH "RULE"	WHAT ACTUALLY HAPPENED	Primary Source	Secondary Source
Voting for conviction and sentencing in a capital case was to be conducted individually beginning with the youngest, so younger members would not be influenced by the voting of the elder members.	The members of the Sanhedrin voted simultaneously and nearly rioted.	Mishnah: Sanhedrin 4:2	Berg, ibid.
Verdicts in capital cases were to be handed down only during daylight hours	The Sanhedrin convicted Yeshua and condemned Him right away, then reconvened the next day to give the appearance of order.	Mishnah: Sanhedrin 4:1	Berg, ibid.
The members of the Sanhedrin were to meet in pairs all night, discuss the case, and reconvene for the purpose of confirming the final verdict and imposing sentence.	We see only a rush to judgment and no indication that the judges met for any reason, least of all to find Yeshua "not guilty."	Mishnah: Sanhedrin 4:1	—
Sentencing in a capital case was not to occur until the following day.	The Sanhedrin convicted Yeshua and condemned Him right away, then reconvened the next day to give the appearance of order.	Mishnah: Sanhedrin 4:1	Berg, ibid.

Adapted from the sermon, "Analysis of a Courtroom Fiasco," by Charles R. Swindoll

Special Communication

On the Physical Death of Jesus Christ

William D. Edwards, MD; Wesley J. Gabel, MDiv; Floyd E. Hosmer, MS, AMI

■ Jesus of Nazareth underwent Jewish and Roman trials, was flogged, and was sentenced to death by crucifixion. The scourging produced deep stripelike lacerations and appreciable blood loss, and it probably set the stage for hypovolemic shock as evidenced by the fact that Jesus was too weakened to carry the crossbar (patibulum) to Golgotha. At the site of crucifixion his wrists were nailed to the patibulum, and after the patibulum was lifted onto the upright post, (stipes) his feet were nailed to the stipes. The major pathophysiologic effect of crucifixion was an interference with normal respirations. Accordingly, death resulted primarily from hypovolemic shock and exhaustion asphyxia. Jesus' death was ensured by the thrust of a soldier's spear into his side. Modern medical interpretation of the historical evidence indicates that Jesus was dead when taken down from the cross.
(*JAMA* 1986; 255:1455-1463)

THE LIFE and teachings of Jesus of Nazareth have formed the basis for a major world religion, (Christianity) have appreciably influenced the course of human history, and, by virtue of a compassionate attitude toward the sick, also have contributed to the development of modern medicine. The eminence of Jesus as a historical figure and the suffering, and controversy associated with his death has stimulated us to investigate, in an interdisciplinary manner, the circumstances surrounding his crucifixion. Accordingly it is our intent to present not a theological treatise but rather a medically, and historically accurate account of the physical death of the one called Jesus Christ.

SOURCES

The source material concerning Christ's death comprises a body of literature and not a physical body or its skeletal remains. Accordingly, the

From the Departments of Pathology (Dr. Edwards) and Medical Graphics (Mr. Hosmer), Mayo Clinic, Rochester, Minn; and the Homestead United Methodist Church, Rochester, Minn, and the West Bethel United Methodist Church, Bethel, Minn (Pastor Gabel).
Reprint requests to Department of Pathology, Mayo Clinic, Rochester, MN 55905 (Dr Edwards).

credibility of any discussion of Jesus' death will be determined primarily by the credibility of one's sources. For this review, the source material includes the writings of ancient Christian and non-Christian authors, the writings of modern authors, and the Shroud of Turin.[1-40] Using the legal-historical method of scientific investigation,[27] scholars have established the reliability and accuracy of the ancient manuscripts.[26,27,29,31]

The most extensive and detailed descriptions of the life and death of Jesus are to be found in the New Testament gospels of Matthew, Mark, Luke, and John.[1] The other 23 books of the New Testament support but do not expand on the details recorded in the gospels. Contemporary Christian, Jewish, and Roman authors provide additional insight concerning the first-century Jewish and Roman legal systems and the details of scourging and crucifixion.[5] Seneca, Livy, Plutarch, and others refer to crucifixion practices in their works.[8,28] Specifically, Jesus (or his crucifixion) is mentioned by the Roman historians Cornelius Tacitus, Pliny the Younger, and Suetonius, by non-Roman historians Thallus and Phlegon, by the satirist Lucian of Samosata, by the Jewish

Talmud, and by the Jewish historian Flavius Josephus, although the authenticity of portions of the latter is problematic.[26]

The Shroud of Turin is considered by many to represent the actual burial cloth of Jesus,[22] and several publications concerning the medical aspects of his death draw conclusions from this assumption.[5,11] The Shroud of Turin and recent archaeological findings provide valuable information concerning Roman crucifixion practices.[22-24] The interpretations of modern writers, based on a knowledge of science and medicine not available in the first century, may offer additional insight concerning the possible mechanisms of Jesus' death.[2-17]

When taken in concert certain facts—the extensive and early testimony of both Christian proponents and opponents, and their universal acceptance of Jesus as a true historical figure; the ethic of the gospel writers, and the shortness of the time interval between the events and the extant manuscripts; and the confirmation of the gospel accounts by historians and archaeological findings[26-27]—ensure a reliable testimony from which a modern medical interpretation of Jesus' death may be made.

GETHSEMANE

After Jesus and his disciples had observed the Passover meal in an upper room in a home in southwest Jerusalem, they traveled to the Mount of Olives, northeast of the city (Fig 1). (Owing to various adjustments to the calendar, the years of Jesus' birth and death remain controversial.[29] However, it is likely that Jesus was born in either 4 or 6 BC and died in 30 AD.[11,29] During the Passover observance in 30 AD, the Last Supper would have been observed on Thursday,

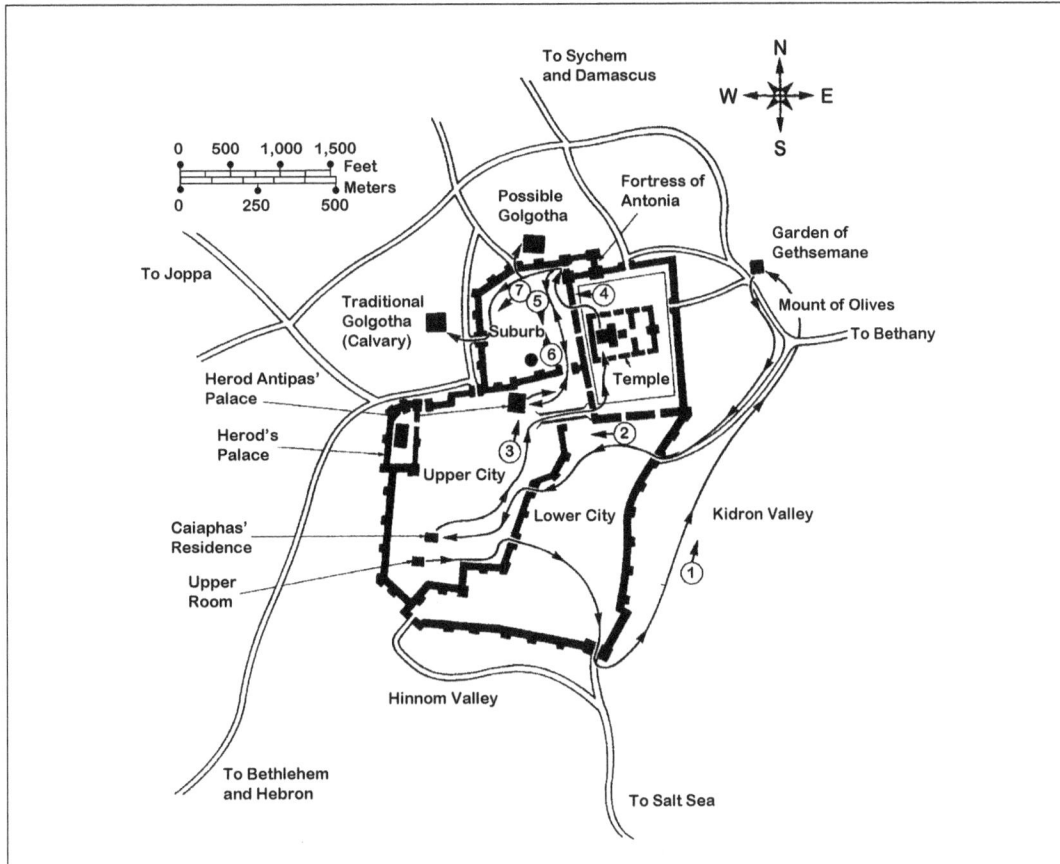

Fig 1.—Map of Jerusalem at time of Christ. Jesus left Upper Room and walked with disciples to Mount of Olives and Garden of Gethsemane (1), where he was arrested and taken first to Annas and then to Caiaphas (2). After first trial before political Sanhedrin at Caiaphas' residence, Jesus was tried again before religious Sanhedrin, probably at Temple (3) Next, he was taken to Pontius Pilate (4), who sent him to Herod Antipas (5). Herod returned Jesus to Pilate (6), and Pilate finally handed over Jesus for scourging at Fortress of Antonia and for crucifixion at Golgotha (7). (Modified from Pfeiffer et al.[30])

April 6 [Nisan 13], and Jesus would have been crucified on Friday, April 7 [Nisan 14].[29]) At nearby Gethsemane, Jesus, apparently knowing that the time of his death was near, suffered great mental anguish, and, as described by the physician Luke, his sweat became like blood.[1]

Although this is a very rare phenomenon, bloody sweat (hematidrosis or hemohidrosis) may occur in highly emotional states or in persons with bleeding disorders.[18-20] As a result of hemorrhage into the sweat glands, the skin becomes fragile and tender.[2,11] Luke's description supports the diagnosis of hematidrosis rather than eccrine chromidrosis (brown or yellow-green sweat) or stigmatization (blood oozing from the palms or elsewhere).[18-21] Although some authors

have suggested that hematidrosis produced hypovolemia, we agree with Bucklin[5] that Jesus' actual blood loss probably was minimal. However, in the cold night air,[1] it may have produced chills.

TRIALS

Jewish Trials

Soon after midnight, Jesus was arrested at Gethsemane by the temple officials and was taken first to Annas and then to Caiaphas, the Jewish high priest for that year (Fig 1).[1] Between 1 AM and daybreak, Jesus was tried before Caiaphas and the political Sanhedrin and was found guilty of blasphemy.[1] The guards then blindfolded Jesus, spat on him, and struck him in the face with their fists.[1] Soon after daybreak, presum-

ably at the temple (Fig 1), Jesus was tried before the religious Sanhedrin (with the Pharisees and the Sadducees) and again was found guilty of blasphemy, a crime punishable by death.[1,5]

Roman Trials

Since permission for an execution had to come from the governing Romans,[1] Jesus was taken early in the morning by the temple officials to the Praetorium of the Fortress of Antonia, the residence and governmental seat of Pontius Pilate, the procurator of Judea (Fig 1). However, Jesus was presented to Pilate not as a blasphemer but rather as a self-appointed king who would undermine the Roman authority.[1] Pilate made no charges against Jesus and sent him to

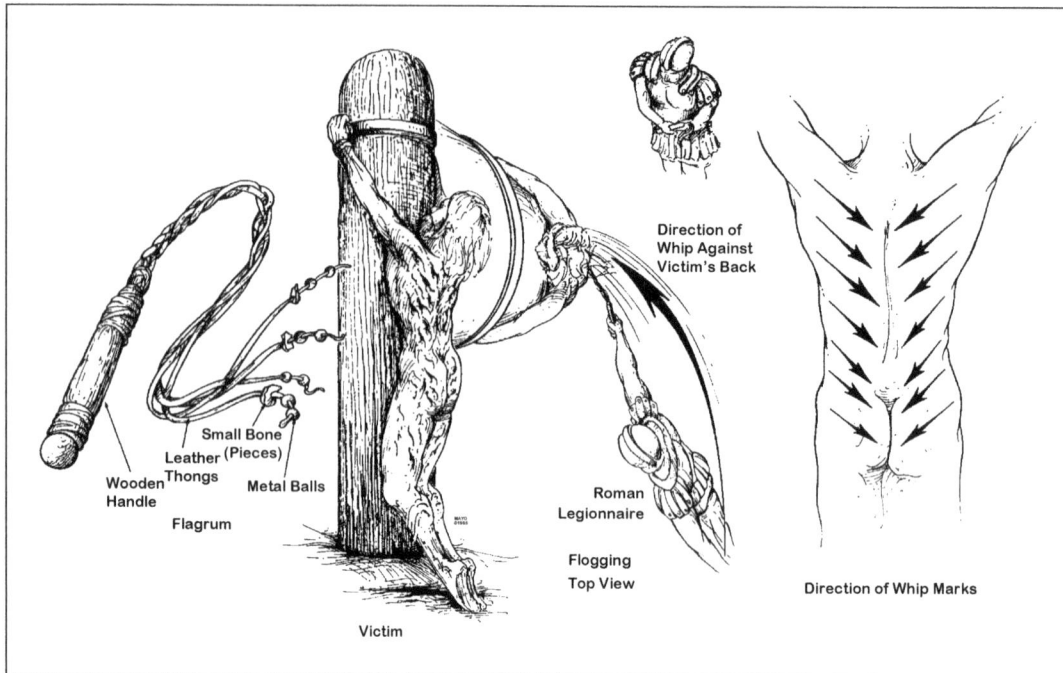

Fig 2.—Scourging. Left, Short whip (flagrum) with lead balls and sheep bones tied into leather thongs. Center left, Naked victim tied to flogging post. Deep stripelike lacerations were usually associated with considerable blood loss. Center right, View from above, showing position of lictors. Right, Inferomedial direction of wounds.

Herod Antipas, the tetrarch of Judea.[1] Herod likewise made no official charges and then returned Jesus to Pilate (Fig 1).[1] Again, Pilate could find no basis for a legal charge against Jesus, but the people persistently demanded crucifixion. Pilate finally granted their demand and handed over Jesus to be flogged (scourged) and crucified. (McDowell[25] has reviewed the prevailing political, religious, and economic climates in Jerusalem at the time of Jesus' death, and Bucklin[5] has described the various illegalities of the Jewish and Roman trials.)

Health of Jesus

The rigors of Jesus' ministry (that is, traveling by foot throughout Palestine) would have precluded any major physical illness or a weak general constitution. Accordingly, it is reasonable to assume that Jesus was in good physical condition before his walk to Gethsemane. However, during the 12 hours between 9 PM Thursday and 9 AM Friday, he had suffered great emotional stress (as evidenced by hematidrosis), abandonment by his closest friends (the disciples), and a physical beating (after the first Jewish trial). Also, in the setting of a traumatic and sleepless night, he had been forced to walk more than 2.5 miles (4.0 km) to and from the sites of the various trials (Fig 1). These physical and emotional factors may have rendered Jesus particularly vulnerable to the adverse hemodynamic effects of the scourging.

SCOURGING

Scourging Practices

Flogging was a legal preliminary to every Roman execution,[28] and only women and Roman senators or soldiers (except in cases of desertion) were exempt.[11] The usual instrument was a short whip (flagellum or flagellum) with several single or braided leather thongs of variable lengths, in which small iron balls or sharp pieces of sheep bones were tied at intervals (Fig 2).[5,7,11] Occasionally, staves also were used.[8,12] For scourging, the man was stripped of his clothing, and his hands were tied to an upright post (Fig 2).[11] The back, buttocks, and legs were flogged either by two soldiers (lictors) or by one who alternated positions.[5,7,11,28] The severity of the scourging depended on the disposition of the lictors and was intended to weaken the victim to a state just short of collapse or death.[8] After the scourging, the soldiers often taunted their victim.[11]

Medical Aspects of Scourging

As the Roman soldiers repeatedly struck the victim's back with full force, the iron balls would cause deep contusions, and the leather thongs and sheep bones would cut into the skin and subcutaneous tissues.[7] Then, as the flogging continued, the lacerations would tear into the underlying skeletal muscles and produce quivering ribbons of bleeding flesh.[2,7,25] Pain and blood loss generally set the stage for circulatory shock.[12] The extent of blood loss may well have determined how long the victim would survive on the cross.[8]

Scourging of Jesus

At the Praetorium, Jesus was severely whipped. (Although the severity of the scourging is not dis-

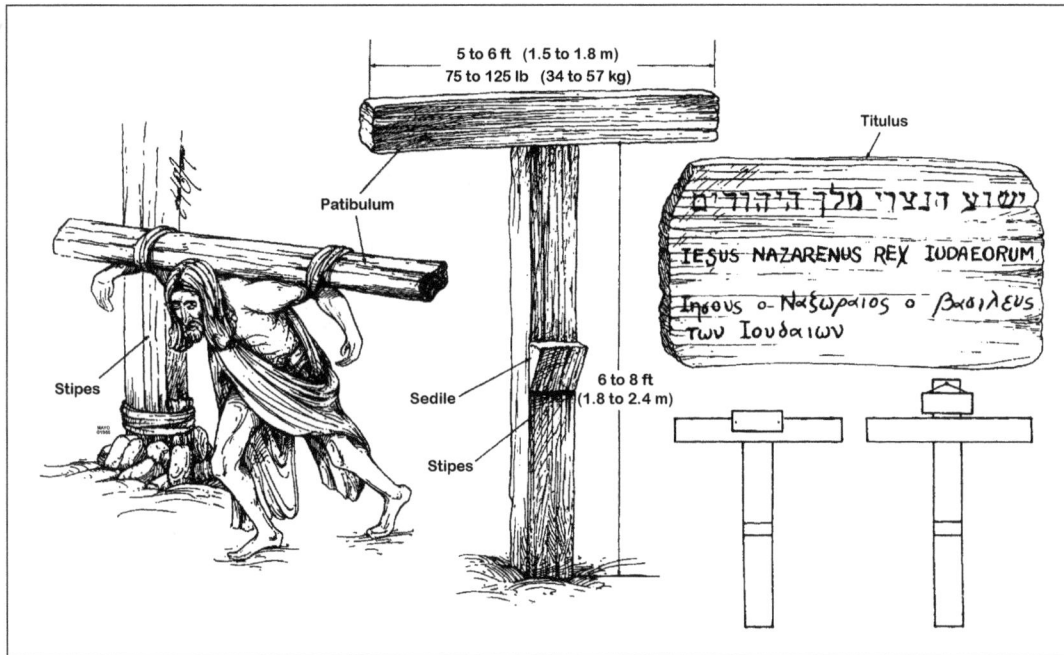

Fig 3.—Cross and titulus. Left, victim carrying crossbar (patibulum) to site of upright post (stipes). Center Low Tau cross (crux commissa), commonly used by Romans at time of Christ. Upper right, Rendition of Jesus' titulus with name and crime—Jesus of Nazareth, King of the Jews—written in Hebrew, Latin, and Greek. Lower right Possible methods for attaching tittles to Tau cross (left) and Latin cross (right).

Variations in Crosses Used for Crucifixion	
Latin Designation	Characteristics
Infelix lignum	Tree
Crux simplex,	Upright post
Crux acuta	
Crux composita	Stipes and patibulum
Crux humilis	Low cross
Crux sublimis	Tall cross
Crux commissa	T-shaped (Tau) cross
Crux immissa	†-shaped (Latin) cross
Crux capitata	†-shaped (Latin) cross
Crux decussata	X-shaped cross

cussed in the four gospel accounts, it is implied in one of the epistles [1 Peter 2:24]. A detailed word study of the ancient Greek text for this verse indicates that the scourging of Jesus was particularly harsh.[33] It is not known whether the number of lashes was limited to 39, in accordance with Jewish law.[5] The Roman soldiers, amused that this weakened man had claimed to be a king, began to mock him by placing a robe on his shoulders, a crown of thorns on his head, and a wooden staff as a scepter in his right hand.[1] Next, they spat on Jesus

and struck him on the head with the wooden staff.[1] Moreover, when the soldiers tore the robe from Jesus' back, they probably reopened the scourging wounds.[7]

The severe scourging, with its intense pain and appreciable blood loss, most probably left Jesus in a preshock state. Moreover, hematidrosis had rendered his skin particularly tender. The physical and mental abuse meted out by the Jews and the Romans, as well as the lack of food, water, and sleep, also contributed to his generally weakened state. Therefore, even before the actual crucifixion, Jesus' physical condition was at least serious and possibly critical.

CRUCIFIXION
Crucifixion Practices

Crucifixion probably first began among the Persians.[34] Alexander the Great introduced the practice to Egypt and Carthage, and the Romans appear to have learned of it from the Carthaginians.[11] Although the Romans did not invent crucifixions they perfected it as a form of torture and capital punishment that was designed to produce a slow death with maxi-

mum pain and suffering.[10,17] It was one of the most disgraceful and cruel methods of execution and usually was reserved only for slaves, foreigners, revolutionaries, and the vilest of criminals.[3,25,28] Roman law usually protected Roman citizens from crucifixion,[5] except perhaps in the ease of desertion by soldiers.

In its earliest form in Persia, the victim was either tied to a tree or was tied to or impaled on an upright post, usually to keep the guilty victim's feet from touching holy ground.[8,11,30,34,38] Only later was a true cross used; it was characterized by an upright post (stipes) and a horizontal crossbar (patibulum), and it had several variations (Table).[11] Although archaeological and historical evidence strongly indicates that the low Tau cross was preferred by the Romans in Palestine at the time of Christ (Fig 3),[2,7,11] crucifixion practices often varied in a given geographic region and in accordance with the imagination of the executioners, and the Latin cross and other forms also may have been used.[28]

It was customary for the condemned man to carry his own cross

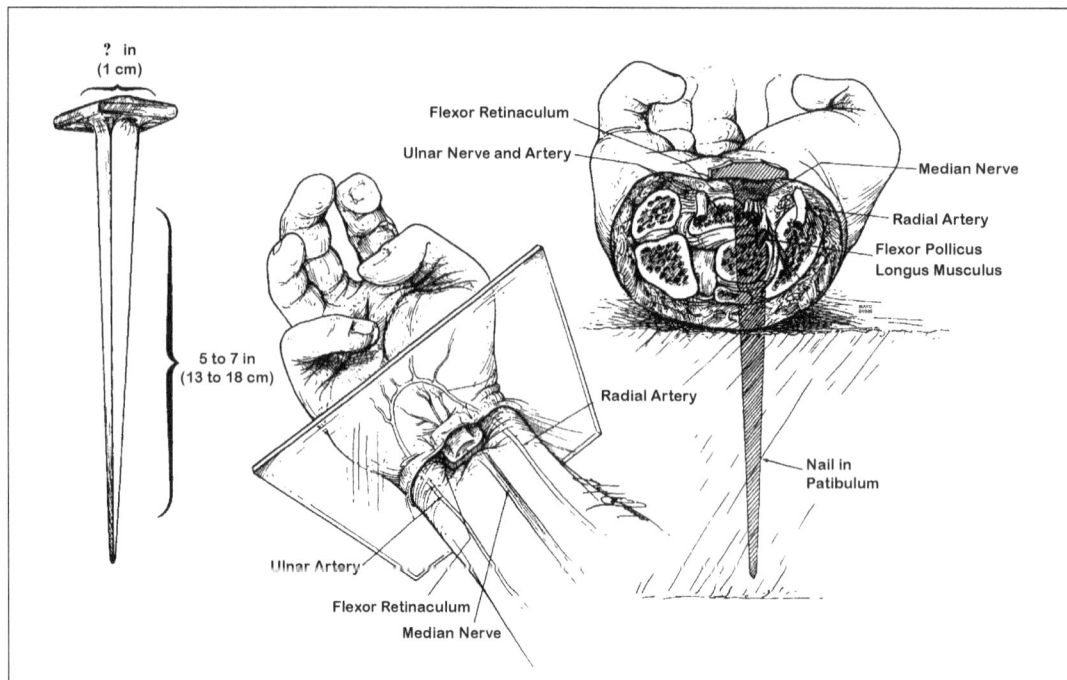

Fig 4.—Nailing of wrists. Left, Size of iron nail. Center, Location of nail in wrist, between carpals and radius. Right, Cross section of wrist, at level of plane indicated at left, showing path of nail, with probable transection of median nerve and impalement of flexor pollicis longus, but without injury to major arterial trunks and without fractures of bones.

from the flogging post to the site of crucifixion outside the city walls.[8,11,30] He was usually naked, unless this was prohibited by local customs.[11] Since the weight of the entire cross was probably well over 300 lb (136 kg), only the crossbar was carried (Fig 3).[11] The patibulum, weighing 75 to 125 lb. (34 to 57 kg),[11,30] was placed across the nape of the victim's neck and balanced along both shoulders. Usually, the outstretched arms then were tied to the crossbar.[7,11] The processional to the site of crucifixion was led by a complete Roman military guard, headed by a centurion.[3,11] One of the soldiers carried a sign (titulus) on which the condemned man's name and crime were displayed (Fig 3).[3,11] Later, the titulus would be attached to the top of the cross.[11] The Roman guard would not leave the victim until they were sure of his death.[9,11]

Outside the city walls was permanently located the heavy upright wooden stipes, on which the patibulum would be secured. In the case of the Tau cross, this was accomplished by means of a mortise and tenon joint, with or without reinforcement

by ropes.[10,11,30] To prolong the crucifixion process, a horizontal wooden block or plank, serving as a crude seat (sedile or sedulum), often was attached midway down the stipes.[3,11,16] Only very rarely, and probably later than the time of Christ, was an additional block (suppedaneum) employed for transfixion of the feet.[9,11]

At the site of execution, by law, the victim was given a bitter drink of wine mixed with myrrh (gall) as a mild analgesic.[7,17] The criminal was then thrown to the ground on his back, with his arms outstretched along the patibulum.[11] The hands could be nailed or tied to the crossbar, but nailing apparently was preferred by the Romans.[8,11] The archaeological remains of a crucified body, found in an ossuary near Jerusalem and dating from the time of Christ, indicate that the nails were tapered iron spikes approximately 5 to 7 in (13 to 18 cm) long with a square shaft ⅜ in (1 cm) across.[23,24,30] Furthermore, ossuary findings and the Shroud of Turin have documented that the nails commonly were driven through the wrists rather than the palms (Fig 4).[22-24,30]

After both arms were fixed to the crossbar, the patibulum and the victim, together, were lifted onto the stipes.[11] On the low cross, four soldiers could accomplish this relatively easily. However, on the tall cross, the soldiers used either wooden forks or ladders.[11]

Next, the feet were fixed to the cross, either by nails or ropes. Ossuary findings and the Shroud of Turin suggest that nailing was the preferred Roman practice.[23,24,30] Although the feet could be fixed to the sides of the stipes or to a wooden footrest (suppedaneum), they usually were nailed directly to the front of the stipes (Fig 5).[11] To accomplish this, flexion of the knees may have been quite prominent, and the bent legs may have been rotated laterally (Fig 6).[23-25,30]

When the nailing was completed, the titulus was attached to the cross, by nails or cords, just above the victim's head.[11] The soldiers and the civilian crowd often taunted and jeered the condemned man, and the soldiers customarily divided up his clothes among themselves[11,25] The

Medical Aspects of Crucifixion

With knowledge of both anatomy and ancient crucifixion practices, one may reconstruct the probable medical aspects of this form of slow execution. Each wound apparently was intended to produce intense agony, and the contributing causes of death were numerous.

The scourging prior to crucifixion served to weaken the condemned man and, if blood loss was considerable, to produce orthostatic hypotension and even hypovolemic shock.[8,12] When the victim was thrown to the ground on his back, in preparation for transfixion of the hands, his scourging wounds most likely would become torn open again and contaminated with dirt.[2,16] Furthermore, with each respiration, the painful scourging wounds would be scraped against the rough wood of the stipes.[7] As a result, blood loss from the back probably would continue throughout the crucifixion ordeal.

With arms outstretched but not taut, the wrists were nailed to the patibulum.[7,11] It has been shown that the ligaments and bones of the wrist can support the weight of a body hanging from them, but the palms cannot.[11] Accordingly, the iron spikes probably were driven between the radius and the carpals or between the two rows of carpal bones,[2,10,11,30] either proximal to or through the strong bandlike flexor retinaculum and the various intercarpal ligaments (Fig 4). Although a nail in either location in the wrist might pass between the bony elements and thereby produce no fractures, the likelihood of painful periosteal injury would seem great. Furthermore, the driven nail would crush or sever the rather large sensorimotor median nerve (Fig 4).[2,7,11] The stimulated nerve would produce excruciating bolts of fiery pain in both arms.[7,9] Although the severed median nerve would result in paralysis of a portion of the hand, ischemic contractures and impalement of various ligaments by the iron spike might produce a clawlike grasp.

Most commonly, the feet were fixed to the front of the stipes by means of an iron spike driven through the first or second intermetatarsal space, just distal to the tarsometatarsal joint.[2,5,8,11,30] It is likely that the deep peroneal nerve and branches of the

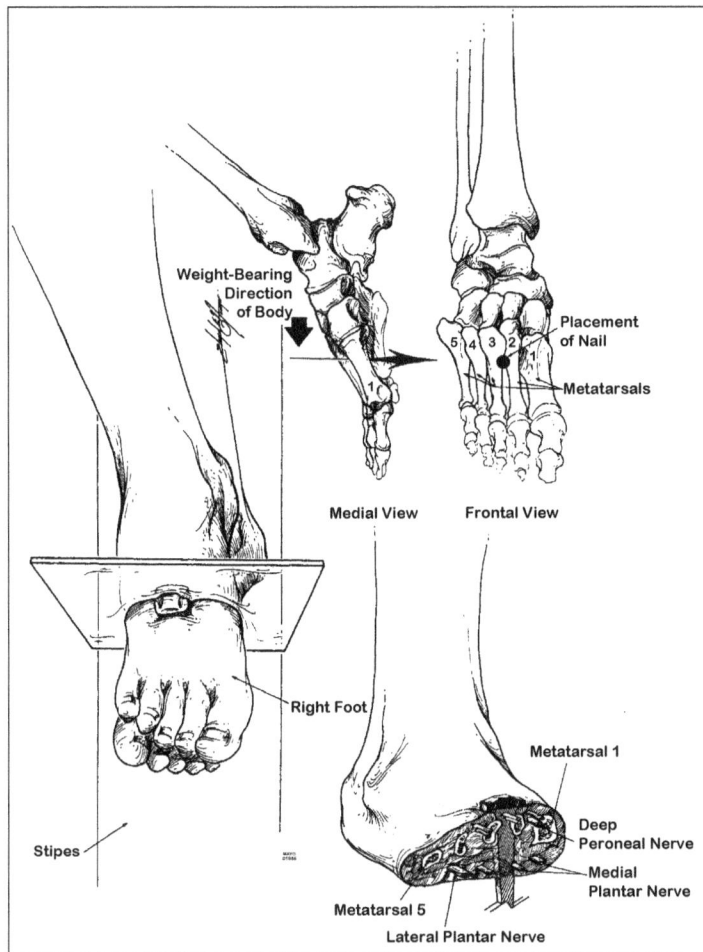

Fig 5.—Nailing of feet. Left, Position of feet atop one another and against stipes. Upper right, Location of nail in second intermetatarsal space. Lower right, Cross section of foot, at plane indicated at left, showing path of nail.

length of survival generally ranged from three or four hours to three or four days and appears to have been inversely related to the severity of the scourging.[8,11] However, even if the scourging had been relatively mild, the Roman soldiers could hasten death by breaking the legs below the knees (crurifragium or skelokopia).[8,11]

Not uncommonly, insects would light upon or burrow into the open wounds or the eyes, ears, and nose of the dying and helpless victim, and birds of prey would tear at these sites.[16] Moreover, it was customary to leave the corpse on the cross to be devoured by predatory animals.[8,11,12,28] However, by Roman law, the family of the condemned could take the body for burial, after obtaining permission from the Roman judge.[11]

Since no one was intended to survive crucifixion, the body was not released to the family until the soldiers were sure that the victim was dead. By custom, one of the Roman guards would pierce the body with a sword or lance.[8,11] Traditionally, this had been considered a spear wound to the heart through the right side of the chest—a fatal wound probably taught to most Roman soldiers.[11] The Shroud of Turin documents this form of injury.[5,11,22] Moreover, the standard infantry spear, which was 5 to 6 ft (1.5 to 1.8 m) long,[30] could easily have reached the chest of a man crucified on the customary low cross.[11]

Death of Christ—Edwards et al

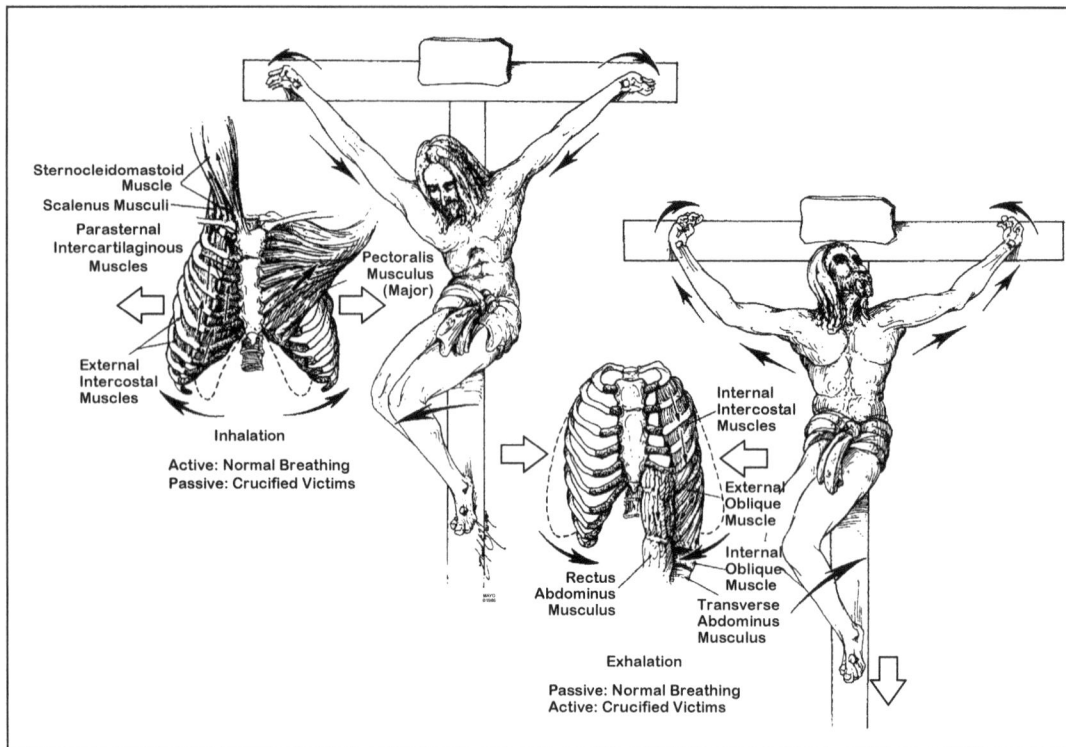

Fig 6—Respirations during crucifixion. Left, Inhalation. With elbows extended and shoulders abducted, respiratory muscles of inhalation are passively stretched and thorax is expanded. Right, Exhalation. With elbows flexed and shoulders adducted and with weight of body on nailed feet, exhalation is accomplished as active, rather than passive, process. Breaking legs below knees would place burden of exhalation on shoulder and arm muscles alone and soon would result in exhaustion asphyxia.

medial and lateral plantar nerves would have been injured by the nails (Fig 5). Although scourging may have resulted in considerable blood loss, crucifixion per se was a relatively bloodless procedure, since no major arteries, other than perhaps the deep plantar arch, pass through the favored anatomic sites of transfixion.[2,10,11]

The major pathophysiologic effect of crucifixion, beyond the excruciating pain, was a marked interference with normal respiration, particularly exhalation (Fig 6). The weight of the body, pulling down on the outstretched arms and shoulders, would tend to fix the intercostal muscles in an inhalation state and thereby hinder passive exhalation.[2,10,11] Accordingly, exhalation was primarily diaphragmatic, and breathing was shallow. It is likely that this form of respiration would not suffice and that hypercarbia would soon result. The onset of muscle cramps or tetanic

contractions, due to fatigue and hypercarbia, would hinder respiration even further.[11]

Adequate exhalation required lifting the body by pushing up on the feet and by flexing the elbows and adducting the shoulders (Fig 6).[2] However, this maneuver would place the entire weight of the body on the tarsals and would produce searing pain.[7] Furthermore, flexion of the elbows would cause rotation of the wrists about the iron nails and cause fiery pain along the damaged median nerves.[7] Lifting of the body would also painfully scrape the scourged back against the rough wooden stipes.[2,7] Muscle cramps and paresthesias of the outstretched and uplifted arms would add to the discomfort.[7] As a result, each respiratory effort would become agonizing and tiring and lead eventually to asphyxia.[2,3,7,10]

The actual cause of death by crucifixion was multifactorial and varied somewhat with each case, but the two

most prominent causes probably were hypovolemic shock and exhaustion asphyxia.[2,3,7,10] Other possible contributing factors included dehydration,[7,16] stress-induced arrhythmias,[3] and congestive heart failure with the rapid accumulation of pericardial and perhaps pleural effusions.[2,7,11] Crucifracture (breaking the legs below the knees), if performed, led to an asphyxic death within minutes.[11] Death by crucifixion was, in every sense of the word, excruciating (Latin, excruciatus, or "out of the cross").

Crucifixion of Jesus

After the scourging and the mocking, at about 9 AM, the Roman soldiers put Jesus' clothes back on him and then led him and two thieves to be crucified.[1] Jesus apparently was so weakened by the severe flogging that he could not carry the patibulum from the Praetorium to the site of crucifixion one third of a mile (600 to

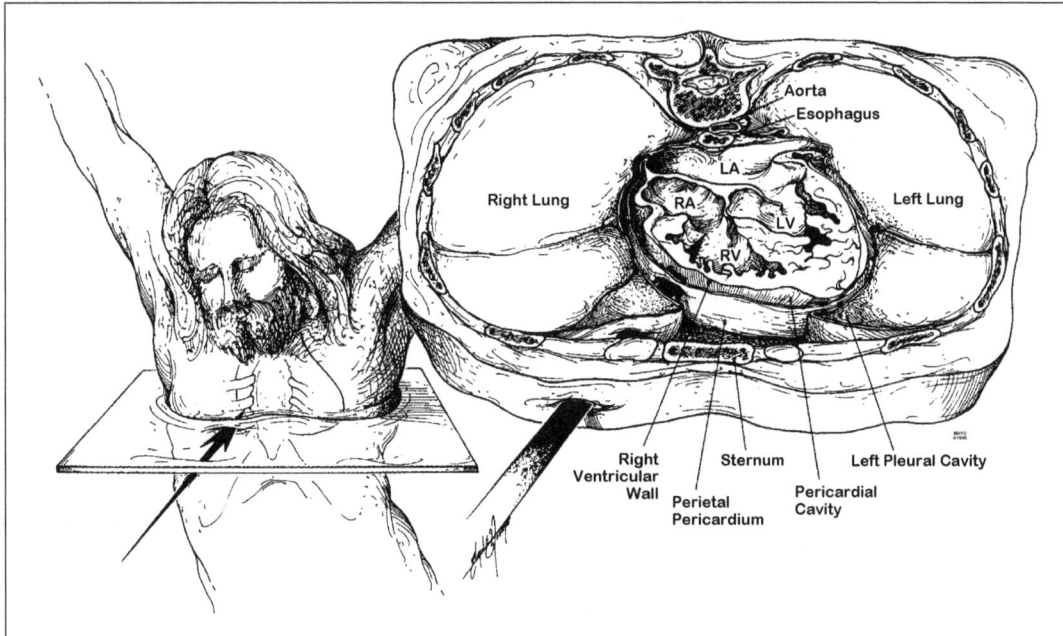

Fig 7.—Spear wound to chest. Left, Probable path of spear. Right, Cross section of thorax, at level of plane indicated at left, showing structures perforated by spear. LA indicates left atrium; LV, left ventricle; RA, right atrium; RV, right ventricle.

650 m) away.[1,3,5,7] Simon of Cyrene was summoned to carry Christ's cross, and the processional then made its way to Golgotha (or Calvary), an established crucifixion site.

Here, Jesus' clothes, except for a linen loincloth, again were removed, thereby probably reopening the scourging wounds. He then was offered a drink of wine mixed with myrrh (gall) but, after tasting it, refused the drink.[1] Finally, Jesus and the two thieves were crucified. Although scriptural references are made to nails in the hands,[1] these are not at odds with the archaeological evidence of wrist wounds, since the ancients customarily considered the wrist to be a part of the hand.[7,11] The titulus (Fig 3) was attached above Jesus' head. It is unclear whether Jesus was crucified on the Tau cross or the Latin cross; archaeological findings favor the former[11] and early tradition the latter.[38] The fact that Jesus later was offered a drink of wine vinegar from a sponge placed on the stalk of the hyssop plant[1] (approximately 20 in, or 50 cm, long) strongly supports the belief that Jesus was crucified on the short cross.[6]

The soldiers and the civilian crowd taunted Jesus throughout the crucifixion ordeal, and the soldiers cast lots for his clothing.[1] Christ spoke seven times from the cross.[1] Since speech occurs during exhalation, these short, terse utterances must have been particularly difficult and painful. At about 3 PM that Friday, Jesus cried out in a loud voice, bowed his head, and died.[1] The Roman soldiers and onlookers recognized his moment of death.[1]

Since the Jews did not want the bodies to remain on the crosses after sunset, the beginning of the Sabbath, they asked Pontius Pilate to order crucifracture to hasten the deaths of the three crucified men.[1] The soldiers broke the legs of the two thieves, but when they came to Jesus and saw that he was already dead, they did not break his legs.[1] Rather, one of the soldiers pierced his side, probably with an infantry spear, and produced a sudden flow of blood and water.[1] Later that day, Jesus' body was taken down from the cross and placed in a tomb.[1]

DEATH OF JESUS

Two aspects of Jesus' death have been the source of great controversy, namely, the nature of the wound in his side[4,6] and the cause of his death after only several hours on the cross.[13-17]

The gospel of John describes the piercing of Jesus' side and emphasizes the sudden flow of blood and water.[1] Some authors have interpreted the flow of water to be ascites[12] or urine, from an abdominal midline perforation of the bladder.[15] However, the Greek word (πλευρα, or pleura)[32,35,36] used by John clearly denoted laterality and often implied the ribs.[6,32,36] Therefore, it seems probable that the wound was in the thorax and well away from the abdominal midline.

Although the side of the wound was not designated by John, it traditionally has been depicted on the right side.[4] Supporting this tradition is the fact that a large flow of blood would be more likely with a perforation of the distended and thin-walled right atrium or ventricle than the thick-walled and contracted left ventricle. Although the side of the wound may never be established with certainty, the right seems more probable than the left.

Some of the skepticism in accepting John's description has arisen from the difficulty in explaining, with medical accuracy, the flow of both blood and water. Part of this difficulty has been based on the assumption that the blood appeared first, then the water. However, in the ancient Greek, the order of words generally denoted prominence and not necessarily a time sequence.[37] Therefore, it seems likely that John was emphasizing the prominence of blood rather than its appearance preceding the water.

Therefore, the water probably represented serous pleural and pericardial fluid,[5-7,11] and would have preceded the flow of blood and been smaller in volume than the blood. Perhaps in the setting of hypovolemia and impending acute heart failure, pleural and pericardial effusions may have developed and would have added to the volume of apparent water.[5,11] The blood, in contrast, may have originated from the right atrium or the right ventricle (Fig 7) or perhaps from a hemopericardium.[5,7,11]

Jesus' death after only three to six hours on the cross surprised even Pontius Pilate.[1] The fact that Jesus cried out in a loud voice and then bowed his head and died suggests the possibility of a catastrophic terminal event. One popular explanation has been that Jesus died of cardiac rupture. In the setting of the scourging and crucifixions with associated hypovolemia, hypoxemia, and perhaps an altered coagulable state, friable non-infective thrombotic vegetations could have formed on the aortic or mitral valve. These then could have dislodged and embolized into the coronary circulation and thereby produced an acute transmural myocardial infarction. Thrombotic valvular vegetations have been reported to develop under analogous acute traumatic conditions.[39] Rupture of the left ventricular free wall may occur, though uncommonly, in the first few hours following infarction.[40]

However, another explanation may be more likely. Jesus' death may have been hastened simply by his state of exhaustion and by the severity of the scourging, with its resultant blood loss and preshock state.[7] The fact that he could not carry his patibulum supports this interpretation. The actual cause of Jesus' death, like that of other crucified victims, may have been multifactorial and related primarily to hypovolemic shock, exhaustion asphyxia, and perhaps acute heart failure.[2,3,5-7,10,11] A fatal cardiac arrhythmia may have accounted for the apparent catastrophic terminal event.

Thus, it remains unsettled whether Jesus died of cardiac rupture or of cardiorespiratory failure. However, the important feature may be not *how* he died but rather *whether* he died. Clearly, the weight of historical and medical evidence indicates that Jesus was dead before the wound to his side was inflicted and supports the traditional view that the spear, thrust between his right ribs, probably perforated not only the right lung but also the pericardium and heart and thereby ensured his death (Fig 7). Accordingly, interpretations based on the assumption that Jesus did not die on the cross appear to be at odds with modern medical knowledge.

References

1. Matthew 26:17-27:61, Mark 14:12-15:47, Luke 22:7-23:56, John 13:1-19:42, in *The Holy Bible* (New International Version). Grand Rapids, Mich, Zondervan Bible Publishers, 1978.
2. Lumpkin R: The physical suffering of Christ. *J Med Assoc Ala* 1978;47:8-10,47.
3. Johnson CD: Medical and cardiological aspects of the passion and crucifixion of Jesus, the Christ. *Bol Assoc Med PR* 1978;70:97-102.
4. Barb AA: The wound in Christ's side. *J Warburg Courtauld Inst* 1971;34:320-321.
5. Bucklin R: The legal and medical aspects of the trial and death of Christ. *Sci Law* 1970;10:14-26.
6. Mikulicz-Radecki FV: The chest wound in the crucified Christ. *Med News* 1966;14:30-40.
7. Davis CT: The crucifixion of Jesus: The passion of Christ from a medical point of view. *Ariz Med* 1965;22:183-187.
8. Tenney SM: On death by crucifixion. *Am Heart J* 1964;68:286-287.
9. Bloomquist ER: A doctor looks at crucifixion. *Christian Herald*, March 1964, pp 35, 46-48.
10. DePasquale NP, Burch GE: Death by crucifixion. *Am Heart J* 1963;66:434-435.
11. Barbet P: *A Doctor at Calvary: The Passion of Our Lord Jesus Christ as Described by a Surgeon*, Earl of Wicklow (trans). Garden City, NY, Doubleday Image Books, 1953, pp 12-18, 37-147, 159-175, 187-208.
12. Primrose WB: A surgeon looks at the crucifixion. *Hibbert J*, 1949, pp 382-388.
13. Bergsma S: Did Jesus die of a broken heart? *Calvin Forum* 1948;14:163-167.
14. Whitaker JR: The physical cause of the death of our Lord. *Cath Manchester Guard* 1937;15:83-91.
15. Clark CCP: What was the physical cause of the death of Jesus Christ? *Med Rec* 1890;38:543. 16.
16. Cooper HC: The agony of death by crucifixion. *NY Med J* 1883;38:150-153.
17. Stroud W: *Treatise on the Physical Cause of the Death of Christ and Its Relation to the Principles and Practice of Christianity*, ed 2. London, Hamilton & Adams, 1871, pp 28-156, 489-494.
18. Allen AC: *The Skin: A Clinicopathological Treatise*, ed 2. New York. Grune & Stratton Inc, 1967, pp 745-747.
19. Sutton RL Jr: *Diseases of the Skin*, ed 11. St Louis, CV Mosby Co, 1956, pp 1393-1394.
20. Scott CT: A case of haematidrosis. *Br Med J* 1918;1:532-533.
21. Klauder JV: Stigmatization. *Arch Dermatol Syphilol* 1938;37:650-659.
22. Weaver KF: The mystery of the shroud. *Natl Geogr* 1980;157:730-753.
23. Tzaferis V: Jewish tombs at and near Giv'at ha-Mivtar, Jerusalem. *Israel Explor J* 1970;20:18-32.
24. Haas N: Anthropological observations on the skeletal remains from Giv'at ha-Mivtar. *Israel Explor J* 1970;20:38-59.
25. McDowell J: *The Resurrection Factor*. San Bernardino, Calif, Here's Life Publishers, 1981, pp 20-53, 75-103.
26. McDowell J: *Evidence That Demands a Verdict: Historical Evidences for the Christian Faith*. San Bernardino, Calif, Here's Life Publishers, 1979, pp 39-87, 141-263.
27. McDowell J: *More Than a Carpenter*. Wheaton, Ill, Tyndale House Publishers, 1977, pp 36-71, 89-100.
28. Hengel M: *Crucifixion in the Ancient World and the Folly of the Message of the Cross*, Bowden J (trans). Philadelphia, Fortress Press, 1977, pp 22-45, 86-90.
29. Ricciotti G: *The Life of Christ*, Zizzamia AI (trans). Milwaukee, Bruce Publishing Co, 1947, pp 29-57, 78-153, 161-167, 586-647.
30. Pfeiffer CF, Vos HF, Rea J (eds): *Wycliffe Bible Encyclopedia*. Chicago, Moody Press, 1975, pp 149-152, 404-405, 713-723, 1173-1174, 1520-1523.
31. Greenleaf S: *An Examination of the Testimony of the Four Evangelists by the Rules of Evidence Administered in the Courts of Justice*. Grand Rapids, Mich, Baker Book House, 1965, p 29.
32. Hatch E, Redpath HA: *A Concordance to the Septuagint and the Other Greek Versions of the Old Testament (Including the Apocryphal Books)*. Graz, Austria, Akademische Druce U Verlagsanstalt, 1975, p 1142.
33. Wuest KS: *Wuest Word Studies From the Greek New Testament for the English Reader*. Grand Rapids, Mich, WB Eerdmans Publisher, 1973, vol 1, p 280.
34. Friedrich G: *Theological Dictionary of the New Testament*, Bremiley G (ed-trans). Grand Rapids, Mich, WB Eerdmans Publisher, 1971, vol 7, pp 572, 573, 632.
35. Arndt WF, Gingrich FW: *A Greek-English Lexicon of the New Testament and Other Early Christian Literature*. University of Chicago Press, 1957, p 673.
36. Brown F, Driver SR, Briggs CA: *A Hebrew and English Lexicon of the Old Testament With an Appendix Containing the Biblical Aramaic*. Oxford, England, Clarendon Press, 1953, pp 841, 854.
37. Robertson AT: *A Grammar of the Greek New Testament in Light of Historical Research*. Nashville, Tenn. Broadman Press, 1931, pp 417-427.
38. Jackson SM (ed): *The New Schaff-Herzog Encyclopedia of Religious Knowledge*. New York, Funk & Wagnalls, 1909, pp 312-314.
39. Kim H-S, Suzuki M, Lie JT, et al: Nonbacterial thrombotic endocarditis (NBTE) and disseminated intravascular coagulation (DIC): Autopsy study of 36 patients. *Arch Pathol Lab Med* 1977;101:65-68.
40. Becker AE, van Mantgem J-P: Cardiac tamponade: A study of 50 hearts. *Eur J Cardiol* 1975;3:349-358.

JAMA March 21, 1986—Vol 255, No. 11

Death of Christ—Edwards et al   **1463**

The Various Types of Biblical Criticism

Biblical criticism is a form of ***Historical Criticism*** that seeks to analyze the ***Bible*** through asking certain questions of the text, such as: Who wrote it? When was it written? To whom was it written? Why was it written? What was the historical, geographical, and cultural setting of the text? How well preserved is the original text? How unified is the text? What sources were used by the author? How was the text transmitted over time? What is the text's genre and from what sociological setting is it derived? When and how did it come to become part of the ***Bible***?

Textual criticism is a branch of ***philology*** that examines the extant manuscript copies of an ***ancient*** or ***medieval*** literary work to produce a ***text*** that is as close as possible to the original. The original is called the ***autograph***.

Source Criticism is an aspect of ***historical criticism***, a method of literary study used especially in the field of ***biblical criticism*** that seeks to understand a literary piece better by attempting to establish the sources used by the author and/or redactor who put the literary piece together. Sometimes biblical scholars use the term ***literary criticism*** as a synonym for source criticism.

Form criticism is a method of ***biblical criticism*** applied as a means of analyzing the typical features of texts, especially their conventional forms or structures, in order to relate them to their sociological contexts. Form criticism begins by identifying a text's genres or conventional literary forms, such as ***parable***s, ***proverb***s, epistles, or ***love poem***s. It goes on to seek the sociological setting for each text's genres, its "situation in life" (German: *Sitz in Leben*). For example, the sociological setting of a law is a court, or the sociological setting of a psalm of praise (hymn) is a worship context, or that of a ***proverb*** might be a father to son admonition. Having identified and analyzed the text's genre-pericopes, form criticism goes on to ask how these smaller genre-pericopes contribute to the purpose of the text as a whole.

Tradition history/criticism is a methodology of ***Biblical criticism*** that was developed by ***Hermann Gunkel***. Tradition history seeks to analyze biblical literature in terms of the process by which biblical traditions passed from stage to stage into its final form, especially how it passed from oral tradition when it was passed down by word of mouth to the final stage in the written form. Tradition History/Criticism is a sister discipline of ***Form Criticism***--also associated with Gunkel who used the results of source and form criticism to develop the history of tradition interpretation. ***Form Criticism*** and Tradition Criticism thus overlap, though the former is more narrow in focus. Tradition History is connected with secular Folklore Studies, especially Alex Olrik's analysis of Scandinavian folklore and the "laws" which he established concerning the nature of such folklore. The stories in the Bible were then analyzed on the basis of these "laws".

taken from: http://www.spiritus-temporis.com/biblical-criticism/types-of-biblical-criticism.html

"Dome of the Rock" — Inscription on the *Outer* Face of the Octagonal Arcade

S: In the name of God the Merciful, the Compassionate. There is no god but God alone, without partner. Say: He is God, One, God, the Everlasting, who has not begotten and has not been begotten. He is without equal. [Qur'an 112] Muhammad is God's messenger, may God bless him.

SW: In the name of God the Merciful, the Compassionate. There is no god but God alone, without partner. Muhammad is God's messenger. God and His angels send blessings on the Prophet.

W: 0 you who believe, send blessings on him and salute him with all respect. [Qur'an 33:56] In the name of God the Merciful, the Compassionate. There is no god but God alone. Praise

NW: to God who has not taken a son and who doesn't have any partner in dominion nor any protector out of humbleness. Magnify Him greatly. [Qur'an 17:111] Muhammad is God's messenger.

N: May God, His angels and His messengers bless him and God grant him peace and mercy. In the name of God the Merciful, the Compassionate. There is no god but God alone, without partner.

NE. To Him belongs dominion and to Him belong praise. He gives life and He makes to die; He is powerful over all things. [conflation of Qur'an 64:1 and 57.2] Muhammad is God's messenger, may God bless him and accept his intercession on the day of resurrection for his community.

E: In the name of God the Merciful, the Compassionate. There is no god but God alone, without partner. Muhammad is God's messenger, may God bless him. There built this dome the servant of God

SE: 'Ab[d al-Malik, commander] of believers, in the year seventy-two, may God accept [it] from him and be pleased with him. Amen. Lord of the worlds. Praise to God.

"Dome of the Rock" — Inscription on the *Inner* Face of the Octagonal Arcade

S: In the name of God the Merciful, the Compassionate. There is no god but God alone, without partner. To Him belongs dominion and to Him belongs praise. He gives life and He makes to die; He is powerful over all things. [conflation of Qur'an 64:1 and 57:2] Muhammad is God's servant and His messenger.

SE. God and His angels send blessings on the Prophet. 0 you who believe, send blessings on him and salute him with all respect. [Qur'an 33:56] May God bless him and grant him peace and mercy. 0 people of the book, do not go beyond the bounds in your religion,

E: nor say anything but the truth about God. The Messiah Jesus son of Mary, was only God's messenger, His word that He committed to Mary, and a spirit proceeding from Him. So believe in God and His messengers. Do not say 'three'. Refrain,

NE: it is better for you. For God is one god. Glory he to Him - that He should have a son! To Him belongs all that is in the heavens and in the earth. God suffices for a guardian [Qur'an 4:171]. The Messiah will not disdain to be

N: God's servant; nor will the angels who are stationed near to Him. Whoever disdains to serve him and waxes proud, He will muster them to Him, all of them. [Qur'an 4:172] 0 God, bless your messenger and servant, Jesus

NW: son of Mary. Peace be upon him the day he was born, the day he dies, and the day he is raised up alive. That is Jesus son of Mary, in word of truth, about which they are doubting. It is not for God to take a son. Glory be to Him.

W: When He decrees a thing, he only says to it 'Be' and it is. God is my lord and your lord. So serve Him. This is a straight path. [Qur'an 19:34-36 paraphrased] God, His angels, and men possessed of knowledge and upholding justice bear witness that there is no god but He. There is no god but He

SW: the all-mighty, the all-wise. The true religion with God is Islam. Those who were given the book did not dissent except after knowledge came to them, when they became envious of each other. Whoever disbelieves in God's-signs, God will swiftly call to account. [Qur'an 3:18-19].

TO THE ENDS OF THE EARTH

Act V – Scenes 1 & 3 of Yahweh's Grand Drama

Hands of Hur Biblical Literacy Series
Part Three

I. UNIT 1 — "Myth, Mystery, and *Misunderstanding*"

   A. Modern Myths About an Ancient Book

      1. Myth #1: The Old Testament is primarily a "Jewish" book, and the New Testament is primarily a "Christian" book.

      2. Myth #2: The Old Testament in built around the principle of obedience (law), and the New Testament is built around the principle of grace (liberty).

      3. Myth #3: The divisions, "Old Testament" and "New Testament" are reasonable and helpful.

   B. Our Invention: A "Three Story" Bible

      1. Old Testament   - the "basement"; the story about the people of Israel

      2. Gospels   - the "ground floor"; the story about Jesus

      3. New Testament   - the "top floor"; the story about the Church

      4. We tend to think in terms of an "old, old, story" and a "new and improved" story:

         a. Christian book titles betray our bias (88% vs 12%).

         b. Question: When I share "the Gospel," who do I start with? Jesus? Abraham? Adam?

         c. Question: When I think of "the Gospel," do I think of a story or a gift?

      5. We seem to privately believe that the Old Testament is more of a "Jewish" book, and the New Testament is a "Christian" book.

         a. Yet, out of the 777,687 words in the Bible, the word, "Jew" appears 286x, and 200 of them are in the New Testament!

         b. Out of the 188,654 words in our New Testament, the word "Christian" only occurs three times!

         c. Of the 66 books of the Bible, 64 of them are written by Jews, including 25 New Testament books.

         d. We mistakenly think of the NT as a book on "how to live" as Christians (getting God into *our* "story"), rather than the record of the *living out* of the one Story (myself into *his* Story).

         e. But the greatest tragedy is that we simply do not *think* in terms of the Story, so we live in terms of our own.

   C. God's Intention: A "One Story" Bible

      1. The Bible contains the one Story of *"the one God and Father of all who is over all, and through all and in all."* **Eph. 4:6**

      2. Believers in that one Story of the one God become part of *"the one Body, the one hope, the one faith, and the one baptism."* **Eph. 4:4-5**

      3. The word that challenges all these misconceptions is the word that turns our "Three Story" Bible back into the one Story of the one God, is the word, "covenant."

      4. Covenant - In Hebrew, is the word, *berith,* and in Greek, the word, *diathēkē.*

         a. Appears 282x in the OT and 34x in the NT; but only 6x in the Gospels and Acts!

         b. Unfortunately, our English Bibles follow the Latin Vulgate's designations: *Vestus Testimentum* and *Novus Testamentum.*

         c. The words "testament" and "covenant" have virtually nothing in common in our modern world, and this is only contributes to our misunderstanding of the one Story.

          "The Abrahamic covenant is the overarching plan that unites God's dealings with his people and bridges the Old and New Testaments. This was God's unconditional plan for his people that he would see through to the end."   **The Journey From Texts to Translation, p 32**

   D. God's Intervention: Editing the "Story" of a Rabid Rabbi

      1. Paul (like us) believed that there was only one "Story"…his!

      2. Saul's conversion and subsequent ministry is a parable of sorts, of the problem.

         a. The details of his conversion are very significant (Acts 9:1-22).

> *"Saul rose from the ground, and although his eyes were opened, he saw nothing. So they led him by the hand and brought him into Damascus.... And immediately something like scales fell from his eyes, and he regained his sight. Then he rose and was baptized;"* **Acts 9:8, 18**

b. Paul's "healing" caused him to realize that the Story began with *Adam*, not Abraham, and ended with all of creation, not merely the Jews (Rom 5:14; 1 Cor 15:22,45; Eph 1:7-10; 2:11-16):

> *"Yet death reigned from Adam to Moses, even over those whose sinning was not like the transgression of Adam, who was a type of the one who was to come."* **Romans 5:14**

> *"For as in Adam all die, so also in Christ shall all be made alive.... Thus it is written, 'The first man Adam became a living being'; the last Adam became a life-giving spirit."* **1 Cor. 15:22, 45**

c. Paul called the Story a *mustērion*, a *"mystery"* hidden until the proper time.[1]

(1) Jesus only used this word *once*, to talk about what he called *"the kingdom"* (Mk 4:11; Mt 13:11; Lk 8:10).

(2) Paul used the word twenty times in four letters to refer to the Story (Romans, 1 Corinthians, Ephesians, Colossians).

(3) Paul's "mystery" was what Jesus, the apostles and the early Church called, "the Gospel."

> *"...and also for me, that words may be given to me in opening my mouth boldly to proclaim the mystery of the gospel,"* **Ephesians 6:19**

- •Jesus preached it to Jews (Matt 9:35; Mk 4:11)
- •Peter preached it to Jews, Samaritans and Gentiles (Acts 2,8,10)
- •Paul preached it to Jews and Gentiles (Acts 14)

d. This "mystery" was something prophets predicted yet didn't comprehend!

> *"Concerning this salvation, the prophets who prophesied about the grace that was to be yours searched and inquired carefully, inquiring what person or time the Spirit of Christ in them was indicating when he predicted the sufferings of Christ and the subsequent glories. It was revealed to them that they were serving not themselves but you, in the things that have now been announced to you through those who preached the good news to you by the Holy Spirit sent from heaven, things into which angels long to look."* **1 Peter 1:10-12**

e. The Story is a "mystery" even to the angelic hosts of heaven and hell! (1 Pet 1:12; Eph 3:8-13).

f. Paul's *"mystery"* had three main components:

(1) It was the playing out of the purposes and will of God; his *"plan for the fulness of time..."*[2]

> *"In him we have redemption through his blood, the forgiveness of our trespasses, according to the riches of his grace, which he lavished upon us, in all wisdom and insight making known to us the mystery of his will, according to his purpose, which he set forth in Christ as a plan for the fullness of time, to unite all things in him, things in heaven and things on earth."* **Ephesians 1:7-10**

(2) It would reunite and restore all of God's creation:

> *"For I consider that the sufferings of this present time are not worth comparing with the glory that is to be revealed to us. For the creation waits with eager longing for the revealing of the sons of God. For the creation was subjected to futility, not willingly, but because of him who subjected it, in hope that the creation itself will be set free from its bondage to decay and obtain the freedom of the glory of the children of God. For we know that the whole creation has been groaning together in the pains of childbirth until now. And not only the creation, but we ourselves, who have the first fruits of the Spirit, groan inwardly as we wait eagerly for adoption as sons, the redemption of our bodies. For in this hope we were saved. Now hope that is seen is not hope. For who hopes for what he sees? But if we hope for what we do not see, we wait for it with patience."* **Romans 8:18-25**

(3) It was centered around and dependent upon the person and the work of Yeshua, the Son of God:

---

[1] *Musterion* is a derivative of *muō*, "to shut the mouth"; the verb only appears once in our New Testament, by Paul in Philippians 4:12, *"I have learned the secret...".* The word came to mean, *"to initiate into the mysteries,"* or *"to teach fully."*

[2] Redemption is much, much larger that simply a solution for humanity's *forensic* problem with God, i.e. our "guilt". In other words, redemption is larger than justification, although it includes it.

"He has delivered us from the domain of darkness and transferred us to the kingdom of his beloved Son, in whom we have redemption, the forgiveness of sins. He is the image of the invisible God, the firstborn of all creation. For by him all things were created, in heaven and on earth, visible and invisible, whether thrones or dominions or rulers or authorities—all things were created through him and for him. And he is before all things, and in him all things hold together. And he is the head of the body, the church. He is the beginning, the firstborn from the dead, that in everything he might be preeminent. For in him all the fullness of God was pleased to dwell, and through him to reconcile to himself all things, whether on earth or in heaven, making peace by the blood of his cross."
Colossians 1:13-20

E. Our Investigation: The Final Chapter of the One Story—Book of the 2nd Covenant

1. Our "Map": The Book of Acts

   a. It is the only book in our New "Testament" that is an "intentional narrative."[1]

   b. It's OK to think of Acts chronicling the "birth of the Church," as long as we see Genesis 3 through Malachi 4 as its "gestation"!

2. The Book of Acts: The *Missing* "Manual"

   a. Luke-Acts is the major component of our New "Testament" (27% compared to Paul's contribution of 24%).

   b. It provides for the New "Testament" what we *lacked* for the Old "Testament"—a vital link between what preceded and followed it.[2]

   c. Acts gives us an amazing look into the collision of the Kingdom of God with three influential cultures of the first century: Greek, Roman and Jewish

   (1) "Jew" - 75x

   (2) "Greek" - 13x

   (3) "Rome/Roman" - 19x

   (4) "Gentile" - 30x

   (5) "Samaritan" - 1x

   d. Without the Book of Acts, we would lack:

   (1) Any record of the fulfillment of Jesus' promised Holy Spirit.

   (2) Any record of who "Paul" is and why he called himself an "apostle."

   (3) Any record of why "churches" replaced synagogues as the focal point of worship.

   (4) Any record of what happened to the apostles after Jesus left.

   (5) Any record of how the Story got to Asia, Greece and Rome.

   (6) The necessary context for all of the writings of the Apostles.

3. The Book of Acts: A *Misused* "Manual"

   a. The genre of the Book of Acts is narrative, *not* didactic; it is historical not theological.

   (1) It contains 676 references to 115 names for 134 people!

   (2) It contains 432 references to 101 names for actual places.[3]

   b. If I am to pull theology from this book, it should come first from the teaching or preaching sections, *not* the narrative sections.[4]

---

[1] The four Gospels, by contrast, are immensely difficult to assign a genre to. Some scholars have used the term "Lives" to describe their unique place in biblical literature. In his Gospel, Luke also clearly tells us his methodology and sources (cf. Lk 1:1-4), which we may assume were also employed in his composition of its "sequel," the Book of Acts.

[2] For example, we have no hint of Pharisees, Sadducees, synagogues, and an enormous Temple in our Old Testament. They simply "appear" in the Gospels. Acts, on the other hand, provides us with a wonderful link between the four Gospels and the Epistles of our

[3] For example, Acts 18 alone lists 8 cities and 7 regions. See chart on page 101 for a full list of place names and personal names.

[4] This is important because *Acts* is *not* "dripping" with the supernatural like some people assume or insist. In a very real sense, *Acts* should be the literal "last place" we go when formulating theology because of its genre. We *should* "go there," but after we've exhausted the teaching sections on the particular doctrine at hand. *Acts* can provide some illustrative perspective.

(1) There are only 9 references to "healing," and 5 references to "tongues" compared to 21 in 1 Corinthians (i.e. 12-14).

(2) The "Holy Spirit" is mentioned 53x, the same number as in the Gospels, and less than half as many times as the rest of the New "Testament" (e.g. 136).

(3) There are only 2 references to people "prophesying" in Acts (2:18; 19:6).

(4) Of the 33 references to "prophets" in Acts, only 4 are for people in the church.

(5) There are 13 *sermons* in Acts, by 3 different people that make up 23% of the entire book (see chart in Appendix Section).

    (a) The theology of Acts was "unfolding before their eyes" in a very real sense.

    (b) The Jewish believers were being forced to rethink everything they had known and believed about Yahweh and his purposes.

    (c) They were, in a very real sense, faced with Jesus' prior teaching on new wine and wineskins and the *"scribe who has been trained for the kingdom of heaven…"* (cf. Matt. 9:17; 13:52).

c. This book chronicles the *unfolding* of a Story 20 centuries old, *not* the telling of something "new."

d. To miss this is to misrepresent the Gospel, misunderstand the purpose of the Church, and possibly waste my life.[1]

*"Therefore I, the prisoner of the Lord, implore you to **walk** in a manner **worthy of the calling** with which you have been called…"*   **Ephesians 4:1**

*"Only **conduct yourselves** in a manner **worthy of the gospel of Christ**, so that whether I come and see you or remain absent, I will hear of you that you are standing firm in one spirit, with one mind striving together for the faith of the gospel;"*   **Philippians 1:27**

*"…so that you will **walk in a manner worthy of the Lord**, to please Him in all respects, bearing fruit in every good work and increasing in the knowledge of God;"*   **Colossians 1:10**

*"…so that you would **walk in a manner worthy of the God** who calls you into His own kingdom and glory."*   **1 Thessalonians 2:12**

*"This is a plain indication of God's righteous judgment so that you will be **considered worthy of the kingdom of God**, for which indeed you are suffering."*   **2 Thessalonians 1:5**

*"To this end also we pray for you always, that our God will count you **worthy of your calling**, and fulfill every desire for goodness and the work of faith with power,"*   **2 Thessalonians 1:11**

e. Acts gives us a look at priorities and values of those caught up in the Story when it first moved from "mystery" to reality.

F. Summing Up: Our Primary Goals For *"To The Ends of the Earth"*

1. To seek to comprehend the enormity of this "Story we find ourselves in."

2. To allow this enlarged view of the Gospel to propel us into a new passion for an informed evangelism.

3. To grow in our commitment to *live out* the Story, not merely know it better (1 Cor 13:2).

II. UNIT 2 — "Clash of the Titans: Making Way for 'The Way'"

A. An Irrelevant Book or an Ignorant Readership?

"'Fear not little flock': this seems apt for those pious watercolor people so long ago, those blameless and endearing shepherds and fishermen, in colorful native garb, whose lives seems pure, because they are not our lives. They were rustics, silent and sunlit, outdoors, whom we sentimentalize and ignore. They are not in our world. They had some nascent sort of money, but not the kind to take seriously. They got their miracles, perhaps, but they died anyway, long ago, and so did their children. Salvation is obviously for them, and so is God, for they are, like the very young and the very old in our world, peripheral. Religion is for outcasts and victims; Jesus made that clear. Religion suits primitives. They have time to work up their touching faith in unverifiable promises, and they might as well, having bugger-all else.…Our lives are complex. There are many things we must consider before we go considering any lilies. There are many things we must fear. We are in charge; we are running things in a world we made; we are nobody's little flock."   **"The Book of Luke"** in *The Annie Dillard Reader.* **page 272**

---

[1] This abbreviated list of scriptural injunctions takes on an elevated seriousness in light of the majesty of the One Story and my role in it.

1. The "irrelevance" of the Bible is more a product of our own ignorance than any insufficiency of scripture.

2. "Relevancy" is really a measure of *"how closely connected or appropriate something is to the matter at hand."*

3. In order to make a judgment on the "relevancy" of the Bible, I need to be as adequately informed about the *ancient past* (the cultural context of composition), *and* the present (cultural context of application).[1]

4. Two vital questions:

    a. What *was* the cultural context that produced our "New Testament"?

    b. What similarity, if any, is there with the culture we find ourselves immersed in?

B. Jesus Might Have Been Born in a Manger…The Church Wasn't!

1. "The Way" (Acts 24:14) emerged in the center of a collision of three global cultures:

    a. GREEK: The influence of Alexander was everywhere in the known world in the form of architecture, language and thought.

    b. ROMAN: The evidence of Rome's military might was everywhere present in the form of prefects, praetoria, and proconsuls.

    c. JEWISH: There were Jewish populations throughout the known world, with special concentrations in N. Africa, Egypt, Syria and Rome.

2. Judaism had more in common with "The Way" than it did with Athens or Rome.

    a. "The Way" was, after all, Jewish in origin, nature and purpose.

    b. "The Way" and Judaism were the only monotheistic religions in a polytheistic and pluralistic world.

    c. While Judaism *opposed* "The Way," it was not its "enemy" in the same sense Athens and Rome were.

C. *The World of Our New Testament — "What Goes Around Comes Around"*

1. Roman culture's one key value: *dignitas* (see "Roman Social Structure" on page A-3)

    a. Status & Image

        (1) *"You are who you appear to be."* (clothing, seating, affiliations)

        (2) The Roman toga could only be worn by citizens.

        (3) Senatorial order, by law, wore a toga with broad purple stripe, sat in front rows at public spectacles and monopolized the religious offices.

        (4) The *minimum* requirement for entry into the Senatorial order was one million sisterces (500,000 denarii; 685 years of work for a day laborer!)

    b. Status and Association

        (1) "You are who you appear with."

        (2) Clients and patrons – the transfer of status by association.[2]

            (a) Status verified by the *number* and "quality" of your clients.

            (b) Housing arrangements in Rome reflected this philosophy (integration versus segregation).[3]

> *"The notion that all people are equal is utterly alien to the ancient Roman mind."*
> **Garrett Fagan, University of Pennsylvania**

---

[1] The principle, I*"God's word to us was first God's word to someone else."* is very relevant as we begin our study of the final pages of our Bible. Understanding the culture that shaped not only the lives, but the *thinking* of those who populate the pages of the New Testament *and* those who actually gave us the New Testament. These men and women were not living or writing in a vacuum. To fail to recognize this is to show a lapse of integrity in our Bible study and teaching.

[2] Patrons often provided financial security as well as status to their clients, in exchange for support in the arenas where the patron would want it (politics, etc.). Clients could also have clients of their own, and be a sort of patron themselves. It is very likely that Theophilus mentioned by Luke, was Luke's patron and financed his research for his Gospel and the Book of Acts.

[3] One's status was not determined or illustrated by where one lived, like it is in the U.S. The world of status in Roman culture needs to be perceived more like a series of intersecting circles rather than a pyramid or hierarchy.

c. Status and Leisure[1]

    (1) "You are what you do."[2]

    (2) Cicero spoke of, *"...craftsmen, petty shopkeepers, and all that filth of the cities."*

                                                                       Pro Flacco, 18

    (3) Consider this graffiti from ancient Rome:

        "I hate poor people. If anyone wants something for nothing, he's a fool. Let him pay up and he'll get it."

        "Baths, wine, and love-making destroy our bodies, yet love-making, wine, and baths make life worth living."

    (4) Slavery in Roman culture was an issue of status, *not* ethnicity.

    (5) Status categories among slaves prevented a "slave identity" from emerging (e.g. there were only 2 slave uprisings in Roman history; one was Spartacus in 75 BC).[3]

    (6) Having the time to enjoy leisure activities and/or the money to provide entertainment facilities and activities for the populace were signs of status.

        "Among ancient peoples, the Romans were the first to develop a genuine culture of public leisure and mass entertainment. The provision of "conveniences" (Latin, commoda) for the enjoyment of the masses was both seen and presented as a cardinal benefit of the central imperial and local regional administrations."

                                                             Garrett Fagan

d. Status and Entitlement

    (1) Upper classes (recognizable by name and appearance) got the best seats at spectacles, larger portions of state allotments, finer food at banquets, smaller fines, and impunity from lawsuits by lower classes.

    (2) Even the expansive aqueduct system brought water into the cities for entertainment and leisure (e.g. public baths), running for miles above the heads of the poor in the fields (at least for 30 of the 260 miles).

2. Greek Culture's Key Value: *anthropos (esp. andrēs!)*

  a. THEOLOGY: *"So man created god in his own likeness."*

    (1) Greek mythology is a *non-revelatory* religious system.[4]

    (2) Greek mythology has no "sacred texts," and therefore no "theology," only an exalted anthropology.

    (3) There are no creeds, therefore no "heresy." (Inquisitions or Fatwas either!)

    (4) The gods and the myths surrounding them could, and did evolve to serve the purposes of the people.

    (5) *"New and interesting"* had precedence over *"absolute and true"* (cf. Acts 17: 21).

  b. RELIGION: No First Amendment Needed

    (1) Greeks made a distinction between religion (public) and faith (private).

    (2) Because of the Greek emphases on the *polis,* (city) and *isonomia* (equal before the law), "religion" was always employed for the social good.[5]

---

[1] Roman culture tended to trust the rich and mistrust the poor because they believed only the rich could "afford" to be honest because they were already secure and didn't need to manipulate people to get something they wanted, but didn't have, like the poor.

[2] Certain members of Roman society, as evidenced in Cicero's comment, were looked down upon simply because of their work. This is a ramped up version of the U.S. distinctions of "white collar" and "blue collar" jobs. The major difference is that in Roman culture, one was actually despised if he performed certain tasks for a living.

[3] Slaves would see themselves as having more in common with slaves that were like them (ancestry, birthplace, cause of enslavement, etc.) than they would with each other as "slaves" in contrast to those who were "non-slaves." In other words, it would be very difficult for an "us" versus "they" mentality to fester, and this is at the heart of any rebellion or revolution.

[4] In Greek mythology, the gods may "speak," but it's to one another or *about* humanity rather than *to* humanity.

[5] Also, because of the polytheistic, anthropomorphic nature of Greek and Roman religion, there was "something for everyone," and a "god" for every occasion.

(3) But, Greek religion was very anthropocentric rather than theocentric.

    (a) The focal point of Greek religious architecture was the *bomos* (altar), not the *naon* (temple).[1]

    (b) Where the sacrifices were performed was more important than where the "god/goddess" dwelt *(agalma)*.

    (c) Greek religious sacrifices were community-wide festivals and feasts often built around the agricultural and astronomical cycles.[2]

c. HOMOSEXUALITY: More than men in tights

    (1) During the Classical Period (prior to Alexander), homosexuality and masculinity were synonymous, as were boyishness and femininity.

    (2) The naked *male* body was the subject of nearly all Greek sculpture during this period. (Female statues were typically clothed.).

    (3) Part of a boy's journey to manhood included being the *eronomos* (beloved) of an older Greek man, the *erastēs* (lover).

    (4) Boys were courted publicly and upon family approval, entered into a homosexual "mentorship" for a season.

    (5) The normative nature of pederasty (pais + erastēs) was tied to many social behaviors: nudity in art and athletics, delayed marriage for aristocratic men, *symposia,* and the seclusion of women.

    (6) This behavior was characteristic of the affluent elite, intellectual, leisure class.

d. WOMEN: *"Be still and know that I am a god!"*

    (1) During the Classical Period and beyond, women were viewed with suspicion, even as evil!

    (2) In The Myth of Pandora (800 BC), the creation of woman is the punishment to men for stealing fire from the gods!

    (3) Another writer in 500 BC compared women to various animals, such as the mare, the bitch, the sow, and the vixen.

    (4) Pericles' closing comment of his funeral oration after the First Peloponnesian War[3] (c. 444 BC) is very revealing:

> *"The living have envy to contend with, while those who are no longer in our path are honored with a good will into which revalry does not enter. On the other hand, if I must say anything on the subject of female excellence to those of you who will now be in widowhood, it will be all comprised in this brief exhortation. Great will be your glory in not falling short of your natural character; and greatest will be hers who is least talked of among men whether for good of for bad."*

    (5) Citizen wives slept in upstairs back bedrooms away from the *andron*, the "man's room" on the ground floor near the front.[4]

    (6) A female slave was one of life's five "necessities" (along with a house, a wife, an ox and a plow).

    (7) The "ideal" Greek wife stayed in the house, bore and raised children, avoided the public and was neither praised nor slandered by men.[5]

    (8) Self-assertion and autonomy among women in Greek culture was reserved for the realm of the prostitute and priestess.[6]

---

[1] This is largely due to the fact that these religious systems involved a lot of "bartering" with the gods; seeking their favor

[2] Think Fourth of July, Labor Day, and New Year's Day parades in towns and cities of the U.S.

[3] This was a war fought between Athens and its empire on the mainland, against the Peloponnesian League led by Sparta.

[4] The *andron* was the part of the house where the Greek *symposia* took place, parties that involved drinking, eating, conversations, and entertainment. Free women were not allowed to attend, but some *symposia* included articulate and well-read prostitutes.

[5] The idealized woman of Proverbs 31 stands as an amazing contrast. She is mobile, visible, and highly regarded for both her service and her skills.

[6] This is an extremely valuable piece of cultural insight for reading and interpreting Paul's Corinthian correspondence. For even though Corinth was a Roman city in many ways, it was still located in the center of Hellenistic culture.

e. WORTH: *"You are what you know."*

(1) Slavery *flourished* in the Greek democracy!

(a) *Not* owning a slave was evidence of extreme destitution.

(b) Greek democracy was built on participation in civic life by the greatest number of citizens possible.

(c) To play the "role" of a citizen demanded time (away from work).

(d) This liberty (i.e. freedom from work) was known as *scholē*.

(e) The existence of a world of free citizen men depended upon a world of slaves (to do the work).

(2) Aristotle: *"I think, therefore I am (not a slave!)"* [340 BC]

(a) Aristotle taught that slavery was "natural," and therefore morally good.

i)   The universe exists in a tension between "dominant" and "subordinate."

ii)   The weaker *should* serve the stronger (e.g. men vs. women).

iii) The better each party is, the better the purpose served (i.e. an excellent slave serving an excellent aristocrat is better than a poor slave serving an excellent aristocrat).

iv) Slavery is the ultimate application of this principle because humans have the most dignity.

v)   According to Aristotle, the *final* proof that a man belongs as a slave is that he *is a slave!*

(3) Schoolwork: The luxury of those with no job!

(a) Superiority was measured inversely by how much one *had* to work.

(b) The pursuit of culture (art, philosophy, poetry, politics, music) became incompatible with labor.

(c) "Low culture" was that done *within* the working class (crafts, pottery, dancing, etc.).

(d) "High culture" was expensive and enjoyed by those with *scholē* (excessive time *away* from labor).

(e) Eventually, *scholē* came to refer to the *activities* one did during leisure time, then it came to mean the *place* where these activities were pursued: "school."

3. Jewish Culture's Key Value: *hagios* (see chart on page A-4)

a. The very nature of Judaism put Jews at odds with the rest of the world.

(1) iconography was blasphemy

(2) a single shrine, altar, and priesthood

(3) all-male priesthood

(4) a single book

(5) exclusivity rather than inclusivity

b. For the Jew, there were two kinds of people in the world: "us" (Jew) and "them" (Gentile). [Jn 4:9]

c. Being marginalized was considered "proof" of holiness and election.

d. Being aloof from culture, especially it's participants and products was seen as a moral good (Lk 18:9-12).

e. Associating only with each other was seen as a moral good.

f. Holiness was the produce of specific *non-behaviors* as well as behaviors (Lk 19:1-7; 18:9-12).

(1) Where they *didn't go:*

(a) gymnasiums

(b) bath houses

(c) theaters

(d) pagan temples/markets

          (e) gentile dwellings/businesses

      (2) What they *didn't do:*

          (a) eat non-kosher food

          (b) work on the sabbath

  D. Revisiting the Question of Relevance

    1. Question: The a world characterized by pluralism, polytheism, paganism, power, pleasure, play, philosophy and Pharisaism have anything in common with the world in which you find yourself?

    2. Do these statements sound familiar?

      a. *"You are who you know."* (the country club vs. the night club)

      b. *"You are what you do."* (white collar vs. blue collar; eating out vs. being a server)

      c. *"You are what you don't do and who you don't know."* (a life that orbits around church rather than the lost; seeing the local church as a "cruise ship" rather than a "mercy ship")

III. UNIT 3 — *"From Mt. Zion to Mt. Vesuvius"*[1] – Intro to The Book of Acts

  A. ACTS: An "Intentional Narrative"

    1. A Historian With Focus Rather Than Family and Fame

      a. Luke *never* mentions himself by name in the Book of Acts.

      b. His name only appears 3x in the entire "New Testament!"

      c. Luke went *without* so that we wouldn't have to:

> *"Luke was a Syrian of Antioch, by profession a physician, the disciple of the apostles, and later a follower of Paul until his martyrdom. He served the Lord without distraction, without a wife, and without children. He died at the age of eighty-four in Boeotia* [region in central Greece], *full of the Holy Spirit."*   **(from the 2nd century, *Anti-Marionite Prologue)***

    2. A Historian With a History of Faithfulness in a World of Fickleness

      a. Everything we read about Luke comes from the imprisoned pen of Paul (Col 4:14; Phm 24: 2 Tim 4:11)[2]:

        (1) He was a physician (Col 4:14; Gk, *iatros*)[3]; 20 of the 38x this word is used, are by Luke himself!

        (2) Luke was a "fellow-worker," part of Paul's elite inner band of "mystery handlers." (Phm 24).

        (3) Luke was a faithful brother to the end (2 Tim 4:11).

        (4) Luke was a "foreigner" to God's covenant people (cf. Col 4:11 and 4:13-14).[4]

    3. Clues Left By Our Reluctant Recorder

      a. Luke was a fastidious researcher (e.g. birth & youth narratives, shepherd report, Martha/Mary, rejection at Nazareth, etc.).

      b. Luke was a "client" of an influential and wealthy "patron" (Gk, *kratistos*; cf. Lk 1:3; Acts 23:26; 26:25)[5].

---

[1] Mt. Vesuvius erupted in AD 79 destroying Pompeii and Herculaneum. It is near Naples, a port city very near Puteoli mentioned in Acts 28:13.

[2] Colossians and Philemon were written at the same time to the same location; Philemon was the owner of the home in which the church at Colossae met. Paul wrote these two letters during his first imprisonment. 2 Timothy was written during Paul's final imprisonment, a time characterized by great danger that proved to be fatal.

[3] The cognate verb of this noun is used in the Septuagint to translate "rapha" (healer), one of the actual names Yahweh takes upon himself in Exodus 15:26.

[4] Paul makes reference to one group of laborers with him as part of "the circumcision." The others (i.e. Luke), by default, are *not* part of "the circumcision," meaning they are not Jews. Luke is obviously in this second group.

[5] The ascription, "most excellent" before Theophilus is the Greek word, *kratistos*. And, both Theophilus and Epaphroditus (Josephus) must be looked upon as patrons of each of the respective writers.

Luke the Historian	Josephus the Historian
"Inasmuch as many have undertaken to compile a narrative of the things that have been accomplished among us, just as those who from the beginning were eyewitnesses and ministers of the word have delivered them to us, it seemed good to me also, having followed all things closely for some time past, to write an orderly account for you, most excellent Theophilus," **Luke, *The Gospel of Luke*, 1:1-3**	"I Suppose that by my books of the Antiquity of the Jews, most excellent Epaphroditus, have made it evident to those who peruse them, that our Jewish nation is of very great antiquity,...However, since I observe a considerable number of people giving ear to the reproaches that are laid against us by those who bear ill-will to us, and will not believe what I have written concerning the antiquity... I therefore have thought myself under an obligation to write somewhat briefly about these subjects, in order to convict those that reproach us of spite and voluntary falsehood, and to correct the ignorance of others, and withal to instruct all those who are desirous of knowing the truth of what great antiquity we really are." **Josephus, *Against Apion*, Book 1:1**
"In the first book, O Theophilus, I have dealt with all that Jesus began to do and teach, until the day when he was taken up, after he had given commands through the Holy Spirit to the apostles whom he had chosen. To them he presented himself alive after his suffering by many proofs, appearing to them during forty days and speaking about the kingdom of God." **Luke, *Acts*, 1:1-3**	"In the former book, most honored Epaphroditus, I have demonstrated our antiquity, and confirmed the truth of what I have said, from the writings of the Phoenicians, and Chaldeans, and Egyptians. I have, moreover, produced many of the Grecian writers as witnesses thereto. I have also made a refutation of Manetho and Cheremon, and of certain others of our enemies. I shall now therefore begin a confutation of the remaining authors who have written any thing against us" **Josephus, *Against Apion*, Book 2:1**

    c. Luke was a "frequent flyer" on Paul's "Gospel ship" (cf. Acts 16:10-17; 20:5-21:18; 27:1-28:16).

4. A History With a Focus Rather Than a Fullness

    a. Though mentioning 134 different people in Acts, Luke focuses on four:

        (1) Holy Spirit – 54x (next largest is Romans - 27x).

        (2) Peter – 62x (he *"drops off the scene"* in chapter 12)

        (3) Jesus[1] – 72x (his name appears in every chapter, except: 12, 14, 23, 27).

        (4) Paul – 158x (he doesn't really *"step onto the scene"* until chapter 9)

    b. In a very real sense, Luke records the fulfillment of Jesus' two final commands associated with the Great Commission: *"go"* and *"wait"* (Matt 28:16-20; Mk 16:14-20; Lk 24:46-49; Acts 1:4-11).[2]

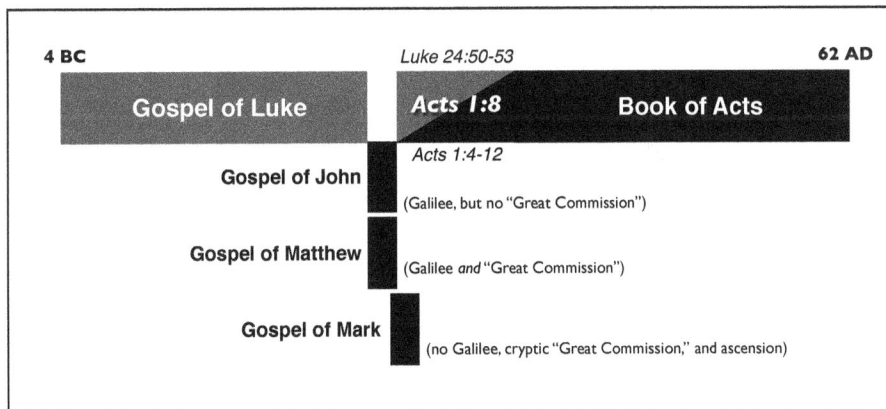

---

[1] One can note a shift in Luke's emphasis though, between Luke and Acts in terms of how he speaks of Jesus. He uses "Jesus" 104x in Luke, but only 72x in Acts, and uses "Christ" 27x in Acts compared to 12x in Luke. He uses the two words together 22x in Acts, but never in Luke. And, the phrase, "the name of Jesus" appears 12x in Acts and not at all in Luke. There is a clear distinction between the resurrected, ascended Lord Jesus Christ in Acts, and the suffering Servant of the Gospels.

[2] It is significant, perhaps, that they are told to "go" and *then* told to "wait." In a very real sense, "wait" is more of a command to "stop from going" then, rather than waiting for some idea of what to do next. They *knew* what was "next." This command to "wait" created both an anticipation as well as an eagerness. The geographical location surrounding each of these two commands is also important, and is often confused. The command to "go" (i.e. the Great Commission) was *not* given at the ascension. It was given in Galilee. The command to "wait," *was* given at the ascension, and it was given on the Mount of Olives just outside Jerusalem.

c. Luke provides us with the context for 56% of our "New Testament," by recording the majority of Paul's life.

d. He provides a *partial* context for the rest of our "New Testament," because he gives us the cultural and geographical matrix for the other nine letters.

e. The Book of Acts forms the "skeleton" upon which we can hang the other 22 books of our "New Testament." (see chart on page 15).

f. Luke stands forever as a testimony to the power of fidelity.

IV. UNIT 4 — *"Caesar's Long Arm"* – The Presence of Rome in Acts

A. LUKE: Our "Link to Latin and Legions"

1. Luke is the best source of insight into the extent of Rome's presence in the life of the young church.

   a. He's the only narrative writer in our "New Testament" to give us Pontius Pilate's fuller name (Lk 3:1; Acts 4:27).

   b. He mentions *three* Roman emperors: Caesar Augustus, Tiberius Caesar, and Claudius (Lk 2:1; 3:1; Acts 18:2).

   c. He provides us with a host of Roman names and political offices[1]:

      (1) Quirinius, "governor" of Syria (Lk 2:2); This was the most powerful Roman position in the Near East.

      (2) Pontius Pilate, "governor" of Judea (Lk 3:1).

      (3) Herod (Antipas), "tetrarch" of Galilee (Lk 3:1).

      (4) (Herod) Philip, "tetrarch" of Iturea and Trachonitis (Lk 3:1).

      (5) Lysanias, "tetrarch" of Abiline (Lk 3:1).

      (6) Cornelius, a "centurion of the Italian cohort" (Acts 10:1).

      (7) Sergius Paulus, proconsul of Cyprus (Acts 13:7).

      (8) Gallio, proconsul of Achaia (Acts 18:12).

      (9) Claudius Lysius, tribune in Jerusalem (Acts 23:26).

      (10) Felix, governor of Judea (Acts 23:23-26).

      (11) Porcius Festus, governor of Judea (Acts 24:27).

      (12) Tertullus, "attorney" in Roman affairs (Gk - *rhetor*) (Acts 24:1)

      (13) Julius, centurion in the Augustan cohort (Acts 27:1).

      (14) Publius, the "leading man" on the island of Malta (Acts 28:7).

   d. He mentions by name, half of the 26 Roman provinces of the first century. (see map on following page):

---

[1] Roman male citizens had a 3-name nomenclature consisting of: (1) *praenomen* - the "forename" or their given name; this was the only name *parents* actually gave and called their child by it. (2) *nomen* - the clan name (group of families). (3) *cognomen* - the family name. This one, along with the *nomen,* were inherited, not given. Examples of this: Gaius Julius Caesar, Marcus Antonium Felix. One would only use all three names if the situation was very "formal."

2. Understanding the "Roman Road to Retirement"

a. *"Cursus Honorum"* was the term for the career path to high status in the world of Roman politics and society.

b. Aristocrats were expected to spend some time in the Roman military on their journey to political office.

c. The Roman military was the Empire's best "propaganda machine," because it, unlike the politicians, was *everywhere*.

3. The Roman military according to Luke[1]

a. Centurion - (10x in Acts); commanded a "century" (100 men)[2]

  - highest rank attainable by a free citizen of the lower class.

  - normal career was 20 years; half died in service

b. *"Primus Pilus"* - centurion of the First Century of a legion (60 centuries)

  - after one year at this rank, could retire with 150,000 denarii bonus ($6 million; eligible for equestrian status)[3]

c. Tribune - commander of a cohort (600 men; six centuries)

d. Praetorian Guard - based in the city of Rome
  - served 16 years instead of 20
  - made triple the salary of a normal legionary soldier[4]
  - immensely powerful and influential to emperors
  - Paul spoke of this elite military band (Phil 1:13)

e. Size of army - there were 150,000 citizen soldiers in the 30 Roman legions
  - there were another 150,000 "auxiliary" non-citizens
  - citizen soldiers could expect to be part of the ruling class of the cities where they retired
  - non-citizen retirees were given full citizenship for themselves and their posterity.

f. "Auxiliaries" - Luke wrote of two: the Italian Cohort and the Augustan Cohort (Acts 10:1; 27:1)

---

[1] Warfare was "big money" for the Roman military. After conquests, slaves were sold and the revenues were given to the generals. After that, what was left was dispersed by rank. In one case, the leading officers received 800,000 denarii and the soldiers 1,500.

[2] Annual salary for Centurions of the 2-10 centuries was 7,500 denarii per year; for centuries 11-60 it was 3,750 denarii per year.

[3] His annual salary was 15,000 denarii.

[4] The salary of a legionary soldier was 225 denarii per year.

4. Roman Citizenship and the book of Acts

    a. Paul used his privileges as a Roman citizen on several occasions to his benefit (Acts 16:37; Acts 21:39; 22:38: 25:11).

THE BOOK OF ACTS & BEYOND

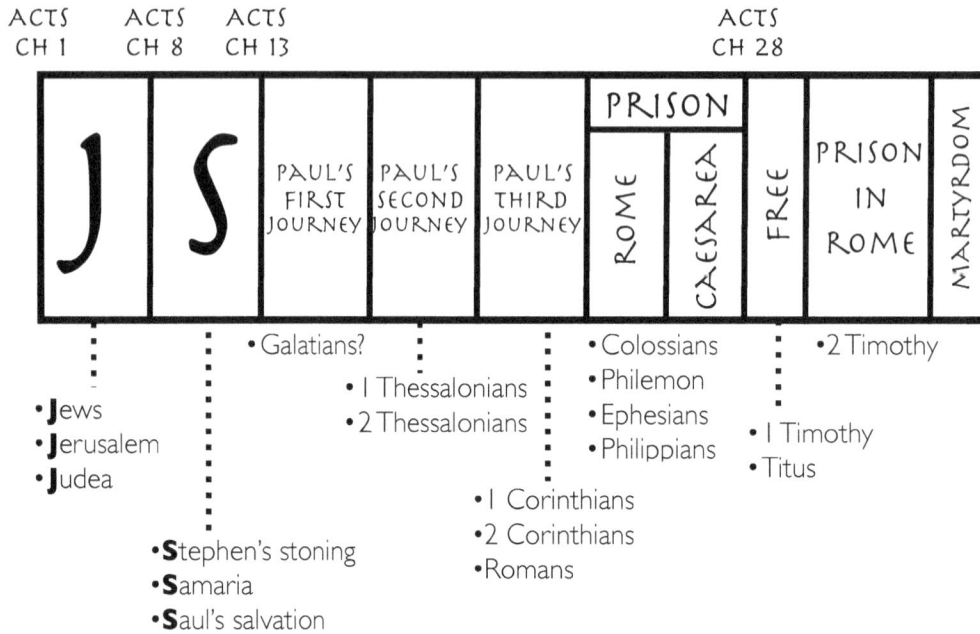

ACTS CH 1   ACTS CH 8   ACTS CH 13   ACTS CH 28

J   S   PAUL'S FIRST JOURNEY   PAUL'S SECOND JOURNEY   PAUL'S THIRD JOURNEY   PRISON / ROME / CAESAREA   FREE   PRISON IN ROME   MARTYRDOM

• Galatians?

• Jews
• Jerusalem
• Judea

• 1 Thessalonians
• 2 Thessalonians

• Colossians
• Philemon
• Ephesians
• Philippians

• 2 Timothy

• 1 Timothy
• Titus

• 1 Corinthians
• 2 Corinthians
• Romans

• **S**tephen's stoning
• **S**amaria
• **S**aul's salvation

V. UNIT 5 — *"Israel's Bar Mitzvah"* – Acts 1 – 5

A. SIX KEY EVENTS: The Spirit Blows Both Ways

1. Jesus' Final Words[1] (ch 1:4-8)

2. Jesus' is "Taken Up" (ch 1:9-11)

3. The First Baptism of the Holy Spirit[2] (ch 2:1-41)

4. The "First Fruits" of the Holy Spirit[3] (2:42-4:37)

5. A "Foul Fruit" of Church Growth (5:1-11)

6. Persecution: God's Unlikely "Missions Conference" (5:12-42)

B. Jesus' Final Words — Acts 1:8

"But you will receive power when the Holy Spirit has come upon you, and you will be my witnesses in Jerusalem and in all Judea and Samaria, and to the end of the earth."   **Acts 1:8**

---

[1] It is interesting that Jesus' final commissioning to his followers is done as a group, but when he "calls" and sends Paul, it is all done in private. Paul, In other words, has no "witness" of his own commissioning. Perhaps that is why he is eager to have his message validated by the Jerusalemite believers later on.

[2] This is the fulfillment of what Jesus predicted would happen to them in Acts 1.

[3] Pentecost is the Jewish Feast of First Fruits; the first "fruits" of the Spirit's presence were power, healing, and evangelism.

1. Jesus' final command is stern and emanates from Jesus the Lord, *not* Jesus the Nazarene — *"stay put!"* (Gk - *paraggello;* same word used by the Sanhedrin in 4:18; 5:28).[1]

2. The disciples' final question is both deflating *and* instructive:

   "So when they had come together, they asked him, "Lord, will you at this time restore the kingdom to Israel?"
   Acts 1:6

   a. They still don't have the Story straight![2]

   b. Jesus' response unveils our perennial problem: missing the present because of a preoccupation with the future (cf. 1:7 and Matt 24:3-5).[3]

3. Jesus' final promise is both prophetic *and* didactic (1:8):

   a. It forms the "outline" for Luke's "second book" (1:1).

   b. It introduces God's principle of "radiating centers":

   (1) Jerusalem (Acts 1-7); "out-in-out."

   (2) Ephesus (Acts 19); the capital city of Asia; Paul is here two years.

   (3) Corinth (Acts 18); leading city of Achaia; Paul is here 18 months.

   (4) Caesarea (Acts 23-26); home of Roman governor of Judea; Paul is here 2 years.

   (5) Rome (Acts 28); the "center" of the world; Paul is here 2 years.

4. Jesus' departure was a necessity:

   a. PHYSICALLY: It ended the possibility of more "appearances" (1:3).

   b. THEOLOGICALLY: It laid the foundation for the close of "The Story" (1:11).

   c. SPIRITUALLY: It left the disciples alone – dependent *and* expectant (1:14).

C. PENTECOST: The "Bar Mitzvah" of Israel[4]

1. The events of Acts 2-5 chronicle God's People "coming of age"

   a. Pentecost (*Shavuot*) was the shortest of the three "pilgrim" festivals (Ex 34:22; Lev 23:15-21; Num 28:26-31; Deut 16:9-12, 16-17).

   b. Every Jewish festival was a celebration of something God had done for them *as a people*. This day would be no different.[5]

   c. Peter's "audience" (Jews from 16 geographical regions) was the result of a long history of suffering (2:5-11).

   d. They had been put "there" *(diaspora)* so they would come "here" (Jerusalem) so they could go back "there."

   e. God was beginning the process of pushing out the boundaries of what it meant to be one of the "chosen people."[6]

---

[1] This verb is used by military commanders and the force of the verb is rooted in the authority associated with the *office* of the one saying it.

[2] They are still thinking way too small, assuming that all that God has in mind involves Israel. The remainder of the Book of Acts will show the disciples/apostles continually having to rethink their theology of the Kingdom.

[3] And, if you roll in the repeated admonitions of the Gospels, we also seem to have a proclivity to be "led astray" when it comes to eschatological issues.

[4] Pentecost is a Greek word. It means a "week of weeks" or 49 days. It officially began 50 days *after* the offering of the first wave offering. It marked the *end* of the spring harvest (May/June). It only lasted one day, compared to Passover/Unleavened Bread which lasted 8 days, and the Feast of Tabernacles lasted a week. Deuteronomy 26 provides us with the ritual prayer that was to be offered at the Feat of Pentecost.

[5] In the Jewish mind, the feasts were *community* celebrations of which the *family* was the basic unit (plural "families" appears 72x in our Old Testament). This reinforced both a shared past *and* a shared identity. It was what Yahweh had done for them as a *group*. Even the phrase that appears in this book, *"signs and wonders,"* is likely a deliberate connection (verbally) to the exodus event and the visible manifestations surrounding it. The exodus event was quite literally the *creation* of the "chosen people," one group extracted *from* a larger group to be set apart (holy) unto Yahweh. The exodus is the portion of Israel's history that is rehearsed more than any other in various parts of our Old Testament (e.g. Ps 105; Hosea 11). Pentecost, and the unfolding of The Story, was also accompanied by "signs and wonders" as Yahweh again extracted one group out of another. This time, *true* "Israel" (cf. Gal 6:16) out of national Israel, and as we shall discover, includes the Gentiles.

[6] In other words, who exactly *were* "the children of promise" in terms of Abraham?

2. Peter was a *Jewish* Evangelist[1]

  a. His second sermon occurred on the Temple Mount on his way to the Jewish time of prayer (3:1-11).

  b. He linked Jesus directly to, *"the God of Abraham, the God of Isaac, the God of Jacob, the God of our fathers…"* and *"all the prophets"* (3:13,18).

  c. He presented Jesus as Moses' promised *"prophet just like me"* (Deut 18:15-19; Acts 3:22).

  d. Peter explained this Pentecost as the fulfillment of an 800-year old prophecy (Joel 2:28-32).

  e. Stephen, Philip, Paul, and James do the same thing throughout this book (i.e., "connect the dots"; Acts 7,8,13,15).

  f. Most importantly, Peter identified Jesus as the fulfillment of the Abrahamic covenant (3:25-26).

D. "Church Lite" — The Dark Side of Growth – Acts 4:36 - 5:11

  1. Making the Straight Story Crooked: Ananias and Sapphira

    a. Their story: *"We're just like Barnabas!"* (4:36 - 5:2).

    b. The real story: *"We're not even IN the story!"*

    c. The apparent miracle: two dead posers

    d. The real miracle: a "church" (1st ref) where sin could not hide.

E. Seven Habits of the *"New"* Jew – Acts 2:42 - 4:37

  1. A hunger to understand the "One Story"[2] — *"the apostles' teaching"*

  2. A commitment to gather for the growth of *others* – *"fellowship"*

  3. A commitment to be in each other's homes for worship[3] – *"the breaking of bread"*

  4. A commitment to regular group prayer in private and public (Temple in 1:14 and 3:1; homes in 4:23).

  5. A commitment to shared resources *and* needs (2:44-45; 4:32-37).

  6. A commitment to *tell* the "One Story"[4] – *"the Lord added to their number daily"* (2:41, 47; 4:4; 5:14).

  7. Genuine basis for community: commitment *to* the "One Story" – *"one heart and mind"* (4:32).

F. Pentecost and the Christian

  1. It is significant that sin entered the Church at a time of numerical growth and relative peace.

  2. When I think of being a Christian, do I think of myself or the Church? The present or the past? Abraham or Paul?

  3. Do I think of biblical community and fellowship in terms of the One Story.

VI. UNIT 6 — "The University of Diversity" — Acts 6 – 12

A. Yahweh's Post-Pentecost CE Curriculum

  1. "Geography 101" – God takes the Story "on the road" to ten cities outside Jerusalem.[5]

  2. "Anthropology 201" – Three distinct and historically hostile ethnic groups discover they have the same Father!

  3. "Theology 301" – God squeezes monotheistic Jews and Samaritans into a primitive trinitarianism, and polytheistic Gentiles into a radical monotheism.

---

[1] The Old Testament figures prominently in the Book of Acts, especially in the preaching of Peter in chapter 2 (cf. Joel 2:28-32; Pss 16:8-11; 110:1), James in chapter 15 (Amos 9:11-12), Stephen in chapter 7 (Amos 5:25-27; Isaiah 66:1-2), Philip in chapter 8 (Isaiah 53:7-8), and Paul in chapters 13 and 28 (Ps. 2:7; 16:10; Isaiah 53:3; Habakkuk 1:5; and Isaiah 6:9-10).

[2] We saw the beginnings of this in Luke's account of the two on the road to Emmaus who said, *"Did not our hearts burn within us, while he talked to us on the road, while he opened to us the Scriptures?"* (Lk 24:32). Jesus, on a number of occasions, took his disciples through the Old Testament, pointing out how *he* was the central topic.

[3] It is quite likely that "the breaking of bread" was the combination of a shared meal and eucharist, comparing Luke 22:19 and 24:35.

[4] This needs to be understood as life-to-life evangelism. There was no local church at this time; just a bunch of Jews who were excited about what God was doing in their midst.

[5] The ten are: Gaza, Azotas, Caesarea (6x), Damascus (7x), Tarsus, Lydda, Joppa, Phoenicia, Cyprus, Antioch. This list will grow to 34 in Acts 13-28!

B. "Geography 101" — Expanding the Story Without Franchising Grace

1. Yahweh had to overcome the inertia of 15 centuries of a "theology of place"[1] (10x in Deuteronomy; e.g. 12:5,11; see also Jn 4:19-24).

2. PHASE I: A Daring Death – the martyrdom of Stephen (Acts 6-7)

   a. Stephen was *not* your "ordinary deacon"…or was he? (*"full of the Holy Spirit, full of wisdom, full of grace, full of power"*; cf. 1 Tim 3:8-10)

   b. The word, "full" means to be covered or permeated with something (Gk - phērēs).[2]

   c. It is used 4x for Stephen!

   d. This "fullness" empowered Stephen to feed widows, preach boldly, heal compassionately, and die peacefully (6:3, 5, 8; 7:55).

   e. Stephen died at the hands of those he had gone to "church" (synagogue) with (6:8-15).

   f. Stephen isolated himself as a "new Jew," one who saw himself as an heir to the Story, not the characters (cf. *"our fathers"* 9x in Jacob-David, but *"your fathers"* 2x at the end).

   g. Stephen condemned himself by agreeing with Jesus' own self-description before this same judiciary (cf. Mt 26:63-66 and Acts 7:54-60).

3. PHASE II: Another Deliberate Diaspora (cf. Acts 8:4 and Jms 1:1)

   a. The "church in Jerusalem" was becoming blinded by the benefits of grace:

   "Now the full number of those who believed were of one heart and soul, and no one said that any of the things that belonged to him was his own, but they had everything in common. And with great power the apostles were giving their testimony to the resurrection of the Lord Jesus, and great grace was upon them all."　　　　**Acts 4:32, 33**

   "And the word of God continued to increase, and the number of the disciples multiplied greatly in Jerusalem, and a great many of the priests became obedient to the faith."　　　　**Acts 6:7**

   b. We see the power of Pentecost in Acts 2, but we see the purpose of Pentecost in Acts 8.[3]

   c. Stephen's death sent the Story to Judea, Samaria, Phoenicia, Syria and Cyprus (8:1; 11:19).

   d. Luke intentionally records Saul's violence as the first stimulus for "foreign missions," *and* the prelude to his own conversion…*outside* Jerusalem! (8:1-3 and 9:1-2).[4]

4. PHASE III: Redirecting a Devout Dissident—Saul's Conversion (9:1-19; 22:3-21; ch 26)

   a. Luke is careful to portray Saul's conversion as a redirection of his passion, *not* a reduction of it (8:3; 9:1, 19-22).

   b. Luke is careful to portray Saul's opposition to the Story as a vital part *of* the Story:[5]

   "But the Lord said to him, "Go, for he is a chosen instrument of mine to carry my name before the Gentiles and kings and the children of Israel. For I will show him how much he must suffer for the sake of my name."　　　　**Acts 9:15, 16**

   "And I said, 'Who are you, Lord?' And the Lord said, 'I am Jesus whom you are persecuting. But rise and stand upon your feet, for I have appeared to you for this purpose, to appoint you as a servant and witness to the things in which you have seen me and to those in which I will appear to you, delivering you from your people and from the Gentiles--to whom I am sending you to open their eyes, so that they may turn from darkness to light and from the power of Satan to God, that they may receive forgiveness of sins and a place among those who are sanctified by faith in me.'"　　　　**Acts 26:15-18**

---

[1] The notion of "place" was nearly essential for monotheism to survive in a polytheistic, pagan culture. More "places" always resulted in more "gods." Removing the notion of a single shrine, and a deity that was *not* limited to space and time was going to make things very "messy."

[2] For example, a leper was considered to be "covered" with leprosy. It's a very comprehensive idea.

[3] The Holy Spirit is most passionate about the *mission* of the Church, not the location of the Church.

[4] The statement about Saul's "violence" in 8:1-3 is interrupted by the amazing work of the Spirit in Samaria for the remainder of chapter 8. Then the "violence" motif is resumed in chapter 9, leading up to Saul's rather "violent" conversion.

[5] God brought Saul to Jerusalem *when* He did, so that Saul could do *what* he did.

      c. Luke creatively gives us Saul's "testimony" in three installments:[1]

        (1) The "flow" of the narrative (9:1-19).

        (2) Via Paul's speech to the Jewish mob in Jerusalem (22:3-21).

        (3) Via Paul's defense before Porcius Festus and Herod Agrippa II (ch 26).

    5. Stephen's Legacy — The First Great Commission Cities

      a. Joppa   -   the only harbor for Jerusalem (until Caesarea) on 170 miles of coastline.

        (1) Jonah had been here 700 years earlier with the exact challenge Peter faced in chapter 10 (Jon 1:3).

        (2) God used the death of Dorcas, as the prelude to taking the Gospel to the Gentiles (9:32-43).

      b. Antioch -   2nd largest city in the Roman Empire with a population of a half million people.[2]

        (1) Capital city of Syrian Province; "home" to 24,000 Roman soldiers.

        (2) Controlled all roads connecting Asia Minor, Egypt, and the Euphrates.

        (3) The "birthplace" of intentional foreign missions (13:1-3).

      c. Tarsus   -   Ranked with Athens and Alexandria as a world intellectual center.

        (1) Saul received his "undergraduate degree" here, then went to Jerusalem for "seminary" training (22:3).

        (2) Sat at the intersection of three major trade routes.

        (3) A free Roman city since 41 BC (tax exempt)

      d. Caesarea   -(Re)built by Herod the Great to spite the people of Joppa.

        (1) Gave land to 6,000 Roman colonists, many soldiers

        (2) Herod Agrippa I was struck dead by Yahweh here (12:19-53).

        (3) "Philip the Evangelist" lived here with his four prophetess daughters (6:5; 21:8-9).

        (4) Peter led Cornelius and a large number of Gentiles to faith in Jesus here (ch 10-11).[3]

C. Anthropology 201 — "Guess Who's Coming to Seder?"

    1. Just as Yahweh had to destroy the "theology of place," in order for the Story to stay true, He had to dismantle the "theology of race."

      a. Stephen and the "Seven" — from Jew to "Step-Jew" (Acts 6)

        (1) The "Seven" were all Greek-speaking Jews, and had their own synagogue in Jerusalem (6:8-9).

        (2) "Seven" was a number pointing towards Gentiles in some first century Jewish thinking (Mk 8:20; Acts 13:19).[4]

      b. Simon "The Great" — from Jew to half-Jew (Acts 8).

        (1) The Jews had "no dealings with Samaritans" (Jn 4:9).

      c. Cornelius the Centurion — from Jew to Gentile (Acts 10-11).

        (1) Jews avoided all contact with Gentiles (Mk 7:3-4; Mr. 10:5; Acts 10:9-16).

D. Theology 301 — "Holy Smoke It's the Holy Ghost!"

    1. The Holy Spirit had always been an integral part of Jewish theology from Genesis to Zechariah (Gen 1:1; Is 63:10; Ps 106:33; Zech 4:6).

---

[1] And, Saul's "testimony" is *truly* a testimony. There are 30 years between Acts 9 and 26, and Saul/Paul is still serving God. A "testimony" that recalls a relatively brief period of time (like many modern "testimonies") is only a story until is validates itself over time.

[2] Rome was the largest city, and Alexandria was third largest.

[3] Peter may very well have planted the first church here through these evangelistic efforts.

[4] This is grounded in Yahweh's promise that they would *"...drive out seven nations more numerous and mightier than you."* (Deuteronomy 7:1). This is further substantiated by Jesus when he feeds the 5,000 on the *eastern* shore of the Sea of Galilee, a region known to be predominately Gentile. In that miracle, they gathered up *seven* baskets of leftovers, compared to *twelve* baskets when he did a similar miracle on the Jewish (i.e. western) side of the Sea.

2. The Holy Spirit's ministry had not changed—revealing the Story and calling God's people back to it—only the extent of it:

"You shall know that I am in the midst of Israel, and that I am the LORD your God and there is none else. And my people shall never again be put to shame. "And it shall come to pass afterward, that I will pour out my Spirit on all flesh; your sons and your daughters shall prophesy, your old men shall dream dreams, and your young men shall see visions. Even on the male and female servants in those days I will pour out my Spirit." **Joel 2:27-29**

3. The Holy Spirit's ministry in the Book of Acts is always the same—*validating* the Story:

"And they were amazed and astonished, saying, "Are not all these who are speaking Galileans? And how is it that we hear, each of us in his own native language?...Men of Israel, hear these words: Jesus of Nazareth, a man attested to you by God with mighty works and wonders and signs that God did through him in your midst, as you yourselves know-- this Jesus, delivered up according to the definite plan and foreknowledge of God, you crucified and killed by the hands of lawless men. God raised him up, loosing the pangs of death, because it was not possible for him to be held by it." **Acts 2:7, 8, 22-24**

"And the crowds with one accord paid attention to what was being said by Philip when they heard him and saw the signs that he did....Now when the apostles at Jerusalem heard that Samaria had received the word of God, they sent to them Peter and John, who came down and prayed for them that they might receive the Holy Spirit, for he had not yet fallen on any of them, but they had only been baptized in the name of the Lord Jesus. Then they laid their hands on them and they received the Holy Spirit. Now when Simon saw that the Spirit was given through the laying on of the apostles' hands, he offered them money," **Acts 8:6, 14-18**

"While Peter was still saying these things, the Holy Spirit fell on all who heard the word. And the believers from among the circumcised who had come with Peter were amazed, because the gift of the Holy Spirit was poured out even on the Gentiles. For they were hearing them speaking in tongues and extolling God. Then Peter declared, "Can anyone withhold water for baptizing these people, who have received the Holy Spirit just as we have?" And he commanded them to be baptized in the name of Jesus Christ. Then they asked him to remain for some days." **Acts 10:44-48**

4. The one common denominator in all the occurrences of speaking in tongues in the Book of Acts is the presence of Jews:

   a. At Pentecost:

      (1) tongues were the sign of the fulfillment of a 700 year-old prophecy (Acts 2; Joel 2:27-29).

      (2) tongues was a sign to the 120 that the time had come to take the Story to the nations.

   b. In Samaria

      (1) tongues are withheld from baptized, converted half-Jews until the Jerusalem Jews can "see" them receive the Holy Spirit.

      (2) tongues verified inclusion in the Story to them as well.

   c. In Caesarea

      (1) tongues are given to converted, *un*baptized Gentiles at their conversion so that the Jerusalem Jews can "see" them receive the Holy Spirit.

      (2) tongues verified inclusion in the Story to them as well.

   d. Saul/Paul:

      (1) It is significant, that in this book, there is no mention of Saul speaking in tongues; there is no need.

E. Acts 6-12 and the 21st Century Church

   1. In these first 12 chapters, the Story had expanded:

      a. geographically

      b. ethnically

      c. theologically

      d. socioeconomically

      e. numerically

   2. Which of these five expansions do *we* value most, 20 centuries later?

   3. What caused *them* to rejoice 20 centuries earlier? (cf. Acts 11:18).

   4. Dorcas and Stephen's deaths force us to rethink our criticism of God for "taking " gifted people when they're at the "top of their game."

VII.UNIT 7 — Paul The Apostle to the "New Jew": Acts 9 – 12 and Galatians

A. Assembling the "Pauline Portrait Puzzle"

1. Paul's life must be "assembled" and sometimes even inferred rather than merely read.

    a. He wrote more letters than we have in our Bibles (Col 4:16; 2 Cor 2:4).

    b. He appears to have been in prison more times than we know, and had many major experiences we have to record of (cf. 2 Cor 11:23-27).[1]

    c. His other letters often give passing "hints" of personal details[2], but Galatians gives us nearly an entire chapter!

    d. This is Paul's only letter that mentions other apostles in a familiar way.

    e. Paul's letter to the Galatians forces us to revisit Acts 9-12 and rework the "Pauline Puzzle."

2. Acts 9-12 in Stereo: The Pens of Luke and Paul:

Scripture	Details of Saul's Life
Acts 9:1-18	• conversion outside Damascus; baptism inside Damascus
Acts 9:19-22	• ministry to Jews in Damascus
Gal 1:16-18	• ministry and retreat into Arabia; return to Damascus
Acts 9:23-25 2 Cor 11:32-33	• life is threatened by the governor of Syria under the direction of King Aretas of Nabatea • lowered from wall in a basket & escapes
Acts 9:26-28 Gal 1:18	• first visit to Jerusalem 3 years later for "apostolic approval" of his conversion • meets Peter and James • Barnabas "sticks his neck out" for Saul • "disputes" with same Jews that killed Stephen (same Gk verb) • stays 15 days
Acts 9:30 Gal 1:22	• Saul sails to Tarsus • ministers in Cilicia and Syria
2 Cor 2:2-7	receives his "thorn in the flesh" (14 years before writing 2 Corinthians)
Acts 11:19-24	Barnabas is sent to Antioch to check on "Gentile revival" (cf. Acts 8:14-25)
Acts 11:25-26	• Barnabas retrieves Saul from Tarsus & they minister in Antioch for one year together.
Gal 2:1-10 Acts 11:27-30	• Saul makes 2nd visit to Jerusalem for "apostolic approval" of his "Gentile Gospel" • Barnabas, him and Titus bring financial help from Syrian believers (*Gentiles!*) after a "revelation" by Agabus.
Acts 12	• Herod kills the apostle James (12:1-2) • God kills the apostate Herod (12:20-23) • Barnabas, Saul and John Mark return to Syria (Antioch)
Acts 13 - 14	• the Holy Spirit sends out "Barnabas and Saul" • ministry on Cyprus, Barnabas' home (13:4-12) • ministry in Galatia (Antioch, Iconium, Lystra, Derbe; 13:13-20) • return through same cities, organizing & equipping (13:21-23) • the Holy Spirit brings back "Paul and Barnabas" (13:26-28)
Gal 2:11-14	• Peter comes to Antioch and is confronted by Paul
—	Paul writes Galatians from Antioch in Syria (c. AD 48-49)

---

[1] For example, in his correspondence with the believers in Corinth, he mentions *three* shipwrecks prior to the only one we have a record of in Acts 27. He also mentions multiple beatings by the Jews, which we also have to clear record of in Acts.

[2] See for example, his brief references to Cephas and James in 1 Corinthains 9:5.

B. BARNABAS: Spotlight on an Unsung Hero

1. It was Barnabas who sought Saul out, listened to his story and defended it before the Jerusalem church (Acts 9:26-27).

2. It was Barnabas who was entrusted with evaluating the first "Gentile revival" the way Peter and John had done the Samaritans (11:19-24).[1]

3. It was Barnabas who sought Saul out again and gave him a ministry position in his own ministry (11:25-26).

4. It was Barnabas who led the first missionary team to Cyprus (13:1-4).

5. It was Barnabas who stepped back and let Paul lead from Cyprus on (13:13,50).

6. It was Barnabas who did for John Mark the same thing he had done for Saul, even though it cost him his ministry (15:36-41).

7. Yet, Barnabas is unknown in our New Testaments apart from his relation to Paul (only 2 of the 24x).

C. GALATIANS: A Letter From the Apostle of the Heart Set Free

1. First Things First: A Basic Primer on New Testament Letters

a. Genre is everything![2]

b. Four questions to have in mind while reading someone else's "mail":

(1) What history exists between writer and reader, if any?

(2) What prompted this letter?[3]

(3) What are the reoccurring words or themes?

(4) How would they have understood it?

2. Second Things Second: A Summary Look at Paul's "Style"

a. When Paul writes *theologically*, he is very "Greek" (i.e. linear; impersonal):

(1) His letters have very few first person pronouns

(2) His letters have two chunks, typically: theology and practice

(a) Romans: ch 1-11 and 12-16 (pronouns - 1%)

(b) Galatians: ch 1-4 and 5-6 (*pronouns - 3.4%*)

(c) Ephesians: ch 1-3 and 4-6 (pronouns - 1%)

(d) Colossians: ch 1-2 and 3-4 (pronouns - 1.5%)

b. When he writes *relationally*, he tends to be more "Hebraic" (i.e. personal and anecdotal):

(1) His letters have more first person pronouns and personal stories:

(a) 1 Corinthians - pronouns - 2.2%

(b) 2 Corinthians - pronouns - 3.7%

(c) Philippians - pronouns - 5.7%

3. Galatians is a unique book because of its content:[4]

a. It is highly theological and highly personal.

---

[1] Barnabas was sent to Antioch by the Jerusalem church to evaluate a larger "turning" of the Gentiles to the gospel. Peter's visit with Cornelius, while a Gentile conversion, must be understood more as an isolated event that what happened in Samaria with Peter and Antioch with Barnabas.

[2] We must continually remind ourselves that even though we *speak of* "the Book of Galatians," it is, in reality, a letter *not* a "book." The same is true of all of the New Testament "epistles."

[3] Re-educating ourselves on this matter is vital. In an age of texting and instantaneous communication—all of it relatively free—we are very far removed from a number of factors that played very large in the first century. It was, for the most part, an illiterate, oral culture. Writing was, for the most part, intended to be *read* aloud to a larger group (e.g., Paul's letter to Philemon is also addressed to *"the church in your house"*). Also, the *cost* of writing a letter was very high because of the rarity of writing materials. This meant letters were both rare *and* expensive.

[4] Galatians and James were likely the first two "books" (i.e. letters) written to 1st century believers. The issues they addressed are two persisting issues *still* facing believers: (1) the relationship of the believer to faith and works (James), and (2) the relationship of the believer to law and grace (Galatians).

b. This would make sense because of how soon the issues in it arose after Paul had planted these churches.

c. It's *opening* is unique among his letters to churches:

PHILIPPIANS	GALATIANS
"Paul and Timothy, servants of Christ Jesus," **Philippians 1:1**	"Paul, an apostle—not from men nor through man, but through Jesus Christ and God the Father, who raised him from the dead—and all the brothers who are with me,… " **Galatians 1:1, 2**
"To all the saints in Christ Jesus who are at Philippi, with the overseers and deacons: Grace to you and peace from God our Father and the Lord Jesus Christ." **Philippians 1:1-2**	"…To the churches of Galatia Grace to you and peace from God our Father and the Lord Jesus Christ, who gave himself for our sins to deliver us from the present evil age, according to the will of our God and Father,"to whom be the glory forever and ever. Amen." **Galatians 1:2-5**
"I thank my God in all my remembrance of you, always in every prayer of mine for you all making my prayer with joy, because of your partnership in the gospel from the first day until now. And I am sure of this, that he who began a good work in you will bring it to completion at the day of Jesus Christ. It is right for me to feel this way about you all, because I hold you in my heart, for you are all partakers with me of grace, both in my imprisonment and in the defense and confirmation of the gospel. For God is my witness, how I yearn for you all with the affection of Christ Jesus. And it is my prayer that your love may abound more and more, with knowledge and all discernment, so that you may approve what is excellent, and so be pure and blameless for the day of Christ, filled with the fruit of righteousness that comes through Jesus Christ, to the glory and praise of God." **Philippians 1:3-11**	"I am astonished that you are so quickly deserting him who called you in the grace of Christ and are turning to a different gospel—not that there is another one, but there are some who trouble you and want to distort the gospel of Christ. But even if we or an angel from heaven should preach to you a gospel contrary to the one we preached to you, let him be accursed. As we have said before, so now I say again: If anyone is preaching to you a gospel contrary to the one you received, let him be accursed." **Galatians 1:6-9**

4. Galatians is an unusual book because of its harsh language:

a. "deserting" in 1:6 (Gk - *metatithēmi*)

(1) Means to transpose two things, to exchange one for the other

(2) In this case, they were exchanging *God* for a totally different Gospel (Gk - *heteros*, different of a different kind, not *allos*, different of the same kind)

b. "accursed" in 1:8-9 (Gk - *anathema*)

(1) This is the same word used repeatedly in the OT for the Hebrew, *cherem*, the "ban" of Joshua 7:15.

c. "bewitched" in 3:1 (Gk - *baskainō*; only use in NT)

(1) An ancient word meaning "to fascinate" or "charm" with one's speech

d. "emasculate" in 5:12 (Gk - *apokoptō*)

(1) Strong word meaning to amputate or cut off

(2) Used of Peter's attack in Gethsemane (Jn 18:10)

(3) Used of Jesus' statement about severity in dealing with sin (Mk 9:43)

5. Galatians is a crucial book because of its subject matter:

a. Paul is playing "hardball" because the Gospel (the Story) is at stake.

b. The issue that has brought on his wrath is circumcision. It is mentioned 16 times in this short letter![1]

c. For Paul, circumcision is a "smokescreen" masking a more insidious attempt to "emasculate" grace:[2]

(1) Paul says making circumcision mandatory chains one to the entire law (5:3).

(2) Returning to the law now is to make the law into something it was never intended to be—a means of justification (3:23-24).[3]

(3) Making the law the centerpiece is to disregard the Cross, grace and the entire Story (2:21; 5:4; 3:18).

d. Paul redraws the lines between a true Jew and Abraham and Moses:

(1) Paul equates Mt. Sinai (Moses & the Law) with Hagar and bondage (4:24-25).

(2) Paul elevates the covenant with Abraham over the covenant with Moses (3:15-18).[4]

(3) Paul says the Abrahamic covenant is the unalterable plan of God that now is fulfilled by Gentile inclusion in "Israel":

"And the Scripture, foreseeing that God would justify the Gentiles by faith, preached the gospel beforehand to Abraham, saying, "In you shall all the nations be blessed." So then, those who are of faith are blessed along with Abraham, the man of faith." **Galatians 3:8, 9**

"...so that in Christ Jesus the blessing of Abraham might come to the Gentiles, so that we might receive the promised Spirit through faith." **Galatians 3:14**

"There is neither Jew nor Greek, there is neither slave nor free, there is neither male nor female, for you are all one in Christ Jesus. And if you are Christ's, then you are Abraham's offspring, heirs according to promise." **Galatians 3:28, 29**

"For neither circumcision counts for anything, nor uncircumcision, but a new creation. And as for all who walk by this rule, peace and mercy be upon them, and upon the Israel of God."

Galatians 6:15, 16

e. Paul lays out the nonnegotiable doctrine that justification is and always has been by faith plus nothing (3:6; 2:20-21).[5]

f. Paul says that the message of the Story is that people of faith are "sons of Abraham," and "sons of God" (3:7, 26); Yahweh is now Abba! (4:6)

D. Galatians is a relevant book for the 21st century because of its sobering theology:

1. The real "enemies" of the Gospel are not those who deny the work of Christ, but those who add to it — this is known as legalism (5:1-9).

2. But, an equal enemy of the Gospel is he who mistakes Christian "liberty" for "license":

a. license - *"I have been "turned loose" to do as I wish!"* (Gal 5:13).

b. liberty - *"I have been set free to do what He enables!"* (Gal 5:22-26).

"For in Christ Jesus neither circumcision nor uncircumcision counts for anything, but only faith working through love." **Galatians 5:6**

VIII. UNIT 8 — James: The Apostle to the *"Old Jew"* — The Letter of James

A. Authorship: Lining Up "The James Gang" (candidates for authorship of this book)

1. James, the father of "Judas-not-Iscariot" (Lk 6:12, 16; Jn 14:22).

---

[1] The place of circumcision in the life of Jewish believers is *not* a small or simple matter. The *extensive* nature of Paul's teaching in this book must *not* be eclipsed by his passion. The language of Yahweh to Abraham in Genesis 17_9-14 is extensive and harsh. Circumcision, for the Jew, was an enormous thing. How does one do away with the *mark* of the Abrahamic covenant without doing away with the covenant itself? Circumcision (along with the sabbath) set the Jews apart from the rest of the world; it was the "sign" of their *election,* not their devotion.

[2] This is much more than a "Jewish" version of the debate over baptism: sprinkling vs. immersion. It cuts to the heart of the work of Christ and the purposes of God regarding Gentile inclusion.

[3] Paul argues that the scripture tells us that "Abraham believed God and it was reckoned to him as righteousness" happened at least 13 years before *he* was circumcised and 400 years before the Law was given at Sinai (cf. Gen. 15; 17:24-25; Gal. 3:15-17).

[4] It is worth noting that Moses is not even mentioned in this book, while Abraham is mentioned nine times.

[5] Paul makes it clear throughout this letter that *everything* is accomplished by the Spirit; beginning to end. The "Spirit" is mentioned 18 times in this letter, and "the flesh" is mentioned sixteen. This is a strong contrast in the mind of Paul.

2. James, the son of Alphaeus; one of "the Twelve" (Lk 6:15; Acts 1:13).

3. James, the son of Zebedee; one of the "sons of thunder," brother of John and one of the Twelve (Mk 3:16-17).

4. James, the son of Joseph; "the Lord's (half) brother," a leader in the Jerusalem Church (Acts 21:17-18; 1 Cor 15:7; Gal 1:18-19).

B. James the Man: A Patchwork Biography

1. Most likely the oldest of Jesus' four brothers (Mat 13:54-55).

2. Did *not* accept Jesus' messianic "delusions" at first (cf. Jn 7:3-5 and Mk 3:4).

3. Received a personal, private appearance from his resurrected brother (1 Cor 15:7).

4. Was a leader in the Jerusalem church when Saul made his first visit there (Gal 1:19).

5. Was recognized by Peter as at least a co-leader in the Jerusalem church (Acts 12:17).[1]

6. The leader of the Jerusalem church at the time of the first major "council" to discuss Gentile inclusion (Acts 15).

7. The one Paul "reported" the results of his missionary journeys to just prior to his arrest in Jerusalem (Acts 21:17ff).

8. Tried to persuade Paul to be "sensitive" to the Jewish Christians desires to remain kosher while he was visiting (Acts 21:17-26).

9. Died as a martyr at the hands of Ananus, the high priest in AD 62 according to Josephus (Antiquities, 20.199-203).

C. James the Letter: A Literary Masterpiece

1. The most "unique" book in our "New Testament."

   a. A "letter" that's a non-letter (no anecdotes, no closing, etc.)

   b. His familiarity with his readers is obvious the result of a shared ethnicity, not a shared history.

   c. Clearly written to Jewish Christians *as Jews*, not "Christians."[2]

   d. Reflects an intimacy with the oral teaching of Jesus and the Old Testament.

      (1) There are over so unmistakeable allusions/citations from his brother's most famous "sermon." (see pages A14-15)

   e. Reflects an amazing literary style and knowledge of Greek:

      (1) More allusions to nature than in all Paul's letters combined (e.g. 1:10; 3:3; 4:14; 5:2).

      (2) Sixty Greek words that appear nowhere else in the NT; some that he even "created" (e.g. "favoritism," prosopolempsia in 2:1).

D. James the Letter: A Protestant Embarrassment

1. There has been no NT letter that has been avoided, minimized, sanitized and demthologized more than the letter of James:

   "Saint John's gospel and St. Paul's epistles, especially that to the Romans, and St. Peter's first epistle are the true pit and marrow of all the books. They should justly be the first books, and every Christian should be advised to read them first and most, and by daily reading to make them as familiar to himself as his daily bread. In them you do not find described many works and miracles of Christ; but you do find depicted in a masterly manner how faith in Christ overcomes sin, death, and hell, and gives life, righteousness, and salvation. This is the real nature of the Gospel ... These books show you Christ and teach you all that is necessary and salutary for you to known even though you were never to see or hear any other book or doctrine. Therefore St. James epistle is really an epistle of straw compared to them, for it lacks this evangelical character."
   Martin Luther

---

[1] Peter gives specific instructions to "tell James…" about his miraculous release from prison, indicating that Peter considered James a leader in the church.

[2] All the illustrations are from the Old Testament; James uses the Greek word for "synagogue" in 2:2, and uses the Old Testament name for Yahweh, "Lord of Hosts" in 5:4.

2. This is a tragedy because it reflects "The Story" in its infancy and closest proximity in time to Yeshua himself.

3. Much of this is due to an artificial contradiction we have created between James and Paul based on similar language:

James	Paul
"Was not Abraham our father justified by works when he offered up his son Isaac on the altar? You see that faith was active along with his works, and faith was completed by his works; and the Scripture was fulfilled that says, "Abraham believed God, and it was counted to him as righteous-ness"—and he was called a friend of God. You see that a person is justified by works and not by faith alone." **James 2:21-24**	*"What then shall we say was gained by Abraham, our forefather according to the flesh? For if Abraham was justified by works, he has something to boast about, but not before God. For what does the Scripture say? "Abraham believed God, and it was counted to him as righteousness." Now to the one who works, his wages are not counted as a gift but as his due."* **Romans 4:1-4**

4. James' intention was to instruct his Jewish brothers on how to live in "the world" in which they found themselves dispersed (Gk - *diaspora*).[1]

E. James the Letter: A Vital Reassessment

1. This letter exposes an ancient and debilitating tendency among God's people that is not ancient — a "divided life."[2]

   "Teach me your way, O LORD, and I will walk in your truth; give me an undivided heart, that I may fear your name." **Psalms 86:11, NIV**

2. Frank Thielman, New Testament scholar entitled the chapter on James in his NT Theology textbook, *"James: The Wisdom of the Undivided Life."*

3. For believers of all ages, our perennial temptation is to separate our lives into "compartments" that are insulated and isolated from the one that contains our "faith."

4. The Letter of James destroys this error forever by showing that faith, if real, is at the heart of *every* facet of my life, and has no life of its own.[3]

5. This is the over-arching purpose and "key" to this letter:

   a. "the faith" and my suffering — 1:2-9; 2:1-13; 5:7-18

   b. "the faith" and my deeds — 1:26-27; 2:14-26

   c. "the faith" and my wealth/possessions — 2:14-16; 5:1-6

   d. "the faith" and my obedience — 1:21-25

   e. "the faith" and my relationships — 2:1-10; 4:1-2; 5:19-20

   f. "the faith" and my plans — 4:13-17

6. James' portrait of a life isolated from faith is tragic and frightening:

   a. whining and grumbling (1:2-4)

   b. agitated and angry (1:19-20; 4:1; 5:4-6)

   c. inner unrest and anxiety (4:2)

   d. prayerlessness and/or self-focused prayer (4:2-3)

   e. envy, lust and hatred (4:2)

---

[1] Realistically, this is no different than living in the 21st century. We too are "dispersed" and need instruction on how to live in "the world" we find ourselves.

[2] In the Bible, the *opposite* of being "whole hearted" is *not* being "half-hearted." It's having a divided heart; a heart that is partially committed to a number of things.

[3] James actually takes this argument a step further and insists that faith that is *not* organically connected to all aspects of a believer's life is actually "dead."

       f.   feeling "at home" in the culture (4:4)

       g.   seeing obedience as "legalism" (4:4,8)

       h.   a recreational attitude towards sin (4:9)

       i.   bigotry and injustice (2:1-4; 5:4)

       j.   arrogance (4:6-7)

       k.   hypocritical speech (3:9-10)

       l.   dishonest/unjust business practices (5:4)

    7.   James is a sobering reminder that *our own* "story" is always waiting in the wings, anxious to become *the* "Story."

  F.   MIXED METAPHORS: "Citizen-Subjects"

    1.   Throughout the centuries, the orthodox Church has tirelessly hammered out some very significant doctrines:

       a.   AD 325 - 681: six ecumenical councils forged our current doctrines of the Trinity and the nature of Jesus Christ

       b.   15th century - the "Reformers" forged our current doctrines of revelation and mediation:

          (1) the authority of scripture

          (2) justification by grace through faith

          (3) the priesthood of all believers

    2.   Our current struggle is to understand "The Story" of kingdom subjects in a covenant community while immersed in a capitalistic democracy.

    3.   We lack the same clarity in five key "Story doctrines," the first of which James sheds amazing light:[1]

       a.   *ergology* - the nature and place of "deeds" in the life of the believer

       b.   *ecclesiology* - the nature and purpose of the Church

       c.   *argurology* - the nature and purpose of wealth

       d.   *huparchology* - the nature and purpose of possessions

       e.   *ptochology* - the nature of poverty and the responsibility to the poor

  G.   Exorcizing the "Demon" of Works[2]

    1.   Learning the ancient language

       a.   the word translated "works" or "deeds" in our Bible is *ergon*.

       b.   These two words are not synonyms in the minds of Christians; "works" is dripping with motive, while "deeds" is not.

       c.   Paul separates these modern meanings in his ancient words:[3]

          a.   "works of the law" (*ergōn nomou*; 6x only by Paul in Galatians and Romans)

> *"For by works of the law no human being will be justified in his sight, since through the law comes knowledge of sin."*
> **Romans 3:20**

> *"yet we know that a person is not justified by works of the law but through faith in Jesus Christ, so we also have believed in Christ Jesus, in order to be justified by faith in Christ and not by works of the law, because by works of the law no one will be justified."*
> **Galatians 2:16**

---

[1] I've named these "doctrines" using a similar nomenclature used by theologians for other key doctrines, namely, using the Greek word that points to the issue as the root, followed by *"-ology"* as the suffix. In the above doctrines, the roots are: "works," "church," "silver (wealth)," "possessions," and "the poor."

[2] We have actually "demonized" works by painting it the enemy of grace and faith. Once something is "demonized" by Christians, we feel free from any sense of responsibility to it or for it. We've done the same thing with the issue of homosexuality.

[3] When Paul speaks of "the works of the law" he is referring to living like a Jew, or one's attitude about the connection between Judaism and the gospel. When he speaks of "works" or "good works," he is referring to our lives as believers. It is very significant that Paul refers to "good works" 8 times in his letters, and *all* of them are instructions to pastors. The implication is clear: he wants this *taught* in the churches.

  b. "good works" (*kala erga* and *ergōn agathōn*)

   "They are to do good, to be rich in good works, to be generous and ready to share," **1 Timothy 6:18**

   "Show yourself in all respects to be a model of good works, and in your teaching show integrity, dignity, and sound speech that cannot be condemned, so that an opponent may be put to shame, having nothing evil to say about us." **Titus 2:7, 8**

  d. "Kala erga" is better translated, "blessed deeds" because "kala" carries with it the idea of beauty and virtue.

  e. Jesus said our "blessed deeds" are the light that others see that causes them to "glorify our Father in heaven" (Mt 5:16).

  f. Jesus and Paul blasted "works of the law" as a means of being justified before Yahweh (Lk 18:9-14; Rom 3:20).

  g. But, the entire New Testament agrees with James that "blessed deeds" are the normal behavior of genuine believers:

  h. "In the same way, let your light shine before others, so that they may see your good works and give glory to your Father who is in heaven." Matthew 5:16

  i. "They are to do good, to be rich in good works, to be generous and ready to share," 1 Timothy 6:18

  j. "The saying is trustworthy, and I want you to insist on these things, so that those who have believed in God may be careful to devote themselves to good works. These things are excellent and profitable for people." Titus 3:8

  k. "And let us consider how to stir up one another to love and good works," Hebrews 10:24

  l. "Keep your conduct among the Gentiles honorable, so that when they speak against you as evildoers, they may see your good deeds and glorify God on the day of visitation." 1 Peter 2:12

2. Unlearning the untruths

  a. "Unbelief" is the opposite of faith, *not* "deeds."

  b. "Merit" is the opposite of grace, *not* "deeds."

  c. The opposite of "blessed deeds" is…disobedience![1]

  d. Unfortunately, in many of our churches, "legalism" has become a euphemism for disobedience!

3. James and the 21st Century

  a. Paul and James agree on two vital points:

   (1) *I* am justified by faith apart from "works of the law."

   (2) My *faith* is justified by "blessed deeds" apart from "works of the law."[2]

  b. Paul *and* James each remind us in our day of a sobering truth:

   (1) Paul tells me that my place in "The Story," the script God has written for me is the very thing the Church has "demonized"!

   "For we are his workmanship, created in Christ Jesus for good works, which God prepared beforehand, that we should walk in them." **Ephesians 2:10**

   (2) James tells me that my "faith," if devoid of *kala erga*, is at best, demonic![3]

   "But someone will say, "You have faith and I have works." Show me your faith apart from your works, and I will show you my faith by my works. You believe that God is one; you do well. Even the demons believe--and shudder!" **James 2:18, 19**

---

[1] The letter of James contains 60 imperatives in 108 verses! There are 1,800 Greek imperatives in our New Testament. That means there are a great number of things God wants us to *do!* Because we have a command to act, the indwelling Holy Spirit to empower, and for the most part the resources to complete the assignment, our only explanation for *not* doing what God tells us is simply that we don't want to.

[2] This effectively dissolves the perceived difficulties typically associated with Jesus' statements in Matthew 25 in his parable about the "sheep and goat judgment." It also supports Jesus' opening comments to five of the seven churches of Asia Minor in the first three chapters of the Book of Revelation (e.g., *"I know your works…"*).

[3] In a rather strange reversal of modern logic, James tells us that faith without deeds is no better than the "faith" of demons. So, rather than "works" being demonic, our faith turns out to be demonic, when it's divorced from deeds.

IX. UNIT 9 — *"How Firm a Foundation"* — Paul's 2nd Missionary Journey

A. It is during this "second missionary journey" that Paul lays the foundation for eight of the letters he will soon write (Philippians, Thessalonians, Corinthians, Ephesians, Colossians, Philemon).

B. Understanding the people and cities he visited will open our hearts to difficulty of his task, and our minds to the content of his words.

C. A Visit With Paul's "Travel Agent": A Patchwork Itinerary *("church plants" are indicated by **)*

 1. Paul decides to make a "follow-up" visit to minister to the churches planted on his 1st journey (Acts 15:36).

 2. After a "sharp disagreement" (Gk, *apōchorizō*; cf Rev 6:14), over John Mark, Paul and Barnabas go opposite directions.

 a. This "parting" produced three leaders, not two: Silas is a replacement for Barnabas, *not* John Mark (Gk used for J.M. both times is *sumparalamanō*, but not for Silas).

 (1) Silas is one of the "leading men" of Jerusalem (15:22).

 (2) He was a prophet and a teacher (15:32).

 3. Paul's "encouragement trip" turns into a 2nd missionary journey of enormous significance — the "Story" goes to Europe (Acts 15:41–18:22).

 a. In Lystra, Paul recruits a young believer from a bi-racial, "mixed" marriage named Timothy (16:1-3).

 b. There is at least the possibility that Paul had Timothy in mind *before* he left Antioch, as he is *very* familiar with Timothy's family and personal history (cf. 2 Tim 1:5-7).

 c. Paul and Silas' ministry here is virtually "exploding" in numbers and power (Gk *episterizō*, *"increasing"* means "constantly overflowing").

 d. Paul goes from total revival to at least a month (450 miles of travel) where God forbids successful ministry (16:6-8).

 e. He arrives at Troas and receives a double "blessing": another helper we know as Luke, *and* an "invitation" to successful ministry (16:8-11).

 f. Makes a 2-day journey by sea (120 miles) from Troas to Neapolis, the official port of Philippi, 10 miles away (16:11-12).

 g. **Paul plants the first church in Europe (Philippi), an enthusiastic, multi-racial, economically mixed group of non-Jewish converts to the Story (16:12-40).

h. **After being beaten and driven out of town by angry Gentiles for economic reasons, he travels nearly 80 miles to the enormous city of Thessalonica.[1]

i. Jews, jealous of a loss in numbers from their synagogue, create a riot and drive Paul out of town (17:1-9).

j. **Paul travels two days to Berea and has the opposite experience as in Thessalonica…for a while at least (17:10-13).[2]

k. Driven from Berea, he goes to Athens (while Silas and Timothy remain); no response from Jews and marginal response from the intellectual elite (17:16-34).[3]

l. Silas and Timothy join Paul in Athens (implied from 1 Th 3:1-2).

m. Paul sends Timothy back to Thessalonica to "check" on the church (1 Th 3:1-5).

n. **Paul moves on to Corinth where he ministers for 18 months, along with fellow tent-makers Aquila and Priscilla (18:1-17).

o. Timothy joins Paul in Corinth with a "mixed" report from Thessalonica (1 Th 3:6).

p. Paul writes 1 Thessalonians.

q. Paul receives a disturbing "oral report" about Thessalonica (2 Th 3:11).

r. Paul writes 2 Thessalonians.

s. Paul leaves Corinth and sails to Ephesus; brief ministry with Aquila and Priscilla (18:18-20).[4]

t. Sails to Caesarea and makes a "silent" visit to Jerusalem (e.g. *"went up"* and *"went down"*) then back to Antioch (18:21-22).[5]

** - *indicates a church plant*

D. *"God's Word to Us Was First God's Word to Someone Else"* – Three Key Cities of Paul

1. **Philippi** — *"a leading city of the district of Macedonia and a Roman colony"*

a. Philippi was a "miniature Rome"

(1) It was the site of one of the most famous and decisive battles in Roman history in 41 BC.[6]

(2) Latin, not Greek was the "official" language (86% of the inscriptions discovered are Latin!).

(3) Grid system for streets, with the Via Egnatia as "main street"!

(4) Roman style Forum at center of city, complete with a "bema."

(5) Nurtured a distrust and distaste for Jews (cf. 16:20. *"…these men are Jews…"*).

(6) Only city mentioned in our "New Testament" as a Roman colony.

b. It could be called "Little Italy": granted *ius Italicum* (Italian Law):

(1) considered Italian "soil"

(2) property tax exemption

(3) citizenship conferred by birth

(4) direct rule by Rome

c. It birthed an amazing church—perhaps Paul's "favorite"

(1) It was an unconventional church in its "launch."

---

[1] This young girl with the "pythonic spirit" which Paul exercised and consequently destroyed their business, was only part of the bondage the poor child endured. She was also a slave to the men who "pimped" her demonic wares to the people of Philippi.

[2] The word "noble" that is applied to the Berean believers (Gk - *eugenēs)* is only used three times in the New Testament. The other two occurrences have to do with actual nobility (cf. Luke 19:11; 1 Corinthians 1:26).

[3] These philosophers, we are told, were similar to us in our obsession with information and our fear of missing out: *"Now all the Athenians and the foreigners who lived there would spend their time in nothing except telling or hearing something new."* (Acts 17:21).

[4] Paul will return to Ephesus on his third missionary journey and spend three years in this city.

[5] There is no other reason for Paul to sail to Caesarea except to visit Jerusalem. Caesarea was Jerusalem's "port." If he was intending only to return to Antioch in Syria, he would like have sailed to a port north of Caesarea.

[6] The Battle of Philippi pitted Marc Anthony and Octavian agains Cassius and Brutus, the assassins of Julius Caesar.

(2) It was a cosmopolitan church in its "membership."

(3) It was a missional church in its "giving" (cf. Phil 4:14-17; 2 Cor 11:9).

(4) It was a miraculous church in its testimony (16:16-18; 25-34).

(5) It was a suffering church from its beginning (16:19-24).[1]

2. **Thessalonica** — "*You turned to God from idols…*" (1 Thess 1:9)

   a. A spiritual "Wal-Mart"

   (1) Archeologists have found remains of temples to at least ten different gods, including Dionysius, Aphrodite, Yahweh, and Cabrius the "patron" god of the city.

   (2) Paul makes it very clear that these conversions were very different from those in Philippi.

   (3) His response among the Jews was abysmal, (especially compared to Berea), and may indicate a fear of losing their "personal peace and affluence."

   b. A financial Wallstreet

   (1) Thessalonica was the most populous and wealthy city in Macedonia, and second in that part of the world.

   (2) It had the best harbor in the Aegean, and sat and the intersection of two major trade routes.

   (3) It was a Roman "free city," able to run its own affairs and mint its own coins.

3. **Corinth** — "*The City That Julius Built*"

   a. Rome destroyed the city in 146 BC, but it was rebuilt by Julius Caesar and made the capital of the province of Achaia.

   b. Over twice the size of Athens, it was the largest and most prosperous city in Southern Greece.

   c. Its two harbors and "roller-road," along with its "full featured" Temple to Aphrodite, made it a magnet for sailors, businessmen and political figures.

   d. Prostitution was highly esteemed in Corinth; Aphrodite's "servants" had the only "house on the hill," and the best "seats in the house."

   e. The cults of Dionysius and Asklepios (and others) had "communal" meals very similar to the Christian "love feast."

   f. The Christian converts in Corinth were wealthy and affluent by comparison, to those in Macedonia and Judea (cf. 2 Cor 8:14).

   g. Athletics were nearly worshipped in Corinth; the Isthmian Games were held near it every two years and involved "victor's crowns, running, wrestling and boxing.

E. Reflections From the Journey: 21st Century Principles from a 1st Century Trip

1. Luke is careful throughout Acts to highlight the principle of "reputation" when it comes to those most responsible for the Story:

   a. The seven "deacons" (6:3).

   b. Cornelius among the Jews in Caesarea (10:2,22).

   c. Barnabas (11:24).

   d. Ananias in Damascus (22:12).

   e. Paul continues this emphasis in his writings from this era and later:

   (1) men who are elders and deacons (1 Tim 3:2,7).

   (2) Paul's passion for himself (Acts 24:16; 2 Cor 1:12).

   (3) believers in general (1 Th 4:11-12; Titus 2:1-10).

   f. Our "testimony" is *not* how we came to be in the Story, it's our life *in* the Story.

---

[1] It is interesting that Paul does not play the "C" card here (Roman citizenship) until *after* he's been beaten and imprisoned. As a Roman colony, this would have been a very powerful "ticket" *out* of suffering, yet he does not take that route.

2. The amazing diversity of the Philippian church was possible because they each wanted into the Story, not into the church.

3. Paul's "open air" evangelism was most likely face-to-face in the context of his work, *not* on the street corners or door-to-door:

> *"After this Paul left Athens and went to Corinth. And he found a Jew named Aquila, a native of Pontus, recently come from Italy with his wife Priscilla, because Claudius had commanded all the Jews to leave Rome. And he went to see them, and because he was of the same trade he stayed with them and worked, for they were tentmakers by trade."* **Acts 18:1-3**

> *"For you remember, brothers, our labor and toil: we worked night and day, that we might not be a burden to any of you, while we proclaimed to you the gospel of God."* **1 Thessalonians 2:9**

4. Some of the characteristics that made the Spirit's work "easier" in these churches are *not* bound to the past:

    a. *mobility* — a willingness to "go," or let someone you love go (Priscilla, Aquila, Paul, Timothy).

    b. *diversity* — a perspective on people that is driven by the Story rather than the characters in it.

    c. *humility*— a willingness to submit my thinking to God's revealed word (the Bereans).

    d. *generosity*— a willingness to have a loose grip on what others need that I do not (Acts 2, 4, 11:27-29; 2 Cor 8:8-15; Phil 4:14-16).

X. UNIT 10 — *"What's Really Been Left Behind!"* — Paul's Thessalonian Letters

  A. Learning About Paul *From* Paul's Pen

    1. Paul was a "prayerful" pastor.

      a. There are 48 references to prayer in all but two of his letters (Galatians & Titus).

      b. Eight are references to Paul's personal prayer life (e.g. Rom 1:10; Phil 1:9).

      c. Paul *may have* used a "list" when he prayed (e.g. "mention" in Rom 1;(; Eph 1:16; 1 th 1:2; Phlm 4).

      d. Paul prayed privately (Rom 1:10) and with others (Col 1:3) for the spiritual growth of his converts.

      e. Paul told others what he was praying for them (1 Th 3:10; 2 Th 1:11; Phil 1:9-11; Col 1:9-14).

      f. Paul prayed the "Prayer of James," not the "Prayer of Jabez" (others and the Story vs. self and comfort).

    2. Paul valued people above power and prestige.

      a. Mature believers were his "crown" of honor in life (1 Th 2:19; Phil 4:1).

      b. Paul ran from the "celebrity" spotlight (1 Th 2:6; 1 Cor 3:5-7).

    3. Paul modeled the behavior he wanted others to embrace:

      a. suffering (1 Th 2:1, 14)

      b. "marrying" one's visible life to the Story (1 Th 2:8)

      c. pursuing a "blameless" life (1 Th 2:10; 4:11-12)

      d. exhorted, comforted and taught, depending upon the need (2:11-12 and 5:14)

      e. a commitment to countercultural holiness (2:10 and 3:13; 4:7)

      f. the discipline of personal prayer for others (1:2 and 2 Th 3:1)

    4. Paul had a shepherd's heart, not just a scholar's mind (e.g. Romans).

      a. He reminds them he was as "gentle" with them as a "nursing mother" (trophos; 1 Th 1:7).

      b. Even his exhortations to them came from the heart of a "father with his children" (2:11).

      c. His affection for them cause him to want to share his own "soul" (psuche) with them, not just the Story (2:8).

  B. Learning About the Thessalonian Church From Paul's Pen

    1. Thessalonica was hostile, not hospitable!

      a. The Story was opposed by Jews *and* Gentiles (1 Th 1:6; 2:14; Acts 17:1-9).

      b. Thessalonica was a place of sexual license, *not* limitation (1 Th 4:3-8).

(1) A statue of Dionysus was discovered ad the Temple of Serapis in Thessalonica.

(2) The cult of Dionysus would have made *both* orthodoxy and orthopraxy confusing at best, nearly impossible at worst:[1]

> *"Born of a mortal mother, Dionysus was fully divine and immortal, yet concealed his divinity in human form."*

> *"Phallophoria was an ancient Greek celebration involving a procession of people carrying images of phalluses in honor of the god, Dionysus."* **Delia Morgan, Dionysian scholar**

(3) Thessalonica was hostile to the hope of the resurrection:

> *"...for this woman had this surname, while she was still among the living. Because of her special disposition and good sense, her devoted husband created this tomb for her and also for himself, in order that later he would have a place to reset together with his dear wife, when he looks upon the end of life that has been spun out for him by the indissoluble threads of the Fates."*

> **Tomb inscription from Thessalonica**

2. The Thessalonian believers had a long way to grow.

   a. Paul wants to "fill up" what is lacking in their faith (1 Th 3:16).

   b. They don't seem to understand or accept church polity (4:12-13).

   c. Some were exploiting either others either because of their wrong theology, or a sense of entitlement (Paul speaks of "idleness" 4x in these letters).

   d. Their theology of the "end times" was immature and had been polluted by popular ideas (1 Th 4:13-5:11; 2 Th 2).

3. They were growing in only *two* of Paul's key "Kingdom Qualities":

   a. Paul makes 11 clear references to their "faith," all positive.

   b. He makes 8 clear references to their "love," all positive.

   c. Paul makes only 2 references to their "hope," and both indicate a struggle (1 Th 1:3; 4:13).

   d. Timothy had brought good news about their "faith" and "love" being intact, but not their "hope" (3:6).

   e. Paul's pastoral passion was that they "abound" in these three qualities:

   > *"Finally, then, brothers, we ask and urge you in the Lord Jesus, that as you received from us how you ought to live and to please God, just as you are doing, that you do so more and more....Now concerning brotherly love you have no need for anyone to write to you, for you yourselves have been taught by God to love one another, for that indeed is what you are doing to all the brothers throughout Macedonia. But we urge you, brothers, to do this more and more,"* **1 Thessalonians 4:1, 9, 10**

   > *"We ought always to give thanks to God for you, brothers, as is right, because your faith is growing abundantly, and the love of every one of you for one another is increasing."* **2 Thessalonians 1:3**

   f. Paul informs them that "hope" does not depend upon "work" or "labor," like faith and love, but upon "steadfastness" *(hupomonē)* and correct doctrine *(agnoeō, 4:13; 1:3).*

4. They may have felt "abandoned" by Paul, based on his repeated reassurances:

   > *"But since we were torn away (apophanizō)from you, brothers, for a short time, in person not in heart, we endeavored the more eagerly and with great desire to see you face to face, because we wanted to come to you—I, Paul, again and again—but Satan hindered us."* **1 Thessalonians 2:17, 18**

   > *"For this reason, when I could bear it no longer, I sent to learn about your faith, for fear that somehow the tempter had tempted you and our labor would be in vain.... as we pray most earnestly night and day that we may see you face to face and supply what is lacking in your faith?"* **1 Thessalonians 3:5, 10**

---

[1] Paul's instruction to Thessalonian men in 1 Thess. 4:4 may point to the preoccupation with sex in the city: *" For this is the will of God, your sanctification: that you abstain from sexual immorality; that each one of you know how to control his own **body** in holiness and honor, not in the passion of lust like the Gentiles who do not know God."* The word for "body" is the word *skeuos* which can be translated "vessel" or "organ," rather than the word *soma* which is always translated "body." Paul *may* be employing a euphemism here for the male genitals, which was actually a parade item in Thessalonica during one of its festivals!

5. SUMMARY: The infant Thessalonian church, though healthy, needed Paul's pastoral care in four key areas:

    (a) Remaining steadfast in the face of ongoing persecution (1:14; 2 Th 1:5-8).

    (b) Understanding holiness in a sexually deviant culture (1 Th 4:3-8).

    (c) Understanding when "helping can be hurting"—idleness vs. helplessness (1 Th 4:11-12; 2 Th 3:6-15).

    (d) Having a theology of Christ's return that balances hope and responsibility.

C. A Closer Look at the Long View: The Return of Christ

1. There was much confusion about this doctrine in the first century:

    a. Jesus, Peter, John, James and Paul all write about it (Mt. 24; 1 Cor 15:49-53; Phil 3:20-21; Col 3:13; Jn 11:25-26; 1 Jn 2:28; 3:2; 2 Pet 3; Jms 5:8).

    b. Paul devotes 25% of his first letter and 45% of his second teaching and *reteaching* on the "end times" (cf. 2 Th 2:5).[1]

    c. Understanding Paul's intentions is essential for our investigation.

        (1) In 1 Thessalonians, his goal is comfort.

        (2) In 2 Thessalonians, his goal is correction.

    d. Understanding their circumstances is essential for our interpretation.

        (1) They were grieving because they assumed (or had been taught) dead believers would not participate in the Day of the Lord with living believers (1 Th 5:13).[2]

        (2) They had been taught that the Day of the Lord had begun and Christ's return was imminent, causing some to become idle and unruly (2 Th 3:6, *ataktōs*).

2. This is still a much confusion about this doctrine in the 21st century.

    a. The *Left Behind* series has outsold the Chronicles of Narnia.

    b. Most of the confusion/conflict hovers around the relationships of two events and two time periods:

        (1) EVENTS: the "rapture" and the "second coming" (neither of these phrases are in our Bibles).

        (2) PERIODS: the "tribulation" and the "millennium" (only the first term is in our Bibles).

    c. Understanding some key words used in the New Testament is a helpful first step:

        (1) "coming" — *parousia*, (24x)

            (a) used by Jesus (3x), Paul (7x), James (2x), Peter and John (1x).

            (b) by the time of the NT, its primary use inside and outside the Church was for the "arrival of royalty."

        (2) "revelation/revealing" — *apokolupsis/apokoluptō* (5x for Jesus)

            (a) used for the "revealing of the sons of God" (Rom 8:19).

            (b) used for the "revealing" of the "mystery of the Gospel (Rom 16:25).

            (c) used for the "revealing" of the "man of lawlessness" (2 Th 2:3,8).

            (d) used for the return of Jesus Christ in (1 Cor 1:7; 2 Th 1:7; 1 Pet 1:7)

        (3) "appearing" — *epiphaneia* (6x, all by Paul, all for Jesus)

            (a) a distinctly "Pauline" word

            (b) Paul directly links this word to the end of the Tribulation (2 Th 2:8).

        (4) "meet" — *apantēsis* (3x, 1 Th 4:17; Mt 25:6; Acts 28:15)

---

[1] In 2 Thessalonians 2:5, Paul uses the imperfect tense when he says *"...I told you..."* indicating an ongoing instruction in the past. There was significant teaching performed while he was there.

[2] Paul lays the foundation for a unique idea here: grief and hope can coexist. They are not mutually exclusive. For the believer who knows the truth of the resurrection and what follows, there need be *neither* "hopeless grief," or "griefless hope."

         (a)   word is always used for a gathering of people to meet and escort an important person someplace.

         (b)   used of the virgins and bridegroom

         (c)   used to describe the Roman believers who had travelled over 50 miles to "meet" Paul the prisoner and escort him to Rome.

    (5)   Paul uses all four of these words 10x in these two letters.

3.   Clarifying what Paul is *NOT* saying will help us understand what he *IS* saying.

    a.   In 1 Thessalonians

       (1)   Paul is makes *no* reference whatsoever to time in his discussion of the "rapture."

       (2)   Paul makes no reference to the "when" of the "great snatch" (Gk *harpazo*), only the details surrounding it (the "what").

       (3)   Paul says the return of Christ will come "like a thief" for unbelievers, *not* believers (cf. 1 Th 5:2,4).

       (4)   Paul makes no mention of the "destination" following the "meeting" with Christ in the air, only *where* the meeting will occur and who's been "invited."

    b.   In 2 Thessalonians

       (1)   There is nothing in Paul's words to allow us to conclude he is referring to two separate events:

          (a)   "*…the revelation of the Lord Jesus from heaven…*" (1:7-8)

          (b)   "*…the coming of our Lord Jesus…*" (2:1)

       (2)   There is nothing in the text to indicate a distinction between the "coming of the Lord Jesus" (2:1) and "the day of the Lord" (2:2).

4.   Paul *is saying* somethings in these letters that *would* provide comfort and correction:

    a.   The living and dead faithful *will* "meet" Jesus together (*episunagoge*) in the clouds, and be with Him from that point on (I.e. wherever Jesus is, they will be).

    b.   The *parousia* will be accompanied by loud and visible activities (angels, trumpet, a loud cry) and the violent destruction of the "man of lawlessness."

    c.   They need to heed Jesus' original teaching on this subject: "Take heed that you are not misled" (Mt 24:4).

    d.   None of this has yet been set in motion because of some vital details they've forgotten (cf. 2 Th 2:5) have to take place first:

       (1)   the "rebellion" (ESV), "apostasy" (NAS) apostasia (Gk)

       (2)   what/who is "holding back" the "man of lawlessness" must cease from "holding" (noun is neuter in 2:6 and masculine in 2:8).

          "Frankly, I confess that the meaning of this [verse] completely escapes me."   **Augustine**

       (3)   the "man of lawlessness" must be revealed.

    e.   Their view of the return of Christ must *never* contribute to a lack of commitment to this life and those in it (I.e. "idleness").

D.   Predictive Prophecy: What's *Really* Been "Left Behind"

    1.   God's purposes for predictive prophecy must always direct our study of it.

    a.   God gives details of the Story *before they happen* to demonstrate that it is truly *His* Story:

    "To whom will you liken me and make me equal, and compare me, that we may be alike? Those who lavish gold from the purse, and weigh out silver in the scales, hire a goldsmith, and he makes it into a god; then they fall down and worship! They lift it to their shoulders, they carry it, they set it in its place, and it stands there; it cannot move from its place. If one cries to it, it does not answer or save him from his trouble. "Remember this and stand firm, recall it to mind, you transgressors, remember the former things of old; for I am God, and there is no other; I am God, and there is none like me, declaring the end from the beginning and from ancient times things not yet done, saying, 'My counsel shall stand, and I will accomplish all my purpose,'"   **Isaiah 46:5-10**

b. God gives us the *end* of the Story so that His children will give their lives *to* the Story:

(1) living a life consistent with the Story - personal holiness

> *"But the day of the Lord will come like a thief, and then the heavens will pass away with a roar, and the heavenly bodies will be burned up and dissolved, and the earth and the works that are done on it will be exposed. Since all these things are thus to be dissolved, what sort of people ought you to be in lives of holiness and godliness, waiting for and hastening the coming of the day of God, because of which the heavens will be set on fire and dissolved, and the heavenly bodies will melt as they burn! But according to his promise we are waiting for new heavens and a new earth in which righteousness dwells."* **2 Peter 3:10-13**

(2) telling the Story to those who haven't heard it yet - evangelism

> *" Now to him who is able to strengthen you according to my gospel and the preaching of Jesus Christ, according to the revelation of the mystery that was kept secret for long ages but has now been disclosed and through the prophetic writings has been made known to all nations, according to the command of the eternal God, to bring about the obedience of faith-- to the only wise God be glory forevermore through Jesus Christ! Amen."* **Romans 16:24-27**

(3) ministering mercy, compassion and love to those we meet

> *"Therefore, stay awake, for you do not know on what day your Lord is coming. But know this, that if the master of the house had known in what part of the night the thief was coming, he would have stayed awake and would not have let his house be broken into. Therefore you also must be ready, for the Son of Man is coming at an hour you do not expect. "Who then is the faithful and wise servant, whom his master has set over his household, to give them their food at the proper time? Blessed is that servant whom his master will find so doing when he comes."*
> **Matthew 24:42-46**

2. Any view of biblical prophecy that reduces my commitment to the one true Story under the guise of "urgency" violates the *purpose* of prophecy.

XI. UNIT 11 — *"The City on a Hill"* — Paul's "First" Letter to Corinth

A. FLASHBACK: The Birth of the Church in Corinth — Acts 18:1-21

1. Getting the Sequence Straight:

a. Paul ministered in Thessalonica *and* Corinth while on his 2nd missionary journey (Acts 15:40-18:21).

b. Corinth was internationally known as a pleasure spot.[1]

c. Paul's ministry in Corinth was long, arduous, and intense:

(1) It lasted 18 months (18:11).

(2) Paul appears to have "worked with his hands" like he did in Thessalonica (1 Cor 4:12; Acts 18:1-3; 1 Th 2:9).

(3) Paul met two fellow tent-making missionaries who became lifelong friends—Aquila and Priscilla—in Corinth (Acts 18:1; 1 Cor 16:19; Rom 16:3; 2 tim 4:19).

(4) Paul's ministry to Corinthian Jews is brief and intense, but abysmal and mutually hostile (18:5-7).[2]

(5) Paul's persecution by Jews in Damascus (Acts 9:22), Jerusalem (9:28-29), Antioch (13:50), Iconium (14:4), Lystra (14:19), Thessalonica (17:5), and Berea (17:13) may have made him want to quit preaching (Gk in 18:90 is "*stop being afraid to speak…*").

(6) Paul's ministry in Corinth results in a predominately "Corinthian" church that will eventually exhibit very *non*-Jewish problems:[3]

---

[1] Its location was nearly unrivaled in the ancient world. Corinth actually had *two* harbors in a world where most cities had none. One faced Rome in the Corinthian Gulf, and the second faced the Mediterranean on the Saronic Gulf in the Aegean Sea. The harbors of Corinth rivaled those of Alexandria in Egypt, Ostia in Rome, and Caesarea in Palestine.

[2] Paul's behavior at times seems a little "over the top" in terms of how worked up he gets. But, this only reinforces the difficulty he had with this church regarding his apostolic authority.

[3] When one looks at the difficulties Paul addresses in these letters in tabular fashion as in this list, it becomes immediately apparent that these are problems typical of Gentiles and *atypical* of Jews as a group.

        (a)   incest (1 Cor 5:1-13)

        (b)   lawsuits in Corinthian courts (6:1-8)

        (c)   using prostitutes (6:12-20)

        (d)   sexual abstinence *within* marriage (7:1-7)

        (e)   idolatry (10:1-22)

        (f)   participation in pagan festivals (10:20-22)

        (g)   culturally accepted immorality and homosexuality (6:910)

    d.   Paul changes his missionary base from Greece to Asia.[1]

       (1) Paul relocated his "base" in Ephesus, along with Aquila and Priscilla, indicating adequate leaders were in place (Acts 18:18-21).

       (2) Paul returned to Syria and spun around on his 3rd missionary journey (18:22-23).

       (3) Aquila & Priscilla trained Apollos and sent him to Corinth to continue the work (18:24-19:1).

       (4) Paul arrived in Ephesus and spent two years of fruitful ministry:

> *"…all the residents of Asia heard the word of the Lord, both Jews and Greeks."*   **Acts 19:10**

    e.   Paul "Shepherds" the Corinthians long distance *(i.e., from Ephesus)*

       (1) Paul writes what is most likely "First Corinthians," which we do *not* have, addressing the issue of sexual immorality in the church (1 Cor 5:9-11).

       (2) Paul receives a sobering oral report on the sad state of affairs from "Chloe's household" (1:11), and a letter bursting with questions about how the Story applies to life in Corinth.[2]

       (3) Paul writes a lengthy second letter to address all these problems. This is likely our "First" Corinthians (c. AD 54).

       (4) Paul makes a short, *undocumented* "painful visit" to Corinth to deal with things face-to-face (4:19; 2 Cor 2:1-2).[3]

       (5) Paul sends a third "tearful letter" (which we do not have)probably with Titus to address a specific disciplinary issue (2 Cor 2:3-9, 13; 7:16).

       (6) Paul goes to Macedonia and is finally joined by Titus (2 Cor 7:16), and writes his *fourth* letter, our "Second Corinthians" (c. AD 55).

       (7) Paul visits Corinth on the last leg of his 3rd journey and stays for three months (Acts 20:2; 2 Cor 12:14).[4]

B. FLASH FORWARD: "First" Corinthians

  1. Going "Back Stage": The Larger Issues

    a.   Corinth is Paul's first truly *cosmopolitan* congregation with no connection to Jewish theology and scripture.

    b.   Paul has to help them forge an identity that is consistent with The Story without the Jewish props of monotheism, covenant history, and a strong written moral code:

> *"You know that when you were pagans (Gk-ethnos) you were led astray to mute idols, however you were led."*   **1 Corinthians 12:2**

    c.   Paul must help them understand the novel idea of an inseparable connection between orthodoxy (right doctrine) and *orthopraxy* (right living) (something Greek religion did not demand).

---

[1] This happens at the *end* of his second missionary journey.

[2] We are informed about this "letter" full of questions specifically by Paul in 7:1, *"Now, concerning the matters about which your wrote…"* Following this opening comment, Paul proceeds to move through their questions in the remainder of the letter. We are alerted to this by his use of the preposition, "now." (cf. 7:25; 8:1; 12:1; 16:1,12).

[3] His statement that he does not want to "make another painful visit" informs us of the *first* "painful visit" for which we have no record in Acts.

[4] It is very likely that Paul wrote Romans from Corinth during this visit.

2. CENTER STAGE: Four Key Players in the Corinthian Drama

   a. "Tribalism" – the Corinthian had adopted a "we-they" mentality based on what was socially sanctioned.

     (1) "dignitas" was of enormous value in Corinth, a very "Roman" city.

     (2) Corinthian social life was rife with "categories" that regulated all their relationships in public and private:

> *"All those workers who are paid for their labor and not for their skill have servile and demeaning employment, for in their case the very wage is a contract to servitude."*   **Cicero, 106-43 BC**

     (3) It's no wonder Paul is *always* having to defend himself to the Corinthians, he was a tent-making *Jew*!

     (4) Crispus, the *archsynagogos* who came to faith, was a "householder" whose servants would have been baptized with him.

     (5) For Corinthians, oratory was art, and those most skilled in it were most esteemed.

     (6) The Corinthians believers had become divided into house churches built around preachers and theology:

> *"For it has been reported to me by Chloe's people that there is quarreling among you, my brothers. What I mean is that each one of you says, "I follow Paul," or "I follow Apollos," or "I follow Cephas," or "I follow Christ."*   **1 Corinthians 1:11, 12**

     (7) Paul makes it clear that this pressure was always hanging over his head, *and* that it is opposed to The Story:

> *"And I, when I came to you, brothers, did not come proclaiming to you the testimony of God with lofty speech or wisdom. For I decided to know nothing among you except Jesus Christ and him crucified. And I was with you in weakness and in fear and much trembling, and my speech and my message were not in plausible words of wisdom, but in demonstration of the Spirit and of power, that your faith might not rest in the wisdom of men but in the power of God."*   **1 Cor. 2:1-5**

     (8) For Paul, the issue is *always* The Story, *not* the "storyteller."

> *"What then is Apollos? What is Paul? Servants through whom you believed, as the Lord assigned to each. I planted, Apollos watered, but God gave the growth. So neither he who plants nor he who waters is anything, but only God who gives the growth."*   **1 Corinthians 3:5-7**

   b. "Worship" – The Corinthian believers had made themselves the center of worship rather than God (14:26-33).

     (1) Worship services had become arenas of self-expression rather than edification (14:12).

     (2) Spiritual gifts had become a form of *dignitas* (12:12-26).

     (3) Fellowship meals had become merely social gatherings reflecting culture rather than revering Christ (11:17-33).

     (4) "Church" had become an opportunity for people to gather with others just like themselves, including where they sat and with whom!

C. OFF STAGE: Unmasking Corinth in America

  1. How much of my identity as a Christian comes from my social or religious "tribe" rather than the Story?

  2. How much of my loyalty as a believers is to a Storyteller rather than the Story?

  3. How much of my theology as a believer is the product of the consensus of the corporate lifestyle of my church rather than a lifetime of study?

XII. UNIT 12 — *"E Pluribus Unum"* — 1ˢᵗ Corinthians, part 2

A. Letter to a Fractured Fellowship: an outline of 1 Corinthians

  1. Greetings and Thanks (1:1-9)

  2. Fractures and Factions (1:10-6:20)

   a. Two ways of "seeing" the Story (1:10-2:16)

b. Two ways of "seeing" the Storytellers (2:17-3:21)

c. Two types of "apostles" (4:1-21)

3. Money, Sex and Power (5:1-6:20)

a. "All in the family": the case of incest (5:1-22)

b. "Suing the Saints": litigation before unbelievers (6:1-11)

c. "Pornology": developing a theology of purity (6:12-20)

4. "Quiz the Wizard: Questions from Corinth" (7:1 - 16:9)

a. "Knot or Noose?": questions about marriage & celibacy (7:1-40)

b. "Meat or Veggies?": questions about meat offered to idols (8:1-11:1)

c. "Chaos or Charismata?": questions about worship (11:2-14:40)

d. "Dead or Alive?": questions about the resurrection[1] (15:1-58)

e. "Pledges and Promises": questions about the "offering" (16:1-5)

5. Wrapping Up: concluding remarks (16:6-24)

B. Paul's Passion for Peace: Shalom *Is* The Story[2]

1. Unity is not a by-product of the Story, it is at the heart of the Story:

a. Jesus prayed for a "trinitarian" quality unity for all believers as the proof of his incarnation (Jn 17:23).

b. Paul made unity the litmus test of whether an individual *or a church* was living "worthy of the Story":

"Only let your manner of life be worthy of the gospel of Christ, so that whether I come and see you or am absent, I may hear of you that you are standing firm in one spirit, with one mind striving side by side for the faith of the gospel," **Philippians 1:27**

"I appeal to you, brothers, by the name of our Lord Jesus Christ, that all of you agree and that there be no divisions (Gk - schisma) among you, but that you be united in the same mind and the same judgment." **1 Corinthians 1:10**

"May the God of endurance and encouragement grant you to live in such harmony with one another, in accord with Christ Jesus, that together you may with one voice glorify the God and Father of our Lord Jesus Christ." **Romans 15:5, 6**

"I therefore, a prisoner for the Lord, urge you to walk in a manner worthy of the calling to which you have been called, with all humility and gentleness, with patience, bearing with one another in love, eager to maintain the unity of the Spirit in the bond of peace." **Ephesians 4:1-3**

c. Divisions among believers is evidence that the Story has stalled, or been hijacked by those in it.

d. The fruit of spiritual gifts, properly deployed, is always unity:[3]

"If I speak in the tongues of men and of angels, but have not love, I am a noisy gong or a clanging cymbal. And if I have prophetic powers, and understand all mysteries and all knowledge, and if I have all faith, so as to remove mountains, but have not love, I am nothing. If I give away all I have, and if I deliver up my body to be burned, but have not love, I gain nothing." **1 Corinthians 13:1-3**

e. Unity is the visible expression of God's shalom, the inevitable fruit of the Story unfolding.

f. The only durable basis for unity among believers is a commitment to the same Story:

(1) There not only *is* only one Story, there *can be* only one Story: His or someone else's.

(2) Each of us longs to "win an Oscar" for "Best Director," or at least for "Best Supporting Actor/Actress."

---

[1] In denying the resurrection, they were *not* denying life after death. The "afterlife" was held by nearly everyone in the Ancient Near East. This is an important distinction between the first century and our modern era. There were no atheists in the first century. Everyone believed in the gods. The Corinthians were denying the unique claim of Christ-followers of a *bodily* resurrection of Jesus *and* all people versus the disembodied immortality of the soul taught by Greek philosophy.

[2] see 1 Corinthians 1:10 (he uses the Greek word *schisma* here to refer to disunity); Philippians 2:1-2; Ephesians 4:1-6; Romans 15:5-6; Colossians 3:12-14

[3] see also Ephesians 4:1-3, 7-13; 1 Corinthians 12:21-28

        (3) Every individual believer, every church, and every Christian organization is either Story-driven, or Story-imposed.

    g. Disunity was inevitable because all three of these have to disengage from the Story to thrive.

    h. Corinth was an affluent, elitist city that glorified the intellect, the emblems of *dignitas*, and personal autonomy (moral *and* relational).[1]

    i. Unity is the underlying theme of this letter because *disunity* had become the "hallmark" of the church!

C. The Reeducation of Corinth: Unpacking "the Mind of Christ" (1 Cor 2:16)

    1. The "Thin Spaces" in the Story

        a. Paul has over 50 references to "power" in ten of his thirteen books.

        b. Half of them are in these books (15x in 1 Cor; 9x in 2 Cor).

        c. The miraculous was a normal part of Paul's ministry, and accompanied his preaching:

> *"For I will not venture to speak of anything except what Christ has accomplished through me to bring the Gentiles to obedience--by word and deed, by the power of signs and wonders, by the power of the Spirit of God--so that from Jerusalem and all the way around to Illyricum I have fulfilled the ministry of the gospel of Christ;"*   **Romans 15:18, 19**

> *"Does he who supplies the Spirit to you and works miracles among you do so by works of the law, or by hearing with faith--"*   **Galatians 3:5**

> *"...because our gospel came to you not only in word, but also in power and in the Holy Spirit and with full conviction. You know what kind of men we proved to be among you for your sake."*   **1 Thessalonians 1:5**

        d. His burden for Corinth is *not* less "power," but less Corinth (ch 12-14).

    2. Worship Gone Wrong: Ad Libbing in Church (14:39-40)

        a. Women were disrupting worship with their clothing (11:2-16).

        b. Women were disrupting worship with their questions (14:33-35, "*keep silent*").

        c. Prophets were disrupting worship with their filibustering (14:30, "*keep silent*")

        d. Tongues speakers were disrupting worship with their self-assertion (14:28, "*keep silent*")

        e. The wealthy were disrupting worship with their posturing and greed (11:17-34).

        f. Bottom Line: There is a wrong way and a right way to worship:

> *"But all things should be done decently and in order."*   **1 Corinthians 14:40**

        (1) Paul uses *euschēmenōs* here, a word that has to do with the right way to live both inside and outside the church (Rom 13:13; 1 Th 4:12).

D. A Closer Look at Controversy: Spiritual Gifts in the Church

    1. There are at least 13 clear references to spiritual gifts in this letter; It is a key subject.

        a. Paul tells them they are not "deficient/inferior/behind" in any gift (1:7).

        b. Paul includes celibacy as one of the "charisma" from God (7:7).

        c. He does not want them to be "agnostics" about "the spiritual" (Gk: *tōn pneumatikōn*; "charisma" is not in the Greek)

        d. Paul links spiritual gifts clearly to the Trinity, not merely the Holy Spirit:

        (1) God the Spirit distributes the *charismatōn* (gifts).

        (2) God the Son directs the *diakoniōn* (service).

        (3) God the Father determines the *energēmatōn* (empowerment).

        e. Therefore, unity can not be based on the "one gift," only the One God, which means the One Story.

---

[1] We have to remind ourselves that this was the ethos of the city where Paul planted a church and then stayed 18 months to try to get it established and healthy. His correspondence reminds us of the intense difficulty of ministry.

    f.   The purpose of the charisma is for the "bringing together" (Gk-sumpherō) or "the common good."

    g.   No one who possesses the Spirit possesses all the gifts (this is the inevitable conclusion of the sum of Paul's seven "all do not" phrases in 12:29-30).

    h.   No one gift possesses *all* those who possess the Spirit (12:29-30).

    i.   Paul's summary is for them to desire "the spiritual" (14:1), but to pursue love.

       (1) "Pursue" is a volatile word that is translated "persecute" 31 of its 47 times in the NT.

       (2) Jesus used this word to address Saul (Acts 9:4,5).

       (3) Paul used it for himself prior to his conversion (Acts 22:4; 1 Cor 15:9).

       (4) Paul used for himself after his conversion for his "one holy passion:

> *"Brothers, I do not consider that I have made it my own. But one thing I do: forgetting what lies behind and straining forward to what lies ahead, I <u>press on</u> toward the goal for the prize of the upward call of God in Christ Jesus."*   **Philippians 3:13, 14**

       (5) Paul tells pastors and churches to pursue righteousness, peace and what makes for edification of others (1 Tim 6:11; Rom 14:19).

E. Paul's Pornology: Developing a Theology of Sexual Purity

    1.   Paul's arguments about sexual purity is scattered throughout chapters 5-10, but is concentrated in 6:12-20.

    2.   There are four Greek words for immorality and prostitution: *porneia, porneuo, pornē,* and *pornos.*

       a. Paul uses all four of these words 14x in his Corinthian letters

       b. Half of them are in this section.

       c. In his response to the report of incest, he merely tells them *what* to do (5:1-5).

       d. But for sexual immorality, the "hobby" of Corinthians, he develops an extensive "pornology":

          (1) Being in the Story involves my body, *not* just my soul (6:13).

          (2) Therefore, my body is as much a part of my spirituality as my soul (6:13).

          (3) This life is *not* all there is, so hedonism is an invalid (or stupid!) ideology (6:12-13).

          (4) Resurrection means there is a continuity of the body from this life to the next (6:14).

          (5) Because redemption (buying back) extends to my body, I no longer own it (6:20).

          (6) My body is also a shrine of Yahweh; His Spirit is present in it (6:19).

          (7) Sex is a serious *spiritual* reality for the Christian (6:15).

          (8) All this is true for married couples as well (7:2-5).

          (9) Immorality *and* adultery for believers is the same: giving away for free something that cost God His Son and I do not own, to someone who has no right to it.

F. Boycotting Corinth: The Mind of Christ in the 21st Century

    1.   We need to understand that unity is the credibility of the Story, and differentiate between "primary" and "secondary" doctrines.

    2.   We need to understand that spiritual gifts are *not* spiritual "presents." They have no purpose apart from the Story, and degenerate into enemies of the Story when abused.

    3.   We need to understand that pornography is prostitution, not recreation.

    4.   We need to pray for the power of God to be manifested in the American church in ways that is foolish and weak.

XIII. REVIEW: LOOKING BACK ON WHERE WE'VE BEEN

A. The One Story of the One God

    1.   Three Un-Truths to Un-Learn

       a. Untruth #1: The Bible is God's record of the Jews in the Old Testament, Jesus in the Gospels, and the Church in the New Testament.

Truth #1: The Bible is the One Story of the One God "to unite all things in heaven and on earth in Christ" (Eph 1:7-10).

The "Old" Testament is as much "Christian" scripture as the "New" Testament.

b. Untruth #2: The New Testament is a book containing God's instructions on how to become and live as a Christian.

Truth #2: The New Testament is the record of "mystery" of The Story *unfolding*, and what it means to be "in" it, and "stewards" of it.

The "Old" Testament is as much "Christian" scripture as the "New" Testament.

c. Untruth #3: The Book of Acts is the story of the birth of "Christianity."

Truth #3: The Book of Acts is the full unveiling of God's "mystery hidden for ages" from prophets and angels—the promise to Abraham is for the nations.

(1) This is the "Gospel" *(euaggelion)* that the apostles, especially Paul, lived, suffered, and died for.

> *"There is one body and one Spirit--just as you were called to the one hope that belongs to your call-- one Lord, one faith, one baptism, one God and Father of all, who is over all and through all and in all."*
> **Ephesians 4:4-6**

> *"And the Scripture, foreseeing that God would justify the Gentiles by faith, preached the gospel beforehand to Abraham, saying, "In you shall all the nations be blessed."*
> **Galatians 3:8**

> *"But you are a chosen race, a royal priesthood, a holy nation, a people for his own possession, that you may proclaim the excellencies of him who called you out of darkness into his marvelous light. Once you were not a people, but now you are God's people; once you had not received mercy, but now you have received mercy."*
> **1 Peter 2:9, 10**

> *"And you shall be to me a kingdom of priests and a holy nation. These are the words that you shall speak to the people of Israel."*
> **Exodus 19:6**

> *"For you are a people holy to the LORD your God. The LORD your God has chosen you to be a people for his treasured possession, out of all the peoples who are on the face of the earth."*
> **Deuteronomy 7:6**

(2) We need to understand that the "new covenant" inaugurated by Jesus was the *fulfillment* of the Abrahamic covenant, *not* its replacement![1]

(3) The Mosaic covenant (i.e. Law) was set aside, *not* the Abrahamic covenant (i.e. Gen 12, 15, 17).

2. One Large Truth to Embrace (1 Cor 4:1; 2 Cor 4:5; 5:17-20)

a. If we truly are God's people, then we are now:

(1) In The Story[2]

(2) Stewards *of* The Story

(3) Agents of the redemption offered *by* The Story

C. Three Cultural "Roadblocks" to the Spread of the One Story[3]

1. The value system of Rome: *"dignitas"* – image, status, and association.

"You are who you know and who knows you."

2. The value system of Greece: *"anthropos"* – males, myths, and the mind.

"You are what you know and what you don't have to do."

3. The value system of Judea: *"hagios"* – separation, tradition, and exclusion.

"You are what you don't do and who you don't know."

---

[1] The persistence of the Abrahamic covenant *unites* what we instinctively have been taught to divide into "Old" and "New."

[2] Seeing myself as "in" the Story rather than "in" the world; seeing myself as "in" Christ who is "in" the Father (John 17) rather than "in" the world; seeing myself as a "citizen of heaven" rather than a resident of earth.

[3] These are not only hostile *to* the gospel, they are dismantled *by* the gospel. These are the manifestations of what Paul calls *"arguments and every lofty opinion raised against the knowledge of God,"* (1 Corinthians 10:5)

D. The First Four Threats to the One Story

   1. *Legalism*: Galatians

      a. The idea that the "Story" is about us rather than Him (tribalism, rules-keeping, and merit vs. grace).[1]

      b. God's solution was Paul, the Apostle to the "New Jew."

      c. Letter of Galatians – destroys the confusion between grace and deeds.

   2. *Autonomy*: James

      a. The idea that The Story has a "place" in my life rather than vice versa.

      b. God's solution was James, the Apostle to the "Old Jew."

      c. Letter of James – breaks the insulation between faith and "living."[2]

   3. *Confusion*: Thessalonians

      a. Losing track of The Story in the face of conflicting voices (pain, persecution, pleasure, and panic).[3]

      b. God's solution was the Thessalonian letters.

      c. Paul reminds them that "hope" depends upon perseverance, and right doctrine, because suffering is unrelenting in this life (1 Th 1:3; 4:13; 2 Th 1:5-7).

      d. Paul reminds them that God has given them the *end* of The Story so *that* they can live for Him in the meantime (2 Th 1:7-12).

   4. *Conformity*: Corinthians

      a. They bought the idea that we can live in *two* "stories" at once: His Story *and* the story of my culture.[4]

      b. God's solution was the Corinthian letters.

      c. Paul reminds them that while they are "in" the story around them, they are no longer a part of it:

> *"For consider your calling, brothers: not many of you were wise according to worldly standards, not many were powerful, not many were of noble birth. But God chose what is foolish in the world to shame the wise; God chose what is weak in the world to shame the strong; God chose what is low and despised in the world, even things that are not, to bring to nothing things that are, so that no human being might boast in the presence of God."* **1 Corinthians 1:26-29**

> *"For the love of Christ controls us, because we have concluded this: that one has died for all, therefore all have died; and he died for all, that those who live might no longer live for themselves but for him who for their sake died and was raised. From now on, therefore, we regard no one according to the flesh. Even though we once regarded Christ according to the flesh, we regard him thus no longer. Therefore, if anyone is in Christ, he is a new creation. The old has passed away; behold, the new has come."* **2 Corinthians 5:14-17**

XIV. UNIT 14 – REVISITING CORINTH

A. Three Vital Interpretive "Keys" For Paul's Corinthian Letters

   1. We must remind ourselves where the meaning of Scripture lies, and where it does *not*:

      a. It does *not* lie in the words on a page or the mind of the reader.

      b. The meaning of Scripture lies in the mind of the author.

      c. Our "job" is, to the best of our ability, to "become" him!

   2. We must remind ourselves that Corinth was a Roman city, not a Greek one!

      a. Corinth was defeated, looted, and "dismantled" by Rome in 146 BC. Its wealth was transported to Rome.

---

[1] "Rules keeping" inevitably leads to self-righteousness when I succeed, hypocrisy when I fail but hide it, or anger/discouragement when I fail. No Kingdom fruit comes from rules-keeping.

[2] In a very real sense, genuine faith "leaks" into all the cracks and crevices of our lives. It can not be contained to the "Jesus Room."

[3] Understanding that *everyone* needs a story should make us aware that there are many counterfeit stories out there to choose from. Our plot hunger makes us easy prey for plot providers.

[4] This human tendency is at the root of Yahweh's continual admonition to his people all throughout the Old Testament to "choose this day" whom they will serve. Or put another way: *"You can only live in one story at a time. Which will it be, mine or the ones around you?"*

    b. It lay desolate for 102 years, and was rebuilt as a Roman colony in 44 BC by Augustus, and populated by Romans.

    c. Everything about Corinth was a reflection of *"Romanitas,"* (collective term used for the values and culture of Rome).

       (1) Inscriptions and coinage for the first 100 years was all in Latin.

       (2) City grid was based on the Roman "centuriation" system.

       (3) All the architecture was modern (i.e. Roman) rather than ancient (i.e. Greek).

       (4) Aphrodite, the patron goddess of Corinth was eclipsed by Venus, the Mother Goddess of Rome, whose statue was in the center of Corinth.

       (5) Corinth in Paul's day was a reflection of its age, not its ancestry.

       (6) 8 of the 17 names mentioned in the Corinthian letters are Roman, *not* Greek.[1]

3. "Discipleship" *(Gk mathētēs)* was neither a Jewish *nor* a Christian invention. It was a term from the sophist movement, which was *flourishing* in Corinth in Paul's day (our words, "sophisticated" is derived from this word).

    a. "Sophists" were virtuoso orators, characterized by:

       (1) they possessed a large following (and wanted one!)

       (2) they participated in the secular public assembly (Gk *ekklesia*) of a city.[2]

       (3) were official spokesmen on embassies sent to the governor or emperor.

       (4) declaimed (argued passionately) on many topics publicly…for a fee

       (5) owned and operated expensive schools to train the children of the social elite how to argue in criminal and civil courts, and in public.

       (6) students were called "disciples" *(Gk mathētēs)*, and their goal was "imitatio" (emulation) in dress, demeanor, and skill.

       (7) Paul spoke specifically of them:[3]

> *"…where is the debater of this age? Has not God made foolish the wisdom of the world?"*
> **1 Corinthians 1:20**

B. *"I Follow Apollos, I Follow Cephas, I Follow Paul…"*

1. Paul's Corinthian letters must be read and understood against the backdrop of Romanitas and Sophistry.

    a. Paul continually admonishes them about issues that stem from the Roman value of *dignitas* (hierarchy of spiritual gifts, cult of celebrity, sophist approach to discipleship, etc.)

    b. Paul deliberately uses *anti-sophist* language in his description of himself and his ministry:

    c. "And I, when I came to you, brothers, did not come proclaiming to you the testimony of God with lofty speech or wisdom. For I decided to know nothing among you except Jesus Christ and him crucified. And I was with you in weakness and in fear and much trembling, and my speech and my message were not in plausible words of wisdom, but in demonstration of the Spirit and of power, that your faith might not rest in the wisdom of men but in the power of God." **1 Corinthians 2:1-5**

Sophists in Corinth	Paul in Corinth
Upon arriving in a city, he sent out invitations telling where and when he would present his credentials and declaim.	"…when I came to you brothers…"

---

[1] Fortunatus, Gaius, Lucius, Priscilla, Acquila, Quartus, Titius Justus, Tertius
[2] This is the same word we translate "church" throughout our English New Testament.
[3] Paul's use of "debater" (Gk *suzētēs*) is used only here in our New Testament.

Sophists in Corinth	Paul in Corinth
At the appointed time, he would address the crowd while seated, using a sort of "liturgy": • an encomium - praise of the city • a covert self-commendation • an invitation to the crowd to pick a topic for him to declaim • if he felt competent to declaim, he would rise but if not, he would return in 24 hours** **(this was the "make" or "break" stage)	"…I did not come proclaiming…with lofty speech or wisdom. For I decided to know nothing among you except Jesus Christ and him crucified.…"
After declaiming, the audience (and city) either embraced or rejected his services for their city.	"And I was with you in weakness and in fear and much trembling, and my speech and my message were not in plausible words of wisdom, but in demonstration of the Spirit and of power, that your faith might not rest in the wisdom of men but in the power of God." **1 Cor 2:1-5**
If they embraced him: • parents of elite children would enroll them in his school • city fathers would award him citizenship to the city (required to debate publicly) • citizens welcomed him as their spokesman for an embassy (if needed)	"For what we proclaim is not ourselves, but Jesus Christ as Lord, with ourselves as your servants for Jesus' sake." **2 Corinthians 4:5** "Therefore, we are ambassadors for Christ, God making his appeal through us. We implore you on behalf of Christ, be reconciled to God." **2 Corinthians 5:20**
Competition was stiff, often malicious, and permanence was never guaranteed and often challenged.	"What I mean is that each one of you says, "I follow Paul," or "I follow Apollos," or "I follow Cephas," or "I follow Christ." **1 Corinthians 1:12** "I have been a fool! You forced me to it, for I ought to have been commended by you. For I was not at all inferior to these super-apostles, even though I am nothing." **2 Corinthians 12:11**
This was an opportunity for "big money" in an affluent city driven by "*dignitas*."	"What then is my reward? That in my preaching I may present the gospel free of charge, so as not to make full use of my right in the gospel." **1 Corinthians 9:18** "Or did I commit a sin in humbling myself so that you might be exalted, because I preached God's gospel to you free of charge?" **2 Corinthians 11:7**

2. Paul's Corinthian letters, especially 2 Corinthians may be the most relevant New Testament books for the 21st century. (Next Unit!)

3. In it we discover the story of the beneficiaries of the Abrahamic covenant trying to live in light of their ancestry instead of their age.

XV. UNIT 15 - CORINTH: PAUL'S "PAINFUL PARISH" (2 Corinthians cont'd)

A. Four Letters to the Same Painful "Zip Code"

   1. Paul's heart for the Corinthians is evident in both the quality *and* quantity of his correspondence with them.[1]

      a. It is likely that he wrote four letters to the Corinthians, even though we only have two of them preserved for us in our Bibles:[2]

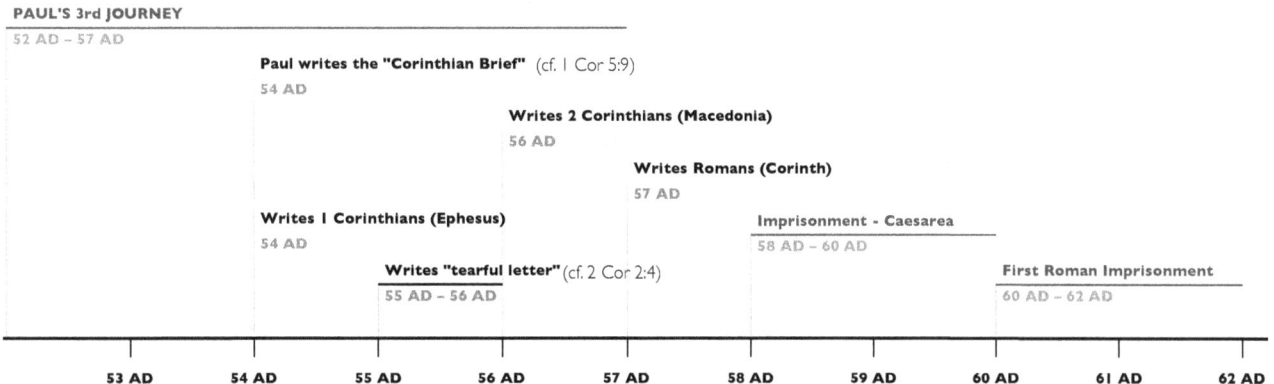

PAUL'S 3rd JOURNEY
52 AD – 57 AD

Paul writes the "Corinthian Brief" (cf. I Cor 5:9) — 54 AD

Writes 2 Corinthians (Macedonia) — 56 AD

Writes Romans (Corinth) — 57 AD

Writes I Corinthians (Ephesus) — 54 AD

Imprisonment - Caesarea — 58 AD – 60 AD

Writes "tearful letter" (cf. 2 Cor 2:4) — 55 AD – 56 AD

First Roman Imprisonment — 60 AD – 62 AD

53 AD | 54 AD | 55 AD | 56 AD | 57 AD | 58 AD | 59 AD | 60 AD | 61 AD | 62 AD

      b. There is no other place in all of Paul's 43,281 words were he is more vulnerable *and* self-disclosing than his Corinthian correspondence.

      c. This becomes clearer when one looks at his use of first person *singular* pronouns (i.e. "I, me, my")versus second person *plural* pronouns (i.e. "you").[3]

Audience	1PSP	P.F.*	T.F.**	2PP
Galatians	106	34	32	99
Thessalonians	9	3	58	168
Corinthians	501	35	35	75
Romans	193	20	23	214
Colossians	30	15	51	98
Ephesians	27	9	27	82
Philemon	39	85	80	37
Philippians	123	57	35	75
Timothy	95	24	15	59
Titus	9	10	9	10

* *"Personal Factor" (PF) based on (#1PSP ÷ #words × 1000)*
** *"Teaching Factor" (TF) based on (#2PP ÷ #words × 1000)*

[1] Merely looking at the *volume* of words is very revealing. Paul's Corinthian correspondence (that we *have*) accounts for 35% of all of Paul's writings. Paul's instruction to them was one and a half times as much as to the leading city in the word—Rome! And, he wrote these three letters at roughly the same time in his ministry, indicating the priority he was placing on the church in Corinth. However, it must also be stated that Corinth also contained the most *unhealthy* church in the New Testament.

[2] There were also very likely personal visits to Paul's churches that we have no record of in Acts. For example, there appears to have been an unrecorded second visit which preceded the "tearful letter" he mentions in 2 Corinthians 2:4.

[3] Another significant word that appears unusually frequently in his Corinthian letters is the word, "apostle." One of Paul's major difficulties with this church was their refusal to accept his apostolic authority. In fact, this is a major theme in our 2 Corinthians. For example, the word "apostle" appears 17 times in the Corinthians letters, compared to 19 times in his other eleven letters combined. And, of the 6 times it appears in 2 Corinthians, 4 of them are in reference to *false* "apostles."

2. Paul's difficulties with the Corinthians stemmed from their insistence on being "*Corinthian* Christians," instead of Christians who happened to live in Corinth.[1]

3. This manifested itself in a number of ways:

   a. Their persistence on maintaining a the expected "social life" of the affluent elite in Corinth, including banquets in idol temples (1 Cor 8; 10:14-22; 2 Cor 6:14 - 7:2).

      (1) There are 51 references to "food" and "drink" in the New Testament; 49 of them are in these letters! (47 in 1 Corinthians).

   b. Their insistence on "picking" their spiritual shepherd (1 Cor 3:1-4; 4:14-16; 2 Cor 1:23-24; 3:1; 7:2-4; 10:1-11; 11:1-6; 13:10).[2]

   c. Their insistence on keeping certain aspects of their personal lives *out* of The Story (e.g. wealth, friendships, patrons, etc.; cf 2 Cor 8-9).

   d. Their obsession with "*dignitas*" (social status in the eyes of their friends):

      (1) The word "boast" appears 34x in these letters, compared to only 12x in the rest of Paul's writings![3]

      (2) Manifested in their constant criticism of Paul's lack of "sophistication" (1 Cor 2:1-5; 2 Cor 10:10).

      (3) Their criticism of Paul (their "teacher") for working with his hands (2 Cor 11:7).

      (4) Their refusal to acknowledge Paul's apostleship because of *his* lack of "*dignitas*."[4]

         (a) The word "apostle" appears 17x in these letters, nearly as much in the other 11 letters of Paul combined!

      (5) Their unwillingness to be associated with the aspects of The Story that their friends would consider "foolish" (i.e. lacking *dignitas*).

         (a) The words "wise" and "foolish" appear 2x as much in these two letters as in all of Paul's other writings combined (19 out of 30)!

B. Getting The Straight "Scoop" on The Story

   1. Paul's closing comments cut to the heart of his "problem parish":[5]

      a. Instead of "examining" themselves and each other by the standards of their social context, they need to examine themselves to determine if they're really in The Story!

      "But with me it is a very small thing that I should be judged by you or by any human court. In fact, I do not even judge myself." **1 Corinthians 4:3**

      "Am I not free? Am I not an apostle? Have I not seen Jesus our Lord? Are not you my workmanship in the Lord? If to others I am not an apostle, at least I am to you, for you are the seal of my apostleship in the Lord. This is my defense to those who would examine me." **1 Corinthians 9:1-3**

      "Not that we dare to classify or compare ourselves with some of those who are commending themselves. But when they measure themselves by one another and compare themselves with one another, they are without understanding." **2 Corinthians 10:12**

      "Examine yourselves, to see whether you are in the faith. Test yourselves. Or do you not realize this about yourselves, that Jesus Christ is in you?--unless indeed you fail to meet the test!" **2 Corinthians 13:5**

---

[1] This issue of "identity" is implicit in Paul's reference to them as having *been* "pagans" (Gk - *ethnos*, the word for Gentiles)! How are they *now*, considering that "Jew" or "Gentile" aren't really viable categories of identity anymore.

[2] We tend to do similar things in the 21st century. In our case, we focus on our own personal sin and justification to the neglect of the larger issues of redemption in all of Creation, which is the heart of the Story.

[3] It is noteworthy, on this topic of *dignitas*, that there are ten references to "commending" in these letters; nine of them in 2 Corinthians alone!

[4] Because of the way *dignitas* operated, Paul's lack of "clout" in the society would have actually eroded *theirs*, if it became known that they were *his* "disciples."

[5] In our age of fickleness and quick abandonment of things that are difficult, Paul's faithfulness to this obstinate, narcissistic church is admirable. He *never* distances himself from them or his responsibility to them as their pastor and "father" in the faith.

2. Paul's "Portrait" of a Genuine Character in "The Story":[1]

Characteristic/Quality	Scripture
someone *"sanctified in Christ Jesus"*	1 Corinthians 1:2
someone *"called to be a saint"*	1:2
[those] *"called into the fellowship of Jesus Christ"*	1:9
"those who are being saved"	1:18; 15:2; 2 Cor 2:15
"those who are called"	1:24
"God's field," "God's building," God's Temple"	3:9,16; 2 Cor 6:16
[those who have been] *"washed, sanctified, justified in the name of Christ Jesus"*	6:11
[those who] *"are not your own...bought with a price"*	6:19-20
[those] *"baptized by one Spirit into one body"*	12:13,27
[those who] *"will bear the image of the man of heaven"*	15:49
[those who] *"will be changed...imperishable"*	15:51
[those who] possess God's Spirit and bear His *"seal"*	2 Corinthians 1:22
[those] "being transformed into the same image from one degree of glory to another"	3:18
[those who are] *"a new creation"*	5:17
[those who are] *"the righteousness of God"*	5:21
[those who are] *"in the faith"*	13:5
[those whom] *"Christ Jesus is in..."*	13:5

3. Paul's "Self-Portrait" of An *unsophisticated* "Story Teller" (1 Cor 4:9-13; 2 Cor 1:8-10; 4:7-9; 6:4; 11:23-12:10)

a. Those *proven* (*apodeiknumi*) by God to be least valued in culture (1Cor 4:9,13; the two words in 4:13 refer to those kept alive only to bear the curses of a city).

"We have become, and are still, like the scum of the world, the refuse of all things". The Greek word which we render filth, is *perikayarmata*, a purgation, or lustrative sacrifice; that which we translate offscouring is *periqhma*, a redemption sacrifice. To understand the full force of these words, as applied by the apostle in this place, we must observe that he alludes to certain customs among the heathens, who, in the time of some public calamity, chose out some unhappy men of the most abject and despicable character to be a public expiation for them; these they maintained a whole year at the public expense; and then they led them out, crowned with flowers, as was customary in sacrifices; and, having heaped all the curses of the country upon their heads, and whipped them seven times, they burned them alive, and afterwards their ashes were thrown into the sea..."

Adam Clarke's Commentary on 1 Corinthians 4:13

b. A "public show" (*theatron*; "spectacle"); a form of entertainment to the world, angels, and people (similar to an execution in the Ancient Near East; cf. 4:9).[2]

c. Considered a weak, foolish and valueless to those outside The Story (4:10).

---

[1] Or put another way, Paul's "salvation vocabulary" in the Corinthian letters.
[2] Even today, consider what sorts of things Christians are made fun of on primetime TV. It's *not* for Story items!

d. Poorly dressed (by comparison), lacking a permanent home[1] and abundant food and drink (4:11; cf. Matt 6).

e. Work long, exhausting hours in The Story (4:12).

f. Endure afflictions crushing enough to induce despondency (2 Cor 1:8-10; the Greek word, *thlipsis* appears 12x in 2 Corinthians).

g. Ordinary "containers" of an extraordinary Story (4:7).

h. Facing "*some of every kind*" (Gk - *pas*) of affliction (4:7).

i. Often uncertain about what to do next (4:8).

j. Aggressively pursued and attacked by those hostile to The Story (4:9).[2]

k. Often dishonored and disgraced (Gk - kataballō "*cast down low*").

l. Continually driven to the point of weakness and powerlessness (4:10-11).

m. A life characterized by needing to endure suffering in general ("afflictions, hardships, calamities), particular types of suffering (beatings, imprisonments, riots), and suffering that is chosen (labors, sleepless nights, hunger). [2 Cor 6:4]

n. A life characterized by virtue that is unaffected by circumstance or audience (6:6-8).

o. A life characterized by spiritual *warfare*, not furlough (6:7).[3]

p. A life whose value system is "foolish" to the culture (6:8-10).

q. Enduring "countless" (Gk - *huperballontos*) beatings (the word implies the use of whips & rods; cf. Acts 16:23-33).

r. Condemned to death *and* executed…twice! (Acts 14:19)

s. Shipwrecked four times (11:25 and Acts 27-28).

t. Every conceivable type of relational and circumstantial "peril."[4]

u. Self-sacrificing, ceaseless toil for the spiritual needs of others (11:27).

v. A deep sense of spiritual responsibility for the spiritual health of those in his life (11:28-29).

w. A deep motivating conviction that God is noticed most when Paul is noticed least (12:9-10).

C. "Corinthian Questions": Learning the Most From the Worst

1. Question: "How much of my own Christian identity and lifestyle is a product of my own address rather than The Story?"

2. Question: "Who am I submitted to within the Body of Christ (i.e. Who is my shepherd?)

3. Question: "What is my current understanding about the place of suffering in the life of a Christian?

4. Question: "Do I see my personal wealth in light of the Mosaic Covenant or the Abrahamic Covenant?" (Deut 28; Lev 26; Gen 12; 2 Cor 8:12-15; 9:6-8).[5]

---

[1] Consider the implications of being "homeless" in our own culture. It's typically thought of as evidence of some personal failure.

[2] Often in the modern world, Christians are attacked by those who are hostile to the "caricature" of the Story that they've seen, rather than the Story itself.

[3] As Christ-followers, we need to realize and constantly remind ourselves and each other that *our* "rest" will take place at the same time that *God* rests again…at the *end* of the Story, not anytime in the midst of it (cf. John 5:17; 9:4).

[4] Paul uses the Greek word, *kindunos*; It appears 9 times in our New Testament, *all* by Paul. Eight of them are in a single verse, 11:26; other is in Paul's litany of things that cannot separate us from the love of Christ in Romans 8:35.

[5] In the Mosaic covenant, wealth was a sign of blessing. In the Abrahamic covenant, wealth was to be the *means* of blessing (others). It is interesting, in this regard, that those who promote the "health and wealth theology" simultaneously teach that the Mosaic Law is not binding on believers. That we are "living under grace, not under law." Yet, it is the Mosaic covenant from which they derive their proof-texts for God's supposed desire to "bless" us with wealth. In Paul's Corinthian correspondence, "giving" is to be regular (1 Cor 16:2), proportional to income (1 Cor 16:2), freely and cheerfully done (2 Cor 9:7), generous and abundant (2 Cor 9:6, and intended to "balance" needs and excesses (2 Cor 8:12-15; 9:11).

XVI. UNIT 16 - PAUL'S "RETIREMENT PLANS": ROME & SPAIN![1]

A. Chasing Paul Across the Mediterranean — A Plausible Timeline

1. **AD 49 -** The Emperor Claudius expels "Jews" from Rome "…because they were constantly rioting at the instigation of Chrestus…" —**Suetonius, in** *Life of Claudius*

    a. Aquila and Priscilla were among these "Jews," indicating that both Hebraic Jews and Messianic Jews were expelled (Acts 18:2).

    b. This would have left a predominately Gentile church in Rome.[2]

    c. Aquila and Priscilla meet Paul in Corinth around this time; he is on his second missionary journey.

2. **AD 51 -** Gallio is appointed as proconsul of Achaia and makes his home in Corinth (cf. Acts 18:18).[3]

3. **AD 52 -** Paul leaves Corinth, and stops at Ephesus on his way back home to Syria. He leaves Aquila and Priscilla in Ephesus where they host a church in their home (Acts 18:19; 1 Cor 16:19).

4. **AD 53 -** Paul returns to Ephesus on his *third* journey and ministers there for three years. He writes 1 Corinthians from here at this time (Acts 19:1,10; 20:17,31).

5. **AD 54 -** Emperor Claudius dies and Jews begin returning to Rome only to find that the "Jewishness" of the city is much more a minority view.

6. **AD 56 -** Paul leaves Ephesus and spends 3 months in Corinth[4] where he writes Romans (Acts 20:1-3):

    a. "Phoebe," a deaconess of the church at Cenchreae, *and* "patron" of many, including Paul, seems to be carrying the letter (Rom 16:1-2).

    b. Gaius, an important Corinthian official, is Paul's host while he is writing Romans (Rom 16:23; 1 Cor 1:14).

7. **AD 57 -** Paul leaves Corinth, heading for Jerusalem via Miletus to address the elders of Ephesus (Acts 20:18-32).

B. Sleuthing The Source — Plausible Reasons for Romans

1. **Reason #1:** Paul seems to be changing "chapters" in his life work:

    a. He makes repeated statements hinting that his "work"[5] in the western Mediterranean basin is over:

    b. Paul lists the "extremities" of his ministry, and says he has *"filled-up to the brim"* the ministry of the Gospel in these areas.

    "…by the power of signs and wonders, by the power of the Spirit of God—so that from Jerusalem and all the way around to Illyricum I have fulfilled the ministry of the gospel of Christ;"   **Romans 15:19[6]**

    "…and thus I make it my ambition to preach the gospel, not where Christ has already been named, lest I build on someone else's foundation…"   **Romans 15:20**

    "Now after these events Paul resolved in the Spirit to pass through Macedonia and Achaia and go to Jerusalem, saying, "After I have been there, I must also see Rome."   **Acts 19:21** *[while on 2ⁿᵈ journey]*

    And when they came to him, he said to them: "You yourselves know how I lived among you the whole time from the first day that I set foot in Asia, serving the Lord with all humility and with tears and with trials that happened to me through the plots of the Jews…And now, behold, I know that none of you among whom I have gone about proclaiming the kingdom will see my face again…Therefore be alert, remembering that for three years I did not cease night or day to admonish everyone with tears. And now I commend you to God and to the word of his grace, which is able to build you up and to give you the inheritance among all those who are sanctified."   **Acts 20:18,19;31-32,25**

---

[1] Paul's idea of "retirement" was *not* to cease from working hard, but to work hard in a new direction. We could learn much from this idea in our modern world designed to work hard then "coast" for the last chapter.

[2] This fact is vital in properly reading and understanding Paul's arguments in this book. His audience determines much of what he says, and how and why he says it.

[3] Much extra-biblical literary evidence, including an inscription found at Delphi mentioning Gallio *and* dated. He was brother to the famous Roman philosopher, Seneca. As proconsul, he had a deep and wide authority.

[4] Priscilla and Aquila are *back* in Rome by this time, hosting another house church (Rom. 16:3-5). There is at least the possibility that they actually returned to the church that had been involved with *prior* to their expulsion in AD 49.

[5] Remember: Paul was more of a church *planter* than a shepherding pastor.

[6] Both the NIV and the NASB have the word, "preaching" in Romans 15:19, but the verb is absent in the Greek.

"...always in my prayers, asking that somehow by God's will I may now at last succeed in coming to you...I want you to know, brothers, that I have often intended to come to you (but thus far have been prevented), in order that I may reap some harvest among you as well as among the rest of the Gentiles...So I am eager to preach the gospel to you also who are in Rome."   **Romans 1:10,13,15**

"This is the reason why I have so often been hindered from coming to you. But now, since I no longer have any room for work in these regions, and since I have longed for many years to come to you, I hope to see you in passing as I go to Spain, and to be helped on my journey there by you, once I have enjoyed your company for a while."   **Romans 15:22-24**

2. **Reason #2:** Paul may be planning to make Rome his western "base" of ministry just like he did Antioch in Syria for the east.

   a. Paul spends the first six verses describing himself and call to ministry to a church he had never visited (Rom 1:1-6).

   b. He may be laying a clear theological basis of his apostleship *and* the gospel he has been preaching for twenty years.

   c. Romans also serves as a sort of "theological memoir" of Paul's past twenty years of ministry—his theology "at its best."

3. **Reason #3:** Paul is seeking *financial* assistance from the church in Rome for this western expansion into Spain.[1]

4. **Reason #4:** The Gentile-Jew tension in the Roman church was both a denial of, and threat to, "The Story."

   a. There are 59 references to "Gentiles"[2] in this book, and only 24 references to "Jews" (i.e. Israel, Jews).

   b. The majority of references to "Jews" is *before* chapter 9!

   c. From beginning to end, Romans is dripping with Paul's unquenchable desire for everyone to understand the "mystery" hidden for ages—that the Abrahamic covenant *is* "The Story."

   d. Paul opens the letter with a clear statement of expansive nature of The Story:

   "For I am not ashamed of the gospel, for it is the power of God for salvation to everyone who believes, to the Jew first (protos; first in succession) *and also to the Greek* (Hellēn).*"*   **Romans 1:16**

   e. His closing doxology of praise is full of "Story" language:

   "Now to him who is able to strengthen you according to my gospel and the preaching of Jesus Christ, according to the revelation of the mystery that was kept secret for long ages but has now been disclosed and through the prophetic writings has been made known to all nations [Gk, ethnos], according to the command of the eternal God, to bring about the obedience of faith—to the only wise God be glory forevermore through Jesus Christ! Amen."   **Romans 16:25-27**

   f. Paul argues that one's ethno-theological preferences must be made subservient to The Story:[3]

   "One person esteems one day as better than another, while another esteems all days alike. Each one should be fully convinced in his own mind. The one who observes the day, observes it in honor of the Lord. The one who eats, eats in honor of the Lord, since he gives thanks to God, while the one who abstains, abstains in honor of the Lord and gives thanks to God."   **Romans 14:5, 6**

   "I know and am persuaded in the Lord Jesus that nothing is unclean in itself, but it is unclean for anyone who thinks it unclean. For if your brother is grieved by what you eat, you are no longer walking in love. By what you eat, do not destroy the one for whom Christ died."   **Romans 14:14, 15**

   g. Paul's doctrine of adoption is inclusive of both Jews and Gentiles, both are "fellow heirs" together with Christ, and can equally address Yahweh as "Abba, Father":

---

[1] Paul uses the Greek word, *propempō* in Rom 15:24, which we translate "helped." But, it implies providing someone with the things *necessary* to make a journey. By implication, Paul is speaking about funding this trip. See, for example: 2 Corinthians 1:16; Titus 3:13; 3 John 6.
[2] Greek is *ethnos*; i.e. Gentile, Greek, nations.
[3] The first two references are in regard to Jews and Gentiles, but the third reference has to do with Gentile arrogance about the "folly" of Jewish dietary restrictions.

> *"For all who are led by the Spirit of God are sons of God. For you did not receive the spirit of slavery to fall back into fear, but you have received the Spirit of adoption as sons, by whom we cry, "Abba! Father!" The Spirit himself bears witness with our spirit that we are children of God, and if children, then heirs--heirs of God and fellow heirs with Christ, provided we suffer with him in order that we may also be glorified with him."* **Romans 8:14-17**

> *"For there is no distinction between Jew and Greek; the same Lord is Lord of all, bestowing his riches on all who call on him."* **Romans 10:12**

    h. The hotly debated chapters dealing with the nation of Israel must be understood beneath the umbrella of "The Story," *not* the doctrine of "election" (cf. ch 9-11).[1]

    i. Paul's argument for perseverance is based on The Story, *not* us studying a few of its key "characters":[2]

> *"For whatever was written in former days was written for our instruction, that through endurance and through the encouragement of the Scriptures we might have hope."* **Romans 15:4**

    j. Paul's closing arguments about Christlikeness and his prayer for them as a church, all reflect this Jew-Gentile tension:

> *"May the God of endurance and encouragement grant you to live in such harmony with one another, in accord with Christ Jesus, that together you may with one voice glorify the God and Father of our Lord Jesus Christ. Therefore welcome one another as Christ has welcomed you, for the glory of God."* **Romans 15:5-7**

  C. SUMMARY: Our "Roman Road" May Not Be Heading in the Right Direction

    1. We must be very careful that what we mean when we say "The Gospel" matches what Paul meant.

    2. What Paul was "not ashamed of" was *not* The Four Spiritual Laws, it was the scandalous news of an inclusive redemption by an exclusive God.

    3. Galatians and Romans are Paul's most convincing arguments that left to ourselves, we will lose the Story in the midst of the script.

XVII. UNIT 17 - PAUL'S LONGEST LETTER TO THE WORLD'S LARGEST CITY

  A. Reading Romans Responsibly

    1. We need to approach the letter to the Romans by admitting that we do *not* know for sure why Paul wrote this letter.

      a. We can only guess at his motivation for writing, content inclusion, and arrangement.[3]

      b. We *can* assume, because of his unbridled use of the Jewish scriptures that his audience had a level of spiritual maturity.

> *"For I long to see you, that I may impart to you some spiritual gift to strengthen you—that is, that we may be mutually encouraged by each other's faith, both yours and mine."* **Romans 1:11, 12**

        (1) Paul's most robust theological vocabulary is in this letter:

•law (73)	•death (25)	•sanctification (3)
•sin (66)	• judgment (22)	•glorification (2)
•righteousness (41)	• justification (15)	•predestination (2)
•faith (40)	• wrath (12)	•redemption (2)
•(Holy) Spirit (31)	•condemnation (9)	•propitiation (1)

      c. It is unavoidably true that one of Paul's goals is to provide a detailed explanation of what he calls, "*my gospel*" (2:16; 16:25).

        (1) It is Paul's longest letter to a church he had yet to visit.

---

[1] Paul's passion was unity *in the Story*, not division over the details of it!

[2] The basis of our hope is *not* the encouragement of studying Old Testament characters who we can "learn" from, but to understand the Story itself. This is the basis of our encouragement; God's faithfulness to see the Story through, *not* the saints' perseverance in the midst of it.

[3] For example, the resurrection is assumed but never mentioned, there is only a hint about the return of Christ, and sexual purity is implied but not a key topic. Because this is a *letter*, we must assume that its recipients' circumstances and environment were instrumental in determining what Paul addresses and what he does not.

        (2) Paul asks 85 questions to which he expects no response.[1]

        (3) Paul uses the Greek word, *oun* ("therefore, then"), a word used to conclude arguments, 39x.

  2. We need to guard ourselves against *using* Romans to support our own "flavor" of theology:

    a. This letter must be read and understood against the backdrop of Paul's passion for the *mustērion* of Yahweh—the One Story of the One God (cf pp 2-3 of syllabus).

    b. Of the 50 names in the letter, only 9 are mentioned more than once, and they are all dead![2]

    c. Paul draws from 13 books in at least 53 citations from the Jewish scriptures.

    d. Paul *appears* to be seeking to build a theological "bridge" between the past and *their* present (i.e. "prove" the Story).

    e. In other words, Paul seems to want them to fully understand The Story, and their place in it:

        (1) Ch 1-11 — the theology of the Story

        (2) Ch 12-16 — the theology because of The Story

  3. "*Our*" Gospel must be developed against the backdrop of Romans, rather than Romans becoming a "Gospel" that fits our age.

B. Getting Inside the "*My Gospel*" of Paul

  1. The "Good News" is only as good as the "bad" it trumps![3]

    a. The "Gospel" is the working of God to save some (i.e. "*those who believe*") from among all people groups (1:16).

    b. The Gospel "reveals" (*apokoluptō*) God's righteousness, which "reveals" His wrath against the sin that "suppresses" (*katechō*, holds back) The Story (1:17-18).

    c. Sin entered the world through Adam, and it and its consequences are now a permanent part of the fabric of life (5:8, 17-18).

    d. Sinful humanity is in a continual retreat from God's glory and left to itself will continually degenerate and corrupt all of creation (1:21-32; 3:23).

    e. Both those *with* the Jewish scriptures and those without them fail to do what they know to be right, and do what they know to be wrong (2:1-3; 3:8; ch 7).

    f. Both those with and without the Jewish scriptures sin because they are sinners, not vice versa (3:9-20).[4]

    g. Both those *with* and *without* the Jewish scriptures are damned because of their Adamic ancestry and its fruit:

"I carried about in me a cut and bleeding soul that could not bear to be carried by me and where I could put it, I could not discover. Not in pleasant groves, not in games and singing, nor in the fragrant corners of a garden. Not in the company of a dinner table, not in the delight of the bed. Not even in my books and poetry. It floundered in a void and fell back on me. I remained in a haunted spot, which gave me no rest, from which I could not escape. For where could my heart flee from my heart? Where could I escape myself? Where would I not dog my own footsteps?" **Augustine of Hippo**

    h. The entire creation has been affected and infected by sin, and it is dying like the human race (8:19-22).

    i. Man's problem is not that he's not "good" (some are! 5:7), it's that he's not righteous (3:20-26; 5:19).

---

[1] This is the very type of rhetoric that he deliberately *avoided* in his Corinthian letters, likely because of the priority the Corinthians placed on one's public speaking and declamation skills.

[2] 36 names appears in chapter 16 alone, and each is used only once.

[3] An anemic doctrine of sin leads to an anemic doctrine of redemption, which results in an "anemic" Jesus.

[4] This stands in stark contrast between the Christian doctrine of sin and that of Islam. In Islam, people are *not* born sinful, but learn sinful behavior, and can also "unlearn" it. In a conversation with a woman who had converted from Islam to Christianity, she told me the distinction between the Muslim's view of sin and that of the Christian is enormous and critical. She took a bowl of oatmeal and sprinkled some raisins in it. Then she took them out, one by one, with a spoon. *"This, is the Islamic view of sin. You just need to work at getting the sinful behaviors and deeds out of your life."* Then, she took another bowl of oatmeal and sprinkled salt in it and stirred it. *"This is the Christian view of sin. You cannot remove it. You need a whole new bowl of oatmeal."*

C. Yahweh: An Equal Opportunity Savior

   1. Yahweh Himself solved this hopeless dilemma of a helpless race through incarnation (1:2-4), execution (3:21-26; 6:3-5), and resurrection (4:24-25; 6:4).

> *"Only the message that another true and obedient human being has come on our behalf, that he has lived for us the kind of life we should live but can't, and that he has paid fully the penalty we deserve for the life we do live but shouldn't—only this message can give assurance that we have peace with God through our Lord Jesus Christ."* **Graeme Goldsworthy**, *Preaching the Whole Gospel as Christian Scripture*

   2. Wrath has been poured out, a death has been exacted, a perfect life has been lived, and every aspect of conscience *and* the Law has been obeyed…on my behalf (3:23-26; 5:8-11; 8:1-4).

   3. This was the merger of *"grace and truth"* (Jn 1:17), the one means back into the One Story.

D. The Gospel is "out of faith into faith" (Gk - *ek pisteō eis pistis;* 1:17).

   1. Those now in the Story are never "out of character."

     a. They have a shared hatred for the "antagonist" (Adam) in them (ch 6-7).[1]

     b. The Author of the Story indwells them, redirecting their values and choices (ch 8).

     c. They are humbled by the *enormity* of the Story, even in *this* life (ch 4-5, 9-11).[2]

     d. The understand that the redemption extended to them reaches even to creation (8:19-23).

     e. They humbly accept their small role, and are committed to a life of understanding it better (ch 12).[3]

     f. They realize that in a world of many political "fictions," there is only one true Story (ch 13).

     g. They are constantly on their guard against the host of minor characters and subplots that threaten to hijack the Story (ch 14).

E. "When in Rome…" — Taking Romans Seriously

   1. We must refuse to relegate the "gospel" to Romans 1-11, as in this modern gospel tract:

     a. *"Here's Hope Roman Road Tract"* (from North American Mission Board of the Southern Baptist Convention)

       (1) Rom 1:16 — "The Gospel: the power of God for Salvation"

       (2) Rom 3:23 — "Change: Necessary For Everyone"

       (3) Rom 5:8 — "God's Love For Us"

       (4) Rom 10:9 — "Your Commitment"

     b. The Gospel that Paul preached, that Christ gave him, is the subject of *all* of the letter to the Romans.

     c. The moral side of our faith (i.e. behavior) *must* have a deep theological explanation behind it that is linked to The Story, *not* culture or family.[4]

     d. The Gospel we proclaim must truly be "good news" to *all* people groups (1:16; 10:12), the poor (Is 61:1; Lk 4:18), and to Creation itself (8:19-22; Hosea 4:1-3).

     e. Understanding and embracing God's Story is the only sufficient foundation for missions.

     f. When we say the "Bible is God's Word," we must have a satisfactory answer to the question, "About what?"

---

[1] Consider this stanza from a popular Christian hymn: *"In my heart there is a treason; One that poisons all my love. Take my heart and consecrate it; wash it in your cleansing blood."*

[2] When one considers that he is actually an integral part of a drama that includes characters like Adam, Abraham, Moses, ancient Israel, Daniel, Paul, etc., he is rightfully humbled. It is an eternal Story of immeasurable magnitude. It is beyond belief that I have been brought into it.

[3] Paul warns them not to think too "highly" of themselves, and to realize that there are "different giftings" in this grand Story. And they are exactly that...gifts!

[4] The consequences of failure on this point are especially disastrous over time. Whenever a believer comes to assume they're only accountable to those around them, or those they love and respect, they lose the sufficient grounds for moral purity over time.

XVIII. UNIT 18 - FOUR LETTERS FROM PAUL'S NEW "OFFICE" IN ROME — part 1

A. Connecting the "Dots" Between Romans and Colossians (Acts 21-28)

1. **Acts 21:1-8** — Paul sails from Miletus in Asia to Caesarea[1] on the coast of Palestine; we discover that Philip from the original seven deacons, now called "the Evangelist" lives in Caesarea along with his four unmarried daughters "who prophesied."

2. **Acts 21:17-26** — Paul travels to Jerusalem, meets with the apostle James and the elders[2] and reports on the ministry to the Gentiles. They are encouraged, and ask Paul to be "sensitive" to the Jews in Jerusalem because his name is very volatile there.

3. **Acts 21:27-22:29** — Paul is arrested by Roman officers after a near riot breaks out, instigated by some Jews from Asia.[3] He is allowed to address the Jewish mob, but when he makes reference to Yahweh's call on his life to go to the Gentiles, another riot breaks out. The Roman officers nearly beat him, but find out he's a citizen.

4. **Acts 22:30-23:22** — Paul defends himself before the Sanhedrin to no avail.[4] He is given assurance by Yahweh that he will testify in Rome, and then discovers a plot to assassinate him in Jerusalem.

5. **Acts 23:23-26:32** — Paul is transported to the governor's headquarters in Caesarea by military escort and *stays there for 2 years* (AD 58-60), and has opportunity to testify before two Roman procurators[5] and Herod Agrippa II. He appeals to Caesar and plans are made for that journey.

6. **Acts 27:1-28:13** — Paul's journey to Rome is interrupted by a shipwreck on an island called Malta, where Paul ministers to the son of a high-ranking Roman official, Publius.

7. **Acts 28:14-31** — Paul is escorted on foot to Rome and is imprisoned in a "minimum security" cell (i.e. house arrest). Luke ends Acts with Paul in prison (AD 60-62).

B. Filling in the "Blanks" Between Acts and Colossians (a plausible chronology)

1. In the mid-50's, Paul spends three years (cf. Acts 20:31) in the city of Ephesus, 120 miles west of Colossae, so that Luke tells us, "*all Asia heard the word of the Lord.*" (19:10).

2. Ephaphras[6], a resident of Colossae, journeys to Ephesus where he was convinced the Jesus was the Messiah, and is discipled by Paul during this time.

3. Ephaphras returns home, bringing the Gospel to Colossae, most likely to the Jewish and god-fearing Colossians associated with a synagogue there (Col 1:6-7).

4. Philemon comes to faith, and hosts a church in his home (Philemon 2).

5. The Story spreads to the neighboring city of Laodecia, where a house church is hosted in the home of Nympha, to whom Paul wrote a letter that is lost (4:15-16).

6. Ephaphras travels to Rome to inform Paul of the status of the church, bringing a mixture of good news and bad. Paul writes our letter of Colossians in response, likely carried by Tychicus (4:7,12).

7. Paul writes to Philemon, his family, and the Colossian church about his runaway slave Onesimus. The letter is carried by Tychicus or perhaps even by Onesimus himself.[7]

---

[1] Caesarea was the headquarters for the Roman presence in Palestine. It was where the procurator (e.g. Pontius Pilate) lived the majority of the year.

[2] It seems a bit odd that Peter is not mentioned by name during this visit.

[3] Luke is careful to let his readers know the areas from which the "troublemakers" came; The areas that had previously rejected Paul; Lystra, Pisidia, etc.

[4] It is during this conflict that Paul shrewdly employs the theological differences between the Pharisees and Sadducees to his advantage (cf. Acts 23:6).

[5] Felix (Acts 24:27) and Festus.

[6] He may very well have been a convert *to* Judaism, In other words, a "god-fearer" who was likely *not* a Hebrew by birth (cf. Colossians 4:11-12).

[7] Nine of the names in both letters are the same!

C. COLOSSIANS: The World *Behind* the Letter — Geography, History, and Heresy

1. Colossae was the *"ugly step-city"* in a tri-city cluster with Laodecia and Hierapolis, its two very affluent and influential neighbors (cf 4:13).[1]

2. These three cities were 6-12 miles from each other, and about 100 miles east of Ephesus.

3. This is the "Laodecia" rebuked by the aged John 30 years later for its arrogance and affluence (Rev 3:14-22).

4. Hierapolis was a recreational center, boasting of healing spas and mineral waters.

5. It had a significant Jewish population, *but* the church was largely Gentile:

   a. Antiochus the Great had relocated 2,000 Jewish families to this area and many others joined them so that Palestinian Jews lamented how many Jews had moved there for the *"...wine and baths of Phrygia."*

   b. Paul used the phrase, *"alienated and hostile in mind"* to describe them, a description he used for Gentiles (1:21).

   c. In the context of speaking of *"...the mystery of Christ among the Gentiles,"* he refers to *"Christ in you, the hope of glory"* (1:27).

   d. In referring to their pre-Story lives, his list of their sins is very "Gentile":

   "Put to death therefore what is earthly in you: sexual immorality, impurity, passion, evil desire, and covetousness, which is idolatry. On account of these the wrath of God is coming. In these you too once walked, when you were living in them.   **Colossians 3:5-7**

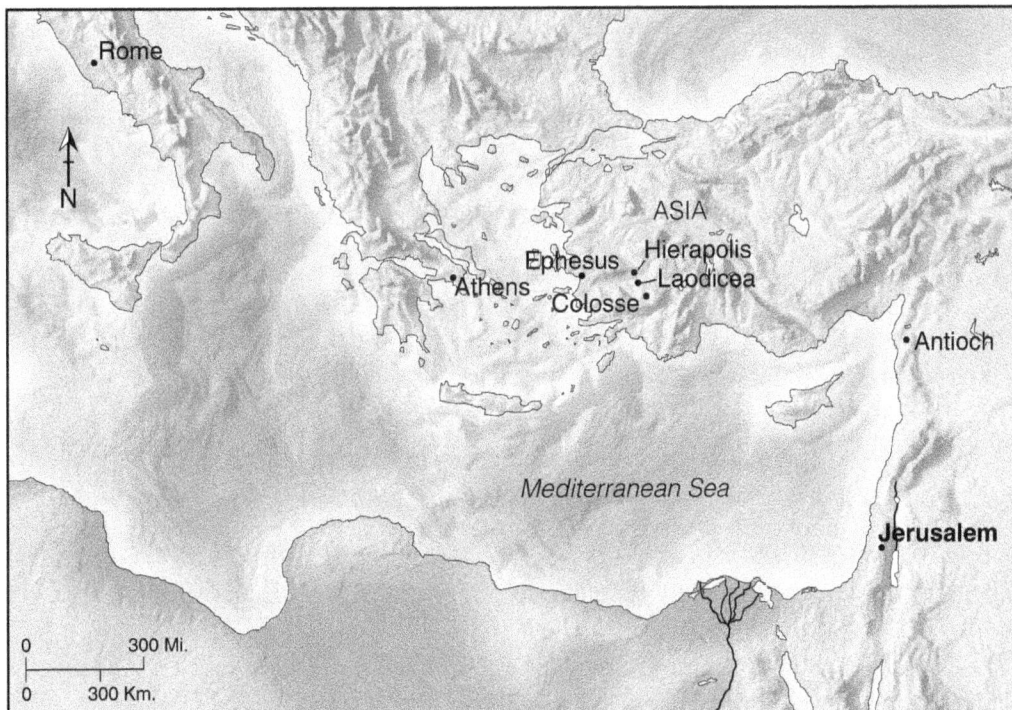

6. Colossae featured an "All-You-Can-Take" *spiritual* smorgasbord that was encroaching on the Story[2]:

   a. Coins minted in Colossae show a veritable "Wal-Mart' of deities in the city:

   (1) Egypt: *Isis* and *Sarapis*

   (2) Greece: *Athena, Demeter, Helios, Hygieia, Tyche*

---

[1] Laodecia once refused government financial aid from Rome following an earthquake, so self-sufficient did the city feel.
[2] This city, perhaps more than others, embodied what we would call "pluralism," a high value on "tolerance" and no sense of exclusivity.

      (3) Ephesian: *Artemis*

      (4) Laodecian: *Zeus*

      (5) Colossian: *Men & Selene* (lunar god and goddess)

  b. Archeological, epigraphic and documentary sources reveal the same:

      (1) Curse Tablets ("*Curses for Dummies*") have been found, detailing how to curse individuals and property.

      (2) Inscriptions have been found that contain prayers to angels (pagan *and* Jewish)

      (3) Spirits, especially demonic spirits, associated with nature, ancestors, stars and planets, were a central part of the mythology of the area.

7. Colossae appears to have been infiltrated by an individual who was serving up a sort of spiritual "smoothie," blending all the local "stories" of the region into a replacement for the One Story:

> "*I say this so that* **no one** *will delude you with persuasive argument.*"   **Col 2:4**

> "*See to it that* **no one** *takes you captive through philosophy and empty deception, according to the tradition of men, according to the elementary principles of the world, rather than according to Christ.*" **Col 2:8**

> "*Therefore* **no one** *is to act as your judge in regard to food or drink or in respect to a festival or a new moon or a Sabbath day-...*"   **Col 2:16**

> "*Let* **no one** *keep defrauding you of your prize by delighting in self-abasement and the worship of the angels, taking his stand on visions he has seen, inflated without cause by his fleshly mind...*" **Col 2:18**

8. This "Smoothie" included:

  a. the worship of angels (2:18)

  b. a fear and preoccupation with the demonic ("rulers and authorities"; 1:16; 2:15).

      (1) Paul uses the word, *stoicheia* to refer to the "*elemental spirits of the world...*" (2:8)

      (2) A 1st century AD Jewish occult document known as The Testament of Solomon sheds tremendous light on the seriousness of Paul's concern:

> "*Then [Solomon] commanded another demon to appear before me. There came to me thirty-six heavenly bodies [stoicheia], their heads like formless dogs...When I, Solomon, saw these things, I asked them saying, 'Well who are you?' All at once, with one voice they said, 'We are thirty-six heavenly bodies [stoicheia] the world rulers of the darkness of this age.*"

  c. Jewish elements of diet, circumcision, and ritualistic self-denial and abuse (2:11,16-17,21-23).

  d. A spiritual "aristocracy" built around knowledge:

      (1) there are 17 references to knowledge and wisdom in all four chapters.

      (2) Paul goes out of his way to dismantle any idea of "elitism"[1] in The Story:

> "*Him we proclaim, warning* **everyone** *[panta] and teaching* **everyone** *[panta] with* **all** *[pasa] wisdom, that we may present* **everyone** *[panta] mature in Christ. For this I toil, struggling with all his energy that he powerfully works within me.*"   **Colossians 1:28, 29**

  e. The most insidious element in this counterfeit story was its relegation of Jesus Christ to a supporting role.

9. Paul's Solution: Recasting the Story Around the Pre-Eminence of Christ

  a. This is Paul's most "Christological" church letter:

      (1) There is no other letter by Paul that exalts Christ more than Colossians.

      (2) Paul's use of "Christ" in comparison to "Jesus" in this letter is nearly 2x in every other letter he wrote.

      (3) Paul's intentional teaching on the person and work of Jesus Christ is the most extensive of all his letters:

         (a) Christ *is* The Story (*musterion*; 2:2)

---

[1] Think of this as a sort of "Christian" *dignitas*.

(b) Christ is the image of the invisible God and in him all fullness dwells[1] (1:15,19)

(c) Christ is the "firstborn of all creation"[2] (1:15; cf Ps 89:27).

(d) By him were all things created (1:16)

(e) In him all things hold together (1:17)

(f) In him are hid all the treasures of wisdom and knowledge[3] (2:2)

(g) In him dwells the fullness of the godhead in bodily form[4] (2:9)

D. The Long "Half-Life" of Colossae's Error

1. Because there can only be One Story, any religious counterfeit has to "fire" the key character.

Islam - *"Jesus was no more than a mortal whom Allah favored and made an example to the Israelites. They are unbelievers who say God is Messiah, Mary's son."*　　　　　　　　　　**Surat al Nisa 4:157-158**

"And because of their saying: we slew the messiah Jesus son of Mary. Allah's messenger-they slew him not nor crucified　　　　　　　　　　**Sura 43:59**

"Such was Jesus, the son of Mary; it is a statement of truth, about which they vainly dispute. It is not befitting to the majesty of God, that He should beget a son. Glory be to Him! When He determines a matter, He only says to it, 'Be' and it is"　　　　　　　　　　**Quran 19:34-35**

"The Messiah (Jesus), son of Mary, was no more than a Messenger before whom many Messengers have passed away; and his mother adhered wholly to truthfulness, and they both ate food (as other mortals do). See how We make Our signs clear to them; and see where they are turning away!"　　　**Quran 5:75**

Jehovah's Witnesses - (Charles Taze Russell) - *"There is Scriptural evidence for concluding that Michael was the name of Jesus Christ before he left heaven and after his return."* (WT 5/15/1969, p. 307) ... *"Michael the great prince is none other than Jesus Christ himself."* (WT 12/15/1984 p29) *"Michael the archangel is no other than the only begotten son of God, now Jesus Christ.."*　　　　**New Heavens and New Earth, pg.30-31**

Mormonism - *"..That Lucifer, the son of the morning, is our elder brother and the brother of Jesus Christ."* (Apostle B. McConkie Mormon doctrine p.163-164) *"...Jesus, our elder brother, was begotten in the flesh by the same character that was in the garden of Eden, and who is our Father in Heaven,"*　　　　　　　　　　**Journal of Discourses, Vol. 1, pp. 50-51**

"Jesus got married at Cana and had many wives Martha, Mary and others he also had many children,"　　　　　**Journal of Discourses, Vol. 1 345-346; Vol. 2 79-82; Vol. 4:259-260; The Seer p.172**

Benny Hinn (televangelist)- *"What was the appearance of God the Father? Like that of a man...God has the likeness of fingers and hands and a face."* (Good Morning Holy Spirit, p. 82) *"Have you been begotten? So was He. Don't let anyone deceive you. Jesus was reborn."* (Our Position 'In Christ,' Part 1 1991), videotape #TV-254. *"God the Father, God the Son, and God the Holy Ghost - three separate individuals, one in essence, one in work - and, may I add, each one of them possesses His own spirit-body."*　　　　**"Praise the Lord", 10/23/92**

E. The World *Before* the Letter: Colossians and the American Church

1. It is very significant, that in Paul's "practical" chapter in this letter (ch 3), he uses "Christ" more than in the others (8x), and makes 16 references to the Lordship of Jesus.[5]

2. His first corrective is for them to remind themselves that they are in The Story (3:1-3).

3. Paul lays out three commands that are to be employed in the meantime:

a. *"Let the peace of Christ rule in your hearts to which indeed you were called in one body. And be thankful."* (3:15)

b. *"Let the word of Christ[6] dwell in you richly...with thankfulness in your hearts to God"* (3:16)

---

[1] In other words, there is nothing "missing."

[2] This title must be understood in the arena of "rank," *not* "birth order" as Jehovahs' Witnesses insist saying the Jesus was the first thing God created and is therefore part of creation and *not* God.

[3] The Story is comprehensive. All that we need to "know" it contains.

[4] Fully God and fully human. This was the "heart" of the Christological debates of the 4th century, out of which our Nicene Creed emerged.

[5] In all our discussion about Christianity, the "practical" aspects of our faith must *never* be separated from the larger canvas of the Story from which they derive their meaning.

[6] This is *not* to be understood as some vague reference to "the Bible." It is a clear admonition that the *words* of Jesus have a home in our lives.

    c. Do everything you do "In the name of Christ[1], giving thank to God the Father through him." (3:17)

  4. Paul then lays out four arenas where these those in The Story are to obey these commands:

    a. husbands and wives (3:18-19)

    b. parents and children (3:20-21)

    c. slaves and masters[2] (3:22 - 4:1)

    d. "insiders" and "outsiders" (4:5-6)

XIX. UNIT 19 - FOUR LETTERS FROM PAUL'S NEW "OFFICE" IN ROME — part 2

  A. EPHESIANS: The "Queen of Epistles" Meets the "Queen of Heaven"

    1. *"The saints who are in Ephesus…"* weren't *always* "saints"!

      a. The "saints who are in Ephesus" are the result of Paul's 3-year ministry there during his second missionary journey (AD 52-55; Acts 19).

      b. Ephesus served as a "radiating hub" from which the Story emanated to the surrounding cities of Hierapolis, Laodecia, Smyrna, Sardis, etc. (Acts 19:8-10).[3]

      c. His ministry here was significant enough to provoke a riot because of a drop in idol worship in the city (cf. Acts 19:21-20:1).[4]

      d. The Ephesian believers appear to be people of passionate, yet practical conviction (e.g. public book burning; 19:19).[5]

      e. Paul is evacuated out of the city, travels through Macedonia and Greece, sails to Jerusalem and is imprisoned for 4 years in Caesarea and Rome (from which he writes this letter).

      f. There are roughly five years between Paul's last encounter with them and this letter.

    2. The City of Ephesus and What Put Her "On the Map"

      a. In 550 BC the Temple of Artemis was completed, after 120 years of construction.[6]

        (1) It was the largest building in the Greek world at the time.

        (2) It was the first building of its size completely made of marble.

        (3) Herodotus listed this temple as one of the Seven Wonders of the World (5th century BC).

        (4) The temple area served as a regional "savings and loan" for the city.

      b. This explains the enormous backlash against Paul when the Story began to affect the silversmith trade:

        [Demetrius the silversmith]: *"And there is danger not only that this trade of ours may come into disrepute but also that the temple of the great goddess Artemis may be counted as nothing, and that she may even be deposed from her magnificence, she whom all Asia and the world worship.* **Acts 19:27**

      c. Ephesus was the third largest city in the known world, with a population close to 250,000 people (Rome and Alexandria were larger).

      d. Asia Minor was the richest region in the Roman empire, and Ephesus was its leading city.

      e. The theater where Paul could have lost his life seated over 20,000 people (Acts 19:28-34).

---

[1] Or put another way, "Live in such a way that your conduct points to the power and truth of the Story and does not contradict it.

[2] Paul's teaching here is explosive. Telling first century slave owners to *"treat your slaves justly and fairly…"* was unheard of! Paul uses the word *isotēs* which points to equality.

[3] The influence of the Ephesian ministry on Heirapolis and Laodecia we know from Paul's own writings. The radiating influence on Smyrna, Sardis, etc. we can surmise with great certainty.

[4] Paul was actually more responsible for a drop is the *sales* of idols in the city. However, a drop in sales would correspond to a decline in the activities associated with the idols as well.

[5] This event, along with the failed exorcism from the seven sons of Sceva, seems to point to a spiritual "darkness" in the city. Paul's extensive teaching on the nature and prescription for spiritual warfare in this book (and not in others) seems to support this idea s well.

[6] It was funded by legendary King Croesus of Lydia, and measured 377' by 180' and had 40' columns.

  f. Timothy is the "pastor" of this city by the time Paul first writes him in AD 64 (1 Tim 1:3), and perhaps even until Paul is executed in AD 67 (cf. 2 Tim 1:18;4:12).[1]

  g. Thirty years later, when the Apostle John writes his letter to the "seven churches of Asia Minor," the Ephesian church isn't doing well:

> *"To the angel of the church in Ephesus write: The words of him who holds the seven stars in his right hand, who walks among the seven golden lampstands. 'I know your works, your toil and your patient endurance, and how you cannot bear with those who are evil, but have tested those who call themselves apostles and are not, and found them to be false. I know you are enduring patiently and bearing up for my name's sake, and you have not grown weary. But I have this against you, that you have abandoned the love you had at first. Remember therefore from where you have fallen; repent, and do the works you did at first. If not, I will come to you and remove your lampstand from its place, unless you repent. Yet this you have: you hate the works of the Nicolaitans, which I also hate.'"*
>
> **Revelation 2:1-6**

3. Postal Confusion: Who Were *"the saints who are at Ephesus"*?

  a. There is overwhelming evidence that the residents of Ephesus were *not* the recipients of this letter:[2]

   (1) Paul gives no personal greeting like his other letters (cf. Phil 1:3-5).

   (2) Paul only mentions one person besides himself (Tychicus), in contrast to his other letters.[3]

   (3) He doesn't address a single location-specific issue like all his other letters (cf. 1 Cor 7:1; Phil 4:2-3).

   (4) He says he has *"heard of their faith in Christ Jesus"* (Eph 1:15).

  b. Ephesus was his longest missionary "stay" on record, *and* people he had a very strong emotional attachment to:

> *"Now from Miletus he sent to Ephesus and called the elders of the church to come to him.…And when he had said these things, he knelt down and prayed with them all. And there was much weeping on the part of all; they embraced Paul and kissed him, being sorrowful most of all because of the word he had spoken, that they would not see his face again. And they accompanied him to the ship."*
>
> **Acts 20:17, 36-38**

  c. It is likely that this was either a "circular" letter for all the regional Gentile congregations surrounding the city.

4. "Ephesian 101" — Learning the Vocabulary of This Letter

  a. This is Paul's most exquisite and exhaustive discussion of The Story.

   (1) The pronouns and verbs in this letter are all plural. This is *not* a letter to or about individuals, it is a letter to and about a group (especially the opening chapter).

   (2) 21 times in the first four chapters, Paul speaks of a group that is "in Christ," where *all* the aspects of the Story are (e.g. spiritual blessings, our election, adoption, forgiveness, inheritance, heavenly position, reconciliation).

   (3) He moves from the cosmic and eternal to the local and personal aspects of the Story (1:3-14).

   (4) He uses his word "mystery" 6 times in this letter, opening and closing with it[4] (1:9; 3:3,4,9; 5:32; 6:19).

   (5) He speaks of Yahweh's "shalom" more frequentlythan any other letter (1:2; 2:14,15,17; 4:3; 6:15,23).[5]

   (6) He speaks of the "church" (Gk, *ekklesia*) as a spiritual reality more than any other letter (9x; 1:22; 3:10,21; 5:23-25,27,29,32).

    (a) He says Christ's relationship to it is a "mystery" (5:25).

  b. Paul's exposes the Story as cosmic, not "Christian" or "Kosher":

---

[1] In writing to Timothy, Paul makes mention of one "Alexander the coppersmith," a trade that has echoes of this Ephesian conflict in it (cf. 2 Timothy 4:14).

[2] Some critical scholars also see this as evidence that Paul was not its author.

[3] He mentions 41 people in Romans, 19 in 2 Timothy, and 11 in Colossians.

[4] Paul uses the word twenty times in is writing, ten of which are in two letters written at nearly the same time: Ephesians and Colossians.

[5] Paul speaks of God's peace ten times in Romans and only 8 times in Ephesians, but Romans is three times as long as Ephesians.

(1) 1:3-10; 3:1-9 – It Yahweh's "eternal purpose," hidden for ages, full of lavish grace and spiritual riches

(2) 1:9-10 – all things in heaven and on earth will be brought back together, "summed up" (Gk, *anakephalaiomai*) in Christ (shalom returns).

(3) 1:15-23 – "Seeing" the fullness of the Story is impossible without revelation from God (just like Paul received!).

(4) 2:11-15 – those "in Christ" are part of a new (Gk, *kainos*) humanity.[1]

(5) 2:14-15 – the shalom of God *is* Christ; *"He himself is our peace…"* (2:14)

(6) 2:19-22 – God is "building" a place where *He* can dwell again; the "church" is *His* holy temple.[2]

  c. An Ephesian "Walkabout": Living in the Grip of the Good News

    (1) Eight times in this letter, Paul refers to how the Ephesians "walk" (Gk, *peripateō*; 2:2,10; 4:1,17; 5:2,8,15).

    (2) He makes it very clear that they cannot be Story tellers and *not* "Story Dwellers."

      (a) Story Dwellers walk "worthy" of the Story, working for shalom.

      (b) Story Dwellers' lives are characterized by sacrificial love and blessed deeds.

      (c) Story Dwellers' "culture" is Christ.[3]

B. The World *Before* the Letter: Being a Story Dweller in Our Age

  1. I need to hold both "halves" of the Story before me at all times:

    a. It is significant that Paul begins every one of his 13 letters the same, *"grace and peace (shalom)"*

    b. Paul's admonished his listeners to *never* stop looking backwards in their place in the Story:[4]

> *"…**remember** [present imperative] that at one time you Gentiles in the flesh…were at that time separated from Christ, alienated from the commonwealth of Israel and strangers to the covenants of promise, having no hope and without God in the world…"*   **Ephesians 2:11-12**

> *"Remember and do not forget how you provoked the LORD your God to wrath in the wilderness. From the day you came out of the land of Egypt until you came to this place, you have been rebellious against the LORD."*   **Deuteronomy 9:7**

  2. I need to see my behavior in marriage, family and work in the context of the Story, not vice versa.

    a. Paul's practical admonitions about human relations in and out of the home in 5:22-6:9 have no meaning apart from his teaching on imitating God and being filled with the Spirit in 5:1-21.

    b. The ministry of the Spirit is *always* in the direction of shalom (4:3).

  3. I need to ask myself, "What is *my* culture?"

> *"I therefore, a prisoner for the Lord, urge you to walk in a manner worthy of the calling to which you have been called, with all humility and gentleness, with patience, bearing with one another in love, eager to maintain the unity of the Spirit in the bond of peace. There is one body and one Spirit—just as you were called to the one hope that belongs to your call—one Lord, one faith, one baptism, one God and Father of all, who is over all and through all and in all."*   **Ephesians 4:1-6**

  4. I need to remind myself that Satan's ultimate target is the Story, not me.

  5. I need to continually remind myself that I can not be a true Story *teller* if I am not a Story *dweller*:[5]

    a. Paul's admonitions about "talk" (4:29-30; 5:4,19-20) are meaningless apart from those about "walk" (4:1,17;5:1, 8, 15).

  6. I need to remind myself that the Story is still mysterious, even though it's no longer a "mystery."

---

[1] This is *not* an "ethnic" distinction, but an anthropological one. Paul is speaking of a "second human race" brought about by the "last Adam."

[2] *This* is Paul's ecclesiology.

[3] Paul tells them that *God* is the one they are to "imitate."

[4] This has *always* been Yahweh's M.O. He trains His people to look backwards because only then will they be reminded that they are part of the larger flow of what Yahweh is doing and has been doing since man's demise in Eden. The entire Jewish agricultural calendar was built around the exodus event and the wilderness wandering. Yahweh never wanted them to forget from whence they had come and what they were a part of. Paul did the same, but *not* because he was a Jew. He sought to remind us to remember because that what *God* wanted.

[5] We should be sobered when we realize that the Ephesian church of John's day (30 years later) had great theology, but their lives were wrong.

    a. Paul's passion in his opening words is to root the Story in the mind of God, *not* to give an explanation about who's "in" and who's "out.

    b. Paul's attitude as a steward of the mystery was *always* one of brokenness and humility:

"To me, though I am the very least of all the saints, this grace was given, to preach to the Gentiles the unsearchable riches of Christ,"   **Ephesians 3:8**

"The saying is trustworthy and deserving of full acceptance, that Christ Jesus came into the world to save sinners, of whom I am the foremost."   **1 Timothy 1:15**

XX. UNIT 20 - FOUR LETTERS FROM PAUL'S NEW "OFFICE" IN ROME — part 3

A. The World *Behind* The Letter: Philippi — "Rome on the Range"

  1. Paul traveled nearly 3,100 miles on this journey alone:

    a. 1,800 miles by land

    b. 1,300 miles by sea

  2. He traveled 500 miles across Asia, doing "follow-up" and strengthening the churches he planted his first journey—*all on foot*!

  3. Going to Philippi was *not* his idea, it was God's!

And they went through the region of Phrygia and Galatia, having been forbidden by the Holy Spirit to speak the word in Asia. And when they had come up to Mysia, they attempted to go into Bithynia, but the Spirit of Jesus did not allow them. So, passing by Mysia, they went down to Troas. And a vision appeared to Paul in the night: a man of Macedonia was standing there, urging him and saying, "Come over to Macedonia and help us." And when Paul had seen the vision, immediately we sought to go on into Macedonia, concluding that God had called us to preach the gospel to them."   **Acts 16:6-10**

  4. Luke joins Paul's team here ("we") and they sail from Troas to the port city of Neapolis.[1]

---

[1] This entailed 2 days of sailing; It took them five days on his *third* journey to make the same trip in reverse!

5. Traveled 9 miles on the military road built by Rome a hundred years earlier, the (Egnatian Way) that connected the city of Rome with Byzantium in Turkey.[1]

6. Between him and the city of Philippi, stood the Symbolum, a 1600' high mountain from which he would have seen the city in the valley below.

7. The plain west of the city is the fate of the world had been decided a hundred years earlier.[2]

8. This battle marked the end of the Republic and the beginning of the Roman Empire; it also made Philippi a Roman colony. *(Did Paul think back on his own native city of Tarsus, knowing the it was in the city where he grew up that Mark Anthony met Cleopatra?)*

9. As Paul entered the city, he would have been struck by how different Philippi was from all the other cities they had ministered in.[3] It was Roman through and through (he didn't arrive in Corinth until Acts 18:1).

   a. He would have noticed the Roman forum, not knowing that he would be on trial there in a few months. He would have seen the many shops in the agora where he would do evangelism.

   b. He would have walked past the Roman baths and seen the temple to Augustus.

   c. The city was full of Latin inscriptions (80%), many people spoke Latin, and wore Roman togas, the sign of citizenship.

   d. He would have *not* heard his native tongue of Aramaic, for there was *no synagogue* in Philippi, because there were not even 10 Jewish men![4]

   e. He would have walked under the *pomerium*, a marble arch which marked the sacred area of Philippi.

   "And on the Sabbath day we went outside the gate to the riverside, where we supposed there was a place of prayer, and we sat down and spoke to the women who had come together." **Acts 16:13**

10. Outside of the city he found a *proseuchē*, or "place of prayer" where a number of woman were gathering to worship.[5] It was here that the Philippian church was birthed:

    a. The first convert in Europe was a woman from Thyatira 250 miles away named Lydia, a wealthy and successful businesswoman. (upper class; female; probably single). Her home became the ministry "base" (Acts 16:15).

    b. A few weeks later in the same place, Paul casts a "pythonic" spirit out of a slave girl who was being exploited by her masters (Acts 16:16-19). (lower class female child; probably orphaned)

    c. A riot breaks out and Paul and Silas are hauled before the Roman magistrates and beaten with rods publicly, and then thrown into the "inner" prison (Acts 16:22-24).[6]

    d. An earthquake frees them, and in the process, the Roman jailer is converted and he and his family are baptized. (working middle class male; probably married)

11. Paul uses his Roman citizenship as a bargaining chip to secure the safety of this infant congregation. He then is asked to leave town, and makes the 100 mile journey to plant a church in the neighboring city of Thessalonica.

12. Luke stays behind; perhaps for 5-7 years to disciple these new believers ("we") until Paul returns on his *third* journey.

---

[1] Rome had defeated Macedonia at the Battle of Pydna in 167 B.C.

[2] This was the Battle of Philippi, fought in 41 B.C., two years after the assassination of Julius Caesar by Brutus and Cassius. These two fought and were defeated at Philippi by Marc Antony and Octavian.

[3] We need to be careful to remember that even though the Corinthian correspondence was *written* before Philippians, Paul actually visited Philippi and planted the church there *prior* to arriving in Corinth (cf. Acts 16 and 18).

[4] There was also an obvious anti-semitism present in Philippi, evidenced by a statement made during the uproar surrounding Paul's visit there. One of the "charges" brought against him and his traveling companions was, *"these men are Jews..."* (Acts 16:20). Compare the *absence* of a synagogue with the other cities where Paul ministered: Damascus, Jerusalem, Pisidian Antioch, Iconium, Thessalonica, Berea, Athens, Corinth, and Ephesus.

[5] Running water was a requirement for a "place of prayer." Most likely because of the water cleansing rituals associated with Jewish worship. (The water was also known as "living water."). It's likely that there were "god-fearers" among this group as well as some Jews. Just not enough Jewish men to form a synagogue.

[6] If Paul wrote these letters from prison in Rome near the end of Acts, we must assume that his conditions in Philippi were much worse than the "house arrest" he found himself under in Rome.

13. Paul's letter, Philippians, is written 10 years *after* he planted the church.

14. The Philippians had provided him with financial support for ten years!

> *"I thank my God in all my remembrance of you, always in every prayer of mine for you all making my prayer with joy, because of your partnership in the gospel from the first day until now. ...And you Philippians yourselves know that in the beginning of the gospel, when I left Macedonia, no church entered into partnership with me in giving and receiving, except you only."* **Philippians 1:3-5; 4:15**

B. The World *Of* The Letter: A "Missionary Support Letter" to Paul's Favorite Church

1. There is no correction for sin, no defense of his apostleship, no serious correctives, instead there is joy and gratitude for their faith and faithfulness:[1]

> *"I thank my God in all my remembrance of you, always in every prayer of mine for you all making my prayer with joy, because of your partnership in the gospel from the first day until now. And I am sure of this, that he who began a good work in you will bring it to completion at the day of Jesus Christ. It is right for me to feel this way about you all, because I hold you in my heart, for you are all partakers with me of grace, both in my imprisonment and in the defense and confirmation of the gospel. For God is my witness, how I yearn for you all with the affection of Christ Jesus. And it is my prayer that your love may abound more and more, with knowledge and all discernment, so that you may approve what is excellent, and so be pure and blameless for the day of Christ, filled with the fruit of righteousness that comes through Jesus Christ, to the glory and praise of God."* **Philippians 1:3-11**

2. What do you say to a group of believers meeting in a home, that are...

   a. Jews, Greeks, and Romans

   b. Men, women, and children

   c. Lower class, middle-class, and upper class

   d. Pagan backgrounds and religious backgrounds

   e. Residents of a city that is hostile to you, them, and the gospel?

3. Paul admonishes them to focus on something that had become very, very dear to him: living a "worthy" life:

> *"I therefore, a prisoner for the Lord, urge you to walk (Gk, peripateō) in a manner worthy of the calling to which you have been called,"* **Ephesians 4:1**

> *"...so as to walk (Gk, peripateō) in a manner worthy of the Lord, fully pleasing to him, bearing fruit in every good work and increasing in the knowledge of God."* **Colossians 1:10**

   a. But, he takes a different "spin" on it in this letter and uses language that is loaded with special meaning for Philippi:

> *"Only let your manner of life be (Gk, politeuomai) worthy of the gospel of Christ, so that whether I come and see you or am absent, I may hear of you that you are standing firm in one spirit, with one mind striving side by side for the faith of the gospel,"* **Philippians 1:27**

> *"But our citizenship (Gk, politeuma) is in heaven, and from it we await a Savior, the Lord Jesus Christ, who will transform our lowly body to be like his glorious body, by the power that enables him even to subject all things to himself."* **Philippians 3:20-21**

   b. Philippi was one of only five cities to be distinguished as *ius Italicum* (free of direct taxation and governed by Roman law).

   c. The word, "citizen" (Gk, *politeuma*), can mean both a group with political rights, *or* a distinct group away from their homeland; a sort of "city within a city."

   d. He says Jesus is "savior," "Lord," and all things are "subject" to him. All three of these attributes were ascribed to Caesar![2]

---

[1] There are seventeen references to "joy" and "rejoicing" in this short letter. It appears in each of the four chapters.

[2] An inscription from Ephesus dated to AD 48, only a few years before Paul wrote Philippians, speaks of Julius Caesar as "a visible god and political savior of human life." Another inscription from Egypt, this time perhaps from a few years after Philippians, calls Emperor Nero "savior and benefactor of the world." Paul wants the Philippians to know that the "Savior" of their "community" (*politeuma*) is none other than Jesus, who will bring "everything under his control" (3:21; cf 2:10).

4. Paul is arguing for a unity based on a shared identity, *not* on a privileged geography.

    a. 1:27 – He told them that "conducting themselves in a manner worthy of the Gospel" would result in them having "one mind" (Gk, *psuchē*).

    b. 2:2 – He speaks of them "same mind (Gk, *sunpsuchē*), having the same love, being in full accord and of one mind."

    c. 2:19-20 – He holds Timothy up as an example of someone who is of the "same soul" with him:

        "But I hope in the Lord Jesus to send Timothy to you shortly, so that I also may be encouraged when I learn of your condition. For I have no one else of kindred spirit (Gk, isopsuchos) who will genuinely be concerned for your welfare. For they all seek after their own interests, not those of Christ Jesus."
        Philippians 2:19-21, NAS

5. But, Paul's supreme example is Jesus Christ himself:

    "Have this mind among yourselves, which is yours in Christ Jesus, who, though he was in the form of God, did not count equality with God a thing to be grasped, but made himself nothing, taking the form of a servant, being born in the likeness of men. And being found in human form, he humbled himself by becoming obedient to the point of death, even death on a cross."
    Philippians 2:5-8

6. Even his arguments about his own Jewish ancestry are best understood against this idea:

    "But whatever gain I had, I counted as loss for the sake of Christ. Indeed, I count everything as loss because of the surpassing worth of knowing Christ Jesus my Lord. For his sake I have suffered the loss of all things and count them as rubbish, in order that I may gain Christ and be found in him, not having a righteousness of my own that comes from the law, but that which comes through faith in Christ, the righteousness from God that depends on faith—that I may know him and the power of his resurrection, and may share his sufferings, becoming like him in his death, that by any means possible I may attain the resurrection from the dead. Not that I have already obtained this or am already perfect, but I press on to make it my own, because Christ Jesus has made me his own. Brothers, I do not consider that I have made it my own. But one thing I do: forgetting what lies behind and straining forward to what lies ahead, I press on toward the goal for the prize of the upward call of God in Christ Jesus. Let those of us who are mature think this way, and if in anything you think otherwise, God will reveal that also to you."
    Philippians 3:7-15

7. Paul wanted for himself what God wanted for him:

    "Not that I have already obtained this or am already perfect, but I press on to make it my own, because Christ Jesus has made me his own."
    Philippians 3:12

8. Paul wants his "one thing" to be their "one thing":

    *"Brothers, I do not consider that I have made it my own. But **one thing I do**: forgetting what lies behind and straining forward (Gk,diōkō) to what lies ahead, I press on toward the goal for the prize (Gk, brabeion) of the upward call of God in Christ Jesus. Let those of us who are mature think this way, and if in anything you think otherwise, God will reveal that also to you. Only let us hold true to what we have attained. Brothers, join in imitating me, and keep your eyes on those who walk according to the example you have in us."*
    Philippians 3:13-17

    a. His language here is strenuous and continuous; this was his one holy passion.

C. The World *Before* the Letter: "Conducting Myself in a Manner Worthy of the Gospel"

1. Paul tells us that our identity will shape what we "run" for, or be shaped by it.
Question: *What* am I running for: dried celery or the crown of life? (1 Cor 9:25; 2 Tim 4:8).

2. Paul tells us that Timothy valued what Jesus valued (Phil 2:19-20).
Question: *Who* am I living for: myself or others?

    "Therefore, my brothers, whom I love and long for, my joy and crown, stand firm thus in the Lord, my beloved."
    Philippians 4:1

    "For what is our hope or joy or crown of boasting before our Lord Jesus at his coming? Is it not you?"
    1 Thessalonians 2:19

    "For what we proclaim is not ourselves, but Jesus Christ as Lord, with ourselves as your servants for Jesus' sake."
    2 Corinthians 4:5

XXI. **UNIT 21 - THREE LETTERS TO TWO YOUNG PASTORS (Timothy & Titus)**

A. The World *Behind* The Letters: "The Best of Times…The Worst of Times"

1. Reconciling Luke's Silence With Paul's Pen

    a. Acts ends with Paul under "house arrest" for two years, awaiting trial before Caesar (Acts 28:30-31).

    b. Demas is *with* Paul during this imprisonment (Col 4:14), but had *deserted* him by the time of the imprisonment mentioned in 2 Timothy (4:10).[1]

    c. This "second imprisonment" idea is supported by the 3rd century church historian, Eusebius:

    > "Festus was sent by Nero to be Felix's successor. Under him, Paul, having made his defense, was sent bound to Rome. Aristarchus was with him, whom he also somewhere in his epistles quite naturally calls his fellow-prisoner. And Luke, who wrote the Acts of the Apostles, brought its history to a close at this point, after stating that Paul spent two whole years at Rome as prisoner at large, and preached the word of God without restraint. Thus, after he had made his defense it is said that the apostle was sent again upon the ministry of preaching, and that upon coming to the same city a second time he suffered martyrdom. In this imprisonment he wrote his second epistle to Timothy, in which he mentions his first defense and his impending death.…But these things have been adduced by us to show that Paul's martyrdom did not take place at the time of that Roman sojourn which Luke records."
    >
    > **Ecclesiastical History, 2.22.1–8**

    d. The 2-year delay was likely due to the absence of the "prosecution" from Jerusalem:

    (1) The Sanhedrin had to send a personal delegation to Rome to present their case against Paul.

    (2) A year earlier, Rome had passed legislation making spurious charges a very serious offense or failed to appear to prosecute.

    (3) But, the political climate in Jerusalem was heating up due to the growing rebellion of the Zealots.

    (4) It is possible that they *never* arrived in Rome, and Paul was therefore released without a stigma on his "record."

    e. After his apparent release, Paul spent more time in Ephesus where he left Timothy to continue the ministry (1 Tim 1:3). He may also have visited Colossae during this time (Philemon 22).[2]

    f. Paul left Ephesus for Macedonia (1 Tim 1:3).

    g. He may have ministered in Philippi (Phil 2:23-24).

    h. Paul ministered *extensively* on the island of Crete, where he had (likely) done ministry while his prison ship was harbored there (cf. Acts 27; Tit1:5).

    i. He left Titus on Crete and travelled to Nicopolis on the western coast of Greece (Titus 1:12).

    j. He spent time in Troas[3] and Miletus in Asia (2 Tim 4:13,20).

2. The *Pax Romana* Was Becoming the *Pox Romana*!

    a. Nero was assassinated in June, AD 68.

    b. That began the "year of four emperors"

    (1) Galba: June 68 – January 69

    (2) Otho: January 69 – March 69

    (3) Vitellius: April 69 – December 69

    (4) Vespasian: December 69 — AD 79

    c. The First Jewish War had begun in AD 66 in Galilee, according to Josephus.[4]

---

[1] This fact effectively rules out Acts 28 as the historical context for the composition of Paul's "pastoral" letters.
[2] Paul's itinerary following release from his first imprisonment is assembled by seeking to construct a timeline using comments made by him in these letters.
[3] Some scholars suggest that this city is where Paul was first imprisoned, citing a "hasty" departure as the reason he left so many things of value there (e.g. cloak, books, and parchments).
[4] The second Jewish war, known as the Bar Kochba Rebellion took place c. AD 132.

    d. Vespasian turned the leadership of the Roman legions over to his son, Titus and returned to Rome in AD 68.

    e. Titus destroyed Jerusalem and the Temple in AD 70.[1]

    f. The last holdouts killed themselves at Masada in AD 73.

    g. Judaism was shattered in Palestine, and the "Hebraic" flavor of The Way was lost as well.

    h. The intense political divisions within Judaism would have infiltrated the early Church as well.

    i. Both Peter and Paul would be martyred before the Temple was destroyed. These were *cataclysmic* times for believers!

  3. In the midst of all this, Paul pens his last three letters, two while free (1 Timothy & Titus) and his final letter as a prisoner, just prior to his martyrdom (2 Timothy).

    a. They are written to two converted Gentiles: Timothy (Acts 16:1) and Titus (Gal 2:3).

    b. Paul wrote more biographically about Titus than any other of his "fellow workers" (12 refs cf. 3 for Timothy).

    c. Timothy was Paul's "senior" disciple.[2]

    d. 1 Timothy and Titus are written at the same time, to two men doing the same thing in two different places.

    e. They provide us with many insights into the life of a 1st century pastor in general and Timothy in particular.

      (1) We are introduced to the requirements of "elder" (*presbuteroi*) or "bishop" (*episkopos*) and "deacon" (*diakonos*) (1 Tim 3 and Titus 2).

      (2) We discover that Timothy was "catechized" by his mother and grandmother (2 Tim 1:5; 3:14-15).

      (3) We discover that Timothy's "fire" was going out (2 Tim 1:6 cf. 1 Tim 4:14).

      (4) We discover that Paul was concerned about the Story being discarded, diminished, and distorted:

> *"...But I am not ashamed, for I know whom I have believed, and I am convinced that he is able to guard until that Day what has been entrusted* [parathēkē] *to me. Follow the pattern of the sound words that you have heard from me, in the faith and love that are in Christ Jesus. By the Holy Spirit who dwells within us, guard the good deposit* [parathēkē] *entrusted to you."*
> **2 Timothy 1:12ᵇ-14**

> *"If anyone teaches a different doctrine and does not agree with the sound words of our Lord Jesus Christ and the teaching that accords with godliness, he is puffed up with conceit and understands nothing. He has an unhealthy craving for controversy and for quarrels about words, which produce envy, dissension, slander, evil suspicions, and constant friction among people who are depraved in mind and deprived of the truth, imagining that godliness is a means of gain."*
> **1 Timothy 6:3-5**

> *"...preach the word; be ready in season and out of season; reprove, rebuke, and exhort, with complete patience and teaching. For the time is coming when people will not endure sound* [healthy] *teaching, but having itching ears they will accumulate for themselves teachers to suit their own passions, and will turn away from listening to the truth and wander off into myths."*
> **2 Timothy 4:2-4**

B. The World *Of* The Letters: Paul's Unique "Pastoral" Vocabulary

  1. "godliness" — (Gk, *eusebeia*) Paul uses this word 11x in these letters and nowhere else in his writings.

  2. "ungodliness" — (Gk, *asebeia*) Paul uses this word once in all 3 letters, and 4x in only one other letter, Romans.

  3. "faith" — (Gk, *pistis*) Paul uses this word twice as much in these letters as he does in all his other letters, but not in reference to justification.

  4. "blessed deeds" — (Gk, *kala erga*) Paul uses this phrase 8 times in 1 Timothy and Titus:

---

[1] This was the final destruction of a Jewish Temple. There has been no Temple since AD 70.
[2] A comprehensive biblical timeline of Timothy's life is on pages 104-5.

      a. he tells Pastor Timothy they should characterize a godly widow (1 Tim 5:10).

      b. he tells Pastor Timothy to teach rich Christians to be "rich" in "blessed deeds" (1 Tim 6:18).

      c. he tells Pastor Titus that his congregation should learn how to do "blessed deeds" from watching him (Titus 2:7).

      d. he tells Pastor Titus that Jesus died to "set apart" for Himself a "people who are zealous for "blessed deeds" (Titus 2:14).

      e. He tells Pastor Titus that "blessed deeds" are to be the normal activity of all believers (Titus 3:8).

5. Paul's "love language"

      a. He tells Pastor Timothy that love that "issues" (Gk, *ek*) from a purified heart, a healthy conscience and a non-phony faith is the goal of all his teaching (1 Tim 1:5).

      b. He uses nine different compound verbs for "love" in these letters:

        (1) *philoxenos* – a "lover of strangers" (1 Tim 3:2; Titus 1:8; "hospitable").

        (2) *phiarguria* – a "lover of silver" (1 Tim 6:10; 2 Tim 3:2; "lover of money").

        (3) *philautoi* – a "lover of oneself" (2 Tim 3:2).

        (4) *philhēdēnoi* – a "lover of pleasure" (2 Tim 3:4).

        (5) *philotheoi* – a "lover of God" (2 Tim 3:4).

        (6) *philagathon* – a "lover of the good" (Titus 1:8).

        (7) *philandros* – a "lover of one's husband" (Titus 2:4).

        (8) *philteknos* – a "lover of children" (Titus 2:4).

        (9) *philanthropia* – a "lover of mankind" (Titus 3:4, speaking of God).

C. The World *Before* The Letters: Letting Paul Pastor Us

1. Paul builds an inseparable bond between The Story and the living out of one's "faith" (i.e. "godliness") in these letters.

"Great indeed, we confess, is the mystery [Gk, mustērion] *of godliness* [Gk, eusebeia]*: He was manifested in the flesh, vindicated by the Spirit, seen by angels, proclaimed among the nations, believed on in the world, taken up in glory."*   **1 Timothy 3:16**

2. He makes an unbroken connection between this life and "the life to come" because the Story doesn't end when this life does.

"Have nothing to do with irreverent, silly myths. Rather train yourself for godliness; for while bodily training is of some value, godliness is of value in every way, as it holds promise for the present life and also for the life to come."   **1 Timothy 4:7, 8**

3. He makes a special connection about which Story we talk about, and what we become:

"O Timothy, guard the deposit [parathēkē] *entrusted to you. Avoid the irreverent babble and contradictions of what is falsely called "knowledge,"*   **1 Timothy 6:20**

"But avoid irreverent babble, for it will lead people into more and more ungodliness [Gk asebeia]*"*   **2 Timothy 2:16**

4. He makes a connection between which Story we spend our time looking at, and what we become:

"For Demas, in love with this present world, has deserted me and gone to Thessalonica..."   **2 Timothy 4:10**

5. He reinforces the place of "blessed deeds" in The Story and those who are truly in it:

"For the grace of God has appeared, bringing salvation for all people, training us to renounce ungodliness and worldly passions, and to live self-controlled, upright, and godly lives in the present age, waiting for our blessed hope, the appearing of the glory of our great God and Savior Jesus Christ, who gave himself for us to redeem us from all lawlessness and to purify for himself a people for his own possession who are zealous for good works."   **Titus 2:11-14**

6. He makes it undeniably clear that those in the Story are to be diligent about training others in The Story:

"and what you have heard from me in the presence of many witnesses entrust to faithful men who will be able to teach others also."   **2 Timothy 2:2**

D. **Three Pastoral Questions:**

1. Which Story do I spend my time studying, the *mustērion* or the *kosmos*?

2. Which Story occupies the majority of my conversation?

3. Who am I intentionally "entrusting" the Story to?

XXII. UNIT 22 - A BURNING BUSH WE'VE PUT UNDER A BUSHEL (Hebrews-pt 1)

A. The "Black Sheep" of the New Testament

1. Hebrews is one of the most important, yet least appreciated facets for truly understanding The Story.

   a. It is under-preached, quickly read, and rarely studied.

   b. Yet, it is Scripture's most expansive description of The Story, and the pitfalls associated with being in it:

   (1) It lays out the entire panarama of The Story from creation to the Second Coming (see 1:2 and 9:28).

   (2) It painstakingly portrays Judaism as a vital but provisional "chapter" in The Story.

   c. Understanding it requires familiarity with the Old Testament:

   (1) It quotes directly from nine Old Testament books,[1] and 11 different psalms.

   (2) Of the 25 proper names in the letter, only 2 are from the New Testament era (Jesus, Timothy).

   (3) Understanding how they lived out their place in The Story is vital to understanding The Story itself.

2. The World *Behind* The Letter: Learning to Live With Silence

   a. The Letter to the Hebrews has been an enigma since the 2nd century regarding both author and audience:

   (1) Eusebius of Caesarea, writing in the 3rd century, cites Origen of Alexandria of the 2nd century:

   > **11** *In addition he makes the following statements in regard to the Epistle to the Hebrews in his Homilies upon it: "That the verbal style of the epistle entitled 'To the Hebrews,' is not rude like the language of the apostle, who acknowledged himself 'rude in speech that is, in expression; but that its diction is purer Greek, any one who has the power to discern differences of phraseology will acknowledge.* **12** *Moreover, that the thoughts of the epistle are admirable, and not inferior to the acknowledged apostolic writings, any one who carefully examines the apostolic text will admit.'* **13** *Farther on he adds: "If I gave my opinion, I should say that the thoughts are those of the apostle, but the diction and phraseology are those of some one who remembered the apostolic teachings, and wrote down at his leisure what had been said by his teacher. Therefore if any church holds that this epistle is by Paul, let it be commended for this. For not without reason have the ancients handed it down as Paul's.* **14** ***But who wrote the epistle, in truth, God knows.*** *The statement of some who have gone before us is that Clement, bishop of the Romans, wrote the epistle, and of others that Luke, the author of the Gospel and the Acts, wrote it. "But let this suffice on these matters."*   **Ecclesiastical History, 2.22.1–8**

3. The "evidence" *against* Paul being the author is worth noting:

   a. The book is anonymous, whereas every one of Paul's 13 letters are ascribed to him (e.g. Rom 1:1; Col 1:1; 1 Tim 1:1, etc.).

   b. The strong emphasis in this letter on the role or relationship of Jesus as "priest/high priest"

   (1) This concept is *totally* foreign to Paul (Rom 15:16 only, a reference to himself!).

   (2) Hebrews has 36 references to the priesthood in 10 different chapters.

   c. There are over 150 Greek vocabulary words that do not appear in Paul's other writings (or anywhere else in the New Testament).

   d. The author's manner of referring to Yahweh's revelation is consistent with Greek-speaking Jewish synagogues, but the opposite of Paul:

---

[1] Genesis, Exodus, Deuteronomy, 2 Samuel, Isaiah, Jeremiah, Habbakuk, Haggai, and Proverbs

    (1) Paul uses the phrase, "*it is written…*" (Gk, *graphō*) 30 times in his writings.[1] It appears only once in Hebrews.

    (2) The writer of Hebrews refers to Yahweh "*speaking*" [Gk, legō] 32x, the same number Paul used in all 13 of his letters (this is 6x that of Paul).

  e. Most importantly, the author of Hebrews makes it clear that he is *not* one of the eye-witnesses of the resurrection that were commissioned by Jesus, the very thing Paul constantly argued for:

"…how shall we escape if we neglect such a great salvation? It was declared at first by the Lord, and it was attested to us by those who heard."   **Hebrews 2:3**

"For I would have you know, brothers, that the gospel that was preached by me is not man's gospel. For I did not receive it from any man, nor was I taught it, but I received it through a revelation of Jesus Christ."   **Galatians 1:11, 12**

  f. The author is skilled in the allegorical interpretive model that was used by the Greek-speaking Jews in Alexandria (e.g. extensive portions on Melchizadek).

  g. Hebrews seems more like a transcript of a sermon than a letter:

"About this we have much to say, and it is hard to explain, since you have become dull of hearing."   **Hebrews 5:11**

"Above it were the cherubim of glory overshadowing the mercy seat. Of these things we cannot now speak in detail."   **Hebrews 9:5**

"And what more shall I say? For time would fail me to tell of Gideon, Barak, Samson, Jephthah, of David and Samuel and the prophets…"   **Hebrews 11:32**

4. The Undeclared Audience of an Unsigned Letter

  a. Our only certainty is that these listeners are Jewish Christians:

    (1) There is no explanation of any of the extensive references to tabernacle worship, the priesthood, or ancient Jewish history.

    (2) There are 39 quotations and some 34 allusions to the Old Testament, *all* taken from the Greek version of the Hebrew Bible.

Hebrews	OT Citation	Hebrews	OT Citation	Hebrews	OT Citation
1:5a	Ps 2:7	3:15	Ps 95:7	10:13	Ps 110:1
1:5b	2 Sam 7:14	4:3	Ps 95:11	10:15	Jer 31:33
1:6	Ps 97:7	4:5	Ps 95:11	10:17	Jer 31:34
1:7	Ps 104:4	4:7	Ps 95:7	10:30	Deut 32:35-36
1:8	Ps 45:6	5:5	Ps 2:7	10:37-38	Hab 2:3-4
1:9	Ps 45:7	5:6	Ps 110:4	11:18	Gen 21:12
1:10	Ps 102:25	6:14	Gen 22:16ff	12:5-6	Prov 3:11-12
1:11-12	Ps 102:26	7:17	Ps 110:4	12:20	Exod 19:12ff
1:13	Ps 110:1	7:21	Ps 110:4	12:26	Hag 2:6
2:6-8	Ps 8:4-6	8:5	Exod 25:40	13:5	Deut 31:6
2:12	Ps 22:22	8:8-12	Jer 31:31-34	13:6	Ps 118:6
2:13	Isaiah 8:17-18	9:20	Exod 24:8	—	—
3:7-11	Ps 95:7-11	10:5-8	Ps 40:6-8		

    (3) There is no warning against circumcision or any references to it, most likely because they already were (cf. 42 refs in Paul, especially Galatians).

    (4) The writer speaks of Temple sacrifices still occurring (7:27; 10:2-3).[2]

---

[1] The phrase only appears 60 times in the entire New Testament. Paul accounts for half of its use.

[2] This inadvertently provides with something of a "date stamp" for this letter. It *had* to be written prior to AD 70 when the final Temple was destroyed by the Romans.

      (5) There is not a single reference to Gentiles or Gentile behavior.

  b. It is very *unlikely* that they are in Palestine:

      (1) The author indicates that they have not yet faced martyrdom (12:3-4).[1]

      (2) The Jerusalem Christians were recipients of financial help, the believers in this letter were givers of help (13:1-5,16).

      (3) The statement, "*...those who came from Italy send greetings*" may be a reference that this Hebrew congregation is in Rome (13:24).

B. The World *Of* The Letter: A Tapestry of High Christology and Ancient Memory

  1. The author's arguments all address a group that is contemplating a unique form of apostasy—returning to Judaism![2]

  2. His basic argument is that returning to Judaism is impossible, because in God's Story, it was only the "trailer" not the film:

    a. Everything that led up to Yeshua was merely a "copy" or "shadow" pointing to Him:

> *"For since the law has but a shadow (Gk, skia) of the good things to come instead of the true form (Gk, eikon) of these realities, it can never, by the same sacrifices that are continually offered every year, make perfect those who draw near."*　　　　　　　　　　**Hebrews 10:1**

    b. This is the same thing Paul had taught those contemplating a "kosher" Christianity in Asia:

> *"He is the image (Gk, eikon) of the invisible God, the firstborn of all creation."*　　　**Colossians 1:15**

> *"Therefore let no one pass judgment on you in questions of food and drink, or with regard to a festival or a new moon or a Sabbath. These are a shadow [Gk, skia] of the things to come, but the substance belongs to Christ."*　　　　　　　　　　**Colossians 2:16, 17**

C. The World *Before* The Letter: Removing Our Sandals

  1. We have four misunderstandings that cause us to "keep our sandals on" when we read God's Story:

    a. We have a casual, not a "kosher" understanding of God's self-disclosure.

      (1) A "talking God" was a terrifying thing to a Jew:

> *"For ask now of the days that are past, which were before you, since the day that God created man on the earth, and ask from one end of heaven to the other, whether such a great thing as this has ever happened or was ever heard of. Did any people ever hear the voice of a god speaking out of the midst of the fire, as you have heard, and still live?"*　　**Deuteronomy 4:32, 33**

> *"Thus says the LORD: "Heaven is my throne, and the earth is my footstool; what is the house that you would build for me, and what is the place of my rest? All these things my hand has made, and so all these things came to be, declares the LORD. But this is the one to whom I will look: he who is humble and contrite in spirit and trembles at my word."*　　**Isaiah 66:1, 2**

> *"See that you do not refuse him who is speaking. For if they did not escape when they refused him who warned them on earth, much less will we escape if we reject him who warns from heaven. At that time his voice shook the earth, but now he has promised, "Yet once more I will shake not only the earth but also the heavens." This phrase, "Yet once more," indicates the removal of things that are shaken--that is, things that have been made--in order that the things that cannot be shaken may remain. Therefore let us be grateful for receiving a kingdom that cannot be shaken, and thus let us offer to God acceptable worship, with reverence and awe, for our God is a consuming fire."*　　**Hebrews 12:25-29**

---

[1] This would not be a true statement if it were speaking of the church in Jerusalem. They had seen the deaths of James and Stephen.

[2] This is very different from the "desertion" or apostasy of Demas Paul speaks of in 2 Timothy 4:10. He was "in love with the world," and so left the faith. These believers are in love with Judaism and so want to return to it.

b. We fail to recognize the supernatural nature of what we read for our "quiet time": the "oracles of Yahweh" mediated to Jews by angels![1]

"This is the Moses who said to the Israelites, 'God will raise up for you a prophet like me from your brothers.' This is the one who was in the congregation in the wilderness with the angel who spoke to him at Mount Sinai, and with our fathers. He received living oracles to give to us." **Acts 7:37, 38**

"For since the message declared by angels proved to be reliable and every transgression or disobedience received a just retribution, how shall we escape if we neglect such a great salvation?..."
Hebrews 2:2

(1) There are over 300 references to angels in The Story.

(2) There are 180 references to angels in 16 books of the New Testament; 11 in the first chapter of Hebrews.[2]

(3) They are in The Story to *serve* us (Heb 1:14).

(4) They see us, have a language of their own, will accompany Jesus on His return, can take human form, invoked fear when seen, mediated the scriptures, yet can *not* fully understand The Story (1 Cor 4:9; 13:1; Gal 3:19; 2 Th 1:7; Heb 13:2; Lk 1:12; 1 Pet 1:12).

c. As as result of all this, we fail to understand the opening lines of this letter:

"Long ago, at many times and in many ways, God spoke to our fathers by the prophets, but in these last days he has spoken to us by his Son, whom he appointed the heir of all things, through whom also he created the world. He is the radiance of the glory of God and the exact imprint of his nature, and he upholds the universe by the word of his power. After making purification for sins, he sat down at the right hand of the Majesty on high, having become as much superior to angels as the name he has inherited is more excellent than theirs."
Hebrews 1:1-4

d. Because we limit the Gospel to be God's solution to our guilt, we neglect one of the greatest purposes of the Incarnation:

(1) Jesus is the fullest and final revelation of Yahweh.

(a) *"the radiance of the glory of God"* (1:3) —[Gk, *apaugasma*]; speaks of the radiant manifestation of God's presence. To see God's glory, was to witness His presence. (I.e. *"The Word became flesh and dwelt among us..."*).

(b) *"...the exact imprint of his nature..."* (1:5) — [Gk, *charaktēr*]; 1x in our NT. Originally used for an engraving tool, a stamp, or even a branding iron. It eventually came to be used of the image or mark itself made, for example on coins or seals.

(2) This was Paul's argument in Philippians 2:1-11.

(3) It was Yeshua's own statement to Andrew in John 14:9.

e. The author of Hebrews opens this letter with the strongest statement in all of Scripture about the role of Yeshua as God's self-disclosure.

f. This book opens, not with a long discourse on angels, but on Yahweh and Yeshua.

g. If you want to know what Yahweh, the "God of the Old Testament" really "was" like, look at Yeshua.

h. This is the proper way to read and understand the Old Testament, Yahweh working all things together for the good of those who love Him, who are called according to His purpose (i.e. The Story).

XXIII. UNIT 23 - "HOLINESS" IS STILL A BIG DEAL TO YAHWEH *(Hebrews-pt 2)*

REVIEW: Looking Back One Unit

A. The Letter to the Hebrews is the New Testament's clearest statement about:

1. The *antiquity* of The Story.

---

[1] Paul reminds us of the enormous privilege of simply having the thoughts of God in our possession in Romans 3:-12, where he speaks of the Jews as the only group of people to be entrusted with "the oracles of God." Hebrews 5:12 seems to intimate that there are "layers" of sorts, to these oracles by speaking of there being "elementary principles" of the oracles. Or, by implication, that there are oracles of God that are *not* "elementary." Peter, in 1 Peter 4:11, referring to spiritual gifts, says that those who have "speaking gifts" should have the attitude that they are speaking "the oracles of God."

[2] There are 10 references in six of Paul's letters, 13 in Hebrews, 52 in the Gospels, 21 in Acts, 7 in Peter/Jude, and 74 in Revelation.

    2. The unbroken connection between our two "Testaments."

    3. The "Jewishness" of Christianity.

    4. The necessity of Old Testament familiarity for New Testament theology.

B. The Old Testament is the unfortunate "stepchild" of Christian scriptures.

    1. It is under-preached, superficially-read, and poorly known.

    2. Not knowing our Old Testament results in not knowing The Story.[1]

    3. It was the true meaning of their own Scriptures that would keep the recipients of this letter (i.e., believers who had come out of a Jewish background) from "hiding" in them.[2]

A DEEPER "REVIEW": Looking Back 182,000 Weeks!

A. Five "Oases" in a Desert of Our Own Making:

    1. Leviticus is the "red letter" book of the Bible, nearly nine out of every ten words come from the mouth of Yahweh! (30x is says, "The LORD spoke to Moses, saying…").

    2. It addresses five vital areas of spirituality that transcend time, geography, and ethnicity:

        a. The holiness of Yahweh (215x; three Hebrew words, qadosh, qodesh, qadash).

        b. The place of holiness within the covenant community (cf. Lev 11:45).

        c. A chronology rooted in their relationship with Yahweh, *not* the solar system.[3]

        d. The place of holiness of the covenant community within culture.

        e. A comprehensive theology of atonement and mediation.

B. *"You Cannot Repair the Temple Curtain's Tear"*

    1. Hebrews is the final commentary on Leviticus.

        a. The Story is non-reversible; to "go back" is to deny it, *not* just "amend" it.

        b. The superiority of Yeshua the Messiah is the result of His finality:[4]

Characteristic	Old Testament High Priest	Our "Great High Priest"
Eligibility	a son of of Aaron (Lev 16:3,32)	*Son of God (Heb 4:14)*
Place of Primary Sacrifice	Holy of Holies (Lev 16:15,16)	*the presence of Yahweh (Heb 9:24)*
Frequency of Sacrifice	once each year (Lev 16:34)	*once for all time (Heb 9:12)*
The Sacrifice	blood of animals (Lev 16:14,15)	*his own blood, i.e. life (Heb 9:12)*
Beneficiaries of sacrifice	Israelite nation (Lev 16:34)	*all who come to Yahweh (Heb 7:25)*
Efficacy of sacrifice	for one year (Lev 16:34)	*forever (Heb 9:12)*
Priest's own preparation	he must atone for his own sin and that of his household (Lev 16:6)	*none; he is sinless (Heb 7:26-28)*

    2. All biblical prophecy is properly understood in its fulfillment, *NOT* in its pronouncement.[5]

        a. Yeshua is the final "commentary" on the Old Testament:

            (1) Passover (Exodus 12)

                "Cleanse out the old leaven that you may be a new lump, as you really are unleavened. For Christ, our Passover lamb, has been sacrificed." **1 Corinthians 5:7**

            (2) The daily Sin Offering (Exodus 29)

                "He has no need, like those high priests, to offer sacrifices daily, first for his own sins and then for those of the people, since he did this once for all when he offered up himself." **Hebrews 7:27**

---

[1] Unfortunately, we often are content with a sort of "Cliff Notes" understanding of the Old Testament, which leads to the unintended consequence of a truncated gospel. One that begins in Bethlehem rather than Eden or Ur.

[2] We tend to do the same thing, "hiding" in our New Testament, by focusing our *own* justification to the neglect of the larger portrait of redemption and God's "plan for the fulness of time to unite all things in heaven and on earth in Christ."

[3] This extended to their entire liturgical, civil, and agricultural calendar, as well as land management, debt management, and their entire economy.

[4] The author of Hebrews builds an "air tight" case for the fact that *nothing* can be added to Yeshua and what he has done.

[5] In fact, Jesus instructs us *not* to listen to those who preach and teach on *unfulfilled* prophecy with an attitude of certainty (cf. Luke 17:23-24; 21:8-9).

(3) Day of Atonement (Leviticus 16)

"Nor was it to offer himself repeatedly, as the high priest enters the holy places every year with blood not his own,…so Christ, having been offered once to bear the sins of many, will appear a second time, not to deal with sin but to save those who are eagerly waiting for him." **Hebrews 9:25, 28**

(4) The entire Old Testament:

"Then he said to them, "These are my words that I spoke to you while I was still with you, that everything written about me in the Law of Moses and the Prophets and the Psalms must be fulfilled." **Luke 24:44**

"You search the Scriptures because you think that in them you have eternal life; and it is they that bear witness about me, yet you refuse to come to me that you may have life." **John 5:39, 40**

C. Leviticus is the "cradle" out of which our most treasured New Testament doctrines were birthed.

 1. What Paul "learned" from Moses and Jesus:

 a. Death — (the "shedding of blood") is the fruit of sin (Lev 17:11 and Rom 5:12).

 b. Imputation — the guilt of a sinner is "transferred" to something/someone else (Lev 16:20-22 and 2 Cor 5:21).

 c. Substitution — something/someone must die in my place (Lev 14:24 and Rom 5:6-8; 8:3).

 d. Mediation — someone else must represent me before Yahweh (Lev 16:17 and Col 1:21-22).

XXIV. Unit 24 - "RUNNING THE RACE: DETOURS AND POTHOLES" *(Hebrews-pt 3)*

A. Replaying the Sermon to Revisit its Purpose

 1. It was intended to be a prophetic sermon:

 a. The writers uses four different words for "therefore" 29 times in this sermon.[1]

 b. He was laboring to confront their thinking and their theology.

 c. It contains six warnings from *their own history* about where they are and where they're headed:[2]

 (1) a warning about "drifting" from the truth they had heard (2:1–4)

 (2) a warning about "disbelief" (3:7–4:13)

 (3) a warning about "dullness of hearing," immaturity and apostasy (5:11–6:20)

 (4) a warning about "deliberate disobedience" (10:26-31)

 (5) a warning about "defiling"[3] others through bitterness (12:12-17)

 (6) a warning against "disregarding" the current voice of Yahweh (12:25-29)

 2. It was intended to be a remedial sermon:

 a. It was intended to reconnect them to The Story by correcting their misunderstanding of it and their place in it.

 (1) Their "Jewishness" — He uses the word, "better" [Gk, *kreittōn*] 14x to compare Yeshua and genuine faith in Him with all the aspects of Judaism (1:4; 6:4-9; 7:14-19,21-23; 8:6-9; 9:23; 10:34; 11:16; 12:24).

 (2) Suffering and Persecution — He builds a masterful panorama of "faith" from *their own history*, that moves from glory to suffering (Heb 11).

 (3) The word "therefore" in 12:1 [Gk, *toigaroun*] he only uses once, indicating his final summation:

 (a) All of Judaism was a preparation for Yeshua who "trumped" it all by *fulfilling* it all.

 (b) Those who drifted, disbelieved, disobeyed, disregarded and disrespected the word of Yahweh faced the consequences. That hasn't changed.

---

[1] I.e., he is drawing a lot of conclusions. This letter must be understood as an argument of sorts.
[2] The cumulative impact of these warnings would have been very sobering because they are all *negative!*
[3] The word "defile" has a long, powerful, and highly nuanced history among Yahweh's covenant people. It is, in a very real sense, a uniquely "Jewish" word. It would have created many thoughts among the hearers that fall upon deaf ears in our largely "Gentile" hearts.

     (c) The "faith of your fathers" involved both believing what Yahweh said, and doing what Yahweh asked. That hasn't changed.

     (d) Persecution and opposition to The Story are actually *part of* The Story, and any who are in it, including Yeshua!

     (e) "*Put on your big boy pants*" and get back into the race!

B. Facing the "Elephant in the Room" Before Looking at the Face in the Mirror

  1. Hebrews 6:4-6 is one of the most difficult *and* sobering passages in our New Testament.

> *"For in the case of those who have once been enlightened and have tasted of the heavenly gift and have been made partakers of the Holy Spirit, and have tasted the good word of God and the powers of the age to come, and then have fallen away, it is impossible to renew them again to repentance, since they again crucify to themselves the Son of God and put Him to open shame."* **Hebrews 6:4-6, NAS**

> *"For it is impossible to restore again to repentance those who have once been enlightened, who have tasted the heavenly gift, and have shared in the Holy Spirit, and have tasted the goodness of the word of God and the powers of the age to come, if they then fall away, since they are crucifying once again the Son of God to their own harm and holding him up to contempt."* **Hebrews 6:4-6, ESV**

  2. There are some very important contextual details to consider in forging a possible interpretation:

    a. The historical context (i.e., original audience) sets the boundaries for what it is saying (In some ways, we're reading "someone else's mail").

    b. The context of the passage itself is spiritual infancy (e.g. "infants") and apathy (5:11-6:3).

    c. The context of the book as a whole sets the boundaries for what it likely means, (i.e., Israel's history of "unbelievers" [ch 3-4] and "believers" [ch 11] *within* the covenant community).

    d. The author shifts his address from his listeners to "those" in vs. 4, and back to his listeners in vs. 9 (this plural article is our only "clue," because the verbs in 4-8 are all participles which have to "person").

     (1) This might be a homiletical tool pointing to a hypothetical situation.

     (2) It might be a description of people they actually know.

     (3) We do know it is *not* a description of them:

> *"...Though we speak in this way, yet in your case, beloved, we feel sure of better things--things that belong to salvation. For God is not so unjust as to overlook your work and the love that you showed for his sake in serving the saints, as you still do. And we desire each one of you to show the same earnestness to have the full assurance of hope until the end, so that you may not be sluggish, but imitators of those who through faith and patience inherit the promises."* **Hebrews 6:9-12**

    e. The "lostness" of the people described here is permanent (Gk *adunatos*, "impossible," is the word used for the likelihood of Yahweh lying in 6:18).

    f. This is certainly a strong warning against "salvation by association," a characteristic of Jewish thinking, *and* the fruit of infantile theology.

  3. In our rush to dismiss the obvious "speck" in other's theology, let's not miss the log in our own:

    a. Imputed righteousness and forgiven guilt are *not* holiness.

    b. As righteous and forgiven children of Yahweh, we are *still* commanded to be holy for the same reason the Israelites were...Yahweh is (Heb 12:14; 1 Pet 1:15-16; Lev 11:44; 19:2; 20:7).

> *"Strive for peace with everyone, and for the holiness without which no one will see the Lord."* **Hebrews 12:14**

     (1) "strive" [Gk, *diōkō*] is an incredibly strong word meaning, "to molest, to persecute, to chase swiftly, to pursue."

     (2) "strive" is a command with no end in sight

(3) "peace" and "holiness" are *both* the object of this verb, "holiness" is *not* the fruit of striving for "peace."[1]

   c. The abolition of the Mosaic covenant in the face of the New Covenant is simply the fulfillment of the Abrahamic covenant:

> *"When Abram was ninety-nine years old the LORD appeared to Abram and said to him, 'I am God Almighty; walk before me, and be blameless,'"*   **Genesis 17:1**

   d. In our theology of salvation, we've confused not fearing the judgment of God with not fearing God, even though the Bible warns otherwise:

> *"So whether we are at home or away, we make it our aim to please him. For we must all appear before the judgment seat of Christ, so that each one may receive what is due for what he has done in the body, whether good or evil. Therefore, knowing the fear of the Lord, we persuade others. But what we are is known to God, and I hope it is known also to your conscience."*   **2 Corinthians 5:9-11**

> *"Therefore, my beloved, as you have always obeyed, so now, not only as in my presence but much more in my absence, work out your own salvation with fear and trembling, for it is God who works in you, both to will and to work for his good pleasure."*   **Philippians 2:12, 13**

> *"And if you call on him as Father who judges impartially according to each one's deeds, conduct yourselves with fear throughout the time of your exile,"*   **1 Peter 1:17**

> *"For we know him who said, 'Vengeance is mine; I will repay.' And again, 'The Lord will judge his people.' It is a fearful thing to fall into the hands of the living God."*   **Hebrews 10:30, 31**

> *"Therefore let us be grateful for receiving a kingdom that cannot be shaken, and thus let us offer to God acceptable worship, with reverence and awe, for our God is a consuming fire."* **Hebrews 12:28, 29**

C. The "Jew" in the Mirror: Letting Hebrews "Preach" to *Me*

   1. This sermon is our most majestic panorama of The Story I'm in, and those who have lived and died in it before me.

   2. The three proper responses to this sermon are gratitude, awe-induced worship, and a sense of Yahweh's empowerment to fulfill my role in The Story:

> *"Therefore let us be grateful for receiving a kingdom that cannot be shaken, and thus let us offer to God acceptable worship, with reverence and awe, for our God is a consuming fire."*   **Hebrews 12:28, 29**

> *"Now may the God of peace who brought again from the dead our Lord Jesus, the great shepherd of the sheep, by the blood of the eternal covenant, equip you with everything good that you may do his will, working in us that which is pleasing in his sight, through Jesus Christ, to whom be glory forever and ever. Amen."*   **Hebrews 13:20, 21**

XXV. UNIT 25 - "SIMON SAYS": The Letters of Peter

A. "Simon the Son of John" (John 1:42)

   1. Simon was a native of Bethsaida, living with his mother-in-law in Capernaum (Jn 1:44; Mt 8:5,14).

   2. He was the brother of Andrew, and fishing partners with him and the "sons of Zebedee, James and John (Mt 4:18; Luke 5:10).

   3. Andrew was a disciple of John the Baptizer, who became a disciple of Jesus (Jn 1:35-40).

   4. It was *Andrew* who introduced his brother, Simon (i.e. "Cephas, Peter"), to Jesus "east of the Jordan" (Jn 1:28-42).

   5. Sometime after the wedding at Cana, the four fishermen responded to Jesus' rabbinic call to discipleship in Capernaum (Jn 2:1-12; Luke 5:1-11).[2]

B. The Inquisitive Peter

   1. Peter gave evidence of having the most curious mind among the Twelve:

---

[1] In Greek, nouns that are the direct object of the main verb are in the accusative case, whereas the subject of the verb is in the nominative case. In this verse, both "peace" and "holiness" are in the accusative case, indicating that they are a compound object of the verb.

[2] John's unique reporting of what is known as the "Early Judean Ministry" of Yeshua informs us that Peter, Andrew, James, and John had already met Yehsua prior to that day on the shores of the Sea of Galilee. Without John's vital insights, it would appear that their decision to follow this new rabbi was rash and irresponsible.

"And Peter answered him, 'Lord, if it is you, command me to come to you on the water.'" **Matthew 14:28**

"Then Peter came up and said to him, 'Lord, how often will my brother sin against me, and I forgive him? As many as seven times?'" **Matthew 18:21**

"Then Peter said in reply, 'See, we have left everything and followed you. What then will we have?'" **Matthew 19:27**

"Peter said, 'Lord, are you telling this parable for us or for all?'" **Luke 12:41**

"Simon Peter answered him, 'Lord, to whom shall we go? You have the words of eternal life,'" **John 6:68**

"He came to Simon Peter, who said to him, 'Lord, do you wash my feet?'" **John 13:6**

"Simon Peter said to him, 'Lord, where are you going?' Jesus answered him, 'Where I am going you cannot follow me now, but you will follow afterward.' Peter said to him, 'Lord, why can I not follow you now? I will lay down my life for you.'" **John 13:36, 37**

C. The Impetuous Peter: *"Shooting from the lip"*

1. Peter boldly declared that he wanted to walk on water (Mt 14:28-31).

2. Peter rebuked Jesus for unveiling the gruesome details of The Story (Mt 16:21-23).

3. Peter blurted out a "game plan" during the Transfiguration (Lk 9:30-33).[1]

4. Peter rebuked Jesus for trying to wash his feet (Jn 13:4-11).

5. Peter boasted he would *never* desert Jesus, but did, *twice*[2] (Mk 14:29; Mt 26:38-40,56; cf Ps 69:20).

6. Peter boasted he would *never* deny Jesus, but he did, three times (Mt 26:34-35, 69-75).

D. The Important Peter

1. Peter's name is listed first in all the "apostolic lists" in the New Testament (Mt. 10:2; Mk 3:16; Lk 6:14-16; Acts 1:13).

2. Peter's name is mentioned 98x in the Gospels, nearly 4x that of the next three most mentioned (James-29, Judas and John - 23).

3. Peter was part of the privileged "apostolic trinity" (Peter, James, John):

   a. Witnessed the raising of Jairus' daughter (Lk 8:51).

   b. Eyes witness of the Transfiguration of Jesus (Mk 9:2-10).

   c. Present in the inner Garden of Gethsemane (Mt 26:37).

4. Jesus made it a *priority* to be privately reconciled to Peter on Easter Sunday (Lk 24:1,34; 1 Cor 15:5).

5. Jesus made it a point to *publicly* "restore" Peter to leadership (Jn 21:15-19).

E. The Inspired Peter

1. He emerged from Pentecost an anointed preacher and miracle-worker (Acts 2-3).

2. He was extruded into leadership of the Jerusalemite believers (Acts 4:5-22; 5:1-11; 8:18-20).[3]

3. He turned the leadership of the Jerusalemite Church over to James and left the area for missionary work (Acts 12:17 and 15:13-21).

4. He (apparently) ministered in Corinth (e.g. "I follow Cephas...", 1 Cor 1:12) and extensively in the region south of the Black Sea (1 Pet 1:1), before martyrdom in Rome.

   "But not to dwell upon ancient examples, let us come to the most recent spiritual heroes. Let us take the noble examples furnished in our own generation. Through envy and jealousy, the greatest and most righteous pillars [of the Church] have been persecuted and put to death. Let us set before our eyes the illustrious apostles. Peter, through unrighteous envy, endured not one or two, but numerous labours and when he had at length suffered martyrdom, departed to the place of glory due to him. Owing to envy, Paul also obtained the reward of patient endurance, after being seven times thrown into captivity, compelled to flee, and stoned. After preaching

---

[1] It is nearly comical to realize that Yahweh had to essentially "interrupt" Peter's monologue in order to speak to the group!

[2] Peter's first "desertion" was the fact that he fell asleep in the Garden of Gethsemane after Yeshua had asked him to stay awake and pray. It would be reasonable to assume that Yeshua was also asking these three men to "stay on guard," knowing what was about to befall him. In military terms, Peter abandoned his post by sleeping.

[3] "Extrusion" is Yahweh's proper path for those he chooses and calls to lead his people. *Seeking* to have authority over others is a clear sign that one is not ready for leadership in the Kingdom.

both in the east and west, he gained the illustrious reputation due to his faith, having taught righteousness to the whole world, and come to the extreme limit of the west, and suffered martyrdom under the prefects. Thus was he removed from the world, and went into the holy place, having proved himself a striking example of patience."   **The First Epistle of Clement to the Corinthians 5; c. AD 88-97**

THE CHURCHES OF PETER'S LETTER

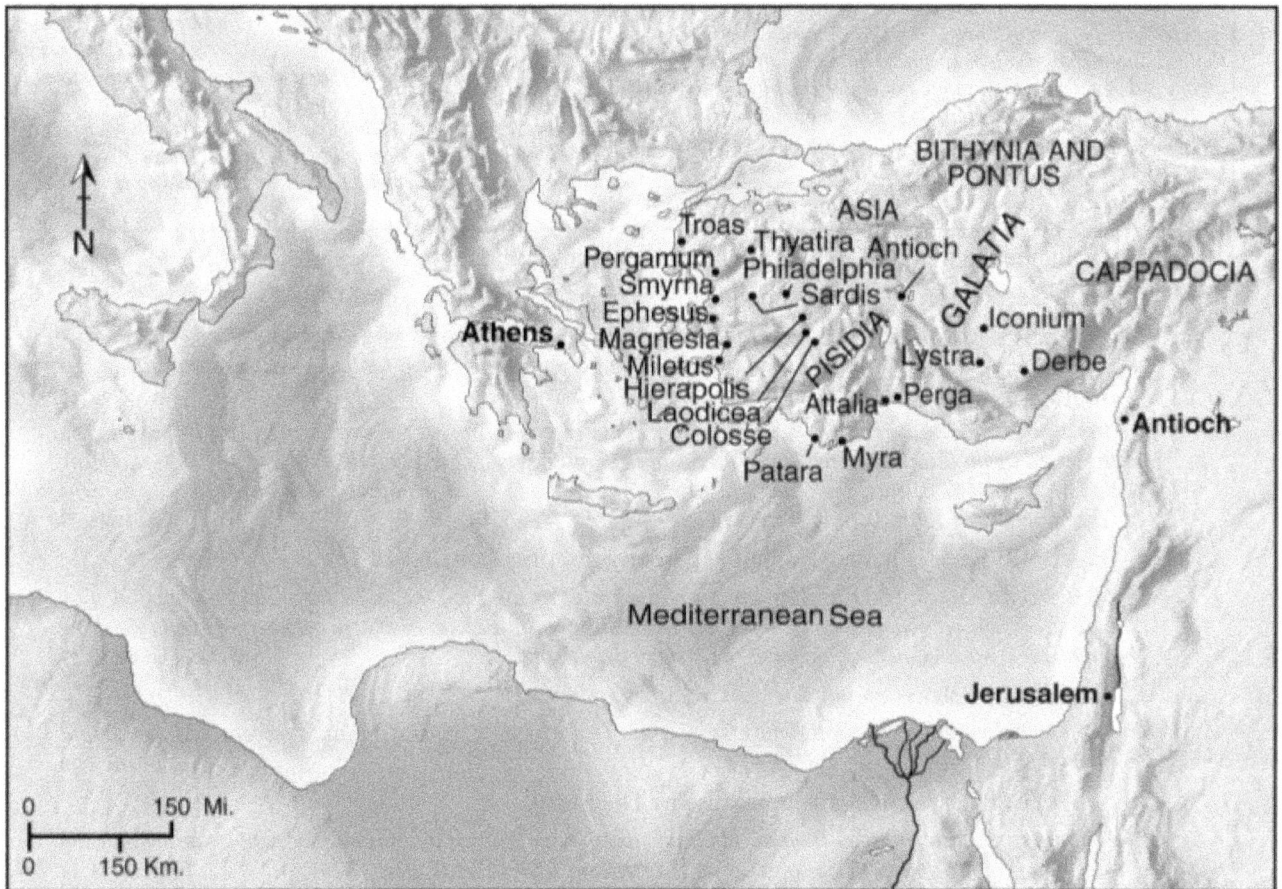

F.   The "Improved" Peter: In his old age, he was wiser and more patient

Peter Near the End	Peter at the Beginning
"Likewise, you who are younger, be subject to the elders. Clothe yourselves, all of you, with humility toward one another, for God opposes the proud but gives grace to the humble." **1 Peter 5:5**	Peter said to him, *"Even though they all fall away, I will not."* **Mark 14:29**
"...so that the tested genuineness of your faith—more precious than gold that perishes though it is tested by fire—may be found to result in praise and glory and honor at the revelation of Jesus Christ." **1 Peter 1:7**	*"Simon, Simon, behold, Satan demanded to have you, that he might sift you like wheat, but I have prayed for you that your faith may not fail. And when you have turned again, strengthen your brothers."* **Luke 22:31, 32**
"...but in your hearts regard Christ the Lord as holy, always being prepared to make a defense to anyone who asks you for a reason for the hope that is in you..." **1 Peter 3:15**	*Now Simon Peter was standing and warming himself. So they said to him, "You also are not one of his disciples, are you?" He denied it and said, "I am not."* **John 18:25**
"The end of all things is at hand; therefore be self-controlled and sober-minded for the sake of your prayers....Be sober-minded; be watchful. Your adversary the devil prowls around like a roaring lion, seeking someone to devour." **1 Peter 4:7; 5:8**	*And he came and found them sleeping, and he said to Peter, "Simon, are you asleep? Could you not watch one hour? Watch and pray that you may not enter into temptation. The spirit indeed is willing, but the flesh is weak."* **Mark 14:37, 38**

Peter Near the End	Peter at the Beginning
"And after you have suffered a little while, the God of all grace, who has called you to his eternal glory in Christ, will himself restore, confirm, strengthen, and establish you." **1 Peter 5:10**	*When they had finished breakfast, Jesus said to Simon Peter, "Simon, son of John, do you love me more than these?" He said to him, "Yes, Lord; you know that I love you." He said to him, "Feed my lambs."* **John 21:15**
"So I exhort the elders among you, as a fellow elder and a witness of the sufferings of Christ, as well as a partaker in the glory that is going to be revealed: shepherd the flock of God that is among you, exercising oversight, not under compulsion, but willingly, as God would have you; not for shameful gain, but eagerly; not domineering over those in your charge, but being examples to the flock." **1 Peter 5:1-3**	*He came to Simon Peter, who said to him, "Lord, do you wash my feet?" Jesus answered him, "What I am doing you do not understand now, but afterward you will understand. ... When he had washed their feet and put on his outer garments and resumed his place, he said to them, "Do you understand what I have done to you? You call me Teacher and Lord, and you are right, for so I am. If I then, your Lord and Teacher, have washed your feet, you also ought to wash one another's feet. For I have given you an example, that you also should do just as I have done to you."* **John 13:6, 7, 12-15**

1. But, his understanding of The Story was gradual, not immediate:

   a. **c. AD 38:** Peter reluctantly responds to Cornelius' invitation (Acts 10):

      While Peter was still saying these things, the Holy Spirit fell on all who heard the word. And the believers from among the circumcised who had come with Peter were amazed, because the gift of the Holy Spirit was poured out even on the Gentiles. **Acts 10:44, 45**

      "As I began to speak, the Holy Spirit fell on them just as on us at the beginning. And I remembered the word of the Lord, how he said, 'John baptized with water, but you will be baptized with the Holy Spirit.' If then God gave the same gift to them as he gave to us when we believed in the Lord Jesus Christ, who was I that I could stand in God's way?" **Acts 11:15-17**

   b. **c. AD 48:** Peter is persuaded, but apparently not fully *convinced*:

      "But when Cephas came to Antioch, I opposed him to his face, because he stood condemned. For before certain men came from James, he was eating with the Gentiles; but when they came he drew back and separated himself, fearing the circumcision party." **Galatians 2:11, 12**

   c. **c. AD 62:** Peter is *consumed* by The Story:

      "Once you were not a people, but now you are God's people; once you had not received mercy, but now you have received mercy." **1 Peter 2:10**

   d. **c. AD 66:** Peter is *condemned* because of The Story:

      "I think it right, as long as I am in this body, to stir you up by way of reminder, since I know that the putting off of my body will be soon, as our Lord Jesus Christ made clear to me." **2 Peter 1:13, 14**

XXVI. UNIT 26: "THE PERPETUAL PETER" — Principles From Peter for the Present

A. A Thorough Theology of Suffering

1. 1 Peter is the most extensive New Testament book on suffering ("suffer" appears 16x in this letter, out of 55 in the entire NT; 14x as much as any other letter).

2. This letter is the *opposite* of Job: little description and much explanation.

3. Peter presents seven profound theological truths about suffering:

   a. It is normal:

      "Beloved, do not be surprised at the fiery trial when it comes upon you to test you, as though something strange were happening to you." **1 Peter 4:12**

   b. It is necessary and purposeful:

      "In this you rejoice, though now for a little while, if necessary, you have been grieved by various trials, so that the tested genuineness of your faith—more precious than gold that perishes though it is tested by fire—may be found to result in praise and glory and honor at the revelation of Jesus Christ. ...Since therefore Christ suffered in the flesh, arm yourselves with the same way of thinking, for whoever has suffered in the flesh has ceased from sin," **1 Peter 1:6, 7; 4:1**

c. It is spiritual in nature and universal in scope:

> *"Resist him, firm in your faith, knowing that the same kinds of suffering are being experienced by your brotherhood throughout the world."*
> **1 Peter 5:9**

d. The *present* persecution of Christ[1] is a source of suffering for those in The Story:

> *"But rejoice insofar as you share Christ's sufferings, that you may also rejoice and be glad when his glory is revealed."*
> **1 Peter 4:13**

> *"Now I rejoice in my sufferings for your sake, and in my flesh I am filling up what is lacking [Gk, husterēma, deficient, need] in Christ's afflictions for the sake of his body, that is, the church,"*
> **Paul, in Colossians 1:24**

> *And falling to the ground he heard a voice saying to him, "Saul, Saul, why are you persecuting me?"*
> **Jesus, in Acts 9:4**

> *"Blessed are you when others revile you and persecute you and utter all kinds of evil against you falsely on my account. Rejoice and be glad, for your reward is great in heaven, for so they persecuted the prophets who were before you."*
> **Jesus, in Matt 5:11-12**

e. The "call" to Christ is a call to suffering. He suffered so we would know how to, not so that we wouldn't *have* to:

> *"For to this you have been called, because Christ also suffered for you, leaving you an example, so that you might follow in his steps. He committed no sin, neither was deceit found in his mouth. When he was reviled, he did not revile in return; when he suffered, he did not threaten, but continued entrusting himself to him who judges justly."*
> **1 Pet 2:21-23**

> *"Since therefore Christ suffered in the flesh, arm yourselves with the same way of thinking, for whoever has suffered in the flesh has ceased from sin, so as to live for the rest of the time in the flesh no longer for human passions but for the will of God."*
> **1 Peter 4:1, 2**

f. The believer's "hope" in times of suffering is the same as in times of shalom: the *end* of The Story:

> *"Blessed be the God and Father of our Lord Jesus Christ! According to his great mercy, he has caused us to be born again to a living hope through the resurrection of Jesus Christ from the dead, to an inheritance that is imperishable, undefiled, and unfading, kept in heaven for you…"*
> **1 Peter 1:3, 4**

> *"Therefore, preparing your minds for action, and being sober-minded, set your hope fully on the grace that will be brought to you at the revelation of Jesus Christ."*
> **1 Peter 1:13**

g. "Apologetics" is to be a reasoned response about my hope in the crucible of suffering, not the details of my theology in the face of skepticism:

> *"But even if you should suffer for righteousness' sake, you will be blessed. Have no fear of them, nor be troubled, but in your hearts regard Christ the Lord as holy, always being prepared to make a defense [Gk, apologia] to anyone who asks you for a reason for the hope that is in you; yet do it with gentleness and respect, having a good conscience, so that, when you are slandered, those who revile your good behavior in Christ may be put to shame. For it is better to suffer for doing good, if that should be God's will, than for doing evil."*
> **1 Peter 3:14-17**

B. A Radical Theology of Identity

1. It is vital to understand that Peter is writing to Gentile converts, *not* Jewish believers (see 1 Pet 4:3-5 ; 2 Pet 2:10-20; these are "non-Jewish" sins).

2. He uses the most majestic Hebrew metaphors to describe *them* as true Israelites, and no longer "Gentiles":

> *"But you are a chosen race, a royal priesthood, a holy nation, a people for his own possession, that you may proclaim the excellencies of him who called you out of darkness into his marvelous light. Once you were not a people, but now you are God's people; once you had not received mercy, but now you have received mercy. Beloved, I urge you as sojourners and exiles to abstain from the passions of the flesh, which wage war against your soul. Keep your conduct among the Gentiles honorable, so that when they speak against you as evildoers, they may see your good deeds and glorify God on the day of visitation."*
> **1 Peter 2:9-12**

---

[1] Yeshua's question to Saul on the road to Damascus informs us that he is still suffering: *"Saul, Saul, why do you persecute me?"* His *propitiatory* suffering is over, but not his suffering experienced in his new "body" the Church.

a. *"You are a chosen race..."* [Deut 10:15]

b. *"You are...a royal priesthood"* [Exodus 19:6]

c. *"You are...a holy nation"* [Exodus 19:6; Rev 1:6]

d. *"You are...a people belonging to God"* [Exodus 19:5; Deut 14:2]

e. *"You were 'not a people, but now you are God's people'"* [Hosea 2:23]

f. *"You had not received mercy, but now you have received mercy"* [Hosea 2:23]

g. He speaks to "Gentile" believers using the strongest covenant language[1] possible, and describes them as the fulfillment of Israel's failed mission:[2]

> *"But you are a chosen race, a royal priesthood, a holy nation, a people for his own possession, that you may proclaim the excellencies of him who called you out of darkness into his marvelous light.*
> **1 Peter 2:9**

> *"Remember not the former things, nor consider the things of old. Behold, I am doing a new thing; now it springs forth, do you not perceive it? I will make a way in the wilderness and rivers in the desert. The wild beasts will honor me, the jackals and the ostriches, for I give water in the wilderness, rivers in the desert, to give drink to my chosen people, the people whom I formed for myself that they might declare my praise."*
> **Isaiah 43:14-21**

3. He uses two powerful Greek words to describe them as *non*-citizens in the counter-Story:[3]

> *"Beloved, I urge you as sojourners [Gk, paroikos] and exiles [Gk, peripidemos] to abstain from the passions of the flesh, which wage war against your soul. Keep your conduct among the Gentiles honorable, so that when they speak against you as evildoers, they may see your good deeds and glorify God on the day of visitation."*
> **1 Peter 2:11, 12**

a. *peripidemos* – someone who is "from someplace else," and lives side-by-side with the citizens of another country; emphasis is on their origin.

b. *paroikos* – someone who is "from someplace else," and lives side-by-side with the citizens of another country; emphasis is on their present location.

4. The writer to the Hebrews describes Jewish believers using the same terms (cf. Heb 11:9,13). This is the identity of anyone in The Story!

5. "Gentiles" are anyone *outside* The Story, including unbelieving Jews[4] (1 Pet 2:12)!

C. A Progressive Theology of Salvation[5]

1. Peter makes it forever clear that one is not "saved" in the modern sense of the word:

> *"...he has granted to us his precious and very great promises, so that through them you may become partakers of the divine nature, having escaped from the corruption that is in the world because of sinful desire. For this very reason, make every effort to supplement your faith with virtue, and virtue with knowledge, and knowledge with self-control, and self-control with steadfastness, and steadfastness with godliness, and godliness with brotherly affection, and brotherly affection with love. For if these qualities are yours and are increasing, they keep you from being ineffective or unfruitful in the knowledge of our Lord Jesus Christ. For whoever lacks these qualities is so nearsighted that he is blind, having forgotten that he was cleansed from his former sins."*
> **2 Peter 1:3-9**

---

[1] cf. Paul in Ephesians 2:11 - 3:12

[2] The Greek word translated "that" in 1 Peter 2:9 is the word *hopōs,* which carries within it the idea of purpose, direction, or desired outcome. Peter is clearly stating that there is a divine purpose that is created by their calling out of darkness into the light. The word "proclaim" is the Greek word, *exaggellō*, which means to "publish" or to "declare." Peter's choice of words in this verse actually serve to make it more of a parallel text to the Isaiah 43:21 that it reflects.

[3] Other than Yeshua's clear teaching in John 15 and 17, this verse along with Hebrews 11:9, 13-16 are the clearest New Testament passages on our identity as believers and participants in the Story.

[4] Looking closer at Paul's metaphor of the olive tree in Romans 11, one sees that the real issue is the "root" of the tree, *not* the "branches" (i.e. Jew or Gentile). The "root" is the Story, or Yahweh's ultimate purposes.

[5] The passage below (2 Peter 1:3-9) should be viewed more of a "chain" than a "list." These characteristics or virtues clearly seem to build upon one another rather than merely *follow* one another in a tabular sense. The starting point is "faith" and the destination point is "love." Also, Peter uses the Greek word *epichorēgein* which is translated "supplement" in the third line above. The word points to a lavish and rich provision. It was a word originally used for a person who financed the choir in the staging of a public drama performance.

D. An Ethical System Rooted in the Power of Narrative Rather Than Precept:[1]

"But the day of the Lord will come like a thief, and then the heavens will pass away with a roar, and the heavenly bodies will be burned up and dissolved, and the earth and the works that are done on it will be exposed. Since all these things are thus to be dissolved, what sort of people ought you to be in lives of holiness and godliness, waiting for and hastening the coming of the day of God, because of which the heavens will be set on fire and dissolved, and the heavenly bodies will melt as they burn! But according to his promise we are waiting for new heavens and a new earth in which righteousness dwells." **2 Peter 3:10-13**

E. A *Civic* Identity That Flows From The Story Rather Than Culture[2]

"Beloved, I urge you as sojourners and exiles to abstain from the passions of the flesh, which wage war against your soul. Keep your conduct among the Gentiles honorable [kalēn}, so that when they speak against you as evildoers, they may see your good deeds [kalōn ergōn] and glorify God on the day of visitation." **1 Peter 2:11, 12**

"In the same way, let your light shine before others, so that they may see your good works [kala erga] and give glory to your Father who is in heaven." **Matthew 5:16**

F. Peter And The Present

1. What comes to mind when someone asks you, *"Where are you from?"*

2. How much is the glory of God the motivation behind your civic responsibility?

3. Have you ever thought of your "salvation" in terms of being *"effective and productive in your "knowledge of the Lord Jesus Christ?"*

G. *"Cliff Notes"* on 2 Peter and Jude

1. These two letters are best understood as strong polemics *against* false Story-tellers and counterfeit Stories.

XXVII. UNIT 27 - "YAHWEH'S FINAL WORD": The Writings of John

A. "SON OF ZEBEDEE—SON OF THUNDER" *"...and John his brother"* (Matt 4:21)

1. Of the 20 times John's name is mentioned in the Gospels, only twice does it appear *before* James (Jairus' daughter in Lk 8:51 and the transfiguration in 9:28).

2. His name is *never* mentioned in the Gospel of John[3] *(neither are Simon the Zealot, both James, and Matthew).*

3. Along with his brother James, was nicknamed, "sons of thunder" by Jesus (Mk 3:17).[4]

And he sent messengers ahead of him, who went and entered a village of the Samaritans, to make preparations for him. But the people did not receive him, because his face was set toward Jerusalem. And when his disciples James and John saw it, they said, "Lord, do you want us to tell fire to come down from heaven and consume them?" But he turned and rebuked them. **Luke 9:52-55**

4. He is almost certainly the "other disciple" and "the disciple Jesus loved" in the Gospel of John (Jn 1:35-40; 13:23; 21:7).

a. Was closest to Jesus at the last supper (Jn 13:23).

b. Seems to have "known" the high priest and had access into his villa (Jn 18:15; verb is imperfect tense).

c. The only apostle stated to have been at the crucifixion (Jn 19:26).

---

[1] We are to behave in a certain way *not* because to do otherwise is to violate a "line" in the script, but rather because our entire lives should reflect and validate the Story itself; in its entirety. I'm *not* to commit adultery, to give generously, and to worship freely because I understand and embrace the Story and affirm that these behaviors are consistent with the Story and my part in it.

[2] Peter provides some excellent advice for how *not* to be a "lightening rod" for attention and criticism as a believer. In other words, he tells us what *not* to have to suffer for as a believer. Unfortunately, much of the criticism and discrimination leveled against modern believers is likely deserved.

[3] This is obviously intentional on his part. But, it is still significant because of the "status" he had in the inner circle of three with Yeshua *and* the unique place he had with Yeshua himself. This is evidenced clearly by the fact that Yeshua's mother is entrusted to his care during the crucifixion.

[4] At least three occasions brought out their "thunder": the inhospitality of Samaritans (Lk 9:54), their desire to forbid "outsiders" from exorcising demons (Lk 9:38,49), and their desire to secure a "place" at the right and left hand of Yeshua (Lk 22:24; Matt 20:20). This rather "either/or" approach to truth permeates John's first epistle. Things were pretty "black and white" to this son of thunder.

     d. The one to whom Jesus entrusted his widowed mother (Jn 19:27).

     e. First male to the empty tomb (Jn 20:4).[1]

     f. Claimed authorship for the "Gospel of John" (Jn 21:24).

5. After the resurrection, he along with Peter are the recognized leaders in the Jerusalemite church (Acts 1:13; 3:1-11; 8:14-16).

6. By the time his own brother James is martyred, John has priority over James (Acts 12:1-2).[2]

7. Paul considered him one of the "pillars" of the Jerusalemite church:

     "...and when James and Cephas and John, who seemed to be pillars, perceived the grace that was given to me, they gave the right hand of fellowship to Barnabas and me, that we should go to the Gentiles and they to the circumcised."

                   Galatians 2:9

8. Many ancient sources list him as the bishop of Ephesus until his exile and death:

     "For in Asia also great lights have fallen asleep, which shall rise again on the last day, at the coming of the Lord, when he shall come with glory from heaven and shall seek out all the saints. Among these are Philip, one of the twelve apostles, who sleeps in Hierapolis, and his two aged virgin daughters, and another daughter who lived in the Holy Spirit and now rests at Ephesus; and moreover John, who was both a witness and a teacher, who reclined upon the bosom of the Lord, and being a priest wore the sacerdotal plate. He also sleeps at Ephesus."

            Polycrates, bishop of Ephesus c. 189-198; cited in Eusebius' *Ecclesiastical History,* **3.31.3**

9. He was the last authoritative voice for Jesus as the first century closed.

     a. John ascribes his eyewitness and apostolic status to his writings:

       "This is the disciple who is bearing witness about these things, and who has written these things, and we know that his testimony is true."

                      John 21:24

       "That which was from the beginning, which we have heard, which we have seen with our eyes, which we looked upon and have touched with our hands, concerning the word of life—the life was made manifest, and we have seen it, and testify to it and proclaim to you the eternal life, which was with the Father and was made manifest to us—that which we have seen and heard we proclaim also to you, so that you too may have fellowship with us; and indeed our fellowship is with the Father and with his Son Jesus Christ."

                      1 John 1:1-3

     b. His Gospel's "uniqueness" is a product of *when* it was written more than by whom it was written.

     c. His five books are indeed God's "final word" to mankind: Gospel of John, 1, 2, 3 John, and The Revelation.

XXVIII. UNIT 28: "THE EPISTLE OF *TOUGH* LOVE" — 1ˢᵗ John

A. The Unique Vocabulary of a "Unique" Apostle[3]

1. John's language in this letter is very *similar* to his Gospel and *dissimilar* from everyone else:

Word/Phrase	1 John	John	Matthew	Mark	Luke
"love"	46	44	9	6	14
"know"	41	143	49	33	55
"true/truth"	27	47	1	3	4
"world"	23	78	9	3	3
"life"	13	36	7	4	5
"light/darkness"	12	31	9	0	6

---

[1] Peter gets the award for "first inside the tomb" by apparently blowing past John while John was looking in from the entrance.

[2] We typically lose sight of this fact because the martyrdom of Stephen tends to eclipse John's rise to authority. Yet, in Acts we see John as a key leader.

[3] There are a number of Story truths buried in the text of 1 John that would be easy to miss. The opening verse informs us that the Story is indeed *ancient,* harkening back to Genesis 1:1. John unpacks a number of Old Testament doctrines that modern believers have unfortunately assumed to be "new" to Yeshua. The first is the idea that "God is love." This truth about God was one of the first things he told Moses about himself (cf. Ex. 15:13; 20:6; 34:6-7). It reappears among the prophets as the motivation for repentence (Is 43:4; Jer 31:3; Hos 11:1; Mal 1:2). Even Yeshua's "new commandment" is truly an old commandment (cf. Lev 19:18). Only now, we *know* what it "looks" like to love our neighbor, because Yeshua tells us to love one another as *he has loved us.* In a very real sense, Yeshua didn't inaugurate this teaching, he inherited it.

Word/Phrase	1 John	John	Matthew	Mark	Luke
"walk" (lifestyle)	10	8	0	1	1
"believe"	9	93	10	15	10
"eternal life"	6	16	3	2	3
"testimony"	6	10	0	3	1

B. Special Times Call For Special People: The "Days of St. John the Divine"

   1. Because of the compressed time period of his writings (i.e. all five books were written within a very short time window; perhaps 5-10 years), John himself is our best source of the spiritual "climate" surrounding this letter:

     a. False teachers: (Ephesus)

     "I know your works, your toil and your patient endurance, and how you cannot bear with those who are evil, but have tested those who call themselves apostles and are not, and found them to be false. I know you are enduring patiently and bearing up for my name's sake, and you have not grown weary. But I have this against you, that you have abandoned the love you had at first." **Revelation 2:2-4**

     b. Sexual Immorality: *(Pergamum)*

     "But I have a few things against you: you have some there who hold the teaching of Balaam, who taught Balak to put a stumbling block before the sons of Israel, so that they might eat food sacrificed to idols and practice sexual immorality. So also you have some who hold the teaching of the Nicolaitans." **Revelation 2:14, 15**

     c. Satanic Theology: (Thyatira)

     "But I have this against you, that you tolerate that woman Jezebel, who calls herself a prophetess and is teaching and seducing my servants to practice sexual immorality and to eat food sacrificed to idols....But to the rest of you in Thyatira, who do not hold this teaching, who have not learned what some call the deep things of Satan, to you I say, I do not lay on you any other burden." **Rev. 2:20, 24**

     d. Moral Laxity:[1] (Sardis)

     "And to the angel of the church in Sardis write: 'The words of him who has the seven spirits of God and the seven stars.' 'I know your works. You have the reputation of being alive, but you are dead. Wake up, and strengthen what remains and is about to die, for I have not found your works complete in the sight of my God." **Revelation 3:1, 2**

     e. Spiritual Blindness:[2] (Laodecia)

     "For you say, I am rich, I have prospered, and I need nothing, not realizing that you are wretched, pitiable, poor, blind, and naked....Behold, I stand at the door and knock. If anyone hears my voice and opens the door, I will come in to him and eat with him, and he with me." **Revelation 3:17, 20**

     f. Hostile Jews: (Philadelphia)

     "Behold, I will make those of the synagogue of Satan who say that they are Jews and are not, but lie —behold, I will make them come and bow down before your feet and they will learn that I have loved you." **Revelation 3:9**

     g. "Proto-Gnosticism": (Ephesus)

     "By this you know the Spirit of God: every spirit that confesses that Jesus Christ has come in the flesh is from God, and every spirit that does not confess Jesus is not from God. This is the spirit of the antichrist, which you heard was coming and now is in the world already." **1 John 4:2, 3**

C. Gnosticism: The Long "Half-Life" of an Old Heresy

   1. "Knowing" as opposed to "being" was becoming the dominant measure of true spirituality. (Gk, *gnōsis*).

     a. Only those who had been initiated into the secret knowledge were truly "in the light."

---

[1] This attitude of "coasting" along, morally, is the opposite of Peter's strong admonition to "add to our faith…" in 2 Peter 1:3-9.

[2] This church's "blindness" is a sobering and fearful thing. "Church" was going along as usual and everyone thought "there's nothing missing from our fellowship." Yeshua crashes this complacency by informing them that *he is missing!* He's on the "outside" knocking to be allowed entrance.

The Spiritual "Weather" of John's Day

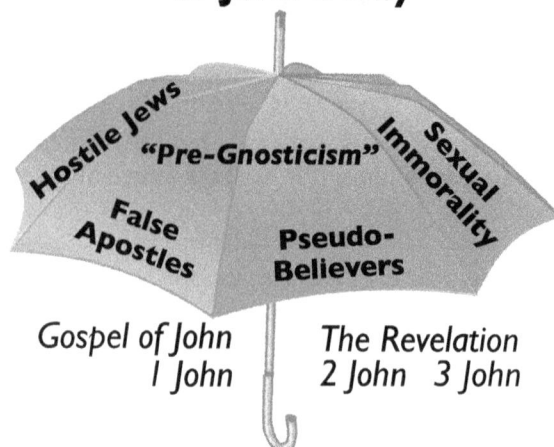

Hostile Jews
"Pre-Gnosticism"
Sexual Immorality
False Apostles
Pseudo-Believers

Gospel of John
1 John

The Revelation
2 John   3 John

   b. Dualism: "A total separation between the "spiritual" and the physical; the closer you got to one the further you were from the other. [1]

   c. The body was evil at worst, unimportant at best, including Yeshua's body! [2]

   d. Total confusion was growing over how to "know" who were the genuine believers.

D. God's Solution: *"The Idiot's Guide to Phony Christians"* (1 John)

   1. John lays out the characteristics of a phony Christian and a genuine one.

      a. *Phony* Christians are those who:

         (1) Put all their focus on what they *profess*, rather than what they *confess*: [3]

"Whoever says "I know him…"	**1 John 2:4**
"…whoever says he abides in him…"	**1 John 2:6**
"Whoever says he is in the light…"	**1 John 2:9**
"If anyone says, "I love God…"	**1 John 4:20**

         (2) Use grace as an excuse for disobedience:

"No one born of God makes a practice of sinning, for God's seed abides in him, and he cannot keep on sinning because he has been born of God."   **1 John 3:9**

"Whoever says "I know him" but does not keep his commandments is a liar, and the truth is not in him,"   **1 John 2:4**

         (3) Believe fellowship with God and fellowship with believers are unrelated:

"If anyone says, "I love God," and hates his brother, he is a liar; for he who does not love his brother whom he has seen cannot love God whom he has not seen."   **1 John 4:20**

---

[1] We still have versions of this dualistic thinking with us today. In the church it's the separation of the "sacred" from the "secular," so certain behaviors are more spiritual and certain vocations more godly. In the secular world, the spheres of "work" and "play" are divided. So, ideas like TGIF imply that we work all week for the reward of the weekend.

[2] This eventually produced two polar opposites in terms of behavior. The first was an asceticism in which believers sought to *withdraw* from the world because of its evil. The opposite was antinomianism, disregarding anything "done in the body" because it was of no spiritual consequence. It wasn't possible for anything done *physically* to affect one spiritually. The offspring of this was immorality, gluttony, and a host of "bodily" behaviors. John's letter addresses both of these errors.

[3] "Profession" has to do with my speech; what I *say* about what I believe. My "confession" has to do with lifestyle and the visible expression of my faith and beliefs. For the genuine believer, the two should be the same. In the days of John (and our own) "profession" became an end in itself.

(4) Remove Christ from the center of The Story:

> *"No one who denies the Son has the Father. Whoever confesses the Son has the Father also."*
> **1 John 2:23**

> *"And we know that the Son of God has come and has given us understanding, so that we may know him who is true; and we are in him who is true, in his Son Jesus Christ. He is the true God and eternal life."*
> **1 John 5:20**

b. *Genuine* Christians are those who:

(1) Put their focus on how they live because of what they confess:

> *"...whoever says he abides in him ought to walk in the same way in which he walked."* **1 John 2:6**

> *"By this we know love, that he laid down his life for us, and we ought to lay down our lives for the brothers."* **1 John 3:16**

> *"But if anyone has the world's goods and sees his brother in need, yet closes his heart against him, how does God's love abide in him?"* **1 John 3:17**

> *"Little children, let us not love in word or talk but in deed and in truth."* **1 John 3:18**

(2) See *obedience* as evidence of salvation (mine and others), *and* the path to intimacy with God ("commandments" appears 18x in this brief letter!):[1]

> *"And by this we know that we have come to know him, if we keep his commandments."* **1 John 2:3**

> *"For this is the love of God, that we keep his commandments. And his commandments are not burdensome."* **1 John 5:3**

(3) Believe that true fellowship is a condition, not an activity; it is something I'm either "in" or "out" of, not something I do or don't do.[2]

> *"...that which we have seen and heard we proclaim also to you, so that you too may have fellowship with us; and indeed our fellowship is with the Father and with his Son Jesus Christ....If we say we have fellowship with him while we walk in darkness, we lie and do not practice the truth. But if we walk in the light, as he is in the light, we have fellowship with one another, and the blood of Jesus his Son cleanses us from all sin."* **1 John 1:3, 6, 7**

> *"Whoever loves his brother abides in the light, and in him there is no cause for stumbling. But whoever hates his brother is in the darkness and walks in the darkness, and does not know where he is going, because the darkness has blinded his eyes."* **1 John 2:10, 11**

(4) Believe that knowing Christ and being known by Him is more important than what you know ("know" appears 42x; there are 59 refs to Jesus Christ and 85 references to God):

> *"See what kind of love the Father has given to us, that we should be called children of God; and so we are. The reason why the world does not **know** us is that it did not **know** him."* **1 John 3:1**

> *"And we **know** that the Son of God has come and has given us understanding, so that we may **know** him who is true; and we are in him who is true, in his Son Jesus Christ. He is the true God and eternal life."* **1 John 5:20**

E. 1st Century John Speaks to the 21st Century Church

1. Grace can easily becomes an euphemism for disobedience when I extract it from The Story.

> *"In this the love of God was made manifest among us, that God sent his only Son into the world, so that we might live through him. In this is love, not that we have loved God but that he loved us and sent his Son to be the propitiation for our sins. Beloved, if God so loved us, we also ought to love one another."*
> **1 John 4:9-11**

---

[1] True believers come to understand the *purpose* of the commandments. They are the correct way to live with the Story of God. We don't complain when someone tells us the correct way to light a gas grill! We simply accept it as "the way things should be."

[2] We erroneously assume that "fellowship" is what happens when Christians gather. We speak of "a time of fellowship" after sporting events or other meetings. We designate certain places as where "fellowship" occurs. We have Fellowship Halls, organizations with the word "fellowship" in them, or churches with the name "fellowship" attached. It's as if we assume that "fellowship" will just "happen" when believers gather in certain places and at certain times. John bursts that notion by informing us that "fellowship" happens when two believers who are *both* in fellowship with God (i.e. "walking in the light") are together. The opposite is sobering. It means two believers, one of which is *not* in fellowship with God (or another believer) can *not* have "fellowship" no matter which room they're in or what time it is. In fact, many "times of fellowship" are the gathering of people who are neither in fellowship with each other or God!

2. I am to *hate* the "counter-Story" (Gk, *kosmos*), but *love* those caught in it:

> *"Do not love the world or the things in the world. If anyone loves the world, the love of the Father is not in him. For all that is in the world—the desires of the flesh and the desires of the eyes and pride in possessions—is not from the Father but is from the world."*   **1 John 2:15, 16**

3. History is linear because life has a narrative (i.e. a Story):

> *"Children, it is the last hour, and as you have heard that antichrist is coming, so now many antichrists have come. Therefore we know that it is the last hour."*   **1 John 2:18**

4. Fellowship is not based on shared interests, shared theology or a shared geography, but a shared condition:

> *If we say we have fellowship with him while we walk in darkness, we lie and do not practice the truth. But if we walk in the light, as he is in the light, we have fellowship with one another, and the blood of Jesus his Son cleanses us from all sin."*   **1 John 1:6**

XXIX. UNIT 29 - THE FINAL WORD: "REVELATION: *PRESCRIPTION, PREDICTION & PORTENT*"

> *"And though St. John the Evangelist saw many strange monsters in his vision, he saw no creature so wild as one of his own commentators. The general fact is simple. Poetry is sane because it floats easily in an infinite sea; reason seeks to cross the infinite sea, and so make it finite. The result is mental exhaustion...The poet only desires exaltation and expansion, a world to stretch himself in. The poet only asks to get his head into the heavens. It is the logician who seeks to get the heavens into his head. And it is his head that splits."*
> **G.K. Chesterton in *Orthodoxy*, pp. 21-22**

> *"The Book of Revelation fascinates and also perplexes the modern reader. For the present generation, it is the most obscure and controversial book in the Bible. Yet...it may well be that with the exception of the Gospels, the Apocalypse is the most profound and moving teaching on Christian doctrine and discipleship found anywhere in the Holy Scripture. Neither the fanaticism of some who have fixed their attention on prophecy buy not on Christ, nor the diversity of interpretive viewpoints should discourage us from pursuing Christian truth in this marvelous book."*   **Allan F. Johnson in *The Expositor's Bible Commentary*, p. 399**

A. Where We *Start* Will Determine Where We Land — Five Vital Factors

1. What are my convictions regarding the nature and scope of "redemption."

2. What are my convictions regarding the nature and scope of the "Gospel."

3. What is my understanding of the nature and purpose of apocalyptic literature.

4. What are my convictions regarding the *purpose* of predictive prophecy.

5. What are my convictions regarding the role of inspiration in the arrangement of the New Testament canon.[1]

B. What We Honestly Admit Will Effect How Much We Can Learn

1. This is a *very* difficult book for even the best of scholars:

   a. There are at least four different "camps" built around its relation to *time*.[2]

   b. There is disagreement regarding its literary genre (epistle, prophetic, Jewish apocalyptic, etc.).

   c. We have no other New Testament literary grid to assist us (the OT books are not much help).

   d. The closest modern genres we have are fantasy (*Lord of the Rings*) and science fiction (*The Matrix*).

2. There is enormous disparity regarding the purpose, sequence, and interrelationship between two periods of time and two events.

   a. Two time periods:

   (1) The Great Tribulation (6:9-11; 7:14; Mt 24:21,29).

---

[1] Is it significant, in other words, that the Book of Revelation is "last" in our Bible? What is it actually the "end" of? Not thinking about this reveals an ignorance of the narrative nature of the Bible.

[2] They are known as the Preterist, which sees the events in the book as complete, all of them occurring in the first few centuries. The second is the Historicist, which sees the events primarily as a progressive past, encompassing the eras of church history. The third is the Futurist, which sees the book describing events that have yet to take place. The final, the Idealist, sees the book as purely symbolic and addressing enormous cosmic issues of good versus evil, etc.

(2) The "Millennium" (ch 20).

   b. Two Events:

     (1) The "rapture" (cf. 1 Th 4:13-18; 1 Cor 15:51-2; no mention in Revelation).

     (2) The Second Coming of Christ (19:11-21; 1 Th 1:9-10; 2 Th 1:5-10).

3. There are at least two views regarding the nature of the "new heavens and earth":

   a. **View #1:** Renewed but *not* destroyed (Gk *kainos* Rev 21:1 and 2 Pet 3:13 can mean "renewed" or "remade").[1]

   b. **View #2:** A totally *new* creation (Gk *kainos* in Rev 3:12; 5:9; 14:3; 21:5 clearly means similar to something pre-existing, but still "new" in the normal sense of the word).

4. We need to assess the reasons for our interest (or lack of it) in this final word from God:

   a. Is it a basis for hope in the face of suffering and a motivation for redemptive living in the present?

   b. Or is it a Nostradamus-like cipher to explain or predict modern events; a sort of Christian "astrology"?[2]

     (1) There are 15,500,000 "hits" on Google for "The Book of Revelation" and "The Revelation of John," nearly 4x as many as for Paul's letter to the Romans.

     (2) Christianbook.com has nearly 1,000 books dealing with Revelation.

     (3) There are a host of Bible teachers all claiming to have "cracked" the book to one degree or another, even though they disagree among themselves.

       • *Because the Time is Near: John MacArthur Explains the Book of Revelation* by John MacArthur

       • *Revelation Unveiled,* by Tim LaHaye

       • *God's Final Word: Understanding Revelation* by Ray C. Stedman

       • *Revelation: Four Views* edited by Steven Gregg

       • *The Book of Revelation: Unlocking the Future - Twenty-first Century Biblical Commentary* by Ed Hindson

       • *The Final Word:* The Book Of Revelation Simply Explained by Steve Wilmshurst

       • *The 12 Gemstones of Revelation:* Unlocking the Significance of the Gemstone Phenomenon by Mary Trask

       • *What the Bible Really Says: Breaking the Apocalypse Code* by Thomas A. Howe

C. The World *Behind* the Text:— Genre The First Step of Bible Study

1. The opening word of the book is an important "clue" — *apokalupsis* (to unveil, to lay bare, to disclose the unknown)

   a. This word does not appear anywhere in Classical Greek literature![3]

   b. "Apocalyptic" was a literary genre that was 300 years old by the time John recorded these visions.

2. Five Characteristics of Apocalyptic Literature (from: www.jewishencyclopedia.com)

   a. Contains revelation of things beyond human knowledge and experience:

     (1) the purposes of God for mankind

     (2) secrets of heaven itself

     (3) angels' (good/evil) characteristics and roles

     (4) impending events (especially those related to Israel)

---

[1] Some argue that "remaking" the current earth tends to glorify God more because it demonstrates that Satan didn't "win" in the sense of God having to start all over.

[2] This motivation is immensely *sinful* because it is rooted in a desire for power; Either power over our own circumstances or power over other people because of what we "know" that they don't know. This desire for power was at the heart of Satan's fall, Adam and Eve's demise, and is also the motivation behind all of the pagan practices Yahweh forbade in the Old Testament (e.g. divination, necromancy, astrology).

[3] The Classical Period is typically understood to be the period of history prior to the rise of Alexander (c. 4th century B.C.). There were surely examples of apocalyptic literature prior to this time, but by the time of John it was an established literary genre.

(5) future of mankind

(6) end of the world, judgment and eternity[1]

b. A *literary* genre consisting of dreams and visions recorded in first person (205 first person pronouns in Revelation).

c. Angels rather than God are key communicators and servants (74 refs to angels; 1 every 6 verses!).

d. Primary chronological focus is the *future*, particularly God's ultimate purposes:[2]

> "...and came to make you understand what is to happen to your people in the latter days. For the vision is for days yet to come."
> **Daniel 10:14**

> "...Come up here, and I will show you what must take place after this."
> **Revelation 4:1ᵇ**

e. Literary and stylistic peculiarities:

(1) Excessive use of numbers (e.g. "seven"- 55 times for 18 different things, "twelve," etc.)

(2) Descriptions of real or mythical creatures (e.g. "lion," "eagle," "dragon," "beast")

(3) Excessive use of symbols (e.g. "horn," "star," "lamp stand," "seals," "bowls," "trumpets,")

(4) The Book of Daniel and The Book of Enoch are examples of Jewish apocalyptic literature:

> "Daniel declared, "I saw in my vision by night, and behold, the four winds of heaven were stirring up the great sea. And four great beasts came up out of the sea, different from one another. The first was like a lion and had eagles' wings. Then as I looked its wings were plucked off, and it was lifted up from the ground and made to stand on two feet like a man, and the mind of a man was given to it."
> **Daniel 7:2-4, c. 550 BC**

> "And after that I saw thousands of thousands and ten thousand times ten thousand, I saw a multitude beyond number and reckoning, who stood before the Lord of Spirits. And on the four sides of the Lord of Spirits I saw four presences, different from those that sleep not, and I learnt their names: for the angel that went with me made known to me their names, and showed me all the hidden things. And I heard the voices of those four presences as they uttered praises before the Lord of glory. The first voice blesses the Lord of Spirits for ever and ever. And the second voice I heard blessing the Elect One and the elect ones who hang upon the Lord of Spirits. And the third voice I heard pray and intercede for those who dwell on the earth and supplicate in the name of the Lord of Spirits. And I heard the fourth voice fending off the Satans and forbidding them to come before the Lord of Spirits to accuse them who dwell on the earth."
> **The Book of Enoch, 40.1-7, c. 120 BC**

D. The World *Of* The Text: Getting Inside John's Apocalyptic Adventure

1. This book is a record of Yahweh's *apokalupsis* to "His bond servants" that was given to Jesus Christ and mediated to John by an angel![3]

> "The revelation of Jesus Christ, which God gave him to show to his servants the things that must soon take place. He made it known by sending his angel to his servant John, who bore witness to the word of God and to the testimony of Jesus Christ, even to all that he saw."
> **Revelation 1:1-2**

2. This is first and foremost a book about Yahweh and His purposes, *not* us and our future:[4]

a. There are 150 references to God and to the Lamb.

---

[1] It is worth noting at this juncture that God's description of Babylon (i.e. Rome) in this book in chapters 17-18 is something of a timeless description and condemnation of the "world," any system that is saturated with sexual sin and economic oppression in the large context of affluence. Any nation or power that "exports" these things and makes itself and other nations wealthy through them, is under the condemnation of God (e.g. Tyre in Ezekiel 27:12-13; Babylon in Jeremiah 50-51, and even Jerusalem in Ezekiel 15-16).

[2] This is a stark difference from the classical prophets (e.g. Isaiah, Jeremiah, Ezekiel, etc.) whose focus was *primarily* on the present and only secondarily on the future. The primary role of the Old Testament classical prophet was to call Yahweh's people (especially the leaders) *back* to covenant faithfulness.

[3] There appears to be something of a progression in this *apokalupsis* as the book unfolds. In 4:1, John says, *"I saw a door standing open in heaven..."* In 11:19 he sees the Temple standing open, and in 19:11 he says, *"I saw heaven standing open..."*

[4] This truth is absolutely vital in keeping our hearts and minds in the right place as we read this book.

b. Of the 10 times God is referred to as "Almighty" in the New Testament, nine are in this book![1] (Heb, *shaddai*, Gk, *pantokrator*)

c. There are 126 references to angels and to beasts and the dragon.

d. There are less than 50 references to saints, prophets and apostles.

e. The book opens with an identical Isaiah-like vision of God's throne room:

> *"And the four living creatures, each of them with six wings, are full of eyes all around and within, and day and night they never cease to say, 'Holy, holy, holy, is the Lord God Almighty, who was and is and is to come!'"* **Revelation 4:8**

> *"In the year that King Uzziah died I saw the Lord sitting upon a throne, high and lifted up; and the train of his robe filled the temple. Above him stood the seraphim. Each had six wings: with two he covered his face, and with two he covered his feet, and with two he flew. And one called to another and said: "Holy, holy, holy is the LORD of hosts; the whole earth is full of his glory!"* **Isaiah 6:1-3**

f. The book closes with Isaiah-like self-descriptions by Yahweh and Jesus:

> *"And he said to me, "It is done! I am the Alpha and the Omega, the beginning and the end. To the thirsty I will give from the spring of the water of life without payment."* **Revelation 21:6**

> *"I am the Alpha and the Omega, the first and the last, the beginning and the end."* **Revelation 22:13**

> *"Thus says the LORD, the King of Israel and his Redeemer, the LORD of hosts: 'I am the first and I am the last; besides me there is no god.'"* **Isaiah 44:6**

3. Because The Story is "*...the mystery of his will, according to his purpose, which he set forth in Christ as a plan for the fullness of time...*" (Eph 1:9, 10), it *too* has an "Alpha and Omega".

a. Yahweh unrolls the whole story in the first eight verses:

Revelation	Old Testament
"To him who loves us and has freed us from our sins by his blood and made us a kingdom, priests to his God and Father, to him be glory and dominion forever and ever. Amen. Behold, he is coming with the clouds, and every eye will see him, even those who pierced him, and all tribes of the earth will wail on account of him. Even so. Amen. "I am the Alpha and the Omega," says the Lord God, "who is and who was and who is to come, the Almighty." **Revelation 1:5-8**	*"...and you shall be to me a kingdom of priests and a holy nation. These are the words that you shall speak to the people of Israel."* **Exodus 19:6**
	"I saw in the night visions, and behold, with the clouds of heaven there came one like a son of man, and he came to the Ancient of Days and was presented before him." **Daniel 7:13**
	"And I will pour out on the house of David and the inhabitants of Jerusalem a spirit of grace and pleas for mercy, so that, when they look on me, on him whom they have pierced, they shall mourn for him, as one mourns for an only child, and weep bitterly over him, as one weeps over a firstborn." **Zechariah 12:10**
	"Listen to me, O Jacob, and Israel, whom I called! I am he; I am the first, and I am the last." **Isaiah 48:12**

b. Even though there isn't a single direct Old Testament citation, there are over 250 *allusions* to the Old Testament "Story" in 404 verses!

c. The Story "ends" where it "began":

   (1) The Tree of Life is present in the new "garden"[2] (Rev 22:2; Gen 2:9; 3:22)

   (2) The River of Life is present again in the new "garden" (Rev 22:1; Gen 2:8-16; Ps 46:4; Joel 3:18; Zech 14:8)

   (3) Yahweh Himself is present in the new "garden" again (Rev 21:2-3)

d. The "Bride" of Christ (i.e. the Lamb) is the New Jerusalem representing all those from both "halves" of the Story:

---

[1] The final occurrence is Paul "citing" what is actually a conflation of Old Testament passages (cf. 2 Corinthians 6:18 with 2 Sam 7:14, 27; Hosea 1:10; and Isaiah 43:6).

[2] Only now, it is available to "all nations" rather than the first couple. (see also Ezekiel 47:12).

> *"Then came one of the seven angels who had the seven bowls full of the seven last plagues and spoke to me, saying, "Come, I will show you the Bride, the wife of the Lamb." And he carried me away in the Spirit to a great, high mountain, and showed me the holy city Jerusalem coming down out of heaven from God, having the glory of God, its radiance like a most rare jewel, like a jasper, clear as crystal. It had a great, high wall, with twelve gates, and at the gates twelve angels, and on the gates the names of the twelve tribes of the sons of Israel were inscribed-- on the east three gates, on the north three gates, on the south three gates, and on the west three gates. And the wall of the city had twelve foundations, and on them were the twelve names of the twelve apostles of the Lamb."*
> **Revelation 21:9-14**

    e. The Story "ends" on earth, *not* in "heaven," with the redemption of everything God originally declared to be "very good," that was corrupted by sin.

E. The World *Before* The Text: Living In Light of the Story

  1. Imagine yourself in a 5-act play:

    a. Act I — Introduction of major characters; (Gen 1-2)

    b. Act II — Conflict Introduced; (Gen 3-11)

    c. Act III — Complication (conflict grows and intensifies; (Gen 12- Malachi)

    d. Act IV — Climax: the turning point in the Story; (Gospels)

    e. Act V — Resolution: all aspects of the conflict are resolved; (Acts - Rev)

    f. Act V has three "scenes" and the second is missing!

      (1) Question: "How Then Shall We Live?"

      (2) Peter's final word tells us:

> *"Since all these things are thus to be dissolved, what sort of people ought you to be in lives of holiness and godliness, waiting for and hastening the coming of the day of God, because of which the heavens will be set on fire and dissolved, and the heavenly bodies will melt as they burn!... Therefore, beloved, since you are waiting for these, be diligent to be found by him without spot or blemish, and at peace."*
> **2 Peter 3:11-12,14**

  2. Of the seven "beatitudes" (i.e. "blessed") in this book, four of them have to do with how I choose to live until Jesus returns (Re 1:3; 14:13; 16:15; 19:9; 20:6; 22:7,14).

  3. The best thing we can seek to do, in the "in between time," is to seek to be able to say the same thing to Yahweh that Jesus did, when we meet Him:

> *"I glorified you on earth, having accomplished the work that you gave me to do."*
> **John 17:4**

CONTRIBUTORS TO OUR NEW TESTAMENT

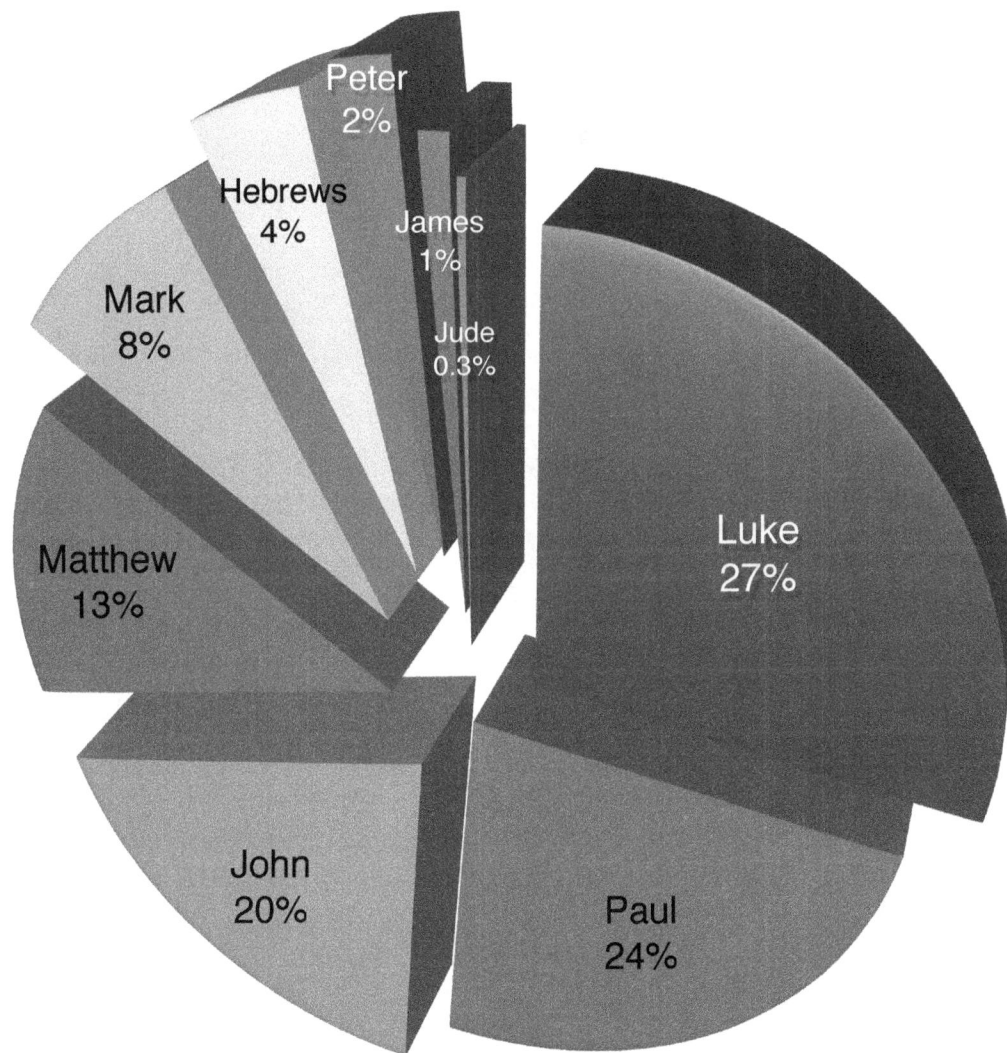

Peter
2%

Hebrews
4%

James
1%

Jude
0.3%

Mark
8%

Matthew
13%

Luke
27%

John
20%

Paul
24%

THE WORLD OF THE APOSTLE PAUL

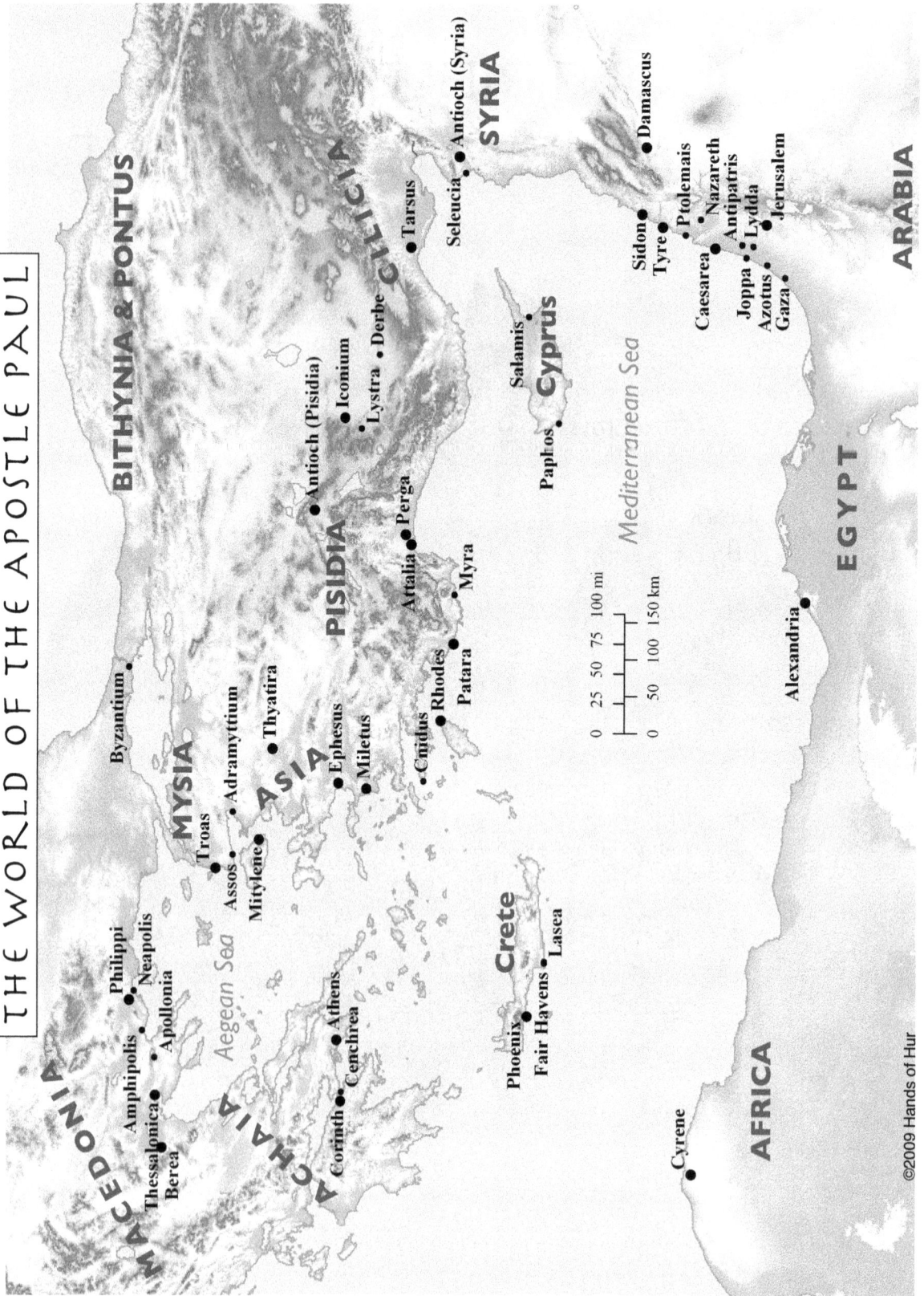

BITHYNIA & PONTUS

MACEDONIA

Byzantium

Philippi
Neapolis
Amphipolis
Apollonia
Thessalonica
Berea

MYSIA
Troas
Assos
Mitylene
Adramyttium
Thyatira

Aegean Sea

ASIA
Ephesus
Miletus

ACHAIA
Athens
Corinth
Cenchrea

CILICIA
Tarsus

PISIDIA
Antioch (Pisidia)
Iconium
Lystra · Derbe

Perga
Attalia

Myra
Patara
Rhodes
Cnidus

Crete
Phoenix
Fair Havens · Lasea

SYRIA
Antioch (Syria)
Seleucia

Damascus

Sidon
Tyre
Ptolemais
Caesarea
Nazareth
Antipatris
Joppa · Lydda
Azotus
Gaza · Jerusalem

ARABIA

Salamis
Cyprus
Paphos

Mediterranean Sea

Alexandria

EGYPT

AFRICA
Cyrene

0 25 50 75 100 mi
0   50 100 150 km

©2009 Hands of Hur

THE "NEW" TESTAMENT LETTERS

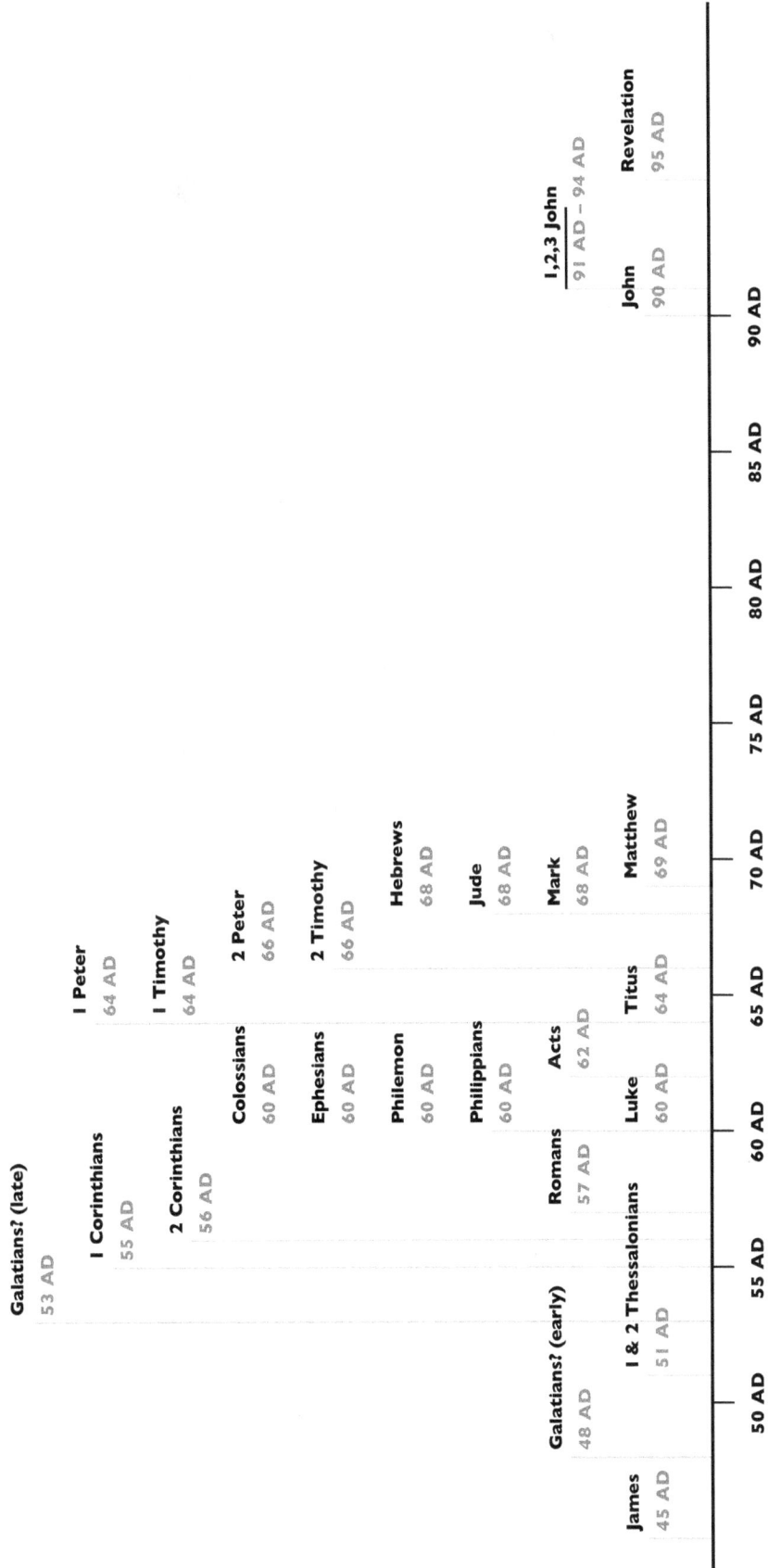

50 AD	55 AD	60 AD	65 AD	70 AD	75 AD	80 AD	85 AD	90 AD

James 45 AD

Galatians? (early) 48 AD

1 & 2 Thessalonians 51 AD

Galatians? (late) 53 AD

1 Corinthians 55 AD

2 Corinthians 56 AD

Romans 57 AD

Colossians 60 AD

Ephesians 60 AD

Philemon 60 AD

Philippians 60 AD

Luke 60 AD

Acts 62 AD

1 Peter 64 AD

1 Timothy 64 AD

Titus 64 AD

2 Peter 66 AD

2 Timothy 66 AD

Hebrews 68 AD

Jude 68 AD

Mark 68 AD

Matthew 69 AD

1,2,3 John 91 AD – 94 AD

John 90 AD

Revelation 95 AD

POLITICAL LEADERS IN THE N.T.

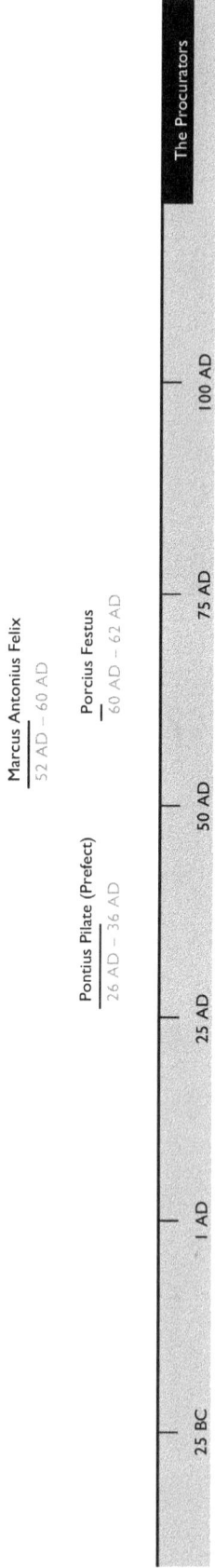

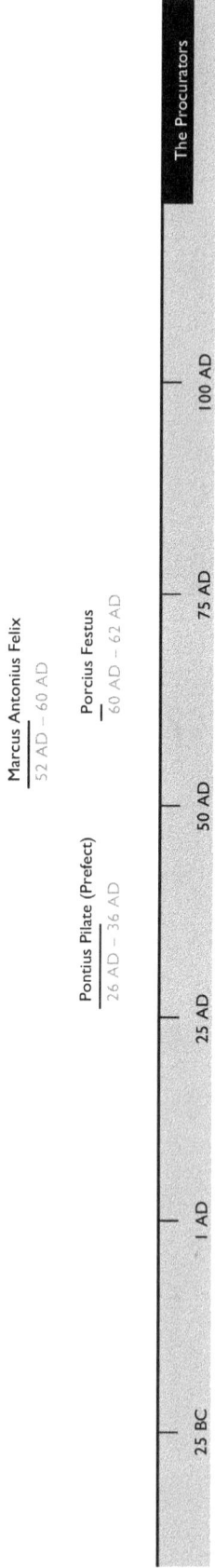

The Procurators

Pontius Pilate (Prefect)
26 AD – 36 AD

Marcus Antonius Felix
52 AD – 60 AD

Porcius Festus
60 AD – 62 AD

25 BC | 1 AD | 25 AD | 50 AD | 75 AD | 100 AD

The Caesars

Caesar Augustus
31 BC – 14 AD

Tiberius
14 AD – 37 AD

Caligula
37 AD – 41 AD

Claudius
41 AD – 54 AD

Nero
54 AD – 68 AD

Vespasian
69 AD – 79 AD

Titus
79 AD – 81 AD

Domitian
81 AD – 96 AD

Nerva
96 AD – 98 AD

Trajan
98 AD – 117 AD

Hadrian
117 AD – 138 AD

25 BC | 1 AD | 25 AD | 50 AD | 75 AD | 100 AD

The Herodian Dynasty

Herod the Great
37 BC – 4 BC

Herod Antipas
4 BC – 39 AD

Herod Archelaus
4 BC – 6 AD

Herod Philip
4 BC – 34 AD

Herod Agrippa I
37 AD

Herod Agrippa I
41 AD – 44 AD

Herod Agrippa II
44 AD – 92 AD

25 BC | 1 AD | 25 AD | 50 AD | 75 AD | 100 AD

PAUL'S UNIQUE VOCABULARY

W.P. Workman's Count of Hapax Legomena in NT Epistles

A *hapax legomenon* is a word that only appears once in the writings of a particular author, or a body of text. The Greek New Testament con-tains 686 hapax legom-ena, of which 62 occur in 1 Peter, and 54 occur in 2 Peter.

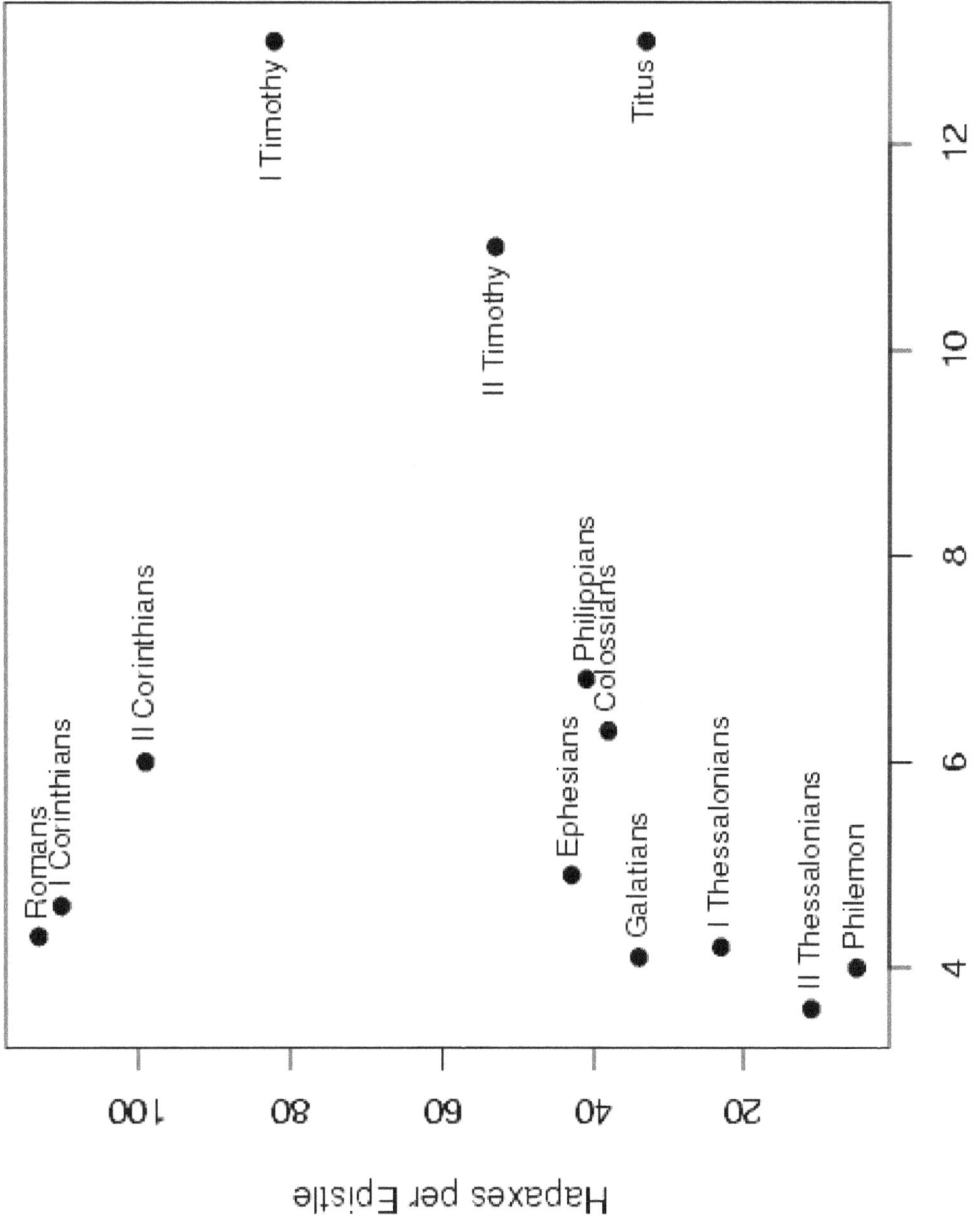

Hapaxes per page of Westcott and Hort

Hapaxes per Epistle

PAUL: LIFE & LETTERS

THE LIFE OF PAUL

- Saul's conversion — 33 AD
- Damascus & Arabia — 34 AD – 37 AD
- 1st meeting w/Peter — 37 AD
- Ministry in Syria, Tarsus, Cilicia — 37 AD – 45 AD
- "Thorn in the flesh" — 42 AD – 44 AD
- 1st missionary journey — 46 AD – 47 AD
- 2nd visit to Jerusalem; famine — 47 AD
- *GALATIANS — 48 AD
- *1 & 2 THESSALONIANS — 49 AD – 51 AD
- 2nd missionary journey — 49 AD – 51 AD
- Jerusalem Council — 49 AD
- Meets Priscilla & Aquila — 49 AD
- Paul before Gallio in Achaia — 51 AD
- *1 CORINTHIANS — 54 AD – 55 AD
- 3rd missionary journey — 52 AD – 57 AD
- ministry in Ephesus — 52 AD – 55 AD
- *2 CORINTHIANS — 55 AD – 56 AD
- *ROMANS — 57 AD
- Arrested in Jerusalem — 57 AD
- Prison in Caesarea — 57 AD – 59 AD
- *COL, PHLM, EPH, PHIL — 60 AD – 62 AD
- Prison in Rome — 60 AD – 62 AD
- *1 TIMOTHY & TITUS — 62 AD – 64 AD
- Free from prison — 62 AD – 64 AD
- Prison in Rome (final) — 64 AD – 67 AD
- *2 TIMOTHY — 66 AD
- Death — 67 AD

"A Prophet Who Was Honored in His Own Home!"

"JESUS" IN JAMES	JESUS IN MATTHEW
"Count it all joy, my brothers, when you meet trials of various kinds," **James 1:2**	*"Blessed are those who are persecuted for righteousness' sake, for theirs is the kingdom of heaven. "Blessed are you when others revile you and persecute you and utter all kinds of evil against you falsely on my account. Rejoice and be glad, for your reward is great in heaven, for so they persecuted the prophets who were before you."* **Matthew 5:10-12**
"And let steadfastness have its full effect, that you may be perfect and complete, lacking in nothing." **James 1:4**	*"You therefore must be perfect, as your heavenly Father is perfect."* **Matthew 5:48**
"If any of you lacks wisdom, let him ask God, who gives generously to all without reproach, and it will be given him." **James 1:5**	*"Ask, and it will be given to you; seek, and you will find; knock, and it will be opened to you. For everyone who asks receives, and the one who seeks finds, and to the one who knocks it will be opened. Or which one of you, if his son asks him for bread, will give him a stone? Or if he asks for a fish, will give him a serpent?"* **Matthew 7:7-10**
"Every good gift and every perfect gift is from above, coming down from the Father of lights with whom there is no variation or shadow due to change." **James 1:17**	*"If you then, who are evil, know how to give good gifts to your children, how much more will your Father who is in heaven give good things to those who ask him!"* **Matthew 7:11**
"for the anger of man does not produce the righteousness that God requires." **James 1:20**	*"But I say to you that everyone who is angry with his brother will be liable to judgment; whoever insults his brother will be liable to the council; and whoever says, 'You fool!' will be liable to the hell of fire."* **Matthew 5:22**
"But be doers of the word, and not hearers only, deceiving yourselves." **James 1:22**	*"Everyone then who hears these words of mine and does them will be like a wise man who built his house on the rock. And the rain fell, and the floods came, and the winds blew and beat on that house, but it did not fall, because it had been founded on the rock. And everyone who hears these words of mine and does not do them will be like a foolish man who built his house on the sand. And the rain fell, and the floods came, and the winds blew and beat against that house, and it fell, and great was the fall of it.""* **Matthew 7:24-27**
"Listen, my beloved brothers, has not God chosen those who are poor in the world to be rich in faith and heirs of the kingdom, which he has promised to those who love him?" **James 2:5**	*"Blessed are the poor in spirit, for theirs is the kingdom of heaven. "Blessed are those who mourn, for they shall be comforted. "Blessed are the meek, for they shall inherit the earth."* **Matthew 5:3-5**
"For whoever keeps the whole law but fails in one point has become accountable for all of it." **James 2:10**	*"Therefore whoever relaxes one of the least of these commandments and teaches others to do the same will be called least in the kingdom of heaven, but whoever does them and teaches them will be called great in the kingdom of heaven."* **Matthew 5:19**
"For judgment is without mercy to one who has shown no mercy. Mercy triumphs over judgment." **James 2:13**	*"Blessed are the merciful, for they shall receive mercy."* **Matthew 5:7**
"Can a fig tree, my brothers, bear olives, or a grapevine produce figs? Neither can a salt pond yield fresh water." **James 3:12**	*"You will recognize them by their fruits. Are grapes gathered from thornbushes, or figs from thistles?"* **Matthew 7:16**
"And a harvest of righteousness is sown in peace by those who make peace." **James 3:18**	*"Blessed are the peacemakers, for they shall be called sons of God."* **Matthew 5:9**
"You desire and do not have, so you murder. You covet and cannot obtain, so you fight and quarrel. You do not have, because you do not ask. You ask and do not receive, because you ask wrongly, to spend it on your passions." **James 4:2, 3**	*""Ask, and it will be given to you; seek, and you will find; knock, and it will be opened to you. For everyone who asks receives, and the one who seeks finds, and to the one who knocks it will be opened."* **Matthew 7:7, 8**
"You adulterous people! Do you not know that friendship with the world is enmity with God? Therefore whoever wishes to be a friend of the world makes himself an enemy of God." **James 4:4**	*""No one can serve two masters, for either he will hate the one and love the other, or he will be devoted to the one and despise the other. You cannot serve God and money."* **Matthew 6:24**

"JESUS" IN JAMES	**JESUS IN MATTHEW**
"Be wretched and mourn and weep. Let your laughter be turned to mourning and your joy to gloom. Humble yourselves before the Lord, and he will exalt you." **James 4:9, 10**	*"Blessed are those who mourn, for they shall be comforted."* **Matthew 5:4** *"Whoever exalts himself will be humbled, and whoever humbles himself will be exalted."* **Matthew 23:12**
"Do not speak evil against one another, brothers. The one who speaks against a brother or judges his brother, speaks evil against the law and judges the law. But if you judge the law, you are not a doer of the law but a judge. There is only one lawgiver and judge, he who is able to save and to destroy. But who are you to judge your neighbor?" **James 4:11, 12**	*"Judge not, that you be not judged. For with the judgment you pronounce you will be judged, and with the measure you use it will be measured to you. Why do you see the speck that is in your brother's eye, but do not notice the log that is in your own eye? Or how can you say to your brother, 'Let me take the speck out of your eye,' when there is the log in your own eye? You hypocrite, first take the log out of your own eye, and then you will see clearly to take the speck out of your brother's eye."* **Matthew 7:1-5**
"Come now, you who say, "Today or tomorrow we will go into such and such a town and spend a year there and trade and make a profit"-- yet you do not know what tomorrow will bring. What is your life? For you are a mist that appears for a little time and then vanishes." **James 4:13, 14**	*"Therefore do not be anxious about tomorrow, for tomorrow will be anxious for itself. Sufficient for the day is its own trouble."* **Matthew 6:34**
"Your riches have rotted and your garments are moth-eaten. Your gold and silver have corroded, and their corrosion will be evidence against you and will eat your flesh like fire. You have laid up treasure in the last days. Behold, the wages of the laborers who mowed your fields, which you kept back by fraud, are crying out against you, and the cries of the harvesters have reached the ears of the Lord of hosts. You have lived on the earth in luxury and in self-indulgence. You have fattened your hearts in a day of slaughter." **James 5:2-5**	*"Do not lay up for yourselves treasures on earth, where moth and rust destroy and where thieves break in and steal,"* **Matthew 6:19**
"As an example of suffering and patience, brothers, take the prophets who spoke in the name of the Lord." **James 5:10**	*"Rejoice and be glad, for your reward is great in heaven, for so they persecuted the prophets who were before you."* **Matthew 5:12**
"…behold, the Judge is standing at the door." **James 5:9**	*"So also, when you see all these things, you know that he is near, at the very gates."* **Matthew 24:33**
"But above all, my brothers, do not swear, either by heaven or by earth or by any other oath, but let your "yes" be yes and your "no" be no, so that you may not fall under condemnation." **James 5:12**	*"Again you have heard that it was said to those of old, 'You shall not swear falsely, but shall perform to the Lord what you have sworn.' But I say to you, Do not take an oath at all, either by heaven, for it is the throne of God, or by the earth, for it is his footstool, or by Jerusalem, for it is the city of the great King. And do not take an oath by your head, for you cannot make one hair white or black. Let what you say be simply 'Yes' or 'No'; anything more than this comes from evil."* **Matthew 5:33-37**

FOUR POSSIBLE NEW TESTAMENT CHRONOLOGIES

Book or Event	Allen P. Ross	John Stott	D.A. Carson/Moo	ESV Study Bible	References
	New Testament Chronology				
	Date By Scholar				References
Crucifixion	**33 A.D.**	**30 A.D.**			
Conversion of Paul	**36 A.D.**	**33 A.D**	**34-35 A.D.**		
First Missionary Journey	**46 A.D.**	**47,48 A.D.**	**46-47 or 47-48 A.D.**		Acts 13:1- 14:28
Galatians *(Early Date)*			47 or 48 A.D.	48 A.D.	
Jerusalem Council	**48 A.D.**	**49 A.D.**	**48 or 49 A.D.**		Acts 15
Second Missionary Journey	**48 A.D.**	**49 A.D.**	**48 or 49-51 A.D.**		Acts 15:36- 18:22
James	45-50 A.D.		Early 40's A.D.	40-45 A.D.	
1 Thessalonians	50-51 A.D.		50/51 A.D.	49-51 A.D.	
2 Thessalonians	51 A.D.			49-51 A.D.	
Third Missionary Journey	**51 A.D.**	**52 A.D.**	**52-57 A.D.**		Acts 18:23- 21:26
Galatians *(Late Date)*	49 or 53 A.D.		47 or 48 A.D.		
1 Corinthians	55 or 56 A.D.		c. 55 A.D.	53-55 A.D.	
2 Corinthians	56 or 57 A.D.		c. 56 A.D.	55-56 A.D.	
Romans	57-58 A.D.		55/56 or 57 A.D.	57 A.D.	
Paul's Trial By Festus	**59 A.D.**	**59 A.D.**			Acts 24-25
Paul's Arrival in Rome	**60 A.D.**	**60 A.D.**	**60 A.D.**		
Ephesians	60 A.D.		c. 60 A.D.	62 A.D.	
Philippians	60 A.D.		59-60 or 61-62 A.D.	62 A.D.	
Colossians	60 A.D.		60/61	62 A.D.	
Philemon	60 A.D.		60's A.D.	62 A.D.	
Luke	60 A.D.			62 A.D.	
Acts	60-64 A.D.		62 A.D.	62 A.D.	
Nero Begins Persecuting Christians	**64 A.D.**				
1 Timothy	64 A.D.		Mid 60's A.D.	62-64 A.D.	
Titus	65 A.D.		Mid 60's A.D.	62-64 A.D.	
1 Peter	65 A.D.			62-63 A.D.	
Second Roman Imprisonment	**66 A.D.**				
2 Timothy	66 A.D.		65-66 A.D.	64-67 A.D.	
2 Peter	66 A.D.		Pre 65 A.D.	64-67 A.D.	
Paul Beheaded	**66 A.D.**		**64-65 A.D.**		
Mark	68 A.D.		50-60 A.D.	Mid to late 50's A.D.	
Hebrews	68 A.D.		Pre-70 A.D.	60-70 A.D.	
Jude	68 A.D.		Late 60's A.D.	Mid-60's A.D.	
Matthew	50 or 70 A.D.?		Pre-70 A.D.	Late 50's Early 60's	
Jerusalem and Temple Destroyed	**70 A.D.**	**70 A.D.**	**70 A.D.**		
John	85-90 A.D.		c. 80 A.D.	70-100 A.D.	
1 John	90-95 A.D.		80-85 A.D.	85-95 A.D.	
2 John	90-95 A.D.		80-85 A.D.	85-95 A.D.	
3 John	90-95 A.D.		80-85 A.D.	85-95 A.D.	
Revelation	95 A.D.		81-96 A.D.	Mid- 90's A.D.	

(This chart was adapted from the ESV Study Bible and other sources.)

THE BOOK OF ACTS

THE PLACES

Achaia	Cappadocia	Greece	Mitylene	Rhodes
Adramyttium	Cauda	Haran	Myra	Rome
Adriatic	Cenchreae	Iconium	Mysia	Salamis
Alexandria	Chaldea(ns)	Israel	Nazareth	Salmone
Amphipolis	Cilicia	Italy	Neapolis	Samaria
Antioch (2)	Cnidus	Jerusalem	Olivet	Samos
Antipatris	Corinth	Joppa	Pamphylia	Samothrace
Apollonia	Cos	Judea	Paphos	Seleucia
Arabia(ns)	Cretans	Lasea	Parthians	Sharon
Areopagus	Cyprus	Libya	Patara	Shechem
Asia	Cyrene	Lycaonia	Perga	Sidon
Assos	Damascus	Lycia	Philippi	Sinai
Athens	Derbe	Lydda	Phoenicia	Syracuse
Attalia	Egypt	Lystra	Phoenix	Syria
Azotus	Elam(ites)	Macedonia	Phrygia	Syrtis
Babylon	Ephesian	Malta	Pisidia	Tarsus
Berea	Epicurean	Medes	Pontus	Thessalonians
Bithynia	Ethiopia(n)	Mesopotamia	Ptolemais	Thyatira
Caesarea	Galatia	Midian	Puteoli	Troas
Canaan	Galilean	Miletus	Rhegium	Tyre

THE PEOPLE

Aaron	Caesar (2)	Hamor	Lysias	Priscilla	Tabitha
Abraham	Caiaphas	Hermes	Manaen	Prochorus	Tertullus
Aeneas	Candace	Herod	Mark	Publius	Theophilus
Agabus	Claudius (2)	Isaac	Mary	Pyrrhus	Theudas
Agrippa (2)	Cornelius	Isaiah	Matthew	Rephan	Thomas
Alexander (2)	Crispus	Jacob	Matthias	Rhoda	Timon
Alphaeus	Damaris	James (4)	Mnason	Samuel	Timothy
Ananias (3)	David	Jason	Moloch	Sapphira	Titius
Andrew	Demetrius	Jesse	Moses	Satan	Trophimus
Annas	Dionysius	Jesus	Nicanor	Saul (2)	Tychicus
Apollos	Dorcas	Joel	Nicolaus	Sceva	Tyrannus
Aquila	Drusilla	John (4)	Niger	Secundus	Zeus
Aristarchus	Elymas	Joseph	Parmenas	Sergius	
Artemis	Erastus	Joshua	Paul	Silas	
Barnabas	Eutychus	Judas	Paulus	Simeon	
Barsabbas	Felix	Julius	Peter	Simon (4)	
Bartholomew	Festus	Justice	Pharaoh	Solomon	
Benjamin	Gaius (3)	Justus	Philip (2)	Sopater	
Bernice	Gallio	Lucius	Pontius Pilate	Sosthenes	
Blastus	Gamaliel	Lydia	Porcius	Stephen	

Note: numbers in parentheses indicate the number of *different* people or places with that name.

SERMONS IN THE BOOK OF ACTS

Preacher	Topic(s)	Location	Length	Scripture
Peter *(Pentecost)*	Jesus, crucified and raised, is the Christ in fulfillment of Scripture	Jerusalem *(Temple area)*	597 words	2:14-41
Peter *(lame man)*	Jesus' death & resurrection is the final fulfillment of God's plans for Israel.	Jerusalem *(Solomon's Portico)*	359 words	3:12-26
Peter	The crucifixion, resurrection of Jesus make Him the only way to salvation.	Jerusalem *(Sanhedrin)*	113 words	4:8-12
Peter *(& the apostles)*	The crucifixion, resurrection and exaltation of Jesus; Salvation is through repentance and belief.	Jerusalem *(high priestly family)*	65 words	5:29-32
Stephen	A historical survey of Israel's refusal to submit to Yahweh's purposes for them.	Jerusalem *(Sanhedrin)*	1,235 words	7:2-53
Peter	The crucified, risen Jesus is judge of all, and offers forgiveness through faith in Him.	Caesarea *(a Gentile household)*	223 words	10:34-43
Paul	• Jesus is the fulfillment of Yahweh's purposes for Israel and the Jews. • Salvation is by faith in the work of the crucified, risen Messiah, Jesus.	Pisidian Antioch	568 words	13:16-41
Paul	The sovereign creator God made all of mankind for Himself and will judge the world by the man whom He appointed (Jesus).	Mars Hill in Athens	264 words	17:22-31
Paul	• Rehearses his 3-year ministry to the Ephesian church. • Warns the elders to be attentive to themselves and their flock against false teachers. • Be servant givers to the ministry.	Miletus *(to the elders of the Ephesian church)*	432 words	20:18-36
Paul	• Gives testimony of his past devotion to Judaism *and* his miracu-lous conversion on the road. • Reminds his Jewish listeners of his long and hateful opposition to the Gospel. • Testifies that God's current purpose for him is to preach to the Gentiles rather than the Jews.	Jerusalem *(angry mob of Jews)*	500 words	22:1-21
Paul	Testifies to the fact that his hope and faith are in the resurrection of the dead—the same hope of every Jew.	Caesarea *(before Felix, a Roman governor)*	259 words	24:10-21
Paul	• The resurrection of the dead is the hope of Israel. • Paul's previous fanaticism against Jesus was well known among Jews. • Testifies about his experience on the road to Damascus. • Connects his message and faith to that of Moses and the prophets—the salvation of all mankind.	Caesarea *(Festus, Herod Agrippa & Bernice)*	720 words	26:2-29
Paul	(after preaching all day about Jesus from Moses and the prophets) Paul confronts the Jews with their blindness and reiterates God's call on his life to preach to the Gentiles.	Rome *(Jewish leaders)*	173 words *(recorded)*	28:23-29

"WHO'S WHO IN THE ANCIENT HEAVENS"

ROMANS	GREEKS	God/Goddess of...
AESCULAPIUS	ASKLEPIOS	the god of healing
APOLLO	APOLLO	the god of youth, music and prophecy *(twin brother of Artemis)*
BACCHUS	DIONYSUS	the god of wine, merriment, madness and debauchery
CASTOR/POL-LUX	CASTOR/POLLUX	the patron twin gods of sailors *(cf. Acts 28:11)*
CERES	DEMETER	the goddess of fertility and grain
DIANA	ARTEMIS	the goddess of the woods (Roman), moon, women and slaves cf. *(Acts 19:35)*
FORTUNA	TYCHE	the goddess of farming (Roman) and good luck
JUNO	HERA	the goddess of women, marriage and childbirth *(wife of Zeus)*
JUPITER	ZEUS	god of the sky and thunder ("father" of all the gods; cf. Acts 14:11-13)
MARS	ARES	the god of war and bloodshed
MERCURY	HERMES	the god of shopkeepers, thieves, eloquence *(the messenger of the gods; Acts 14:11-13)*
MINERVA	ATHENA	the goddess of crafts and war
NEPTUNE	POSEIDON	the god of the sea and earthquakes
VENUS	APHRODITE	the goddess of love
VESTA	HESTIA	the goddess of the hearth and household activities
VULCAN	HEPHAESTUS	the god of fire and smiths

JEWS	the One God who...
ץﬡﬔﬠﬓ (YAHWEH)	• *"...made the world and everything in it..."* • *"...is Lord of heaven and earth..."* • *"...does not live in temples..."* • *"...is not served by human hands..."* • *"...gives to all mankind life and breath and everything."* • *"...made from one man every nation of mankind to live on all the face of the earth..."* • *"...determined allotted periods and the boundaries of their dwelling places..."* • *"...is not far from each of us..."* • *"...is NOT like gold or silver or stone or an image formed by art and imagination..."* • *"...commands all people to repent..."* • *"...has fixed a day on which he will judge the world in righteousness by a man whom he has...raised from the dead."* **[Paul's description of Yahweh to the Greek philosophers in Athens, Acts 17:22-34]**

chart of Roman/Greek deities adapted from: *The Greco-Roman World of the New Testament,* James Jeffers, IVP, ©1999, pg. 93.

A TIMOTHY TIMELINE

- **(Acts 14:8-21/2 Tim 3:11)** Paul makes his first missionary journey through Asia Minor and enters the region of Lyconia and the city of Lystra (A.D. 47-49). While in Lystra, is it possible that he stayed in the home owned by Timothy's mother, Eunice. While in this city, Timothy would have witnessed Paul's healing of a lame man and the worship that was offered to him by the pagans who saw it. He would have seen the Jews who came from the neighboring cities create a riot and watch as Paul was stoned to death for preaching the Gospel. He would have also seen Paul miraculously raised up, perhaps from the dead. Timothy had no romantic ideas of what it meant to be a minister of the Gospel. Timothy and his mother and grandmother were most likely converted at this time, even though it is not stated.

- **(Acts 16:1-2/2 Tim 1:5; 3:15)** Paul is now on his second missionary journey A.D. 49-52). This time he asks Timothy to join him as a disciple. We find out a great deal about Timothy's family at this point. He was Paul's total opposite: raised in a rural area, relatively uneducated in a formal sense, an ethnic half-breed, and one who grew-up in a home divided by religion. We also discover that in the two or three years since Paul's first visit, Timothy has distinguished himself among the Christians in the entire area. He has a magnificent testimony. His conversion and confession of faith at his baptism apparently made a profound impact on all who heard it (cf. 1 Tim 6:12).

- **(Acts 16:3/1 Tim 1:8)** Timothy is publicly "set apart" for the Gospel ministry, and this appointment is affirmed by the Holy Spirit, just like it was for Paul at the church in Syrian Antioch prior to his first journey. Timothy's mother understands that she may never see her son again. The greatest commitment an adult can make to world missions is not from their pocketbook, it is from their nursery. Timothy's life would never be the same! He was leaving the quiet, rural and safe life in the Lycus valley for danger, uncertainty and travel to some of the largest cities in the world. (Thessalonica was 200k, Corinth 500k and Rome 1 million at this time.) Timothy is most likely college-age at this time.

- **(Acts 16:4-)** The group ministers towards the coast and ended-up in a city called Troas. This appears to be Luke's hometown. In response to a vision, the group travels across the Aegaen Sea to Macedonia where they minister in the Roman province of Philippi where Paul was beaten and imprisoned. From here they went to Thessalonica were a riot broke-out from Paul's preaching and he was snuck out of the city at night. From there they moved to the neighboring city of Berea were Paul was welcomed by some of the most noble students of Scripture in the Bible. Timothy's name is absent from this account all the way from Troas to Thessalonica. His name appears again in Berea.

- **(Acts 17:13-14)** When the Jews arrive in Berea, Paul leaves for Athens, but tells Silas and Timothy to remain to help this brand new church get stabilized. This is an incredible statement of confidence in Silas and Timothy by the apostle Paul. It is also a sobering thing to realize that Paul left them in the face of great persecution—great enough for Paul to have to leave Thessalonica for his life! Paul tells the Berean brothers to have Silas and Timothy join him in Athens at their earliest convenience.

- **(1 Thess 3:1-2/2:18)** Even though Luke is silent about this (in Acts), we discover from Paul's letter to the Thessalonians that Timothy did join Paul in Athens and brought him vital news about the Jewish persecution of the Berean and Thessalonian believers. We also find out that Paul sent Timothy back to Thessalonica to find out how they were faring under the intense persecution.

- **(1 Thess 3:2-5)** Timothy was to assess the "damage" and also invest himself in the believers there. This is Timothy's first "solo" ministry, right into the "storm center" of persecution. We cannot underestimate the significance of this first "assignment," in its difficulty and the confidence that Paul had in this young "man of God."

- **(Acts 18:5)** Timothy returns from Thessalonica to Paul (who has moved on to Corinth from Athens) with good news about the Thessalonian Christians. Much relieved, Paul writes the letter, 1 Thessalonians (cf. 3:6). A few months later, Paul pens 2 Thessalonians. In both letters, Timothy is listed in the greeting. Already, he is an important part of Paul's "team," and has proven himself as an able minister of the Gospel.

- **(Acts 18:4)** Paul began his preaching ministry alone in Corinth while Timothy was back in Macedonia. But, we learn from Paul in 2 Cor. 1:19 that Timothy (and Silas) also were involved in the preaching ministry in Corinth. Here is our twenty-something young man, preaching in a city of 500,000 people. And, this city was the most significant cities in the known world, even more than than Athens.

- **(Acts 19:22)** Paul is now on his third journey (A.D. 52-57). Timothy's name appears here in Ephesus, but there is no prior mention of him since Corinth on Paul's second journey. Some think he stayed behind in Corinth when Paul left.

- **(Acts 20:31)** This section of Paul's third journey lasted three years. All of the province of Asia heard the Gospel. It is very likely that Timothy ministered personally in the city of Colossae during this time (cf. Col 1:1 and Philemon 1).

- **(1 Cor. 4:16-17)** Paul sends Timothy to the city of Corinth to address and handle the problems that the church is having. He was sending Timothy into a veritable "hornets' nest" (cf. 16:10-11).

- **(Acts 20:23)** Paul and Timothy arrive at Corinth (on the 3rd journey). Paul wrote the letter to the Romans at this time. Timothy is with him when he writes it (Rom 16:21).

- **(Acts 21:29)** Paul sails for Jerusalem. Timothy accompanies him on this final journey, but then is not mentioned by name for at least 3 years. Paul's 2-year stay in the prison at Caesarea (A.D. 58-60) and his journey to Rome seem to occur without Timothy.

- **(Col. 1:1/Philemon 1)** Timothy's name is mentioned with Paul's, so he is apparently now in Rome with Paul. During this time, Paul most likely wrote his "prison letters" (Colossians, Philemon, Ephesians and Philippians).

- While in prison in Rome, Paul writes the church at Philippi. This letter contains what is perhaps his most complimentary statement about Timothy: "I have no one else like him" (2:19-23). The Greek word Paul uses here, "*isopsuchē*" means to "have the same soul." Paul also places Timothy on the same plane as himself in the greeting, "Paul and Timothy, servants of Jesus Christ…" (1:1).

- **(1 Tim 1:3)** Paul and Timothy minister together for a while in Ephesus, then Paul apparently left for Macedonia.

- **(2 Timothy)** Paul is again in prison, but this time is facing death under the reign of Nero. The Neronian persecution threatened the very existence of Christianity. Paul was leaving this life and wanted to pass the baton to Timothy at perhaps the most perilous time in the history of the Church.

- **(Heb 13:23)** Timothy himself was apparently imprisoned and released. The details are not provided.

- **(Rev. 2:1-6)** There is some speculation that Timothy is the "angel" of the church in Ephesus that Jesus addresses in this section of scripture. This church's "angel" is described in terms that fit Timothy very well. If so, Paul would have been dead for about thirty years by this time, and Timothy himself would now be close to Paul's age when he was martyred.

ROMAN SOCIAL STRUCTURE

CLASS – (Latin, *ordo*) the group of persons into which I was born, and (with few exceptions), that in which I will die. The number of privileges and amount of honor bestowed upon me by those *under* me is determined by my *ordo*.

SENATORIAL ORDER

· Senatorial wealth was nearly unimaginable; a young man born into a senatorial family could *join* the Senate when he had property worth 250,000 denarii (685 years of work at daily wage!)

· The 2 largest senatorial fortunes known were each worth $20 billion.

· Pliny the Younger (governor of Bithynia, late 1st century) was 21st on a list of known wealthy Romans; his worth was 5 million denarii.

· Agriculture was the only acceptable trade for a senator.

New Testament: Sergius Paulus of Cyprus, Annaeus Gallio of Achaia, and the *proconsuls* spoken of in Acts were all of senatorial order (Acts 13:7-8,12; 18:12-17; 19:"38).

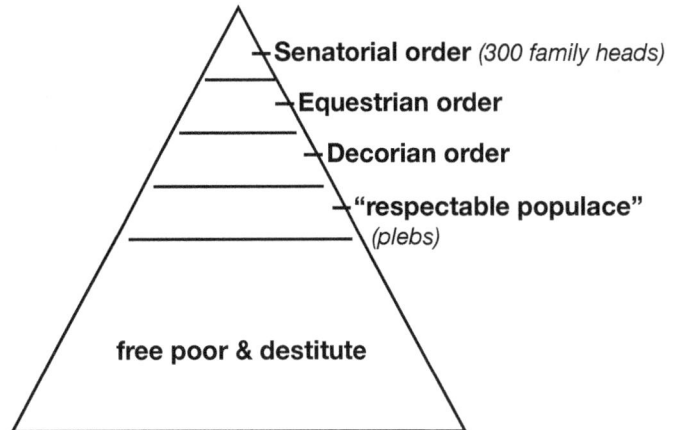

[Pyramid diagram with labels, top to bottom:]
Senatorial order *(300 family heads)*
Equestrian order
Decorian order
"respectable populace" *(plebs)*
free poor & destitute

EQUESTRIAN ORDER

· This order originated with the military; any citizen serving on horseback in the Roman army had to provide his own horse, weapons, and other supplies!

· The sons of senators were automatically enrolled in the equestrian order.

· The "entrance requirements" were: moral excellence, 100,000 denarii, proof of free birth for 2 generations.

·Agriculture was the only acceptable trade for a senator.

New Testament: The *tribune* Claudius Lysius in Jerusalem, and the *procurators* Pontius Pilate, Marcus Antonius Felix and Porcius Festus were all of the equestrian order (Luke 3:1; Acts 23 and 24).

DECORION ORDER

· These were the aristocrats of cities around the Empire, and the lowest of the top three orders.

· They ruled the cities of Italy, Roman colonies and other cities seeking to emulate Rome.

· Sometimes called "municipal senators" because they served in local, municipal senates.

· Unlike senators and equestrians however, there was great *inequality* among them from city to city, and even within cities.

· In the Eastern Mediterranean world, most decorions were Greeks or hellenized people.

· Imperial Rome allowed decorions to keep their wealth as long as they helped keep the *Pax Romana* and collected taxes for Rome.

New Testament: Dionysius the Areopagite in Athens and Erastus the treasurer of Corinth were of the decorion order (Acts 17:34 and Rom 16:23).

RESPECTABLE POOR

· (Latin, *populus integer*) Comprised of small land owners, shopkeepers, and craftsmen. Their status was assigned roughly by how much work they "did" through *others*.

POOR & DESTITUTE

· These were those completely dependent upon others either for opportunities to work, or for welfare.

· Rome provided next to nothing for the aged, widows, orphans, disabled or infirm.

· There were high concentrations in urban centers throughout the Empire; estimates for Rome were over 300,000!

·

STATUS –(Latin, *dignitas*) the net sum of the categories of honor I hold (e.g. a well-educated, wealthy, non-citizen, former slave had less *dignitas* than a poor, uneducated freeborn citizen).

1. The status of a member of the elite was identifiable through status symbols, themselves legally restricted to the different ranks.
   a. Senators had the right by law, to wear a toga with a broad purple stripe, wore a gold ring, and sat in the front seats at spectacles and public events; they also monopolized all the important priesthoods at Rome.
   b. Equestrians wore a toga with a narrow purple stripe, wore a gold ring, were given a horse at public expense which they could display during parades, and occupied seats behind the senators at spectacles.
   c. The usurpation of any of these status symbols was taken very seriously by the authorities (that is, the elite) and many laws, empire-wide and local, protected their usage strictly.
2. The topography of the typical Roman town reflects this social order, with the houses of the important and less important evenly distributed throughout rather than grouped into high-class neighborhoods and ghettos. The homes of clients were often in close proximity to their patron's home.

NOTE: *Even wealth had "categories," according to Cicero: inherited wealth had more honor than wealth gained in one's lifetime, but now enjoyed, which had more honor than wealth still being accumulated.*

ROMAN PROVINCIAL GOVERNMENT

The Roman Empire was made up of several geographic territories called provinces. Each province fell under the control of a provincial governor. There were 3 types of provinces and several classifications of governor. In 180 AD Provincial governors were still mainly drawn from the Senate. The provincial types were broken down as follows:

Imperial Provinces Governed by Senators

The emperor was the Proconsul of all provinces with any significant military force, with the exceptions of Africa and Aegyptus. In 180 AD there appears to have been 28 Imperial provinces. Those provinces with at least one legion stationed in them had a senatorial governor called a *Legatus Propraetore Augusti* (imperial legate of praetorian rank). The imperial governors were technically below the level of a senatorial proconsul and had five lictors instead of six.

This formal distinction had no real significance since the legate was the representative of the governor, but officially they were lower in rank because they were subordinates of the Emperor, who was theoretically the actual governor. In provinces with one legion, the legate in charge of the province (normally of praetorian rank) also controlled the legion himself. In provinces with more than one legion, like the Germanies, Syria and Cappadocia, each legion was commanded by its own legate of praetorian rank, while the province as a whole was commanded by a legate of consular rank who could dictate general control over the entire army stationed there. These governorships were completely at the whim of the Emperor and could serve anywhere from 1 to 5 years.

Imperial Provinces Governed by Equestrians

The Emperor also had under his control a number of smaller, but potentially difficult provinces that did not need an entire legion. These provinces were put under the control of governors of equestrian status. Under the early Empire their title was *Praefectus* like that of the governor of Egypt, but later the title became procurator. New conquests generally fell into this equestrian category but most were later changed in status to reflect varying conditions in Roman control. Like the other Imperial provinces, the governors could serve any length of time up to 5 years or longer.

Much like the Senatorial province of Africa, the equestrian province of Aegyptus was an exception to the rule of Legions stationed only in Imperial provinces. Egypt was not a normal province like any other. It was considered the personal possession of the Emperor and the governor, the *Praefectus Aegytpi* was considered the highest ranking equestrian post during the early empire. Later, the post would fall second to that of the *Praetorian* command, but its position was still very prestigious.

Duties of the Governor

The governor of any Roman province had four major tasks.

Taxes and financial concerns: As the emperor's personal, or the Senate's financial agent, he had to supervise the local authorities and the private tax collectors. A governor could mint coins and negotiate with wealthy institutions like temples and money-lenders that could advance the money.

Chief accountant: He inspected the books of major cities and various operations and supervised large scale building projects.

The province's supreme judge: The governor had the sole right to inflict the death penalty and capital cases were normally tried before him. Appeal was not impossible, but getting to Rome and an audience with the Emperor was expensive. Appeal was unlikely to change matters anyway, as a Governor wouldn't generally take the chance of convicting someone who the Emperor would not like to be convicted. The governor was also supposed to travel through the main districts of his province to administer justice in the major towns.

Commanded an army: In the more important provinces, this could consist of legions; but elsewhere, there were only auxiliaries. As a part of his standing orders, the governor had the authority to use his legion to stamp out organized brigands in the area without need for Imperial approval.

Every governor had at his disposal a various number of advisers and staff, who were known as his *comites* ('companions'), the number depending on his social standing and rank. Military Legates relied heavily upon their *Tribunus Augusticlavii* and others could have Senatorial Quaestors or non magistrate Procurators.

ORGANIZATION OF THE ROMAN IMPERIAL LEGION

A full strength legion was officially made up of 6,000 men, but typically all legions were organized at under strength and generally consisted of approximately 5,300 fighting men including officers. It is difficult to determine whether non-combatants like field surgeons and clerks were included in the 5,300 or helped bring the total number of men up to the official 6,000.

The basic structure of the army is as follows:

Contubernium: (tent group) consisted of 8 men.

Centuria: (century) was made up of 10 contubernium with a total of 80 men commanded by a centurion

Cohorts: (cohort) included 6 *centuriae* or a total of 480 fighting men, not including officers. In addition the first cohort was double strength but with only 5 *centuriae* instead of the normal 6.

Legio: (Legion) consisted of 10 cohorts. Additionally each Legion had a 120 man *Alae* (cavalry unit) called the *Eques Legionis* permanently attached to it possibly to be used as scouts and messengers.

Therefore the total fighting strength of a Legion:

The First Cohort totaling 800 men (5 double-strength centuries with 160 men each) 9 Cohors (with 6 centuries at 80 men each) for a total 4,320, and an additional 120 man cavalry for a grand total of 5,240 men not including all the officers.

The basic designation of the 10 cohorts was the same throughout all the Legions. They were arranged in battle so that the strongest and weakest units would be mixed throughout the formation maximizing moral and effectiveness

Cohort I: Was made up of the elite troops. Its direct commander was the *Primus Pilus*, the highest ranking and most respected of all the Centurions.

Cohort II: Consisted of some of the weaker or newest troops.

Cohort III: No special designation for this unit.

Cohort IV: Another of the four weak cohorts.

Cohort V: Again, no special designation.

Cohort VI: Made up of "The Finest of the Young Men".

Cohort VII: One of the four weak cohorts and a likely place to find trainees and raw recruits.

Cohort VIII: Contained "The Selected Troops".

Cohort IX: One of the four weak cohorts and a likely place to find trainees and raw recruits.

Cohort X: Made up of "The Good Troops".

Roman Legionary Ranks

The following list indicates ranks from highest command to lowest common soldier:

Senior Officers of the Roman Legion

Legatus Legionis: The overall Legionary commander. This post was generally appointed by the emperor, was a former Tribune and held command for 3 or 4 years, although could serve for a much longer period. In a province with only one legion, the Legatus was also the provincial governor and in provinces with multiple legions, each legion has a Legatus and the provincial governor has overall command of them all.

Tribunus Laticlavius: Named for the broad striped toga worn by men of senatorial rank. This tribune was appointed by the Emperor or the Senate. Though generally quite young and less experienced than the *Tribuni Angusticlavii*, he served as second in command of the legion, behind the Legate.

Praefectus Castrorum: The camp Prefect. Generally he was a long serving veteran who had been promoted through the ranks of the centurions and was 3rd in overall command.

Tribuni Angusticlavii: Each legion had 5 military tribunes of equestrian (knight) class citizens. They were in many cases career officers and served many of the important administrative tasks of the Legion, but still served in a full tactical command function during engagements.

Primus Pilus: The "First File" was the commanding centurion of the first cohort and the senior centurion of the entire Legion. Service in this position also allowed entry into the equestrian social class upon retirement.

Mid-Level Officers in the Roman Legion

Centurions: Each Legion had 59 or 60 centurions, one to command each *centuria* of the 10 cohorts. They were the backbone of the professional army and were the career soldiers who ran the day to day life of the soldiers as well as issuing commands in the field. They were generally moved up from the ranks, but in some cases could be direct appointments from the Emperor or other higher ranking officials. The cohorts were ranked from the First to the Tenth and the *Centuria* within each cohort ranked from 1 to 6, with only 5 Centuria in the First Cohort (For a total of 59 *Centuria* and the *Primus Pilus*). The *Centuria* that each Centurion commanded was a direct reflection of his rank. (Command of the First *Centuria* of the First Cohort was the highest and the 6th *Centuria* of the 10th Cohort was the lowest). The 5 Centurions of the First Cohort were called the *Primi Ordines*, and included the *Primus Pilus*. Additional ranks are highlighted here:

Pilus Prior: The commander of the first cohort of each Centuria (except the first).

(**taken from:** http://www.unrv.com/military/legion.php (a website dedicated to the history of ancient Rome. In particular, this URL gives a detailed explanation of the Roman military structure.)

ROMAN GOVERNANCE OF JUDEA

Form	Title	Leaders	Dates
Client kingdom	King	Herod the Great	37 – 4 BC
	Ethnarch	Archelaus	4 BC – AD 6
Roman Province	Prefect	Coponius	AD 6 – 9
	Prefect	Marcus Ambivius	AD 9 – 12
	Prefect	Annius Rufus	AD 12 – 15
	Prefect	Valerius Gratus	AD 15 – 26
	Prefect	Pontius Pilate	AD 26 – 36
	Prefect	Marullus	AD 37 – 41
Client kingdom	King	Herod Arippa I	AD 41 – 44
Roman Province	Procurator	Cuspius Fadus	AD 44 – 46
	Procurator	Cumanus	AD 48 – 52
	Procurator	Marcus Antonius Felix	AD 52 – 59?
	Procurator	Porcius Festus	AD 59 – 62?
	Procurator	Albinus	AD 62 – 64
	Procurator	Gessius Florus	AD 64 – 66

"LIFE CYCLE OF AN EMPIRE"

"A G E O F ..."	S A L I E N T C H A R A C T E R I S T I C S
"Pioneers"	•people typically poor, hardy, enterprising, aggressive
"Conquests"	•sudden outburst •extraordinary display of energy and courage •readiness to improvise and experiment *(i.e. few established traditions)* •general optimism and confidence •strong religious commitment
"Commerce"	•travel or goods stimulated by the new markets opened up by conquest •commerce stimulated by the general tranquility of the area under domination
"Affluence"	•increase in art and luxury as expressions of wealth •new forms of wealth develop

"Intellect"	•money replaces honor/duty as a chief social objective
	•growth of "intellectualism" evidenced by:
	    •*education transformed into a means of obtaining wealth*
	    •*universalism in higher education*
	    •*dependence on ideas and dialogue for solutions*
	•denunciation of military aggressiveness
	•growth of pacifism
	•increasing civil dissent & internal political hatred and divisions

"Decadence"	•defensiveness due to desire to maintain wealth and luxury •universal pessimism •frivolity (*"eat, drink, be merry"*) •materialism •influx of foreigners unrelated to original conquerers •welfare state; lavish spending on its own benevolence •decline in religion *(lays seeds for religious revival)* •cult of worship of athletes, actors and musicians •increase of influence in public life by women and homosexuals

N A T I O N	RISE & FALL DATES	DURATION
Assyria	859 – 612 BC	247 years
Persia (Cyrus and descendants)	538 – 330 BC	208 years
Greece (Alexander and descendants)	331 – 100 BC	231 years
Roman Republic	260 – 27 BC	233 years
Roman Empire	27 BC – AD 180	207 years
Arab Empire	634 – 880	246 years
Marmeluke Empire	1250 – 1517	267 years
Ottoman Empire	1320 – 1570	250 years
Spain	1500 – 1750	250 years
Romanov Russia	1682 – 1916	234 years
Britain	1700 – 1950	250 years

The "Life Cycle of an Empire" chart was distilled from the book, *The Fate of Empires,* by Sir John Glubb. Edinburgh, Wm. Blackwood Publishers, ©1976. The chart of nations and dates was extracted from the book itself.